The Financial Crisis and White Collar Crime – Legislative and Policy Responses

This book offers a commentary on the responses to white collar crime since the financial crisis. The book brings together experts from academia and practice to analyse the legal and policy responses that have been put in place following the 2008 financial crisis. The book looks at a range of topics including: the low priority and resources allocated to fraud; EU regulatory efforts to fight financial crime; protecting whistleblowers in the financial industry; the criminality of the rogue trader; the evolution of financial crime in cryptocurrencies; and the levying of financial penalties against banks and corporations by the US Department of Justice and Securities and Exchange Commission.

Nicholas Ryder is Professor in Financial Crime at the University of West England, UK.

Jon Tucker is Professor of Finance and the Director for the Centre for Global Finance at the University of the West of England, UK.

Umut Turksen is Professor of Law and Business at Kingston University, UK.

The Law of Financial Crime
Series Editor: Nicholas Ryder

Available titles in this series include:

Fighting Financial Crime in the Global Economic Crisis
Nicholas Ryder, Umut Turksen and Sabine Hassler

The Financial War on Terror
A review of counter-terrorist financing strategies since 2001
Nicholas Ryder

The Financial Crisis and White Collar Crime – Legislative and Policy Responses
A critical assessment
Edited by Nicholas Ryder, Jon Tucker and Umut Turksen

Forthcoming titles in this series include:

Stemming Terrorist Finance
The regulation of hawala and alternative remittance systems
Karen Cooper

The Financial Crisis and White Collar Crime – Legislative and Policy Responses

A critical assessment

Edited by Nicholas Ryder, Jon Tucker and Umut Turksen

Routledge
Taylor & Francis Group
LONDON AND NEW YORK

First published 2017 by Routledge

2 Park Square, Milton Park, Abingdon, Oxfordshire OX14 4RN
711 Third Avenue, New York, NY 10017

Routledge is an imprint of the Taylor & Francis Group, an informa business

First issued in paperback 2018

British Library Cataloguing in Publication Data
A catalogue record for this book is available from the British Library

Library of Congress Cataloging in Publication Data
Names: Ryder, Nicholas, editor. | Tucker, Jonathan, 1968– editor. | Turksen, Umut, editor.
Title: The financial crisis and white collar crime – legislative and policy responses: a critical assessment / Edited by Nicholas Ryder, Jon Tucker and Umut Turksen.
Description: New York : Routledge, [2016] |
Series: The law of financial crime | Includes bibliographical references and index.
Identifiers: LCCN 2016035256 | ISBN 9781138119970 (hbk) | ISBN 9781315652009 (ebk)
Subjects: LCSH: White collar crimes—Law and legislation. | Commercial crimes—Law and legislation. | Financial institutions—Law and legislation—Criminal provisions. | Financial crises.
Classification: LCC K5215. F56 2016 | DDC 345/.0268—dc23
LC record available at https://lccn.loc.gov/2016035256

ISBN: 978-1-138-11997-0 (hbk)
ISBN: 978-0-367-03031-5 (pbk)

Typeset in Galliard
by Keystroke, Neville Lodge, Tettenhall, Wolverhampton

Contents

Notes on contributors

Andrew H. Baker

Andrew Baker is a Senior Lecturer in Law at Liverpool John Moores University. His research interests include contract law, regulation of financial services, financial crime, particularly money laundering and market abuse, and corporate social responsibility of banks. Andrew engages in teaching in bank and financial services regulation, the law relating to financial crime and company law, and is currently undertaking a doctorate assessing bank regulation in the United Kingdom.

Mark Button

Professor Mark Button is Director of the Centre for Counter Fraud Studies at the Institute of Criminal Justice Studies, University of Portsmouth. Mark has written extensively on counter fraud and private policing issues, publishing many articles, chapters and completing eight books. His latest book (co-authored with Martin Tunley, Andrew Whittacker and Jim Gee) is titled *The Accredited Counter Fraud Specialist Handbook* (Wiley, 2014). Some of the most significant research projects include leading the research on behalf of the National Fraud Authority and ACPO on fraud victims, the Department for International Development on fraud measurement, Acromas (AA and Saga) on 'Cash-for-Crash fraudsters', the Midlands Fraud Forum, Eversheds and PKF on 'Sanctioning Fraudsters'. Mark has also acted as a consultant for the United Nations Offices on Drugs and Crime and the United Nations Development Programme/European Union on enhancing civilian oversight of the Turkish private security industry.

Dionysios Demetis

Dr Dionysios Demetis is a Lecturer in Law and Management Systems at the Business School of the University of Hull. He holds a PhD from the London School of Economics. He has been an Associate Staff member of the Information Systems Innovation Group of the LSE, as well as an Adjunct Professor at the Thomas Jefferson School of Law. He is the author of two books and a number of journal publications, while his book on anti-money laundering, entitled *Technology and Anti-Money Laundering*, is the first book to provide a coherent theoretical structure for AML research and practice, based on Systems Theory. While at the LSE, he has contributed widely to a number projects for the European Commission.

Rhian Dow

Rhian Dow is Senior Lecturer in Law and Accounting and Finance at the University of the West of England, Bristol, and teaches corporate governance and accountability. She is a Fellow of the Institute of Chartered Accountants in England and Wales, with a background in auditing and assurance in both the private and public sectors, having worked for a Big Four accounting firm and the National Audit Office in London. Before qualifying as an accountant, she worked for some years as a financial journalist, reporting corporate news and results.

Andrew Haynes

As well as being a Professor of Law at the University of Wolverhampton, Andrew Haynes is a visiting Professor of Law at the University of Macau, People's Republic of China, and a Senior Visiting Research Fellow at the Institute of Advanced Legal Studies. The second edition of his book *The Law Relating to International Banking* will be published in 2016 (Bloomsbury Professional). Andrew is also Chairman of the Market Abuse Association and he lectures on the law relating to international banking and capital markets, financial services and financial crime, and corporate finance law. He also holds a number of editorial positions, including for *The Company Lawyer*, the *Journal of Financial Crime* and the *International Journal of Disclosure and Compliance.*

Daniel Jasinski

Daniel Jasinski was formerly an Associate Lecturer in Law at the University of the West of England. His research interests include banking regulation, consumer protection, criminal law and commercial law. Daniel completed his LLM under the supervision of Professor Nicholas Ryder at the University of the West of England and was called to the Bar of England and Wales in 2015.

Paul Keenan

Paul Keenan is a Visiting Practitioner Professor in Financial Regulation, University of the West of England, Bristol, Chartered MCSI, and Managing Director, Keenan Regulatory Consulting Ltd. He graduated in Economics and Statistics from the University of Exeter in 1972, and has followed a number of career paths, including secondary school teaching, university lecturing, government service, investment banking and, latterly, financial market regulation, with a focus on the international aspects of all of those areas of activity. Most recently, Paul has been retained in various expert witness roles, both in the UK and internationally, assisting in cases involving the market practice in, and regulation of, the complex products in financial markets. He is a respected speaker on regulatory and compliance issues at financial market seminars and conferences.

Alison Lui

Dr Alison Lui, Senior Lecturer at Liverpool John Moores University, is a Max Planck Fellow, a Winston Churchill Fellow and an Academic Fellow of the Honourable Inner Temple. Her research interests are financial regulation and corporate governance. She has published several journal articles and a monograph entitled *Financial Stability and Prudential Regulation: A Comparison between the Regulators and Central Banks of the United Kingdom, the United States, Canada, Australia and Germany* (Routledge, 2016). Alison has presented papers at numerous national and international conferences, including the World Bank High Level Meeting on Governance of Bank Subsidiaries in Vienna and the International Corporate Governance Network Meeting in Amsterdam.

Axel Palmer

Dr Axel Palmer is a specialist in the field of economic crime research. Formerly a Head of Debt Management and Head of Litigation at a major international bank, he lectures and publishes on international commercial disputes law, banking and finance law, and fraud, bribery and corruption law.

Christopher Recker

Christopher is a solicitor with insurance litigation law firm BLM. While studying for his LLB, Christopher developed a strong interest in commercial, company and financial crime law. Christopher elected to complete a research-based dissertation to analyse the National Crime Agency and the UK's response to financial crime. Christopher regularly acts and assists on cases involving allegations of fraud (from a claimant and defendant perspective) and has experience of obtaining freezing injunctions, tracing assets and recovering the proceeds of fraud. Christopher also has extensive experience of interpreting insurance policies and providing advice on policy responses to allegations of dishonesty and misappropriation.

Nicholas Ryder

Dr Nicholas Ryder is a Professor in Financial Crime in the Department of Law at the University of the West of England, Bristol. His research has been published in prestigious journals and he is the founder and series editor of the Routledge series, The Law of Financial Crime. Nicholas is a member of several editorial boards, including *Goode: Consumer Credit Law and Practice*, and he is the senior managing editor for the *British Journal of White Collar Crime*. His research has been sponsored by the Economic and Social Research Council, the City of London Police Force, ICT Wilmington Risk & Compliance, Universities South West, France Telecom Group and the European Social Fund.

Gauri Sinha

Dr Gauri Sinha holds a PhD specialising in anti-money laundering compliance and works as a Lecturer in Law at Kingston University, London. Her research interests include financial crime, financial regulation and corporate accountability. Gauri also consults on AML issues, and has advised the Government of Jamaica on financial sanctions and asset-freezing related to weapons proliferation. Prior to joining Kingston University, Gauri was working at PricewaterhouseCoopers as a Senior Associate in the forensic department, where she consulted several global banks and commercial organisations. In addition, she has worked with the World

Bank as a financial crime specialist, to design a 'Know Your Customer' security framework for a carbon-trading platform.

Jon Tucker

Jon Tucker is a Professor of Finance and the Director of the Centre for Global Finance at the University of the West of England, Bristol. He has published widely in the fields of financial markets, corporate finance, banking, corporate financial reporting, and financial crime, and is on the editorial board and review panel of a wide range of accounting and finance journals. Jon engages in teaching finance at master's level and supervising PhD students, and is actively involved in business engagement and consultancy. He is a member of the Chartered Institute for Securities & Investment, and has worked in the banking and accounting professions.

Martin Tunley

Dr Martin Tunley, Senior Lecturer, is an academic criminologist based at the Centre for Counter Fraud Studies in the Institute of Criminal Justice Studies, University of Portsmouth. He has published in academic journals on fraud loss measurement and benefit fraud, and his book, *Mandating the Measurement of Fraud*, based on his doctoral studies at the University of Portsmouth, has been published by Palgrave (2014). He has also co-authored *The Accredited Counter Fraud Specialist Handbook*, published by Wiley. Martin serves on the editorial board of the *Internet Journal of Criminology*, and is Deputy Head of the Secretariat of the Counter Fraud Professional Accreditation Board.

Umut Turksen

Dr Umut Turksen is a Professor of Law and Business at Kingston University, London, a Visiting Professor at the University of the West of England, Bristol, and an executive of the Commonwealth Legal Education Association. Umut teaches WTO law, international institutional law and EU law. Mostly based on comparative legal research, Umut has numerous publications in the area of international trade law, energy security, financial crime and ethics of counter-terrorism. He provides consultancy and CPD training to prestigious international businesses and government projects. In addition to his expertise in financial crime and compliance, he has extensive knowledge of, and practice in, international trade law, energy law and security, and digital assets.

Sarah Wilson

Dr Sarah Wilson, Senior Lecturer, University of York, is a specialist in financial crime. Her other research interests include trusts law and the regulatory aftermath of the 2007–2008 financial crisis. Sarah's 2014 monograph, *The Origins of Modern Financial Crime in Britain: Historical Foundations and Current Problems*, was published by Routledge. Sarah has also published in many prestigious journals, including the *Journal of Financial Crime*, *Law Crime and History* and the *British Journal of Criminology*. Sarah has held academic posts at Keele University, the University of Leeds and the University of Wales, Swansea.

Acknowledgements

This edited collection is the culmination of several years of patience and hard work. First, we would like to thank our research students and colleagues at the Centre for Global Finance and Commercial Law Research Unit for their inspiration and feedback. Second, we would like to thank the University of the West of England, Bristol, and Kingston University, London, for their ongoing support. Finally, we would also like to thank Katie Carpenter and the staff from Routledge for their continued understanding and support (thanks for the extension or two) during the completion of this project. Nicholas Ryder would like to thank Ruth and Ethan for putting up with another book. Jon Tucker would like to thank his wife, Mihaela, and his son, Bobby, for their support during the development of the book. Umut Turksen would like to thank his wife, Jo, and his children, Melike, Evren and Kyra, for having the patience with him for taking on yet another book project.

1 Introduction

Nicholas Ryder, Umut Turksen and Jon Tucker

In September 2007, the collapse of the United States (US) sub-prime mortgage market resulted in the global meltdown of the financial markets. This in turn led to the collapse of many international financial institutions including Northern Rock, Bradford and Bingley, American Insurance Group, Freddy Mac, Fannie Mae and Lehman Brothers. The G20 countries responded with a plethora of financial stimulus packages aimed at combating the largest global financial problem since the Wall Street Crash in October 1929 and the Great Depression. Many commentators, regulatory agencies and politicians have argued that the financial crisis was the result of numerous interrelated factors which resulted in nation states introducing a raft of legislative measures to protect their economies.

However, the purpose of this collection is to highlight the impact of another, perhaps even more significant, trigger event – financial crime. There is an increasing amount of evidence from the Federal Bureau of Investigation (FBI), the Securities and Exchange Commission (SEC), the Financial Conduct Authority (FCA) and the Serious Fraud Office (SFO) which highlights the increase in financial crime. Therefore, the aim of this collection is to provide a unique commentary on the response to white collar crime since the financial crisis. It seeks to contribute to this vast area of law by providing a unique review from a wide range of experts from academia and practice. The collection is based on a series of papers that were presented at a one-day conference that was held at the University of the West of England Bristol in July 2014 on the legislative and enforcement responses to white collar crime and the financial crisis. It seeks to build on the earlier findings of *Fighting Financial Crime in the Global Economic Crisis*, published in November 2014, which identified the link between the 2008 financial crisis and white collar crime. In the first edited collection for the Law of Financial Crime series, the contributors attempted to illustrate the link or association between the most recent financial crisis and financial crime. That edited collection presented a significant amount of evidence that suggested that financial crime was at least a contributory factor. Since its publication, an impressive array of scholars and commentators have conducted research on the association between the financial crisis and financial crime.[1] However, it is important to note that not all commentators would agree that financial crime was a factor that contributed towards the financial crisis.[2]

Contents overview

Chapter 2 of this collection is written by Professor Mark Button and Dr Martin Tunley and is entitled 'The 2008 financial crisis and fraud: the roles of immoral phlegmatism, deviancy attenuation and de-labelling'. Here the authors argue that the extent of fraud that has been uncovered since the financial crisis and the scale of the damage done would lead some to believe that many should be held to account through the most serious sanctions the state has to hand, criminal prosecution. The reality, however, is that in criminal terms, at least, the financial institutions and persons responsible have not been held to account. This chapter argues that there is a variety of reasons to explain this, and will use new counter theories such as de-labelling, deviancy attenuation and immoral phlegmatism as the lenses through which to explore these events.[3] This chapter begins by briefly outlining moral panics, deviancy amplification and labelling, the theories these counter-theories are built upon, before using the example of benefits fraud in the UK, which, it is argued, fits with many of these well-established theories. The chapter will then set out the counter-theories: de-labelling, deviancy attenuation and immoral phlegmatism, and then use the financial crisis of 2008 to explore them.

In Chapter 3, Dr Alison Lui uses a combination of the doctrinal approach and interview data. The interview data consists of two former employees of HBOS and Lloyds TSB. The first interviewee is Paul Moore, the former Head of Regulatory Risk at HBOS (2002–2004). The second is Ian Taplin, a former

1 See, for example: R. Tomasic, 'The financial crisis and the haphazard pursuit of financial crime' (2011) *Journal of Financial Crime* 18(1), 7; N. Ryder, *The Financial Crisis and White Collar Crime: The Perfect Storm?* (Cheltenham: Edward Elgar, 2014); N. Ryder, U. Turksen and S. Hassler (eds), *Fighting Financial Crime in the Global Economic Crisis: Policy, Trends and Sanctions* (New York: Routledge, 2014); W. Huisman, 'White-collar crime and the economic crisis' (2012/2013) *Newsletter of the European Society on Criminology* 11; M. Deflem (ed.), *Economic Crisis and Crime* (Bingley, West Yorks: Emerald Group Publishing, 2011); O. Osoka, A. Trakkidi, J. Fisher, M. Blottiaux, S. Daniel, H. Oliveira and D. Green, 'The global financial crisis: the case for a stronger criminal response' (2013) *Law & Financial Markets Review* 7(3), 159; E. Herlin-Karnell, 'White-collar crime and European financial crises: getting tough on EU market abuse' (2012) *European Law Review* 37(4), 481; P. Hardouin, 'The aftermath of the financial crisis' (2011) *Journal of Financial Crime* 18(2), 148; A. Creseney, G. Eng and S. Nuttal, 'Regulatory investigations and the credit crisis: the search for villains' (2009) *American Criminal Law Review* 46, 225; E. Posner and A. Vermeule, 'Crisis governance in the administrative state: 9/11 and the financial meltdown of 2008' (2009) *University of Chicago Law Review* 76, 1613.

2 See, for example: M. Gill, 'Fraud and recessions: views from fraudsters and fraud managers' (2011) *International Journal of Law, Crime and Justice*, 39, 204–214.

3 M. Button and M. Tunley, 'Explaining fraud deviancy attenuation in the United Kingdom' (2015) *Crime, Law and Social Change* 63, 49–64.

employee in the Wealth and Private Bank of Lloyds TSB (2005–2010). The chapter demonstrates that banks such as HBOS and Lloyds TSB did not pay sufficient attention to consumer protection. The pursuit of profits by such banks prevailed over consumer protection. Although legislation and FSA guidelines prior to the financial crisis highlighted the importance of consumer protection, it will be demonstrated that they were insufficient. Subsequent reforms in the law have improved protection given to whistle-blowers in the financial industry, but corporate governance is still the driving force behind changing the culture of organisations. Whistle-blowers can play an important role in improving corporate governance due to the information asymmetry problem in the financial sector. Whistle-blowers did not prevent the scandals linked to the financial crisis of 2007–2009,[4] but they have contributed towards more regulatory intervention as a result of exposing weaknesses in corporate governance and regulation.[5] They thus play important roles in uncovering financial misconduct in Potemkin villages.

Chapter 4 is written from a practitioner's perspective by Professor Paul Keenan and is entitled 'Rogues in the City'. In this chapter, Professor Keenan concentrates on rogue traders and the question of criminal intent and concentrates on a number of cases studies including that of Jerome Kerviel. Chapter 5 has been written by Dr Dionysios Demetis, who seeks to examine the role of information systems (IS) in creating financial instability by automating critical decision-making processes. By following a systems theoretical approach by Lee and Demetis[6] and based on a few fundamental systems principles, the chapter identifies theoretical propositions about the nature of technology in constructing financial markets, and by extension, financial crises. The chapter draws from a few instances of the Dow Jones Industrial Average crisis of 2010, also known as the Flash Crash of 2:45 where $1trillion was lost in market value within a few minutes. This is used as an example of technology out of control, where algorithmic trading creates contingencies that affect how different stakeholders interact and react. Based on the entanglement of systems principles and technological interference, the main hypothesis developed in this chapter is that technology is largely set to lead in the creation of future instabilities and amplify the degree of uncertainty in markets. Ultimately, this aims to highlight the broader role of technology in the financial system, not as a tool that can be strictly harnessed to support transacting, but as a system in itself that has both emergent and unintended consequences, one of which escalates to the concept of a financial crisis.

4 See: R. Posner, *The Crisis of Capitalist Democracy* (Cambridge, MA: Harvard University Press, 2011); J. Stiglitz, *Freefall: America, Free Markets, and the Sinking of the World Economy* (New York: Norton, 2010).

5 Ibid. Also see National Commission on the Causes of the Financial and Economic Crisis in the United States, *The Financial Crisis Inquiry Report* (New York: Public Affairs, 2011).

6 A. Lee and D. Demetis, *Crafting Theory to Satisfy the Requirements of Systems Science* (2016) 49th Hawaii International Conference on System Sciences, IEEE: 5075–5084.

Chapter 6, by Professor Jon Tucker, examines the financial crisis and financial crime from a finance industry perspective. It explores the structure of the industry, the instruments traded and the role of the key players in an attempt to understand the basis for their interactions and the motivations for individual actions. The chapter explores the central importance of financial markets and institutions to a successful economy and society, and seeks to understand the inherent institutional challenges around scale, complexity and information asymmetry. The chapter goes on to consider the incentives of key players and the possible causes of things 'going wrong', such as systemic problems, poorly designed incentive structures, negligence, lack of training, unforeseen circumstances and, of course, criminal activity. Finally, the chapter examines how key actors in the finance industry such as regulators, financial institutions and professional bodies have set in place systems and approaches around not just compliance but also integrity and ethics in an attempt to reduce the possibility of a similar crisis in the next decade. In brief, the chapter underlines the importance of the finance industry, the imperative for balanced discussion of the issues around financial crime, the central role of integrity and ethics in modern institutions, and an end to 'banker bashing'.

In Chapter 7, Andrew H. Baker assesses how the market abuse regime of the Financial Services and Markets Act 2000 attempts to deal with the risk posed to financial markets by the misuse of information by market participants. The chapter analyses the risks posed by the misuse of information, with some focus on insider dealing under both the civil and criminal provisions. The purpose is to assess whether the regime in its amended form is capable of ensuring that the UK financial markets are free from abusive practices and continue to operate in a fair and open manner.

Chapter 8, by Daniel Jasinski, offers an alternative stance on the response to the financial crisis, in which he seeks to analyse the Financial Conduct Authority's approach to regulating the market from a consumer protection perspective. The chapter provides an analysis of the Consumer Credit Act 1974, and in particular the elements that can be invoked by consumers in order to seek redress for harm caused to them by financial institutions. The next section reflects on the powers and performance of the Office of Fair Trading and compares it with the Financial Services Authority. The chapter pays particular attention to predatory lending and other illegal lending mechanisms, and draws comparisons with the United States of America.

In Chapter 9, Professor Andrew Haynes concentrates on money laundering and provides a summary of the manner in which the law has developed, and is continuing to develop, and its causes. The chapter then moves on to concentrate on market abuse and insider dealing. The final part considers the quandary that this has created. Is the role of such laws and regulations to combat crime effectively, or is it to look as though something is being done, when in effect little is? Is there an alternative approach, and, if so, what is it?

Chapter 10, by Rhian Dow and Professor Umut Turksen, comments on whether and to what extent accountants and auditors in the EU are protected when they blow the whistle and report suspicious (financial crime) activity in the context of money laundering. In the confines of this chapter, it is not possible to consider all Member States of the EU. Rather, the authors have chosen several Member States in a hope to depict the general state of affairs across the EU and highlight the main differences therein.

In Chapter 11, Dr Gauri Sinha seeks to answer a number of important questions, including: Has a stricter regime led to more effective regulation in financial crime? The answer lies in the analysis of the 'credible deterrence strategy' followed by the Financial Conduct Authority in the United Kingdom that has led to an inefficient 'comply or explain' approach on the part of the regulated sector. The chapter argues that a move towards this tougher regulation is purely cosmetic and encourages regulated entities to follow a 'tick-box' approach. The underlying objective of the author is to counter the belief that excessive regulation leads to more efficient compliance of financial crime laws, and therefore a more stable financial system. Looking at the crisis from the other side of the coin, why are individual prosecutions almost non-existent? Contributory factors such as a lack of resources within law enforcement agencies may give part of the answer; however, the author contends that it is definitely not the most crucial factor. In analysing the above issues, the focus of the chapter remains the United Kingdom; however, in discussing the financial crisis and the (lack of) prosecutions, it is inevitable to traverse through the reaction of law enforcement to the issue of corporate accountability in the United States.

In Chapter 12, Dr Axel Palmer critically assesses the response of the United States of America to financial crime, a key component of the financial crisis. This chapter begins with the issues faced by President George W. Bush in the closing months of his administration, moves on to examine the response of President Barack Obama, and then considers how the Department of Justice and the Securities and Exchange Commission undertook their roles to supervise, regulate and protect consumers and individuals from financial abuse.

In Chapter 13, Chris Recker seeks to discuss and critically assess the role of the National Crime Agency and the wider battle against financial crime. This chapter first provides an overview of the legislative framework that governs fraud, money laundering, bribery and corruption, and then introduces the regulators and law enforcement agencies of financial crime in the United Kingdom. This chapter then considers the future of fraud, money laundering and bribery, and corruption regulation. The chapter concludes with a balanced commentary on the success of the National Crime Agency and the extent to which it has impacted the United Kingdom's financial crime policy.

In the final chapter of this collection, Dr Sarah Wilson seeks to draw inspiration from how the financial crisis has produced a rich and voluminous academic commentary on the 'first crisis of globalisation'. It also takes its lead from how academic scholarship on the financial crisis is also exhibiting burgeoning interest in exploring connections between financial crises and financial crime. Within this emergent body of literature, identifiable focal points are already readily apparent, with interest concentrating centrally on how financial distress and instability provide a context for financial impropriety, which occurs in violation of criminal law, such that it is precipitating debate on the adequacy of existing criminal liability. This discernible academic interest in associations between the financial crisis and financial crime is also readily apparent in UK debates on regulatory reform alongside commentary responses, and this chapter draws extensively on both. In focusing particularly on the apparent significance of criminal enforcement in current discourses, the chapter considers current perceptions of in/adequacy, linking these closely with normative questions arising from what role the criminal law should have in promoting propriety within financial systems, as these are seen by academics and regulators alike. Two key academic studies help to frame this discussion, one of which has been written more generally around the financial crisis, with the other being more specifically focused on financial crime. The chapter explores the lexiconic qualities of Reinhart and Rogoff's '"this time is different" syndrome' and Friedrichs' thesis of 'transformative understandings' of crime, regarding them as invaluable tools for analysing the current state of play. Both works are also used to explain how the interactions between financial crises and financial crime can be analysed historically, with the chapter also pointing to the manifest importance for the current context of them being so.

2 The 2008 financial crisis and fraud: the roles of immoral phlegmatism, deviancy attenuation and de-labelling

Mark Button and Martin Tunley

Introduction

The financial crisis beginning in 2008 triggered in many countries the worst economic recession since the Great Depression of the 1930s. This economic downturn was unique, not just for its size and severity, but also because a significant cause of it was fraud. Much of the blame for the crisis has been attributed to the collapse of the sub-prime mortgage market in the USA, and the demise of this sector has been substantially linked to what most would regard as fraud. The scandal of sub-prime mortgages was built upon a base of dishonest applicants applying for mortgages they should never have been given, brokers turning a blind eye to them or even helping to fabricate such applications, and ultimately to the bankers at the top of the pyramid dicing them up into complex securities which were then marketed as low-risk investments and sold throughout the world.[1] The cost of the global financial crisis of 2008–09 has been estimated at $12.8 trillion to the US economy alone.[2] The extent of fraud that has been uncovered and the scale of the damage done would lead some to believe that many should be held to account through the most serious sanctions the state has to hand, criminal prosecution. The reality, however, is that, in criminal terms at least, the financial institutions and persons responsible have not been held to account. This chapter will argue that there are a variety of reasons to explain this and will use new counter-theories such as de-labelling, deviancy attenuation and immoral phlegmatism as the lenses through which to explore these events.[3] This chapter will begin by briefly outlining moral panics, deviancy amplification and labelling, the theories these counter-theories are built upon, before using the example of

1 See, for example, National Commission on the Causes of the Financial and Economic Crisis in the United States (2011). *Financial Crisis Inquiry Report*, Seattle, WA: Pacific Publishing Studio (hereinafter 'National Commission'); N. Ferguson (2008) *The Ascent of Money*, London: Penguin.

2 Bloomberg Business (2012). Tallying the Full Cost of the Financial Crisis. Available at: http://www.bloomberg.com/news/articles/2012-09-14/tallying-the-full-cost-of-the-financial-crisis.

3 Button, M. and Tunley, M. (2015). Explaining fraud deviancy attenuation in the United Kingdom. *Crime, Law and Social Change*, 63, 49–64.

benefits fraud in the UK, which, it is argued, fits with many of these well-established theories. The chapter will then set out the counter-theories: de-labelling, deviancy attenuation and immoral phlegmatism, and then use the financial crisis of 2008 to explore them.

Moral panics, deviancy amplification and labelling

Before we explore some of the new counter-theories, let us first examine some of the theories these are built upon. Labelling theory, or the labelling 'perspective', as it is more commonly known, formed the basis of early social reaction theory and is an integral component of what is often referred to as the 'new deviancy theory', otherwise known as 'interactionist' theory.[4] Accordingly, labelling is an accepted criminological model by which certain behaviours and individuals become labelled respectively as crimes and criminals by the wider community, as well as by organisations and official institutions. Labelling theory therefore poses two specific questions: first, why do certain types of behaviour become labelled as deviant or criminal? Second, what are the effects of such a process on those who are labelled? The answer to the first question can be found within two concepts that have emerged out of labelling theory, these being moral panics and deviancy amplification, both of which will be discussed shortly. This has implications for those who are thus 'labelled', in terms of their future behaviours and the resources and the priority society and the legislature put in place to deal with them. Labelling is often associated with social problems such as drug-taking and juvenile delinquency, to name but two.[5] According to labelling theorists, the deviant is 'someone who has to be managed, and should be managed better by a bureaucratic apparatus of official care-takers'.[6] As will be evidenced later in this chapter, however, in relation to fraud, these official care-takers appear to be lacking when it comes to fulfilling this role. We will now explore moral panics, before moving on to examine deviancy and the concept of deviancy amplification.

Historically, media representations of crime often 'exaggerate certain risks'.[7] This style of media representation resulted in the development of the concept of a 'moral panic',[8] which occurs when 'a condition, episode, person or group of persons become defined as a threat to societal values and interests'.[9] The concept

4 See Rubington, E. and Weinberg, M. (eds) (1987). *Deviance: The Interactionist Perspective*. New York: Macmillan.

5 See Becker, H. (1963). *Outsiders: Studies in the Sociology of Deviance*. London: Macmillan; Wilkins, L. (1964). *Social Deviance: Social Policy, Action and Research*. London: Tavistock.

6 Gouldner, A. W. (1975). *For Sociology: Renewal and Critique in Sociology Today*. Harmondsworth: Pelican Books, at 38.

7 Newburn, T. (2007). *Criminology*. Cullompton, Devon: Willan, at 93.

8 See Cohen, S. (1972). *Folk Devils and Moral Panics: The Creation of the Mods and Rockers*. London: MacGibbon and Kee, at 8.

9 See Cohen, S. (1980). *Folk Devils and Moral Panics* (2nd edn). London: Martin Robertson, at 9.

of moral panics actually emerged as a result of research into deviance which adopted an interactionist approach.[10] These studies focused on the process by which particular groups, usually associated with youth culture, became labelled as a problem and were presented as such to the rest of society, and culminated in a spiral of over-reaction.[11] The research conducted paid particular attention to the role of the media, which from time to time created 'panics' about certain groups within the community that were considered to pose a threat to the remainder. As a consequence, labelling theory was 'recast into moral panic theory'.[12] Moral panics developed as a result of societal reaction to a perceived problem, which was influenced by a convergence of a number of forces concentrating on the young, including police targeting, media scaremongering, outcry from local communities and councillors, condemnation from politicians and, finally, criminalisation of deviance, which accordingly perpetuated the cycle. The media, however, was the main catalyst, frequently condemning the perceived threat that it had actually helped to create. Interestingly, according to Pearson,[13] examples of moral panics can be found as far back as the nineteenth century, where reference can be found to threats from youth cultures and comparisons with better times.

Deviance is something that is not accounted for by applied criminology and, in fact, may be considered to be wider than crime itself, manifesting itself as any form of behaviour that falls outside societal norms or conventional behaviour. The development of the term 'deviancy' was, in fact, an attempt to merge the process of criminalisation with the more indistinct process by which certain behaviours are afforded the nomenclature 'unconventional'. This notion is further developed within the conflict model of deviance, whereby there exist superordinates that create and enforce rules, and subordinates whose behaviour is subject to those rules.[14] Initially developed by Wilkins,[15] deviancy amplification takes the concept of moral panics one stage further, whereby the process of labelling certain groups as a threat or a problem actually results in either the creation of that problem or exacerbating what may, in reality, be a minor issue so that it becomes a problem that is far worse than it actually is. The concept of deviancy amplification

10 See Young, J. (1970). *The Drugtakers*. London: McGibbon and Kee; Cohen, above n. 8.

11 Murji, K. (2001). *Moral Panic*. In McLaughlin, E. and Muncie, J. (eds), *The Sage Dictionary of Criminology*. London: Sage.

12 See Young, J. (1998). Breaking windows: situating the new criminology. In Walton, P. and Young, J. (eds), *The New Criminology Revisited* (pp. 14–46). Basingstoke: Palgrave Macmillan, at 21.

13 Pearson, G. (1983). *Hooligan: A History of Respectable Fears*. Oxford: Blackwell.

14 See Horowitz, I. L. and Liebowitz, M. (1968). Social deviance and political marginality: towards a redefinition of the relation between sociology and politics. *Social Problems*, 15(3), 280–296 (at 282–283).

15 Wilkins, L. (1964). *Social Deviance: Social Policy, Action and Research*. London: Tavistock.

occurs therefore when an act that is believed to be deviant is considered worthy of attention and 'responded to punitively'.[16]

The case of benefits fraud in the UK

A good way to illustrate these concepts is to look at one of the few exceptions among frauds, that of benefits fraud. In contrast to the complacent and often ambivalent attitudes to most frauds, which will be illustrated shortly, there is one significant exception, this being benefits fraud. Politicians, the media and the public get very worked up over social security fraud.[17] It is the one type of fraud for which there is widespread disapproval, with aspirations and initiatives to do something about it.

The media and sensational reporting are central to moral panics, and for benefits fraud this is very important to the hype. The media frequently report on benefit cheats with 'luxurious lifestyles' funded by defrauding the system.[18] The tabloid newspaper *The Sun* has been very proactive in reporting this problem. In May 2013 it launched a campaign to 'beat the cheats', encouraging readers to contact them with information about suspected benefit cheats. Their campaign has yielded many spectacular cases which have been published in the papers in great detail, including a woman working as a pole dancer while claiming incapacity benefit for depression, a man claiming disability allowance while riding speedway motorbikes, and another running a window-cleaning business while claiming benefits related to an inability to go outside, to name some of the more extreme.

It is not just *The Sun* which campaigns on this issue; all the other tabloid press cover these cases, as do the 'quality' media outlets too, in part. BBC News, for example, regularly covers social security fraud cases, and the topic of benefits fraud also receives regular coverage on television programmes such as *Saints and Scroungers*[19] and *Benefits Street.*[20] Furthermore, in recent years media attention on

16 Cohen, S. (2002). *Folk Devils and Moral Panics* (30th anniversary edn). London: Routledge, at 8.

17 See, for example, Golding, P. and Middleton, S. (1982). *Images of Welfare.* Oxford: Martin Robertson; Golding, P. (1999). Thinking the unthinkable: welfare reform and the media. In Franklin, B. (ed.), *Social Policy, the Media and Misrepresentation* (pp. 146–159). London: Routledge; Connor, S. (2007). We're onto you: a critical examination of the Department for Work and Pensions' 'Targeting Benefit Fraud' campaign. *Critical Social Policy,* 27, 231–252; Grover, C. (2005). Advertising social security fraud. *Benefits,* 13, 199–205; Tunley, M. (2011). Need, greed or opportunity? An examination of who commits benefit fraud and why they do it. *Security Journal,* 24, 302–319.

18 See Golding, P. (1999). Thinking the unthinkable: welfare reform and the media. In Franklin, B. (ed.), *Social Policy, the Media and Misrepresentation* (pp. 146–159). London: Routledge.

19 See Gordon, M. (Executive Producer) and Littlewood, D. (Presenter) (2013). Jones/Stuart [Television series episode]. In Kreps, A. (Series Producer), *Saints and Scroungers.* London: BBC 2.

20 Love Productions (Series Producer) (2014). *Benefits Street.* [Television series]. Birmingham: Channel 4.

benefit fraud has begun to introduce the notion that it is the taxpayer's money that is being lost to fraud. For example, the *Daily Mail* reported on a 'benefit cheat' who had paid for a luxury Spanish holiday home 'with £66,000 of taxpayers' money'.[21] This shift in focus certainly achieves the desired effect of further exacerbating the moral panic through the suggestion of collective victimisation. This variety of media reporting on 'welfare cheats' can be contrasted with general fraud, where there is much less media interest. Frauds do get reported in the media, but they tend to focus upon staff frauds with some additional salacious factor, such as the money was used for gambling or prostitutes, or someone famous is linked to the story. This should be contrasted with the specialist media which Levi has noted does tend to cover fraud, but in a different way.[22]

The moral panic about benefit fraud is fuelled even further by the government's imbalanced approach, which is best illustrated by comparing the resources dedicated to fraud in general with those allocated to benefits fraud. Several academics have noted the different way social security fraud is dealt with compared with other offences.[23] The government has also been willing to invest in additional resources in the counter-fraud infrastructure for this problem, funding an additional 200 officers[24] at a time where numbers of policing personnel have generally been cut. Indeed, research conducted by Button, Blackbourn and Tunley illustrates that there were 2,708 counter-fraud staff employed by the Department for Work and Pensions to deal with this problem.[25] If those 2,708 staff were compared with the 43 police forces in England and Wales, that staff would be bigger than over a dozen police forces and far exceed the 1,061 police officers and civilian staff across all forces identified in the aforementioned research as being dedicated to all aspects of economic crime. It is interesting to then juxtapose these figures with the size of the problem, which for benefits fraud is also measured very accurately using statistically valid fraud loss measurement techniques. In 2013 the National Fraud Authority estimated the total identified

21 See *Daily Mail* (2014). Benefits cheat, 57, paid for luxury Spanish holiday home with £66,000 of taxpayers' money (and at £7.20 a week it'll take her 176 years to pay it back). Available at: http://www.dailymail.co.uk/news/article-2584159/Benefits-cheat-paid-luxury-Spanish-holiday-home-66-000-taxpayers-money.html (accessed 24 September 2015).

22 See Levi, M. (2006). The media construction of financial white-collar crimes. *British Journal of Criminology*, 46, 1037–1057.

23 See, for example, Doig, A. and Levi, M. (2009). Inter-agency work and the UK public sector investigation of fraud, 1996–2006: joined-up rhetoric and disjointed reality *Policing and Society*, 19(3), 199–215.

24 Cook, D. (1989). *Rich Law, Poor Law: Different Responses to Tax and Supplementary Benefit Fraud*. Oxford: Oxford University Press; Cook, D. (1997). Social divisions of welfare: tax and social security fraud. In Robertson, A. (ed.), *Unemployment, Social Security and the Social Division of Welfare: A Festschrift in Honour of Adrian Sinfield*. Edinburgh: University of Edinburgh; Dean, H. and Melrose, M. (1997). Manageable discord: fraud and resistance in the social security system. *Social Policy and Administration*, 31, 103–118.

25 Button, M., Blackbourn, D. and Tunley, M. (2015). 'The not so thin blue line after all?' Investigative resources dedicated to fighting fraud/economic crime in the United Kingdom. *Policing: A Journal of Policy and Practice*, 9(2), 129–142.

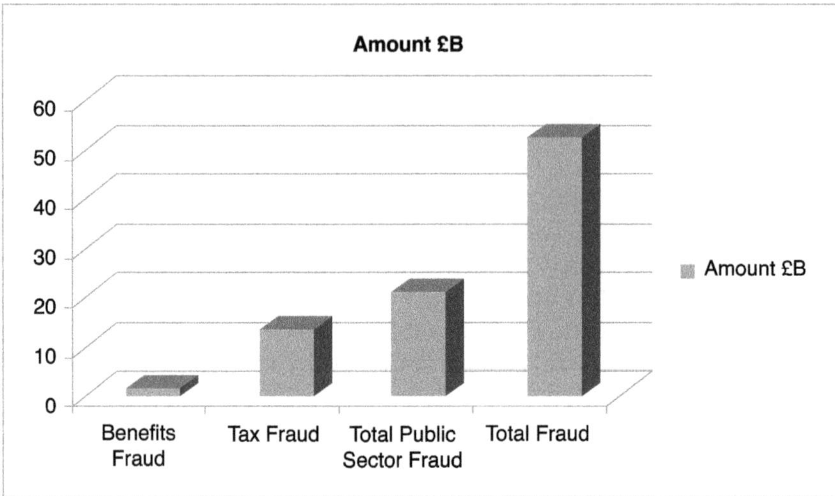

Figure 2.1 The cost of benefits fraud in the UK in comparison with others (adapted from National Fraud Authority (2013))

and hidden fraud in the UK amounted to £52 billion, with just under £21 billion in the public sector. In that scenario, benefits fraud amounts to £1.2 billion, with a further £670 million tax credit fraud. By comparison, tax fraud is estimated as a £14 billion problem[26] (see Figure 2.1). It could be suggested that benefit fraud is low because resources are devoted to investigating it, and should these be directed elsewhere, there is a likelihood that the figures would increase. However, it important to emphasise that devoting this amount of resources to benefit fraud is a political choice by government as the fraud they are going to squeeze, and presents yet another example of those in power seeking 'populism'.[27] It could also be suggested that this level of resource further evidences the Marxist view that it is a lower-class crime punished by the powerful. In further support of this assertion are the observations of Wood[28] that in addition to manipulating benefit statistics 'for media consumption – encouraging public hostility towards benefit scroungers', they even go so far as to use official government data bulletins, such as the one on how income tax was spent, 'to perpetuate the same myth'.

Furthermore, it is also worth noting that contrary to the moral panic perpetuated by the government and the media, latest statistics at the time of writing show that

26 See National Fraud Authority (2013). *Annual Fraud Indicator*. London: National Fraud Authority.

27 See Tunley, M. (2011). COUNTERBLAST: Another case of old wine in new bottles? The coalition's misguided strategy to reduce benefit fraud. *The Howard Journal of Criminal Justice*, 50(3), 314–317.

28 See Wood, C. (2014). Back to basics. *Public Finance*, December 2014, 35–37, at 36.

the number of people leaving the welfare system is higher than the number of new claims being received.[29] Consequently, this means a reduction in the overall welfare budget due to a decrease in the number of claims overall, which, in turn, arguably lessens the potential amount of fraud within the benefits system. Interestingly, at this point it is worth exploring the findings of an Ipsos MORI research project on public perceptions of welfare expenditure that further evidences the contention that there is a continuing public moral panic concerning benefit fraud.[30] The finding of note is that the public estimate that £24 out of every £100 spent on benefits is claimed fraudulently, whereas official estimates suggest it is closer to £0.70 in every £100 spent. This misconception and general lack of knowledge is understandable, as the print media frequently portrays benefit recipients as 'spongers' or 'scroungers' who are 'fiddling' the state.[31]

The antithesis of these concepts

Drawing upon the work of Button and Tunley,[32] this chapter will now develop the counter-theories that are the antithesis to labelling, moral panics and deviancy amplification. The section ends by using the financial crisis of 2008 and the build-up and response to it, to illustrate these theories.

De-labelling fraud

As discussed in the previous section, labelling is an acknowledged criminological concept by which certain behaviours and individuals become labelled respectively as crimes and criminals by the wider community and official institutions. For most volume crimes, definitions are fairly straightforward. There is a definition in statute or the common law of an offence, and offenders who perform such behaviours are prosecuted against those definitions through the criminal justice system. A simple legalistic view would be the mere fact that many of these deviant acts are not dealt with as criminal means they are not.[33] However, the reality is that for fraud it is a much more complex issue. There are behaviours committed by individuals and organisations which contain the basic foundations of the criminal act of fraud. However, those same acts are treated differently according to the victim and the enforcement body involved. It is common to find similar organisations dealing with similar occupational frauds in very different ways. Some might sack the employee only, some will do this and seek criminal prosecution, and some

29 See Department for Work and Pensions above, n. 17.

30 Ipsos MORI (2013). *Perceptions Are Not Reality: The Top Ten We Get Wrong*. Available at: https://www.ipsos-mori.com/researchpublications/researcharchive/3188/Perceptions-are-not-reality.aspx (accessed 24 September 2015).

31 See Baillie, R. (2011). An examination of public discourse on benefit claimants in the media. *Journal of Poverty and Social Justice*, 19(1), 67–70.

32 See Button and Tunley above, n. 3.

33 See Slapper, G. and Tombs, S. (1999). *Corporate Crime*. Harlow: Pearson Education Limited.

will do both of these and also pursue civil or regulatory sanctions. Frequently, for those who are sacked only, it will not be for fraud, but for 'not following procedures', 'misconduct', 'breach of contract', etc.[34]

In England and Wales a criminal definition of the offence is set out under the Fraud Act 2006 (among many other fraud-related offences). However, unlike the other volume criminal offences, the use of criminal definitions and the criminal justice system represent the tip of the iceberg. There are many more options for pursuing sanctions for fraudulent behaviours through a 'fraud justice network', involving the civil law, regulatory sanctions and private mechanisms, which create their own nomenclature, where the word 'fraud' is often removed.[35] Arguably, the creation of so many non-criminal alternatives could be linked to the ability of the powerful to influence the response to crimes which may affect them. There are also a number of justice and regulatory routes for dealing with fraud which apply other labels. The deceptive behaviours which fall under fraud are therefore much more elastic in what they can be defined as. Consequently, behaviours, prima facie for most, would be considered as the criminal act of fraud. If resources and commitment were available people could be pursued in the criminal justice system, often become defined as something else and dealt with through different structures. Fraud is therefore a crime, which is frequently de-labelled.

Immoral phlegmatism

As discussed earlier in the chapter, the term 'moral panic' is frequently used in criminology and wider circles to describe the response to certain types of deviance, which is a threat to social values, out of proportion to the reality of the problem, culminating in a spiral of over-reaction.[36] This chapter will argue that there is an antithesis and it can be found with most fraud offences, bar the exception of benefits fraud already discussed. This concept is defined as 'immoral phlegmatism',[37] which is a large social problem, but for which the response to deal with it is disproportionately low, and that lack of an appropriate response can be considered immoral – it is important to stress the immoral aspect. Speeding could be seen as another major problem, about which much more could be done, such as increasing the numbers of speed cameras and police officers patrolling. However, for most, someone getting away with speeding would not be considered immoral,

34 See Button, M., Blackbourn, D., Lewis, C. and Shepherd, D. (2015). Uncovering the hidden cost of staff fraud: an assessment of 45 cases in the UK. *Journal of Financial Crime*, 22(2), 170–183.

35 See Levi, M. (1987). *Regulating Fraud: White Collar Crime and the Criminal Process.* London: Routledge; Button, M., Tapley, J. and Lewis, C. (2013). The 'fraud justice network' and the infra-structure of support for individual fraud victims in England and Wales. *Criminology and Criminal Justice,* 13, 37–61.

36 See Tunley, M. J. (2015). Mandating the measurement of public sector fraud. *Public Sector Digest*, 26–33; Murji above, n. 11.

37 And Button and Tunley above, n. 3.

compared with fraud, where someone getting away with defrauding a person or organisation would be.[38]

To develop this immoral aspect further, not tackling fraud with an appropriate-level response could be considered immoral for a number of reasons. First, fraud in most cases is stealing money or resources through deception. Second, frauds against organisations ultimately impact upon society; for example, frauds against insurers lead to higher premiums and frauds against the government lead to inadequate public services and/or higher taxes. Third, frauds can have a devastating impact upon wider society, as will be illustrated later in the chapter. Finally, frauds are more associated with higher-status individuals, and applying different standards to frauds, compared with other volume crimes usually associated with persons of lower social status, is unfair.

It could be argued, as it is by many writers on white collar crime, that one of the reasons for the lower priority given to fraud is business interests seeking to minimise the risk of possible sharp-practice undertaken by themselves, and that it is restricted to state 'regulatory' enforcement, rather than 'criminal' enforcement.[39] Such arguments are plausible for crimes and fraud perpetrated by corporate bodies, of which there is much evidence.[40] However, corporate bodies are victims of fraud too and lose out substantially in financial terms and in the lack of interest of state institutions. Immoral phlegmatism is therefore manifested in the following key ways:

- lack of interest of leaders in the problem;
- lack of accurate measurement of the problem;
- lack of resources dedicated to the problem; and
- lack of punishment of those committing such acts.

Deviancy attenuation

The consequences of de-labelling and immoral phlegmatism is a process of deviancy attenuation, whereby a big problem is attenuated to become a small problem. If we commence at 'one pm on the clock' on Figure 2.2, the process begins with the narrowing of behaviours defined as the crime of fraud. Added to this is a lack of accurate measurement, leading to performance statistics at national, industry and organisational levels which do not show fraud as a problem. This

38 See Association of British Insurers (2003). *What Is Dishonest?* Available at: http://www.abi.org.uk /Publications/24810.pdf (accessed 26 November 2007); Karstedt, S. and Farrall, S. (2006). The moral economy of everyday life. *British Journal of Criminology*, 46(6), 1011–1036.

39 See Levi above, n. 35.

40 See Braithwaite, J. (1989). *Crime, Shame and Integration*. Cambridge: Cambridge University Press; Tombs, S. and Whyte, D. (2007). *Safety Crimes*. Cullompton, Devon: Willan; Barak, G. (2012). *Theft of a Nation: Wall Street Looting and Federal Regulatory Colluding*. Lanham, MD: Rowman and Littlefield.

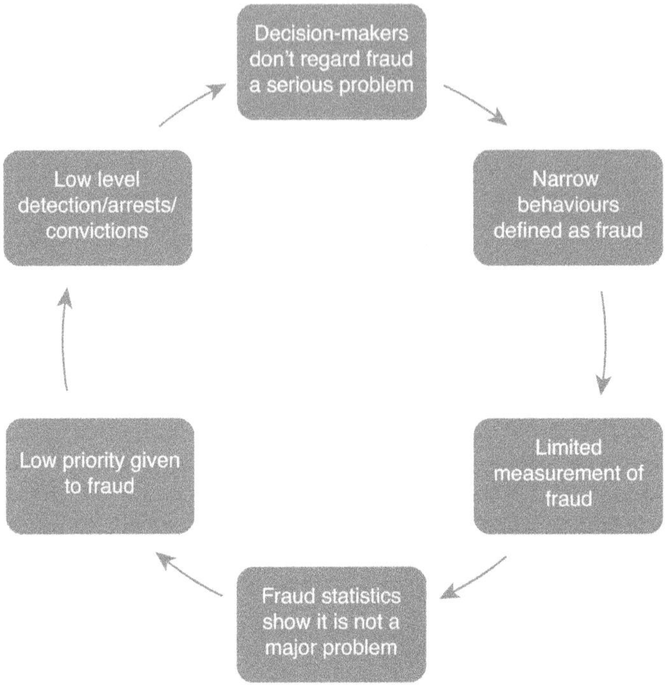

Figure 2.2 Deviancy attenuation

leads to a low priority given to fraud which culminates in fewer resources dedicated to it, thus less fraud is detected and reported, reinforcing to decision-makers that fraud is no longer a problem.

The financial crash of 2008 through the lens of the counter-theories

This chapter will now explore these counter-theories by considering the financial crisis of 2008. The first important thing to note is that the financial crisis had a very large impact and caused significant problems. The cost of this resultant global financial crisis in the US alone has been estimated at $12.8 trillion.[41] Other research has suggested a loss of just under 1% of GDP for many countries.[42] This

41 See Bloomberg Business (2012). Tallying the Full Cost of the Financial Crisis. Available at: http://www.bloomberg.com/news/articles/2012-09-14/tallying-the-full-cost-of-the-financial-crisis.

42 See Deutsche Bank Research (2010). *The Direct Financial Cost of the Fiscal Crisis*. Frankfurt: Deutsche Bank Research.

US crisis has had an international impact,[43] being described by Morris as 'the first big boulder in an avalanche of asset write-downs'.[44] It has also been felt by the wider society, with millions of Americans being in danger of losing their homes,[45] metropolitan areas experiencing higher unemployment rates,[46] and many households experiencing a decline in net wealth combined with reduced access to credit.[47] The size and impact of the crisis is not in doubt.

Central to deviancy attenuation is a large problem, which is diminished to a smaller problem. Nobody doubts the size of the problems caused by the financial crash. The important point to note in terms of the counter-theories is the contribution of fraud to the crisis. Fraud played a significant part in the cause of the crisis, but for a variety of reasons that fraud was attenuated through a variety of processes and only became a more important issue once the crisis unfolded. Even then the response has not been commensurate with the size of the problem.

Let us begin the analysis by exploring what went wrong. The National Commission states:

> We conclude this financial crisis was avoidable. The crisis was the result of human action and inaction, not of Mother Nature or computer models gone haywire. The report catalogues the rising incidence of mortgage fraud, which flourished in an environment of collapsing lending standards and lax regulation. As irresponsible lending, including predatory and fraudulent practices, became more prevalent, the Federal Reserve and other regulators and authorities heard warnings from many quarters.[48]

According to Pontell *et al.*, 'the global meltdown that began in 2008 was influenced by a number of factors, including flawed financial policies, law breaking, greed, irresponsibility, and not an inconsiderable amount of concerted ignorance and outright stupidity'.[49] The sub-prime mortgage sector in the USA has been considered to be a significant contributor to the crisis and much of this can be attributed to fraud. From brokers exaggerating their clients' prospects, to ultimately a system of mortgages which was certainly built upon negligence, if not a great deal of fraud, this all culminated to creating a growth in mortgages,

43 Friedman, H. H., Friedman, L. W. and Kass-Shraibman, F. (2008). Ethical Imperatives of CEOs: creating the virtuous corporation. *Journal of Business Systems, Governance and Ethics*, 3(4), 31–42, at 31.

44 See Morris, C. R. (2008). *The Trillion Dollar Meltdown*. New York: Public Affairs.

45 Ibid.

46 See National Commission above, n. 1, at 23.

47 Ibid., at 391.

48 See National Commission above, n. 1, at xv–xx.

49 See Pontell, H. N., Black, W. K. and Geis, G. (2014). Too big to fail, too powerful to jail? On the absence of criminal prosecutions after the 2008 financial meltdown. *Crime, Law and Social Change*, 61(1) 1–13, at 1.

which were doomed to default.[50] Nguyen and Pontell suggest that this sub-prime mortgage crisis was

> a real estate and financial disaster marked by an unprecedented rate of mortgage delinquencies and foreclosures brought on by factors that include lax lending policies, poor underwriting standards, inadequate regulatory structure, and government oversight – entails significant amount of fraud at various institutional levels.[51]

Investigations conducted by the FBI support this contention, their findings identifying that there was a significant amount of lending fraud involved, and mortgages based on fraudulent misrepresentations about the financial status of borrowers, which included overstating income and/or assets, based upon false or counterfeit employment records or exaggerating property values.[52]

At the next level up, the toxic mix of mortgages were then bundled together with other financial products of varying risk and sold as low-risk financial products. There was clearly evidence that some of those doing the dicing, slicing and mixing knew what they were up to. As Eisinger (2013) noted:

> On March 16, 2007, Morgan Stanley employees working on one of the toxic assets that helped blow up the world economy discussed what to name it. Among the team members' suggestions: 'Subprime Meltdown,' 'Hitman,' 'Nuclear Holocaust,' 'Mike Tyson's Punchout,' and the simple-yet-direct: 'Shitbag.' Ha ha. Those hilarious investment bankers. Then they gave it its real name and sold it to a Chinese bank.[53]

The National Commission on the Causes of the Financial and Economic Crisis in the United States clearly demonstrated there was much concern in organisations at the scale of the fraud problem.[54] However, those decision-makers in a position of power to define the response failed to act, even though signs of the coming crisis were there several years before its impact. News reports suggested that mortgage fraud was an increasing problem and a news conference held by a senior FBI investigator claimed that mortgage fraud had the potential for an 'epidemic'. Yet former US Attorney General, Alberto Gonzales,

50 See National Commission above, n. 1; Ferguson above, n. 1.

51 See Nguyen, T. H. and Pontell, H. N. (2010). Mortgage origination fraud and the global economic crisis. *Criminology and Public Policy*, 9(3), 591–612.

52 See Federal Bureau of Investigation (2008). *2007 Mortgage Fraud Report.* Available at: https://www.fbi.gov/stats-services/publications/mortgage-fraud-2008 (accessed 24 September 2015).

53 See Eisiner, J. (2013) Explosive Charge: Morgan Stanley Peddled Security Its Own Employee Called 'Nuclear Holocaust'. Available at: https://www.propublica.org/thetrade/item/explosive-charge-morgan-stanley-peddled-security-its-own-employee-called-nu (accessed 22 March 2016).

54 See National Commission above, n. 1.

> who served from February 2005 to 2007, told the FCIC he could not remember the press conferences or news reports about mortgage fraud. Both Gonzales and his successor Michael Mukasey, who served as attorney general in 2007 and 2008, told the FCIC that mortgage fraud had never been communicated to them as a top priority. 'National security . . . was an overriding' concern, Mukasey said.[55]

Indeed, the Commission also discovered that those who did note what was happening and tried to address the issue did not fare well. For example,

> the former head of Ameriquest's Mortgage Fraud Investigations Department told the Commission that he detected fraud at the company within one month of starting his job there in January 2003, but senior management did nothing with the reports he sent. He heard that other departments were complaining he 'looked too much' into the loans. In November 2005 he was downgraded from 'manager' to 'supervisor,' and was laid off in May 2006.[56]

In another comment in relation to federal enforcement officials the Commission noted:

> Fed officials seemed impervious to what the consumer advocates were saying. The Fed governors politely listened and said little, she recalled. 'They had their economic models, and their economic models did not see this coming,' she said. 'We kept getting back, "This is all anecdotal"'.'[57]

Another important dimension to note is the lack of accurate measurement of fraud in this sector. One of the most accurate means to measure fraud is through fraud loss measurement. Under this approach a set of similar transactions are subject to a random sample, which are then investigated to determine whether they are fraudulent, errors or acceptable. From this sample it is then possible to extrapolate within a statistical range and level of confidence the level of fraud and error. In the USA the federal government mandates such approaches in a wide variety of areas of federal expenditure under the federal improper payments legislation.[58] Such approaches have not been mandated for the financial services sector, nor have such institutions sought to use such methods. There has therefore been very little accurate measure of fraud in this sector, other than detected levels of fraud. And detected levels of fraud are flawed because they are

55 Ibid., at 15.

56 See National Commission above, n. 1, at 12.

57 Ibid., at 16.

58 See Tunley, M. (2014). *Mandating the Measurement of Fraud: Legislating Against Loss.* Basingstoke: Palgrave Macmillan; Tunley, M. J. (2015). Mandating the measurement of public sector fraud. *Public Sector Digest*, 26–33.

ultimately linked to the effort of an organisation to uncover and detect fraud. Large organisations can therefore seek to expose or reduce levels of fraud.

The picture so far demonstrates a number of these counter-theories at work. First, the above discussion has shown there were warning signs, despite the lack of accurate measurement, of major problems brewing in the sub-prime mortgage sector. However, there was evidence that senior managers in the financial institutions, the regulators and law enforcement did little to take these warnings seriously. There was therefore clearly a degree of phlegmatism at work among these decision-makers. The lack of accurate measurement also contributed to a lack of understanding of the true size of the problem. Further actions such as the dismissal of staff who were 'looking too much', as cited above, served to further undermine the potential to identify the scale of the problem. All of this combined to attenuate what was a large problem of fraud to a small one.

These processes have still been prevalent in the response to the financial crisis after 2008, with the de-labelling of this crisis from criminal to regulatory. As noted above, there is little doubt that fraud played a major part in contributing to the crisis. Fraud is a criminal act under various statutes in the USA, as in many other countries. Fraud, however, can also be dealt with – and is – by regulatory means outside the criminal justice system. Often when it is dealt with by such non-criminal means, the act is relabelled. Table 2.1 below from the US Securities and Exchange Commission (SEC) details the actions that have been taken up to January 2016 in response to the behaviours by many individuals and organisations at the centre of the crisis.

It is also interesting to note that many of the regulatory actions noted by the SEC use a lexicon dominated by terms such as 'misleading investors', 'filing mis-stated financial reports', 'making faulty disclosures', 'compromising independent judgement', 'using dummy assets', 'maintaining inaccurate books and records', and so on. Morgan Stanley, which was noted above, was charged under Section 17 of the Securities Act 1933, which covers 'Fraudulent Interstate Transactions'. The bank agreed to pay $275 million, without admitting or denying the allegation. The press release issued by the SEC is entitled 'Morgan Stanley to Pay $275 Million for Misleading Investors in Subprime RMBS Offerings' and contains no mention of the word 'fraud'.[59] The SEC has used the word 'fraud' in some of its actions. However, what have been missing are criminal convictions for fraud.

There has only been one criminal prosecution in the US resulting in imprisonment – for Kareem Serageldin, a senior trader at Credit Suisse, who in 2014 was given a 30-month sentence for 'inflating the value of mortgage bonds in his trading portfolio, allowing them to appear more valuable than they

59 See SEC (2014). Morgan Stanley to Pay $275 Million for Misleading Investors in Subprime RMBS Offerings. Available at: http://www.sec.gov/News/PressRelease/Detail/PressRelease/1370542355594.

really were' (two of his subordinates also pleaded guilty).[60] As Table 2.1 below notes, the SEC has pursued many actions, but the bulk of these have been regulatory and voluntary settlements based upon large financial settlements with financial institutions. The statute of limitations for fraud cases in the financial sector in the USA is five years, which in 2013 led one news outlet to run the headlines 'The Untouchables' and 'As Deadlines Loom for Financial Crisis Cases, Prosecutors Weigh Their Options'.[61] The reasons for the lack of criminal prosecutions can be linked to a number of factors, such as the difficulty of proving such offences against alleged perpetrators who can draw upon high-quality legal defence teams; the reduction in law enforcement resources such as in the FBI (where staff were redeployed to counter terrorism); and, of course, the focus upon high-value settlements with the financial institutions, which yield substantial payments and are easier to achieve than a criminal prosecution. The latter is a very persuasive argument, but it does yield significant consequences beyond the financial services sector. For if a banker can get away with behaviours that many would regard as fraud, which involve substantial sums of money, and this de-labelling of fraud is juxtaposed with the poor social security claimant, who misleads the government to secure a relatively small extra income, is caught, prosecuted in the criminal courts and sent to jail, a fundamental injustice in society is exposed. If we were to use Rawls' very useful veil of ignorance and strip the actors and acts of all distinguishing marks, we are essentially dealing with people who are submitting misleading information to secure a payment.[62] Yet one is treated as a criminal and the other through regulatory action.

Table 2.1 Actions by the SEC after the 2008 financial crisis up to 13 January 2016[63]

Actions	*Numbers*
Number of entities and individuals charged	198
Number of CEOs, CFOs and other corporate officers charged	89
Number of individuals who have received officer and director bars, industry bars or commission suspensions	53
Penalties ordered or agreed to	>$1.93 billion
Disgorgement and prejudgement interest ordered and agreed to	>$1.47 billion
Additional monetary relief obtained by harmed investors	$418 million
Total penalties, disgorgement and other monetary relief	>$3.76 billion

60 See Cohan, W. D. (2015). How Wall Street's bankers stayed out of jail. *The Atlantic*, September. Available at: http://www.theatlantic.com/magazine/archive/2015/09/how-wall-streets-bankers-stayed-out-of-jail/399368 (accessed 24 September 2015).

61 PBS (2013). As Deadlines Loom for Financial Crisis Cases, Prosecutors Weigh Their Options. Available at: http://www.pbs.org/wgbh/frontline/article/as-deadlines-loom-for-financial-crisis-cases-prosecutors-weigh-their-options.

62 Rawls, J. (1971). *A Theory of Justice*. Cambridge, MA: Harvard University Press.

63 SEC (2016). SEC Enforcement Actions. Available at: http://www.sec.gov/spotlight/enf-actions-fc.shtml.

Conclusion

This chapter began by outlining the criminological theories of labelling, moral panics and deviancy amplification, upon which the counter-theories introduced are based. We then moved on to offer the example of benefits fraud in the UK and argued that this is the exception to the manner in which fraud is both viewed and dealt with generally and thus presents a case study offering empirical evidence of the three aforementioned criminological theories. Specifically, media reporting of the fraud typology has created a moral panic which, in turn, has fuelled amplification of the perceived problem, the end result being that all benefit claimants are labelled as potential fraudsters.

The chapter then introduced the counter-theories which we have developed, commencing with the process of de-labelling, which leads to frauds not only being defined as something not criminal, but also called by other names. The chapter has also shown that there is an immoral phlegmatism dominant among those in positions of power at a national and organisational level. It has shown that fraud is not accurately measured and that the resources dedicated to dealing with it are not commensurate with the size of the problem. All of these processes combine to attenuate the problem of fraud, leading to a circle of attenuation.

The financial crash of 2008 was then viewed through the lens of the counter-theories previously discussed in the chapter. In reviewing the information that was available, the chapter identified the significant part played by fraud, in particular sub-prime mortgage fraud, as a root cause of the financial crisis. We then moved on to offer empirical evidence that the response to the crisis, and more importantly the role played by fraudulent transactions facilitated by irresponsible brokers, has not been commensurate with the size of the problem, thus offering empirical evidence of the counter-theories developed within this chapter.

3 The importance of whistle-blowers in uncovering financial misconduct in Potemkin villages[1]

Alison Lui

3.1 Introduction

Regulating financial markets can be justified by four reasons according to the World Bank Global Financial Development Report.[2] These are; anti-competitive behaviour, market misconduct, information asymmetries and systemic instability. The cost of financial misconduct is significant. Since 2009, UK banks have paid almost £30 billion in fines and redress costs.[3] This amount is approximately the level of capital that UK banks raised during 2009–2015. Financial misconduct includes misselling payment protection insurance, manipulating the London Inter Bank Lending Rate (LIBOR) and failing to observe money-laundering rules.[4] The costs are likely to increase. In November 2014, the UK Supreme Court ruled in *Plevin v Paragon Personal Finance Ltd* that non-disclosure of a big commission on a payment protection insurance policy rendered the relationship between the lender and customer unfair.[5] The Financial Conduct Authority (FCA) is therefore considering whether it should implement more guidance and/or rules to deal with complaints regarding payment protection insurance. Further, several overseas regulators are investigating some UK banks. Following a $2 billion settlement between nine global banks and investors in America in August 2015 for alleged manipulation of the foreign exchange rate, UK banks are preparing themselves for similar civil claims from investors.[6] It is therefore understandable that we need regulation to minimise market misconduct, to ensure that participants act with

1 Potemkin village: an impressive facade designed to mask undesirable facts and conditions.
2 The World Bank (2013). *Global Financial Development Report 2013*. Washington, DC: The World Bank.
3 The Bank of England (2015). *Financial Stability Report*. London: The Bank of England, p. 37.
4 For a more detailed discussion, see: Ryder, N. (2014). *The Financial Crisis and White Collar Crime: The Perfect Storm?* Cheltenham: Edward Elgar.
5 [2014] UKSC 61, Supreme Court.
6 Dunkley, E. and Fortado, L. (2015). Banks braced for billions in civil claims over forex rate rigging. *Financial Times*, 17 August. Available at: https://next.ft.com/content/3b19f516-44e2-11e5-af2f-4d6e0e5eda22 (accessed 2 August 2016).

integrity and that consumers have adequate and relevant information to make informed decisions.[7]

The lack of timely information received by consumers is a key factor of information asymmetry. Information asymmetry in financial markets is due to the complexity and opaqueness of financial products and processes such as securitisation.[8] The traditional problems resulting from information asymmetry in securitisation are adverse selection and moral hazard. Securitisation exacerbates the problem of adverse selection due to the principal–agent problems. Adverse selection takes place when the original lender has more information on the borrower's credit history than the parties in securitisation and so the latter find it very difficult to differentiate between the qualities of products. Under the traditional 'originate-to-hold' model, banks have access to information on the borrower's credit history, so they can pick and choose customers. In the 'originate-to-distribute' model, however, the transfer of ownership from the originator to a special purpose vehicle means that banks have less incentive to screen customers. This encourages originators to take on more bad loans from the beginning under the 'originate-to-distribute' model because they can pass them along the chain. Stiglitz and Weiss highlighted the twin issues of moral hazard and adverse selection in the credit and insurance markets.[9] In particular, the issue of information and price hurdles faced by some customers is interesting. In the financial sector, information problems facing consumers include: 'product complexity, unknown quality, opaque pricing, and complex disclosures and financial illiteracy'.[10] However, these limitations are further aggravated when financial institutions do not disclose sufficient information to customers about complex financial products. Unless lenders explain financial products to customers in a simple manner, disclosure per se would not entirely assist.[11]

In the period before the most recent financial crisis, some customers signed contracts without fully understanding them because they felt that they did not have many options.[12] This is mainly due to the problem of access to the financial market, which has not been equal in some cases as a result of higher prices charged to customers with lower salaries. There is evidence in the UK that customers with lower salaries have to pay more for banking services and products because of

7 The World Bank (2014). *Global Financial Development Report 2014.* Washington, DC: The World Bank.

8 Dewing, I. and P. Russell (2014). Whistleblowing, governance and regulation before the financial crisis: the case of HBOS. *Journal of Business Ethics.* DOI: 10.1007/s10551-014-2407-1.

9 Stiglitz, J. and Weiss, A. (1981). Credit rationing in markets with imperfect information. *American Economic Review* 71: 393–410.

10 Lumpkin, S. (2010). Consumer protection and financial innovation: a few basic propositions. *OECD Financial Market Trends* 1: 1–23.

11 Brennan, L., Zevallos, Z. and Binney, W. (2011). Vulnerable consumers and debt: can social marketing assist? *Australasian Marketing Journal* 19(3): 203–211.

12 Wilson, T., Howell, N. and Sheehan, G. (2009). Protecting the most vulnerable in consumer credit transactions. *Journal of Consumer Policy* 32(3): 117–140.

restricted access to credit due to lower credit scores.[13] This 'poverty premium' phenomenon will be demonstrated later in the account of Ian Taplin, who worked for Lloyds TSB. There is also a poor understanding of capital risks among some customers because of a change in financial products.[14]

In this chapter, the author uses a combination of the doctrinal approach and interview data. The interview data is from two former employees of HBOS and Lloyds TSB. The first interviewee is Paul Moore, the former Head of Regulatory Risk at HBOS (2002–2004). The second is Ian Taplin, a former employee in the Wealth and Private Bank of Lloyds TSB (2005–2010). The author will demonstrate that banks such as HBOS and Lloyds TSB did not pay sufficient attention to consumer protection. The pursuit of profits by such banks prevailed over consumer protection. Although legislation and FSA guidelines prior to the financial crisis of 2007–2009 highlighted the importance of consumer protection, it will be demonstrated that they were insufficient. Subsequent reforms in the law have improved protection given to whistle-blowers in the financial industry but corporate governance is still the driving force behind change in the culture of organisations. Whistle-blowers can play an important role in improving corporate governance due to the information asymmetry problem in the financial sector. Whistle-blowers did not prevent the scandals linked to the financial crisis of 2007–2009,[15] but they have contributed towards more regulatory intervention as a result of exposing weaknesses in corporate governance and regulation.[16] They thus play important roles in uncovering financial misconduct in Potemkin villages.

3.2 Lack of consumer protection at HBOS

HBOS was formed in 2001 when Halifax Plc and the Governor and Company of the Bank of Scotland merged. At the end of 2006, HBOS was the fourth-largest UK bank in terms of assets.[17] According to the 2007 HBOS Annual Report, it held 20% of the mortgage market and 16% of the savings market.[18] Like many other banks, HBOS experienced rapid growth between 2003 and 2008. However, its debt increased from £112 billion in 2003 to £231 billion in 2007 and total

13 The European Commission (2016). *Consumer Vulnerability Across Key Markets in the European Union – Final Report.* Brussels: The European Commission.

14 See Dewing and Russell above, n. 8; Taplin, I. (2014). Banking Standards – written evidence from Ian Taplin. Available at: http://www.publications.parliament.uk/pa/jt201314/jtselect/jtpcbs/27/27v_we40.htm (accessed 8 June 2016).

15 See Posner, R. (2010). *The Crisis of Capitalist Democracy.* Cambridge, MA: Harvard University Press; Stiglitz, J. (2010). *Freefall: America, Free Markets, and the Sinking of the World Economy.* New York; Norton.

16 Ibid. See also: National Commission on the Causes of the Financial and Economic Crisis in the United States (2011). *The Financial Crisis Inquiry Report.* New York: Public Affairs.

17 Milne, A. and Wood, G. (2008). Shattered on the rock? British financial stability from 1866 to 2007. Paper presented at the conference in honour of Ted Balbach, Federal Reserve Bank of St Louis, 3 March.

18 HBOS Plc (2007). *Annual Report and Accounts 2007.* London.

assets increased from £408 billion in 2003 to £667 billion in 2007. Rapid growth came at a cost, since a sales culture prevailed over HBOS. HBOS was regulated by the Financial Services Authority (FSA) prior to the financial crisis of 2007–2009. Consumer protection was a regulatory objective of the FSA, the predecessor of the Financial Conduct Authority (FCA). The objective of consumer protection in the Financial Services and Markets Act 2000 (FSMA 2000) conflicted with the principles of the FSA facilitating financial innovation and competition.[19] The use of innovative, securitised products combined with a risky business model and sales culture at HBOS and Lloyds TSB illustrates that customers were treated as products and not individuals. Using HBOS and Lloyds TSB as examples, this chapter will demonstrate that these banks have breached Principles for Businesses under high-level standards of the FSA Handbook and Principle 6 of the FSA's Treating Customers Fairly Initiative. Further, it will be seen that poor corporate governance defeated the statutory duties of a whistle-blower, namely Paul Moore, in his communication with the FSA regarding the sales culture of HBOS.

Despite the objective of consumer protection being enshrined in UK legislation and FSA handbooks, HBOS's customers suffered because of its prevalent sales culture (Moore 2010).[20] Ellis and Taylor provide an interesting account of the culture at HBOS from Margaret Taylor, an ex-employee of HBOS who is also a political activist.[21] Taylor has three reasons for why HBOS went wrong. First, the incentive structure has changed from a simple pay package to individualised, performance-driven pay. Second, deregulation in the 1980s encouraged retail organisations to expand into banking. This led to a more sales-driven approach in banking and increased emphasis on marketing. Gardener and Howcroft concur with this view.[22] In their paper, they conducted a case study into the evolution of retail banking in the UK. They found that since the mid-1970s, banks have become more market-orientated. Promotion and marketing became more important.[23] Finally, technological advances had replaced human labour.[24] Paul Moore, the former Head of Regulatory Risk at HBOS between 2002 and 2005, described HBOS staff as 'being forced to sell things; sell credit; sell mortgages; sell insurance products that were simply not in the best interests of the customer'. The Head of Risk in the division said to Moore that 'they [HBOS directors] pay no attention to risk management here at all. The only thing that counts is sales

19 For a general discussion of the statutory objectives of the FSA, see: Ryder, N. (2001). Two plus two equals financial education – the Financial Services Authority and consumer education. *The Law Teacher*, 35(2): 216–32,

20 BBC News (2009). 'HBOS whistle-blower statement', 10 February. Available at: http://news.bbc.co.uk/1/hi/uk_politics/7882581.stm (accessed 5 August 2016).

21 Ellis, V. and Taylor, M. (2010). Banks, bailouts and bonuses: a personal account of working in Halifax Bank of Scotland during the financial crisis. *Work Employment Society* 24: 803–813.

22 Gardener, E. and Howcroft, J. (1999). The new retail banking revolution. *The Service Industries Journal* 19(2): 83–100.

23 Ibid.

24 See Ellis and Taylor above, n. 21.

and you know, they are animals around here.'[25] From 2004, there was evidence that at HBOS 'leadership and focus on risk matters has had no priority'; 'sales were regarded as more important than anything else' and 'risk was not seen as a core business imperative or competency'.[26]

Wisskirchen *et al.* support the argument that HBOS pursued a sales policy. Their main submission is that many retail banks adopted an innovative and short-term sales approach to attract new customers, since it was more difficult to achieve the same effect through long-term growth and profitability.[27] They mentioned, in particular, the innovative approach that HBOS adopted. In order to compete with the other major UK retail banks, HBOS advertised heavily their simple yet innovative products. An example is an interest-bearing current account, which paid more interest on deposits than any other account on the market at that time. HBOS trained all its customer assistants in helping new customers to transfer their bank details and accounts. HBOS then rewarded the assistants who achieved their sales targets.[28] HBOS managed to increase its overall share of current accounts from 9% to 14% between 2002 and 2006.[29] Wisskirchen *et al.* revealed that most retail banks are aware that developing a strong customer relationship is very important.[30] The authors used a study in 2004 by Bain & Company which showed that UK banks performed worst in customer relationships. There is therefore a significant area for improvement in this field. Although Wisskirchen *et al.*[31] provide a more sympathetic view of HBOS's sales policy than Paul Moore does, the fact that customer assistants are rewarded for hitting their sales targets corresponds with Ellis and Taylor's submission that individualised, performance-driven pay is one of the reasons why HBOS failed.[32]

3.3 HBOS – Paul Moore's whistle-blowing journey

Paul Moore tried to raise concerns about HBOS's sales culture, but a major weakness at HBOS was the reluctance of certain directors and the Group Audit Committee to cooperate with him. As the Head of Regulatory Risk, Moore was responsible for reviewing corporate bond fund sales and the sales culture at HBOS. With the former, key staff in the regulated insurance products and investments team did not want the review to go ahead.[33] Moore found it very

25 Moore, P. (2009). *Memorandum of Additional Evidence to the House of Commons Treasury Select Committee Relating to the Banking Crisis.* House of Commons Treasury Committee. UK, s.n.

26 Ibid.

27 Wisskirchen, C., Vater, D., Wright, T., De Backer, P. and Detrick, C. (2006). The customer-led bank: converting customers from defectors into fans. *Strategy & Leadership* 34(2): 10–20.

28 Ibid.

29 Ibid., n 26.

30 Ibid.

31 Ibid., n 26.

32 See Ellis and Taylor above, n. 21.

33 See Dewing and Russell above, n. 8.

difficult to carry out his role and to raise his concerns within the formal channels of HBOS. Increasingly anxious about the customers' lack of understanding of the capital risks tied to corporate bond funds, Moore wanted to undertake a review into corporate bond fund sales. Corporate bond funds were sold to customers at HBOS when the yield rates decreased on their standard deposit accounts. Moore did not have the support of the Chief Financial Officer and, at times, his team was 'threatened' when they carried out the review.[34]

Undertaking the sales culture review proved to be more straightforward because reviewing the sales culture was not an issue. Reporting the findings to the directors, the Group Audit Committee and the board, however, was an issue. Moore was strongly reprimanded by Mike Ellis for

> tabling at a Group Audit Committee meeting the full version of a critical report by my department making it clear that the systems and controls, risk management and compliance were inadequate in the Halifax to control its 'over-eager' sales culture.[35]

Moore merely performed his job as the Head of Regulatory Risk. He was aware of his duties as an 'approved person' under section 59 of FSMA 2000 to perform 'controlled functions'. The 'approved person' regime imposes a *duty* on Moore to blow the whistle internally and also externally to the FSA (Statement of Principle 4). This is in contrast to the less onerous concept under the Public Interest Disclosure Act 1998, where Moore had the *option* to make a protected disclosure.

Moore[36] argued that he tried to blow the whistle externally after he was notified that he would be made redundant. The matter concerned the appointment of Jo Dawson as his successor. An interesting choice, thought Moore,[37] since Dawson had never been a risk manager before. The Chief Executive Officer personally made that appointment and against the wishes of the other directors.[38] Moore questioned whether the Chief Executive Officer has breached his fiduciary duties and the FSA's 'Principles for Approved Persons' as a result of this personal appointment. Before he ceased working at HBOS, Moore informed the FSA of his concern about the appointment as well as the results of the two reviews mentioned above. Moore was, after all, obliged to do so under the 'approved person' regime. The FSA and HBOS subsequently commissioned KPMG to produce a report on Moore's allegations. KPMG are the auditors of HBOS. The appointment of KPMG therefore seemed unfair when Moore faced difficulties when blowing the whistle to the Group Audit Committee. Besides, the KPMG

34 Ibid.
35 See Moore above, n. 25.
36 Ibid.
37 Ibid.
38 Ibid.

report was damning of Moore's allegations and character. It portrayed him as an 'emotional, not reasoned and overly aggressive' individual.[39] The FSA dismissed Moore's claim, stating that it was without merit. The FSA's findings are extraordinary, given that when Moore subsequently revealed the HBOS reviews publicly to the House of Commons Treasury Select Committee and on television, it is clear that his account of events is credible. Besides, the FSA later asked PricewaterhouseCoopers (PwC) to carry out a 'skilled persons report' in accordance with section 166 of FSMA 2000. The 'skilled persons report' revealed that HBOS needed to improve its risk management system.[40] Therefore, this information corroborates Moore's account of events.

The HBOS whistle-blowing episode is significant for two reasons. First, it reveals that HBOS's internal controls were weak. The bank subsequently had to contact their customers to explain the capital risks and offered a free transfer back to standard deposit accounts. HBOS thus failed to protect its consumers. Second, and more importantly, the law failed to protect whistle-blowers such as Moore. Although he owed a common law implied duty of good faith and fidelity to his employer, Moore also owed a fiduciary duty to clients to act in their best interests. In theory, the scope of the common law implied duty of good faith and fidelity is wide. Hepple believes that this imposes a duty of respect for the employee's human rights.[41] In the case of *Heinisch v Germany*, the European Court of Human Rights found that where a whistle-blower is dismissed, this could amount to a breach of the right to freedom of expression under Article 10 of the European Convention of Human Rights, unless it was 'prescribed by law, pursues a legitimate aim and is necessary in a democratic society for achievement of such an aim' and, in particular, where the interference was a proportionate response to the aim pursued.[42] Here, it was held that Mrs Heinisch disclosed information of public interest; she acted in good faith, she had not knowingly reported false information and she had tried disclosing internally but management did not indicate when a solution would be available. This protects whistle-blowers' freedom of expression but does little to protect their employment status.[43]

With the common law duty of good faith and fidelity, the employee has to take account of the employer's interests but does not owe a duty to act in the latter's interests. The equitable principle is one-sided, since the fiduciary owes an absolute duty to his/her employer or client. Therefore, the equitable principle of fiduciary duties imposes a higher burden on employees. Moore owed an equitable principle to his employer but his disclosure of HBOS's excessive risk strategy and breach of FSA rules was not welcomed by his employers. Moore also alleged that several

39 See Dewing and Russell above, n. 8.

40 Lui, A. (2012). Single or twin? The UK financial regulatory landscape after the financial crisis of 2007–2009. *Journal of Banking Regulation* 13(1): 24–35.

41 Hepple, B. (1998). Human rights and employment law. *Amicua Curiae* 18: 19–23.

42 28274/08, [2011] ECHR 1175, [2011] IRLR 922, (2014) 58 EHRR 31, 32 BHRC 252.

43 Lui, A. (2014). Protecting whistle-blowers in the UK financial industry. *International Journal of Disclosure and Governance* 11(3): 195–210.

directors of HBOS breached their fiduciary duties when he blew the whistle. The equitable principle failed to protect Moore.[44] Common law provided inadequate protection to whistle-blowers.[45]

Nor did legislation assist significantly. The Public Interest Disclosure Act 1998 (PIDA) aims to protect whistle-blowers. However, it does not actively encourage them to whistle-blow and there is no obligation to blow the whistle. Prior to the amendments made by the Enterprise and Regulatory Reform Act 2013, whistle-blowers are protected if they informed on their employers where they made a 'qualifying disclosure' under section 43B (1) PIDA in good faith (section 43D) and satisfied the conditions in section 43G. The requirements in section 43G are that the whistle-blower reasonably believes that the information disclosed and any allegation contained in it is substantially true and s/he does not make the disclosure for purposes of personal gain. The principle of 'protected disclosure' is difficult to fulfil, especially in relation to external disclosures. In *Goode v Marks and Spencer Plc*, the employee's communication to *The Times* did not qualify as 'protected disclosure', since his external disclosure was dissimilar to the internal one.[46] However, the PIDA will protect employees in exceptionally serious circumstances where they disclose confidential information externally to the media. The case of *Holbrook v Queen Mary Sidcup NHS Trust* suggests that the whistle-blower should raise his/her concerns internally first before contacting the media.[47]

The statutory 'approved persons' regime under FSMA 2000, which obliged Moore to raise his concerns internally and externally, was swept aside when it became evident that the directors and Chief Financial Officer did not cooperate with Moore.[48] This is a clear example of the negative impact of deregulation and lobbying. Placing too much trust in banks has led to the hegemony of a weak corporate governance culture over the statutory obligation of whistle-blowers to challenge management in the HBOS episode. Regulators can fail to react to whistle-blowers due to political influence and pressure: Moore's experience is an example.[49] No amount of statutory legislation can protect whistle-blowers if the internal culture of banks is not receptive to challenge for the better protection of consumers. It will be seen later in this chapter that, despite some improvements made to protection of whistle-blowers in new legislation, whistle-blowers are still vulnerable because the culture in the financial sector remains a problem.[50]

44 Ibid.

45 See Jubb, P. (1999). Whistleblowing: a restrictive definition and interpretation. *Journal of Business Ethics* 21: 77–94; Collins, H., Ewing, K. and McColgan, A. (2005). *Labour Law Text and Materials*. Oxford: Hart Publishing.

46 UKEAT/0442/09/DM. 442/09, UKEAT.

47 ET/1101904/06.

48 See Dewing and Russell above, n. 8.

49 Nielsen, R. (2013). Whistle-blowing methods for navigating within and helping reform regulatory institutions. *Journal of Business Ethics* 112: 385–395.

50 See Taplin above, n. 14.

3.4 Ian Taplin's whistle-blowing experience at Lloyds TSB

In many ways, Ian Taplin's whistle-blowing encounter at Lloyds TSB is different to Paul Moore's at HBOS. Taplin was a former employee in the Wealth and Private department of Lloyds TSB between 2005 and 2010. He raised two formal grievances internally at Lloyds TSB in 2009 after his initial concerns were not addressed in 2007.[51] His grievances are in relation to intimidation by management and an unfair sales policy called 'segmentation'.[52] Taplin was dismissed in August 2010. Although Taplin was neither the Head of Regulatory Risk nor had any regulatory role, he was an 'approved person' under section 59 of FSMA 2000. Similarly to Moore, therefore, Taplin was under a statutory duty to blow the whistle internally and externally. Their fates were, unfortunately, similar. In Taplin's case, he stated that when he first raised his concerns about the unfair sales policy, he had an initial meeting with his sales director, his manager and an adviser from human resources. Taplin submits that he was forced to sign the meeting notes but the notes were not reflective of the discussion.[53] In December 2009, Taplin filed a grievance regarding the sales segmentation policy and another meeting was held in January 2010. In this meeting, Taplin was asked to talk about his personal history. When he started discussing the sales segmentation policy, the director offered him a settlement agreement, which Taplin declined because he did not want to drop the complaint and sign a gagging clause.[54]

Taplin's main grievance concerns the unfair sales segmentation policy. Consumer protection at Lloyds TSB was manifested by segregating customers into three classes: very wealthy customers, called the 'Mayfair' category; the middle category, the 'mass affluent'; and the bottom category, the 'mass market'. Taplin argues that this segregation was unfair for the following reasons. First, the 'mass market' customers were most vulnerable and needed the most protection, but they were offered the least advice. They had 'five lines of advice when the wealthy people had twelve lines of advice'.[55] Second, staff advising the 'mass market' class had fewer qualifications, and customers' access to financial products was restricted. The practical effect is that 'mass market' customers were sold more expensive financial products compared with 'mass affluent' customers purchasing the same products. 'Mass affluent' sales advisers earned the most, since they were well qualified and sold the most expensive commission products, such as insurance bonds, which generated a commission of 5–7%.[56] The segregation sales policy essentially discriminated against 'mass market' customers and ignored the principle of 'Putting Customers First' in Lloyds TSB's Code of Conduct.

51 Ibid.
52 Ibid.
53 Ibid.
54 Ibid.
55 Ibid.
56 Ibid.

An important feature raised in the Taplin episode is that he had to raise grievances rather than blow the whistle because Lloyds TSB did not have a whistle-blowing policy in place at the time. The PIDA does not require employers to put in place organisational whistle-blowing policies. According to the 2009 report by Public Concern at Work (an independent authority on whistle-blowing), only 38% of employers had a whistle-blowing policy in place. Under the UK Corporate Governance Code, companies listed in the UK are obliged to have whistle-blowing arrangements or explain why they do not. Corporate governance plays an important role when it comes to regulating human behaviour. Therefore, Codes of Conduct and internal whistle-blowing policies should provide detailed information to protect employees who may want to blow the whistle. This is not the case at Lloyds TSB. In the annual report of 2007, Lloyds TSB mention that they had 'a whistle blowing policy setting out the procedure by which people can raise, in confidence, any matters of concern. A whistle blowing line enables employees to raise any concerns and for such matters to be independently investigated'.[57] There was nothing on whistle-blowing in the 2008 or 2009 annual reports.[58] In 2010 and 2011, Lloyds stated in their annual report that they had reviewed the Group's whistle-blowing procedures and incidents.[59] Lloyds had a Code of Conduct, but whistle-blowing was not mentioned in Taplin's case. This is why Taplin had to use the grievance procedure to raise his formal complaints, even though they related to regulatory breaches. It was seven months after he submitted his grievances that Lloyds TSB notified Taplin of the whistle-blowing procedure.[60] Taplin submits that the grievance channel in his case worked conveniently for Lloyds TSB because grievances could be dealt with by staff in the sales and human resources departments. If Taplin blew the whistle, compliance staff would have to deal with the matter, since they had the requisite approval and qualifications. By keeping the grievances away from the compliance staff, Taplin had an uphill struggle in raising and discussing the regulatory breaches. Sales staff had little incentive to listen to his regulatory concerns when they were under pressure to achieve sales targets. Further, there was is a conflict of interest between sales targets and compliance targets of 'treating customers fairly'. The financial rewards attached to the former outweighed the latter.[61]

It is therefore evident that Taplin's experience highlights the deficiencies in the law to protect whistle-blowers. The PIDA does not actively encourage

57 Lloyds Banking Group Plc (2007). *Annual Report and Accounts: Building Long-term Relationships*. London: Lloyds Banking Group Plc.

58 See Lloyds Banking Group Plc (2009). *Annual Report and Accounts 2009: Creating the UK's Best Financial Services Provider*. London: Lloyds Banking Group Plc.

59 See Lloyds Banking Group Plc (2011). *Annual Report and Accounts 2011: Becoming the Best Bank for Customers*. London: Lloyds Banking Group Plc; Lloyds Banking Group Plc (2010). *Annual Report and Accounts 2010: Creating the UK's Best Financial Services Provider*. London: Lloyds Banking Group Plc.

60 See Taplin above, n. 14.

61 Ibid.

whistle-blowing. Besides, it is usually applicable after whistle-blowers have been dismissed because it then protects them from automatically unfair dismissals. This, however, is too late. Whistle-blowers need protection before they are dismissed. They often suffer professional and psychological issues after blowing the whistle.[62] The guise of employment law giving automatic unfair dismissal protection is not practical, because whistle-blowers often find it very difficult to gain employment again.[63] Dyck *et al.* concluded that 82% of whistle-blowers are dismissed, forced to quit their jobs or face limited job opportunities after blowing the whistle.[64] Moore, Taplin and Martin Woods of Wachovia Bank are all examples of whistle-blowers whose careers have been destroyed.[65] The FSA Guidelines Senior Management Arrangements, Systems and Controls 18.2.2 clause 1 does encourage staff to air their concerns by adopting relevant procedures: 'Firms are encouraged to consider adopting appropriate procedures which will encourage workers with concerns', but these are merely guidelines of persuasive force.[66] Self-regulation under the UK Corporate Governance Code prior to the financial crisis of 2007–2009 was not effective in this instance either. The 'comply or explain' principle in the Corporate Governance Code carries no binding effect on listed companies due to the nature of soft law. In this instance, Taplin suffered because he was only informed of the Lloyds TSB whistle-blowing policy after he filed his grievances. Further, the fact that the sales staff had little incentive to be sympathetic towards whistle-blowing concerns due to the incentive and business models at Lloyds created more hurdles for Taplin. Reliance on internal procedures is insufficient.[67] When one person in senior management undermines the whistle-blower, the whole internal procedure falls apart.

Taplin, a founder member of Whistle-blowers UK, has with other members developed a new registration system for protecting whistle-blowers. Under the registration system, whistle-blowers register an entry of public interest with the regulator on a specific date. The date is recorded and the regulator cannot act yet because they do not have any information. However, any potential misconduct by the bank after the date entered may be considered as bad practice. Whistle-blowers can withdraw the entry at any time because it is essentially a non-event

62 Tippett, E. (2007). The promise of compelled whistleblowing: what the corporate governance provisions of Sarbanes Oxley mean for employment law. *Employee Rights and Employment Policy Journal* 11(1): 1–42.

63 Dyck, A., Morse, A. and Zingales, L. (2010). Who blows the whistle on corporate fraud? *Journal of Finance* 65: 2213–2253.

64 Ibid.

65 See Taplin above, n. 14.

66 Financial Services Authority (2012). FSA publishes censure against Bank of Scotland plc in respect of failings within its Corporate Division between January 2006 and December 2008. Available at: http://www.fsa.gov.uk/library/communication/pr/2012/024.shtml (accessed 6 June 2015).

67 McHale, J. (1995). Whistleblowing in American health care. In: Hunt, G. (ed.) *Whistleblowing in the Health Service*. London: Edward Arnold, pp. 116–132.

apart from the date. Yet whistle-blowers can inform their employers about the entry in order to forewarn them. The system empowers whistle-blowers and the regulator. According to Taplin, the FCA liked the system when Whistleblowers UK presented it to them, but it has not been implemented.[68] The charity Public Concern at Work was not supportive, because it believes that the registration scheme externalises the whistle-blowing procedure.[69] Without the support of the law and regulator, Taplin was vulnerable. However, he was pleased to find assistance from a high-profile politician, who has been instrumental in challenging the Financial Conduct Authority's handling of the sales segmentation policy.[70]

Despite the difficulties Moore and Taplin encountered, their actions have produced results. In March 2012, the FSA took enforcement action and censured HBOS's corporate division for 'very serious misconduct' during 2006–2008.[71] This is because HBOS failed to comply with Principle 3 of the FSA's Principles for Businesses, which says: 'A firm must take reasonable care to organise and control its affairs responsibly and effectively, with adequate risk management systems.' HBOS pursued an aggressive growth strategy even in the period of 2006–2008 when the other UK banks scaled back their lending to corporate borrowers. More importantly, the FSA held that HBOS had a culture of focusing on profit at the expense of assessing risks properly. The FSA's censure of HBOS is a public one. It wanted to 'name and shame' the bank and act as a lesson on risk management failures. In 2013, Lloyds Banking Group was fined £28,038,800 for serious failures in their incentive schemes. Sales advisers at Lloyds were selling products to customers that they did not require or want because advisers were under pressure to hit targets.[72] The FCA increased the fine by 10% because the FSA had given several warnings to Lloyds Banking Group in the past for poorly managed incentive schemes. Lloyds also had a previous fine from the FSA for unsuitable sale of bonds in 2003 which was caused partly by the sales targets. It appears that Lloyds Banking Group had not learnt from its previous mistakes and therefore the hefty fine in 2013 was intended to act as a deterrent. Credit goes to both the FSA and FCA for taking enforcement action against Lloyds for breach of the FSMA's objective of consumer protection and Principle 3 of the Principles of Businesses.

68 See Taplin above, n. 14.

69 Ibid.

70 Ibid.

71 Financial Services Authority above, n. 66.

72 Financial Conduct Authority (2013). FCA fines Lloyds Banking Group firms a total of £28,038,800 for serious sales incentive failings. Available at: http://www.fca.org.uk/news/press-releases/fca-fines-lloyds-banking-group-firms-for-serious-sales-incentive-failings (accessed 12 June 2015).

3.5 New legislation to protect whistle-blowers

3.5.1 Amendments to the PIDA

Whistle-blowers are messengers of protected disclosures. Marshall McLuhan, a philosopher of communication theory, argues that 'the medium is the message' – a seemingly paradoxical statement, meaning that the focus should be on the technological process rather than the content of the message.[73] The shift from earlier oral cultures to more visual, print-based cultures has given rise to mass communication via the medium of the global internet. The medium has thus changed individuals and societies. In the whistle-blowing context, the main task of whistle-blowers such as Taplin was to 'present information in such a way that the regulator cannot ignore it any more'.[74] Tactics and power should be the focus of whistle-blowers. The medium, in the form of the press media, can be powerful if journalists report the whistle-blowers' concerns. When McLuhan first received the hard copy of his book *Understanding Media: The Extensions of Man*, there was a mistake in the title of chapter 1. It read 'The medium is the *massage*', but McLuhan liked the new title so much he kept it. The word pun of 'massage' and 'mass age' is visionary: McLuhan knew that the internet would revolutionise communication. As seen earlier, however, *Holbrook v Queen Mary Sidcup NHS Trust* suggests that the whistle-blower should raise his/her concerns internally first before contacting the media. The American position is similar; this is demonstrated in the case of *Tides v Boeing Co.*, where the court refused to provide protection to those whistle-blowing to the media.[75] This is a pity because studies have shown that whistle-blowers approach the media when they feel powerless within their organisations to make change happen, and when their concerns are not taken seriously internally.[76]

Besides, the media is often driven by circulation and other factors such as newsworthiness. Just because a whistle-blower's story is worth publishing does not mean that it is in the public's interest.[77] A new amendment to the PIDA favours a 'public interest' element. Under the Enterprise and Regulatory Reform Act 2013 (ERRA), the phrase 'is made in the public interest' is inserted after 'in the reasonable belief of the worker making the disclosure' into section 43B of the Employment Rights Act 1996 (ERA). After the Court in *Parkins v Sodexho Limited* held that failure to comply with legal obligations under section 43B (1)(b)

73 McLuhan, M. and Lapham, L. (eds) (1994). *Understanding Media: The Extensions of Man*. Cambridge, MA: MIT Press.

74 See Taplin above, n. 14.

75 644 F.3d 809 (9th Circuit 2011).

76 Dworkin, T. and Callaghan, E. (1993). Employee disclosures to the media: When is a 'source' a 'sourcerer'? *Hastings Communications and Entertainment Law Journal* 15: 357–397.

77 Dworkin, T. and Brown, A. (2013). The money or the media? Lessons from contrasting developments in US and Australian whistleblowing laws. *Seattle Journal for Social Justice* 11(2): 653–715.

ERA could be considered as a protected disclosure, the inclusion of the 'public requirement' is to be welcomed in theory.[78] Supperstone J in *Chesterton Global Ltd and Anor v Nurmohamed* reaffirmed this position:

> The words 'in the public interest' inserted into section 43B (1) of the 1996 Act by the 2013 Act were intended to reverse the effect of *Parkins v Sodexho Ltd* in which it was held that a breach of a legal obligation owed by an employer to an employee under his or her own contract of employment may constitute a protected disclosure.[79]

Ashton mentioned that some potential whistle-blowers may be discouraged from blowing the whistle, as they might perceive the 'public interest' requirement as an additional hurdle. Recent court interpretation of the 'public interest' test may alleviate this concern. In *Morgan v Royal MENCAP Society*, the Employment Appeal Tribunal held that it is for a tribunal to determine whether a claimant's subjectively held belief that the disclosures were in the public interest was reasonable when objectively viewed.[80] This issue is dependent on the facts of each case. In *Morgan*, the claimant's complaint regarding cramped working conditions constituted a 'public interest' disclosure on health and safety grounds. Arguably, the 'public interest' threshold is low. Cramped conditions at a charity are unlikely to affect many employees in comparison with breaches in the healthcare sector. Nevertheless, the claimant in *Morgan* demonstrated that other employees could be affected by the same or similar cramped working conditions.[81] She also included several ways in which the public interest may be affected. Therefore, it would appear that the low 'public interest' threshold should not discourage whistle-blowers to blow the whistle.

The author submits that even if there is an increase in whistle-blowing claims in the future, employment law in practice favours settlement. Since 6 May 2014, early conciliation is necessary before a claimant can bring a claim in front of an employment tribunal. Early conciliation is an attempt to resolve an employment dispute between the parties before a claimant files a claim. If the parties agree to a settlement, the dispute is resolved outside a tribunal. The Employment Tribunal *Thomas v Nationwide Building Society* rejected the claimant's whistle-blowing claim because she failed to use the compulsory early conciliation scheme.[82] The judge, however, said that the mistake can be rectified retrospectively, so that the claim may continue once it is rectified. From a practical perspective, settlement is helpful since it saves time and money. Nevertheless, whistle-blowers who sign

78 [2002] IRLR 109.

79 UKEAT/0335/14.

80 Ashton, J. (2015). 15 years of whistleblowing protection under the Public Interest Disclosure Act 1998: are we still shooting the messenger? *Industrial Law Journal* 44(1): 29–52. See UKEAT/0272/15/LA.

81 UKEAT/0272/15/LA.

82 1601342/2014.

settlement agreements often will be bound by gagging clauses. Therefore, the 'public interest' requirement is rendered futile in reality. The removal of the good faith requirement from the PIDA by the ERA is therefore also futile, because there is now an express requirement to act in the public interest. Whistle-blowers now do not need to show that the protected disclosure is made in good faith, although a tribunal may increase the compensatory award by up to 25% if the disclosure is found to be made in bad faith (section 49 PIDA). Since 2012/13, there has been a steady decline of unfair dismissal claims heard by employment tribunals. In 2012/13, there were 49,036 claims, in 2013/14, there were 28,528 claims, and in 2014/15, there were 12,652 claims.[83] The combination of early conciliation, the introduction of tribunal fees and cuts in legal aid funding have contributed to the decline in the number of claims. It is therefore submitted that the amendments to the PIDA are mainly academic.

3.5.2 PRA Rulebook and FCA Handbook

The Prudential Regulatory Authority (PRA) and FCA have implemented some useful reforms through the FCA's Senior Management Arrangements, Systems and Controls handbook and the PRA's Supervisory Statement SS39/15. The new rules affect UK deposit takers with assets of £250 million or more (including banks, building societies and credit unions), PRA-designated investment firms, insurance and reinsurance firms within the scope of Solvency 2 and the Society of Lloyd's and managing agents. Rule 18.5.1R of the FCA Handbook sets out the requirement for settlement agreements to include a clause explaining workers' legal rights in making protected disclosures. Yet the contractual clause merely enshrines and clarifies the statutory protection: it does not provide additional protection to whistle-blowers' rights in making protected disclosures. Rule 18.5.3R of the FCA Handbook prohibits relevant firms from asking workers signing settlement agreements to state whether they have made a protected disclosure or that they know of no information that could form the basis of a protected disclosure. The PRA goes further and includes employment contracts, whereas the FCA only mentions settlement agreements. There is, however, nothing in the rules to ban gagging clauses. Whistle-blowers are essentially encouraged to make protected disclosures but cannot criticise their employers in public after they have made such disclosures. Although rules 18.4.4 and 18.5.3(1) prevent victimisation and breach of warranties against whistle-blowers, there should be a clause prohibiting gagging clauses so that matters of public interest can be made known.[84]

83 Her Majesty's Courts and Tribunals Service (2015). *Employment Tribunal and Employment Appeals Tribunal Statistics.* London: Her Majesty's Courts and Tribuals Service.

84 Prudential Regulatory Authority (2015). Policy Statement PS24/15 Whistleblowing in deposit-takers, PRA-designated investment firms and insurers. London: Prudential Regulatory Authority.

The appointment of a whistle-blowing champion (rule 18.4.1 FCA Handbook) is to be welcomed. Having a non-executive director should improve the effectiveness of the internal whistle-blowing procedures which will be more robust under rule 18.3.6 and protect whistle-blowers from victimisation (rule 18.2.2). The whistle-blowing champion has to produce an annual report to the board of directors and notify the FCA if the firm was unsuccessful in a whistle-blowing claim (rule 18.3.1(f)). Financial institutions have the flexibility to decide on the precise responsibilities of the whistle-blowing champion. Institutions should exercise this discretion cautiously. As discussed earlier, McHale noted that if one person in senior management undermines the whistle-blower, the internal procedure falls apart.[85] Whistle-blowers are protected by rule 18.3.2(a)(i) on confidential and anonymous disclosure of information to their employers. Anonymity is not always possible due to the nature of the information provided. Anonymity can also create practical difficulties such as gathering information and identifying relevant participants if the whistle-blower's identity is concealed. It will, however, give a 'veil of ignorance',[86] which is a safeguard to whistle-blowers since the employment protection given to them is unsatisfactory. One of the most difficult issues for employers and regulators to determine is whether a concern reported is genuine. Since anonymity provides protection to the whistle-blowers' identities, one might question their motives in blowing the whistle. Ultimately, if there is alleged wrongdoing, then the motive of the whistle-blower should not be the deciding factor in investigating the allegation. However, the credibility of the whistle-blower *may* be called into question if the practical process of obtaining data is difficult[87] and the evidence provided is less accurate than when whistle-blowers' identities are known.[88] Naturally, if the anonymous whistle-blower can provide concrete and reliable evidence, then credibility should not be an issue. Interestingly, research by Nayir and Herzig revealed that among 329 Turkish managers, the statement that had the highest consensus is the desire for anonymity if they blow the whistle. Regulators also have to observe anonymity under section 43FA PIDA.[89] This requires regulators who receive whistle-blowing disclosures to report annually on the disclosures they receive. Regulators will have to disclose how many whistle-blowing complaints they have received and any action taken in response. The identity of the whistle-blowers and employers will be protected.

85 See McHale above, n. 67.

86 Elliston, F. (1982). Anonymity and whistleblowing. *Journal of Business Ethics* 1(3): 167–177.

87 Ayers, S. and Kaplan, S. (2005). Wrongdoing by consultants: an examination of employees' reporting intentions. *Journal of Business Ethics* 57(2): 121–137.

88 Price, A. (1998). Anonymity and pseudonymity in whistleblowing to the U.S. Office of Research Integrity. *Academic Medicine* 73(5): 461–472.

89 Nayir, D. and Herzig, C. (2012). Value orientations as determinants of preference for external and anonymous whistleblowing. *Journal of Business Ethics* 107: 197–213.

3.5.3 Senior managers and certification regime

The experiences of Moore and Taplin are clear examples that the 'approved persons' regime under the FSA failed to work. The Parliamentary Commission for Banking Standards described the 'approved persons' regime' as a 'complex and confused mess . . . It fails to perform any of its varied roles to the necessary standard.'[90] As a result of this, Parliament passed the Financial Services (Banking Reform) Act 2013 ('the 2013 Act') to improve the culture and professional standards of the UK financial sector. The 2013 Act incorporates the changes suggested by the Parliamentary Commission on Banking Standards' *Changing Banking for Good* report. The Financial Services (Banking Reform) Act 2013 introduces the Senior Managers and Certification Regime ('SMCR'). The SMCR is divided into parts. Under the first part of the senior managers' regime, there is a statutory duty for senior managers to take reasonable steps to prevent regulatory breaches by the firms in which they work.[91] Further, senior managers' qualifications and conduct will be subject to stricter scrutiny since the firms which the senior managers work for have to submit documents outlining their responsibilities. The regulator will continue to play a part in approving senior managers under this regime. Senior managers will also have to comply with the Rules of Conduct. The SMCR is to be welcomed since it should raise the standard and conduct of senior managers. Several banks in the UK, notably the ones which required governmental assistance, had senior managers who were not qualified in finance or economics. Senior bankers are professionals and they should be subject to conduct rules similar to other professions. The second part of the SMCR is the certification regime. The regulator does not need to pre-approve, so the onus is on individual firms to assess the suitability and fitness of staff annually. Firms are responsible and accountable for the internal procedures to the regulator to that effect. The rationale is for the FCA to concentrate on the senior managers' regime and delegate the certification regime to individual firms to monitor.[92]

There are some positive reforms under the SMCR. The whistle-blowing champion is a non-executive director who will be subject to the senior managers' regime and will therefore be personally accountable if a whistle-blower is victimised. Personal accountability and sanctions imposed on whistle-blowing

90 House of Commons Treasury Committee (2013). *Changing Banking for Good: Report of the Parliamentary Commission on Banking Standards. Volume I: Summary, and Conclusions and Recommendations.* London: The Stationery Office Limited. Available at: https://www.parliament.uk/documents/banking-commission/Banking-final-report-volume-i.pdf (accessed 3 August 2016).

91 HM Treasury (2015). *Senior Managers and Certification Regime: Extension to All FSMA Authorised Persons.* London: HM Treasury. Available at: https://www.gov.uk/government/uploads/system/uploads/attachment_data/file/468328/SMCR_policy_paper_final_15102015.pdf (accessed 3 August 2016).

92 Financial Conduct Authority (2015). *Financial Conduct Authority Confirms Approach to Improving Responsibility and Accountability in the Banking Sector.* London: Financial Conduct Authority.

champions should act as powerful deterrents not to victimise whistle-blowers. Section 36 of the 2013 Act provides that individual senior managers of banks and building societies may be prosecuted by the PRA or FCA for taking a decision that causes their institution to fail. For the offence to have been committed, the senior manager must have been aware of a risk that its implementation may cause the institution to fail at the time the decision was taken. Moreover, the senior manager's conduct in relation to the decision must fall far below what could reasonably be expected of someone in their position (section 36(1)(c) 2013 Act). A controversial issue is the burden of proof in the SMCR. Originally, senior managers would have to demonstrate that they had discharged their responsibilities. Reversal of the burden of proof means that regulators now have to demonstrate that senior managers had not discharged their responsibilities. This burden of proof is in line with other regulatory enforcement actions. The original reverse burden of proof can be understood against the background of public anger. However, the reversal seems to demonstrate the Treasury's attempt to dilute the personal accountability of senior managers. The PRA said that the change is merely procedural rather than substantive.[93] Regulators may need more time and resources to deal with investigations into personal accountability with the reversal in the burden of proof. If the approval procedure of senior managers and high standards are observed, there should be less likelihood of misconduct. However, when misconduct does take place, it is important that the regulators have sufficient resources for fair and thorough investigations. Otherwise, it would be a shame to introduce a new offence for senior managers when in reality it is difficult and expensive to operate.

Following an initial heavy crackdown on financial crime after the financial crisis, the FCA abandoned an industry review into the culture of banks in 2016. The FCA decided that it was difficult to compare culture across different banks. Instead, it launched a review in January 2016 into Lloyds Banking Group as to whether the latter has manipulated the price of government bonds.[94] The Shadow Chancellor criticised this move: in his view, the FCA was softening its approach towards banks.[95] The Walker Review of 2010 investigated corporate governance weaknesses of banks after the global financial crisis and made 39 recommendations. It would be appropriate to have an industry review of banking culture since the Walker Review to see whether banks have made improvements since its implementation. It is hoped that the FCA will remain robust and thorough in adopting an individualistic style when reviewing the culture of banks.

93 Treanor, J. (2015). UK government waters down financial regulation regime. *Guardian*, 15 October. Available at: https://www.theguardian.com/business/2015/oct/15/financial-accountability-regime-will-not-be-fully-operational-until-2018 (accessed 2 August 2016).

94 Treanor, J. (2016). Lloyds under investigation by FCA over possible market rigging. *Guardian*, 6 January. Available at: https://www.theguardian.com/business/2016/jan/06/lloyds-under-investigation-fca-market-rigging (accessed 2 August 2016).

95 See BBC (2015). Banking culture inquiry shelved by regulator FCA. BBC, 31 December. Available at: http://www.bbc.co.uk/news/uk-35204010 (accessed 5 January 2016).

3.6 Conclusion

> The financial crisis, and multiple conduct failures, have exposed serious flaws in governance. Potemkin villages were created in firms, giving the appearance of effective control and oversight without the reality . . . Poor governance and controls are illustrated by the rarity of whistle-blowing, either within or beyond the firm, even where, such as in the case of LIBOR manipulation, prolonged and blatant misconduct has been evident.[96]

The Parliamentary Commission on Banking Standards are correct to identify the underlying factor of poor corporate governance practice in the financial industry. Whistle-blowers Moore and Taplin confronted internal and external hurdles when they raised legitimate concerns about sales practices, policies and culture at HBOS and Lloyds TSB. The common law, the PIDA, FSA guidelines and the UK Corporate Governance Code all failed to provide support and protection to Moore and Taplin. Reforms to whistle-blowers' protection are thus long overdue, especially when they play important roles in corporate governance and regulation. As it stands, it is submitted that the PRA Rulebook, FCA Handbook and the Senior Managers and Certification Regime are more far-reaching than the amendments made to the PIDA. The practical emphasis on settling employment law disputes, including whistle-blowing claims, means that the addition of the 'public interest' test and the removal of the 'good faith' element in disclosure are academic. With the increased personal accountability and possible sanctions imposed on whistle-blowing champions for the victimisation of whistle-blowers, uncovering financial misconduct in Potemkin villages should be less traumatic for whistle-blowers. Ultimately, consumers will benefit from a more transparent, responsible and accountable financial sector.

96 House of Commons Treasury Committee above, n. 90.

4 Rogues in the City

Paul Keenan

Rogue traders and the question of criminal intent

Perhaps 'Rogues in the City' as a title does not have the same immediate audience appeal as 'Sex in the City' – but, to some, the thought of a 'Rogue' is just as appealing as that of Sarah Jessica Parker – and some 'Rogues' do become even more famous. The rogues I am looking at here are, of course, the so-called 'Rogue Traders', who have lost billions of dollars for their firms, and the 'Rogues Gallery' becomes more populated every year. A quick trawl of the internet using any search engine reveals a long list of famous – even notorious – names. Table 4.1 presents a list from several internet sources, all from publicly available information, of recent losses in excess of US$ 1 billion.

What these cases have in common is that they all involve traders who were acting for their institution itself, rather than for any customers, and that all were trading complex or sophisticated products which carried higher than normal risk, and which were difficult to value from available price feeds or stock exchange information. I am looking at this as a former Compliance Officer in charge of the Compliance function for a department which was trading in these complex products and derivatives (both for customers and for the bank's own account), and what I see is a list of traders who were active with permission from, and in the name of, their respective institutions. But when I look more closely, I must draw the conclusion that they were not adequately monitored or controlled, and they may well have had less than adequate training in the products for which they took (and were given) responsibility. All such complex products have even more complex risk management, monitoring, accounting and valuation systems, which also may not have been up to an adequate standard.

Trading activity, of whatever kind, carries an Operational Risk, and Operational Risk is an area where Risk Management is just as important as (some say more important than) any other kind of risk. In fact, because Operational Risk is more difficult to define, the systems in place to manage it probably need to be more sophisticated, rather than, as I have observed to be usual, left as an afterthought to the trading strategy, and developed ad hoc, as trading moves forward into ever newer, more untested and more complex territory. The traders listed in Table 4.1 were all blamed for the losses, which, in most cases, did

Table 4.1 Examples of rogue traders 1993 to date

Rogue trader(s)	*Total loss (USD)*	*Country*	*Company*	*Instrument traded*	*Year*
Howie Hubler	9 bn	USA	Morgan Stanley	Credit default swaps	2008
Jérôme Kerviel	7.22 bn	France	Société Générale	European Index futures	2008
Brian Hunter	6.50 bn	USA	Amaranth Advisors	Gas futures	2006
Bruno Iksil	5.80 bn	UK	JPMorgan Chase	Credit default swaps	2012
John Meriwether	4.6 bn	USA	Long Term Capital Management	Interest rate and equity Derivatives	1998
Yasuo Hamanaka	2.62 bn	Japan	Sumitomo Corporation	Copper futures	1996
Isac Zagury, Rafael Sotero	2.52 bn	Brazil	Aracruz	FX Options	2008
Kweku Adoboli	2 bn	UK	UBS	Equities ETF and Delta 1	2011
Frances Yung	1.89 bn	China	CITIC Pacific	Foreign exchange trading	2008
Boaz Weinstein	1.8 bn	USA	Deutsche Bank	Derivatives	2008
Robert Citron	1.7 bn	USA	Orange County	Leveraged bond investments	1994
Heinz Schimmelbusch	1.59 bn	Germany	Metallgesellschaft	Oil futures	1993
Nick Leeson	1.31 bn	Singapore	Barings Bank	Nikkei futures	1995
Wolfgang Flöttl, Helmut Elsner	1.29 bn	Austria	BAWAG	Foreign exchange trading	2000
Toshihide Iguchi	1.10 bn	Japan	Daiwa Bank	Bonds	1995
Boris Picano-Nacci	1.10 bn	France	Groupe Caisse d'Epargne	Derivatives	2008
Adriano Ferreira, Álvaro Ballejo	1.09 bn	Brazil	Sadia	FX and credit options	2008

Sources: various internet sources.

irreparable damage to their institutions' balance sheets (and thus share prices); some were prosecuted, some spent time in jail. But, in all cases, these traders had been active over a considerable time period and had lost a considerable amount of capital before they were 'caught'.

My key question for this analysis is: did these traders have criminal intent which would justify the soubriquet 'Rogue'? Should we investigate what other factors created an environment where these traders could act in the way they did? Also, while it was right to blame them for their own losses, were they the only ones to blame? I believe there were several factors in play. First and foremost, there was probably an element of greed (who can forget Gordon Gecko's mantra 'Greed is good'?[1]). Traders are paid to make money; therefore, they have an almost automatic impulse to make money by any means – first for their institution, but also, and importantly, to create a profit pool which then filters down to their salaries and bonuses. The institutions want them to make money to enhance their balance sheets, the traders want to make money to enhance their lifestyles. The second factor is inertia. Traders have always taken risks, so there is an attitude that they should be allowed to continue to take risks on the basis that the positive and negative vagaries of securities markets usually leave profits at the end of it. Then there is incompetence. The traders just get it wrong, and their management does not understand how they get it wrong (or, worse, do not even realise that the traders have got it wrong). There is fear. Traders do have a constant worry that they might lose, and so keep trading to improve the 'odds' of making more than they lose (that is, they just follow the age-old and much-decried practice of roulette players of 'doubling up' in the hope of covering previous losses). And, of course, there is the real fear of losing their job if their trading losses are discovered before they can 'win' them back. We must also consider ignorance as a factor. Empirical evidence certainly shows that in many cases, these traders, their managers and their institutions did not fully understand what they were doing. Finally, an answer that traders might give when asked why they do what they do is 'Because I can!' No one could or should offer any of these factors as an excuse for what went wrong in the respective institutions, but, importantly, neither would I point to any of them as indicating a specific 'criminal intent'. I want to look at this in more detail in the case study that follows.

The case of Jerome Kerviel

I have chosen the case of Jerome Kerviel, the trader at Société Générale (SG), who in January 2008 was revealed to have made what is listed as the second-largest loss ever by a 'Rogue Trader' – US$7.2 billion. This case is interesting not only because it brought about one of the biggest bank losses through this sort of activity, but because SG itself has made details of the case very public, and so there

1 *Wall Street* (1987), film by Oliver Stone and Stanley Weiser, Twentieth Century Fox Film Corporation.

is a lot more information available than is usual in such cases. Kerviel was initially charged with fraud, but eventually charged with and convicted of abuse of confidence and illegal access to computers. He was found guilty and received a prison sentence of five years, of which he served three. In addition, his sentence included the condition that he make restitution to his employer, and so now Kerviel is said to be 'the most indebted person in the world', as he still owes SG over $6 billion. As I will bring out below, the total loss was even greater.

But I want to go back to 24 January 2008, when police were first made aware of the SG loss. It appears to me that France takes a much more serious and proactive view of these events than do other jurisdictions. On being notified, the police immediately entered SG premises, interviewed top management about their knowledge of events, took Kerviel's computers and records, and raided Kerviel's flat – all gathering evidence as promptly as they could, before it could be lost or destroyed. Within days, SG appointed three senior independent (non-executive) directors – Jean Martin Folz, Jean Azema, and Antoine Jeancourt-Galignani – to undertake an inquiry, with Folz as Chairman of this Special Committee. The Committee appointed PricewaterhouseCoopers (PwC) to undertake the extensive independent analysis of the situation that would be necessary.

That Committee reported very quickly, and before the end of February 2008 issued their *Progress Report of the Special Committee of the Board of Directors* (the Report),[2] which revealed a set of circumstances, which, to me, indicate that the problem was more to do with the systems surrounding Kerviel, his management and the communication channels surrounding his business, than with any specific 'rogue' ideas or intent of Kerviel himself. To their credit, SG made the initial *Progress Report* by the Folz Committee available to all via the internet, which has added greatly to our understanding of what went wrong. Other financial institutions should take note!

The Report starts by advising that 'criminal proceedings were opened on January 28th 2008' (a mere four days after the loss was discovered). Further, in this introductory section, it goes on to say that the purpose of the Committee's audit was to 'establish the chronology of the fraudulent positions'.[3] However, it is the main body of the Report that I find more interesting, and it is on that part I would like to dwell for a while, and, in doing so, look at the 'criminality' of the events. There is, in the Report, what I consider to be a little obfuscation in discussing the difference between client trading and proprietary trading. Certainly, client trading is far more regulated in all European financial markets, and losses made in a client's name are regarded very seriously by the law and by the financial regulators. However, Kerviel's trading involved no client funds, and so discussion of such has no bearing on his activity.

2 See http://www.societegenerale.com/sites/default/files/pressrelase/comiteSpecialFevrier08gb.pdf.

3 Ibid.

So, we are left to look at the sort of trading Kerviel did undertake. His mandate was to trade only for the bank's own account, risking the bank's own capital (proprietary trading), and included the ability to take 'arbitrage positions' – that is, take positions where a market holding (a 'long' position) might be balanced by a sale of similar securities (a 'short' position). Such positions were expected in normal market circumstances to have an equivalent (equal and opposite) response to market movement. Therefore, the total portfolio position would, in these 'normal circumstances', be immunised against either an upward or a downward general market movement in total value. The long and the short positions have a positive/negative symmetry, which balance each other out. The specific purpose of Kerviel's activity, in order to make money, was to look for and to take advantage of anomalies where financial products which have, ostensibly, similar features actually respond asymmetrically to market movement, thus offering an advantage on one side over the other (the strategy being to be long of the one responding well, and short of the one responding poorly.) This mandate did not include taking directional positions – that is, positions which were merely a bet on market direction – without any compensating arbitrage position.

Now, the products which were the subject of Kerviel's activity were complex, and had complex purchase and delivery features, including forward sales or purchases and deferred payments, as well as derivative internal cash-flow features, making valuations difficult. For the sake of this analysis it is not important to understand those intricacies; they were a normal feature of the derivative product markets for which Kerviel had authorisation.

It is certainly true that Kerviel manipulated, and even overstretched, his mandate, took positions that were not technically authorised and traded beyond his set limits. But was it fair to start from an assumption of criminality and fraudulent intent? That is what I will examine here. The Report makes a very telling observation when it states that 'the controls provided by the support and control functions were carried out in accordance with the procedures but did not make it possible to identify the fraud before January 18th 2008'.[4]

My main interest, from a compliance point of view, however, and where I will focus most of my attention, is in the next statement of the Report:

> failure to identify the fraud can be attributed firstly to the variety and efficiency of the concealment techniques employed by the fraudster [*sic*], secondly to the fact that operating staff did not systematically carry out more detailed checks, and finally to the absence of certain controls that were not provided for and which might have identified the fraud.[5]

Again, I note that fraud is presumed from the start. This indicates a predisposition of the Committee to prove fraud, rather than seek to discover what really

4 Ibid.
5 Ibid.

happened (which was certainly and undeniably irregular) and why it went unnoticed for so long.

The first 'intermediary conclusion' of the Report was that directional positions were being taken – and, I note from PwC's data, were found to have been taken in 2005–2006, some two or three years before the losses were discovered. Yet within this conclusion is a statement that 'on the whole, the controls provided by the support and control functions were carried out in accordance with the procedures, but did not make it possible to identify the fraud before 2008'.[6]

The Committee does excuse itself from drawing a more damning conclusion which might have judged the 'Control Function', by citing the constraints because of ongoing legal investigation. This section of the Report ends with a statement that there was no evidence of embezzlement, or internal or external complicity.

The Report then presents a summary of the findings of PwC, presenting a diagrammatic representation of Kerviel's trading, reproduced below in Figure 4.1, which is of interest to me primarily because it is able to display all positions taken and reported by Kerviel going back to 2007, indicating that everything Kerviel did was logged and recorded somewhere on SG's systems, and therefore could have been seen by managers and controllers.

This analysis, as I would expect, appears to show that Kerviel had opened arbitrage positions, whereby profits in one area were balanced (almost in mirror image) by losses in another. It also clearly indicates that this information was available and could have been scrutinised in the SG systems throughout that period. The actual position is said to be the first graph, and the second graph is said to be 'fictional positions'. Thus the losses in the first graph were realised, but the profits of the second never were. It is never explained why this anomaly was not picked up between March 2007 and July 2007, when, even if they were real, the arbitrage positions would appear to have exceeded limits, and losses were significant and sustained. We must accept that Kerviel was trying to hide his losses, was desperate, even, to be given time to return to profit before any losses were noticed, and thus engaged in desperate measures.

Why were they never noticed? PwC then examines the activities that might have revealed Kerviel's activity if they had been picked up by the monitoring systems and controls. Systems and controls (SYSC) are a key requirement of financial market regulators, with the general rule being to the effect that a firm's SYSC arrangements should be such as to furnish its governing body with all the information it needs to play its part in identifying, measuring, managing and controlling risks within its business activity that might be of regulatory concern. Regulators are concerned about a firm's own balance sheet trading, as a decline in capital adequacy can create instability in the sector.

Three key factors to determine the adequacy of SYSC will be the relevance, reliability and timeliness of the information gathered to enable effective management of the firm's business. In framing SYSC rules, regulators aim to

6 Ibid.

Exhibit no. 2: **The trader manages to hide his actual P&L, showing an "official" P&L which is very low in comparison.**

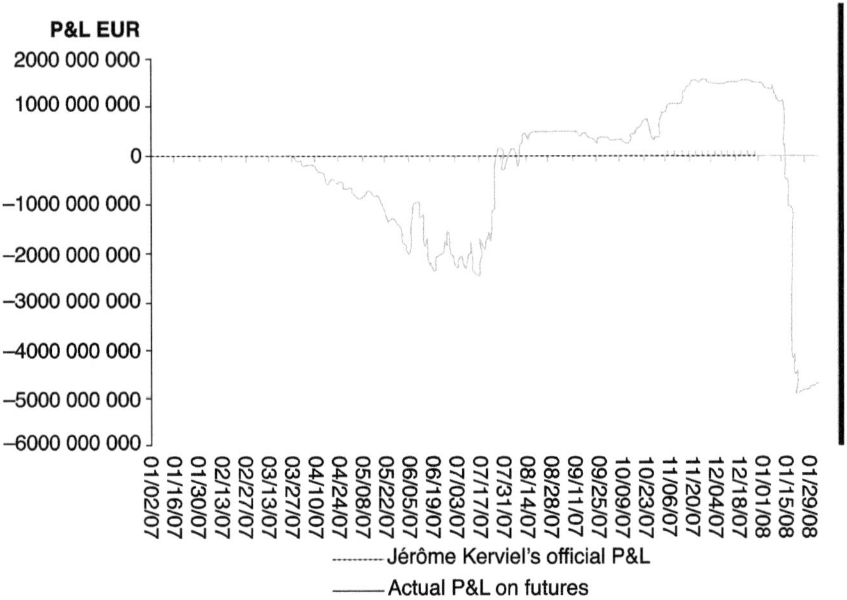

The P&L profile generated by the fictitious transactions is parallel to that of the fraudulent P&L:

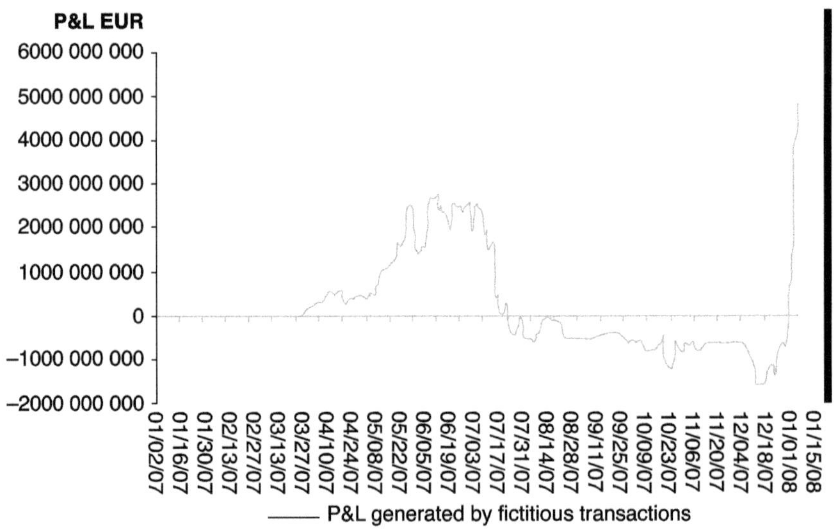

Figure 4.1 Diagrams of Kerviel positions in the Report

(Source: *Progress Report of the Special Committee of the Board of Directors of Société Générale*, 20 February 2008)[7]

7 Ibid.

ensure that complex businesses have measures in place sophisticated enough to monitor and control the complexities, while 'simple' businesses are not burdened by undue costs of complex systems.

The areas picked up by PwC are as follows (all in the year 1 January 2007 to 1 January 2008):

- 'JK *appears to have used* forged emails on *seven* occasions.'[8]
- Supervisors did not systematically extend controls beyond what was called for by procedures, which resulted in:
    - *six alerts* of irregular deal input being left unverified;
    - *13 alerts* of irregular counterparty gateways uninvestigated;
    - *13 alerts* of front-to-back office anomalies in data;
    - *five alerts* of intra-group reconciliation not pursued;
    - *seven alerts* of accounting review variations not pursued;
    - *two alerts* of counterparty risk monitoring not pursued;
    - *24 alerts* picked up by risk monitoring systems attributed to data processing problems.

These damning observations, derived from SG's own systems, appear to contradict the statement in the introduction that 'failure to identify the fraud until that date [18 January 2008] can be attributed firstly to the variety and efficiency of the concealment techniques employed by the fraudster'.[9]

In my view, 70 alerts (that we know about) would indicate a lack of efficiency and ineffective concealment by Kerviel, but, indeed, an even greater lack of efficiency by the systems and control mechanisms (or the managers responsible for operating those mechanisms), and the lack of effectiveness in following up alerts (and, probably, a lack of understanding of what the alerts were identifying).

There are mitigating factors which can, to some extent, support the controllers. Kerviel had worked in the back-office on the systems before he was promoted to the trading floor, so he knew his way around those systems. He could talk about the systems perhaps more knowledgeably than some of the controllers who picked up the alerts and questioned him, and so perhaps give them some (false) comfort that 'everything will be all right'; but a lack of knowledge and training of the controllers should not be cited as an excuse for missing so many opportunities to pick up the anomalies. In particular, it is not explained why Internal Audit, and Senior Management who would see the reports, albeit later, did not ask pertinent questions.

In their detailed examination of the handling of all the alerts, PwC made comments such as:

- '. . . the next level of superiors failed to react when notified'
- '. . . no initiative was taken'

8 Ibid., emphasis added.
9 Ibid.

- '. . . contented itself with an email from operations indicating trades to be cancelled'
- '. . . did not cast a critical eye'
- '. . . did not seek to understand the explanation given by JK'
- '. . . attributes cause of anomalies to recurring problems in computer systems'.[10]

PwC further observed that they did not find any indication of 'embezzlement of funds', and did not identify any signs of internal or external collusion. It is reasonable to conclude, as an outside observer, therefore, that the Committee's only real accusation stated in the report was that Kerviel was 'able to increase indirectly the amount of flexible compensation' – that is, his inflated statement of profits would have had a positive effect on his bonus. But, in my opinion, the damning criticisms of the failure of systems and controls for more than a year, and possibly for as long as three years, may well outweigh that, especially as those systems, if they had been operated effectively, would have revealed an 'uninflated' statement. Certainly, following the full investigation, senior managers were dismissed, retired or quietly moved aside, and SYSC within SG was dramatically improved – but by then the horse had bolted.

A major element *not* covered in the Committee's report is the total effect of the operational risk element of this discovery. We know the headline figure, that Kerviel's losses amounted to US$7.2 billion, but these may well have been overshadowed by the Operational Risk (OR) losses. OR is the risk that does not flow from the business, but from the people involved in (or 'operating') the business. In this case, Kerviel was certainly an OR factor, but also everyone involved in management of his activity and in operating the SYSC mechanisms were each an OR factor. How do we judge the OR effect? The easiest way is to look at SG's share price (both a measure of the trust the market has in the company and an indirect indication of its capital value).

In the case of SG, there was a dramatic fall in share price when this news broke in January 2008, as indicated in Figure 4.2. At the beginning of January 2008, the shares were trading at over €90, and as the news broke they rapidly lost one-third of their value and dropped to €60. As the story continued to unfold throughout the year, they dropped further, so that by January 2009 they were only worth €20, less than a quarter of their value a year earlier. Even after that, recovery proved difficult. Certainly, by then there were other factors, both in the international economy and with international banking in general, which also contributed, but there can be no doubt that the news of Kerviel's losses was the start of SG's woes.

But was Kerviel a 'Rogue'? His actions have been judged 'criminal', in that he was convicted and sentenced by a court. But the blame also needs to be apportioned to those who failed to respond to control alerts, who failed to manage

10 Ibid.

Figure 4.2 Société Générale Group closing share price 1 January 2008–30 May 2016 (in euros) (data from Yahoo Finance France)

Kerviel's trading within his mandate, and who failed to notice, for more than a year, that Kerviel's trading pattern was 'unusual', to say the least. If Kerviel had been right in his guesses as to where the market was going, he might well have been a 'Star Trader' rather than a 'Rogue Trader', so is the difference merely a matter of luck?

All we can really derive from this is a 'formula' for business in general:

Rogue/Incompetence + Supervision Failure + Systems Failure = Loss of Reputation

Loss of Reputation = Loss of Value

The problems of Kerviel were not, of course, unique to SG. As Table 4.1 shows, many banks in many countries have suffered what are called 'Rogue Trader' losses. I prefer to call them 'Operational Risk losses' – arising because the Operational Risk was a risk that was left either inadequately managed or not managed at all.

The current international banking system

Now, if we scroll forward from 2008 to 2016, we see that the international banking system is having to recover from a seismic shock, not least because of huge losses resulting from the banks' investments in complex derivatives and structured products (even the well-managed and correctly valued derivatives were losing). These 'operational risk' losses (no longer blamed solely on 'rogues'), have been building up so that banks have had to have governmental support for their capital, or else be forced into mergers or into closure.

In the UK, a Parliamentary Commission addressed the problems which arose and issued their report in 2013.[11] The introductory summary of what was to be addressed in the report could almost be a summary of the lapses of 'Rogue Traders' and SYSC failures detailed above.

> The UK banking sector's ability both to perform its crucial role in support of the real economy and to maintain international pre-eminence has been eroded by a profound loss of trust born of profound lapses in banking standards. The Commission makes proposals to enable trust to be restored in banking. These proposals have five themes:
>
> - making individual responsibility in banking a reality, especially at the most senior levels;

11 House of Commons Treasury Committee (2013). *Changing Banking for Good: Report of the Parliamentary Commission on Banking Standards. Volume I: Summary, and Conclusions and Recommendations.* London: The Stationery Office Limited. Available at: https://www.parliament.uk/documents/banking-commission/Banking-final-report-volume-i.pdf (accessed 3 August 2016).

- reforming governance within banks to reinforce each bank's responsibility for its own safety and soundness and for the maintenance of standards;
- creating better functioning and more diverse banking markets in order to empower consumers and provide greater discipline on banks to raise standards;
- reinforcing the responsibilities of regulators in the exercise of judgement in deploying their current and proposed new powers; and
- specifying the responsibilities of the Government and of future Governments and Parliaments.

> No single change, however dramatic, will address the problems of banking standards. Reform across several fronts is badly needed, and in ways that will endure when memories of recent crises and scandals fade.[12]

The Commission's report also made a telling remark in its conclusion, which I find appropriate to any study of the effect of 'Rogue Trader' losses and SYSC failures:

> Banks in the UK have failed in many respects. They have failed taxpayers, who had to bail out a number of banks including some major institutions, with a cash outlay peaking at £133 billion, equivalent to more than £2,000 for every person in the UK. They have failed many retail customers, with widespread product mis-selling. They have failed their own shareholders, by delivering poor long-term returns and destroying shareholder value.[13]

Regulators in the UK have been 'consulting' on the problem for some years and, following this Parliamentary Commission report, issued a Consultation Paper to the industry for comment in 2014,[14] and followed up in 2015.[15] These consultation papers give the industry an opportunity to let the regulator know what they think of the regulatory environment and how the proposed changes might affect their businesses. The regulator then takes the responses into account before deciding on final policy.

These papers cover management of SYSC and Operational Risk, among other management issues now being addressed by regulators, and in March 2016 the FCA and PRA delivered their final policies and introduced a 'Senior Managers

12 Ibid.

13 Ibid.

14 CP14/13: Strengthening Accountability in Banking: A New Regulatory Framework for Individuals (30 July 2014). Available at: https://www.fca.org.uk/news/cp14-13-strengthening-accountability-in-banking (accessed 3 August 2016).

15 CP15/22: Strengthening Accountability in Banking: Final Rules (Including Feedback on CP14/31 and CP15/5) and Consultation on Extending the Certification Regime to Wholesale Market Activities) (7 July 2015). Available at: https://www.fca.org.uk/news/cp15-22-strengthening-accountability-in-banking-final-rules (accessed 3 August 2016).

Regime' and 'Certification Regime',[16] which will have the effect of making senior management directly responsible for the actions of staff who enter into risk positions on behalf of the bank or for clients, and will introduce a regime where SYSC is backed up by evidence of qualification and continuous training of the senior management who have the responsibility to apply and monitor controls.

Back in 2008, when sizeable, capital-damaging, losses started to become apparent, there was a popular 'joke' circulating within banking circles:

> Who is the odd one out in this list: Lord Stevenson, Chairman of HBOS; Andy Hornby, CEO of HBOS; Sir Tom McKillop, Chairman of RBS; Fred Goodwin, CEO of RBS; Gordon Brown, Chancellor/PM; Sir Terry Wogan, TV and radio presenter?

The answer, of course, was:

> Sir Terry Wogan – he was the only one who had a banking qualification!

So many people were in senior positions in the banking and finance industry who had got to the top executive positions without any formal qualifications to justify their place there. It was to be expected that these were all very experienced people who had earned their places at the top of corporate entities through knowledge and previous successes, but perhaps their experiences were not suitable for the 2007–2008 crisis environment in the banking industry, and previous successes in 'bull markets' offered no experience which would help in a 'bear market'. There was also a suspicion, however, that there were occasions when a senior director was appointed because his/her prominent name could enhance the bank's headed notepaper!

The Financial Services Authority (FSA) and other international regulators had always focused on the banks' customers, and so had always required a more formal qualification regime for any professional in the financial markets sector who was responsible for advising, or even talking to, private customers, as that was where they saw the need for protection.

The FSA had a series of 'Control Functions' (CF),[17] which identified the various officers of a financial institution who have important roles (in the view of the regulator), and logged them on an FSA Register as 'Approved Persons'. In 2008 they ranged from CF1, the Chief Executive Function, to CF30, the Customer Function (though recently two more have been added to cover officers

16 FCA Policy Statement 16/6 of 2 March 2016 (https://www.fca.org.uk/news/ps16-06-consequential-changes-to-the-senior-managers-regime); FCA Policy Statement 16/3 of 4 February 2016 (https://www.fca.org.uk/news/ps16-03-strengthening-banking-accountability) and PRA Policy Statement 13/16 of March 2016 (http://www.bankofengland.co.uk/pra/Documents/publications/ps/2016/ps1316.pdf).

17 See https://www.the-fca.org.uk/approved-persons/controlled-functions?field_fcasf_sector=unset&field_fcasf_page_category=unset.

responsible for devising and reporting benchmarks). But it was only the CF30 who required specific formal qualifications, documented and carefully checked, to become an Approved Person. (Note: most of those employees undertaking solely a 'trading' function, which did not involve any communication with customers, did not require any sort of regulatory approval.)

The FSA, predecessor to the Financial Conduct Authority (FCA) and Prudential Regulation Authority (PRA), had started looking at the roles of directors as long ago as the early 2000s, and had been consulted on the report of Derek Higgs, which was published in January 2003 (The Higgs Report).[18]

The Higgs Report was addressed to the Chancellor of the Exchequer and gave an assessment of the boardroom directorial governance of the corporate sector in general – the FSA looked at its application to the banking and finance industry, and so, as long ago as 2003, started considering how the senior management structure of financial institutions might be brought into the registration regime, which has required until now only that officers dealing directly with customers prove their qualifications and maintain their knowledge via regular training. Other senior staff had to be approved by the FSA, but only in so far as background checks revealed no criminal records, personal financial problems or previous regulatory mishaps.

Both the PRA (responsible for monitoring the financial stability of firms in the financial sector) and the FCA (responsible for monitoring the conduct and market practices of firms in the financial sector) have now issued policy statements, which include rules that require prior approval by the regulator of Chairmen, Senior Independent Directors and the Chairs of Audit, Remuneration and Risk Committees.

The Parliamentary Commission's report focused on the damage done to the economy by the banking sector's failures. The FCA addressed this in its Consultation Papers and Policy Statements and introduced the term 'significant harm' to describe how major losses and SYSC failures have a wider effect on the stability of the financial markets beyond the failing institution. In describing its policy, the FCA says:

> A key aspect of the Certification Regime is the importance it places on firms assessing for themselves the fitness and propriety of staff who carry out 'significant harm functions' (SHF) both at the point of recruitment and on an ongoing basis.[19]

So, a key aspect of the new Senior Management Regime is this 'significant harm function', which should identify, and highlight for special management supervision,

18 Higgs, D. (2003). *Review of the Role and Effectiveness of Non-executive Directors.* London: The Stationery Office. Available at: http://www.ecgi.org/codes/documents/higgsreport.pdf (accessed 3 August 2016).
19 See CP15/22 above, n. 15.

the staff who could pose a risk of significant harm to the firm or to any of its customers. This would cover proprietary traders such as Kerviel who can do significant harm to a bank's balance sheet and, importantly, its reputation, but also investment advisers, brokers and the staff who administer benchmarks (such as LIBOR) which have a bearing on the financial markets as a whole.

Thus, the FCA is making it clear that its rules are intended to address the SYSC failures and that the senior management of any firm will now have to take personal responsibility for failures and, further, must be qualified and trained to take such responsibility. In this way we might see headlines in the future which no longer shout about a 'Rogue Trader', but maybe an 'Unsupervised Trader' or a 'Mismanaged Trader'. The word 'Rogue' can then be reserved for the real criminals, those who devise systems specifically intended to defraud, such as Michael Milken in the 1980s or, more recently, Bernie Madoff.

This new regulatory regime, which started in March 2016 by being applied to the major financial institutions, has a transition period of 12 months before it applies to all firms. In its Policy Statement, the FCA has set out a basic standard of behaviour that it expects from financial market participants, and has put the onus on the firms' management to take responsibility for ensuring compliance with the new rules, and for applying suitable systems to control their businesses. A key instruction from the regulator to the firms is that it is the firms that will be expected to ensure that the relevant staff members are made aware of the new conduct rules and how those rules apply to the different kinds of businesses.

Firms were always responsible for ensuring that they had suitable staff in each aspect of their business, but relied on the FCA giving its endorsement by qualifying them as 'Approved Persons' (a qualification that throughout a financial market participant's career might pass from one firm to another, as that person's job changed, without ever being reassessed), but never before was the onus put on firms to undertake what is almost a 'positive vetting' of their staff, with an annual review and confirmation of continuing qualification. In the past they could, for instance, rely on academic qualifications such as a CFA, or membership of a professional body such as the Chartered Institute for Securities and Investment or the Institute of Chartered Accountants as a 'proof' of ability (passed once, never reassessed!). Now firms must check on and verify the 'fit and proper' status of staff before they put them forward for approval by the FCA, and they must confirm continuing qualification with annual checks, to ensure that training and knowledge is maintained and kept up to date.

This new approach by the FCA is set out in its 'Principles of Good Regulation' (as stated on the FCA website in January 2015),[20] in which it states clearly what is expected of senior management in firms. The Principle relating to senior management responsibility has three components:

20 See http://www.fca.org.uk/about/operate/principles.

> A firm's senior management is responsible for the firm's activities and for ensuring that its business complies with regulatory requirements. This secures an adequate but proportionate level of regulatory intervention by holding senior management responsible for the risk management and controls within firms. Firms must make it clear who has what responsibility and ensure that its business can be adequately monitored and controlled.[21]

In presenting this new regime in a speech at the time of the Consultation, in July 2015, Martin Wheatley, then CEO of FCA, said, very simply: '[W]e should have nothing to fear from high standards.'[22]

As the process developed from consultation to policy, Tracy McDermott, then Acting CEO of FCA, said in December 2015:

> There are two major priorities here.
>
> - The first is that there is a clear focus from firms on meeting the spirit of the new rules, rather than approaching this with a narrow focus on what the letter of the law requires.
> - The second, linked task is that firms must take ownership of the regime and embrace the opportunities it presents for their business.[23]

This is an important, if pithy, announcement. It requires firms to understand the *intention and required outcome* of the rules, and to apply them to achieve that end. We can only hope that this will mean that firms will adjust their business practices to meet this intention and requirement of the rules, rather than, as has too often been the case in the past, acquire legal interpretations of the rules to fit their business model!

Finally, as the new Policy Statements and rules were introduced, Anthony Browne of the British Bankers Association (BBA), when commenting on the FCA's policy, chose to quote Uncle Ben's advice to Spider-Man: 'With great power comes great responsibility.'[24]

It is to be hoped, therefore, that the new regime will see people in positions of senior responsibility being held to account for failures within their areas of management and control.

Summary and outlook

There can be little doubt that we will still see large losses in firms when their traders get it wrong, or when they make poor judgements and do loss-making

21 Ibid.
22 See https://www.fca.org.uk/news/accountability-from-debate-to-reality.
23 See https://www.fca.org.uk/news/personal-accountability.
24 See https://www.bba.org.uk/news/insight/chief-executives-newsletter-march-2016.

deals. There can also be little doubt that criminals (or 'rogues') will still try to make money from banks and their customers. But the new regulatory regime appears to be designed to ensure that responsibility for errors, misreporting or systems and control failures will lie firmly where it belongs – with the management of those activities or management of the systems meant to monitor and control the activities.

Even as these new policies and rules are being introduced, however, we are seeing new 'roguish' activity being identified – LIBOR benchmark-fixing, foreign exchange (FX) trading irregularities and the like.

All we can hope for is that the 'rogues' find it more difficult to operate and that the SYSC develops to control businesses and catch any roguish activity earlier, before what is now called 'significant harm' is done.

5 The systemic role of technology in financial instability

Dionysios Demetis

5.1 Introduction and review

The role of technology in shaping financial crises is both fundamental and systemic. This chapter develops a theoretical model for such technological interference in the financial markets, based on principles of *systems theory*. This is done by the extraction of a set of theoretical propositions (designated as P_1, P_2, P_3, P_n) that will be synthesised in the discussion. The case of the Flash Crash of the Dow Jones Industrial Average (DJIA) is also utilised for this purpose; deriving from it, additional propositions are extracted for exploring the role of technology in this context.

Of course, in the academic literature, scholars have explored the intersection of technology/crashes from a number of different perspectives. For example, Brandt and Neumann[1] explore the role of information technology in causing ambiguities by employing hyper game theory and render flash crashes on the actions of rational agents. Bréhier[2] considers the role of technology (and its evolution) as a threat for the financial markets and prompts us to reflect on the variety of regulatory measures that need to be introduced (e.g. by revising the Market in Financial Instruments Directive (MiFID2)[3] and the Market Abuse Directive (MAD2)).[4] In a similar trajectory, the importance of a regulatory intervention for market stabilisation is stressed by Brewer *et al.*,[5] as well as Ciallella,[6] who tracks the regulatory evolution of high-frequency trading (HFT) and considers MiFID2. This is

1 Brandt, T. and Neumann, D. (2015) Chasing lemmings: modeling IT-induced misperceptions about the strategic situation as a reason for flash crashes. *Journal of Management Information Systems* 31(4): 88–108.
2 Bréhier, B. (2013) High frequency trading: should technological developments be considered a potential threat to financial markets and be subject to specific regulation?, *ERA Forum* 14(1): 69–80.
3 Markets in Financial Instruments Directive (Directive 2004/39/EC).
4 Market Abuse Directive (EU) 2015/2392 of 17 December 2015.
5 Brewer, P. *et al.* (2013) Market microstructure design and flash crashes: a simulation approach. *Journal of Applied Economics* 16(2): 223–250.
6 Ciallella, G. (2015) Describing and regulating high-frequency trading: a European perspective. *Handbook of High Frequency Trading*, pp. 95–110.

extended by Moosa and Ramiah[7] who explore this in an Asian context where regulators considered imposing restrictions on high-frequency trading.

Baxter and Cartlidge[8] reflect on the interactions between large-scale (technological) systems and the financial markets by pointing out that the level of complexity has risen significantly in how automation affects the financial system. In exploring the role of technology for the Flash Crash, Bethel *et al.* take a 'technology vs technology' approach: they explore the deployment of supercomputers to detect the problems that algorithmic traders may generate; this is directed towards the development of an automated 'early warning system' that would generate alerts towards unusual market conditions.[9] At a micro-level, others propose risk-averse reinforcement learning for algorithmic trading,[10] thereby placing technological emphasis on the individual 'rationality' of distinct algorithmic players. This approach does not seem to be shared by other scholars who view the Flash Crash as a disastrous consequence of computerised trading systems.[11] Moosa dismisses the criticism directed at high-frequency trading[12] while Stoll views such developments as side-effects towards a path of more liquid and less costly markets.[13] In turn, this is contradicted by an examination of how news affects electronic systems, whereby Cai *et al.* find that electronic markets are prone to greater stealth trading and post-trade volatility (expressing also concern for the proliferation of algorithmic trading and short-term volatility).[14] At the same time, Treleave *et al.* view algorithmic trading as a 'secretive community where implementation details are difficult to find'.[15]

With the debate on the role of technology in the development of crises (like the Flash Crash) showing no signs of relaxation, this chapter positions itself in the context of this literature by taking a *systems theoretical* approach. While every recent financial crisis has largely been accelerated by technology (through the

7 Moosa, I. and Ramiah, V. (2014) The regulation of high-frequency trading: an Asian perspective. *Handbook of Asian Finance: REITs, Trading, and Fund Performance* 2: 153–170.
8 Baxter, G. and Cartlidge, J. (2013) *Flying by the Seat of Their Pants: What Can High Frequency Trading Learn from Aviation?* ACM International Conference Proceeding Series.
9 Bethel, E. W. *et al.* (2011) *Federal Market Information Technology in the Post Flash Crash Era: Roles for Supercomputing.* WHPCF'11 – Proceedings of the 4th Workshop on High Performance Computational Finance, Co-located with SC'11.
10 Shen, Y. *et al.* (2014) *Risk-averse Reinforcement Learning for Algorithmic Trading.* IEEE/IAFE Conference on Computational Intelligence for Financial Engineering, Proceedings (CIFEr).
11 Edwards, C. (2010) Flash and burn. *Engineering and Technology* 5(13): 50–53.
12 Moosa, I. (2015) The regulation of high-frequency trading: a pragmatic view. *Journal of Banking Regulation* 16(1): 72–88.
13 Stoll, H. R. (2014) High speed equities trading: 1993–2012. *Asia-Pacific Journal of Financial Studies* 43(6): 767–797.
14 Cai, C. X. *et al.* (2015) Informed trading and market structure. *European Financial Management* 21: 148–177.
15 Treleaven, P. *et al.* (2013) Algorithmic trading review. *Communications of the ACM* 56(11): 76–85.

sheer speed of communication), the financial world has now reached a stage where the *systemic* role of technology is *en route* to dominate how the next financial crises will unravel. Behind all of the underlying complexity, the reason for this is rather simple (albeit phrased in its extreme form): human beings are no longer making financial decisions. Algorithms have replaced human decision-making to a large extent. Nowadays,

> the majority of volume is traded electronically, based on systematic computer algorithms. The ultra-high-speed version of algorithmic trading, high frequency trading, is estimated to account for over 77% of transactions in the UK market according to Tabb Group.[16]

For example, in the foreign exchange market since 2009, it has been estimated that more than 85 per cent of all trading is conducted by algorithms alone: in their study published by the board of governors of the Federal Reserve, Chaboud *et al.* called this the 'Rise of the Machines'.[17] This creates the following (intensifying) condition:

P_1: In the financial markets, algorithms dominate financial decisions and have largely replaced human decisions.

While several technological and financial forces are responsible for this development, one question that may immediately come to mind could be phrased as follows: Are not the designers of algorithms humans? Therefore, could not we think of algorithms (and technology in general when applied to the financial system) as an extension, an abstraction even, of human decisions? As we will see in the example further on with the Flash Crash in the Dow Jones Index, there are several obstacles to thinking about the role of technology in this way and several elements that complicate the circumstances further. In brief, the idea of technology as a force that imposes linearity and cause-and-effect relationships needs to abandoned.[18] While technology at a micro-scale is controllable, technology at a macro-scale creates non-linear emergent phenomena that infect any corresponding

16 Sornette, D. and Becke, S. v. d. (2011) *Crashes and High Frequency Trading: An Evaluation of Risks Posed by High-Speed Algorithmic Trading.* UK Government Foresight Project, The Future of Computer Trading in Financial Markets, p. 5. Available at: https://www.gov.uk/government/uploads/system/uploads/attachment_data/file/289016/11-1226-dr7-crashes-and-high-frequency-trading.pdf (accessed 3 August 2016).

17 Chaboud, A. *et al.* (2009) *Rise of the Machines: Algorithmic Trading in the Foreign Exchange Market.* International Finance Discussion Papers 980. Board of Governors of the Federal Reserve System. Available at: https://www.federalreserve.gov/pubs/ifdp/2009/980/ifdp980.pdf (accessed 3 August 2016).

18 Reichel, A. (2011) Technology as system: towards an autopoietic theory of technology. *International Journal of Innovation and Sustainable Development* 5(2/3): 105–118.

application domain with uncertainty and unpredictability.[19] There is a clear systemic role to technology within the global financial sector and it is increasingly expected that algorithms will be autonomous in their actions. This inevitably raises significant moral and ethical issues in the 'machine world'.[20]

The same pattern towards algorithmic dominance can be observed across multiple financial markets. Speed of transacting has become not only essential but also constitutive of the way markets behave under algorithmic guidance. The role of algorithms in financial decisions has become so central that they are guarded as 'state secrets' due to their potential impact on the markets. A good example of this is the background to the story of Sergey Aleynikov, a Russian computer programmer who was working for Goldman Sachs and was subsequently arrested by the FBI for stealing part of the algorithmic trading code. In the proceedings of this case before the United States Southern District Court of New York, the US attorney representing the government stated the following (in the context of the severity of this incident and the dangers from the stolen computer code): –

> The bank's profit margin will be eroded – and I'll explain why in a minute – by the other competitive activity. In addition, because of the way this software interfaces with the various markets and exchanges, *the bank has raised a possibility that there is a danger that somebody who knew how to use this program could use it to manipulate markets in unfair ways.*
>
> What this program does is connect and draw information from stock exchanges around the country, and it draws them in very small increments of time. One of the bank officers described it as *milliseconds of time.* And it is very efficient at processing that stock information and sending to the bank's programs that conduct trades based upon algorithms that are developed by mathematicians and physicists.[21]

What is rather evident – and astonishing – is that *the same technological/algorithmic development* that is used for profit-making from one financial institution is depicted (by government officials!) as a perceived danger of 'unfair market manipulation' in the hands of someone else (based on the information the bank itself gave the government). So a major financial institution such as Goldman Sachs can be entrusted to use this algorithmic technology in a sensible way, but in the hands of someone else it could amount to manipulation? Of course, the real question

19 Backhouse, J. *et al.* (2005) Spotlight: new approaches to fighting money-laundering. demetis.wordpress.com; Demetis, D. and Angell, I. (2006) AML-related technologies: a systemic risk. *Journal of Money Laundering Control* 9(2): 157–172.

20 Van Lier, B. (2016) From high frequency trading to self-organizing moral machines. *International Journal of Technoethics* 7(1): 34–50.

21 United States District Court Southern District of New York (2009) US against Sergey Aleynikov, Proceedings before Magistrate Judge Kevin N. Fox. Available at: http://www.securityprivacyandthelaw.com/uploads/file/Transcript (US v_ Aleynikov).pdf (accessed 3 August 2016), pp. 7–8, emphasis added.

behind this is as follows: Would regulators be in a position to unpack the *effects* of algorithms designed by mathematicians and physicists that operate across markets over milliseconds and *en masse*? The answer to that as we shall see is to the negative – this is a *complex system* where the multiplicity of interactions remains invisible. But in light of the aforementioned case and the significance of a single algorithmic platform (guided and executed by a single market player), the following proposition can be put forward:

P_2: Through algorithmic trading, a single market player can create considerable effects in an extremely limited time-span.

Another consequence of these dynamics that are illustrated in the case above is the importance of *security* in protecting these algorithms. This opens up the possibility of 'computer hacking' in the financial markets and algorithmic-generated crises, not by debilitating the financial system in itself but by trading within its algorithmic confines.

From the few examples discussed already we can see how the role of technology in the financial system is characterised by deep penetration effects instead of superficial technological use. The following section builds on this idea and extracts several propositions based on systems theory.

5.2 Basics of systems theory and reflections for the financial *system*

In what way is the financial system a *system* and in what way is a financial crisis a *systemic* phenomenon? This section approaches systems as objects of study in general and identifies further propositions that emerge directly from prominent scholars in the field of systems theory. This will help us connect the role of technology in dominating financial decision-making and develop the conceptual synthesis that ties in technology and financial instability.

First, it is important to recognise that the vision for the development of systems theory came in the early 1950s with the Society for General Systems Research. Bertalanffy,[22] Boulding,[23] Rapoport[24] and then Miller[25] sought to develop a meta-theory that would be used to describe different phenomena and apply across different fields. The whole endeavour has been called a *science of synthesis*[26] and

22 Bertalanffy, L. V. (1950) An outline of general system theory. *British Journal for the Philosophy of Science* 1(2): 134–165.

23 Boulding, K. E. (1956) General systems theory – the skeleton of science. *Management Science* 2(3): 197–208.

24 Rapoport, A. (1950) *Science and the Goals of Man; A Study in Semantic Orientation* (Harper).

25 Miller, J. G. (1978) *Living Systems* (McGraw-Hill).

26 Hammond, D. (2003) *The Science of Synthesis: Exploring the Social Implications of General Systems Theory* (University Press of Colorado).

applied across many fields: physics, biology, sociology, law, finance, etc. The generality of systems theory can be perceived as:

> the skeleton of science in the sense that it aims to provide a framework or structure of systems on which to hang the flesh and blood of particular disciplines and particular subject matters in an orderly and coherent corpus of knowledge.[27]

A system can be defined as a 'complex of interacting elements e_1, e_2 . . . e_n. Interaction means that the elements stand in a certain relation, R, so that their behaviour in R is different from their behavior in an another relation, R'.'[28] Another way to think about this is that a system is constituted of its subsystems (and by these sub-subsystems, *ad infinitum*). This definition of a system must also be put into the context of the primary distinction that can be recognised across several branches of systems theory – that is the recognition that any system must be distinguished from its *environment*; the distinction between system/environment is fundamental. No system can exist without an environment[29] and for any defined system, the environment is always more complex.[30] These very few starting principles are identified below as ST_1, ST_2, ST_3, . . . and they have major ramifications analysed by Skyttner[31] and expanded below with insights developed by other systems theoreticians such as Von Foerster,[32] Bateson,[33] Beer[34] and Luhmann:[35]

ST_1: **Interdependence**: A system is constituted of elements and relations (or of subsystems, sub-subsystems, etc.). It is the interrelationship and interdependence of objects and their attributes that is significant; unrelated and independent elements can never constitute a system.

ST_2: **Holism**: Holistic properties (at the level of the system itself) cannot possibly be detected by any analysis of the 'components' of the systems. However, it is still possible to define such holistic properties in the system. Properties that can be found at the level of the system but are spawned from the

27 Boulding, p. 208 (see above, n. 23).

28 Bertalanffy, p. 143 (see above, n. 22).

29 Bertalanffy, L. (1969) *General System Theory* (George Braziller, Inc.); Luhmann, N. (1995) *Social Systems* (Stanford University Press); and Luhmann, N. (2006) System as difference. *Organization* 13(1): 37–57.

30 Luhmann, N. (2002) *Deconstruction as Second-Order Observing. Theories of Distinction: Redescribing the Descriptions of Modernity* (Stanford University Press), pp. 94–112.

31 Skyttner, L. (2005) *General Systems Theory: Problems, Perspectives, Practice* (World Scientific), p. 53.

32 Von Foerster, H. (1951) *Cybernetics, Circular Causal and Feedback Mechanisms in Biological and Social Systems: Transactions* (Josiah Macy, Jr. Foundation).

33 Bateson, G. (1972) *Steps to an Ecology of Mind* (Ballantine Books).

34 Beer, S. (1985) *Diagnosing the System for Organizations* (Wiley).

35 Luhmann, N. (1995) *Social Systems* (Stanford University Press).

complex interactions of the system's components (and as such they cannot be reduced to the study of those components) are called *emergent properties.*

ST_3: Goal seeking: Systemic interaction must result in some goal or final state to be reached or some equilibrium point being approached. However, within each system there are subsystems with different (and distinct) goals, and due to the complexity of the environment, there is always uncertainty that cannot allow strict controllability of systems. Still, the system (e.g. an organisation) identifies itself with a strategic goal.

ST_4: Transformation process: All systems, if they are to attain their goal, must transform inputs into outputs. In living systems this transformation is mainly of a cyclical nature.

ST_5: Inputs and outputs: In a closed system the inputs are determined once and for all; in an open system additional inputs are admitted from its environment. In today's business environment, organisations can be conceived of as complex open systems.

ST_6: Regulation: The interrelated objects constituting the system must be regulated in some fashion so that its goals can be realised. Regulation implies that necessary deviations will be detected and corrected. One can extend this at an operational level and think of such systems as *self-regulating systems*: systems that have the capacity to adapt themselves based on a set of rules and conditions.

ST_7: Hierarchy: Systems are generally complex wholes made up of smaller subsystems. This nesting of systems within other systems is what is implied by hierarchy. As mentioned already, this would follow the form of: systems → subsystems → sub-subsystems, *ad infinitum.*

ST_8: Differentiation: In complex systems, specialised units perform specialised functions. This is a characteristic of all complex systems and may also be called specialisation or division of labour.

ST_9: Equifinality and **multifinality**: Open systems have equally valid alternative ways of attaining the same objectives from different initial conditions (convergence) or, from a given initial state, obtain different and mutually exclusive objectives (divergence).

What propositions can we extract from the above high-level systems theoretical principles for the financial system and the concept of the financial crisis itself? We will take the above aspects and expand on them for the identification of such propositions. First, what we could identify as a *financial system* commences with the interrelationship and interdependence of the system's different elements. Hence, from **ST_1** we can consider the financial *system* as constituted of complex interdependencies that are significant for the system itself. From this, we can consider that:

P_3: A financial crisis is a holistic property of the financial system and constitutes an emergent phenomenon. A crisis emerges out of the interaction of several interdependent components and cannot be attributable to a single transacting element.

Portrayed this way, the concept of financial crisis is viewed as an expression of the system itself. There may be an initial stimulus (that will lead to a financial crisis eventually), but neither the 'stimulus' (and how that is spawned) nor the pathway towards a financial crisis can be determined. A financial crisis is not something that can be predicted uniquely so that meaningful action can be taken – to a degree that it will stop the crisis from ever manifesting. The evidence for this is everywhere but mostly on the realisation that *no advanced mathematical/statistical technique, big data analysis or market interpretation* has ever predicted a crisis (or its effects and unravelling extent). Ironically, the financial *system* itself, when reaching the realisation that it generates contradictory descriptions of itself that lead to its own destabilisation, has sought a way to create financial instruments for de-risking. The second-order derivatives market can be seen as a paradoxical manifestation of this. But, of course, one may 'mention the volatility of the financial market with its new derivative instruments for simultaneously maximising security and risk with unpredictable effects'.[36]

Risk and unpredictability are also present in the context of any system. If we take a specific organisation as an example of our **ST_3** principle on goal-seeking, then we may observe that different organisations (if we define those as our systems) will have different goal-seeking strategies. These are always time-dependent and depend also on complex system/environment interactions, and on the degree in which the system allows feedback from its environment in shaping its goal-seeking strategies. If we take a trading algorithm as the system to be examined, then we can consider that:

P_4: Algorithms launched from different financial players will have different goal-seeking strategies. When they are activated and become part of the financial system, algorithms find themselves in a much more complex environment. They affect and are affected by that environment (in which other algorithms reside) in unpredictable ways. While each algorithm 'controls' its actions, the effects for the financial system as a whole are emergent.

Based on **ST_4** and **ST_5**, all systems transform inputs into outputs. This takes a number of varieties in the context of the financial system, but there are several examples that can reflect this further. Given the conceptual focus of this chapter in algorithmic processing, we can look at this process through that context. In algorithmic trading, selected *inputs* (such as the *price of a stock* or the trading *volume*) can be chosen from an algorithm; the *output* then is an *automated decision* (e.g. buy/sell an X amount of that stock at that price). Even though such a

36 Luhmann, N. (1997) Globalization or world society: how to conceive of modern society. *International Review of Sociology* 7(1): 13–67.

transformation process seems to be controllable, there are environmental stimuli that algorithms consider automatically without human interference. Decision algorithms now take input from:

a) the system of *mass media* – the algorithms deconstruct and analyse news automatically about the companies they are monitoring; for example, Bloomberg uses sentiment analysis of company news in order to classify news items as 'negative' news for a company;[37] the algorithm can act on that 'automated' news feed and trigger a sequence of further automated buy/sell decisions;
b) the wider system of the *economy*, where trading patterns are being monitored and fed into automated trading decisions that use numerical thresholds; and
c) the system of *law*, where legislative initiatives or guidelines (e.g. issued by the Securities and Exchange Commission) are deconstructed as logical restrictions, thereby forbidding certain courses of action for the trading algorithms (e.g. do not engage in abusive short-selling).

Based on the exposition described above,

P_5: Algorithms take *inputs* from the financial system in various ways (e.g. price, volume, news, restrictions) and transform these inputs into *outputs that take the form of algorithmic decisions.*

Based on **P_5** as stated above (and extrapolated from the preceding analysis), it is worth emphasising that *inputs* are allowed from the *environment* of each algorithm. This renders the totality of algorithmic trading as a complex open system; it also implies that any cause-and-effect relationships embodied by individual algorithms (through a strict rational logic in the form of: *if* this event occurs *then* execute a specified sequence) cannot be followed through at a macro-scale. Inputs from the environment are unpredictable and, while each algorithm usually underpins specific thresholds through which the automated execution of decisions will be manifested, this is not always the case. As we will see in the case of the Flash Crash of 2:45 of the Dow Jones Index, at least one algorithm did not consider price fluctuations at all in its automated decision-making, but only volume.

This shift towards algorithmic decision-making has implications for **ST_6**, **ST_7**, **ST_8** and **ST_9** (regulation, hierarchy, differentiation and equafinality). While each algorithm is self-regulating (and human intervention may take place in critical parts of the process as and when required), the effects of algorithms become part of the environment (and then feed back as stimuli to the algorithms themselves). This circularity requires both differentiation and hierarchy to be dealt with, but

37 Bloomberg (2015). Sentiment analysis of financial news and social media. Available at: http://www.bloomberglabs.com/data-science/projects/sentiment-analysis-financial-news-social-media.

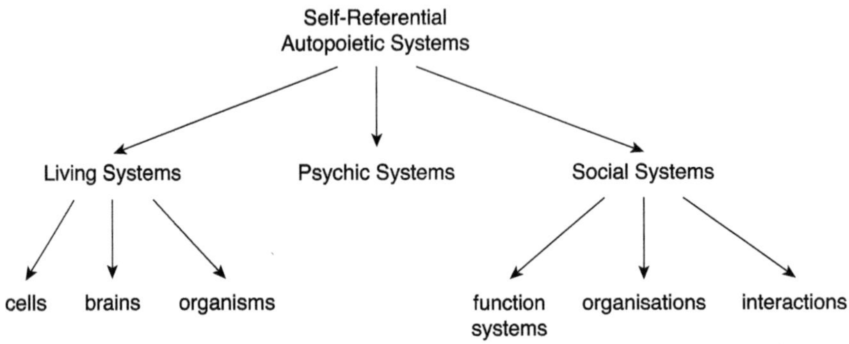

Figure 5.1 Classification of systems

can never be accounted for, as the complexity in the financial system supersedes any attempt at controlling the market.

The implications of the previous propositions can now be considered in light of further systemic elaborations. This is based on systems theorist Niklas Luhmann, who developed systems science further and applied it to society and its subsystems (law, economics, politics, media, etc.). While Luhmann's work is complicated, a basic diagram can assist us in conceptualising his classification of systems (Figure 5.1 above).[38]

'Living systems' refer to biological entities, while 'psychic systems' refer to the minds of human individuals. Our focus here is 'social systems'. For Luhmann, the only function that is primary at the level of society itself is *communication*. Hence, social systems can be conceived of as communication systems; communication involves 'a unity of announcement (*Mitteilung*) or "utterance" based on information (*Information*),[39] and understanding (*Verstehen*)'.[40] Any act of communication within social systems (or subsystems of society such as the *financial system*) involves these three elements. Financial communication in particular can be considered as:

1. *announcements/utterances* where stakeholders initiate buy/sell decisions; these utterances are considered as
2. *information* from other stakeholders that engage with them, and then, based on their
3. *understanding* (a cognitive interpretation of the received information), the latter decide to act and initiate their own 'utterances'.

38 Luhmann, N. (1990) *Essays on Self Reference* (Columbia University Press); Moeller, H.-G. (2006) *Luhmann Explained* (Carus Publishing Company).
39 Seidl, D. (2006) Organizations as distinction generating and processing systems: Niklas Luhmann's contribution to organization studies. *Organization* 13(1): 9–35.
40 Moeller, p. 22 (see above, n. 38).

With the development of algorithmic trading, this fundamental model of communication has changed drastically since the last part – ***cognitively interpreting*** the received information – is missing. We can no longer speak of ***understanding*** (*Verstehen*) in communication through algorithmic processing. Accordingly, this allows us to consider that:

P$_6$: The development of algorithmic trading is based on a faster form of communication that eliminates the step of cognitive understanding in the process of communicating. This is replaced by ***algorithmic 'understanding'*** – a limited logical type that collapses understanding to mere information processing.

This shift in how humans communicate (with the assistance of technology) to how algorithms communicate (in the absence of human interference) has additional implications for how we can depict financial interactions between stakeholders. For example, in the economic system, any interactions that can be considered as economic communications involve the 'satisfaction of needs'; the meaning (or what Luhmann calls the 'code') of the economic system is expressed through the unity of the distinction between 'payment/non-payment'. Similar conditions arise for other subsystems of society (Luhmann calls these function systems) like the legal system, where communication involves the 'regulation of conflicts' and the code is expressed based on the distinction between 'legal/illegal'.[41] In this regard, 'codes' are binary distinctions that encapsulate the identity of a core system in society and support communication across all of their subsystems. 'Organisations', as another form of social system, also conduct communication, but Luhmann specifically conceptualises organisations as conducting the communication of decisions, and hence are 'systems of decisions'.[42]

In considering each social subsystem (such as the financial system) through an expression of a fundamental 'binary code', Luhmann depicts such a code as the fundamental basis upon which the identities of these subsystems rest. This fundamental code cannot be resolved – such a process would result in a paradox. For example, paradoxically, the legal system cannot define what is legal or illegal – this is defined through operations:

> [W]hile the distinction between legal and illegal can be maintained for individual coding, the legal system as a unity can never decide the basis of what is legal or illegal. It can never apply the code to itself as a system. There is no foundational value establishing what is legal or illegal, only operations.[43]

41 Moeller, p. 29 (see above, n. 38).
42 Moeller, p. 31 (see above, n. 38).
43 Luhmann, N. (2004) *Law as a Social System* (Oxford University Press).

This creates a unique self-reference that is always underpinned by a paradox: 'this enables the legal system to operate legally (!) by declaring that something is legal or against the law'.[44]

Hence, the basic relationship behind the 'code' of the financial system and technology can be expressed as follows.

P_7: Technology as it is currently being used in the financial system creates a meta-organisation: a system of automated decisions that shape the 'code' of the financial system itself and influence the primary distinction of payment/non-payment.

In other words, technology itself imposes its logic in shaping the very *identity* of the financial system. Through technologically induced automated decisions, the code of the financial system (payment/non-payment) is expressed. Algorithmic operations constitute the basis for these expressions at an operational level.

Additional theoretical aspects of systems can help us to establish further general propositions upon which we can build reflections for the role of technology in the development of financial crises (following the March 2010 event descriptions in the next section). Another important aspect that has already been mentioned and is emphasised further here is the distinction between system and environment. For Luhmann, the environment is not a residual category (here system, there environment), but constitutive of the existence of the system. Between any defined system (and its environment) there is a structural coupling and one cannot exist without the other. This ontological binding between system and environment has considerable implications if applied to the role of technology in the financial system. If technology underpins the financial system as a *system*, then what is its environment? Where does the technologically driven *financial system* receive its information from? There are several possibilities here, but other function systems in society (such as the legal system or the system of mass media) would be the appropriate candidates, as already mentioned. This drives the need for further automation in the financial system itself (and an unstoppable excessive reliance on technology) as the precondition for system/environment interactions now becomes the automation of the environment, or, indeed, the automation of specific information-dependency paths from the environment of the financial system. This force has created several contingencies and few examples can be found here: one that has already been mentioned is the integration of *sentiment analysis* by automated means in order to filter negative news of companies. As Hendershott *et al.* frame it:

> [S]ome algorithms are designed to sniff out other algorithms or otherwise identify order flow and other information patterns in the data. For example, if an algorithm identifies a sequence of buys in the data and concludes that

44 Ibid.

> more buys are coming, an algorithmic liquidity supplier might adjust its ask price upward. Information in newswires can even be parsed electronically in order to adjust trading algorithms.[45]

And what if the information in newswires is also computer-generated (or is an error or ambiguous)? How can we perceive the function of technology then? In May 2014, the Associated Press (AP) announced that the majority of stories about US earnings for business news reports would eventually be produced by using automated technology. Lou Ferrara, Vice President and Managing Director of AP, stated that in this way 'instead of providing 300 stories manually, we can provide up to 4,400 automatically for companies throughout the United States each quarter'.[46]

So automation in one function system (mass media) is being used as input for automation in another function system (financial system). This level of *automated couplings* should really concern us, along with the fact that automated decision-taking is occurring in each case. In fact, automated decision-taking is being used as input for further automated decision-taking. This process of 'automation out of automation' across the financial system indicates the self-referential character of this condition and how technology is starting to hijack financial decision-making. Through the medium of algorithms, automation re-inserts itself into . . . itself. In systems terminology this is known as an *autopoietic* system: 'a system that produces itself'.[47] It is perhaps best understood in contrast to an allopoietic system, such as a factory, 'which takes in materials and uses them to produce something other than itself'.[48] But in the case of the financial system with its current use of technology, *automated decisions* produce *further automated decisions.*

An incredible example of this over-reliance on algorithmic computerisation comes from a recent example of an automated robot (i.e. an online 'bot') that scanned websites to extract investor-relevant information from the public domain. An early posting about Twitter's Q1 results on their investor relationship website (managed by Nasdaq) was mistakenly placed online for a mere 45 seconds – plenty of time for the algorithms of Selerity (a company based in the US) to scan and tweet them on without any human intervention. That single tweet wiped $8bn off Twitter's value in a single day.[49] The above reflections demarcate a

45 Hendershott, T. *et al.* (2011) Does algorithmic trading improve liquidity?' *The Journal of Finance* LXVI(1).

46 Colford, P. (2014) A leap forward in quarterly earnings stories. Available at: http://blog.ap.org/2014/06/30/a-leap-forward-in-quarterly-earnings-stories.

47 Maturana, H. and Varela, F. (1998) *The Tree of Knowledge: The Biological Roots of Human Understanding* (Shambhala).

48 Buchanan, I. (2010) *A Dictionary of Critical Theory* (Oxford University Press).

49 Simmons, D. (2015) How one tweet wiped $8bn off Twitter's value. Available at: http://www.bbc.co.uk/news/technology-32511932.

unique space for how technology in the financial system affects other technology in a self-referential way with real and serious consequences.

P$_8$: Technological interactions in the financial system are developing into autonomous interdependencies that affect each other in a self-referential manner.

Self-reference (which remains part of the core theoretical architecture of Luhmann's Systems Theory[50]) denotes the ability of systems to refer to themselves and replicate the system/environment distinction internally. Conceptualising technology in this way reinforces the description of technology as a system that collects information about its own functioning and this in turn can contribute towards a change of its functioning.[51]

A fascinating expression or example of the above contingencies can be found in the context of the Flash Crash of the Dow Jones Index. Through this example, we will extract additional propositions for our discussion.

5.3 Flash Crashing the Dow Jones Index: a new role for technology and developing a financial crisis

While a complete reconstruction of the market events of 6 May 2010 (what has become known as the 'Flash Crash of 2:45') is beyond the scope of this chapter, several critical aspects that relate to the role of technology in its development will be reviewed here. An important aspect is that the complexity of the case itself, and the multi-dimensional role of algorithmic traders within it, have made the case almost impossible to deconstruct in its totality – this is admitted in several official reports (e.g. the first source listed below). Once again, the purpose of this section is to extract propositions from this case, which, combined with those extracted above from systems theory, will allow us to synthesise the development of the conceptual construct for the (current and future) role of technology in financial crises. The main sources being used for extracting quotations/propositions and the main findings of the Flash Crash include:

- the Report of the Staffs of the US Commodity Futures Trading Commission (CFTC) and Securities & Exchange Commission (SEC) to the Joint Advisory Committee on Emerging Regulatory Issues;
- the UK report on crashes and high-frequency trading from the Government Office for Science (*The Future of Computer Trading in Financial Markets – Foresight Driver Review* – DR 7);

50 Luhmann, N. (1993) *Risk: A Sociological Theory* (Transaction Publishers); Luhmann, N. (1995), *Social Systems* (Stanford University Press); Luhmann, N. (2002) *Deconstruction as Second-Order Observing Theories of Distinction: Redescribing the Descriptions of Modernity* (Stanford University Press), pp. 94–112; Luhmann, N. (2004) *Law as a Social System* (Oxford University Press).

51 Geyer, F. (2002) The march of self-reference. *Kybernetes* 31(7): 1021–1042.

- a perspective for Certified Public Accountants when Advising Investors entitled *Understanding the 'Flash Crash'*, which summarises the basic characteristics of the Flash Crash in a succinct way.[52]

First, in order to illustrate the pivotal role technology played in the Flash Crash, it is important that we put this in some context. Following uncertainty and generalised market turmoil about the possibility that the Greek government might default on their sovereign debt, market sentiment was broadly negative and 'was already affecting an increase in the price volatility of some individual securities'.[53] The key trends in the timeline before the 2:45pm Crash are as follows.

1) Around 1pm, a number of volatility pauses were triggered on the New York Stock Exchange (NYSE); individual equities began to increase above average levels.
2) The S&P 500 volatility index rose at 22.5% by 2.30pm. Investors engaged in 'flight to quality', and the Dow Jones Industrial Average (DJIA) was down by 2.5% due to the selling pressure.
3) Buy-side liquidity in the 'E-mini' and the 'SPY' (the E-mini S&P 500 futures contracts and the S&P 500 SPDR exchange traded fund) had suffered 55% and 20% declines respectively.
4) At 2.32pm, a large fundamental trader (a mutual fund complex) 'initiated a sell program to sell a total of 75,000 E-mini contracts (valued at approximately $4.1billion) as a hedge to an existing equity position'.[54]

Perhaps the last of these steps is considered to be one of the critical interventions, as the large trade was conducted via an ***automated execution algorithm***. While the single fundamental trader is not solely responsible for the Flash Crash (and the exact reason is not known), it is important to examine this further. Usually, a customer makes a choice of how much human judgement is involved when executing the trade. Also, a customer can choose to enter orders manually into the market or engage a third party that will execute a block trade and manage the position. However, in this case, the trader 'chose to execute this sell program via a [. . .] "*Sell Algorithm*" that was programmed to feed orders [. . .] but without regard to price or time'.[55] The algorithm only took volume into consideration. But while the initial problems were indeed created by the algorithm of the fundamental trader, they were then 'amplified by the strategic behavior of the HFT'.[56] This created a self-referential phenomenon: a circularity where

52 Betancourt, L., *et al.* (2011) Understanding the 'Flash Crash'. *The CPA Journal* (January): 40–45.
53 CFTC/SEC (2010) *Findings Regarding the Market Events of May 6, 2010: Report of the Staffs of the CFTC and SEC to the Joint Advisory Committee on Emerging Regulatory Issues*, p. 1.
54 Ibid., p. 2.
55 Ibid., pp. 2–3.
56 Sornette and Becke, p. 11 (see above, n. 16).

technology A excited *technology B* and then that fed back to *technology A* recursively. Indeed, as the initial sell pressure created by the 'Sell Algorithm' was absorbed by HFTs – at about 2.44pm – HFTs started to sell contracts aggressively and traded about 33% of the total trading volume. Then the

> Sell Algorithm used by the large trader responded to the increased volume *by increasing the rate at which it was feeding the orders into the market, even though orders that it already sent to the market were arguably not yet fully absorbed*.[57]

This can be perceived as a 'negative spiraling effect [where] HFT may have had a destabilising effect through its endogenous self-excitation nature within the (small) pool of participants'.[58] From this, we can infer that:

P_9: A technological subsystem such as the *Sell Algorithm* can excite another technological subsystem (e.g. HFTs) and the effects can recursively affect the *Sell Algorithm*.

The events that unfolded in the stock market saw the biggest daily stock market collapse of the Dow Jones Industrial Average on Thursday 6 May 2010 – popularly known as the Flash Crash of 2:45. The DJIA plunged 998.5 points, and following almost five months of investigations, the Security and Exchange Commission (SEC) along with the Commodity Futures Trading Commission (CFTC), attributed the decline to, almost exclusively, the automated execution of orders. Nevertheless, it is important to stress that

> the exact reason or reasons for the so-called flash crash remain *obscured by the* mechanics of the electronic trading systems that execute millions of buy and sell orders during the course of a single trading day. Some initially blamed the crash on a 'fat finger,' while others contend that essentially unregulated electronic trading platforms were the culprit. Others even questioned whether terrorists or hackers were behind the dramatic drop.[59]

The key lesson from this is that the crash cannot be attributed to any single algorithm or system in isolation. It is a *systemic phenomenon* that emerges out of the complex interaction of multiple automated execution technologies.

Consequently, whatever the complex automated configuration that created the conditions for the crash, it is quite clear that without the possibility for algorithmic trading at that scale, the Flash Crash would not have been possible. According to the testimony of SEC Chairman Mary Schapiro to the US Congress, this was

57 CFTC/SEC, p. 3 (see above, n. 53), emphasis added.
58 Sornette and Becke, p. 11 (see above, n. 16).
59 Betancourt, pp. 40–41 (see above, n. 52), emphasis added.

mostly due to the 'automated trading systems [that] will follow their coded logic regardless of outcome, while human involvement likely would have prevented these orders from executing at absurd prices'.[60]

Of course, the financial markets are not the only ones that suffer from such conditions. Another example involves Amazon.com Inc.[61] The *algorithmic* definition of prices on Amazon.com faced similar 'feedback loop' effects; Amazon vendors 'use algorithmic pricing to ensure that they can automatically change their product prices based on a competitor'.[62] This led to a book titled *The Making of a Fly* by evolutionary biologist Peter Lawrence to be priced at $23,698,655.93 (plus $3.99 shipping)! The unpredictability with which automated algorithms feed off each other creates emergent conditions that can destabilise any system that technology itself penetrates.

For the financial system, the implications are clear.

P_{10}: Automated systems follow their coded logic regardless of outcome. The demand for millisecond transacting creates another version of the financial system that will be drawn into a war between algorithms.

Whereas in the crash of 1987 (on 19 October), some Wall Street brokers simply declined to pick up their phones to avoid orders from their customers, in the new conditions imposed by technology, *algorithms themselves become 'responsible'* for shielding the market against further crash. For example, while the chaotic behaviour was continuing in the Flash Crash, the *Stop Logic Functionality* of the Chicago Mercantile Exchange (CME) was triggered in order to stop any further decline. This means that:

P_{11}: In order to address the emergent uncertainties from the automated behaviour of buy algorithms and sell algorithms, there is now a need to include both *Stop and Pause* algorithms.

Further complications can be considered about how *more technology* is actually emerging in order to deal with (and also exploit) the unpredictability and instability spawned by technological interactions. For example, new 'crash algorithms will likely be developed to trade during periods of market stresses in order to profit from these periods'.[63] One can consider here that algorithms which are designed to find the digital footprint of each other and collaborate in specific

60 Schapiro, M. (2010) *Testimony Concerning the Severe Market Disruption on May 6, 2010*, p. 7. Available at: http://www.sec.gov/news/testimony/2010/ts051110mls.htm.

61 Amazon.com is a multinational online retailer (with a revenue of US$107 billion in 2015) of books, movies, music and games along with electronics, toys, apparel, sports, tools, groceries and general home and garden items.

62 Solon, O. (2011) How a book about flies came to be priced $24 million on Amazon. Available at: http://www.wired.com/2011/04/amazon-flies-24-million.

63 Sornette and Becke, p. 4 (see above, n. 16).

market conditions thereby create unfair *algorithmic* competition. Inevitably, with the increasing attention that has been given to information security and cyber security breaches,[64] automated financial trading may become subject to hackers or terrorists who will seek to create financial instability deliberately (e.g. by deactivating or modifying a stop algorithm). This is certainly a real possibility and it would be devastating if cybercriminals managed to conduct a malicious flash crash attack.[65] Whatever the destabilisation effect, the speed of such transacting and the practical elimination of the human factor leads to an *algorithmic financial war*, where the algorithms will structure not only the market (by automated execution) but also the crisis (by creating complexity in automated transacting), the exploitation of the crisis (by crash algorithms) and the response to the crisis (by stop/pause algorithms). The net effect of these contingencies is bound to lead to several high-level conditions for the systemic function of technology in financial markets; subsequently, these will form the basis for examining the systemic role of technology in financial crises.

Hence, it is important to recognise that the very ontology of a 'financial crisis' is inextricably bound with the concept of the market as a *system*. A financial crisis is not necessarily the result of bad decision-making. In the financial sector, a decision often involves taking one risk over another risk. The development of new financial products/instruments/techniques accentuates this contingency. Thus, any financial decision is an approach that signifies the immediate need to cut down on the complexity of the market – simplify the uncertainty – and make a *selection*. From all the noise of the market, such a selection is unavoidable, as no single entity (human or algorithm) can monitor concurrently all financial interactions taking place at any given point, or account for the myriad complex (and often invisible) organisational phenomena before these come to be announced and reflected on stock market prices.

This sequence of complexity-reduction to unavoidable risk highlights the contingency that crises are systemic and are not – strictly speaking – controllable.

5.4 Discussion

From the aforementioned analysis, the following propositions have been developed for the systemic role of technology in financial crisis. These are consolidated below in Table 5.1.

The above propositions suggest a rather bleak scenario where financial crises may be starting from environmental stimuli (of real conditions and uncertainty

64 Dhillon, G. and Backhouse, J. (2000) Information system security management in the new millennium. *Communications of the ACM* 43(7): 125–128.

65 Erra, R. (2011) Malicious flash crash attacks by quote stuffing: This is the way the (financial) world could end. 10th European Conference on Information Warfare and Security 2011, ECIW 2011.

Table 5.1 Extracted propositions based on systems theory

Propositions developed
P_1: In the financial markets, algorithms dominate financial decisions and have largely replaced human decisions.
P_2: Through algorithmic trading, a single market player can create considerable effects in an extremely limited time-span.
P_3: A financial crisis is a holistic property of the financial system and constitutes an emergent phenomenon. A crisis emerges out of the interaction of several interdependent components and cannot be attributable to a single transacting element.
P_4: Algorithms launched from different financial players will have different goal-seeking strategies. When they are activated and become part of the financial system, algorithms find themselves in a much more complex environment. They affect and are affected by that environment (in which other algorithms reside) in unpredictable ways. While each algorithm 'controls' its actions, the effects for the financial system as a whole are emergent.
P_5: Algorithms take *inputs* from the financial system in various ways (e.g. price, volume, news, restrictions) and transform these inputs into *outputs that take the form of algorithmic decisions.*
P_6: The development of algorithmic trading is based on a faster form of communication that eliminates the step of cognitive understanding in the process of communicating. This is replaced by *algorithmic 'understanding'* – a limited logical type that collapses understanding to mere information processing.
P_7: Technology as it is currently being used in the financial system creates a meta-organisation: a system of automated decisions that shape the 'code' of the financial system itself and influence the primary distinction of payment/non-payment.
P_8: Technological interactions in the financial system are developing into autonomous interdependencies that affect each other in a self-referential manner.
P_9: A technological subsystem such as the *Sell Algorithm* can excite another technological subsystem (e.g. HFTs) and the effects can recursively affect the *Sell Algorithm.*
P_{10}: Automated systems follow their coded logic regardless of outcome. The demand for millisecond transacting creates another version of the financial system that will be drawn into a war between algorithms.
P_{11}: In order to address the emergent uncertainties from the automated behaviour of buy algorithms and sell algorithms, there is now a need to include both *Stop and Pause* algorithms.

– e.g. the Greek crisis), but then become part of hyper-complex millisecond transacting system that is largely uncontrollable at a macro-level. At the basis of this condition is the delusion behind the use of such information and communication technologies (ICTs) – and their broader role in the financial system. Unfortunately, ICTs are usually considered to be a 'tool' that can be strictly controlled; however, the belief that the deployment of technology is largely controllable is not justified.[66] In fact, 'technology is widely depicted as an unproblematically beneficial force for human progress [. . .] technology is widely understood as simply applied science'.[67]

Technology, however, in light of the systemic description and the propositions put forward in this chapter, can be considered to 'irritate society in a way that social reality is created by technology'.[68] This re-description has profound implications for the financial system, as it is not the human decision-makers who use technology as a tool in order to make financial decisions. Based on the propositions extracted theoretically (and from our example of the Flash Crash), the situation seems to be reversed: *technology dominates* financial decision-making and human beings are there as the back-up plan to 'recalibrate the systems' when that is required. Ironically, one of the things that humans reassess in cases where automated trading needs to pause is: 'the ability of their (automated) systems to handle the very high volume of trades and orders that they were processing'.[69] In this context, we can reconceptualise technology in the financial system[70] and claim that technology is shaping the market itself through a complex nexus of (almost invisible) automated decisions. Consequently, technology is bound to shape the future of financial crises by assuming a more central role in how financial decisions are made with minimal (or no) human intervention.

In order to consider the implications of technological domination in an ever-expanding number of social systems (such as the financial system), we need to reflect on how the automated replacement for human decisions substitutes for human decision-making. As shown in the case of the Flash Crash of the DJIA, technology initiates *non-controllable events;* these emerge from complex interactions and feedback loops that develop very quickly (in our case, over milliseconds). By allowing complex configurations of manual decisions to be automated, we (as humanity) have allowed technology to take responsibility over financial (and other) decisions. At the same time, technology is providing a proxy for shifting responsibility to automated decisions. This also 'makes it very difficult for regulators to understand what is happening in the market',[71] a contingency that is rather desirable for many individual investors and financial institutions. If little or no human involvement takes place, then humanity can be considered to be an afterthought in the *society of computers*, in which computers largely shape, construct, reconstruct and observe financial reality. This leaves us

66 Dreyfus, H. L. *et al.* (1986) *Mind over Machine : The Power of Human Intuition and Expertise in the Era of the Computer* (Basil Blackwell); Angell, I. (1993) Intelligence: logical or biological. *Communications of the ACM* 36(7): 15–16 and 119.

67 Scharff, R. and Dusek, V. (eds) (2014) *Philosophy of Technology: The Technological Condition, An Anthology* (Wiley Blackwell), p. 9.

68 Reichel, A. (2011) Technology as system: towards an autopoietic theory of technology. *International Journal of Innovation and Sustainable Development* 5(2/3): 105–118, p. 105.

69 CFTC/SEC, p. 4 (see above, n. 53).

70 Reichel (see above, n. 68).

71 Betancourt, p. 42 (see above, n. 52).

with a condition where humanity can only react to *how computers shape financial reality*.

In this context, it would appear that the original designs of the algorithmic/computer logic are considered almost irrelevant. Indeed, an additional lesson from the Flash Crash is that 'there was no "big glitch", no fat-finger *error* or unforeseen computer error that triggered the crash. Instead, nearly every firm in the market at the time did precisely what it thought was rational according to current regulations.'[72] It could therefore be argued that while every human designer of algorithmic practices had 'imbued' rational behaviour into the automated decision-making processes, the emergent uncertainty from complex interactions created instability. The type of algorithmic complexity created at the level of the market cannot be simply 'unpacked' and examined; it is impossible to monitor the algorithmic logic of each automated buy/sell decision and the network of interactions that are technologically facilitated.

Against this background, technology becomes the critical proxy through which the financial system also observes itself. Technology is set up in order to assist in the automated execution of tasks, but is then recursively affected by the output of such automated executions; it 'accepts' such output as if the financial transactions represent an un-interfered financial reality of *strictly controlled* technological operations. Algorithms, in effect, have become patterns of decisions and not merely the proxies through which decisions are manually controlled. In systems theoretical terms,[73] it can be said that algorithms decide what becomes automated and unavoidable, and, at the same time, what is left un-automated. Coupled with a complex domain such as the financial system, it is clear that the automated/non-automated decisions prescribed by algorithms are transcending into the financial system itself, into the social sphere, thereby designating what is criminal/non-criminal, what is marketable/non-marketable, what is public/private, and even what is legal/non-legal. In other words, algorithms cut down the complexity that is unmanageable by human beings, and, in doing so, impose their presuppositions via the 'logic' they are given by their creators.

Where this global reliance on technology will lead is anyone's guess. Systemic automation adds to the problem of potential systemic failure that lies in the wings of complexity and chaos. Any system of sufficient complexity exhibits these characteristics, and controlling such a system in the causal sense is merely wishful thinking. Much to the peril of those who momentarily thought they were on top of the concept of *risk*, the financial crisis of 2008 came to demonstrate that the monitoring of *risk* is ultimately rendered impossible. In fact, the very utterance of 'monitoring risk' constitutes a paradox since risk is by default designated to *indicate the residual category* of what can be controlled and monitored – that is,

72 Arnuk, S. and Saluzzi, J. (2012) *Broken Markets: How High Frequency Trading and Predatory Practices on Wall Street Are Destroying Investor Confidence and Your Portfolio* (FT Press), p. 179.

73 Luhmann (1993) (see above, n. 50).

the exact opposite. Technology adds to the risk and does so not only by establishing a 'technology risk' that affects other problem domains, but also by a systemic automation that reconstructs the operational basis of the financial system. Furthermore, the trajectory depicted in the propositions extracted in this chapter should trouble us gravely: they illustrate a space where prediction systems such as those suggested by Bethel *et al.* are – to some degree – of little consequence.[74] Finding ways to develop a magnifying glass of automated transactions is not likely to offer a solution when automated decisions are forming an ever-increasing tsunami. Similarly, the very concept of risk-averse algorithms violates the emergence of uncertainty and cannot account for the uncontrollable side-effects developed by technological interference.[75]

Through the conceptual model developed in this chapter as it is depicted in the set of propositions in Table 5.1 and in the model of Figure 5.1, it becomes clearer that deep technological penetration in the financial system reconstructs our use of it as well as its future application. Technology is not merely a tool that can be strictly controlled. It is a complex system of *automated decision-making processes* that override human behaviour. Technology alters the basic organisational structure through which financial decisions are executed and distorts the structure through which financial crises emerge. Accordingly, law and politics can attempt to deal with only the aftermath of such crises.

74 Bethel, E. W. *et al.* (2011) *Federal Market Information Technology in the Post Flash Crash Era: Roles for Supercomputing.* WHPCF'11 – Proceedings of the 4th Workshop on High Performance Computational Finance, Co-located with SC'11.

75 Shen, Y. *et al.* (2014) Risk-averse reinforcement learning for algorithmic trading. IEEE/IAFE Conference on Computational Intelligence for Financial Engineering, Proceedings (CIFEr).

6 The finance industry perspective

Jon Tucker

6.1 Introduction

This chapter examines the financial crisis and financial crime from a finance industry perspective. It explores the structure of the industry, the instruments traded and the role of the key players in an attempt to understand the basis for their interactions and the motivations for individual actions. The chapter explores the central importance of financial markets and institutions to a successful economy and society, and seeks to understand the inherent institutional challenges around scale, complexity and information asymmetry. The chapter goes on to consider the incentives of key players and the possible causes of things 'going wrong', such as systemic problems, poorly designed incentive structures, negligence, lack of training, unforeseen circumstances and, of course, criminal activity. Finally, the chapter examines how key actors in the finance industry, such as regulators, financial institutions and professional bodies, have set in place systems and approaches around not just compliance but also integrity and ethics, in an attempt to reduce the possibility of a similar crisis in the next decade. In brief, the chapter underlines the importance of the finance industry, the imperative for balanced discussion of the issues around financial crime, the central role of integrity and ethics in modern institutions, and an end to 'banker bashing'.

Before we are in a position to discuss the nature of the finance industry, it is important to be more precise concerning one of its most prominent failures in recent decades – the financial crisis. A financial crisis refers to a rapid financial disintermediation due to financial panic.[1] In practice, this involves a flight to quality, where savers attempt to liquidate the assets they hold in financial institutions due to a sudden increase in their perceived risk, moving their savings to safer assets (to different countries or markets, or even to different asset classes). While we will discuss some of the causes of the financial crisis in far greater detail later in the chapter, the core underlying driver of the 2007 financial crisis was excessive leverage, in common with previous crises. The American economist Hyman Minsky

1 Aizenman, J. 'Financial crisis' in *Princeton Encyclopedia of the World Economy* (Princeton, NJ: Princeton University Press, 2007).

argued back in the 1960s that long periods of economic stability encourage investors in general, and financial institutions in particular, to take on more risk.[2] This led to the curious assertion that after a certain passage of time, stability becomes destabilising.[3] There exists a vicious cycle evident in successive financial crises, whereby financial institutions and investors borrow too much and pay too much in turn for financial assets. Investors perceive this erroneously as a virtuous circle of increasing asset prices and improving personal balance sheets, which reinforces their confidence to 'leverage up' further and invest more, at least until the bubble eventually bursts. Therefore, was the finance industry entirely to blame for the financial crisis? Was there evidence of poor behaviour, a lack of professionalism, or even criminal activity? Mervyn King, the former Governor of the Bank of England, reflected in his recent book: 'No doubt there were bankers who were indeed wicked and central bankers who were incompetent, though the vast majority of both whom I met during the crisis were neither.'[4]

6.2 The structure of the finance industry and its key players

While modern financial markets may be perceived by many to be impenetrable and opaque, existing only to serve the purposes of market professionals and their institution employers, the role of the finance industry in its broadest economic and societal sense is to match those with funds to invest with those who require funding. By investors here, we may refer to institutional investors, whom we might reasonably assume to be technical finance 'experts', or retail/private investors who may have very little appreciation of the true underlying merits of the alternative investment choices. The finance industry operates via financial markets, which constitute a marketplace where buyers and sellers are brought together to trade in financial investments (instruments or assets). Financial markets, such as the London Stock Exchange or the New York Stock Exchange, are largely electronic entities where the market participants interact only in a virtual sense through computer-based trading. Such markets have the advantage of being highly regulated, largely transparent and with prices determined by the interaction of investors with other market participants – in this sense, the prices at which assets are traded are in general meaningful and have been derived efficiently through the forces of supply and demand. There are primary and secondary markets, where the former deal with the issue of new securities (e.g. by companies issuing shares) and the purchase by investors, and the latter deal with the buying and selling of such securities between investors and other market

2 Minsky, H. 'Longer waves in financial relations: financial factors in the more severe depressions', 54 (1964) *American Economic Review*, 324–355.

3 Ibid. See also BBC News Magazine, Did Hyman Minsky find the secret behind financial crashes?, 24 March 2014, available from http://www.bbc.co.uk/news/magazine-26680993, accessed 2 June 2016.

4 King, M., *The End of Alchemy: Money, Banking and the Future of the Global Economy* (London: Little, Brown, 2016).

participants subsequent to the initial issue. There are also third markets which involve over-the-counter (OTC) trades between broker-dealers and large institutions, and even so-called fourth markets which involve transactions solely between large institutions. An OTC market here is a dealer market where trading in small stocks is facilitated.[5]

When we think of financial markets, we often think about the financial intermediaries, such as banks, insurance companies and investment companies, which are positioned between investors and the companies. They require funds to enable them to invest and grow, and of course between investors and other market participants. These intermediaries deal with policy holders, depositors and investors, accepting their funds in exchange for an obligation to provide a stream of funds at some future date. Intermediaries also deal with companies, providing them with funds in exchange for an obligation by the company to provide a stream of funds plus returns at some future date (e.g. loans or bond issues) or to provide investors with an equity interest in the company's fortunes (e.g. company stocks/shares). The precise stream of funds and the returns depend on the form of financial instrument employed; for example, a financial intermediary such as a bank provides an investor with a deposit account which pays periodic interest and then the repayment of the capital to the investor at maturity or upon withdrawal. The funds from depositors are then pooled and lent to a company which is expected to pay periodic interest to the intermediary and repay the capital at maturity. The investor–intermediary relationship and the intermediary–company relationship are both examples of a debt relationship, where the intermediary is the debtor in the former and the company is the debtor in the latter. The role of banks here is particularly important as they provide the payment mechanism, facilitate borrowing and lending, and pool risk, the latter allowing investors and firms to diversify their risks.[6] Banks also provide an essential maturity transformation mechanism by collecting short-term deposits funds and money market funds and transforming these into long-term loans, such as mortgages.[7]

The financial assets or instruments traded within financial markets include stocks (shares), bonds, money markets instruments (a form of short-term debt), cash (the spot market), financial derivatives (such as futures and options), foreign exchange (currencies) and interbank instruments. Furthermore, a wide range of non-financial instruments are traded on such markets, including commodities, such as oil and copper, and a vast range of insurance products. Large financial intermediaries will typically be involved in all market types, and in most instrument and commodity types, albeit there are some variations across institutions around

5 For further explanation of how markets work, see 'Types of financial markets and their roles', Investopedia.com, available from http://www.investopedia.com/walkthrough/corporate-finance/1/financial-markets.aspx, accessed 9 January 2016.

6 Brealey, R., Myers, S. and Allen, F., *Principles of Corporate Finance*, 9th edition (New York: McGraw Hill, 2008).

7 'Maturity transformation', *Money Week*, 20 May 2013, available from http://moneyweek.com/glossary/maturity-transformation, accessed 26 March 2016.

their particular focus and expertise. World financial markets are truly immense in magnitude, scope and reach. Indeed, an estimate by Deutsche Bank's Sanjeev Sanyal placed the value of the world market in 2014 at $294 trillion, including a $69 trillion stock market, $58 trillion of public debts securities, $60 trillion of outstanding institutional bonds, and the remainder consisting of corporate bonds and loans.[8] In terms of the impact of the banking sector on the UK economy, it is estimated that it contributes almost 5 per cent of the UK's Gross Value Added, employs 405,000 people, and contributed £31bn to tax receipts in 2014.[9]

6.3 Economies need strong financial markets

Financial markets are an essential component of a modern and successful economy. Such markets enable:

(i) the production of information sufficient to facilitate the surplus funds of investors to be matched with the funding needs of others, particularly corporations;
(ii) capital formation by underpinning corporate capital investment;
(iii) income generation from otherwise non-productive surplus funds;
(iv) channels for both investment and saving to supplement conventional banking;
(v) established, trusted and low-cost mechanisms to enable the buying and selling of financial assets;
(vi) price discovery through the innate actions of market participants, particularly in developed, efficient markets;
(vii) economic growth-enhancing credit creation; and
(viii) liquidity provision, maturity transformation and financial product innovation.

Many of the benefits of financial markets relate to economic growth – in the absence of financial markets, economic growth would be constrained to the detriment of societies. Indeed, countries at an early stage of financial market development tend to rely almost entirely on conventional banking structures, and do not benefit from the scope of the financial instruments available in more developed financial markets or the flexibility that they confer. Very much related to growth is competitiveness, whereby more financially developed and competitive countries are better able to maintain higher economic growth, as funds should be more readily available and cheaper, and there should be far less mismatch between

8 Sam Ro, 'Here's what the $294 trillion market of global financial assets looks like', *Business Insider UK*, 12 February 2015, available from http://uk.businessinsider.com/global-financial-assets-2015-2?r=US&IR=T, accessed 19 March 2016.

9 British Bankers Association (BBA), *Winning the Global Race: The Competitiveness of the UK as a Centre for International Banking* (London: British Bankers Association, November 2015).

investors and companies, and thus far less need for political patronage to access financing. In this sense, financial market development democratises economies, leading to a potentially wider distribution of economic gains. In the absence of developed financial markets, industrial development would simply be slower and more haphazard as developed markets link investors to the most profitable and worthwhile opportunities to which they may apply their funds and thereby support the best-quality investment projects offered by firms.

While the integration of global financial markets has brought with it significant welfare gains to society through improvements in both the allocation of resources and in the rate of economic growth, the downside of this evolutionary process has been a periodic increase in systemic fragility, as evidenced by the global financial crisis.[10] Thus, financial market development also brings with it some serious risks to countries and their constituent corporations and investors, most markedly brought into focus when things go wrong. In principle, and in general, markets are an effective and efficient mechanism for arriving at an optimal allocation of resources to competing uses. So what do we mean when we contend that markets sporadically 'go wrong'? Financial markets in recent decades have been characterised by significant market volatility and associated upheaval driven in turn by:

(i) market booms followed by busts;
(ii) the ever-increasing speed of capital market flows;
(iii) the misalignment of asset prices with underlying fundamental values; and
(iv) poor behaviour on the part of market participants.

Added to this is the observation by many market-watchers that the western world has embarked inexorably on a road towards greater financialisation, a trend not always welcomed by all.

Boom followed by bust is a pattern that has tended to characterise western financial markets since they were established. By 'boom' we mean economic expansion, job market expansion and high investor returns, and by 'bust' we mean economic contraction, labour market shrinkage and investor losses.[11] Booms tend to be exemplified by periods of excessive investment, as interest rates are effectively too low, leading ultimately to an excess supply of financial assets, property and so on, requiring a sharp correction (or bust) as asset prices fall, companies cut back on investment and jobs, and economic growth slows or even turns negative. Boom and bust periods arguably occur due to excessive optimism, herding behaviour, irrational exuberance or simple financial naïveté. Whatever the

10 Acharya, V., Phillipon, T., Richardson, M. and Roubini, N., 'The financial crisis of 2007–2009: causes and remedies', 18 (2009) *Financial Markets, Institutions & Instruments*, 89–137.

11 'Boom and bust cycle', Investopedia.com, available from http://www.investopedia.com/terms/b/boom-and-bust-cycle.asp, accessed 19 March 2016.

underlying cause, leverage tends to oil the wheels of this cyclical phenomenon – excessive leverage resulting from interest rates which are too low leads to 'surplus liquidity' finding a home in financial or real assets, boosting their price to a level far in excess of that implied by their fundamentals (those characteristics which drive their intrinsic value).

With the advent of super-fast computer and communications technology, capital markets now move at lightning speeds. High-frequency trading (HFT) involves large financial institutions, such as hedge funds and investment banks, using powerful computer algorithms to execute trading orders up to a million times per second.[12] The massive investment in computer technology by the financial institutions gives them a timing edge over other investors as any patterns or anomalies may be traded out almost instantly. As stock markets are a zero-sum game, the gains of the experts are in general financed by the loss of naïve retail investors. Some argue that the advantage of HFT is that it provides additional market liquidity and helps the market to discover asset prices more quickly though others argue that it simply creates an unfair advantage for larger investors to the cost of smaller investors and institutions.[13] Further, if computers are trading against computers, with little human intervention once the algorithms are set in play, then asset bubbles can easily emerge.[14]

In a utopian world of rational economic man and perfect information, financial asset prices will be driven solely by the future cash flows that the asset provides to the investor, discounted by an appropriate cost of capital, the latter driven by the location of an asset on the risk–return spectrum. However, the valuation of stocks illustrates that asset valuation can be tricky in the real world. Stocks are valued in relation to the stream of dividends that they pay (discounted dividend model), by benchmarking the company's stock market value against similar companies (price multiples valuation) or projecting a company's financial statements to determine the cash flows available to the firm (free cash-flow valuation). Aside from the dividend-based valuation approach, which focuses solely on the pay-offs to investors in the form of dividends, most other valuation approaches focus on measures drawn from a firm's accounting balance sheet or income statement. The price multiples approach values the firm by multiplying a firm financial figure, such as earnings, by an industry multiple, such as price to earnings (PE). The free

12 Alan Tovey, 'High frequency trading: when milliseconds mean millions', *The Telegraph*, 2 April 2014, available from http://www.telegraph.co.uk/finance/newsbysector/banksandfinance/10736960/High-frequency-trading-when-milliseconds-mean-millions.html, accessed 19 March 2016.

13 For a critical discussion, see McGowan, M. J., 'The rise of computerised high frequency trading: use and controversy' 16 (2010) *Duke Law and Technology Review*, 2; Arnuk, S. and Saluzzi, J., *Broken Markets: How High Frequency Trading and Predatory Practices on Wall Street Are Destroying Investor Confidence and Your Portfolio* (Indianapolis, IN: FT Press, 2012).

14 See, for example, the case of the 'Flash Crash' as discussed in 'Wall Street's flash crash trader will be extradited to the U.S.', *Fortune*, 23 March 2016, available from http://fortune.com/2016/03/23/flash-crash-trader-extradited-u-s, accessed 23 March 2016.

cash-flow approach values the firm by discounting the free cash flows to the firm (derived from profit after tax) to their present value to arrive at enterprise value. However, investors will soon observe that whatever valuation approach they employ, stock prices are often misaligned with fundamental (accounting-referenced) values, particularly during market booms. Worse still, the accounting values themselves do not always provide a firm base upon which to derive company, and thus individual, stock values due to creative accounting, earnings management, accounting error, fraud and so on.[15]

While financial market development is generally held to be for the economic good of society, the degree of financialisation appears to be a more contentious byproduct. Financialisation may be defined as an increase in the size and importance of a country's financial sector relative to its overall economy.[16] Alternatively, a seminal definition with a more political undertone is provided by Epstein: 'Financialization refers to the increasing importance of financial markets, financial motives, financial institutions, and financial elites in the operation of the economy and its governing institutions, both at the national and international level.'[17] It is argued that financialisation has grown concomitantly with market appreciation of the importance of agency theory.[18] The agency imperative of managers (the agents) in the business world is to act so as to maximise the profits of the company's shareholders (the principals).[19] Widespread acceptance of the importance of agency theory led to an explosion in both the scope and scale of manager compensation in an attempt to address the underlying incentive problem of aligning managers' actions with shareholders' wishes, while fomenting the rise of takeovers and the growth of the private equity industry. The other issue with the agency approach is that the sole purpose of corporations, while simply a societal construction, is to maximise shareholder returns within the confines of the law. The result of this is to cede control over managers to shareholders at the cost of other stakeholders. To deal with the problems associated with financialisation, a range of measures are advocated by regulators and market commentators, such as tackling excessive CEO pay and incentive issues, requiring corporations to become more cognisant of wider stakeholder needs, and breaking the economic–power–policy feedback cycle.

15 See, for example, Mulford, C. and Comiskey, E., *The Financial Numbers Game: Detecting Creative Accounting Practices* (New York: John Wiley & Sons, 2002).

16 See 'Financialization', Investopedia.com, available from http://www.investopedia.com/terms/f/financialization.asp, accessed 19 March 2016.

17 Epstein, G., *Financialization, Rentier Interests and Central Bank Policy*, Department of Economics Working Paper, December 2001, University of Massachusetts, Amherst, MA.

18 Palley, T., *Financialization: What It Is and Why It Matters*, Working Paper Series No. 153, 2007, Political Economy Research Institute, Amherst, MA.

19 For a seminal paper on agency theory, see Jensen, M. and Meckling, W., 'Theory of the firm: managerial behaviour, agency costs and ownership structure', 3 (1976) *Journal of Financial Economics*, 305–360.

6.4 The financial crisis and its institutional foundations

The broad facts underlying the global financial crisis are far less disputed or even discussed than its institutional foundations. Few would disagree that the seeds of the financial crisis were sown when the US housing market began to slow in early 2006, exacerbated by the prevalence of loans to subprime borrowers in that market.[20] The balloon payment financing of such loans was evidently sustainable while house prices continued to rise, but quickly led to borrower defaults from late 2006 when this run of luck came to an end, in turn precipitating a raft of subprime lender failures. Hedge funds that were heavily invested in subprime debt began to fail, leading to an expansion of credit spreads on riskier debt instruments such as collateralised debt obligations, with a knock-on negative effect on the carry trade (making money from interest-rate differentials between countries). This led in turn to wider concerns over the transparency of information across debt markets more generally, with short-term markets beginning to freeze. At this point, it was argued that investors could not discern between 'toxic' and high-quality debt, giving rise to further market seizure and additional subprime lenders failing. Liquidity was then hoarded by banks as a defensive strategy, and lending to the real economy plummeted. While Bear-Stearns was saved through an acquisition by JP Morgan, Lehman Brothers was 'allowed' to fail, and the US government was forced to step in to support other financial institutions to prevent wider systemic collapse. The clear failure of debt markets in the US gave rise to contagion across markets, leading to bank runs and failures, full or partial nationalisation bailouts of large banks, and the wholesale withdrawal of liquidity to corporations. In turn, this led to many advanced western economies slowing, real investment stalling, stock markets crashing and significant upheaval across all financial and real investment markets. 'Risk on' evidently turned to 'risk off', with investors redirecting their investment attention to low-risk assets such as government bonds.[21]

The first phase of the financial crisis, which we might term the 'credit crunch', then led to a series of shocks to the real economy, in the absence of short-term debt provision and requisite market liquidity. The most prominent of these 'aftershocks' was the European sovereign debt crisis, 'in which several European countries faced the collapse of financial institutions, high government debt and rapidly rising bond yield spreads in government securities'.[22] This phase of the crisis commenced in 2008 with the collapse of the banking system in Iceland,

20 Acharya, V., Phillipon, T., Richardson, M. and Roubini, N., 'The financial crisis of 2007–2009: causes and remedies', 18 (2009) *Financial Markets, Institutions & Instruments*, 89–137.

21 'Risk on/risk off', Buttonwood's Notebook, *The Economist*, 11 November 2010, available from http://www.economist.com/blogs/buttonwood/2010/11/financial_markets_and_economy, accessed 23 March 2016.

22 'European sovereign debt crisis', Investopedia.com, available from http://www.investopedia.com/terms/e/european-sovereign-debt-crisis.asp, accessed 19 March 2016.

spreading to countries such as Portugal, Italy, Ireland, Greece and Spain, thereby illustrating the role of contagion in the propagation of crises.[23] Following the credit crunch, real economic growth slowed (and in many cases economies contracted sharply) so that governments could neither 'roll over' nor repay government debt, nor afford to bail out their failing banks given already hard-pressed reserves and existing large government debts. This necessitated the financial assistance of the International Monetary Fund, the European Central Bank and the European Financial Stability Facility. The result for Greece and others was spiralling required return rates for investors in order to retain their interest in the sovereign debt proposition. The fact that the Greek government admitted to misreporting government budget data added to a lack of trust not just in banks but also now in governments, which further exacerbated their dealings with international monetary bodies.[24]

We turn next to the range of institutional factors which provided both the foundations for, and mechanisms characterising, the financial crisis, including:

(i) asset market bubbles;
(ii) the problem of information asymmetry;
(iii) market, bank and financial instrument complexity;
(iv) a lack of adequate regulatory oversight and banks circumventing regulations;
(v) market interconnectedness; and
(vi) the presence of megabanks which are too 'big to fail'.

Booms and bubbles are a core mechanism leading to financial crises. It may be argued that the main cause of the financial crisis was the credit boom and the housing bubble.[25] These two phenomena might be explained quite simply in terms of mispricing (where risk was effectively incorrectly priced) or as a result of failures by the Federal Reserve and other central banks (where interest rates were kept too low for too long, and thus debt was too easily accessed). Bubbles are simply periods of (economic) expansion followed by sharp contractions. In terms of financial securities, bubbles occur when securities prices move above their intrinsic value and continue on this path until prices correct sharply downwards ('the bubble bursts').[26] Howard Davies, formerly of the Bank of England and Financial

23 These countries were at the time referred to by the pejorative acronym PIGS or PIIGS, a discussion of which is found in the following article: 'Europe's PIGS: Country by country', BBC News, 11 February 2010, available from http://news.bbc.co.uk/1/hi/business/8510603.stm, accessed 23 March 2016.

24 Barber, T., 'Greece condemned for falsifying data', *Financial Times*, 12 January 2010, available from http://www.ft.com/cms/s/0/33b0a48c-ff7e-11de-8f53-00144feabdc0.html#axzz43jI5te1S (accessed 23 March 2016; subscription needed).

25 Acharya, V., Phillipon, T., Richardson, M. and Roubini, N., 'The Financial Crisis of 2007–2009: Causes and Remedies' 18 (2009) *Financial Markets, Institutions & Instruments*, 89–137.

26 'Bubble', Investopedia.com, available from http://www.investopedia.com/terms/b/bubble.asp, accessed 21 March 2016.

Services Authority, notes the argument of Alan Greenspan, former US Federal Reserve Chairman, that any attempt to prick financial bubbles in advance is doomed to fail – and thus attention should be focused on clean-up rather than prevention.[27] He reviews the alternatives for pre-emptive actions when we see liquidity and credit building up dangerously. He explores the policy options from focusing the attention of central banks on overseeing financial institutions to more robust countercyclical capital buffers (macroprudential regulation).

Information asymmetry arises where one party to a transaction has more or better-quality information than the other. This imbalance of power can lead to problems such as moral hazard or adverse selection. In a banking setting, moral hazard occurs where banks may behave more recklessly as they believe they are insured (too big to fail) by governments or central banks. Thus, banks internalise the benefits to risky activities, whereas if the bank is 'bailed out' as a result of such activities going wrong, then the costs are borne by society (they are externalised or socialised).[28] Adverse selection occurs where one party to a transaction cannot discriminate between good and bad counterparties, and we can see how this was a contributing factor to the financial crisis, particularly when it comes to debt-related contracts, such as collateralised debt obligations.[29]

The problem of complexity is developed by Alex Pollock writing for the American Enterprise Institute, who argues that we are not able to avoid repeated mistakes such as the subprime crisis and the European sovereign debt crisis, as 'financial markets are governed by a recursive system of interconnected decisions, theories, strategies, predictions, actions, and expectations that lead to booms and busts'.[30] Effectively, the interactions within financial markets are just too complex to be predictable. Further, finance markets are part of a connected system, which is recursive in the respect of feedback loops, which no one can reasonably foresee or even understand after the event. Drawing on logic explored by John Maynard Keynes, Pollock sees each person's behaviour as being based on one another's predictions of one another's behaviour – clearly such behaviour is very difficult to comprehend, let alone capture. Thus, the financial system cannot be understood in the same way that science helps us to explain the universe, as human interaction is at the root of the complexity.

27 Davies, H., 'The trouble with financial bubbles', *Guardian*, 19 October 2015, available from http://www.theguardian.com/business/2015/oct/19/the-trouble-with-financial-bubbles, accessed 21 March 2016.

28 Krugman, P., *The Return of Depression Economics and the Crisis of 2008* (W.W. Norton Company Limited: London, 2009).

29 Akerlof, G.A., 'The market for "lemons": quality uncertainty and the market mechanism', 84 (1970) *Quarterly Journal of Economics*, 488–500.

30 Pollock, A.J., 'Financial markets and "system effects": complexity, recursiveness, uncertainty, and mistakes in finance', American Enterprise Institute, 24 July 2012, available from https://www.aei.org/publication/financial-markets-and-system-effects-complexity-recursiveness-uncertainty-and-mistakes-in-finance, accessed 21 March 2016.

At the nub of the issue of complexity is the almost unimaginably complex nexus of entities in the financial system. In a seminal NBER paper, Caballero and Simsek argue that

> the whole financial system is a complex network of linkages which functions smoothly in the environments that it is designed to handle, even though no bank knows with certainty all the many possible connections within the network (that is, each bank knows the identities of the other banks but not their exposures).[31]

They show in their model that, in the normal course of business, banks carefully monitor the health of their trading partners in order to ensure their financial soundness. However, when financial distress becomes more prevalent, banks will also need to check the financial health of the trading partners of their partners. This process becomes so difficult that, at some stage, the banks cannot afford the cost of information-gathering (monitoring) and decide to withdraw from loan commitments and illiquid positions. Complexity therefore leads to a flight-to-quality and deepening of crisis. There is evidence from the US that more complex banks (in terms of the number of activities they perform) exhibit a higher profitability, lower risk and higher market share, and thus there are many in the industry that will counter the argument that bank complexity is bad per se.[32]

Building on this theme, Mark Buchanan argues that in order to understand finance, we need to embrace complexity.[33] He argues that the interconnections between the world's banks and other financial institutions, by means of ordinary loans and derivatives, are characterised by extreme complexity. For example, financial institutions create and sell new derivatives, even where they deliver no benefits to the market and actually exacerbate financial instability. He further argues that financial institutions find use in complexity, as it helps them to hide the risk that they create. Thus, he explains that how financial systems are 'wired' plays a crucial role in financial stability.

Not only are financial markets themselves complex, but so too are the financial instruments that the markets offer to buy or sell. Many argue that with the onset of the financial crisis, investors were misled by offerings of instruments such as collateralised debt obligations and other structured instruments. However, it is argued that instruments such as these are not intrinsically more complex than, say, equities (shares), and the problem rather lies more in the bounded rationality of investors who are not always best placed to adequately assess pay-offs due to

31 Caballero, R.J. and Simsek, A., *Complexity and Financial Panics*, NBER Working Paper No. 14997, May/June 2009.

32 Liu, F.H., Norden, L. and Spargoli, F., 'Why banks want to be complex', paper presented to the Southern Finance Association 2015 Meeting.

33 Mark Buchanan, 'To understand finance, embrace complexity', Bloomberg View, 27 March 2010, available from http://www.bloombergview.com/articles/2013-03-10/to-understand-finance-embrace-complexity, accessed 21 March 2016.

issues such as information overload.[34] Thus, markets, participant interactions and financial instruments are by their very nature complex. Complexity itself is not a bad thing, provided that regulators and others have sufficient oversight.

In the real world, however, it is unlikely that anyone, including regulators, has true oversight of the entire financial system. There are many reasons for this:

(i) the system is extremely complex, given its size and interconnectedness;
(ii) much of the system lacks transparency, due to proprietary systems, client confidentiality, Chinese walls, and so on;
(iii) most of the component parts of financial markets are virtual and are therefore difficult to observe;
(iv) markets are international and subject to different regulations, laws and jurisdictions;
(v) market professionals are rewarded for being specialists in one part of the system (e.g. for specific asset classes) rather than for their knowledge of the wider markets;
(vi) even the academics who study financial markets over decades necessarily focus on just one small part of the system;
(vii) markets tend to disclose outcomes in the form of prices and volumes rather than trades, leading to little understanding of who is trading with whom;
(viii) we can only measure 'average' behaviour, which is an aggregate of many thousands or millions of transactions in a given period rather than individual transactions; and
(ix) all transactions in markets are driven by humans whose behaviour is not always very predictable.

Whatever the degree of oversight of regulators and others in financial markets may have, banks will always be one step ahead and far better placed to circumvent restrictions in their activities. The 'poachers' simply have far greater expertise and higher-quality data than the 'gamekeepers'. Simon Carr noted that the then Governor of the Bank of England, Mervyn King, saw financial regulation as far too legalistic and impenetrable, 'mainly because every time a regulation is made the banks invent a new product to get round it'.[35]

While large banks are essentially corporations, they are far from typical in many respects. The most important difference between such banks and large corporations is understood best when the banks approach a situation of financial distress. When

34 Brunnermeier, M. and Oehmke, M., 'Complexity in financial markets', paper presented to the 2009 EEA Meetings and the 2008 ECB-Chicago Fed Conference.

35 Simon Carr, 'The Sketch: Finance – it's so complicated that even the head of the Bank of England can't figure it out', *Independent*, 4 November 2011, available from http://www.independent.co.uk/voices/commentators/simon-carr/the-sketch-finance-its-so-complicated-that-even-the-head-of-the-bank-of-england-cant-figure-it-out-6256928.html, accessed 19 March 2016.

a large non-bank corporation gets into financial trouble and it is unable to meet its obligations, then the company might:

(i) seek additional financing;
(ii) accept a takeover from another corporation;
(iii) seek protection under bankruptcy law to reorganise its finances, and continue in business; or
(iv) become insolvent, with the company being broken up, its assets sold off, and its creditors receiving a small proportion of the resources owed to them by the corporation.

Let us contrast this with the case of a high street big-four bank when it gets into financial trouble. In this case, the government and central bank will step in to seek a buyer or will take a large equity investment in the bank to provide some new liquidity in the short to medium term. The reason why authorities do this is to prevent systemic failure; otherwise there would be a run not only on the distressed bank but also on similar large banks, leading to systemic failure. Such failure would lead to the collapse of the banking system and confidence in the national currency, cash hoarding by citizens, an economic slump, business failures and potentially even civil unrest! So general corporate failure leads to loss of equity investor capital and some losses to the corporations' creditors, whereas large bank failure may far more dramatically lead to the collapse of the financial system.

The interconnectedness of banks has recently become a topic of considerable interest to international bank regulators. Banks are interconnected in many different ways, and that greater interconnectedness leads to stresses spreading more rapidly throughout the financial system in times of financial shock. Banks may be directly connected via bilateral transactions, and thus default from one bank can cause contagion to other banks. A small number of core banks exist within each country, whereby distress in one could be propagated extensively throughout the rest of the banking network. Banks may also be interconnected via less direct channels, such as fire sales by a distressed bank leading to asset price falls and mark-to-market losses for other banks. There is evidence that since the financial crisis direct interconnectedness has decreased and indirect interconnectedness has increased.[36]

A common issue identified by governments and regulators is the growth and sheer scale of the 'megabanks'. William Emmons, a St Louis Fed economist, argues that misbehaviour of the megabanks was not picked up by federal regulators in advance of them becoming problematic, due to the complexity of supervising such banks. He explains that the problems occurred due to (i) many regulators across the world supervising the same banks; and (ii) the fact that there is no

36 Liu, Z., Qulet, S. and Roth, B. 'Banking sector interconnectedness: what is it, how can we measure it and why does it matter?', Q2 (2015) *Bank of England Quarterly Bulletin*.

globally unified framework for regulating international banks.[37] He compares the corporate governance mechanisms of the best US corporations with those in 'megabanks', and observes relative shortcomings in the latter, in terms of both internal and external governance effectiveness. With regard to internal governance, the mechanism of managerial self-interest was seen to be present in the megabanks, while both corporate culture and board oversight were seen to be inadequate. In relation to external governance, the megabanks performed reasonably well against supervision and regulation, product market discipline and shareholder discipline criteria, though depositor/bondholder/counterparty discipline was found to be ineffective.

The term 'too big to fail', which has now become ubiquitous in discussions of banking risk, is commonly understood to have become popularised after its use by US Congressman Stewart McKinney during a 1984 Congressional hearing. The too big to fail (TBTF) argument is that certain companies, and in particular financial institutions, have such a large scale and are characterised by such wide and complex interconnections with other entities in an economy that their failure would be unacceptable, given the potential resulting systemic risk, so that governments (and therefore ultimately taxpayers) and/or central banks will feel coerced to step in to support them. A TBTF bank, if allowed to fail, might lead to a collapse in payments systems, runs on the wider banking sector, the failure in turn of client companies and individuals, significant losses by bank equity investors and so on.

While the avoidance of systemic financial collapse through bank failures is clearly desirable both in terms of the economy and in terms of wider societal welfare, the undesirable consequence of TBTF is that such companies then believe that they have the 'licence to behave badly'. The moral hazard problem here is that banks will thus engage in higher-risk activities than they otherwise would have done to earn higher returns, knowing that there is a safety net in case their risk–return strategies fail. Part of the issue here is the vast scale of banks, begging the question: how have banks become so big? To explain this phenomenon, it is important to understand that banks operate on relatively small margins which produce material profits only on very large volumes, and thus greater absolute profits and ultimately greater profitability demand greater scale. Further, the larger entities become, the lower is their cost of capital, and this relation is strengthened yet further for TBTF banks. Thus, there is no such thing as a bank which is 'too big' in terms of bank business models. Banking sectors in western economies are typically dominated by four or five very large, long-established banks, each of which may be considered too big to fail. Various solutions are seen to potentially address this issue:

37 Emmons, W., 'In-depth: the big banks: too complex to manage?', Federal Reserve Bank of St. Louis, Winter 2012, available from https://www.stlouisfed.org/publications/central-banker/winter-2012/the-big-banks-too-complex-to-manage, accessed 13 March 2016.

(i) breaking up the banks to reduce their power and size;
(ii) increasing the monitoring of banks;
(iii) greater regulation to limit risk taking; and
(iv) creating a firewall between investment and retail banking activities.

6.5 The behavioural context of the financial crisis

The financial crisis ultimately arose from the collective behaviour of market participants, including both finance market professionals and investors. Certain practitioner behavioural traits and norms can help to explain how the crisis unfolded without reference to criminal intent, including finance professional psychology, the extant theoretical frameworks within which market professionals work and the culture of complacency. However, blame may indeed be levelled squarely at market participants in the case of poor behaviour, negligence, financial crime and insider behaviour.

We turn first to certain behavioural traits that can lead to financial crises in the absence of malice. The recent financial crisis happened, many would argue, due to the greed of investment bankers – put simply, this is the argument that bankers have a predisposition to bad behaviour. While the behaviour of market participants clearly made some contribution to the financial crisis, it is not clear that bankers behaved any worse than other actors in the business world or, indeed, in the general populace. In terms of psychology, there is a fairly strong argument that emotional responses such as greed and fear can 'short-circuit' the more complex decision-making faculties, such as those required in active portfolio management, thereby leading to poorer trading performance. However, the link between psychological factors and trading performance in day-traders has been examined by researchers, who found that there is little correlation between personality traits and trading performance.[38] Nevertheless, there is indeed some evidence that physiological mechanisms can drive financial bubbles and, in particular, of the surge in testosterone experienced by men when they are 'winning', which causes them to take even riskier positions in their investments.[39] Bankers who succeed are not necessarily different from the rest of us and their behaviour may be entirely hormonal!

Some authors argue that the intellectual, and thus ultimately the behavioural, origins of the global financial crisis are explained in 'blind spots' emanating from

38 Lo, A.W., Repin, D.V. and Steenbarger, B.N., *Fear and Greed in Financial Markets: A Clinical Study of Day Traders*, NBER Working Paper 11243, March 2005, National Bureau of Economic Research, Cambridge, MA.
39 'What traders' testosterone tells us about markets', Bloomberg View, 10 June 2012, available from http://www.bloombergview.com/articles/2012-06-10/what-traders-testosterone-tells-us-about-markets, accessed 28 March 2016.

within conventional financial theory.[40] The basic building-blocks of financial economics, including modern portfolio theory, the capital structure irrelevance proposition, the capital asset pricing model and the efficient market hypothesis, were originally developed as empirically testable propositions, but became over recent decades 'central articles of faith'. The effect of this is to make market actors believe that the prevailing mechanisms will produce optimal allocations of resources, as they are self-correcting opportunity arbitrageurs, and financial regulation is developed predicated upon this belief. However, this faith may be misplaced, as financial market theory is arguably incomplete, particularly in its inability to incorporate both complexity and financial innovation. Complexity in financial markets exists in terms of high information costs, deeply embedded information and expertise asymmetries, and thus acute agency problems. Innovation is in turn found in the development of new financial products and services. Conventional finance theory has therefore presented both a straitjacket to financial thinking and an immutable foundation on which to build further complexity and innovation. Effectively, finance theory became a doctrine around which its practitioner adherents practised their religion.

A behavioural trait of complacency also played a pivotal role in the financial crisis. The culture of complacency strengthens during periods of economic stability and growth, leading at times to some departure from rational investment decisions, an effect which is then compounded by herding behaviour. Complacency is argued to be both institutional and institutionalised, underpinned by the irrational belief that each crisis is unique and thus cannot be identified either in advance or as it is emerging.[41]

We must allow that a potential contributing factor to the financial crisis was the poor behaviour of at least some market players, but what does this mean precisely? The overriding mandate of financial market employees is to generate profitable activity for their clients, and thus ultimately for their financial institutions. The pursuit of profit is to be expected and indeed rewarded in a capitalist system, though if this is undertaken to the detriment of other stakeholders, and in particular client customers, then we might reasonably question the integrity and ethics of both the individual and their organisation. As discussed above, most market participants only see one narrow part of the overall financial system, and they may further lack an understanding of the broader context of their activity (i.e. where and how their involvement impacts upon the wider financial world). Is this negligent? Probably not, given the inability of anyone to have clear oversight of the whole system, including banking and financial market regulators.

We turn next to how negligence is dealt with in financial institutions. If an employee of a financial institution is negligent (failure to exercise care that a

40 Awrey, D. 'Complexity, innovation, and the regulation of modern financial markets', 2 (2009) *Harvard Business Law Review*, 235–294.

41 Tucker, J., 'Financial crises: a culture of complacency', 7 (2010) *Journal of Organizational Transformation and Social Change*, 7–23.

prudent person would exercise in such circumstances, which subsequently leads to damage) on a minor scale, then they will be reprimanded and probably subject to some additional training. However, on a more material scale, negligence will most likely result in the termination of employment. Given the interconnectedness within financial institutions and the organisation of many, if not most, activities in teams, the question of precisely who has been negligent when things go wrong can be far from clear. The difficulty here is one of locus of control – who was ultimately responsible when a negligent action was taken? Team negligence will typically be addressed with a missed or reduced bonus pot for that part of the organisation – this 'light touch' approach can potentially lead to negligence/mistakes recurring without remedy into perpetuity.

A far more serious form of poor behaviour is financial crime. The Financial Conduct Authority identifies the following as the paramount forms of financial crime: money laundering, fraud, sanctions breaches, bribery and corruption.[42] Money laundering involves the process of transforming the proceeds of crime into 'legitimate' money and assets. Fraud is effectively criminal deception for financial or personal gain. Sanctions breaches involve conducting transactions with entities that are embargoed by governments. Corruption is the abuse of a position of entrusted power for illegitimate personal gain, whereas bribery involves the giving or receipt of something of value in order to influence the judgement of a person in charge of a public or legal duty. Each of these is clearly defined in both law and financial regulation, and where there are clear cases of criminal actions, then offenders should, in theory, be prosecuted. However, as the prosecution of employees may lead to significant reputation loss for an institution, the criminal justice system will be avoided at all costs. Many players in financial markets may engage in poor behaviour which does not benefit them directly – such behaviour may solely benefit their clients or financial institutions. Further, some activity which is ultimately criminal, such as not spotting money laundering by clients, may simply be the result of negligence, lack of information, inability to monitor with given resources and so on.

Insider trading is an ambiguous area in financial markets. Insider trading may be defined as 'the buying or selling of a security by someone who has access to material, non-public information about the security'.[43] Investopedia explains that the legality or otherwise of insider trading depends on when the insider makes the trade.[44] Trading is illegal when the material information remains 'non-public' – this is unfair to other investors who do not have the insider information. You might reasonably envisage insider information to emerge through the intrinsic process of investment analysis, particularly through the contact of investment

42 McDermott, T., 'Financial crime in the FCA world', Financial Conduct Authority, available from http://www.fca.org.uk/news/speeches/financial-crime-in-the-fca-world, accessed 21 March 2016.

43 'Insider trading', Investopedia.com, available from http://www.investopedia.com/terms/i/insidertrading.asp, accessed 18 March 2016.

44 Ibid.

analysts with the top management of companies. Indeed, the role of professional investment analysts is to spot underpriced or overpriced shares – not making the most of the information researched on a particular company in guiding both proprietary and client trading may be considered by many professionals to constitute a dereliction of their professional duties.

6.6 How might financial market professionals mislead others?

In addition to activities that are clearly illegal, there are many ways in which market professionals may instead mislead others (market players, investors, institutions and so on), including:

(i) underplaying potential risk or overplaying potential returns;
(ii) charging excessive transactions or management costs;
(iii) the unnecessary bundling of financial products;
(iv) misselling financial products;
(v) taking advantage of the financially naïve; and
(vi) 'tipster' behaviour.

There exists a positive relationship between risk and return referred to as the 'risk–return trade-off'.[45] It is a trade-off in the sense that when exposed to additional risk, investors expect to be compensated commensurately for bearing that risk. In dealings between market professionals and other market players and investors, there frequently occurs an information asymmetry in terms of gauging risk. This is particularly the case when a financial asset has been created by a market professional which is then sold to others. If the true underlying risk is in some way downplayed, then the investor will effectively be accepting a return which is too low for the risk borne. This will also involve the investor overpaying for the investment as the asset's cash flows are discounted at an artificially low rate. Similarly, market professionals may overstate the potential returns (and/or cash flows) of an investment – this is particularly the case for risk-class assets, such as equities or equity portfolios. Given that markets are in general held to be efficient, past trends of returns will not be a useful predictor of future returns, so promising returns on past good asset performance may be a simple way of misleading investors.

Market professionals can also mislead investors in terms of the transparency of transactions costs or management fees charged on financial investments. Transactions costs will be incurred by the investor whenever an investment is bought or sold, whereas management fees are most likely to be incurred on an

45 For further information on the risk–return trade-off, see 'Risk–return tradeoff', Nasdaq, available from http://www.nasdaq.com/investing/glossary/r/risk-return-trade-off, accessed 28 March 2016.

ongoing basis. In fund management, even modest management fees may lead to returns being 'wiped out' in a given period, unless the underlying asset markets are performing very strongly. Transaction fees may also lead to returns being reduced dramatically in fund management, leading to a well-founded criticism of fund managers that they have conducted an inappropriately high volume of transactions during a period, thereby incrementally eroding investor returns.

It is also the case that many financial products are 'bundled' in modern financial services, such that an investment vehicle is sold with loss of income insurance, downside protection or other complementary financial products. It may be very difficult for the investor to discern the relative merits of the individual components, given that they are presented only as an overall packaged product; that is, investors may find it impossible to 'unbundle' the individual package components. The subject of financial misselling has come to the fore in the last decade, particularly in relation to unwanted payment protection insurance (PPI), the selling of derivative-based products to financially unsophisticated clients such as small businesses, the selling of whole-life insurance to an elderly person with no dependants or spouse, and so on. Misselling is defined as 'the ethically questionable practice of a salesperson misrepresenting or misleading an investor about the characteristics of a product or service'.[46] It is therefore misleading to sell financial products to investors without their knowledge (unfair bundling) or products that they simply do not need (misselling).

It has long been recognised in financial markets that investors vary in ability from the 'expert' through to the financially 'naïve'. There exists an asymmetry not only with respect to information, then, but also with respect to ability to understand financial markets and their constituent asset classes. Financial assets or products are by definition very complex, providing a stream of cash flows to the investor over time, which, when discounted back to their present value, may be used to value them. This sounds straightforward, until we understand that, for many financial products, the future (realised) stream of cash flows may vary from current expectations. We also do not know the precise discount rate to be applied to the cash flows to discount them through time, as this depends on the expectation of returns on other financial market assets. The degree of uncertainty with financial assets or products is therefore significant – while financial market professionals are trained to assess and deal with this uncertainty and the underlying complexity of products, naïve investors are not, and so will simply assume that the market has 'got it right' when it comes to the price of a financial investment. If the latter is the case, and markets are indeed efficient, perhaps we should all leave it to markets, which will arrive at a fair intrinsic price for financial assets. However, the collapse of asset prices in the wake of the financial crisis shows that even markets collectively get it very badly wrong on occasion (markets are not as efficient as we might think).

46 'Misselling', Investopedia.com, available from http://www.investopedia.com/terms/m/misselling.asp#axzz1phhWenym, accessed 14 March 2016.

Finally, many news channels and newspapers traditionally provide tips on stocks. However, in so doing, the 'tipsters' find themselves in a position of real power, particularly if they have a large following. All that it requires to make significant gains is for the tipster to trade in advance of providing the tip advice – buying shares in advance of a favourable tip or short-selling shares in advance of an unfavourable tip. However, this activity is clearly illegal. A classic case of such behaviour was the *Daily Mirror*'s 'City Slickers' tipster column, whereby three of the paper's tipsters were convicted of market manipulation following a six-year criminal investigation by the UK Department of Trade and Industry.[47] The risk of this type of activity has increased dramatically now that many investors follow online rather than print press tipsters.

6.7 The response of the industry to these challenges

In addition to advances on the regulatory front, financial institutions and professional bodies have set in place systems and approaches around not just compliance but also integrity and ethics, in an attempt to reduce the possibility of a similar crisis taking place and, of course, to address practitioner malfeasance, misfeasance and nonfeasance.

In terms of the regulatory response to the financial crisis, we can observe an evolution in emphasis over recent years, commencing with governance and behaviour change and moving towards more robust structural reform. In February 2009, David Walker was asked by the UK government to conduct a review of the corporate governance of UK banks in response to the failures of the banking system following the financial crisis. The resulting report, *A Review of Corporate Governance in UK Banks and Other Financial Industry Entities*, was published in November 2009.[48] The argument here was that governance failures within banks contributed materially to the crisis, particularly in relation to excessive risk-taking. It was recognised that the behavioural change required could not be achieved through improved supervision and regulation alone, but that improved corporate governance was of central importance.

The Independent Commission on Banking (ICB), which followed in 2010, was conducted by Sir John Vickers to consider structural reform of the banking sector, with the final report published in September 2011.[49] The report recommended that UK banks should 'ring-fence' their retail banking divisions

47 Simon Bowers, 'Three face jail over Mirror share fraud', *Guardian*, 8 December 2005, available from http://www.theguardian.com/media/2005/dec/08/pressandpublishing.mirror1, accessed 14 March 2016.

48 David Walker, *A Review of Corporate Governance in UK Banks and Other Financial Industry Entities*, London: HM Treasury, 26 November 2009, available from http://webarchive.nationalarchives.gov.uk/20130129110402/http://www.hm-treasury.gov.uk/d/walker_review_261109.pdf, accessed 18 March 2016.

49 Independent Commission on Banking, *Final Report Recommendations*, September 2011, available from http://bankingcommission.independent.gov.uk, accessed 18 March 2016.

from their global wholesale investment banking activities, and that banks should have more prudent capital requirements and greater loss-absorbing capacity. The proposed ring-fencing was seen as preferable to total separation of banks' business segments. The loss-absorption proposal effectively involves greater equity to risk-weighted assets, a higher primary loss-absorbing capacity and a higher ranking of deposits over other unsecured debt. Thus, we can see progression here, from a focus on less tangible governance towards more concrete structural reforms around greater risk capital, loss-absorption capacity and cordoning off the so-called 'casino banking' investment arms of banks from their other business.

In 2013, the Parliamentary Commission on Banking Standards published its report entitled *Changing Banking for Good*, with the aim of restoring trust in the banking sector.[50] The report proposals made the following recommendations to address the problems of the banking industry:

(i) to establish individual responsibility in banking, particularly at senior levels;
(ii) to reform governance within banks in relation to standards and safety;
(iii) to encourage more diverse banking markets and empower customers;
(iv) to reinforce the responsibilities of regulators in exercising their new powers; and
(v) to specify more precisely the role of government.

The emphasis on individual banking professionals focuses on the attribution of responsibility, better incentive schemes in terms of remuneration, and improved enforcement against individuals. Improved governance should take the form of increased accountability, improved lines of communication and the clear demarcation of responsibilities. There was a desire to make markets function better to open up competition within the banking sector and, importantly, to change the structure of the big banks, particularly those bailed out by the government. The serious regulatory failures around the crisis were to be addressed by a move away from box-ticking to the greater exercise of judgement, along with greater oversight and more powerful regulatory tools. The responsibility of government in this was seen to extend from ensuring greater competition and better functioning of bank lending going forward, to holding regulators to account over their decisions and standing up to the powerful lobbying of the industry in its resistance to change. Thus, we can see wide-ranging measures emerging to address the problems of banks, focusing not just on governance or 'optimal' banking structures, but also on the underlying responsibilities of all parties from banks, to regulators and to the government.

50 Parliamentary Commission on Banking Standards, *Changing Banking for Good*, 12 June 2013, available from http://www.parliament.uk/business/committees/committees-a-z/joint-select/professional-standards-in-the-banking-industry/news/changing-banking-for-good-report, accessed 10 March 2016.

The Banking Reform Act 2013 implements the recommendations of both the Independent Commission on Banking and the Parliamentary Commission on Banking Standards.[51] HM Treasury noted that the four key areas of reform since the crisis were: (i) supervision; (ii) structure; (iii) culture; and (iv) competition.[52] In effect, the Act placed the Bank of England back at the centre of the supervisory regime in the UK, introduced greater separation between retail and investment banking, placed more emphasis on stricter banking standards in terms of behaviour and sanctions, and sought to encourage better competition within the sector. Thus, the Act brought the different elements together into law, ranging from softer behavioural aspects through to market aspects such as structure and supervision.

The Financial Conduct Authority is now placed at the very centre of moves to reform the banking sector. The FCA was established by the Financial Services Act 2012 with three objectives: (i) to protect consumers; (ii) to protect financial markets; and (iii) to promote competition.[53] The FCA stated that 'we want consumers to be able to trust that the firms we regulate have their best interests at heart by providing them with appropriate products and services'.[54] So from this we can observe the interests of consumers being placed at the heart of the banking system. The role of the FCA is undertaken in conjunction with the Prudential Regulation Authority (the prudential regulator for deposit-takers, insurers and investment firms), the Bank of England (performs the central bank role), the Financial Policy Committee (monitors risks and weaknesses in the financial system) and the Treasury (responsible for legislation under which the FCA operates). The approach of the FCA is broadly to focus on higher-risk areas, and their activities involve the authorisation of firms and individuals to operate within markets, the supervision of firms to ensure that they operate with integrity and are financially sound, and enforcement to protect consumers and markets from those who 'do not follow the rules'.

In addition to the newly reformed regulatory environment, what advances have financial institutions and their respective professional bodies made towards improving the operation and safety of the finance sector? We direct our attention to changing banker behaviour and culture, a renewed focus on integrity and ethics, staff development and training initiatives, and a renewed emphasis on compliance.

51 Financial Services (Banking Reform) Act 2013, Chapter 33, The Stationery Office, available from http://www.legislation.gov.uk/ukpga/2013/33/pdfs/ukpga_20130033_en.pdf, accessed 5 August 2016.

52 HM Treasury, 'Government completes banking reforms', 5 March 2015, available from https://www.gov.uk/government/news/government-completes-banking-reforms, accessed 18 March 2016.

53 Financial Services Act 2012, The Stationery Office, available from http://www.legislation.gov.uk/ukpga/2012/21/pdfs/ukpga_20120021_en.pdf, accessed 25 March 2016.

54 Financial Conduct Authority, 'What we do', available from http://www.fca.org.uk/about/what, accessed 14 March 2016.

Clearly, one important way of addressing the problems associated with the financial crisis is to achieve behaviour change in the finance sector. The behaviour that was clearly problematic and contributed to the financial crisis was arguably the fact that many financial market participants were driven by personal goals, without full regard to the potential societal losses arising from their actions. But how might we deter financial actors from 'behaving badly'? Logically, banks might achieve this through:

(i) cultural realignment;
(ii) more selective recruitment;
(iii) education and training of the workforce;
(iv) monitoring and enforcement;
(v) effective compliance processes;
(vi) a focus on stakeholder needs rather than merely selling services;
(vii) incentive structures that do not reward risk-taking per se.

However, we might reasonably argue that those attracted to the finance industry are self-selecting individuals with a predisposition to risk-seeking and self-advancement, and, further, the business model of banks is predicated upon this profile of employee type. The simple fact is that, consistent with the broader dynamics of a capitalist system, the pursuit of profit is the clearest objective – when employees get this right, they gain, the bank gains, and shareholders are content. If we introduce objectives other than profit maximisation, then such goals are likely to be more complex, success against them is extremely difficult to gauge, and firms will suffer a decline in performance in a highly competitive international banking market.

The crisis has drawn attention to the internal governance mechanisms and values of modern financial institutions, particularly as there remains a temptation for market actors to return to their pre-crisis behaviours. Poor behaviour observed since the crisis includes:

(i) lobbying against the closer scrutiny of financial firms' business models;
(ii) political pressure to maintain the 'business-friendly' profile of key world financial centres;
(iii) the policy-formulation process being led by senior bankers and business leaders rather than other stakeholders;
(iv) the reluctance of regulators to bring civil let alone criminal cases against corporations;
(v) banks remaining too big to fail and governments recognising this; and
(vi) senior bankers merely apologising rather than accepting personal responsibility for the events leading up to the crisis.[55]

The FCA explains the importance of culture as follows: '[C]ulture drives individual behaviours which in turn affect day-to-day practices in firms and their interaction

55 Tomasic, R. 'The financial crisis and the haphazard pursuit of financial crime', 18 (2011) *Journal of Financial Crime*, 7–31.

with customers and other market participants.'[56] To effect what they refer to as long-term culture change, they argue that it is essential for firms and regulators to work together. They argue that firms should be managed in a way that reflects good governance and promotes the right behaviour for the benefit of consumers and markets, and those who manage firms must be held accountable and their remuneration should be appropriate for the decisions they take. The focus of the FCA going forward is on improved supervision within banks, the clearer attribution of accountability and responsibility within banks, adherence to conduct rules, and an enhanced environment for employees to engage in whistleblowing to challenge poor behaviour and practice.

Given the central importance of instilling the right culture and behavioural norms in the banking sector, it was somewhat surprising to many commentators that, in late December 2015, we learned that the FCA would not be proceeding further with the inquiry into the culture, pay and behaviour of staff in the banking sector, as promised in their 2015/16 Business Plan, following the completion of only its first phase.[57] The inquiry examined whether certain aspects of employment such as remuneration, appraisal (incentives) and promotion structures were linked to financial scandals. On this news, many financial commentators argued that the decision characterised a broader shift in attitude towards a more favourable treatment of the banks, particularly given the continued importance of the City of London as a world financial centre. Perhaps this presaged the end of 'banker bashing'.

However, one aspect of changing behaviour and culture in the finance sector that we can readily observe is the renewed focus on integrity and ethics within both financial institutions and their professional bodies. The term 'integrity' may be defined as 'the quality of being honest and having strong moral principles'.[58] In the setting of the finance industry, some fundamental principles should characterise an ethical financial services industry, including:

(i) not pursuing profit at the expense of all else;
(ii) behaviour in the best interests of clients;
(iii) delivering technical excellence;
(iv) prioritising good ethics over client instructions;
(v) making sure ethics take precedence over legality; and
(vi) the promotion of positive ethical behaviour across the industry.[59]

56 Financial Conduct Authority, 'Culture in banking', available from https://www.fca.org.uk/static/documents/foi/foi4350-information-provided.pdf, accessed 4 March 2016.
57 'Banking culture inquiry shelved by regulator FCA', BBC website, 31 December 2015, available from http://www.bbc.co.uk/news/uk-35204010, accessed 9 January 2016.
58 'Integrity', Oxford Dictionaries, available from http://www.oxforddictionaries.com/definition/english/integrity, accessed 14 March 2016.
59 Black, J. and Anderson, K., *Creating an Ethical Framework for the Financial Services Industry*, Herbert Smith Freehills LLP and London School of Economics, January 2013.

John Hendry argues that the finance sector has such a bad reputation for illegal and unethical behaviour partly because of ignorance and prejudice, with lending, borrowing and speculation seen as morally distasteful.[60] However, he also argues that the sector is more susceptible to ethical lapses than other sectors in the economy. He does not see fraudsters and cheats such as Madoff and Levine at the heart of the problem – in such cases, criminal intent was easy to discern. Instead, he notes that many cases of ethical lapses are unintentional – that is, moral oversight or neglect rather than intentional wrongdoing. He sees certain ethical lapses as arising from:

(i) focusing on technical rather than moral norms;
(ii) not understanding the services offered or thinking through the consequences of offering a particular service to customers; and
(iii) the powerful ability of the sector to extract financial wealth from the rest of the economy.

He argues that the cause of ethical lapses lies in the fact that financial sector activities are detached from physical and moral communities, and that money is inherently demoralising, with the values and obligations of human interactions lost.

Some commentators believe that if bankers are unreliable in terms of committing to more ethical behaviour, then they should be obliged to do so. The Virtuous Banking report launched in July 2014 by ResPublica suggested *inter alia* that bankers should swear a Hippocratic oath to signal their commitment to the pursuit of greater professionalism.[61] Drawing upon the example of Dutch bankers, such an oath might focus on the needs of customers, the quality of service, conducting business in an ethical manner, the responsible creation of value, and committing to a duty of care which exceeds that required by law. A further mechanism for ensuring greater adherence to both regulations and expected behaviours is to facilitate practitioner 'whistleblowing' when poor behaviour is encountered. In October 2015, the Financial Conduct Authority, along with the Prudential Regulation Authority, published new rules in relation to whistleblowing, following the recommendations of the Parliamentary Commission on Banking Standards.[62] The acting Chief Executive of the FCA, Tracy Dermott, commented:

60 Hendry, K., 'Ethics in finance: why is it such a problem?', *European Financial Review* (20 October), available from http://www.europeanfinancialreview.com/?p=4904, accessed 16 March 2016.

61 Llewellyn, D., Steare, R. and Trevellick, R., *Virtuous Banking: Placing Ethos and Purpose at the Heart of Finance* (ResPublica Trust: Lincoln, 2014), available from http://www.respublica.org.uk/wp-content/uploads/2014/07/ueq_Virtuous-Banking-Final-new.pdf, accessed 5 August 2016.

62 FCA, 'PS15/24: Whistleblowing in deposit-takers, PRA-designated investment firms and insurers', Financial Conduct Authority Policy Statement, 6 October 2015, available from https://www.fca.org.uk/news/ps15-24-whistleblowing-in-deposit-takers-pra-designated-investment-firms-and-insurers, accessed 5 August 2016.

'Whistleblowers play an important role in exposing poor practice in firms and they have in the past few years contributed intelligence crucial to action taken against firms and individuals.'[63] The rules set out mechanisms for firms to encourage finance sector workers to come forward with concerns and to challenge poor behaviour and practice.[64] So the new behavioural norm is for finance practitioners to act ethically and to ensure that their organisations and colleagues also act in such a manner.

The role of professional bodies is arguably pivotal in achieving both cultural and behavioural change in financial institutions. For example, the US-based Chartered Financial Analysts (CFA) Institute gives a similar set of aims, focusing on 'ethics, education, and professional excellence', though importantly it also adds the words 'for the ultimate benefit of society'.[65] The UK-based Chartered Institute for Securities & Investment (CISI) states that its aim is to set standards of professional excellence and integrity within the finance industry, and to provide qualifications to promote the highest level of competence in its members.[66] The Chartered Insurance Institute (CII) focuses again on similar words around the highest standards of integrity and technical competence, but also adds that it seeks to promote 'business capability'.[67] So while the primary focus of finance industry professional bodies is still to promote the technical ability and professional excellence of their members, integrity now features prominently in their mission statements.

Perhaps more revealing is the code of ethics to which professional body members have to adhere. The CFA Institute *Standards of Practice Handbook 2014* importantly updated its code of Code of Ethics Principle, adding to the words '(to) promote the integrity and viability of the global capital markets' the important emphasis 'for the ultimate benefit of society'.[68] In addition to more operational matters around professional–client relations, the handbook focuses on professionalism, integrity in capital markets, duties to clients and so on. The headings of the handbook themselves are quite revealing in terms of the areas

63 AIA, 'The FCA rules for whistleblowing at financial firms', Association of International Accountants guidelines, 27 January 2016, available from https://www.aiaworldwide.com/news/fca-rules-whistleblowing-financial-firms, accessed 5 August 2016.

64 FCA, 'FCA introduces new rules on whistleblowing', Financial Conduct Authority press release, 6 October 2015, available from https://www.fca.org.uk/news/fca-introduces-new-rules-on-whistleblowing, accessed 18 March 2016.

65 CFA Institute, 'Mission & vision', available from https://www.cfainstitute.org/about/vision/Pages/index.aspx, accessed 14 March 2016.

66 Chartered Institute for Securities and Investment, 'Professionalism, integrity, excellence', available from http://www.cisi.org/cisiweb2/cisi-website/about-us, accessed 14 March 2016.

67 Chartered Insurance Institute, 'About the Chartered Insurance Institute', available from http://www.cii.co.uk/about/about-the-cii, accessed 14 March 2016.

68 CFA Institute, *Standards of Practice Handbook*, 11th edition (Charlottesville, VA: CFA Institute, 2014), available from https://www.cfainstitute.org/learning/products/publications/ccb/Pages/ccb.v2014.n4.1.aspx, accessed 9 January 2016.

on which the CFA Institute wish to focus their attention going forward. 'Professionalism' focuses on knowledge of the law; independence and objectivity; and misrepresentation and misconduct. 'Integrity of capital markets' focuses on material non-public information and market manipulation. 'Duties to clients' focuses on loyalty, prudence and care; fair dealing; suitability; performance presentation; and the preservation of confidentiality.

In a UK setting, the CISI *Code of Conduct* similarly recognises that '[p]rofessionals within the securities and investment industry owe important duties to their clients, the market, the industry and society at large'.[69] In brief, the principles contained within require members:

(i) to act honestly and fairly as stewards of their clients' interests;
(ii) to act with integrity in conducting their responsibilities;
(iii) to observe law, regulations and conduct standards in their activities;
(iv) to observe good practice and conduct standards in market dealings;
(v) to deal fairly with conflicts of interest;
(vi) to attain and maintain professional competence;
(vii) to not act in matters where members do not have competence; and
(viii) to always uphold the highest personal and professional standards.

It is notable that the concept of stewardship is emphasised here to complement behaviours which are ethical and professional.

Staff development and training have also come into sharp focus, particularly following the Financial Services Authority's Retail Distribution Review (RDR), which came into effect at the end of 2012. The aim of the RDR is to provide better protection to consumers by 'establishing a resilient, effective and attractive retail investment market that consumers can have confidence in and trust at a time when they need more help and advice than ever with their retirement and investment planning'.[70] The initiative is a good example of how market practitioners, in this case retail investment professionals, now understand in no uncertain terms that the focus of their role is to be transparent and professional and to act ethically in relation to their clients. More specifically, from 2013, investment advisers (IFAs), whether independent or restricted, were required to become more highly qualified. In effect, a higher minimum standard of qualification was instituted for those wanting to give investment advice – so the focus here was on increasing knowledge and understanding of the individual professional,

69 Chartered Institute for Securities and Investment, 'Code of conduct', available from http://www.cisi.org/cisiweb2/docs/default-source/cisi-website/ethics/code-of-conduct-2011a5-without.pdf?sfvrsn=2, accessed 8 February 2016.

70 Financial Services Authority, 'Retail Distribution Review', Financial Services Authority, 17 February 2009, available from http://www.fsa.gov.uk/pages/about/what/rdr/index.shtml, accessed 20 March 2016.

as well as increasing the level of their professionalism.[71] How did this affect investment advisers in the UK? It required new investment advisers to become qualified to a higher level, existing investment advisers to fill in the gaps in their qualifications portfolio to ensure they can continue to practise, and all advisers to commit to significant continuing professional development (CPD) training each year. Clearly professional bodies such as the CISI or CII were well placed to help professionals fill the gaps. Evidence shows that the RDR initiative led to a significant reduction in the number of UK financial advisers and higher average levels of qualifications for those remaining.[72] The disruption to financial institutions and IFAs from this aspect of the RDR was, interestingly enough, one of the most tangible changes in the post-crisis financial world, given its emphasis on individual practitioner credibility.

Finally, professionals in the finance industry of today will readily tell you that some of their best-paid and most powerful colleagues now work in the area of compliance. Compliance now takes centre-stage within all financial institutions, and as such has grown significantly in importance, from being merely a 'tick-box' exercise before the financial crisis. The compliance function within a financial institution, as the title implies, works to ensure that the institution complies with all applicable regulations, rules and laws. Sam Fleming of the *Financial Times* wrote that 'the age of the compliance officer is upon us', given the raft of regulatory initiatives and the threat of huge fines in the wake of the financial crisis.[73] Indeed, Andy Haldane, now Chief Economist at the Bank of England, estimated in 2012 that 70,000 new jobs would need to be created in Europe to comply with Basel III requirements alone.[74] Compliance officers focus their attention on preventing conflicts of interest, monitoring the institution's trading activities, ensuring compliance with regulations, guarding against money laundering and helping to prevent tax evasion, among other duties. Failure to take compliance seriously can lead to loss of reputation, fines and sanctions against a financial institution. Thus we see that the financial sector is now facing new structures and far tighter regulation, at the same time having to foster a culture which places customers' needs at the centre of its business. It will be some years before we can determine how successfully the financial sector has embraced this change.

71 'The Retail Distribution Review or "RDR" explained', Adviser-Hub, available from http://www.adviser-hub.co.uk/Better-Business/RDR/RDR-explained, accessed 25 March 2016.

72 Clare, A., Thomas, S., Walgama, O. and Makris, C., *The Impact of the RDR on the UK's Market for Financial Advice: Challenge and Opportunity*, Cass Consulting, June 2013, available from https://www.cass.city.ac.uk/__data/assets/pdf_file/0016/202336/The-impact-of-RDR-Cass-version.pdf, accessed 25 March 2016.

73 Fleming, S., 'The age of the compliance officer arrives', FT.com, 23 April 2014, http://staging.app.ft.com/cms/s/cadd54a6-c3bd-11e3-a8e0-00144feabdc0.html, accessed 14 March 2016 (subscription needed).

74 Ibid.

6.8 Summary

This chapter set out to examine the financial crisis and financial crime from the perspective of the finance industry, in so doing seeking to explain the structures, institutional factors, behaviours and shortcomings that led to the financial crisis. We started by examining the nature of financial crises more generally, and questioning whether financial stability is of itself inherently destabilising, given the natural tendency of financial asset markets to bubble, fuelled by excessive leverage. Understanding the scale, function and structure of the finance industry is important if we want to elucidate the role of its key agents. The industry is composed of primary through to fourth markets, the array of financial intermediaries that occupy them, and a range of asset classes. Global financial markets are almost unimaginably large, and their importance to UK GDP and employment is significant.

We saw that a well-functioning finance industry is pivotal to the development, growth and success of modern capitalist economies, such that they facilitate the optimal allocation of surplus funds to corporations and others with a funding requirement, in addition to many further welfare-enhancing functions. However, advanced financial markets also suffer from welfare-destroying phenomena, such as boom–bust cycles; irrational, computer-based high-frequency trading bubbles and crashes; sharp asset price departure from fundamentals; and so on. The ability of individuals to avoid the effects of these phenomena has rapidly diminished with the unremitting pace of financialisation. There is almost universal agreement on the transmission mechanism of the credit crunch and the sovereign debt crisis that followed, while there is less consensus regarding the precise contribution of institutional factors. Booms and bubbles, information asymmetry, market, institutional and financial instrument complexity, a lack of true regulatory oversight, bank interconnectedness and the presence of megabanks all arguably played an important role in the crisis. With the onset of a financial crisis, it quickly becomes apparent that banks are not like other corporations, and a number of prominent banks have become, and indeed remain, 'too big to fail', due to the systemic failure that would be precipitated in the absence of government support.

We then moved on to consider the behavioural context of the financial crisis. Certain behavioural traits and norms within the finance sector contributed to the crisis which were entirely unrelated to criminal intent or activity. Bankers do not have psychological stereotypes or profiles that are any different to the general populace, while their physiological reactions to taking risk positions are shown to be innate. Part of the problem may be found in the shortcomings of finance theory on which market activity is predicated, which is at times far removed from empirical reality. Slavishly adhering to such theory creates blind spots in practitioner cognition of financial market dynamics, delaying adequate responses and compounding the belief that the crisis could not have been anticipated. Institutional complacency can similarly lead to departure from rational decisions in markets. We must always keep in mind that capitalism not only encourages but demands that bankers and other finance practitioners maximise profits – this mechanism is itself dispassionate and largely 'moral-free'. During the crisis there have been incidences of negligence across the sector, though mitigation rests on the difficult job of establishing a clear locus of control in a predominantly team-orientated operating environment. As in all walks of business life, criminal activity such as fraud and corruption occurred before, during and indeed after the crisis. Such activity may be dealt with in the criminal justice system, in the hope that it will dissuade others from taking this avenue, though the risk of financial institution reputational loss may mean that this course of action is not always taken.

We may observe over recent years a myriad of press stories involving finance sector practitioners misleading investors, most notably in relation to the mis-selling of payment protection insurance or derivative-based loan products. A tiny minority of bankers and other industry practitioners do misbehave, and sometimes on a staggering scale. Misleading behaviour can take the form of misinforming investors of the true risk–return trade-off, being less than transparent regarding transaction and management costs, the unwelcome bundling of financial products, selling investors inappropriate financial products, trading on investor naïveté or information asymmetries, or even tipster-trading. However, over the same period, investors have become more savvy and regulators have become less tolerant, leading to increasingly material compensation claims and an appetite for criminal prosecutions.

The response of the industry, encouraged by both the 'carrot' of moral suasion and the 'stick' of regulatory control, has varied from less meaningful acts of public contrition through to more robust structural change. The regulatory response since the crisis has sought to address banking governance issues (Walker Review) and structural weaknesses in the banking industry (Independent Commission on Banking), to strengthen the overall approach to bank monitoring and governance across stakeholders (Parliamentary Commission on Banking Standards), and to establish the majority of these reforms in law (Banking Reform Act 2013). The key supervisory role is now vested in the Financial Conduct Authority, with their mandate to protect consumers and financial markets, while at the same time promoting competition – this is a tricky balancing act if London wishes to retain its position as a leading world financial market.

In addition to the new tougher, tighter regulatory environment, financial institutions have themselves made significant advances towards improving the safety and probity of their business operations. Such institutions have largely recognised the need for behaviour change, starting with 'getting the culture right' and feeding through to individual practitioner cultural alignment. The emphasis is now to instil an organisational culture, which, taken together with improved governance structures and stricter compliance, will promote integrity and adherence to strong moral principles in their dealings with customers and other stakeholders – put simply, profit should not be pursued at the expense of all else. We probably do not have to go as far as to insist upon bankers taking a Hippocratic oath, as temporarily satisfying as this might be, but instead need to create an environment within financial institutions where 'doing the right thing' becomes instinctive. Professional bodies are making good progress to facilitate not only a good compliance regime within institutions but also a renewed emphasis on integrity and ethics in their membership, recognising that one key component of professionalism is a duty of care to clients. This is enshrined in revisions to professional codes of conduct, professional qualifications levels and structures following the RDR, and the more stringent requirements for continuing professional development placed on market professionals.

In sum, the time for 'banker bashing' has now passed; governments and regulators are now sufficiently equipped to enforce a far more stringent market environment, and financial institutions and their professional bodies have embraced the need for improved integrity and ethics in their dealings with stakeholders. Bankers are ordinary business people, performing a vital economic function by engaging their professional skills within a complex and mutable environment – they must, of course, still focus primarily on the profit maximisation of their institutions, though at all times bearing in mind their duty of care to their clients and wider society. The vast majority of financial market practitioners never encounter criminal intent in their daily work lives, but many will on occasion find themselves in a situation where 'doing the right thing' may be difficult to discern, given their training, ability, experience, institutional setting and the scope of their information universe.

7 Market abuse and the risk to the financial markets

Andrew H. Baker

Introduction

Information is key in a wide variety of circumstances. Those who possess information are placed at a significant advantage over those who do not possess the same information. This has been a particular point of debate with respect to the market for securities and now in a wider financial services context following the LIBOR (London Interbank Offered Rate) and FOREX (Foreign Exchange) scandals. In the securities market, information is one, if not the, most valuable commodity that a trader can possess and use. The interpretation of information can allow traders to make significant profits or avoid significant losses, depending on the nature of the information, and the speed with which information can be obtained amplifies the outcome from the information. This is why some market participants are willing to use what is termed 'inside information' – that is, information of a privileged nature that is not available to all participants, such information therefore placing advantage on those in whose possession the information resides. The fact that this information is not publicly available makes it privileged and prohibited from use – this is insider dealing. While insider dealing is a form of market abuse, market abuse is a significantly wider term, covering a broader range of activities. A useful descriptor of market abuse can be gleaned from the UK's provisions dealing with such activity, namely Part VIII of the Financial Services and Market Act 2000 (FSMA 2000), where, in addition to insider dealing, the legislation advances five other prohibited activities in relation to misuse of information, manipulation and distortion.

History and background

Market abuse is an umbrella term that can be used to describe a range of activity and behaviour associated with market conduct, or, maybe more accurately, conduct on a market or in respect of securities traded on a market. The primary activity associated with market abuse has been insider dealing; however, improper market conduct goes much further than merely trading securities using non-public privileged information. The traditional approach has been to deal with such activity under criminal law, through specific offences of insider dealing, misleading statements or fraud generally.

The UK's regime against insider dealing and market abuse is a relatively recent addition to measures dealing with financial aspects of criminal behaviour. The first real measure criminalising insider dealing was contained in the Companies Act 1980, and later the Company Securities (Insider Dealing) Act 1985. The evolution of the UK's approach to this offence came in the shape of Part V of the Criminal Justice Act 1993. In addition to the specific offence of insider dealing, misconduct by market participants was also dealt with via Section 47 of the Financial Services Act 1986 (FSA 1986), making it an offence to make misleading statements, alongside the broader deception offences contained in the Theft Acts. The real momentous change came with the enactment of the Financial Services and Markets Act 2000 (FSMA 2000), when, in addition to the criminal offences already on the statute book, a civil remedy for market abuse was introduced. The civil offence covered a broader range of activities than the existing regime, moving beyond the mere use of information into market manipulation and distortion, and to a wider range of actors – not just individuals, but corporate entities as well – and without the requirement of intent to commit the offence.

The management of risk

Regulation is undoubtedly a process of managing risk and the contemporary approach to regulation is to operate a risk-based approach. Black notes that this demands that 'the regulator should clearly identify its objectives and the risks that the regulated organizations may present to the achieving of those objectives'[1] and has become a 'significant organising principle of government and a distinct unit of governance'.[2] Risk-based approaches to regulation reflect the need to prioritise regulatory activity; any authority tasked with control will have finite resources to meet the objectives set and therefore needs to target those resources in a way most likely to achieve set objectives. A second clear advantage to risk-based regulation is noted by Simonova, who observes that risk-based regulation refers to 'flexible regulation', allowing rules to be tailored to fit the particular risk profile presented by a particular industry.[3] It is clear to see the attraction of risk-based approaches in complex areas requiring regulators with finite resources with which to regulate.

The original FSMA 2000 created specific statutory objectives to be considered by the regulator, the Financial Services Authority (FSA), a key objective being to reduce financial crime. This objective and, indeed, all the objectives are at the core of managing risk, and the risk of financial crime undermining positive economic activity received high priority in the formulation of the financial services

1 Black, J. 2010. In Baldwin, R., Cave, M. and Lodge, M. *The Oxford Handbook of Regulation*. Oxford University Press, at 281.
2 Ibid., at 302.
3 Simonova, A. 2015. EU Banking law: developments and challenges. *International Company and Commercial Law Review* 26(2), 51–62.

regulation following the New Labour election victory in May 1997. Section 6 of the FSMA clearly articulated the financial crime risk profile being targeted, focusing the regulatory authority on the three classes of financial crime that pose the greatest danger to the financial wellbeing of the UK: fraud or dishonesty;[4] misconduct in, or misuse of information relating to, a financial market;[5] and handling the proceeds of crime.[6] The second of the triumvirate has arguably proven to be the most novel of the measures dealt with by the FSMA 2000, and identifies the risk evident in unclean financial markets.

The global financial crisis that emerged during 2007/08 has profoundly impacted the nature of regulation and has seen wholesale reform of the regulatory structure. The focus on principles-based regulation has made way for greater focus on outcomes of regulatory activity; however, the application of a risk-based approach remains central. Finite resources dictate that regulatory authorities cannot have eyes everywhere and so are forced into focusing those resources where risk is greatest. The previous statutory objectives provided for in the FSMA 2000 have made way for more focused objectives relevant to the regulatory roles of the new regulators, the Prudential Regulation Authority (PRA) and the Financial Conduct Authority (FCA).

With regard to the old financial crime objective and, in particular, the control of market abuse, the FCA is now the lead authority, with the FSA's responsibility in this area transferring on 1 April 2013. The FCA operates under a strategic objective of ensuring that the relevant markets function well, and is supported by operational objectives of ensuring consumer protection, market integrity and competition, with a continuity objective added later.

The elements of the Section are now operationalised within the integrity objective, which states that its aim is protecting and enhancing the integrity of the UK financial system, and includes that system not being used for a purpose connected with financial crime and not being affected by behaviour that amounts to market abuse. It is clear that that these elements pose significant risk to the orderly operation and integrity of the UK financial markets and thus require significant resources.

The FCA 'expects the financial sector to manage risk';[7] however, it is a key function of the FCA that it manages risk also: it states that it 'will detect and act on risks' and 'identify potential problems early', in order to meet its statutory objectives. With respect to the FCA's position, this was the objective of the previous regime under the FSA, the difference being that the FCA will intervene at an earlier stage and will generally be more intrusive now that the era of

4 Financial Services and Markets Act 2000, s.6(3)(a).
5 Financial Services and Markets Act 2000, s.6(3)(b).
6 Financial Services and Markets Act 2000, s.6(3)(c).
7 FCA 2013. *The FCA's Approach to Advancing its Obligations*. Financial Conduct Authority, London.

light-touch regulation is over.[8] This move highlights the failure of regulators to apply regulations in the period preceding the global financial crisis.

The risks inherent in market abuse are clearly shown in the case of *Fleurose v The Securities and Futures Authority*.[9] To avoid payment under options, contract traders at JP Morgan had engaged in large-scale selling of securities to move the market in a downward direction by 38 points in the last six seconds of trading. This was in breach of the London Stock Exchange rules, which prohibit a member firm from engaging in conduct the sole intention of which is to move the value of the index in question, and is a clear example of market abuse.

By setting standards, the market abuse regime, as contained in the FSMA 2000 and administered by the relevant authority, is tasked with ensuring that such risk is reduced and that the markets are free from abusive practices, and open and available to all users. The very real risk is that unclean markets will discourage investors into the market with significant impact on economic activity generally, and by setting the offence in broad terms it allows the regulatory authority to ensure that good behaviour is expected from market participants, leading to clean and efficient markets[10]

The philosophical difficulties

One of the key issues in relation to the wider subject of market abuse, in particular, has been the debate about whether there should be an offence of insider trading in the first place. It is not universally recognised that the trading of securities on the basis of non-public privileged information should be prohibited, and to some it should be encouraged as a way of improving the information flow and of remunerating insiders.[11] While the arguments against the prohibition have not found favour among law makers, there is a strong persuasive strand to the proposition. The seminal work on this was Professor Henry Manne's 1966 book, *Insider Trading and the Stock Market*.[12] The argument is posited on a number of strands. A key element of his argument is that insider trading is a victimless crime,[13] that where insider dealing occurs there is no impact on the firm, the shareholders

8 Turner, A. 2009. *The Turner Review: A Regulatory Response to the Global Banking Crisis*. FSA, London. Available at: http://www.fsa.gov.uk/pubs/other/turner_review.pdf, accessed 1 March 2016.

9 (2001) EWCA Civ 2015.

10 Alexander, K. 2013. UK insider dealing and market abuse law: strengthening regulatory law to combat market misconduct. In Bainbridge, S. M. (ed.) *Research Handbook on Insider Trading*. Edward Elgar.

11 Bainbridge, S. M. 2008. *Manne on Insider Trading*. UCLA Law and Economics Research Paper Series, Research Paper No. 08–04. Available at: http://papers.ssrn.com/sol3/papers.cfm?abstract_id=1096259, accessed 3 April 2016.

12 Manne, H. G. 1966. *Insider Trading and the Stock Market*. New York Free Press.

13 Manne, H. G. 1985. Insider trading and property rights in new information. *Cato Journal* 4(3), 933–943

or wider groups; however, this standpoint is rebutted by others,[14] who term it an 'abominable fraud' and 'cheating'.[15] His other primary argument states that the price of a security will move in the same direction whether or not there is insider trading, as the information has the character to move the security price up or down irrespective of the date of information disclosure. In fact, it is argued that insiders trading on inside information will, in effect, improve the flow of information to the market, allowing other market participants to make more informed decisions in respect of a company's securities, therefore 'stimulating efficiency'.[16] This undermines a major argument in favour of prohibition, that insider dealing creates information asymmetries, with insiders at a distinct advantage over outsiders, further undermining the argument that insider dealing is a risk to the financial system, the securities markets and those who use them. If it actually provides better information flow to markets, how can it add to the risk profile?

To illustrate his point, Manne refers to the landmark US insider dealing case of *SEC v Texas Gulf Sulphur*, where the shares in TGS were trading at around $18 per share, rising to $31 per share following disclosure and jumping to $58 per share thereafter.[17] This would suggest, and as Manne's argument posits, that securities traded on the basis of inside information will move in the same direction as they would if the information were public, and that they would move in a more steady pattern, instead of spikes associated with securities prices following information disclosure; thus, insider dealing actually improves information flow to the market.[18]

While the arguments against absolute prohibition are strong in certain respects and refuse to go away, it is clear that the arguments in favour of prohibition are stronger and have prevailed. From a shaky start, the prohibition of insider dealing has developed through a proactive securities regulator and a general willingness of the US courts. From initial doubts as to whether the Securities and Exchange Act 1934 prohibited insider dealing, the US courts, through a series of cases, from *SEC v Capital Gains Research Bureau*,[19] *Re Cady Roberts*,[20] through *Texas Gulf Sulphur*[21] and on to *Chiarella*[22] and *Carpenter*, and subsequently *Dirks* and *O'Hagan*, were supported by the Securities and Exchange Commission to

14 Kripke, H. 1985. Manne's insider trading thesis and other failures of conservative economics. *Cato Journal* 4(3), 945–957.
15 Rider, B. A. K. 2010. An abominable fraud. Editorial. *Company Lawyer* 31(7), 197–198.
16 McGee, R. W. 1988. Insider trading: an economic and philosophical analysis. *The Mid Atlantic Journal of Business* 25(1), 35–48.
17 401 F.2d 833 (2d Cir. 1968).
18 See Manne above, n. 12.
19 375 U.S. 180 (1963).
20 40 S.E.C. 907 (1961).
21 401 F.2d 833 (2d Cir. 1968).
22 445 U.S. 222 (1980).

ensure that the prohibition is clearly articulated to market participants in the United States.

The fierce debate in this area suggests that, at least in cases of insider dealing, the risks to the financial sector are exaggerated and that allowing the use of information by insiders in advance of disclosure will provide an efficient method of disseminating such information to market participants. This, however, fails to get round the argument that trading on restricted information is at its base unfair and morally unacceptable, that some market participants will be using information as a result of privileged positions with regard to the securities in question, such as in Texas Gulf Sulphur.[23] A better approach could be to alter disclosure rules to encourage quicker release of price-sensitive information.

A further issue is that Manne's position can only really apply to pure insiders, those who are able to access or acquire the information directly through their position within the issuer of the security. Manne's position is arguably correct in respect of the entrepreneur who generates the price-sensitive information themselves; however, the argument seems to weaken, the further away from the information originator the trading takes place, and is weakened further when the entrepreneur passes that information to outsiders. The argument is eroded completely when that information is misappropriated in some way rather than acquired in the usual pursuit of association with the security issuer.

The criminal provisions

After decades of piecemeal provisions to deal with insider dealing,[24] the legislation dealing with the offence in the UK is now contained in Part V of the Criminal Justice Act 1993, which gave effect to EU Directive 89/592.[25] In essence, the legislation creates three offences of insider dealing, punishable by a maximum sentence of seven years on indictment: namely, dealing by an 'insider' in price-affected securities, encouraging another to deal in price-affected securities, and an offence to disclose inside information to another otherwise than in the performance of employment. The offence is relatively narrow in that the prohibition only applies to 'insiders' who are in possession of 'inside information', with the important point that the 'inside information' has not yet been made public, and that the 'insider' knows that the information is inside information, and that the information is from an inside source. It is arguable that keeping the required components of the offence within narrow confines showed a concern regarding the potential scope of the offence and concern that an over-officious offence would negatively affect trading on the market. Alternatively, the narrowness of

23 McVea, H. 1995. What is wrong with insider dealing? *Legal Studies* 15, 390.

24 Davies, J. 2015. From gentlemanly expectations to regulatory principles: a history of insider dealing in the UK: Part 1. *Company Lawyer*, 36(5), 132–143.

25 Bainbridge, S. M. 2008. *Manne on Insider Trading*. UCLA Law and Economics Research Paper Series, Research Paper No. 08–04. Available at: http://papers.ssrn.com/sol3/papers.cfm?abstract_id=1096259, accessed 3 April 2016.

the offence could indicate a worry that insider dealing was 'rampant' and a comprehensive offence would catch a lot of market participants.[26]

The key elements in respect of market abuse and inside information is the information itself, its possession and use. In *Spector Photo Group NV v Commissie voor het Bank*,[27] CJEU, the European Court of Justice, gave judgment that a person in possession of inside information who deals in financial instruments creates a presumption that they use that information to commit the offence, subject to the ability to rebut the presumption.[28] As noted above, information needs to be 'inside information', meaning that the information has particular characteristics that bring it within the offence. The information needs to be in relation to particular securities or to a particular issuer or issuers of securities, excluding a more general approach. In addition, the information has to be specific or precise and has not been made public, and if it were made public, the nature of the information would have a significant effect on the price of the relevant securities. This is reinforced by the requirement that the information is 'price sensitive information' and the securities are 'price affected securities'.

Both the issues of specific or precise and made public are interesting. In respect of the former, the use of 'or' suggests an either/or position to be adopted and as such provides the prosecutor with a wider application where the inside information is not sufficiently specific, but is precise enough to form the offence. Lomnicka notes that this would allow an offence to succeed on the basis that information indicates that profits will exceed expectation and yet lacks the specificity of by how much; to focus on the latter would have placed too high a burden on the offence.[29]

The offence is not committed where the information has been made public. The specifics are set out in Section 58 CJA 1993 in some detail and this provides guidance on the issue. Timing is key and it is not hard to understand why the offence has suffered some problems in terms of success when an assessment of this issue is made. To be made public, information does not have to be announced in a statement; a better way is to see the information as being available to the public or in the public domain, which suggests that the information could be buried in a report, perhaps even an obscure report on a company website, and picked up by a single investor, who, on the strength of the report's content, deals in the securities of the firm. In this respect, the legislation does not penalise for quality of research or the researcher: as long as the information is available to everyone in some form, then no offence has been committed.

26 See Alexander above, n. 10.

27 C-45/08 (2010) 2 CMLR 30, 822.

28 Ashe, M. 2010. Possession and use of inside information. Case Comment. *Company Lawyer* 31(4), 97.

29 Lomnicka, E. 1994. The new insider dealing provisions: Criminal Justice Act 1993, Part V. *Journal of Business Law* March, 173–188.

The civil regime and market abuse as a wider concept

It is clear from the preceding discussion that the criminal offences contained in the CJA 1993 are quite narrow and this has resulted in few successful prosecutions.[30] Davies notes that the large-scale use of the criminal provisions 'proved impossible', with the criminal standard of proof required proving overly burdensome for prosecutors.[31]

The answer lay in a new and innovative approach to the issue of the misuse of information and more generally in the actions and behaviour of market participants, although Davies[32] notes that civil actions were mooted prior to the enactment of the CJA 1993 and were an option open to US authorities for some time.[33] The action to 'fill the regulatory gap'[34] left by an unsuccessful criminal prosecution regime was the introduction of a wholly civil regime based on administrative sanctions rather than criminal ones, with a sanction of an unlimited fine for a breach of the provisions,[35] designed to run in parallel and complement the existing criminal regime.[36] The regime was contained in the Financial Services and Markets Act 2000 (FSMA 2000), Part VIII, to be administered by the Financial Services Authority (FSA). The new 'regime' and the focus on the language of market abuse creates a wider ambit of activity to be covered than the narrow offence of insider dealing, notwithstanding that the first element of the market abuse regime is insider dealing. What is clear is that the market abuse regime was created to provide the relevant authority a high degree of flexibility in respect of dealing with the risks that improper use of information and now improper actions of market participants could have on the market and wider economy. To achieve this, the FSMA 2000 gave significant rule-making powers to the FSA and, more significantly, reduced the standard of proof to the civil standard for actions brought under Part VIII. It is therefore not surprising that the regime has attracted much attention, described as 'novel',[37] 'controversial'[38] and a 'new witchcraft',[39] at least in respect to the civil standard approach; maybe a more accurate description

30 See Davies above, n. 24.

31 Davies, P. L. 2008. *Gower and Davies Principles of Modern Company Law*, 8th edition. Sweet & Maxwell.

32 Davies, J. 2015. From gentlemanly expectations to regulatory principles: a history of insider dealing in the UK: Part 2. *Company Lawyer* 36(6), 163–174.

33 See Rider above, n. 15.

34 Filby, M. 2004. Part VIII Financial Services and Markets Act: filling insider dealing's regulatory gaps. *Company Lawyer* 23(12), 363–370.

35 Haynes, A. 2007. Market abuse: an analysis of its nature and regulation. *Company Lawyer* 28(11), 323–335.

36 Sykes, A. 1999. Market abuse: a civil revolution. *Journal of International Financial Markets* 1(2), 59–67.

37 Linklater, L. 2001. The market abuse regime: setting standards in the twenty-first century. *Company Lawyer* 22(9), 267–272.

38 Alcock, A. 2002. Market abuse. *Company Lawyer* 23(5), 142–150.

39 Alcock, A. 2001. Market abuse – the new witchcraft. *New Law Journal* 151, 1398, 28 September.

in respect of the use of powers in this area is a new alchemy in respect of market behaviour, although the idea of civil measures has been around for some time.[40]

The provisions of the Act set the 'outer limits' of the regime;[41] however, to support the primary provisions and the standard-setting rationale of the regime, the FSMA 2000 requires the relevant authority to create and maintain a Code of Market Conduct (MAR), a detailed list of rules and guidance that sets out the specifics of the regime, allowing market participants to clearly understand the aims and expected outcomes of the market abuse regime. The code is not exhaustive, but it does lay out a wide range of guidance in its attempt to set the required standard. MAR is arguably the embodiment of the risk-based approach regulation, as it provides detailed guidance on what is expected of market participants, placing the burden on those individuals and firms to act in an appropriate manner.

The market abuse regime is much more focused on managing the risk profile of market abuse as compared with that of insider dealing as a criminal measure. The elements of the market abuse regime are essentially focused on dealing with those issues that present a risk to the integrity and proper functioning of the market and to participants in the market. The civil market abuse regime concentrates on setting and managing the behaviour of market participants and the markets in which they participate, thus allowing the market abuse regime to sit within a civil process, but this is not without controversy.

The original iteration of the market abuse regime focused on three categories of abuse: misuse of information;[42] creating false and misleading impressions;[43] and distorting the market.[44] It would seem clear that these three issues represent the most significant risk profile in respect of behaviour that could impact securities and securities markets. Indeed, the FSA's successor, the FCA, specifically notes that they 'work to reduce the risks posed by the spreading of false information that misleads the market' in addition to those posed by insider dealing.[45] The behaviour to which the provisions apply needs to occur in relation to qualifying investments admitted to trading or requested for admission to trade on a prescribed market, with a very wide interpretation to this provision given by the Financial Services and Markets Tribunal in *Jabre v FSA*,[46] where trades made on the Tokyo Stock Exchange were still held to amount to market abuse, focusing on the behaviour of Mr Jabre,[47] again proving the standard-setting nature of the legislation.

To support the application of the provisions, the market abuse regime introduced the regular user approach to assess whether the behaviour amounted

40 See Davies above, n. 24.
41 See Alcock above, n. 39.
42 Financial Services and Markets Act 2000, s. 118(2)(a).
43 Financial Services and Markets Act 2000, s. 118(2)(b).
44 Financial Services and Markets Act 2000, s. 118(2)(c).
45 Financial Conduct Authority above, n. 7.
46 (2006) FSMT 035.
47 See Alexander above, n. 10.

to market abuse. This is when the behaviour in question falls below the standards expected of a

> regular user of that market who is aware of the behaviour as a failure on the part of the person or persons concerned observe the standard behaviour reasonably expected of a person in his or their position in relation to the market.[48]

The regular user test set a hypothetical and objective test based on the hypothetical market participant, a sophisticated version of the Man on the Clapham Omnibus, against which the relevant authority and market participants can judge behaviour.

It is worth noting at this point that the language of the market abuse regime attempts to deliberately avoid connotations with criminal activity. The word 'behaviour' is used to describe activity, in contrast to the word 'offence'; however, it is arguable that this is merely a matter of semantics, as in at least one case the behaviour that is under scrutiny is insider dealing, which exists on both sides of the criminal/civil market abuse divide.

In 2005 the three original behaviours became seven by virtue of the entering into force on 1 July 2005 of the Market Abuse Directive (MAD), given effect by the Financial Services and Markets Act 2000 (Market Abuse) Regulations 2005.[49] The broad elements of the original three forms of behaviour (misuse of information, false and misleading impressions and market distortion) are still identifiable; however, MAD outlines some specific issues in its recitals.

Under the banner of misuse of information, the first and second behaviours caught by the regime are insider dealing and improper disclosure. The former catches an 'insider' who deals, or attempts to deal, on the basis of inside information (Section 118(2)), with the latter catching the insider who discloses information to another person without permission (Section 118(3)). These provisions closely mirror the criminal provisions contained in the CJA 1993, but are broader in their overall remit.

The third behaviour (Section 118(4)) that was covered by the market abuse regime was relevant information not generally available (RINGA). This was an interesting provision as it is not one provided for by MAD and was one of the provisions retained by UK authorities when MAD was implemented. The provision goes further than the Directive requires and potentially catches a wider range of activity, referring to relevant information not generally available. This suggests that, unlike the first two provisions, the information need not be precise or have a significant effect of the price of a security; it only needs to be relevant to the investor to form the offence. However, this is subject to the proviso that it is only usable where the MAD equivalents do not apply and is subject to the regular user test. This provision is termed 'super-equivalent' and has been subject to a sunset

48 Financial Services and Markets Act, s. 118(1))(c).
49 SI2005/381.

clause originally set to end on 30 June 2008, but extended on a number of occasions. However, the provision was repealed by statutory instrument effective on 31 December 2014.[50]

It is arguable that the repeal of the provision weakens the available tools in respect of the misuse of information and increases the risk of abusive practices slipping through the net. At the time, the FSA noted that the retention of the RINGA provision gave the UK a flexible approach and 'enabled action to be taken in relation to behaviour based on information which would be taken into account by investors but is not sufficiently precise to be inside information', and that this flexibility is now lost.[51]

In common with the criminal provision under CJA 1993, the definition of inside information is key, needing to be information that is of a precise nature not generally available, that relates to one or more issuers of qualifying investments, and would if generally available be likely to have a significant effect on the price of those qualifying investments.[52] The regulators' approach to this element was unsuccessfully challenged in *Massey v Financial Services Authority*, where Massey questioned whether the behaviour he was accused of had a significant effect on the price of a qualifying investment. Even though the Tribunal struggled with the interpretation of the statute in places, particularly in relation to the issue of precision, it still found that the information was 'of a kind which a reasonable investor would be likely to use as part of the basis of his investment decisions', and therefore Mr Massey dealt on the basis of inside information.[53] It would seem clear from the Tribunal's decision that the legislation, while not perfect, is being applied in a manner which broadly supports the standard-setting and integrity maintenance aims of the promoter's intentions, although the decision in Massey is not universally popular.[54]

The next behaviour classification caught by the regime moves away from the misuse of information elements and focuses on manipulating behaviour so as to give a false and misleading impression. The first deals with manipulating transactions that give a false or misleading impression as to supply or demand of investments, and the second deals with the use of manipulating devices such as the employment of fictitious devices designed to deceive; for example, giving false and misleading information following the purchase of shares with a view to increasing the value of those shares, thus giving a false impression to other investors regarding the true value of the shares.[55] The next behaviour caught by

50 Sheikh, S. 2008. FSMA market abuse regime: a review of the sunset clauses. *International Company and Commercial Law Review* 19(7), 234–236.

51 FSA. 2004. UK Implementation of the EU Market Abuse Directive (Directive 2003/6/EC): A Consultation Document, June 2004. Available at: http://www.fsa.goc.uk/pubs/other/eu_mad.pdf.

52 Financial Services and Markets Act 2000, s.118(c).

53 (2011) UKUT 49 TCC.

54 See Davies above, n. 32.

55 Financial Services and Markets Act 2000, s.118(5) and (6).

the regime is improper dissemination, where false or misleading impressions are presented regarding a security or issuer of security in the full knowledge that the information is false.[56]

The final behaviour is the second of the super-equivalent measures retained from the pre-MAD market abuse regime, making it a breach to give false and misleading impressions of either the supply or demand of securities, or behaviour that distorts the market in securities.[57] This measure is subject to a sunset clause which was to trigger on 30 June 2008 and was subsequently extended on a number of occasions; it will now cease to operate when the Market Abuse Regulation enters into force on 6 July 2016. Like the now repealed super-equivalent provision in relation to RINGA, this measure utilises the regular user test to assess whether market abuse has been committed.

An interesting element of the civil market abuse regime is that the provision makes the definition of using and possessing inside information a subjective exercise, and that no intent on the market participant is required, unlike the obvious requirement for the criminal offence of insider trading. This suggests that market abuse could be committed negligently, to ensure the focus is on the integrity of the markets.[58] A challenge on this issue was dismissed by the Court of Appeal in *Winterflood Securities v The Financial Services Aurthority*,[59] and follows the line of argument posited during the FSMA 2000 transit through parliament, where the Law Society's concerns about the severity of outcomes as a result of no mental element were answered with reassurances that the proposal was not intended to prosecute persons for accidental breaches of the regime. This emphasises that the rationale behind the measure is to set standards and not to make judgement on the 'moral culpability of individual players in the market', and that 'markets can be affected by the effects of a player's conduct even if this is not the player's intention'. It is worth noting as a discussion point here the decision of *Massey v Financial Services Authority*, where the Upper Tribunal struggled with the interpretation of the statute, and where it would seem that there is debate regarding the intention of Mr Massey in committing market abuse.

The difficulties of the civil regime

Just calling something civil does not necessarily make it civil in nature, and this difficulty has proved problematic for the market abuse regime from the start, prompting Alcock (2001) to call the introduction of the civil regime 'half baked' and its implementation a 'compromise'.[60] The rationale for the regime was to provide a workable alternative to the criminal regime, which was facing significant

56 Financial Services and Markets Act 2000, s.118(7).
57 Financial Services and Markets Act 2000, s.118(8).
58 Horan, S. 2011. *Corporate Crime.* Bloomsbury Professional, West Sussex.
59 (2010) EWCA Civ 423.
60 See Alcock above, n. 39.

challenges in proving the elements of the crime to the criminal standard. A move to a civil standard will allow the regulatory authorities much more flexibility in cleaning up securities markets, setting higher standards and avoiding the types of scandals that emerged under predecessor legislation. However, the move to a lower standard of proof is replete with controversy, especially as the first of the civil offences is insider dealing.

The argument revolves around whether the bringing of an action in respect of insider dealing within Part VIII FSMA 2000 is the equivalent of bringing a new criminal charge. If this is the case, then the defendant will be able to avail themselves of the protections afforded under Article 6 of the European Convention on Human Rights (ECHR), as incorporated in the Human Rights Act 1998 (HRA98), which at its heart provides that anyone charged with a criminal offence has the right to a fair trial and due process of law. There is little difficulty with Article 6(1) ECHR; however, more difficulty is inherent in Articles 6(2) and 6(3).

This issue has caused considerable uncertainty in the application of the regime and continues to prove the greatest challenge, as it does for sibling legislation in respect of confiscation of criminally obtained assets. The primary challenge to this point came in the case of *R (On the application of Fleurose) v Securities and Futures Authority* (2001),[61] where the Court of Appeal dismissed a claim by Fleurose for judicial review of the decision of the disciplinary appeal tribunal of the forerunner of the FSA in respect of securities markets, the Securities and Futures Authority, holding that the proceedings had not involved the determination of a criminal charge and that proceedings against him were not unfair. The case affirms that the process under Part VIII is civil in nature and that the civil standard of proof is to be applied. A problem, however, emerged from the application of that civil standard in the Financial Services and Markets Tribunal, which seemed to struggle with how to actually apply the standard to specific market abuse cases.

In the Tribunal decisions in *Davidson* and *Tatham*, and particularly in *Parker*, the Tribunal seemed to lay down a sliding scale standard of proof, concluding that while there is a single standard of proof, the balance of probabilities, it is flexible in its application, so that the more serious the alleged market abuse is, the 'stronger must be the evidence before we should find the allegation proven on the balance of probabilities', with the Tribunal in *Parker* noting that 'it is difficult to draw a meaningful distinction between the standard we must apply and the criminal standard'. This confusion in application creates a significant challenge for the regulator, in that a simple interpretation of the two cases brings the conclusion that, depending on the severity of the alleged market abuse, the prosecuting authority may need to effectively prove to a criminal standard that the offence has been committed, notwithstanding that the allegation is brought under the Part VIII provisions. If the civil market abuse regime was intended to act as gap filler to complement a failing criminal regime, then the tribunal's decisions put significant restrictions on the regime to achieve its goals.

61 EWCA Civ 2015.

The issue of the standard of proof has now been resolved in the Upper Tribunal decision of *Hannam v The Financial Conduct Authority* (2014),[62] which reviewed the authorities on this issue, including the House of Lords decisions in *Re B* (2009).[63] In light of these authorities, the Upper Tribunal concluded that 'the approach which allowed for a "sliding scale" in the civil standard, by which it varied according to the seriousness of what has to be proved, has been exposed as a heresy'.[64] The decision of the Upper Tribunal, citing binding authority, is a significant victory for the prosecuting authority. The decision in *Hannam* arguably resets the requirements placed on the FCA to a much more manageable limit, thus allowing the authority to implement the regime as intended; the standard is the civil standard on the balance of probabilities.

The Market Abuse Regulation and MAD II

That European Union legislators are convinced that market abuse remains a significant risk to markets is evidenced by the upcoming legislative changes and reflects the evolving nature of securities trading.[65] It shows a determination of the Commission to get tough on market abuse and, by framing the reforms with a Regulation, shows a commitment to ensure Europe-wide harmonisation of anti-abusive practices.[66] This Market Abuse Regulation, along with other reforms (MiFID II, MiFIR and EMIR), evidence the concern that market abuse poses risks to the efficient running of the markets across the European Union and the desire to ensure against regulatory arbitrage creeping in. The Market Abuse Regulation came into force on 6 July 2016 across the member states of the European Union (including the UK for the time being) and will widen the scope of the market abuse regime to new trading platforms that have developed since the original directive. It is interesting that the original draft of the regulation contained a proposal that was very similar to the RINGA provisions contained in the pre-MAD UK regime, in which the necessity of precision was significantly watered down. However, this did not make it through to the final version, ultimately narrowing the scope of the regime, but at the same time providing some greater levels of certainty.

In addition to the regulation, the Commission has brought forward a second Market Abuse Directive, implementing a range of criminal sanctions alongside the civil regime of the 2005 Directive. However, the UK government is opting out of MAD II (more accurately termed Criminal Sanctions MAD), presumably on

62 UKUT 0233 (TCC).

63 1 AC 11.

64 Ibid.

65 Baber, G. 2013. A critical examination of the legislative response in banking and financial regulation to issues related to misconduct in the context of the crisis of 2007–2009. *Journal of Financial Crime* 20(2), 237–252.

66 European Commission. 2011. Press Release. Getting tough on insider dealing and market manipulation. IP/11/1217.

the basis that the UK already has a mature criminal sanctions regime in respect of market abuse.

Market abuse outside the CJA 1993 and Part VIII FSMA 2000

As noted above, market abuse is an umbrella term for activity that covers a broad range of behaviour considered to pose risk to the efficient operation and integrity of securities markets. Prior to the enactment of the FSMA 2000 provisions, the concept of a wider approach to market abuse existed beyond the scope of the insider dealing provisions within the CJA 1993. It was an offence under Section 47 of the Financial Services Act 1986 to make misleading statements or give misleading impressions in order to induce others to deal in investments. This section deals with more general market abuse than insider dealing and looks much more into the general integrity of investments, and it is clearly designed to tackle the same issues as the contemporary market abuse provisions, namely to protect market integrity.[67] The section was replicated in the FSMA 2000 Section 397 to run parallel with the civil regime contained in Part VIII, with sporadic use following enactment, and is now contained in Sections 89–90 of the Financial Services Act 2012.[68]

The LIBOR manipulation scandal arguably placed the market abuse regime in the spotlight and it is surprising that manipulation of a benchmark interest rate was not included either in the Section 397 offence or within the civil market abuse regime. Presumably, the prospect of manipulating such a fundamental benchmark was not thought to be a risk factor during the debate and drafting of the original provisions or following updates, but was dealt with as a breach of Principles.[69] The Wheatley Review into the LIBOR scandal identified a number of failings and presented recommendations to avoid repetition.[70] On the sanctions side of the LIBOR scandal, the lacuna presented by the lack of criminal or civil offences available against individuals was corrected by the addition of a criminal offence to manipulate a benchmark contrary to Section 91 of the Financial Services Act 2012. While this was originally to apply only to the LIBOR benchmark, it has been subsequently expanded to cover a wider range of

67 Barnett, W. 1996. Fraud enforcement in the Financial Services Act 1986: an analysis and discussion of s.47. *Company Lawyer* 17(7), 203–210.

68 Callaghan, V. and Ullah, Z. 2013. Legislative comment: the LIBOR scandal – the UK's legislative response. *Journal of International Banking Law and Regulation* 28(4), 160–165.

69 Ibid.

70 Wheatley, M. 2012. The Wheatley Review of LIBOR: Final Report. Available at: https://www.gov.uk/government/uploads/system/uploads/attachment_data/file/191762/wheatley_review_libor_finalreport_280912.pdf, accessed 20 March 2016.

benchmarks.[71] This is in addition to the use of the common law conspiracy to defraud offence, which has been the only avenue of sanction against individuals in respect of LIBOR manipulation.[72]

Getting tough

The global financial crisis has resulted in a refocus of the regulatory approach to financial services and financial markets. Adair Turner, as Chairman of the FSA, noted an 'end to light touch regulation',[73] and while the cross-hairs of this statement were aimed at the regulation of banks, the scope of the new regulatory engagement extended to the wider financial services sector. During the period since the enactment of the FSMA 2000, the focus had been on using the civil regime to clean up the markets, using the range of enforcement mechanisms to deal with abusive practices. Following the emergence of the banking crisis, the FSA turned increasingly to its criminal prosecutorial powers to meet its financial crime objective and this has been continued by the FCA in meeting its integrity objective. In *R v McQuoid*, the FSA secured its first conviction under the CJA 1993 and, since then, the FSA and FCA between them have secured a further 26 convictions, the latest on 15 March 2016, with a number of further prosecutions yet to be tried.[74] Arguably, the switch back to the criminal process is based on three primary assertions. First, the whole regulatory process for financial services was stung by the breadth of the global financial crisis, and the public clamour to reign in the excesses of the financial services sector, and, in particular, criticisms of the FSA's approach.[75] Second, the emergence of technology in the securities trading industry exploded in the latter part of the 1990s and into the twenty-first century. The use of electronic means of exchange and algorithmic trading has arguably made easier the task of the enforcement authority to track trades and then follow them back into the hands of the trader. The explosion in trading technology has made it harder for insiders to remain inside. Finally, it is also arguable that the application of the sliding scale of proof resulting from decisions in the Financial Services and Markets Tribunal forced the FSA, and now the FCA, into using the criminal process, on the basis that if they have to prove guilt to a criminal standard, they may as well try to get the criminal sanction as well. The rejection of the sliding scale in *Hannam* may now see the options open to the regulator widen in the future.

71 Anon. 2015. Manipulation of further key benchmarks to be made a criminal offence. *Company Lawyer* 36(3), 72.

72 *Daily Telegraph*. 2015. Libor scandal: former City trader gets 14 years for rigging rates. 3 August. Available at: http://www.telegraph.co.uk/finance/financial-crime/11767437/Libor-trial-Tom-Hayes-found-guilty-of-rigging-rates.html, accessed 19 March 2016.

73 See Turner above, n. 8.

74 (2009) EWCA Crim 1301.

75 Haines, J. D. 2008. FSA determined to improve the cleanliness of markets: custodial sentences continue to be a real threat. *Company Lawyer* 29(12), 370.

Conclusion

The subject of market abuse has generated much debate since the FSMA 2000 came into force. The creation of a civil regime to complement the existing criminal regime has added several layers of flexibility to the armoury of regulators in dealing with the risks posed by market abuse. The real issue is how that flexibility is applied in practice. The headline offence remains insider dealing, supported by the other market abuse offences within Part VIII FSMA 2000 and the other offences both within the FSMA 2000 and within other acts, such as the Financial Services Act 2012, the Fraud Act 2006 and the Proceeds of Crime Act 2002. With respect to insider dealing, the application of the offence has seen changing priorities affect the way in which the offence is prosecuted from a wholly criminal process until the FSMA 2000 came fully into force, followed by an almost wholly civil regime between 2000 and 2009, when, partly stung by the global financial crisis, the criminal process has again found favour. It is to be hoped that, following decisions in the Upper Tribunal and Court of Appeal, the regulatory authorities will embrace both processes in the future to ensure a flexible approach to the risks posed by market abuse, in order to eliminate them to the fullest possible extent.

8 The FCA: protecting consumers of the consumer credit market in the wake of the global financial crisis

Daniel Jasinski

8.1 Introduction

Over the last fifty years, the western world has seen a dramatic change in how goods are purchased. Gone are the days of arduous saving in order to purchase the family car, television or living-room suite. Society now depends much more on the 'buy now – pay later' schemes that are frequently waved before consumers to attract their business.[1] Whether in the form of payment breaks,[2] interest-free credit,[3] hire-purchase agreements,[4] credit cards[5] or store cards,[6] a consumer can forgo the wait until they can afford the goods that they want, purchase such goods and mitigate the worry arising from having to pay for these products with the enjoyment of using them.[7] It is not denied that, even before the introduction of

1 Gordon Borrie, 'The credit society: its benefits and burdens' [1986] May *JBL* 181 at 189. A modern example of this is BrightHouse. See BrightHouse 'Buy-now-pay-later electricals' <http://www.brighthouse.co.uk/buy-now-pay-later-electricals>, accessed 23 March 2016; these are also known as rent-to-own schemes; see Helen Clifton, 'Drowning in debt: how irresponsible lenders are cresting a tidal wave of misery' <http://www.church-poverty.org.uk/drowningindebt/report/drowningindebt/drowningindebtpdf>, accessed 23 March 2016, 5.

2 For example, DFS allow a payment break of up to one year followed by four years' interest-free credit. See: DFS 'Your guide to interest free credit' <http://www.dfs.co.uk/content/inspiration-and-help/finance>, accessed 23 March 2016.

3 Ibid.

4 For an overview in relation to the purchase of vehicles in this manner, see: Lisa Bachelor 'New car finance means you can drive a really hard bargain', *Observer* (17 February 2013, London) <http://www.theguardian.com/money/2013/feb/17/motoring-consumer-affairs>, accessed 23 March 2016.

5 Barclays Bank 'Credit cards' <http://www.barclays.co.uk/Creditcards/P1242557963445>, accessed 23 March 2016.

6 Interestingly, clothing retailer Next uses a high-interest credit account as the default option if a customer's card is declined when making purchases online. See further: Matt Clear 'Surprise! You just opened a Next Credit Account' <http://conversation.which.co.uk/money/next-account-card-interest-rate-directory>, accessed 23 March 2016.

7 Christine Ironfield-Smith, Kevin Keasey, Barbara Summers, Darren Duxbury, Robert Hudson 'Consumer debt in the UK: attitudes and implications' (2005) 13(2) *JFR&C* 132, 133. Indeed, the purchase of goods on credit has been described as a good form of 'forced saving'. See: C. Scott and J. Black *Cranston's Consumers and the Law* (London: Butterworths, 2000),

the first Barclaycard in 1966,[8] products were purchased on a post-pay basis. For example, it was common practice to have a weekly visit from the 'Tallyman', coming to collect the instalment due for products purchased in this manner.[9] While, on the face of it, this appears a seemingly fair and friendly way of purchasing products on credit, the contrary appears to be true. The Tallyman was often feared,[10] and falling behind on payments had the potential to leave families in ruin.[11]

In more recent times, the Tallyman has arguably been replaced as the consumers' lender of last resort[12] by shop-based alternatives; where consumers can purchase goods and pay for them through 'seductively affordable . . . weekly instalments'.[13] This means that customers can purchase many products at the same time, without stretching too far beyond their means. However, akin to the Tallyman, such 'seductively affordable' payment methods can lead to the devastation of a family's finances.[14]

As early as 2003, the Department for Trade and Industry[15] noted a vast growth in the number of different methods that could be employed to obtain credit products.[16] Beyond knocking on a bank manager's door during business hours,[17] credit can be obtained through the use of internet banking or even an app on a mobile telephone,[18] where it is promised that £400 can be sent within five minutes of approval, available twenty-four hours a day, seven days a week.[19] With such easy

at 231, as cited by Nicholas Ryder, Margaret Griffiths and Lachmi Singh *Commercial Law: Principles and Policy* (Cambridge: Cambridge University Press: 2012), 499.

8 Barclays Bank 'Barclaycard marks 45 years of credit cards in the UK' <http://www.newsroom.barclays.co.uk/Press-releases/Barclaycard-marks-45-years-of-credit-cards-in-the-UK-7e0.aspx>, accessed 23 March 2016.

9 I.D. Fenton 'The tallyman' 1869 (May) *The Quiver* 521–523.

10 Laura Marcus 'We had to hide from the tally man' (3 November 2012, *Guardian*) <http://www.theguardian.com/lifeandstyle/2012/nov/03/laura-marcus-parents-hidden-poverty>, accessed 23 March 2016.

11 An interesting example of this is outlined by I.D. Fenton (n. 9).

12 As described by: Howard Johnston 'Fair credit' (1991) 10(6) *IBFL* 94, 94.

13 For example, a washing machine can be purchased for £10 per week. See: Amelia Gentleman 'Buy now regret later? The secret of BrightHouse's success' *The Guardian* (4 October 2013, London) <http://www.theguardian.com/society/2013/oct/04/brighthouse-consumer-poverty-high-street>, accessed 23 March 2016.

14 Impact 'One hundred million pounds being sucked out of our poorest communities' <http://www.impactsheffield.plus.com/WATCHDOG.HTM>, accessed 23 March 2016.

15 Hereafter DTI.

16 Department for Trade and Industry *Fair, Clear and Competitive: The Consumer Credit Market in the 21st Century* (Cmd 6040, 2003) paras 1.8 and 1.12–1.27.

17 Ryder, Griffiths and Singh (n. 7), 498.

18 Wonga.com 'Choose Wonga over a typical fast cash advance' <https://www.wonga.com/money/fast-cash-advance-alternative>, accessed 23 March 2016. Jayne Atherton 'The iPhone app that gives you a 3000% loan' <http://metro.co.uk/2010/01/15/wonga-iphone-app-gives-you-a-3000-loan-32289>, accessed 23 March 2016. See further: Daniel M. Collins 'Payday loans: why one shouldn't ask for more' (2013) 28(2) *JIBLR* 55, 55.

19 Ibid.

access to credit products, it comes as little surprise that consumers have made the most of their ability to access 'convenient credit'.[20] The most recent estimate suggests that the average household owes over £6,000 on loans and credit cards.[21] If mortgages are included, the average adult owes nearly £29,000.[22] This massive black hole in household finances could arguably be linked to the rise in house prices in the last twenty years,[23] but it can also be attributed to a change in consumer spending habits,[24] coupled with the increased availability of the products, both in type and method, as outlined above.[25] What is clear is that in modern society many cannot resist the temptation to live beyond their means. Buffet noted that 'it is only when the economic tide goes out that you learn who's been swimming naked'.[26] Indeed, the wake of the 2008 financial crisis revealed just how many people were swimming without swimsuits in the context of their personal finances, revealing that many were borrowing money that they simply could not afford to repay.

By giving in to temptation, consumers have fuelled a multi-billion pound[27] industry benefiting those clever enough to fund debt living. The biggest concern, however, is not the merely level of debt that families are finding themselves in, but the ever-increasing trend towards relying on borrowed money to purchase the necessities of everyday life.[28] Indeed, while the increased availability of credit was initially considered to have raised the living standards of many,[29] it is clear that many now rely upon credit to make ends meet.

The wide range of credit products allows even the least favourable of potential debtors to obtain credit, giving rise to the emergence of high-cost credit as a

20 Convenient credit is defined as 'credit that is granted to the creditor with very little reference to the credit worthiness of the debtor'. See: Nicholas Ryder and Rachel Thomas 'Convenient credit and consumer protection – a critical review of the responses of the Labour and Coalition governments' (2011) 33(1) *JSWFL* 85, 85.

21 The Money Charity 'Debt Statistics June 2014' <http://themoneycharity.org.uk/debt-statistics>, accessed 23 March 2016.

22 Ibid.

23 Due to people borrowing more to purchase their houses. For a discussion of this argument, see: Stephanie Flanders 'The truth about UK debt' <http://www.bbc.co.uk/news/business-17398014>, accessed 23 March 2016.

24 Financial Conduct Authority 'Consumer credit countdown – review into debt collection practices of payday lenders starts on day one of FCA regulation. Note 3' <http://www.fca.org.uk/news/consumer-credit-countdown-review-into-debt-collection-practices-of-payday-lenders-starts-on-day-one-of-fca-regulation>, accessed 23 March 2016.

25 Ryder and Thomas (n. 20) 85–90. See also: Collins (n. 18) 55–56.

26 As cited by Roman Tomasic and Folarin Akinbami 'Towards a new corporate governance after the global financial crisis' (2011) 22(8) *ICCLR* 237 at 247.

27 See n. 24.

28 For example, it has been cited that one in five people have gone into debt to pay for everyday essentials such as food. See: Nikki Whiteman 'Going into debt for food – how has the recession affected you?' <http://conversation.which.co.uk/money/how-has-the-recession-affected-your-spending-habits>, accessed 23 March 2016.

29 Roy Goode 'A credit law for Europe?' (1974) 23 *ICLQ* 227, 231.

consequence of lenders reflecting the risk of lending to an individual in the interest they charge.[30] In his 1974 article, Goode discussed the fact that the increase in banks providing credit products would lead to this high-risk, high-cost lending.[31] However, he went on to state that 'the implications for the bottom rung of borrowers [was] yet to be determined'.[32] Forty years later, these implications are now more visible than ever. Indeed, the dangerous combination of moneylenders hungry to make a 'quick buck' by lending their capital to a vulnerable prey who are seeing their monthly earnings stretched further and further has given rise to the emergence of the payday loan in the UK.[33]

A payday loan can be defined as a 'small [high-cost] loan taken over a short period . . . to balance household finances or to cover emergency domestic or personal'.[34] Akin to the modern Tallyman (firms such as BrightHouse), loans have the potential to cause a great deal of damage to the financial well-being of already financially vulnerable families.[35] Indeed, a payday loan is aimed at consumers who require the monies because they are unable to meet their outgoings for the month.[36] Noted as a 'quick fix' as opposed to a long-term debt solution,[37] such loans have been described as a shortcut to the gutter.[38]

It is due to the clear exploitation of the poor that a rigorous consumer protection regime is needed to prevent more and more families being sucked into the 'seductively affordable' and 'quick fix' credit products that are available to them. It is these new products, along with the already established mainstream loans and credit-card market that highlighted the deficiencies[39] in the regulatory regime that

30 Roy Goode 'Introductory Survey' in Roy Goode (ed.) *Consumer Credit* (United Kingdom Comparative Law Series Sijthoff, 1978) 14. See also: Borrie (n. 1) 186.

31 Goode (n. 29) 232. A similar point can be made in relation to the emergence of the sub-prime mortgage market in the United States. For an interesting overview of the development of the sub-prime market and its catalytic impact on the on the credit crisis, see: Jonathan Jarvis 'The credit crisis explained' <http://www.youtube.com/watch?v=bx_LWm6_6tA>, accessed 23 March 2016.

32 Goode (n. 28) 232.

33 Indeed, it has been noted that payday loans are often used, even with the availability of other options, due to their convenience. See: Collins (n. 18) 55–56.

34 Collins (n. 18) 55.

35 Simon Read 'Disastrous impact of payday loans laid bare with 82 per cent increase in people seeking help in just one year' *Independent* (27 February 2014, London) <http://www.independent.co.uk/money/loans-credit/disastrous-impact-of-payday-loans-laid-bare-with-82-per-cent-increase-in-people-seeking-help-in-just-one-year-9155415.html>, accessed 23 March 2016.

36 Cannon Finance 'How does Cannon Finance work?' <http://www.cannonfinance.co.uk/how-it-works>, accessed 23 March 2016.

37 Gavin Newsham 'The hard sell: QuickQuid' *Guardian* (29 May 2010, London) <http://www.theguardian.com/tv-and-radio/2010/may/29/the-hard-sell-quickquid>, accessed 23 March 2016.

38 Ibid.

39 Discussed further below.

has governed the consumer credit market, albeit with some amendments, over the previous forty years.[40]

On 1 April 2014, the new Financial Conduct Authority[41] took over the regulation of the consumer credit market.[42] This new Authority encompasses much of the conduct-based regulatory responsibility of the Financial Services Authority,[43] coupled with the responsibility for both the prudence and conduct of 23,000 financial services providers.[44] In the context of the consumer credit market, and from the perspective of consumer protection, the FCA faces a difficult challenge. It has to deal not only with the increasing variety of methods with which a consumer can obtain credit, but also with ruthless providers willing to lend to anyone, with little concern as to whether or not that person can repay their loan.[45] The Authority must ensure that moneylenders provide credit in a manner that is not socially harmful,[46] and punish effectively those lenders who are guilty of irresponsible lending.[47] This task, however, is made increasingly difficult by the potential consequences faced through 'over-regulation'. Indeed, Borrie[48] provides the example that an inability to enforce credit agreements in court could reduce the willingness of moneylenders to lend to higher-risk consumers, pushing those consumers into the hands of lenders who use the 'strong-arm methods of debt collection'[49] in order to recover monies owed. Furthermore, the costs of over-burdensome regulation will merely be passed on to borrowers,[50] increasing the cost of credit and possibly pricing some out of the market. Essentially, the FCA has the task of ensuring that consumers who need credit are not prevented from securing it due to their regulatory practices. As such, the potential issues caused by over-regulation are, by and large, borne in mind throughout this chapter.

40 The Consumer Credit Act 1974 was enacted following the 1971 Crowther Committee on Consumer Credit. For further discussion, see: Ryder, Griffiths and Singh (n. 7) 522–523.
41 Hereafter FCA.
42 Andrew Barber, Emma Radmore and Juan Jose Manchado 'Taking the credit – the transfer of consumer credit regulation' <http://www.compliancemonitor.com/uk-regulation/regulatory-structure/taking-the-credit--the-transfer-of-consumer-credit-regulation-64192.htm>, accessed 23 March 2016.
43 Hereafter FSA. See generally: James Perry, Rob Moulton, Glyn Barwick, Richard Small, Jake Green and Nicola Kay 'The new UK regulatory landscape' [2011] 84 *COB* 1, 4.
44 Financial Conduct Authority 'Business Plan 2014/2015' <http://www.fca.org.uk/static/documents/corporate/business-plan-2014-2015-interactive.pdf>, accessed 23 March 2016.
45 Indeed, payday lenders have been cited as lending to people with just £12 per day to live on. See the comments of Neera Sharma, the Assistant Director of Barnardo's, in: Simon Read 'Payday lenders target vulnerable over Christmas' *Independent* (23 November 2012, London) <http://www.independent.co.uk/news/uk/home-news/payday-lenders-target-vulnerable-over-christmas-8307387.html>, accessed 23 March 2016.
46 Anon. 'A little more, a little less' [1992] (Jul/Aug) *Conv* 231, 233.
47 Ryder and Thomas (n. 20) 87–89.
48 Borrie (n. 1) 189–190.
49 Ibid.
50 Arthur Rogerson 'The Consumer Credit Act 1974' (1975) 38 *MLR* 435, 436.

The purpose of this chapter is to analyse the FCA's approach to regulating the market from a consumer protection perspective. In order to do this, the remainder of the discussion is split into five further sections. Section 8.2 provides an analysis of the Consumer Credit Act 1974 (as amended), in particular the elements that can be invoked by consumers in order to seek redress for harm caused to them by financial institutions.[51] Section 8.3 reflects on the powers and performance of the Office of Fair Trading,[52] with particular reference to the comparable elements of the FSMA[53] regime, enforced by the FSA. Section 8.4 considers the approach of the FCA and section 8.5 consists of an analysis of the approach to the regulation of consumer credit market by the United States. Finally, section 8.6 provides conclusions and recommendations based on the discussion throughout this chapter.

8.2 The consumer protection provisions under the Consumer Credit Act 1974: consumer-led redress mechanisms

This section analyses the main consumer protection provisions that are invoked by consumers against creditors contained within the original Consumer Credit Act 1974,[54] in addition to the amendments made by the Consumer Credit Act 2006.[55] Ryder *et al.* outline that there are five key elements to the consumer protection provisions under the original CCA74.[56] The analysis of the 1974 statutory provisions is centred on one of these elements, namely the protection afforded to consumers if they were considered to be party to an extortionate credit bargain.[57] The further consumer protection provisions that are assessed arise mainly from the amendments made by the CCA06: specifically, the removal of the extortionate credit bargain provisions, and replacing them with a new test for 'fairness',[58] in addition to the provision of jurisdiction to the Financial Ombudsman Service[59] in consumer credit matters. The reason for considering

51 The Consumer Credit Act 1974 was amended by the Consumer Credit Act 2006. Hereafter, the amended version will be referred to as the CCA74. Where the original provisions are considered, this will be made clear. Where the Consumer Credit Act 2006 is specifically referred to, this will be cited as CCA06.

52 Hereafter OFT.

53 Financial Services and Markets Act 2000.

54 The Consumer Credit Act 2006 amended the Consumer Credit Act 1974. Hereafter, the amended version will be referred to as the CCA74. Where the original provisions are considered, this will be made clear. Where the Consumer Credit Act 2006 is specifically referred to, this will be cited as CCA06.

55 Hereafter CCA06.

56 Nicholas Ryder, Margaret Griffiths and Lachmi Singh *Commercial Law: Principles and Policy* (Cambridge: Cambridge University Press, 2012), 524.

57 Consumer Credit Act 1974 (unamended) ss137–140.

58 Consumer Credit Act 1974 ss140A–140D (Inserted by the Consumer Credit Act 2006 ss 19–22).

59 Hereafter FOS.

merely three out of the seven[60] key elements is that these are the three *main* areas with which the Financial Conduct Authority[61] appears to be concerned: namely, that tackling the unfair treatment of debtors will help reduce irresponsible lending and assist the FCA in protecting vulnerable customers against greedy lenders.[62]

In order to analyse the aforementioned consumer protection provisions, this section is split into three further sections. The next section analyses the effectiveness of the 'extortionate credit bargain' test in greater detail. Following this, the amendments to the 1974 Act by the 2006 Act are considered. Then the impact of the 'unfair relationship test' is discussed, considering cases where the court has or has not been willing to intervene with a credit relationship under these rules. The final section examines the impact of the FOS on the level of protection afforded to consumers under the CCA74 (as amended).

8.2.1 Extortionate credit bargain

In a similar vein to the Moneylenders Acts 1900–1927, the Consumer Credit Act 1974 granted to the court[63] the discretionary[64] power to adjust any credit agreement[65] which it considered to be extortionate.[66] A credit agreement is extortionate when:

- it requires the debtor . . . to make payments . . . which are *grossly exorbitant*; or
- otherwise grossly contravenes ordinary principles of fair dealing.[67]

When establishing whether or not a credit bargain is extortionate, the court was able to consider a wide range of factors.[68] These factors included the prevailing

60 Despite the fact that the extortionate credit relationship provisions were replaced by unfair credit relationship test, for a full analysis of these elements it is sensible to consider them separately.
61 Hereafter FCA.
62 See further: DWF 'The clock is ticking . . . . and now is a good time to review your treating customers fairly (TCF) policies' <http://fcaconsumercredit.info/the-clock-is-ticking-and-now-is-a-good-time-to-review-your-treating-customer-fairly-tcf-policies>, accessed 23 March 2016.
63 Consumer Credit Act 1974 (unamended) s139.
64 Geraint Howells and Lionel Bently 'Judicial treatment of extortionate credit bargains: Part 1' [1989] (May–Jun) *Conv* 164, 173.
65 Whether or not the agreement was a regulated agreement for the purposes of the act: Consumer Credit Act 1974 (unamended) s137(1) and confirmed by the wording in s139(5). (See generally Consumer Credit Act 1974 (unamended) ss137–140.) See further: Ryder, Griffiths and Singh (n. 56) 544.
66 The previous legal regime allowed the courts to intervene in transactions 'on the ground that interest was excessive . . . or otherwise harsh and unconscionable' See: Roy Goode 'Introductory Survey' in Roy Goode (ed.) *Consumer Credit* (United Kingdom Comparative Law Series Sijthoff, 1978) 14.
67 Consumer Credit Act 1974 (unamended) s138(1). Emphasis added.
68 Ibid. ss138(2)–(5).

interest rate at the time the bargain was made,[69] the characteristics of the borrower[70] and the risk taken by the creditor in providing the credit.[71] It is arguable that the purpose of these provisions was to both discourage creditors from entering into extortionate credit bargains and to afford a mechanism of redress to consumers who were subject to such bargains.[72] In pursuit of these objectives, while the provisions have been described as both 'wide ranging'[73] and 'far reaching',[74] they are largely considered to have been 'ineffective',[75] 'innocuous'[76] and 'primitive'.[77] Howells and Bently highlighted three key reasons for the ineffectiveness of the extortionate credit bargain test. These were: that it was down to the debtor to enforce the extortionate bargain provisions against the lender; that judges were seemingly cautious when it came to interfering with contractual relationships entered into by private individuals; and a lack of any real definition of what constituted an extortionate credit bargain.[78] In order to provide a structure to the analysis of the extortionate credit bargain provisions, these issues are now considered in greater depth.

8.2.2 Extortionate credit bargains before the courts: lack of cases and lack of judicial action

The extortionate credit bargain provisions were long criticised for the low yield of cases in which the test was invoked, successfully or otherwise.[79] Shockingly, the DTI stated that a mere thirty cases were known to have been brought before the courts in nearly thirty years.[80] In their 1999 review of extortionate credit for the UK DTI, Kempson and Whyley highlight many reasons for this being so.[81] In particular, many debtors are unlikely to be in a position to pay lawyers to represent them in court, in addition to the fact that undesirable borrowers may have been reluctant to take action against a lender which may be their only source

69 Ibid. s138(2)(a).
70 Ibid. s138(3).
71 Ibid. s138(4).
72 Richard Mawrey and Tobias Riley-Smith *Blackstones Guide to The Consumer Credit Act 2006* (Oxford University Press, 2006).
73 Dennis Rosenthal *Guide to: Consumer Credit Law and Practice* (2nd edn, Butterworth LexisNexis, 2002) 255.
74 Ryder, Griffiths and Singh (n. 56) 545.
75 Ibid. 544.
76 Rosenthal (n. 73) 255.
77 Eva Lomnicka 'The reform of consumer credit in the UK' [2004] (Jan) *JBL* 129, 137.
78 Geraint Howells and Lionel Bently 'Loansharks and extortionate credit bargains part 2' [1987] (Jul–Aug) *Conv* 234, 234–235.
79 Ibid. at 235. Elaine Kempson and Claire Whyley 'Extortionate credit in the UK: a report to the DTI' <http://www.bris.ac.uk/geography/research/pfrc/themes/credit-debt/pfrc9903.pdf>, accessed 23 March 2016.
80 Department for Trade and Industry *Fair Clear and Competitive: Consumer Credit in the 21st Century* (White Paper Cm 6040, 2003) para 3.29.
81 Kempson and Whyley (n. 79) 31–32.

of credit in a future time of need.[82] Further, as demonstrated by the case *Director General of Fair Trading v First National Bank*,[83] the fact that there was no obligation to provide consumers with information regarding the forms of redress available to them directly results in consumers having a lack of awareness of their own rights.[84]

Of the thirty or so cases that made it to court, a mere ten are cited to have been successful.[85] While it is clear that these legislative provisions had the potential to be far-reaching, the fact these provisions have been relied upon in only a very few cases, let alone successfully, clearly undermines these provisions as an effective legislative tool for protecting consumers.

8.2.3 When is a credit bargain extortionate?

One of the key criticisms of the extortionate credit bargain test relates to the ambiguity with which the term 'extortionate' is defined, making it 'difficult for district judges to use the act effectively'.[86] Indeed, the multitude of factors that could be taken into consideration in determining whether payments are grossly exorbitant, or contrary to the ordinary principles of fair dealings, arguably led to each case turning on its facts, not least because a wide range of factors could be used to mitigate one another.[87] For example, in *Ketley v Scott*,[88] the risk adopted by the creditor was successfully used to mitigate an interest rate of 48 per cent in a short-term loan.[89] This ambiguity in the wording has been attributed to the low number of cases involving the provisions, as outlined above.[90] The apparent lack of clarity in the wording of the provisions, in conjunction with the differing approaches that were taken in order to establish whether credit bargains were extortionate,[91] would have clearly made it challenging for lawyers to advise clients in relation to whether their credit bargain would be considered extortionate by the court.[92]

82 Ibid.

83 [2001] UKHL 52, albeit with regard to ss 129 and 136 Consumer Credit Act 1974 (unamended) in this case, the same can be said for the extortionate credit bargain provisions. See: Kempson and Whyley (n. 79) 31–32.31.

84 *Director General of Fair Trading v First National Bank* [2001] UKHL 52. Albeit with regard to Ss 129 and 137 Consumer Credit Act 1974 in this case.

85 Department for Trade and Industry (n. 80) para 3.29.

86 Kempson and Whyley (n. 79) 32.

87 Ryder, Griffiths and Singh (n. 56) 545–546.

88 *Ketley Ltd v Scott* [1981] ICR 241.

89 Ibid. 247.

90 Kempson and Whyley (n. 79) 31.

91 Geraint Howells and Lionel Bently 'Judicial treatment of extortionate credit bargains: Part 1' [1989] (May–Jun) *Conv* 169.

92 Citizens Advice Bureau 'Daylight Robbery' <http://www.citizensadvice.org.uk/pdf_drob.pdf>, accessed 21 June 2014, 30.

Largely due to the reasons outlined above, the extortionate credit provisions were considered to provide 'little protection to the most vulnerable people in society . . . on low incomes who are most likely to fall prey to . . . lenders on the margins of the market'.[93] In the context of today's credit market, the lack of accessibility to redress, the clear reluctance of judges to use the powers conferred upon them and the absence of a definitive list of situations in which a credit bargain would be considered extortionate would leave desperate debtors without any real hope of redress, in particular the vulnerable prey of high-cost lenders.

8.2.4 Unfair credit relationships

Following a detailed review of the original CCA74,[94] the government introduced the CCA2006.[95] While this change of law has been deemed to lack 'root-and-branch reform',[96] it has led to a dramatic adjustment to the circumstances in which consumers can seek redress in relation to an unsatisfactory credit bargain. The reforms have been described as increasingly consumer-focused, particularly in relation to the protection of the 'vulnerable consumer [from] unfair creditor behaviour'.[97] This has been achieved, in part, through the replacement of the extortionate credit bargain provisions with the unfair credit relationship test.[98] This test remains in force today, as the FCA has decided to take a 'lift and shift' approach and retain much of the CCA74, for the time being at least.[99] It is therefore necessary to analyse the unfair relationship test in greater detail.

The unfair relationship test operates in a similar way to the extortionate credit bargain provisions. It provides the court with the jurisdiction to intervene with a credit agreement,[100] should the court deem that agreement to be unfair.[101] The similarities continue, as the current test remains reliant on the consumer to

93 Richard Mawrey and Tobias Riley-Smith *Blackstones Guide to The Consumer Credit Act 2006* (Oxford University Press, 2006), 90.
94 See: Department for Trade and Industry (n. 80) particularly section 3. See also: Kempson and Whyley (n. 79).
95 Hereafter CCA06.
96 Mawrey and Riley-Smith (n. 93) 90.9.
97 Sarah Brown 'The unfair relationship test, consumer credit transactions and the long arm of the law' [2009] (1) *LMCLQ* 90, 90.
98 Consumer Credit Act 1974 (as amended) ss 140A–140C, Inserted by Consumer Credit Act 2006 ss19–20.
99 Eva Lomnicka 'The future of consumer credit regulation: a chance to rationalise sanctions for breaches of financial services regulatory regimes?' (2013) 34(1) *Comp Law* 13, 20. In particular, the Consumer Credit Act 1974 (as amended) s140B is discussed in the new Consumer Credit Source Book. See Financial Conduct Authority, *Consumer Credit Source Book* at App. 1.4.6.
100 Consumer Credit Act 1974 (as amended) s140B.
101 Ibid.

invoke the provisions during litigation,[102] whether relied on as a cause of action[103] or utilised as a defence to enforcement action by a creditor.[104] Should a debtor set forth the argument that their credit relationship is unfair, it is for the creditor to rebut this by showing that the relationship was, in fact, fair.[105] This 'reverse' burden of proof arguably highlights the consumer-focused nature of this provision.

Unlike the extortionate credit bargain provisions, an unfair relationship can be considered to have arisen from a multitude of factors and related transactions.[106] These factors may have arisen before, during and after the making of the credit agreement,[107] and it is very much down to the court to decide which factors to take into consideration.[108] Indeed, 'what the court has to determine under s.140A is not whether the relevant credit agreement is unfair, but whether the relationship arriving out of the agreement is unfair'.[109] A noteworthy example of this occurred in the case of *Patel v Patel*, where the failure of a creditor to actively pursue repayment of a loan was deemed to contribute to an original loan of £56,450 rising to an outstanding debt of over £6m.[110] The now Mr Justice George Leggatt saw fit to re-open the credit agreement and reduce the amount owed, from the £4,556,181 sought by the claimant to just £207,565.[111] In reaching his conclusion, he considered many factors. This included the fact that by not pursuing repayment of the loan, the creditor had caused the relationship to become increasingly profitable for himself, and therefore increasingly unfair,[112] clearly highlighting that it is the ensuing relationship and not merely the agreement(s) that matter. In addition, it is noteworthy that the judge also considered the value of the benefits obtained by the debtor as a result of having the loan made available to him, including the fact that it was unlikely that he would have been provided credit by another source, preventing him from building

102 See further: Paul Dobson and Rob Stokes *Commercial Law* (Sweet and Maxwell, 2012) 447.

103 See, for example: *Scotland v British Credit Trust* [2014] EWCA Civ 790 and *Robert Shaw v Nine Regions Loans Ltd* [2009] EWHC 3514 (QB).

104 Such as in the case of *Patel v Patel* [2009] EWHC 3264 (QB) and *Swift Advances Plc v Okokenu* [2015] CTLC 302.

105 Consumer Credit Act 1974 (as amended) s140B(9); *Scotland v British Credit Trust* [2014] EWCA Civ 790 [26].

106 For an interesting overview of this, see: Brown (n. 97) 95–108.

107 See further: Mawrey and Riley-Smith (n. 93) 90.95.

108 Consumer Credit Act 1974 (as amended) s140A(2). See further: John Bruce 'The Consumer Credit Act – unfairness as justice?' <http://www.kennedys-law.com/article/consumercreditact1974/>, accessed 30 June 2014, citing Lord Tomlinson in *Harrison v Black Horse Ltd* [2011] EWCA (Civ) 1128, para 37.

109 *Patel v Patel* [2009] EWHC 3264 (QB) [63].

110 Indeed, Mr Justice Leggatt stated that the claimant, by allowing the defendant to not regularly make payments, influenced the way in which the debt snowballed, ultimately for his own benefit. This action was deemed to contribute to the unfairness of the relationship. See: *Patel v Patel* [2009] EWHC 3264 (QB) 250 and 271–272.

111 *Patel v Patel* [2009] EWHC 3264 (QB) [83].

112 Ibid. [73].

two successful businesses.[113] This highlights that deducing the fairness of a credit relationship is a balancing exercise, considering the benefits and burdens of the relationship to both parties.

Additionally, the broad range of factors that can be taken into consideration by the courts when deducing the fairness of a credit bargain are complemented by a far-reaching discretion in relation to the remedies that can be provided to consumers who are deemed to have been treated unfairly during the course of a credit relationship.[114] This can range from the reduction of the amount payable by the debtor under the agreement or any related agreement,[115] to an order for the return of monies paid by a debtor pursuant to an unfair credit relationship.[116]

Initially, it was felt that the unfair credit relationships would lead to a large number of consumers relying on the amended CCA74, with wider powers encouraging the courts to more readily intervene.[117] However, while it is accepted that the provisions have provided an avenue for redress for some consumers,[118] the protective impact of the provisions remains limited. The reasons for this will now be considered in greater detail.

8.2.5 The unfair relationship test: certain uncertainty

An often-stated characteristic of the unfair relationship provisions is the fact that the term 'unfair' is not defined within the Consumer Credit Act.[119] It is noteworthy that governments and legislators are seemingly reluctant to define what is meant by the word 'unfair', highlighting that this would 'impede the courts' ability to justice in every case',[120] as fairness should be judged 'according to the

113 See further: Henderson Chambers 'Unfair relationships' <http://www.hendersonchambers.co.uk/resources/articles/unfair-relationships>, accessed 23 March 2016.
114 Consumer Credit Act 1974 (as amended) s140B.
115 Ibid. s140B(1)(f). See, for example: *Patel v Patel* [2009] EWHC 3264 (QB) 275.
116 Consumer Credit Act 1974 (as amended) s140B(1)(a). See, for example: *Scotland v British Credit Trust* [2014] EWCA Civ 790 [4], [14], where a creditor was ordered to repay the value of a PPI premium, in addition to the interest paid by the debtor pursuant to that premium, on the basis that the credit relationship was unfair due to the debtor being told that PPI was necessary in order to secure credit.
117 Mawrey and Riley-Smith (n. 93) 96.
118 Such as *Scotland v British Credit Trust* [2014] EWCA Civ 790 (above); *Patel v Patel* [2009] EWHC 3264 (QB) (above) and *Melbourne Mortgages v Berry* [2013] NI Master, 3, in which a repossession order was set aside.
119 See for example: Nicola Hoskins 'Unfair relationships in the consumer credit acts' <https://360.optimalegal.co.uk/2011/unfair-relationships-in-the-consumer-credit-acts/>, accessed 23 March 2016. Ross Fentam and Lucy Walker 'Crunching credit agreements: forms, formalities and reformation in consumer credit practice' <http://www.guildhallchambers.co.uk/files/theConsumerCreditActThePitfallsPracticalitiesLWRF.pdf>, accessed 23 March 2016, 40. See also: Dobson and Stokes (n. 102) 449.
120 Julie Patient 'The Consumer Credit Act 2006' [2006] 21(6) *JIBLR* 309, 312–313.

facts of each case'.[121] Indeed, Dobson and Stokes highlight that the evaluation of the fairness of a credit relationship will depend greatly on the facts of each individual case.[122] According to Patient,[123] this presents a problem for creditors, due to the lack of a benchmark against which to set their practices, to ensure that they are treating consumers fairly.[124] There is much guidance in relation to the meaning of unfair in the context of unfair relationships.[125] However, such guidance is usually accompanied by the caveat that the courts need not follow the guidance, if referring to it at all.[126] Indeed, it is arguable that, as with the extortionate credit bargain provisions, the unfair relationship test presents issues for lawyers when providing advice to their consumer clients, with the wide range of potential outcomes due to the wide range of remedies available to the courts, and the lack of direction provided to the courts,[127] rendering cases unpredictable.

8.2.6 Unfair relationship test and payment protection insurance

It could be argued that the unfair credit relationship test may have suffered the same lack of use as the extortionate credit bargain provisions outlined above. However, it is arguable that the misselling of payment protection insurance has contributed to the amended provisions being more widely used.[128] Indeed, the broadness of the unfair relationship test has allowed misselling of payment protection insurance[129] to fall within the remit of the unfair relationship test as a linked transaction.[130] However, despite this flexibility, Lomincka notes that the provisions 'have not proved a significant . . . avenue for redress'[131] in PPI cases.

121 Ibid., citing a speech in the House of Commons by Gerry Sutcliffe MP: HC Deb 9 June 2005, vol. 434, col. 1411.

122 Dobson and Stokes (n. 102) 450.

123 Patient (n. 120) 312.

124 Ibid. 312–314.

125 For example, from the Office of Fair Trading: *Enforcement Actions under Part 8 of the Enterprise Act 2002* (OFT854Rev, updated August 2011).

126 Ibid. 7.

127 Brown (n. 97) 91.

128 It has been noted that a large amount of the litigation centred around the unfair credit provisions is due to the PPI misselling scandal. See: Eversheds 'Unfair relationships – what does the future hold' <http://www.eversheds.com/global/en/what/articles/index.page?ArticleID=en/Financial_institutions/Unfair_relationships_what_does_the_future_hold>, accessed 23 March 2016. See further: *Scotland v British Credit Trust* [2014] EWCA Civ 790 (above).

129 Hereafter PPI.

130 John Briggs and James Boddy 'Payment protection insurance claims and insolvency' (2013) 26(5) *Insolvency Intelligence* 65, 65. This is mentioned in the case of as *Scotland v British Credit Trust* [2014] EWCA Civ 790 [68], but deemed not to be relevant due to the specific facts of that case. See also Eva Lomnicka 'Unfair credit relationships: five years on' [2008] 8 *JBL* 713, 717.

131 Ibid. 726.

Such cases have been more successfully pursued through the banks' internal complaints procedures, and the FOS.[132]

Some cases brought before the courts in this regard have been unsuccessful. Most noteworthy is the recent disclosure of the levels of commission being paid by insurers to creditors for the sale of PPI. For example, in *Harrison v Black Horse Ltd*,[133] the debtors sought to rely on the fact that the credit agreement was unfair on the basis that the amount of commission to be paid to the creditor was not disclosed to them.[134] Tomlinson LJ described the level of commission paid to Black Horse as 'startling'[135] and admitted that 'there would be many who would regard it as unacceptable'.[136] Despite this, the court held that, due to there being no statutory requirement of the creditor to disclose the level of commission to be paid to the lender by the insurer following the sale of a PPI policy,[137] the relationship was not unfair to the debtor.[138] This arguably illustrates that lenders were able to profit from 'startling' and 'unacceptable' linked credit transactions in the credit context. This fact was underpinned in the case of *Conlon v Black Horse Ltd*,[139] in which the debtor argued that that she would have sought a better, and arguably fairer, deal, had the level of commission been disclosed.[140] It was stated in argument that, not least due to the level of commission received by Black Horse, the price paid for the policy was three times that of stand-alone cover.[141] However, in the face of this, it was held that the failure to disclose the commission to be received, even if it 'would have caused to a borrower to do anything different, does not create unfairness in a relationship'.[142] It seemed therefore that, once

132 This is Money 'Your PPI claim success stories' <http://www.thisismoney.co.uk/money/cardsloans/article-1615484/Your-PPI-claim-success-stories.html>, accessed 23 March 2016. Although there have been reports that banks are not complying with awards sanctioned by the FOS. See, for example: Miles Brignall 'Can I bank on Barclays to pay my PPI refund?' *Guardian* (24 August 2014, London) <http://www.theguardian.com/money/2013/aug/26/barclays-pay-ppi-refund>, accessed 23 March 2016.

133 [2011] EWCA (Civ) 1128.

134 Ibid. [48].

135 Ibid. [58].

136 Ibid.

137 Reference was made to the Financial Services Authority's Insurers Conduct of Business Rules (ICOB) rules. Reference to such measures in these cases arguably exemplifies the broadness of materials that can be taken into account when seeking to enforce, or indeed refute, the unfair credit relationship provisions.

138 *Harrison v Black Horse Ltd* [2011] EWCA (Civ) 1128 [58]–[63].
For further discussion see: Kennedys Law 'The Consumer Credit Act 1974 – unfairness as justice?' <http://www.kennedys-law.com/article/consumercreditact1974/>, accessed 23 March 2016.

139 [2012] CTLC 193.

140 *Conlon v Black Horse Ltd* [2012] CTLC 193 [24].

141 Ibid. [23] citing the Judgment of Mr Recorder Atherton following the County Court hearing.

142 Russel Kelsall and Stephanie Clarke 'Appeal judge makes first decision reversing "unfair relationship" finding: Conlon v Black Horse Limited' <http://www.lexology.com/library/detail.aspx?g=6b71bd43-2020-468c-8deb-964765d310ce>, accessed 23 March 2016.

again, the unfair credit relationship provisions would not provide a suitable avenue of redress for those who feel wronged by lenders.

However, the Supreme Court has recently shown a marked change in this view. Indeed, in *Plevin v Paragon Personal Finance Ltd*,[143] Lord Sumption concluded that 'the non-disclosure of the amount of commissions made Paragon's relationship with Mrs Plevin unfair . . . enough to justify the reopening of the transaction under section 140A' CCA74.[144] This groundbreaking judgment sparked such interest that the Regulator has included it in a key part of its review of the handling of PPI complaints.[145] At the time of writing, the response to the FCA's consultation paper has not yet been published.

8.2.7 Unfair relationships in the modern era: providing high-cost credit to the financially untouchable[146]

Initially, it is somewhat striking that there appears to be no reported case law relating to the unfair relationship provisions and the companies such as BrightHouse and Wonga, outlined in section 8.1. However, after further consideration of this matter, the reasoning becomes clear. One of the key similarities of both business entities is the high cost of credit products sold by them. For example, the critics of BrightHouse frequently highlight how customers are paying two to three times the price they would for goods, in comparison with the price that would be paid if the products were purchased at an alternative retailer at the cash price.[147] In addition, a well-known fact relating to payday lenders is the four-figure APR levels attached to loan agreements.[148] Additionally, expensive credit products are aimed at consumers who have little or, indeed, no income from

143 [2014] UKSC 61.
144 Ibid. at 41.
145 Financial Conduct Authority *Consultation Paper: Rules and Guidance on Payment Protection Insurance Complaints* (Financial Conduct Authority, CP15/39, November 2015).
146 As described by Dr Stephen Ladyman MP in a Parliamentary debate relating to credit: HC Deb 18 June 2008, vol. 477, col. 1053.
147 For an interesting overview of this, see: Amelia Gentleman 'Buy now regret later? The secret of BrightHouse's success' *Guardian* (4 October 2013, London) <http://www.theguardian.com/society/2013/oct/04/brighthouse-consumer-poverty-high-street>, accessed 23 March 2016. A particularly striking example is where a television with a recommended retail price of £1,499.99 will cost over £3,700 if purchased under the BrightHouse model. See also: Helen Clifton 'Drowning in debt: how irresponsible lenders are cresting a tidal wave of misery' <http://www.church-poverty.org.uk/drowningindebt/report/drowningindebt/drowningindebtpdf>, accessed 23 March 2016, 7.
148 For example, see: Wonga 'Welcome to Wonga' <https://www.wonga.com>, accessed 23 March 2016, which, at the time of writing, was advertising loans with an APR in excess of 5,000 per cent. While the calculation of APR in this regard is often criticised, the aforementioned page quotes actual interest at 365 per cent. See: John Moorwood 'Wonga responds to US debt comparison jibes' <http://www.moneysavingexpert.com/news/loans/2011/09/wonga-responds-to-us-debt-comparison-jibes?_ga=1.140454707.1886219551.1401817751>, accessed 23 March 2016.

employment.[149] It is easy to draw inferences in relation to the characteristics of the commercial relationships that arise in the high-cost/low-income market, in particular a high default rate, where the fragile circumstances of their consumers change, rendering them incapable of repaying their loan. This therefore begs the question: Why are these agreements not regularly challenged under the unfair credit provisions? Such agreements are clearly covered by the broad nature of the provision.

The answer to this is arguably found in case law. The main reason that payday loans are targeted as an undesirable form of credit is the cost attached to them. However, as noted above, these products are generally provided to high-risk consumers. Indeed, Lomnicka notes, there remains reluctance by the courts to find unfairness in a relationship, even where the cost of credit is seemingly high.[150] It is clearly accepted that, both in relation to the extortionate credit bargain test,[151] and the unfair relationship test,[152] that a high rate of interest may be charged in order to counteract a high level of risk taken by a lender in providing credit to the financially undesirable borrower,[153] in particular where the interest charged is the same as that to a similar borrower, in similar circumstances, in a similar market.[154]

Furthermore, both the actual amount to be repaid by the debtor and the total cost of the credit for high-cost products are clearly presented to the consumer prior to entering into such agreements. Wonga makes use of 'sliders' to highlight the amount to be repaid, in addition to providing clearly the representative APR.[155] In addition, BrightHouse utilises clear advertisements to present this information in their stores and online,[156] satisfying requirements of a fair credit relationship in this regard.[157] Aside from the agreement itself, as outlined above, the post-contractual activities of the lender lead to the credit relationship being considered unfair by the court.[158] A recent example of this in the context of high-cost credit relates to the treatment of customers in arrears by Wonga, where the lender falsified letters from fake law firms, adding these fabricated legal costs to the accounts of already debt-ridden consumers.[159] The FCA imposed redress on behalf of wronged consumers, in a similar manner to those regulated by the FSA

149 Kempson and Whyley (n. 79) 16.
150 Eva Lomnicka 'Unfair credit relationships: five years on' [2008] 8 *JBL* 722–723.
151 See, for example: *Ketley Ltd v Scott* [1981] ICR 241.
152 See, for example: *Nine Regions (t/a log book loans) v Sadeer* (official transcript available on LexisNexis).
153 See further: Daniel Collins 'Payday loans: why one shouldn't ask for more' (2013) 28(2) *JIBLR* 55, 58–60.
154 See n. 152 [41].
155 Wonga 'Welcome to Wonga' <https://www.wonga.com>, accessed 23 March 2016.
156 Such as that found at appendix 1.
157 See further: Collins (n. 153) 637.
158 See discussion regarding *Patel v Patel* [2009] EWHC 3264 (QB).
159 BBC News 'Wonga chased debt using fake law firms, says FCA' <http://www.bbc.co.uk/news/business-28015456>, accessed 23 March 2016.

under the old FSMA regime,[160] with 45,000 Wonga customers receiving their share of a compensation pot, possibly in excess of £2.6m.[161] However, actions such as this may, to some extent, dilute further the necessary existence of the unfair relationship provisions, with the regulator taking firm action against creditors, seeking pecuniary redress on behalf of debtors.[162]

8.2.8 Financial Ombudsman Service

A discussion relating to consumer-led action in the consumer credit context would not be complete without discussion of the Financial Ombudsman Service.[163] As with the introduction of the unfair relationship provisions, the CCA06 is responsible for bringing all consumer credit matters within the jurisdiction of the FOS.[164] The FOS can be described as a form of alternative dispute resolution,[165] acting in disputes between consumers and financial institutions.[166] One of the main benefits of utilising the services of the FOS, rather than litigation, is the fact that the FOS is free to consumers,[167] a feature that makes this avenue of redress more attractive to consumers of the high-cost credit market, where the low amounts involved may be outweighed by the fees and costs attached to litigation.[168] Further, while the FOS may look at matters similar to those covered by the unfair credit relationship test, the Ombudsman is not bound to enforce any particular law or legal regime.[169] The FOS has autonomous power to do what it thinks best to resolve a dispute, subject only to the assessment of its decision through complex judicial review proceedings.[170]

While the FOS appears to have a broad jurisdiction to do right in consumer credit agreements, its prerogatives are somewhat limited by a financial ceiling. Indeed, the *FSA Handbook* states that the maximum the FOS can award to a

160 See section 8.3 below.

161 Financial Conduct Authority 'Wonga to pay redress for unfair debt collection practices' <http://www.fca.org.uk/news/wonga-redress-unfair-debt-collection-practices>, accessed 23 March 2016.

162 Such action was beyond the powers of the OFT. This is discussed further in section 8.3.

163 Hereafter FOS.

164 Consumer Credit Act 2006 s59, amending the Financial Services and Markets Act 2000.

165 See: Citizens Advice Bureau 'Alternative Dispute Resolution (ADR)' <www.adviceguide.org.uk/wales/c_alternative_dispute_resolution.pdf>, accessed 23 March 2016.

166 The FOS is also able to handle complaints small businesses. See: Financial Ombudsman Service 'Frequently asked questions: complaints from businesses, charities and trusts' <http://www.financial-ombudsman.org.uk/faq/answers/complaints_a9.html>, accessed 23 March 2016.

167 See further: Financial Ombudsman Service 'Information for businesses covered by the ombudsman service: why consumers do not pay' <http://www.financial-ombudsman.org.uk/faq/businesses/answers/funding_a9.html>, accessed 23 March 2016.

168 Fiona Hayles 'Does Wonga need a pay day loan?' <https://www.hcrlaw.com/blog/does-wonga-need-a-pay-day-loan>, accessed 25 March 2016.

169 Brown (n. 97) 108–109 citing *R (on the application of IFG Financial Services Ltd) v Financial Ombudsman Service* [2005] *EWHC* 1153 (Admin).

170 Brown (n. 97) 109.

disgruntled consumer is £150,000.[171] This clearly renders the FOS unsuitable for high value credit relationships such as that in *Patel v Patel*,[172] as the debtor in this case was relieved of nearly £5.8m worth of debt liability.[173]

In the context of payday loans, the FOS has an ever-growing caseload in this regard,[174] with the year to end April 2013 giving rise to an increase in cases filed of 75 per cent, compared with the previous financial year.[175] More recently, an increase from 297 (2011–12) to 794 (2013–2014) was recorded by the FOS.[176] The Service worryingly stated that this is figure 'merely the tip of the iceberg',[177] with the Citizens Advice Bureau stating that three in four payday loans could have a case worthy of intervention by the FOS.[178] This has been realised, with the number of complaints about payday lenders rising by around 46 per cent year on year in the two years preceding April 2015.[179] What is evident is that the FOS is dealing with an increasing number of cases on behalf of consumers who feel unfairly treated by payday lenders. However, there are many consumers who may be entitled to remedy from the Ombudsman that are not forthcoming with their complaint. Indeed, it could be argued that the effectiveness of the FOS as a consumer protection tool is undermined by the fact that consumers are ashamed by their over-indebtedness.[180]

This section set out to analyse the consumer-led consumer protection elements of the previous consumer credit regime, in particular those carried forward into the new era of credit regulation under the FCA. It is clear that the unfair relationship test still has some place in the future of consumer credit regulation,

171 Financial Conduct Authority *FCA Handbook* (London: Financial Conduct Authority, 2013) at DISP 3.7.4. Although it has been noted that it is possible to take the £150,000 redress offer and then sue for the remainder in court. See: RPC 'FOS respondents still at risk of further action despite *Clark v In Focus* ruling' <http://www.rpc.co.uk/components/com_flexicontent/uploads/fos-respondents-still-at-risk.pdf>, accessed 23 March 2016

172 [2009] EWHC 3264 (QB) (above).

173 It is duly noted that the debtor in this case was a business user. The case is merely used to highlight the fact that there are some cases above the financial ceiling, and therefore beyond the remit of the FOS as an effective remedy.

174 Ellis Ferran 'Regulatory lessons from the payment protection mis-selling scandal in the UK' (2012) 12(2) *EBOR* 247, 255.

175 Financial Ombudsman Service 'Ombudsman news: payday lending' <http://www.financial-ombudsman.org.uk/publications/ombudsman-news/109/109-payday-lending.html>, accessed 23 March 2016.

176 Andrew Trotman 'Payday lender complaints more than double' *Telegraph* (8 July 2014, London) <http://www.telegraph.co.uk/finance/personalfinance/borrowing/10952770/Payday-lender-complaints-more-than-double.html>, accessed 23 March 2016.

177 Ibid.

178 Citizens Advice Bureau '3 in 4 loans could have cause for complaint to the Ombudsman' <http://www.citizensadvice.org.uk/index/pressoffice/press_index/press_office-20130805.htm>, accessed 23 March 2016.

179 Financial Ombudsman Service 'Annual review 2014/2015: what the complaints were about' <http://www.financial-ombudsman.org.uk/publications/ar15/about.html>, accessed 30 March 2016.

180 Trotman (n. 176).

despite the lack of accessibility and aura of uncertainty surrounding the test. Indeed, the ability of the consumer to challenge the fairness of a credit relationship, no matter how infrequently it is used, is important, particularly as a defence in enforcement proceedings. Furthermore, the FOS provides an invaluable, free, avenue of redress to consumers in credit agreements below the £150,000 ceiling. Indeed, the future activity of the FOS will be interesting to follow as an increasing number of disgruntled consumers come forward to challenge their payday loan agreements. However, it is clear that consumers cannot be merely left to their own devices when challenging the unfair practices of lenders. There is also a need for a stringent regulator-led enforcement regime that is capable of seeking redress and actively protect consumers from unscrupulous lenders. Therefore, the following two sections will analyse the performance of the OFT and provide an overview of the FCA's performance so far, in order to consider whether there will be greater protection for consumers.

8.3 The Office of Fair Trading[181] and consumer protection

This section analyses the performance of the OFT in its role as the market regulator for consumer credit. Under the Consumer Credit Act[182] regime, the OFT was the regulator for the majority[183] of consumer credit products until the taking over of market regulation by the FCA, on 1 April 2014.[184] This move brought the consumer credit market under the auspices of the same conduct watchdog as the wider financial market for the first time since the beginning of regulation of the market by an independent regulator.[185] Indeed, it has been noted that the fact there was a separate regulator for consumer credit was a mere 'accident of history'.[186] However, this 'accident' has arguably had a dramatic impact on consumer protection, as is explored throughout this section. The section is split into two parts. The first part analyses the performance of the OFT from a control-based perspective, considering the measures taken by the OFT as a

181 Hereafter OFT.

182 Consumer Credit Act 1974 (as amended), hereafter CCA74.

183 There were some exclusions, such as first mortgages regulated under the FSMA regime, regulated by the FSA. Consumer Credit Act 1974 (as amended) s16.

184 Ignition Credit 'FCA takes over regulation of consumer credit firms' <http://www.ignitioncredit.co.uk/fca-takes-regulation-consumer-credit-firms>, accessed 23 March 2016.

185 Indeed, Lomnicka noted that the FSA was to be the new 'super regulator' responsible for the entire financial market, initially overlooking the fact that the consumer credit market was to be left out. See: Eva Z. Lomnicka 'Reforming UK financial services regulation: the creation of a single regulator' [1999] (Sep) *JBL* 480. However, the fact that the consumer credit market was separated in a regulatory context became a frequent topic for the commentator. See, for example: Eva Lomnicka 'The future of consumer credit regulation. A chance to rationalize sanctions for breaches of the financial services regulatory regimes?' (2013) 34(1) *Comp Law* 13; and Eva Lomnicka 'The reform of consumer credit in the UK' [2004] *JBL* 129.

186 Lomnicka (2013) (n. 185) 14.

regulator under the authority of the CCA74 seeking to protect consumers by preventing their coming to harm. The second part considers the regulator-led mechanisms of redress available to the OFT in order to compensate consumers who have lost out at the hands of unscrupulous credit providers. At times, comparisons will be made with the Financial Services Authority,[187] operating under the FSMA regime.[188] This is justified on the grounds that the two regulators were focused on achieving the same consumer protection goals, most notably ensuring the fair treatment of consumers by the regulated firms.[189]

8.3.1 Control and guidance over the credit market

This section considers the ways in which the OFT sought to protect consumers by controlling the behaviour of market actors. Specifically, the regulator acted as gatekeeper to the market through solely holding the power to grant licences.[190] In addition, the OFT sought, albeit somewhat loosely, to control the actions of licence holders by issuing guidance as to how they should operate within the regulated market. The effectiveness of these two control mechanisms is now considered in greater depth. The OFT operated under the licensing regime of the CCA74,[191] controlling those who have access to the credit market as providers and, arguably, seeking to ensure that only those who are likely to lend responsibly and treat their customers fairly are able to operate legally in the consumer credit market.[192] Indeed, prior to the transfer of credit regulation to the FCA, for a business to provide credit, it was required to be licensed by the OFT, with the supply of credit without a licence giving rise to criminal liability.[193] In order to gain a licence, the prospective credit provider[194] was assessed by the OFT in order to establish whether or not the business was fit[195] to provide credit.

187 Hereafter FSA.

188 Financial Services and Markets Act 2000.

189 An argument frequently expressed by Professor Lomnicka. See Lomnicka (2013) (n. 185) 13. See also Lomnicka [2004] (n. 185) 130–131.

190 Credit Strategy 'OFT to scrutinise "high risk" collectors' <http://creditstrategy.co.uk/article/6843/online-news/oft-to-scrutinise-high-risk-collectors>, accessed 23 March 2016. The OFT recognised the importance of their role of granting licences from a consumer protection perspective. See: Office of Fair Trading 'Consumer Credit Licenses: Guidance for holders and applicants' <http://www.norfolk.gov.uk/consumption/groups/public/documents/general_resources/ncc048312.pdf>, accessed 23 March 2016, 3.

191 Consumer Credit Act 1974 (as amended) Part 3.

192 Sarah Brown 'Using the law as a usury law: definitions and recent developments in the regulation of unfair charges in consumer credit transactions' [2011] *JBL* 91, 100.

193 Consumer Credit Act 1974 (as amended) s39.

194 It is recognised that there are many different types of licence available, the type issued being dependent on the nature of the business with which the applicant is engaged within the wider context of credit market. See further: Paul Dobson and Rob Stokes, *Commercial Law* (Sweet and Maxwell, 2012) 327–373. For the purposes of this discussion, the distinction between the types of licence is moot.

195 Consumer Credit Act 1974 (as amended) s24A.

While assessing the fitness of applicants, the OFT considered a wide range of characteristics, such as the knowledge and skills of an applicant,[196] any previous contravention of the CCA74 regime,[197] evidence that the applicant has acted in a discriminatory manner relating to a protected characteristic in connection with the business of consumer credit,[198] or had previously engaged in practices that appeared to the OFT 'to be deceitful, oppressive or otherwise unfair or improper (whether unlawful or not)'.[199] It is therefore evident that the OFT had a broad range of reasons that could be employed in order to refuse to grant a credit licence, providing a strong basis for ensuring that persons who are likely to cause harm to consumers do not gain access to the market. One would be forgiven for assuming that with such broad and strong powers to do so, a great number of applications for licences to operate within the credit market would be refused. However, research highlights that the powers have not been put to great use. Indeed, in the year to end April 2014, there were in excess of 19,000 applications either to obtain a licence or to vary an existing licence,[200] with the OFT refusing to grant a mere twenty-six licences.[201] Further, despite the fact that the fitness test was supposedly more stringent than the previous regime,[202] in the year prior to the enactment of the CCA 2006, the number of licences refused was more than double than the year 2013–2014.[203]

In addition to the granting of a credit licence, the OFT also had the power to revoke[204] or suspend[205] a credit licence, should it deem that a licence holder is no longer fit to operate within the consumer credit market.[206] Interestingly, the wording of s32 directs the OFT to consider whether they would grant the creditor

196 Ibid. s25(2)(a).
197 Ibid. s25(2A)(b)(i).
198 Ibid. s25(2A)(d).
199 Ibid. s25(2A)(e). See further: Nicholas Ryder, Margaret Griffiths and Lachmi Singh *Commercial Law: Principles and Policy* (Cambridge: Cambridge University Press, 2012) 541; Office of Fair Trading *Consumer Credit Licensing: General Guidance for Licensees and Applications on Fitness and Requirements* (OFT969, Jan 2008), 3; Kerry Broomfield and Nicholas Ryder 'Payday lending and the Consumer Credit Act' [2013] Feb *FRI* 14.
200 Office of Fair Trading *Annual Report 2013–14* (HC27) <https://www.gov.uk/government/uploads/system/uploads/attachment_data/file/322820/9988-2901757-TSO-OfT_Annual_Report_Web_ACCESSIBLE.pdf>, accessed 23 March 2016, 29.
201 Ibid.
202 Prior to the amendment of the licensing provisions of the 1974 Act by the 2006 Act, it was the ease of obtaining a credit licence that was a central issue. See: HC Deb 30 October 2002, vol. 412, cols 275WH–297WH.
203 Office of Fair Trading *Annual Report 2005–06* (HC1213) <https://www.gov.uk/government/uploads/system/uploads/attachment_data/file/231729/1213.pdf>, accessed 23 March 2016.
204 For example, see: BBC News 'Credit broker Yes Loans stripped of licence by OFT' <http://www.bbc.co.uk/news/business-17298515>, accessed 23 July 2014.
205 Robert Cooper 'OFT uses new powers to suspend consumer credit licence for first time' <http://www.scottrobert.co.uk/oft-uses-new-powers-to-suspend-consumer-credit-licence-for-first-time>, accessed 23 July 2014.
206 Consumer Credit Act 1974 (as amended) s32(1).

a licence in the current circumstances, and should the Office decide that it would not, action should be taken to revoke or suspend a licence.[207] Once again, this appears to be a very strong power that the OFT held in order ensure that consumers of the credit market are safe and well protected from unfair treatment. However, the ability to revoke or suspend a licence also rears its head as another underused power vested in the hands of the OFT. Indeed, in the year to end April 2014, the OFT revoked a mere ten licences, in addition to suspending a further four.[208] Further, it was noted that £450m worth of harm caused to consumers has gone without scrutiny, due to the inadequacies of the OFT's enforcement of the consumer protection regime under the CCA74.[209]

Furthermore, whereas the revocation of a licence should be a metaphorical death sentence to those operating improperly within the market, the contrary appears to be true. It was noted in a report[210] by the Public Accounts Committee that the process that was required to revoke a licence was cumbersome[211] and, more shockingly, that a person who has been deemed unfit to hold a credit licence can easily re-enter the market with a relative or employee heading up their new business entity.[212] This is arguably due to the fact that, as noted in the aforementioned report, the OFT lacked the power to ban a person from operating within the regulated market,[213] undermining the OFT's role as gatekeeper as they are unable to prevent those who have caused harm to consumers from having an active role in the market.

Akin to that of the OFT regime, the FSA had a similar role, acting as gatekeeper for the wider financial services market.[214] Those conducting activities regulated by the FSA, such as banks, independent financial advisers and mortgage brokers, required authorisation by the regulator.[215] Analogous to the OFT's power to revoke credit licences, the FSA could withdraw authorisation, should it, for example, deem an authorised person as falling foul of its rules, or even failing to comply with an FOS award.[216] However, unlike the OFT, the FSA had the power

207 Ibid.

208 Office of Fair Trading, *Enforcement Actions under Part 8 of the Enterprise Act 2002* (OFT854Rev, updated August 2011), 7.

209 National Audit Office *Office of Fair Trading* (HC, 2012–2013, 685) 8.

210 Public Accounts Committee *Regulating Consumer Credit* (HC, 2012–2013, 165).

211 Ibid. [10].

212 Ibid. [5]. See further: Hilary Osborne 'OFT criticized over "ineffectual" payday loans policing' *Guardian* (31 May 2013, London) <http://www.theguardian.com/money/2013/may/31/oft-criticised-ineffectual-payday-loans-policing>, accessed 23 March 2016.

213 Public Accounts Committee (n. 210) [5].

214 Stuart Bazely 'The Financial Services Authority, risk based regulation, principles based rules and accountability' (2008) 23(8) *JIBLR* 422, 434.

215 See in particular: Financial Services and Markets Act 2000 s22 and Financial Services and Markets Act 2000 Schedule 2.

216 Financial Services and Markets Act 2000 s33. See further: Mashood Iqbal 'Interaction between the FSA, FSCS and FOS' <http://www.londonviewchambers.co.uk/Interaction-between-FSA.html>, accessed 31 July 2014. For example, Tudor House Financial Services had their authorisation removed for not complying with FOS awards. See further: Money

to ban individual persons from operating within the regulated market in any capacity,[217] meaning that those who had once caused harm to consumers were unable to do so again – a clear solution to the problem outlined above.

Aside from the power to issue and revoke licences, the OFT had the authority to regulate the conduct of operators within the consumer credit market through the imposition of requirements entailing either positive action by a business or instructing a business to abstain from conduct with which the Office was dissatisfied.[218] For example, the OFT imposed a requirement upon Mackenzie Hall Ltd that the company could not conduct debt collection activities should the debt be disputed.[219] Furthermore, should the business not follow the instructions of the OFT, the Office had the power to impose a penalty on that institution of up to £50,000.[220]

This is arguably similar to the power of the FSA, which could impose unlimited fines for breaches of the FSMA regime,[221] but the OFT was required to take an initial step of instructing each individual licensee with details of the action the Office requires them to take prior to the imposition of the fine. By contrast, the FSA had the power to impose an unlimited penalty payment for any breach of FSMA, or of the *FSA Handbook*.[222] Indeed, the CAB make an interesting comparison, where they identify that the 'FSA could . . . fine a credit firm £1m for mis-selling PPI, the OFT [was] limited in its powers to fine the same firm only £50,000 for mis-selling the associated credit'.[223] Clearly, the powers of the FSA to impose financial penalties were far greater than that of the OFT, and may have acted as a greater deterrent to firms mistreating consumers in the consumer credit market, should the FSA have been the market regulator from the outset.

Finally, it is necessary to consider the mechanisms used by the OFT to influence the way in which businesses operated within the consumer credit market.

Marketing 'Firms lose authorisation for flouting watchdog' <http://www.moneymarketing.co.uk/firms-lose-authorisation-for-flouting-watchdog/56954.article>, accessed 23 March 2016.

217 Financial Services and Markets Act 2000 s56.

218 Consumer Credit Act 1974 (as amended) s33A(2).

219 Office of Fair Trading 'Requirements relating to Mackenzie Hall Ltd' <http://webarchive.nationalarchives.gov.uk/20140402142426/http://www.oft.gov.uk/shared_oft/business_leaflets/consumer_credit/requirements.pdf>, accessed 23 March 2016.

220 Consumer Credit Act 1974 (as amended) s39A. Wonga could have faced such action following the imposition by the OFT of requirements to abstain from oppressive debt-collection tactics. See: National Forum for Financial Inclusion 'OFT warn Wonga over aggressive debt collection tactics' <http://transact.org.uk/news.aspx?itemid=1360&itemTitle=OFT+warn+Wonga+over+aggressive+debt+collection+tactics&sitesectionid=29&sitesectiontitle=News>, accessed 23 March 2016. See further: Ryder, Griffiths and Singh (n. 199) 543.

221 Financial Services and Markets Act 2000 s206.

222 See discussion in relation to Willis Ltd below.

223 Citizens Advice Bureau 'Briefing: The Consumer White Paper – Citizens Advice's ideas for BERR' <http://www.citizensadvice.org.uk/consumer_white_paper_citizens_advice_s_ideas_for_berr.web_copy.pdf>, accessed 23 March 2016, 5.

In general, the OFT sought to achieve this through the publication of guidance documents. For example, the OFT published guidance in relation to what it considered to constitute irresponsible lending.[224] While such guidance was not considered to be directly enforceable, it was noted in the guidance that irresponsible lending could constitute a reason for the revocation of a consumer credit licence.[225] As such, had the OFT used its powers to revoke licences more readily, the guidance documents had the potential to be very influential in the protection of consumers in the consumer credit market.[226] By contrast, the FSA was granted rule-making powers by FSMA,[227] enabling the Authority to create a handbook, the contents of which could be directly enforced against those authorised to operate within the regulated market.[228] For example, in 2011, the FSA fined insurance broker Willis Limited £6.9m as a direct result of the firm's breaches of the *FSA Handbook*.[229] More importantly, the FSA has used this power to take action against institutions whose breaches of the handbook could have led to the unfair treatment of consumers.[230] It is therefore arguable that the FSA, through the use of their rule-making and enforcement powers, were able to more effectively influence the conduct of authorised entities in the context of consumer protection than the OFT's published guidance. This is not least due to the fact that there appears to have been no licence revocations by the OFT as a result of irresponsible lending practices, despite being clear in its guidance that this would be reason for doing so.[231] Indeed, this is yet another example of where the OFT has failed to use its

224 Office of Fair Trading *Irresponsible Lending – Guidance for Creditors* (OFT 1107, February 2011).
225 Ibid. para 1.12.
226 See above discussion in relation to the OFT's lack of use of their power to revoke consumer credit licences.
227 Financial Services and Markets Act 2000 s138.
228 Financial Services Authority *FSA Handbook* (London: Financial Services Authority, 2012) 2.1.1.6. For example, see: Financial Services Authority 'FSA fines Combined Insurance Company of America £2.8m for putting its customers at risk of being treated unfairly' <http://www.fsa.gov.uk/library/communication/pr/2011/fsa-fines-combined-insurance-company-of-america-28-million-for-putting-its-customers-at-risk-of-being-treated-unfairly>, accessed 31 July 2014.
229 Financial Service Authority 'Willis Ltd – Final Notice' <http://www.fsa.gov.uk/pubs/final/willis_ltd.pdf>, accessed 23 March 2016.
See further: Amy Ellis 'Willis fined record £6.9m for handbook breaches' <http://www.postonline.co.uk/post/news/2095688/willis-fined-gbp69m-fsa-handbook-breaches>, accessed 23 March 2016.
230 For example, see: Financial Services Authority 'FSA fines Combined Insurance Company of America £2.8m for putting its customers at risk of being treated unfairly' <http://www.fsa.gov.uk/library/communication/pr/2011/fsa-fines-combined-insurance-company-of-america-28-million-for-putting-its-customers-at-risk-of-being-treated-unfairly>, accessed 31 July 2014. CICA were found to be in breach of Principle 6 of the FSA's principles for business, in that they failed to protect the interests of consumers.
231 Although such revocations were threatened against some payday lenders. See: BBC News 'Payday lenders told to improve by the OFT' <http://www.bbc.co.uk/news/business-21683739>, accessed 23 March 2016.

powers to protect consumers from the greedy lenders that were showing little concern for the damage their products caused to vulnerable consumers.

As it is clear that the OFT had wide powers to control who operated within the consumer credit market, but failed to do so, it is necessary to consider the cause of the lack of effectiveness of these seemingly strong enforcement powers. With an estimated budget of £11.5m for consumer credit regulation,[232] the Office has considered itself good value for money, saving the average customer £8.60 for every £1 spent.[233] A similar comparison can be drawn, not with the FSA, but with the Serious Fraud Office, fighting fraud that causes a £52bn loss to the UK economy[234] with only a budget of £37m.[235] Akin to the OFT, the SFO has been described as providing excellent value for money,[236] costing each person in the UK little over 60p each year, [237] but also ineffective in the fight against serious fraud.[238] Indeed, value for money does not constitute effective consumer protection, and considering that the consumer credit market was estimated to be worth £176bn,[239] with a budget of £11.5m, a mere £4.5m being spent on enforcement,[240] it is unsurprising that £450m of harm caused to consumers has gone without sanction.[241] Lomnicka noted that the FSA was much better resourced than the OFT in their pursuit to prevent unfit persons from operating within the regulated market.[242] Perhaps this alone could be considered reason enough to bring the consumer credit market within the remit of the then FSA, newly branded as the FCA.

With the FCA bringing the consumer credit market within the remit of a regime based on credible deterrence,[243] it is reasonable to analyse whether the licensing regime under the CCA74, as enforced by the OFT, operated to deter greedy lenders from targeting the most vulnerable of consumers. Indeed, Cartwright highlights that, where proceeds of breaching the regulatory regime exceed the possible punishment for doing so, the 'corporate criminal is likely to take the

232 See n. 209. National Audit Office *Office of Fair Trading* (HC, 2012–13, 685), 30.
233 Ibid. 4.
234 Estimate in July 2013. See: National Fraud Authority 'Annual Fraud Indicator' <https://www.gov.uk/government/uploads/system/uploads/attachment_data/file/206552/nfa-annual-fraud-indicator-2013.pdf>, accessed 23 March 2016, 56.
235 The 2012–2013 budget of the SFO. See: Serious Fraud Office, *Annual Reports and Accounts 2012 & 2013* (HC 9, March 2013), 8.
236 Rosalind Wright 'Fraud after Roskill: a view from the serious fraud office' (2003) 11(1) *JFC* 10, 12.
237 See n. 235, 6.
238 See generally: Jessica DeGrazia 'Review of the Serious Fraud Office: final report' <http://www.sfo.gov.uk/media/99271/jdegrazia_final_review_of_sfo.pdf>, accessed 23 March 2016.
239 National Audit Office (n. 209) 4.
240 Ibid. 30.
241 Ibid. 7.
242 Lomnicka [2004] (n. 185) 139.
243 Financial Conduct Authority 'Enforcement' <http://www.fca.org.uk/firms/firm-types/consumer-credit/regulation/enforcement>, accessed 23 March 2016.

risk'.[244] With the aforementioned ability to continue trading under a different directorship, in addition to the limited fine that could be imposed and the infrequency of sanctions and revocations by the OFT, it is clear that the lack of use of their enforcement powers, arguably due to budgetary constraints, has contributed to the continued mistreatment of consumers by greedy lenders, undermining the licensing and control aspect of the regime as an active, credible deterrent.

8.3.2 Regulator-led redress

Lomnicka notes that one of the key benefits of the CCA74 over the FSMA regime is the fact that consumers have a mechanism with which to take direct action against creditors 'that have no analogies in the present FSMA regime'.[245] However, as noted in section 8.2 this mechanism appears to have achieved very little redress for unfairly treated debtors at the hands of unscrupulous lenders. That aside, a considerable disadvantage to regulation by the OFT is arguably the lack of a regulator-led redress regime, where the regulator is able to order the payment of financial redress to consumers by the lender, a power enjoyed and utilised by the FSA.[246]

For example, the FSA ordered sub-prime lender Swift 1st Ltd to pay £2.4m to consumers where the FSA deemed the lender to have failed to treat consumers fairly.[247] The interesting issue arising here is that a major contributor to the FSA's decision was the poor treatment and unfair charges imposed upon consumers in arrears.[248] This is not dissimilar to the reasons a licence could be revoked on the grounds of irresponsible lending,[249] yet the OFT did not have the ability to seek redress on behalf of consumers in the same manner as the FSA. Indeed, whereas the above discussion relates to strong powers that the OFT did not use, this

244 Peter Cartwright 'Credible deterrence and consumer protection through the imposition of financial penalties' in Nicholas Ryder, Sabine Hassler and Umut Turksen, *Fighting Financial Crime in the Economic Crisis* (Routledge, 2015).

245 Eva Lomnicka 'The future of consumer credit regulation: a chance to rationalise sanctions for breaches of financial services regulatory regimes?' (2013) 34(1) *Comp Law* 14, referring to the current provisions under Consumer Credit Act 1974 (as amended) s140A.

246 It is duly noted that agreements regulated by the OFT can be subject to such redress under the auspices of the FOS, as outlined above. However, this still requires the matter to be brought before the FOS by the consumer, unlike regulator-led redress under the FSMA regime, outlined below.

247 Financial Service Authority 'Swift 1st Ltd – Final Notice' <http://www.fsa.gov.uk/pubs/final/swift_1st.pdf>, accessed 23 March 2016. See further: Mortgage Solutions 'Fifth mortgage lender fined by FSA' <http://www.mortgagesolutions.co.uk/mortgage-solutions/news/2107756/fifth-mortgage-lender-fined-fsa>, accessed 23 March 2016.

248 Financial Service Authority 'Swift 1st Ltd – Final Notice' <http://www.fsa.gov.uk/pubs/final/swift_1st.pdf>, accessed 23 March 2016, [2.1]–[2.7]. Mortgage Solutions 'Fifth Mortgage Lender Fined by FSA' <http://www.mortgagesolutions.co.uk/mortgage-solutions/news/2107756/fifth-mortgage-lender-fined-fsa>, accessed 23 March 2016.

249 Specifically in relation to charges, see: Office of Fair Trading (n. 224) para 7.15.

example highlights an issue where the OFT did not have the power to take action on behalf of consumers.[250]

This section has highlighted key issues where the Office of Fair Trading has failed to protect consumers for two key reasons. First, despite having strong statutory powers to control those who enter and operate within the consumer credit market, the OFT did not effectively use its powers to prevent consumers being harmed at the hands of unscrupulous lenders. Although some action has been taken to revoke the licences of payday lenders,[251] there are still many who go without redress. In addition, the OFT lacked the power to secure redress on behalf of consumers, nor could it prevent people entering and operating the market in different roles following the revocation of previous licences. Where the OFT has struggled to provide redress to consumers, the FSA had a great deal more success, securing millions of pounds of financial compensation for unfairly treated consumers, with the power to impose requirements on a business to pay consumers they have wronged. This alone arguably supports the idea that the consumer credit market should have been handed over to the FSA from the outset, with stronger action and more direct redress being afforded to vulnerable consumers, the FSA being the more powerful and better-resourced market regulator. Indeed, while this 'accident of history' has led to this disparity in consumer protection and redress, with the ability to reflect upon this difference of regulatory effectiveness, it is no accident that the market has been brought under the auspices of the new Financial Conduct Authority. The next section analyses the approach of the FCA and considers whether lessons have been learnt, and whether the new regime will afford greater protection to consumers.

8.4 Consumer credit regulation: in the hands of the FCA

The Financial Conduct Authority[252] assumed regulatory control of the consumer credit market on 1 April 2014. This section analyses the approach of the FSA in the supervision of consumer credit firms from a consumer protection perspective, and it is noteworthy that, akin to the FSA, the FCA has a key objective; the protection of consumers.[253] One of the underlying themes of the FCA's

250 It is duly noted that under Part 8 of the Enterprise Act 2002, the OFT could take action where it considered a group of consumers to be at risk of harm. However, the powers are limited to use in the public interest context, as opposed to consumer redress. These powers therefore add little to the armoury of the OFT in this regard. See further: Ryder, Griffiths and Singh (n. 199) 541.

251 See, for example: Robert Cooper 'OFT uses new powers to suspend consumer credit license for first time' <http://www.scottrobert.co.uk/oft-uses-new-powers-to-suspend-consumer-credit-licence-for-first-time/>, accessed 23 July 2014.

252 Hereafter FCA.

253 The FCA has this as an 'Operational Objective': Financial Services and Markets Act 2000 as amended by the Financial Services Act 2012, s1B(3)(c). The FSA had the statutory objective of the protection of consumers by virtue of Financial Services and Markets Act 2000, s5. This has since been repealed.

approach to this objective is that the efforts to protect consumers need to be ‘appropriate’,[254] in that the Authority ‘aims to create a regime that protects consumers and allows businesses to operate’.[255] Throughout this section, reference is made to the flaws in the previous regime, in order to establish whether the new regime will offer greater protection to consumers. Indeed, it is not unreasonable to suggest that the FCA will bring some FSA ‘style’ regulation to actors and products previously regulated under the CCA74 regime, due to the similarities in the powers of the FCA and FSA.[256] This section seeks to discuss the extent to which consumers will be better protected against greedy actors in the consumer credit market under the watchful eye of the Financial Conduct Authority.

The section is split into three further sections. Section two considers the FCA’s approach to their gatekeeper role, [257] considering the effectiveness of the authorisation regime in preventing unfit persons operating within the market. Section three analyses the way in which the FCA supervises and takes enforcement action against firms, in addition to its ability to secure redress on behalf of consumers. Finally, section four examines the FCA’s approach to the regulation of high-cost credit.

8.4.1 The FCA as gatekeeper to the consumer credit market

As noted in the previous section, while the OFT appeared to hold strong powers to control who was permitted to enter the market, the underuse of those powers rendered them ineffective.[258] However, following the undertaking of market regulation by the FCA, new entrants[259] to the consumer credit market will

254 Financial Conduct Authority ‘Business plan 2014/15’ <http://www.fca.org.uk/static/documents/corporate/business-plan-2014-2015.pdf>, accessed 25 March 2016, 17.

255 Comments of FCA Director Martin Wheatley: ‘The FCA sets out in detail how it will regulate consumer credit when it over responsibility in April 2014’ <http://www.fca.org.uk/news/firms/consumer-credit-detail>, accessed 25 March 2016.

256 Some consider the creation of the FCA to be purely a name change. See Anon. ‘Reform of financial regulation gathers pace with son of FSA’ (2011) *Co LN* 1 at 1. However, FCA Director Martin Wheatley is adamant that the FCA will be different, due to losing some responsibility for the supervision of prudence and an increased focus on conduct. See: Guy Anker ‘“We will be different to the FSA”, says new regulator, the FCA, as regime changes today’ <http://www.moneysavingexpert.com/news/banking/2013/04/we-will-be-different-to-the-fsa-says-regulator-as-regime-changes-today>, accessed 25 March 2016. Lomnicka highlights that bringing the consumer credit market under the auspices of the FCA will not merely be a case of making consumer credit business regulated for the purposes of FSMA. See: Lomnicka (2013) (n. 245) 13, 13–14. However, it appears that this will largely be the case, as discussed further below.

257 As described in the FCA’s webinar on consumer credit. See: Financial Conduct Authority ‘FCA Consumer Credit Authorisations Webinar’ <http://play.buto.tv/JGGrN>, accessed 25 March 2016 (video link).

258 See section 8.3, above.

259 During the transition, those firms who held licences issued by the OFT could apply for interim permission, as opposed to seeking full authorisation from the outset. See: Financial

be subject to the new FCA authorisation regime, in which the onus is placed on firms[260] to illustrate that they conform to a detailed set of threshold conditions.[261] These conditions are stated as a minimum standard,[262] and circumstances such as the contravention of the current or previous financial services regimes, holding a criminal record or being subject to enforcement proceedings at the hands of the FCA, or its predecessors, could lead to the Authority's refusal to grant authorisation.[263] The aforementioned circumstances relate to one particular condition, namely whether the firm would be deemed *suitable*, and therefore fit and proper to conduct regulated activities within the consumer credit market.[264] In the consumer credit context, this is deemed to mean that a firm must 'demonstrate . . . that [their] affairs are conducted in an appropriate manner regarding the interests of consumers and the integrity of the UK financial system'.[265] It is clear that the FCA regards the protection of consumers as a top priority and that it is prepared to meticulously audit each application to ensure that only those who will treat customers fairly are active in the market.[266]

It is arguable, however, that such a stringent authorisation regime may have a negative impact on consumers. Considering the wider financial services markets, an issue that is already giving rise to criticism of the new regime due to extended

Conduct Authority 'Interim permission' <http://www.fca.org.uk/firms/firm-types/consumer-credit/consumer-credit-interim>, accessed 25 March 2016. See further: Simon Lovegrove, Anushka Heathe, Charlotte Henry and Matthew Gregory 'The New FCA consumer credit regime' [2014] (May) *Finance and Credit Law* 5.

260 Financial Conduct Authority 'Being regulated by the FCA: Guide for consumer credit firms' <http://www.fca.org.uk/your-fca/documents/consumer-credit-being-regulated>, accessed 25 March 2016, 15.

261 Financial Conduct Authority, *FCA Handbook* (Financial Conduct Authority: London 2014), COND 2. This test is not dissimilar to the old FSA threshold test. See: Financial Services Authority, *FSA Handbook* (London: Financial Services Authority, 2012), COND 2. For a brief overview, see: British Insurance Brokers Association 'Threshold Conditions (COND)' <http://www.biba.org.uk/pdffiles/condlist.pdf>, accessed 25 March 2016.

262 Financial Conduct Authority 'Preparing for authorisation' <http://www.fca.org.uk/firms/firm-types/consumer-credit/authorisation/prepare>, accessed 25 March 2016.

263 Financial Conduct Authority, *FCA Handbook* (London: Financial Conduct Authority, 2013) COND 2.5.6. Financial Conduct Authority 'FCA Consumer Credit Authorisations Webinar' <http://play.buto.tv/JGGrN>, accessed 25 March 2016 (video link).

264 Financial Conduct Authority, *FCA Handbook* (London: Financial Conduct Authority, 2013) COND 2.5.

265 Financial Conduct Authority 'Being regulated by the FCA: guide for consumer credit firms' <http://www.fca.org.uk/your-fca/documents/consumer-credit-being-regulated>, accessed 25 March 2016.

266 See: Financial Conduct Authority 'Treating customers fairly' <http://www.fca.org.uk/firms/being-regulated/meeting-your-obligations/fair-treatment-of-customers>, accessed 25 March 2016, in particular Outcome 1, which states: 'Consumers can be confident that they are dealing with firms where the fair treatment of customers is central to the corporate culture.' See also: Financial Conduct Authority 'Business plan 2014/15' <http://www.fca.org.uk/static/documents/corporate/business-plan-2014-2015.pdf>, accessed 25 March 2016, 17.

authorisation processes, is that new businesses are being prevented from quickly entering the markets across the financial sector, reducing competition and therefore having a negative impact on consumers' choice, and therefore the cost they pay for products.[267] Interestingly, slow authorisation has been attributed to resources being exhausted on applications from 'high risk' firms,[268] which are scrutinised more closely during the authorisation process.[269] It is therefore apparent from the outset that, despite having a much bigger budget,[270] the FCA may be plagued by similar resource issues as the OFT. As the discussion in the previous section demonstrates, such lack of resources can render even the strongest of powers ineffective.

Bringing the discussion back to the context of consumer credit, even without such resource issues, it is evident that firms will have to wait much longer for authorisation than they would have for their licence application when regulated by the OFT. Following the completion of a complex form, the FCA has stated that they aim to provide a decision on applications for authorisation within six months of that application being submitted.[271] By contrast, under the OFT, licences were generally granted within twenty-five working days.[272] Interestingly, current reports appear to suggest that the first granting of consumer credit authorisation was on 12 August 2014, over four months after the FCA had responsibility for controlling new entrants to the market.[273]

267 This was seen as an issue for the FCA prior to taking on the regulation of the consumer credit market. See: Laura Miller 'FCA drags heels in six month delay to authorize firms' <http://www.professionaladviser.com/ifaonline/news/2297516/fca-drags-its-heels-in-six-month-delays-to-authorise-new-firms>, accessed 25 March 2016. Lomnicka highlights that over-burdensome regulation could cause firms to exit the market, leading to a similar effect. See: Lomnicka (2013) (n. 245) 14.

268 Tessa Norman 'FCA approvals fall for retail firms' <http://www.moneymarketing.co.uk/news-and-analysis/regulation/fca-authorisation-approvals-fall-for-retail-firms/2012908.article>, accessed 25 March 2016.

269 Financial Conduct Authority 'Being regulated by the FCA: guide for consumer credit firms' <http://www.fca.org.uk/your-fca/documents/consumer-credit-being-regulated>, accessed 25 March 2016, 11–12.

270 For the regulation of consumer credit alone, in 2014/2015, the FCA has a budget of £41m, a £30m increase on the budget of the OFT. See: Financial Conduct Authority 'Business plan 2014/15' <http://www.fca.org.uk/static/documents/corporate/business-plan-2014-2015.pdf>, accessed 25 March 2016, 41.

271 Financial Conduct Authority 'Being regulated by the FCA: Guide for consumer credit firms' <http://www.fca.org.uk/your-fca/documents/consumer-credit-being-regulated>, accessed 25 March 2016, 16.

272 Scott Robert 'Consumer Credit (Category A) Licence' <http://www.scottrobert.co.uk/consumer-credit-category-a-licence>, accessed 25 March 2016.

273 See: Robyn Hall 'Ingard pips Tenet to the post' <http://www.mortgageintroducer.com/mortgages/250460/5/Industry_in_depth/Ingard_pips_Tenet_to_the_post.htm>, accessed 27 August 2014. Initially, it was thought that Tenet had been the first Consumer Credit firm to be granted authorisation. See: Peter Walker 'Tenet first network to get full FCA credit licence' <http://www.ftadviser.com/2014/08/21/ifa-industry/companies-

Therefore, keeping the words of Martin Wheatley in mind,[274] while the close scrutiny of businesses applying for authorisation will arguably reduce the likelihood of firms with the potential to harm consumers from jumping the fence, the consequences of a prolonged authorisation process, not least due to a lack of resources, may itself cause harm to consumers and render the FCA an 'inappropriate' choice to mind the gate to the consumer credit market. Indeed, Mr Wheatley noted that there was a balance to be struck. Whereas the OFT clearly tipped too far towards the freedom of the operator, the FCA is arguably running the risk of being overprotective.

8.4.2 Protecting consumers – post authorisation

This section considers the ways in which the FCA will supervise firms that are authorised to operate within the consumer credit market. In addition, government policy and proposed changes to the law are discussed, due to the fact that policy will influence, and the law will assist, the Authority in the pursuit of its consumer protection objective. In particular, this section analyses the extent to which FSMA-style supervision and enforcement will improve the levels of protection afforded to consumers, particularly considering whether or not the FCA's approach to supervision and enforcement will act as a credible deterrent to market actors from mistreating consumers. In addition, the potential impact of the imminent increase in product regulation is considered.

8.4.3 Supervision and enforcement

From the outset, it is interesting to note that the OFT considered itself a licensing regime, relying on information from third parties in order to initiate regulatory activity, as opposed to actively supervising those holding a consumer credit licence.[275] By contrast, the FCA is adamant that it will adopt a more supervisory approach, stating: 'Our supervision of firms will be hands on and we will closely monitor how providers treat their customers, in particular those operating in higher risk sectors such as credit cards, debt management and payday [lenders].'[276] This is arguably a positive move from a consumer protection perspective, as such an approach may lead to the more frequent discovery of malpractice, in addition to deterring firms from harming consumers due to this increased chance of being caught. However, should one delve deeper into the way in which the FCA will conduct such supervision, this assertion could be considered somewhat optimistic.

and-people/tenet-first-network-to-get-full-fca-credit-licence-ynL2qyBiVX7nsvXrTia86M/article.html>, accessed 25 March 2016.

274 See n. 255.

275 Public Accounts Committee *Regulating Consumer Credit* (HC, 2012–2013, 165) [8].

276 Financial Conduct Authority 'FCA confirms tough new rules for £200bn consumer credit market' <http://www.fca.org.uk/news/fca-confirms-tough-new-rules-for-200bn-consumer-credit-market>, accessed 25 March 2016.

It seems that observations will initially take place via telephone from the comfort of the FCA's offices, with on-site visits only occurring should the Authority consider firms to present a risk to its objectives, with most consumer credit firms only being subject to inspection every four years.[277] This is due to consumer credit firms, in general, being deemed to pose the lowest risk to the FCA's objectives,[278] and therefore arguably much less risk to consumers.[279] This inference is drawn from the fact that one of the FCA's operational objectives is the protection of consumers and that, as the Authority deems consumer credit firms to be of low risk generally, it is arguable that the FCA deems such firms to be of a lower risk to consumers. Lomnicka goes some way to rationalise this point by stating:

> [M]oney lending has a very different risk profile from . . . FSMA 'regulated activities' (for example, taking deposits, dealing, advising, managing investments). Thus, when lending money, the regulated firms put their money at risk whereas in most FSMA-regulated activities, the consumer normally does.[280]

While an interesting argument, it is questionable whether this should mean that lending businesses pose less risk to consumer welfare than deposit-taking institutions. It is noteworthy that there exists an increased layer of protection for the vast majority[281] of consumers with deposits in FSMA-regulated financial institutions by virtue of the Financial Services Compensation Scheme,[282] where deposits of up to £85,000 are protected, should an institution become insolvent.[283] While the near-collapse of Northern Rock highlighted both the ineffectiveness of the scheme[284] and the impact that the demise of a financial institution has on the macro-economic environment,[285] there is still a level of

277 Financial Conduct Authority 'Being regulated by the FCA: Guide for consumer credit firms' <http://www.fca.org.uk/your-fca/documents/consumer-credit-being-regulated>, accessed 25 March 2016, 25.

278 Ibid.

279 Indeed, when the Authority uses the term 'risk', it appears to refer to the risk posed to its objectives. See: Ibid. 22.

280 Lomnicka (n. 245) 14.

281 This assumption is based on the fact that the average person has circa £20,000 in savings. See: Harry Glass 'Cash-strapped Britain puts a little more aside, as savings increase to an average of £90 a month' <http://www.thisismoney.co.uk/money/saving/article-2248215/Savings-levels-increase-people-set-aside-average-90-monthly-income.html>, accessed 25 March 2016.

282 Hereafter FSCS.

283 Financial Services Compensation Scheme 'Banks/ building societies' <http://www.fscs.org.uk/what-we-cover/products/banks-building-societies/>, accessed 25 March 2016.

284 It was noted that the FSCS, following the near-collapse of Northern Rock, could not have coped with the failure of a large financial institution. See: Treasury Select Committee, *Run on the Rock* (HC, 2007–2008, 56–1) 76.

285 Indeed, Chambers describes the collapse of Northern Rock as a 'catalyst for the banking crisis in the UK': Clare Chambers 'Banking on reform in 2010: is regulatory change ever

protection that is available to customers in credit, but not to those in debt with the same financial institution.

What's more, the near-collapse of Northern Rock also highlighted the fallacies of a risk-based approach to regulating the financial sector.[286] Indeed, even if it is ultimately the lenders' funds that are at risk, it is arguable that effective protection from unscrupulous lenders may not be delivered; such a light-touch, long-distance approach may not reveal malpractice as effectively as previously thought, with reliance on complaints from consumers possibly remaining the key trigger for regulatory enforcement, as it was under the OFT regime.[287] That being said, the way in which the Authority polices the market itself, as opposed to the firms directly, may prove a more effective way of protecting consumers. For example, it has been noted that the FCA has recently identified 227 examples of instances where firms are not complying with the regime's advertising standards.[288] If strong regulatory enforcement action is taken against these firms, this may go some way to mitigate the seemingly relaxed approach taken to the supervision of individual firms.

While concerns can be raised in relation to the supervisory approach of the FCA, consumer protection will almost certainly be improved due to the stronger enforcement powers afforded to the FCA, which can be used against firms who fall foul of their regime. The FCA have created a set of enforceable rules specifically aimed at consumer credit firms within their regulatory handbook, a tool that was effectively used by the FSA in other areas of the financial services market prior to handing over the reigns to the new Conduct Authority.[289] Speaking about the new rules, Martin Wheatley stated: '[The FCA's] new rules will help us protect consumers and give us strong new powers to tackle any firm found to be

enough and will the general election hold the answers for the financial services industry' [2010] 44(2) *The Law Teacher* 218, 219–220.

286 See generally: Treasury Select Committee (n. 284) 21–34 and Joanna Gray 'Is it time to highlight the limits of risk-based financial regulation?' (2009) 4(1) *CMLJ* 50.

287 Public Accounts Committee (n. 275) [8].

288 Donia O'Loughlin 'FCA opens 227 investigations over credit promotions' *FT Advisor* (13 August 2014, London) <http://www.ftadviser.com/2014/08/13/regulation/regulators/fca-opens-investigations-over-credit-promotions-A4e3TIB6PYSJ3aBaPbFhEI/article.html>, accessed 25 March 2016.

289 See, for example: Financial Services Authority 'Willis Ltd – Final Notice' <http://www.fsa.gov.uk/pubs/final/willis_ltd.pdf>, accessed 25 March 2016. Willis were fined £6.9m for breaching the FSA's Principles for Business and rules relating to senior management and control requirements, both of which were contained within the *FSA Handbook*. The *FSA Handbook* was also used to punish Barclays Bank for their part in the LIBOR and EURIBOR rigging scandal. See: Financial Services Authority 'Barclays Bank Plc – Final Notice' <http://www.fsa.gov.uk/static/pubs/final/barclays-jun12.pdf>, accessed 25 March 2016. Where the sanctions were imposed for various breaches of the FSA's Principles for Business, contained within the *FSA Handbook*.

overstepping the line'.[290] As noted by Patient,[291] the new CONC rules are generated from elements of the previous statutory rules,[292] in addition to the guidance provided by the OFT under the CCA74 regime.[293] Essentially, by virtue of s206 FSMA, consumer credit firms will feel the wrath of the FCA's power to impose unlimited fines[294] for breaches of the previous OFT regime, where the OFT were limited to the imposition of fines of up to £50,000.[295] Most noteworthy is the fact that the requirement to assess the creditworthiness of a borrower is now easily enforceable by the regulator, with the CONC rules specifically stating that lenders are to '[take] reasonable steps to assess the customer's ability to meet repayments under the a regulated credit agreement',[296] highlighting the importance of the affordability of credit products in the new regime.[297]

In addition, Patient highlights that consumer credit firms will now face such penalties should they fall foul of the FCA's Principles for Business,[298] within which there is a requirement to act in the best interest of consumers,[299] a principle that the FSA at least readily fined authorised firms for breaching.[300] Finally, individual persons within companies can be both fined and banned from taking part in regulated activities for the improper treatment of customers within the consumer credit market.[301] It is arguable that these increased enforcement powers of the FCA will act as a deterrent to firms acting against the interests of consumers. The

290 Financial Conduct Authority 'FCA confirms tough new rules for £200bn consumer credit market' <http://www.fca.org.uk/news/fca-confirms-tough-new-rules-for-200bn-consumer-credit-market>, accessed 25 March 2016.

291 Julie Patient 'Consumer Credit: FCA takes over regulation' <http://uk.practicallaw.com/9-561-9266>, accessed 25 March 2016

292 Under the Consumer Credit Act 1974 (as amended).

293 Patient (n. 291).

294 Financial Services and Markets Act 2006 s206.

295 See section 8.3 above.

296 Financial Conduct Authority *FCA Handbook* (Financial Conduct Authority, 2014), CONC 5.3.1(2).

297 Financial Conduct Authority 'FCA confirms tough new rules for £200bn consumer credit market' <http://www.fca.org.uk/news/fca-confirms-tough-new-rules-for-200bn-consumer-credit-market>, accessed 25 March 2016.

298 Patient (n. 291).

299 Financial Conduct Authority *FCA Handbook* (Financial Conduct Authority, 2014), PRIN 2.1.1.6.

300 For example, Combined Insurance Company of America were fined £3m, partly due to Principle 6 failings. See: Financial Services Authority 'Combined Insurance Company of America – Final Notice' <http://www.fsa.gov.uk/static/FsaWeb/OCD/cica.pdf>, accessed 25 March 2016 [5.2(2)].

301 For an example of this power being used by the FSA, see: Financial Services Authority 'Andrew Lawton – Final Notice' <http://www.fsa.gov.uk/static/pubs/final/andrew-lawton.pdf>, accessed 25 March 2016, where Andrew Lawton was fined £13,500 and banned from holding a similar role in the future. See further: Simon Read 'FSA fines lender over poor treatment of consumers' *Independent* (11 December 2012, London) <http://www.independent.co.uk/money/mortgages/fsa-fines-lender-12m--over-poor-treatment-of-customers-8399802.html>, accessed 25 March 2016.

fact that practices such as irresponsible lending and the failure to treat customers fairly will now be punishable through the imposition of an unlimited fine, when weighing up whether breaching the regulatory regime is worth the consequence,[302] it is to be hoped that these new sanctions will ensure that businesses think twice.

8.4.4 Redress

One of the key issues outlined in the previous section was the fact that the OFT lacked the power to actively seek redress on behalf of a group of consumers who had suffered harm at the hands of a licensed person. By contrast, following the enactment of the Financial Services Act 2010, the FCA has the power to impose redress requirements on behalf of consumers who have been unfairly treated at the hands of regulated firms.[303] For example, the FSA secured nearly £1.1m of redress for the consumers of Kensington Mortgage Company, who, for example, failed to ensure that customers who were in arrears with their mortgage repayments had repayment plans tailored to their circumstances, which was deemed to breach Principle 6: the requirement to act in the best interest of the consumer.[304] While this type of enforcement will arguably have a similar deterrent effect to the ability of the FCA to impose unlimited fines, it comes with the added bonus of putting cash back into the pockets of harmed consumers.

Indeed, unlike its powers under s206 FSMA, the FCA has used the power to seek redress on behalf of consumers upon a payday lender who has mistreated consumers. As outlined above, the FCA ordered Wonga to pay £2.6m to consumers that the lender sent letters to that were from fake law firms.[305] This is arguably the most powerful message so far from the FCA: to firms, that they are going to take tough action against those who mistreat consumers; and to consumers, that the FCA will ensure that when they are unfairly treated, money will be put back into their pockets.[306]

302 And, as such, identifying whether the FCA's regime acts as a deterrent. See: Peter Cartwright 'Credible deterrence and consumer protection through the imposition of financial penalties' in Nicholas Ryder, Sabine Hassler and Umut Turksen *Fighting Financial Crime in the Economic Crisis,* (Routledge, 2014) 31.

303 Financial Services and Markets Act 2000 s404 as amended by the Financial Services Act 2010. See further: Pinsent Masons 'Law change lets FSA impose consumer redress schemes' <http://www.out-law.com/page-11445>, accessed 25 March 2016. [2.3(3)].

304 Financial Services Authority 'Kensington Mortgage Company – Final Notice' <http://www.fsa.gov.uk/pubs/final/kensington.pdf>, accessed 25 March 2016 [2.3(3)]. See also: Financial Services Authority 'Final Notice – DB mortgages' <http://www.fsa.gov.uk/pubs/final/db_uk.pdf>, accessed 25 March 2016. [2.5]–[2.5], where the redress secured was estimated at £60m.

305 See section 8.2 above.

306 It is noteworthy that this will apply where a number of consumers have been harmed. Individual consumers still have the option to seek redress in the courts by virtue of the unfair credit relationship provisions, and through the use of the FOS: see section 8.2 above.

It is somewhat disappointing that the FCA was unable to fine Wonga under s206 FSMA, which was due to the fact that the misconduct occurred prior to the FCA taking over regulation of the sector.[307] Indeed, this has been identified as a possible weakness in the FCA's regulation of the payday lending market, as it is an escape route from misconduct that occurred prior to the FCA undertaking responsibility for the payday-lending sector.[308] In addition, it has been highlighted that the FCA has not issued a notice in respect of this incident, detailing the specific reasons for the action being taken against Wonga.[309] This has been considered preventing 'the public from knowing why [the] fakery took place',[310] which is arguably important if consumers are to be fully aware of the businesses that they are trusting with their financial well-being. That being said, the imposition of redress of such magnitude by the Authority upon a payday lender is certainly a positive move by the FCA in pursuit of their objective to protect consumers and should go some way to address the £450m redress gap identified above.[311]

8.4.5 High-cost credit: are cost caps the answer?

Finally, this section considers the powers of the FCA to regulate the credit products that are offered for sale by market actors to consumers, in particular the FCA's power to regulate the cost of credit.[312] This is important for this section due to the fact much of the discussion relating to the new powers of the FCA, prior to it undertaking regulation of the consumer credit market, related to the ability to impose cost caps on credit products, directly affecting the products that could be offered for sale by payday lenders.[313]

307 BBC 'Wonga chased debt using fake law firms, says FCA' <http://www.bbc.co.uk/news/business-28015456>, accessed 25 March 2016.

308 Jim Armitage 'Wonga scandal and subsequent let-off calls for full parliamentary inquiry' *Independent* (26 June 2014, London) <http://www.independent.co.uk/news/business/comment/wonga-scandal-and-subsequent-letoff-calls-for-a-full-parliamentary-inquiry-9563833.html>, accessed 25 March 2016.

309 Ibid.

310 Ibid.

311 See section 8.3 above.

312 Financial Services and Markets Act 2000 s137C, as inserted by Financial Services Act 2012 s24.

313 See, for example: Denise Roland 'Payday lenders to face interest rate Cap from City regulator' *Telegraph* (25 November 2013, London) <http://www.telegraph.co.uk/finance/newsbysector/banksandfinance/10471982/Payday-lenders-to-face-interest-rate-cap-from-City-regulator.html>, accessed 25 March 2016. See also: Matt West 'Payday lenders face cap on interest charges from next year as City Watchdog takes control of credit industry' <http://www.thisismoney.co.uk/money/bills/article-2578978/Payday-lenders-face-cap-charges-year-City-Watchdog-takes-control-consumer-credit-industry.html>, accessed 25 March 2016.

Following the undertaking of responsibility for the regulation of the payday loans market, the FCA proposed a cap on the cost of payday loans,[314] stating that loans should not cost more than 0.8 per cent per day in interest charges, [315] in addition to a cap on the amount a consumer will repay, set at 100 per cent of the original loan amount.[316] This cap is designed to protect consumers of the payday loans market,[317] and is set to have a dramatic impact on the profitability on the payday loans industry, possibly reducing profits for lenders by up to 42 per cent.[318] The cap came into force in January 2015.[319]

While on its face this appears to be a victory for consumer protection, reducing the opportunity for consumers to suffer the horrifying over-indebtedness due to the defaulting on payday loans, the FCA's seemingly arbitrary approach to product regulation has the potential to cause more harm than good. Indeed, in April 2013, the FCA itself suggested that interest-rate caps may not be imposed, as it considered some consumers 'might be made worse off by caps on APR', due to this being the only form of loan available to some, particularly in emergencies.[320] Dr Sarah Brown, at a symposium at the University of the West of England, made the point that in the absence of high-cost credit products, high-risk borrowers may have to turn to illegal sources of credit, putting them in even greater danger.[321] As with the authorisation and supervision of consumer credit

314 See generally: Financial Conduct Authority *Consultation Paper: Proposals for a Price Cap on High-cost Credit* (Financial Conduct Authority, CP14/10, July 2014).

315 Which still represents an APR in excess of 1,000 per cent: Financial Conduct Authority 'Consumer Credit Countdown – Review into debt collection practices of payday lenders starts on day one of FCA regulation. Note 3' <http://www.fca.org.uk/news/consumer-credit-countdown-review-into-debt-collection-practices-of-payday-lenders-starts-on-day-one-of-fca-regulation> accessed 23rd March 2016.

316 Financial Conduct Authority 'FCA proposes price cap for payday lenders' <http://www.fca.org.uk/news/fca-proposes-price-cap-for-payday-lenders>, accessed 25 March 2016.

317 Financial Conduct Authority (n. 314).

318 BBC News 'FCA proposes payday loan cap of 0.8% per day' <http://www.bbc.co.uk/news/business-28305886>, accessed 25 March 2016.

319 Rupert Jones 'Payday loan caps come into force' *Guardian* (2 January 2015, London) <http://www.theguardian.com/money/2015/jan/02/payday-loans-caps-fca>, accessed 25 March 2016.

320 Samuel Dale 'FCA says it may stay its hand on payday rate caps' <http://www.mortgagestrategy.co.uk/news-and-features/latest-news/fca-says-it-may-stay-its-hand-on-payday-rate-caps/1069405.article>, accessed 25 March 2016. The consultation paper suggests that around 11 per cent of current payday loans consumers would no longer be able to access these loans: Financial Conduct Authority (n. 314) para 5.15.

321 Dr Sarah Brown at the symposium on Convenient Credit and Consumer Protection at the University of the West of England, 28 March 2012. See also: Damon Gibbons 'Tackling the high cost credit problem: the importance of real-time regulatory databases' <http://www.responsible-credit.org.uk/uimages/File/Tackling%20the%20high%20cost%20credit%20problem,%20importance%20of%20regulatory%20databases%20final.pdf>, accessed 25 March 2016) 12–13. This is due to the fact that, as noted above, cost is often used to mitigate risk. See further: Daniel Collins 'Payday loans: why one shouldn't ask for more' (2013) 28(2) *JBL* 55, 57.

firms, there is certainly a balance to be struck when regulating the cost of consumer credit products.[322]

It seems that the FCA is not necessarily concerned with the detrimental impact of an arbitrary cost of credit cap, and their approach may cause harm to consumers, rather than protecting them. In the wake of the financial crisis, many consumers have needed to rely on payday loans to purchase necessary goods, such as food, or to cover housing costs.[323] In 2013, Daniel Collins suggested that, despite the potential of interest-rate caps, 'the future of payday lenders appears bright and profitable'.[324] However, following the FCA's proposals to cap interest rates and the total cost of credit, this no longer appears to be the case. Unfortunately, the same could arguably be said for the high-risk consumer.

8.4.6 Regulating high-cost credit: what about rent-to-own?

The FCA appears to have missed the financial destruction caused by rent-to-own companies such as BrightHouse.[325] For example, customers have been sold more than one rent-to-own scheme simultaneously, which can cause devastation when a consumer falls into arrears. [326] The FCA appears to have taken no action to regulate this market. It is arguable that this oversight is due the fact that there is less publicity attached the indebtedness caused by BrightHouse, in comparison with payday lenders.[327] From the outset, the FCA needed to be seen taking tough action against companies that cause consumer harm. It seems that taking action against payday lenders, as opposed to rent-to-own credit providers, gives them this limelight.

This section has analysed the FCA's approach to the regulation of consumer credit so far. It is clear from the outset that the FCA will take a tougher approach to the regulation of the consumer credit market, through tighter scrutiny of those the gatekeeper allows into the market, in addition to having much tougher enforcement powers than the OFT under the previous regime. However, from a consumer protection perspective, some notable concerns have been raised. First, the more stringent authorisation regime is a great deal slower, delaying new firms

322 See further: Paul Ali, Cosima McRae and Ian Ramsay 'Payday lending regulation and borrower vulnerability in the UK and Australia' (2015) 3 *JBL* 223.

323 Hilary Osbourne 'Payday loans being used to feed desperate families, charity says', *Guardian* (1 October 2013, London) <http://www.theguardian.com/money/2013/oct/01/payday-loans-feed-families-report>, accessed 25 March 2016.

324 Collins (n. 321) 60.

325 Even debt charities and campaign groups often consider the two products in conjunction with each other: Helen Clifton 'Drowning in debt: how irresponsible lenders are cresting a tidal wave of misery' <http://www.church-poverty.org.uk/drowningindebt/report/drowningindebt/drowningindebtpdf>, accessed 25 March 2016, 8.

326 Amelia Gentleman 'Buy now regret later? The secret of BrightHouse's success' (4 October 2013, *Guardian*) available at <http://www.theguardian.com/society/2013/oct/04/brighthouse-consumer-poverty-high-street>, accessed 25 March 2016.

327 It has been noted that regulators have neglected other credit products due to the focus on payday lending. Damon Gibbons (n. 321) 73.

entering the market, possibly leading to a negative impact on competition, and therefore the consumer. Second, the imposition of a price cap, while reducing over-indebtedness, may lead to consumers seeking loans from illicit sources, who may use 'strong-arm'[328] tactics to recover debts, placing consumers in further danger. By contrast, the FCA's ability to impose redress on behalf of consumers is a definite improvement, and, by putting cash back into the pockets of wronged consumers, should reduce the number of people who are treated unfairly by market actors and go without redress.

8.5 The regulation of payday loans: lessons from the United States?[329]

This section seeks to explore whether lessons can be learned and implemented from the US approach to the regulation of 'predatory lending', specifically the payday loans market. This section is split into two further sections. The first discusses payday lending as a form of predatory lending. The second considers whether there are US regulatory practices that could benefit the UK borrower in the payday loans market from a consumer protection perspective.

8.5.1 Payday lending as predatory lending

Some commentators note that the term 'predatory lending' lacks definition.[330] However, it is arguable that a 'victim'[331] of predatory lending will have one or more of the following characteristics:

1) Victims of predatory lending commonly find themselves in financial difficulty, not because of changes in their personal circumstances during the course of the credit agreement, but because the products sold to them were not suitable for their financial needs at the outset.[332]

328 As described by: Gordon Borrie 'The credit society: its benefits and burdens' [1986] May *JBL* 181 at 189.

329 In carrying out its research into the impact of capping the price of a payday loan, the FCA used the US as one comparison country. See: Financial Conduct Authority, *Consultation Paper: Proposals for a Price Cap on High-cost Credit* (Financial Conduct Authority, CP14/10, July 2014): Annex 4 paras 39–60.

330 See, for example: Hirsh Ament 'Predatory lending: what will stop it' [2009] 4 *J Bus & Tech* 371, 371; John Relman, Fred Rivera, Meera Trehan and Shilpa S. Stoskar 'Designing federal legislation that works: legal remedies for predatory lending' in Gregory D. Squires (ed.) *How to Stop Predatory Lending* (Prager Publishers, 2004) 153; Kathleen Engel and Patricia McCoy 'A tale of three markets: the law and economics of predatory lending' (2002) 80(6) *Texas Law Review* 1255, 1259–1260.

331 The term 'victim' is used here to denote a person who has been subject to predatory lending and is not necessarily the victim of a crime.

332 Nicholas Ryder and Kerry Broomfield 'Predatory lending and white collar crime: a critical reflection' (2014) 25(9) *ICCLR* 287, 291 citing: Marita Shelley and Margaret

2) Victims are sold products with the lender's profit in mind, with little consideration of consumer affordability and need.[333]
3) It is generally accepted that illegal[334] predatory lending is linked to some form of criminal activity on the part of the lender,[335] whether this is the 'fraudulent inducement [of a consumer] to sign a loan document'[336] or encouraging potential debtor to enter false information on their application.[337] Thus, the victim of predatory lending may also be a victim of crime.

For the purpose of this chapter, it is necessary to consider the term 'predatory lending' in the context of payday lending. It is noteworthy that payday loans in any form are not presently illegal in the UK, no matter how high the interest rate, due to there being no cap on the cost of credit.[338] Nor is there any law against the provision of short-term loans that are repayable in a single instalment, so long as the business is authorised by the FCA[339] and is compliant with other regulatory requirements, such as cost disclosure rules.[340] However, it is clear that payday loans can fall within the first two of the above three characteristics. Indeed, in September 2013, Helen Clifton noted that 'more than 150 debt advisors . . . said that the loans were unaffordable from the outset'.[341] Furthermore, it is argued that payday loans are not there to assist consumers, but instead used to exploit

Jackson 'Sub prime lending, its deficiencies and government responses' (2008) 28(10) *JIBLR* 523, 534.

333 Debt.org 'Predatory lending' <http://www.debt.org/credit/predatory-lending/>, accessed 28 March 2016.

334 US law recognises that not all predatory lending practices are illegal. This has been cited as an issue that inhibits consumers when seeking redress; see: Ament (n. 330) 373.

335 Relman *et al.* (n. 330) 166; Nicholas Ryder *The Financial Crisis and White Collar Crime: A Perfect Storm?* (Edward Elgar Publishing, 2014) 75. US General Accounting Office 'Report to the Chairman and Ranking Minority Member, Special Committee on Aging, U.S. Senate: Consumer Protection Federal and Sate Agencies face challenged in combating predatory lending' <http://www.gao.gov/new.items/d04280.pdf>, accessed 28 March 2016 33.

336 Relman *et al.* (n. 330) 156.

337 Engel and McCoy (n. 330) 1268.

338 Indeed, even following the introduction of an interest-rate cap (section 8.4 above), payday loans will still continue to provide an opportunity for high-cost credit products to be sold to vulnerable consumers. In fact, this cap has been considered to condone predatory lending by 'legitimis[ing] . . . high prices and incentivise irresponsible and extortionate lending'. CCRmagazine.com 'FCA's price cap would only legitimize predatory lending' <http://www.ccrmagazine.com/index.php?option=com_content&task=view&id=11648&Itemid=35>, accessed 28 March 2016, citing the Director of the Centre for Responsible Credit, Damon Gibbons.

339 See section 8.4 above.

340 Financial Conduct Authority *FCA Handbook* (Financial Conduct Authority, 2014), COND 4.2.5(2).

341 Helen Clifton 'Drowning in debt: how irresponsible lenders are cresting a tidal wave of misery' <http://www.church-poverty.org.uk/drowningindebt/report/drowningindebt/drowningindebtpdf>, accessed 28 March 2016, 8.

the vulnerable, with lenders happy to see loans roll over and generate extra profits.[342] Therefore, while the practice of offering payday loans is not illegal, it is clearly predatory, falling into the definition 'a predatory lender is one who, for personal profit, takes advantage of another by unfair, albeit technically legal, means'.[343]

8.5.2 The regulation of payday lending: lessons from the US?

In the US, there is an abundance of federal statutes, each aimed at tackling small elements of predatory lending.[344] Much like the consumer protection regime in the UK, there is particular emphasis on the fair treatment of the consumer during the making of the loan agreement,[345] in addition to the protection of consumers who find themselves in arrears.[346] However, due to the fallout of the sub-prime market in the US, much of the focus in relation to predatory lending has been on the sub-prime mortgage market, arguably allowing issues within non-mortgage-based credit market to go largely unnoticed.[347] It is therefore arguable that federal law does not effectively tackle payday lending,[348] and states have taken it upon themselves to attempt to deal with the harm caused by high-cost, short-term credit.[349] As a result, in order to identify whether the UK can take lessons from the US in the regulation of payday lending, this discussion will now

342 Debt.org 'Payday lenders' <http://www.debt.org/credit/payday-lenders>, accessed 28 March 2016.

343 Creola Johnson 'Payday Loans: Shrewd business or predatory lending' (2002–03) 97(1) *Minn L Rev* 1, 5.

344 As outlined by Ryder (n. 335) 75. For an interesting visual comparison of the different practices that each of the US statutes can be invoked to challenge, see: US General Accounting Office 'Report to the Chairman and Ranking Minority Member, Special Committee on Aging, U.S. Senate: Consumer Protection Federal and State Agencies face challenged in combating predatory lending' <http://www.gao.gov/new.items/d04280.pdf>, accessed 29 March 2016, 31.

345 Such as the rules relating to the transparency of the cost of credit under the Truth in Lending Act 15 U.S.C. §§ 1601–1693 (2000) as cited by: Pearl Chin 'Payday loans: the case for federal legislation' [2004] *U Ill L Rev* 723, 730.

346 Such as the Fair Debt Collection Practices Act (15 U.S.C. 1629).

347 As noted, with particular regard to the credit card market, by: William Stadler 'Predatory lending: is the Credit Card Act enough?' (2012) 19(1) *JFC* 99, 99.

348 Indeed, US writers express the need for an effective federal law that specifically regulates payday lending. See: Johnson (n. 343); Chin (n. 345).

349 David Dayen 'The loans with 350% interest and a grip on America', *Guardian* (24 March 2013 London) <http://www.theguardian.com/money/2014/mar/23/payday-lending-interest-banks-advantage-congress>, accessed 4 September 2014. Indeed, at the time of writing, a Bill aimed at the limiting the federal regulation of payday loans by the Consumer Financial Protection Bureau where states have measures in place is being considered in the House of Representatives. See further: Barbara S. Mishkin 'DNC chair supporting bill to curb CFPB payday loan rulemaking authority' <https://www.cfpbmonitor.com/2016/03/10/dnc-chair-supporting-bill-to-curb-cfpb-payday-loan-rulemaking-authority>, accessed 4 April 2016.

consider the approach of US states in pursuit of protecting consumers from payday lenders.[350]

It is noteworthy from the outset that states adopt a variety of different approaches to the regulation of payday lending, as illustrated by the PEW Charitable Trusts, which carried out research across the US and provided information in relation to each state.[351] PEW grouped the states into three categories, ranging from so-called 'permissive' states such as South Dakota, where the only restriction placed upon lenders is a limit on the advanced amount of $500,[352] to 'restrictive' states, such as Georgia and North Carolina, which either outlaw payday loans in their entirety or 'have price caps low enough to eliminate payday lending in the state'.[353] Between the two ends of the spectrum there are a number of 'hybrid' states, which generally have some form of price cap that '[is] lower than most states, but still permit loans to be issued with triple-digit APRs'.[354] As such, when analysing the US approach, it is important to bear in mind that the lessons learned are from a particular state, or group of states, as opposed to the unified US approach to the regulation of payday lending.

One common characteristic of nearly all states that allow payday loans is that they place a limit on the maximum value of the payday loan. Some states utilise a cash amount to cap the amount that can be advanced[355] while others are limited by way of their monthly income: a payday lender is only allowed to lend up to a set percentage of that income.[356] The latter approach is preferable, not least due to the fact that it places a positive obligation upon the lender to determine the income of the prospective borrower, promoting the importance of the lender understanding the needs and limits of a consumer in payday loan transactions.

There is currently no cap on the amount that can be advanced in a payday loan transaction in the UK.[357] In fact, the FCA dismissed this idea as a mechanism

350 For an interactive state-by-state outline of the position of states in relation to payday loans, see: Pew Charitable Trusts 'Data visualisation: state payday loan regulation and usage rates' <http://www.pewtrusts.org/en/multimedia/data-visualizations/2014/state-payday-loan-regulation-and-usage-rates>, accessed 4 April 2016.

351 Ibid.

352 Ibid. There is no restriction placed on the cost of the payday loan in these states. See: Colin Morgan-Cross and Marieka Klawitter 'Effects of state payday loans and price caps and regulation' <http://depts.washington.edu/wcpc/sites/default/files/papers/Payday%20Lending%20Brief.pdf>, accessed 4 April 2016, 3.

353 Pew Charitable Trusts (n. 350).

354 Ibid.

355 These generally range from $500 to $1,000. See further: National Conference of State Legislatures 'Payday lending statutes' <http://www.ncsl.org/research/financial-services-and-commerce/payday-lending-state-statutes.aspx>, accessed 4 April 2016.

356 These are Washington, New Mexico, Illinois and Nevada. Ibid.

357 It is possible to obtain a loan of £2m in a high-cost, short-term loan transaction in the UK. See: Borro 'Personal asset loans' <http://www.borro.com/uk/personal-asset-loans>, accessed 4 April 2016. Interest rates at Borro can be up to 6.99 per cent per month, an APR of nearly 125 per cent.

for circumventing affordability assessments.[358] This argument can be accepted for caps of a specific value, as capping a loan at $500 does not identify whether that person can afford to repay the $500. However, utilising a percentage of a consumer's income has the potential to form an important criterion within an affordability assessment, better protecting consumers from borrowing more than they can afford to repay.

However, a key flaw with this approach is that even if the original loan amount is only 25 per cent of the borrower's income, if the consumer fails to repay the loan fees and charges that are added to the loan, this will raise the amount owed to what may be a less affordable level. Therefore, this salary-linked cap on the value to be advanced alone is not an effective method with which to protect the consumers of the market, arguably highlighted by the fact that these four states impose further cost caps.[359]

A further significant issue in relation to the UK payday loans market is the 'all or nothing' approach taken to the repayment of the loan. That is to say that, when coming to the end of the loan period, if the borrower can only afford to repay part of the loan, the full loan will be rolled over. In fact, part of the FCA's proposals to regulate the payday loan market is to prohibit the part-payment of a loan in order 'to ensure that firms only lend to borrowers who can afford it'.[360] By contrast, prior to the prohibition of payday lending in Arkansas, state law allowed the part-payment of a loan, permitting debtors to pay off debts 'bit by bit'.[361] While the part-payment of the loan will clearly involve the re-financing of the remainder, it is arguably preferable to allow this practice, thus extending the repayment period of a high-cost loan, as opposed to pricing consumers out of the regulated market and driving them to illicit sources of finance.

The majority of states that permit the offering of payday loans have some form of restriction on the cost of the loan, similar to the cost cap proposed by the FCA.[362] Research in the US can be used to support the assertion made in section 8.4 above: that capping the cost of payday loans could cause more harm to consumers than protection. For example, Oregon recently capped interest rates on payday loans at 36 per cent, with the impact of this appearing negative, as more people failed to make bill payments and increased the use of credit products that cost more than the fee of a payday loan.[363] As such, a payday loan would have been

358 Indeed, the cap is used as one criterion which the FCA states Florida uses to protect consumers, rather than impose affordability assessments: Financial Conduct Authority (n. 315) para 7.6.
359 National Conference of State Legislatures (n. 355).
360 Financial Conduct Authority (n. 315) para 7.28.
361 Megan Knize 'Payday lending in Louisiana, Mississippi and Arkansas: toward effective protections for borrowers' (2008–09) 69 *La L Rev* 317, 341.
362 See further: National Conference of State Legislatures (n. 355). A notable exception to this is South Dakota, which has no such limit.
363 Jonathan Zinman 'Restricting consumer credit access: Household survey evidence on effects around the Oregon rate cap' <http://ac.els-cdn.com/S0378426609002283/1-s2.0-S0378426609002283-main.pdf?_tid=394fc36c-37ac-11e4-8bda-00000aacb361&acdnat=1410217536_33b27f7cd83b3fb4969831cc0dc41149>, accessed 4 April 2016; Adam

a better, cheaper option for affected consumers. It is noteworthy that the FCA's proposed cap is much higher than the cap in Oregon and, in fact, there is no similar cap in the US nationwide.[364] Indeed, it will be interesting to see whether the FCA's impact assessment is accurate,[365] and whether their interest-rate cap will push consumers to using higher-priced alternatives.

While, as noted above, there is very little effective legislation at federal level to regulate the payday loans market, under federal law loans with interest rates above 36 per cent may not be provided to members of the military.[366] This is, in part, due to the fact that members of the military who utilised payday loans were deemed to be underperforming when on duty, due to the stress caused by payday loans.[367] While this cap has caused 'the near extinction of any form of payday lending to members of the military',[368] it has also highlighted the importance of more affordable credit products aimed at this particular target audience. Indeed, My Green Loans offers loans ranging from 6 per cent to 35 per cent specifically for military personnel.[369]

The lesson that the UK, and the indeed the FCA, can take from this is the need to facilitate the expansion of alternatives to payday lending to ensure that the impact of the cost cap is mitigated. This is arguably being achieved through the raising of the interest rate cap from 2 per cent to 3 per cent per month[370] on credit products provided by credit unions, enabling credit unions to 'lend to a wider spectrum of borrowers',[371] including those they consider to pose a higher risk of default.[372] Interestingly, a Bill aimed at the establishment of a credit union specifically for members of the British armed forces recently failed to go through

Summers 'Payday lending: protecting or harming consumers' <http://reason.org/files/payday_lending_regulation.pdf>, accessed 4 April 2016

364 States with interest-rate caps are in hundreds of per cent, whereas the FCA's proposed daily rate will give rise to an APR in excess of 1,000 per cent. Jennifer Rankin 'Watchdog plans cap on payday loan charges' *Guardian* (15 July 2014, London) <http://www.theguardian.com/business/2014/jul/15/fca-imposes-cap-on-payday-loans>, accessed 4 April 2016.

365 As outlined in section 8.4 above.

366 Morgan-Cross and Klawitter (n. 352) 2.

367 Scott Carell and Jonathan Zinman 'In harm's way? Payday loan access and military personnel performance' (28 May 2014) <http://rfs.oxfordjournals.org/content/early/2014/05/28/rfs.hhu034.full.pdf>, accessed 4 April 2016, 3–4.

368 Morgan-Cross and Klawitter (n. 352) 2.

369 My Green Loans 'Military loans' <http://www.mygreenloans.com/military-loans>, accessed 4 April 2016.

370 Giving rise to an APR of 42.6 per cent: Adam Uren 'Interest cap for credit unions lifted so they can compete with payday lenders for short-term borrowers' <http://www.thisismoney.co.uk/money/cardsloans/article-2340943/Interest-rate-cap-credit-union-raised.html>, accessed 4 April 2016.

371 HM Treasury 'Raising the maximum interest rate cap: response to consultation' available at <https://www.gov.uk/government/uploads/system/uploads/attachment_data/file/206091/raising_the_maximum_interest_rate_cap_response_to_consultation_110613.pdf>, accessed 4 April 2016, para 2.1.

372 Ibid. para 2.2.

parliament.[373] If revisited, the formation of the Armed Forces Credit Union, in addition to the ability of that union to charge an interest rate to cover the cost of a higher-risk loan, will arguably provide the members of the British military with a more affordable alternative, rather than having to turn to payday lenders in times of need.[374] However, a pilot scheme highlighted that, in order to break even on a payday loan, a credit union would need to charge an APR of 95 per cent.[375] Therefore, it is clear that the raising of the APR cap on credit products offered by credit unions to 42.6 per cent does not go far enough to render the expansion of the credit union market a viable alternative to payday lending for credit unions themselves.

It is also interesting to note the applicability of the criminal law to the payday lending market by states in the US. In a similar vein to those acting outside the old CCA74 licensing regime, there is the possibility of criminal prosecution for acting outside legal lending laws in some states. For example, in Georgia, persons offering loans that are less than $3,000 and interest rates in excess of 16 per cent[376] are liable for a $5,000 fine and a one-year prison sentence, for every loan agreement made that does not comply with state usury laws.[377] Over and above the infringement of the regulatory regime, there is the possibility that other criminal laws could be used to sanction payday lenders who deceive consumers. Indeed, commentators highlight the role of fraud in predatory lending[378] and that the Federal Trade Commission Act has been utilised 'to address predatory lending abuses when borrowers have been misled or deceived about their loan terms'.[379] Indeed, such deceptive practices have been highlighted in Ohio, where a 'survey

373 This is due to the Bill not being passed within the session See: Parliament UK 'Credit Unions Armed Forces Bill 2013–14' <http://services.parliament.uk/bills/2013-14/creditunionarmedforces.html>, accessed 4 April 2016.

374 It has been noted that payday lenders in the UK also target the British armed forces. See: Rosie Murray-West 'Legal loansharks are targeting the military, warns MP for Walthamstow Stella Creasy' *Telegraph* (11 November 2011) <http://www.telegraph.co.uk/finance/personalfinance/borrowing/8884178/Legal-loansharks-are-targeting-the-military-warns-MP-for-Walthamstow-Stella-Creas.html>, accessed 4 April 2016.

375 Damon Gibbons 'Tackling the high cost credit problem: the importance of real-time regulatory databases' <http://www.responsible-credit.org.uk/uimages/File/Tackling%20the%20high%20cost%20credit%20problem,%20importance%20of%20regulatory%20databases%20final.pdf>, accessed 4 April 2016, 70.

376 Georgia Code § 16–17–1(a)(1)(G).

377 Governor's Office of Consumer Protection 'Payday loans' <http://consumer.georgia.gov/consumer-topics/payday-loans>, accessed 4 April 2016.

378 Ryder (n. 335) 75. Ryder further notes that 'the link between predatory lending and fraud has [. . .] been recognized by the [US] judiciary'; see also: Ament (n. 330) 379.

379 US General Accounting Office 'Report to the Chairman and Ranking Minority Member, Special Committee on Aging, U.S. Senate: Consumer Protection Federal and Sate Agencies face challenged in combating predatory lending' <http://www.gao.gov/new.items/d04280.pdf>, accessed 4 April 2016, 33.

revealed . . . [lenders were] giving consumers false or misleading information about the cost of credit'.[380]

In the UK payday loans market, costs and terms of credit are generally presented to the consumer at the point of sale.[381] However, as noted in previous sections, Wonga have misled consumers during the debt-recovery process. Indeed, by sending letters from fake law firms, it has been noted that Wonga are potentially liable for fraud or impersonating a solicitor.[382] It will be interesting to see whether the FCA will be willing to take action in the criminal courts against Wonga. The FSA was renowned for the negligible use of its powers to prosecute for offences that did not arise from FSMA.[383] Indeed, such action could be what the FCA needs to take to show the payday loans market that it means business.[384]

Finally, once again the issue of resources raises its head. Indeed, it has been noted that 'many states do not have the resources to regulate and monitor the payday lending industry'.[385] In a similar vein to the OFT, payday lenders appear to be able to harm consumers due to the lack of funds that states have to enforce their regimes.[386] This underpins the argument that, in order to have an effective consumer protection regime that actively deters breach of that regime, a regulator needs not only strong powers but also resources to enforce those powers.

This section has considered the approach of the US, predominantly at state level, to the regulation of the payday lending market. It is clear that the approach of some states had influence on the proposals of the FCA in relation to their approach to the regulation of payday lending. Potential accessibility to credit issues linked to the FCA's cost caps are realised in the US, although the impact in the UK may not be quite as severe as the consequences of the caps have been on the other side of the Atlantic. The possible application of the criminal law presents an interesting opportunity to curtail the deceptive practices of payday lenders. However, given the history of UK regulators' lack of willingness to use

380 Johnson (n. 343) 32.

381 For example, see: Wonga 'Welcome to Wonga' available at <https://www.wonga.com>, accessed 23 March 2016.

382 As outlined by Dan Bunting 'The payday loan firm and the fake law firms – has Wonga committed a criminal offence? <http://www.legalweek.com/legal-week/blog-post/2352556/the-loan-firm-and-the-fake-law-firms-has-wonga-commited-a-criminal-offence>, accessed 4 April 2016.

383 The then Director of Enforcement and Financial Crime at the FSA, Tracey McDermott, suggested that this was not what the FSA was paid to do. Treasury Select Committee 'Fixing LIBOR: some preliminary findings' available at <http://www.publications.parliament.uk/pa/cm201213/cmselect/cmtreasy/481/48109.htm>, accessed 4 April 2016) para 201. The power of the regulator to prosecute offences outside of FSMA was confirmed in: *R v Rollins* [2010] *UKSC* 39 [20].

384 This term has been used to describe the civil action taken against Wonga by the FCA. See: Kieran Duignan 'Wonga – a sign that the Financial Conduct Authority mean business' <http://www.pannone.com/media-centre/blog/financial-conduct-authority-blog/wonga-—-sign-financial-conduct-authority-mean>, accessed 4 April 2016.

385 Knize (n. 361) 330.

386 Ibid.

their powers of criminal prosecution, it is unlikely that this will present a realistic tool in the pursuit of predatory, payday lender.

8.6 Conclusions and recommendations

This chapter sought to analyse whether customers of the consumer credit market will be better protected under the regulatory eye of the FCA, predominantly enforcing FSMA, than they were under the previous CCA74-backed OFT regime. Section 8.2 began by discussing the avenues of redress available to consumers who have been harmed by unscrupulous lenders. It was highlighted that the expense of litigation and the lack of clarity in the legal provisions of the CCA74, both before and after the amendments by the CCA06, acted as a barrier to recovery. With no similar consumer-led redress mechanism under FSMA, as enforced by the FCA, the unfair relationships provisions remain in force to allow consumers to take action against market actors or to be used as a defence when debts are being recovered by lenders through the courts. Therefore, it appears that there will be no significant improvement in the ability for unfairly treated consumers to obtain redress through litigation. On the other hand, the FOS will continue to be a fundamental mechanism for harmed consumers to gain compensation, not least for users of the high-cost credit market.

Section 8.3 continued with an analysis of the level of protection regime, which highlighted two key issues causing hindrance to the Office's performance as market regulator. First, a stark lack of funding limited the enforcement action that the OFT could take in pursuit of the protection of consumers, leaving many who had suffered unfair treatment at the hands of unscrupulous lenders without redress. Second, the OFT did not have a legal mechanism to take action on behalf of consumers that would see money put back into their pockets. As such, the OFT was plagued by both a lack of funding and inadequate legal powers with which to protect consumers. This led to approximately £450m worth of consumer harm going without compensation. By contrast, the FSA, backed by FSMA, had the power to impose redress requirements on authorised financial institutions that failed to treat their customers fairly. This ethos, and indeed legal power, has been brought forward to the FCA's regime, and such action has already been seen in the consumer credit context against Wonga in the 'fake lawyers' incident. This positive action will, arguably, assist the protection of consumers, not least due to the fact that they will not necessarily be required to engage expensive legal services in order to seek redress. Furthermore, the fact that the FSA can now directly fine those who mistreat credit market consumers and are in breach of the handbook will arguably deter market actors from treating consumers unfairly. There are, however, issues with the stringent nature of the authorisation regime, which appears to be taking too long in enabling new actors to enter the market, having a negative impact on competition and therefore a negative impact on consumers. Indeed, from an overarching regulatory point of view, there is a need to focus on ensuring that actions that are intended to secure an appropriate level of consumer protection do just that.

Specifically, in relation to high-cost, short-term lending, the FCA's proposed cost cap on payday lending may drive consumers to higher-cost credit products, or even illegitimate sources of credit, the latter coming with the added problem of a lack of any regulatory protection for borrowers. These issues are supported by reference to research into capping the cost of credit in the US and have also been recognised by the FCA. As such, where the FCA is clearly committed to ensuring that credit products offered to consumers are affordable, it is submitted that a cost cap is not the best option. Therefore, there is a need, following the introduction of the cost cap in January 2015, to periodically review the impact of the cap to ensure that it is not having a negative impact on the welfare of consumers. In order to protect consumers of the high-cost, short-term credit market, there are three clear alternative options the FCA could pursue.

First, rather than capping the cost of credit, and therefore pricing some consumers out of the market, the FCA could limit the amount of credit that can be advanced to a borrower, based on a percentage of their income. While this will clearly lead to some borrowers reaching the limit, and therefore being unable to access credit, this decision is based on the financial situation of the individual borrower, rather than what the FCA believes to be an affordable cost level for all consumers. Second, there is a need to ensure that lower-cost alternatives to payday loans are available. As noted above, this may be achieved through deregulation of the credit union market. However, more action needs to be taken to ensure that credit unions can offer such products, in a manner that both benefits the consumer and is profitable for their business. Third, there is a need to increase flexibility in the payday loans market with regards to the repayment of loans. The FCA proposes to prevent the refinancing of part of a loan. However, surely it is better to allow a borrower to repay part of the loan and fees, rather than default on the loan altogether. For example, under the FCA's proposed cost cap, there will be a limit of £24 per month, per £100 advanced. If a borrower enters into an agreement for £100 for one month, she will repay £124 at the end of that month. Under the proposed rules, should that borrower be unable to repay the loan for two months, she will incur a maximum £15 default charge, in addition to a further £24 in interest. Therefore, this loan would cost a total of £163 by the end of the two-month period. By contrast, if the government implemented legislation which required lenders to accept a minimum of 50 per cent of the loan amount, in addition to the interest charged that month, £74 in this example, with a view to the borrower repaying the other 50 per cent of the loan plus another month's worth of interest on the outstanding amount, the total paid back by the borrower over the two months would be £136; the second month's repayment being £62. This would encourage borrowers, should they only be in a position to repay part of their loan, to take positive action and make the lender aware of this, as opposed to feeling there is no option but to default on the loan. This 'bit by bit' approach arguably facilitates a more cooperative relationship between lender and borrower, in addition to helping a borrower to pay their debts. This is something that will appropriately protect consumers, while providing freedom for them to engage in credit products and allowing businesses to operate profitably in the provision of such products.

While lenders may despair at offering this level of flexibility, they need to be mindful of the characteristics of the consumer they are dealing with. Indeed, if they want to continue to profit by lending money to consumers who are struggling to make ends meet, lenders need to be prepared to make some sacrifices too. At the beginning of this chapter, reference was made to the modern Tallyman, the rent-to-own market, that is causing devastation to family finances due to tying them into multiple 'seductively' affordable repayment plans. Research for this chapter has yielded very little information with regard to how the FCA will tackle this problem. It is recommended that, once the FCA finishes enjoying the publicity of tackling a topical issue, it must focus on the hard-selling of everyday goods on extortionate finance packages which tie consumers into repayments, often for longer than the product actually lasts. The commission-driven sales tactics within this market are arguably as shameful as that of the PPI misselling scandal, and should be dealt with in a similar manner.

Finally, in Section 8.5, there was mention of the applicability of criminal sanctions to those engaged in predatory lending. As noted, the FCA could rely on existing laws to take action against lenders who act in a manner that amounts to the deception of the consumer. In this vein, more needs to be done to protect consumers from instances where the provision of financial products is done in a manner that exploits the consumers' vulnerable position. Therefore, the FCA should consider criminalising the gravest examples of exploitation, such as where affordability assessments are misrepresented to the consumer by the lender in order to obtain personal commission. This could arguably amount to the offence of fraud by false representation, or obtaining property by deception, but the FCA would need to grow stronger teeth than the FSA, and make use of the powers afforded to it. It is currently too soon to categorically state whether or not the FCA is achieving its objective in securing an appropriate level of protection for consumers. Its bigger teeth are certainly having a deterrent effect, causing those who feel they may fall foul of the regime to exit the market. However, it remains to be seen whether reduced market actors and more tightly regulated products will, on balance, positively affect customers.

9 Legislation and regulation in response to financial crime – pursuing ghosts?

Andrew Haynes

Introduction

The areas of financial crime where legislation and regulation have had the greatest potential impact on society at large are money laundering and market abuse/ insider dealing. Both are areas where large amounts of time and money have been spent developing laws and regulations that have had little impact on reducing the crimes concerned. This is in large measure due to the difficulty in prosecuting such crimes because in most cases it is difficult to prove that the offence has occurred at all. There seems to be no evidence in the evolution of the anti-laundering laws that those drafting them are cognisant of this fact. It is also worth remembering this when considering the anti-laundering laws and regulations as they represent a very significant intrusion into civil liberties.

In the case of market abuse, the whole basis of enforcement through disciplinary procedures and civil action was designed to reduce the difficulties of successfully bringing criminal prosecutions, but there has been limited impact. Very significant operating costs have been imposed on businesses, as with the anti-laundering laws, but the benefits remain very limited. Both sets of laws and regulations will therefore be examined to determine what they seek to achieve and to consider their utility.

Money laundering

The laws in this area really emerged[1] in the late 1980s[2] for political reasons. The drug trade had emerged as a significant criminal and political issue, and the approach of trying to combat the crime by focusing on importation, sales and consumption had shown limited effect. It was therefore believed that a focus on the proceeds of drug sales might be more productive. In addition, it was believed that it might weaken the drugs syndicates if their wealth-based protection

1 UN Convention on Psychotropic Drugs and Narcotic Substances 1988
2 See Drug Trafficking Offences Act 1986

could be stripped away. There was also an expectation that attacking the financial benefits of the crimes would provide a line of attack against the drug gang bosses.

It was an era when there was also a change in the criminological climate that led to a new focus in combating criminal gangs. It was believed that the traditional approach of trying to capture or kill the gang boss was ineffective.[3] Although it has provided the happy ending for most James Bond films, the reality is that the gang leader is quickly replaced by one of his former henchmen, who then proceeds to try to improve his 'business' operations so that he does not go the way of his predecessor.[4]

The Reagan- and Thatcher-driven economic environment of the 1980s also proved fertile ground for this approach. The proceeds of crime could be seized and used to finance initiatives to combat crime. The state's law enforcement costs would therefore be partly financed from the seizure of the proceeds of crime.

The laws in this area are largely the same throughout the world, as all states base their laws in this area on the relevant UN Conventions[5] and the Financial Action Task Force (FATF) Principles. There are key differences, though. Some nations, such as the United States and Australia, have a bulk-transaction reporting system as well as a suspicion-based one, but most nations do not. The UK system is found in the Proceeds of Crime Act 2002, which creates laundering offences in sections 327 to 339. This Act has been amended by the Serious Organised Crime and Police Act 2005 and the Serious Crimes Act 2015. In addition, there are two other relevant statutes: the Terrorism Act 2000 (TA) and the Anti-terrorism, Crime and Security Act 2001, which together with the Terrorism (United Nations) Order 2001[6] determine the position with relation to funds that are suspected of being used to further the ends of terrorism. To this has been added the Money Laundering Regulations 2007, a statutory instrument which has seen a number of updates and additions.

Core offences

The Proceeds of Crime Act 2002 has created three core offences: concealing (etc.) the proceeds of crime;[7] entering into or becoming concerned in an arrangement which that person knows, or suspects, facilitates the retention, use or control

3 It did, however, work well with the Medellin drug cartels in Colombia, where the bodyguards replaced the arrested bosses and proved considerably less adept than their predecessors, losing much of the cocaine market to the Cali cartels.

4 Indeed, this has given rise to a belief that the optimal way of improving the effectiveness of a large criminal operation is to arrest or kill its leader every 18 months, as that is the time frame in which any operational improvements tend to be made.

5 In particular, the UN Convention of Narcotic Drugs and Psychotropic Substances 1988 and the UN Transnational Organised Crime Convention 2000.

6 SI 2001/3365

7 S.327 Proceeds of Crime Act 2002

or criminal property;[8] and, finally, acquiring, using or having possession of criminal property.[9] These are now considered in turn, along with the equivalent parts of the statute relating to terrorist finance.

It is an offence under s.327 to conceal, disguise, convert, transfer or remove criminal property from the jurisdiction. This extends to concealing (etc.) its nature, source, location, disposition, movement, ownership or any rights in relation to it. There are defences, in as much that it is not an offence if the person concerned has made a protected disclosure under s.338, usually to the National Crimes Agency (the NCA), and has been given consent to continue to act; likewise if s/he was going to make such a disclosure but there was 'a reasonable excuse' for not doing so. There is, unfortunately, a lack of clarity in that no definition has been provided to determine what a 'reasonable excuse' is, nor is there yet any relevant case law to assist. Finally, there is a third defence, where the act that has been done consists of carrying out a function s/he has in relation to enforcing any provision of the Proceeds of Crime Act 2002 or of any other statute relating to criminal conduct or benefiting therefrom. 'Criminal property' is defined by s.340(3) as being someone's benefit from criminal conduct where the alleged offender knows or suspects that it represents such a benefit. The recent case of *R v Ogden and others*[10] suggests that the Court of Appeal does not see any hidden complexities in the section. There is an equivalent provision in s.16(2) TA of being in possession of money, intending, or having reasonable cause to suspect, that it may be used for the purposes of terrorism.

It is an offence under s.328 to enter into, or become concerned in an arrangement which that person knows, or suspects, facilitates the retention, use or control of criminal property.[11] Since the case of *Bowman v Fels*[12] it has been clear that an 'arrangement' will cover the relationship between professionals and their clients. This case arose as a result of a property dispute between ex-cohabitees. Shortly before a hearing in the County Court, the solicitor for one party submitted a suspicious transaction report concerning the other party. The legal adviser to that party then requested an adjournment because 'appropriate consent' was not anticipated. The Law Society intervened, seeking clarification on the meaning of 'arrangements' under s.328 Proceeds of Crime Act in the context of solicitors' privilege. The Bar Council and the NCIS[13] (the earliest forerunners of the NCA) were given permission to intervene.

8 S.328 Proceeds of Crime Act 2002

9 S.329 Proceeds of Crime Act 2002

10 *R v Ogden (Neil), Logan, Wilson, Martin, Atkinson, Brough and Ogden (Stephen)* [2016] EWCA Crim 6. For discussion of the case, see *Arch Rev* 2016, vol. 2, issue 2.

11 There are equivalent offences relating to terrorism in sections 19 and 20 of the Terrorism Act 2000.

12 (2005) EWCA CiV 225–6

13 National Criminal Intelligence Service

The original claim was settled out of court, but the resulting Court of Appeal decision arose from the court wishing to provide clarification on how the Proceeds of Crime Act impacted on litigation. The case determined that the following are immune from the section: litigation files, cases where injunctions are being sought, freezing orders and dividing assets in accordance with a judgment or settlement even where those assets are criminal property. The decision did not specifically refer to alternative dispute resolution arrangements, which is unfortunate as this was an obvious example of a case where a detailed *obiter* would have been of assistance. The most rational conclusion would be that they are caught by the judgment as well.

The effect of this is that the privilege exception means that litigation files are not to be regarded as 'arrangements' under s.328. There would be an exception to this where the privilege was being abused by a client; for example, because false litigation was taking place. This might occur where one party had control over two companies, but the ownership was not originally apparent to the legal advisers. A course of action may exist where litigation was commenced by one company against the other so that one party could later settle out of court, and this arrangement might be used as a vehicle for one party laundering to the other.

However, any property dealt with after the judgment could still be criminal property under s.340(3) (an interpretation section). As a result, a suspicious transaction report would have to be made at that stage. There was no analysis by the court of the situation regarding advice as opposed to litigation privilege, but it is rational to assume that it is also not overridden by the Act.

There is a degree of irrationality in this decision, as privilege lasts indefinitely, yet the Court of Appeal has determined that as far as making reports to the NCA are concerned, it evaporates as soon as any property disposition ordered by the judge has been put in place. It is logical to see this as an attempt by the judges to head off the risk of the government pushing through changes to the law to override the privilege exception. There are three defences which are the same as those for s.327.

The courts have not shown any appetite to interpret the section widely. In *R v Geary*,[14] the Court of Appeal held that it is not a breach of s.328 where the assets involved in the transaction are lawful. The facts were that a man who was not getting on well with his wife, and who feared divorce, asked a friend to hold some of his money so that it would not be involved in any later property dispute as part of a divorce case. At the time no divorce proceedings had been instigated and it later transpired that his wife was not contemplating divorce. As a consequence, the court held that the party holding the money was not in possession of funds that were the proceeds of crime. The 'arrangement', that the man's friend would hold and return money, could not be separated from the lawfulness of the money itself. The case would undoubtedly have gone the other way if a divorce hearing

14 30 July 2010

was taking place, as then the money would have been transferred to obstruct the course of justice.

Dare v Crown Prosecution Service[15] continued this restrictive approach. The case involved the proposed sale of a car from a dealer for £800 to Mr Dare. He was aware that the proposed vendor had a past record of selling stolen cars, but nonetheless test-drove the car and then asked for a price reduction and time to raise the finance to buy it. In the end no sale occurred, though Mr Dare's plan had been to buy it and sell it on at a profit. He was originally found guilty of entering into an arrangement under s.328(1) of the Proceeds of Crime Act 2002 on the basis that the car was stolen and thus criminal property, and that the second meeting between the parties amounted to an 'arrangement' for the purposes of the section. Therefore, as he knew or at least had grounds to suppose that it was stolen, and he intended to sell it on for profit, it was argued that he was facilitating the acquisition of criminal property by whoever bought the car from him. The High Court overturned the conviction on the grounds that found this interpretation of s.328 was too wide. It was pointed out that s.328 says that the arrangement must be one which the defendant knows or suspects 'facilitates' the acquisition of criminal property by another, not 'will facilitate'. Therefore, no 'arrangement' had taken place and the conviction was overturned. The logic was continued by the Supreme Court in the case of *R v GH.*[16] The facts were that G and H had both opened bank accounts for X to utilise for funds he was to receive later from advertising fictional insurance policies on five websites. G and H's defence to a charge under s.328 was that no fraud had occurred at the time they opened the accounts, and therefore there was no criminal property for them to have entered into an 'arrangement' with. The Supreme Court determined that it was clear that the property described in s.328 (and for that matter ss.327 and 329 as well) had to be criminal property at the time of the alleged offence. Any alternative approach would make matters extremely difficult for banks and financial services firms. This continued the logic which had been seen in earlier cases,[17] where it had been held that the alternative would mean any case involving stolen goods with a view to resale would also amount to an offence under s.328 (1).[18]

S.329 of the POCA provides the third of the three main offences, namely that it is an offence for someone to acquire, use or have possession of criminal property.[19] While obviously aimed at criminals who receive stolen property from others, it also poses a threat to professionals such as solicitors, accountants and

15 [2012] EWCA Crim 1925, [2012] EWHC 2074 (Admin) and [2012] Lloyd's Rep FC 718

16 [2015] 1 WLR 2126

17 See, for example, *R v Akhtar*, *R v Amir* [2011] EWCA Crim 146.

18 For further discussion of this, see *Crim L R* 2013, 5, 413–414 and *C L & J* 2012, 176 (30), 451.

19 There is a roughly equivalent provision in s.15(2) TA, which states that it is an offence to receive money or other property with the intention that it be used, or where there is reasonable cause to believe it will be used, for the purposes of terrorism.

stockbrokers, as well as banks and financial institutions who will all receive money from clients. The same defences are available to this section as also apply to ss.327 and 328. There is also a fourth, namely where the person acquiring, using or having possession obtained the property for adequate consideration. This is to protect traders who buy goods and are not therefore under a duty to question the source of the money. It would not extend to a situation where the goods or services were being knowingly provided to assist in the carrying out of a crime, or where there was suspicion.

The first useful case on this section was *R v Hogan*,[20] where the person charged under s.329 had purchased some scaffolding from his former employers in cash for about one-sixth of its commercial value, without a receipt. A key issue that arose was whether he had paid 'adequate consideration'. It was determined by the court that the adequacy of the consideration was an objective question of fact to be decided by a jury. The court added that the issue of whether the consideration was adequate was separate from the defendant's state of mind and this necessitated a second test. S.329(2)(c) determined that where the court had concluded that adequate consideration had been given for the acquisition of property, no offence would be exist under this Act even if the offender had known that the property had been stolen. Other criminal offences might have been committed, but they are irrelevant for the purposes of an analysis of the money-laundering laws.

Reporting requirements

The reporting requirement under s.330 arises when someone has reasonable grounds for knowing or suspecting that someone else is engaged in money laundering, where that knowledge or suspicion came into that person's possession in the course of their business in the regulated sector. This last element is not entirely logical. It may well be the case that a professional acting for a client may become suspicious because of information they received socially, or at least outside the parameters of their work environment, which makes the professional activity being carried out seem suspicious in the light of that knowledge. The disclosure should be made to the firm's money-laundering reporting officer and consist of details of the person's identity, where the laundered property is and any other information on which this knowledge is based.

There is a defence[21] where the person concerned has a reasonable excuse for not making the required disclosure, or where he is a professional legal adviser and knows the relevant information because of information coming into his hands in privileged circumstances. This last point is discussed above under s.328.[22] There

20 [2007] EWHC (Admin) 978
21 S.330(6) Proceeds of Crime Act 2002
22 See *Bowman v Fels* (2005) EWCA CiV 225–226.

is a further defence, which is useful for newer members of staff and applies where they have not been provided with money-laundering training by their employer, and that person does not know or suspect that the client is engaged in money laundering as a result of their ensuing ignorance. This will then be presumed to be the cause of the former, if the person concerned has not realised the transaction is suspicious.

The money-laundering reporting officer is expected not simply to forward internal suspicious transaction reporting forms to the NCA, but to bring a degree of value added to the process and to make this disclosure as soon as practicable after they first know or suspect that laundering is taking place, and this should be done in the prescribed format.[23] In institutions such as large banks, there are going to be a large number of internal reports that are likely to be rejected by the laundering officer (or, in a large firm, the laundering department), because of the limited contact with customers and the limited training and knowledge of front-desk staff. On the other hand, a solicitor or accountant has a much better chance of examining the client and the surrounding financial circumstances, is generally better educated and is better able to make an assessment, and so it should be expected that a much higher percentage of internal reports would be passed on by the laundering reporting officer.[24]

Oddly, ss.331 and 332 apply whether the transaction has respectively taken place in or outside the 'regulated sector' – that is, the range of business activities covered by the Money Laundering Regulations 2007 (as amended).[25] The sections are worded almost identically and there seems no obvious reason why they could not have been combined with the reporting requirement being applicable 'regardless of whether or not the reporting body is in the regulated sector'.

There is a defence if the person who should have made a report has a 'reasonable excuse'[26] for not doing so. Unfortunately, this is not defined and it would be wise to interpret it narrowly, pending judicial guidance through future case law.

There is also a tipping-off offence under s.333A,[27] where someone is involved in the regulated sector and they know or suspect that a report to the NCA or other appropriate person along the lines set out above has been made, and that person then makes a disclosure which is likely to prejudice an investigation. There is a rather limited defence that applies where the person responsible can show that they did not know or suspect that the disclosure was likely to be prejudicial. This would almost never be applicable. There is a second defence that applies where the disclosure is made in carrying out a function that person has relating to the enforcement of the Proceeds of Crime Act

23 S.338 Proceeds of Crime Act 2002

24 For a useful set of guidelines, see NCA, 'Submitting a suspicious activity report within the regulated sector.' Guidance Note, February 2015.

25 Equivalent provisions are found in s.21 TA.

26 S.331(6) Proceeds of Crime Act 2002

27 Inserted by SI 2007/3398 Sch. 2, para. 4

2002 or a related statute. Finally, there is a third defence of legal privilege, which applies where information needs to be released as part of constructing a legal defence.

Consent to act

Once a report has been made, the reporting party can only continue acting where the NCA has given consent. Consent to act is automatic where seven days have passed without a response from the NCA. If they communicate that they wish to examine the matter, the reporting firm cannot act until the NCA gives consent or until a further 31 days have elapsed.[28] This is not terribly practical, as in many instances the delay in dealing with a transaction will effectively tip off the client that a suspicious transaction report has been made, though this would obviously not amount to a breach of s.333.

Not surprisingly, it is an offence if someone falsifies, conceals or disposes of documents which are likely to prejudice an investigation or civil recovery action. There is a defence to this, where the person does not know or suspect that this is likely to prejudice such an investigation. Again, the person concerned is legally protected where the action is required by a relevant statute or s/he is a professional legal adviser giving advice in relation to legal proceedings. In either situation, it is difficult to see situations arising where s.342 would be broken in the first place if the person was acting honestly. There is another defence, where the person destroying documents does not know or suspect that they are relevant to an investigation or does not intend to conceal any facts contained in the documents.[29]

The potential consequences for breaching these provisions are serious. Breach of ss.327–329 on summary conviction can lead to a sentence of up to six months in prison and/or a fine. As the three main predicate offences, they have the potential to result in an indictment and this raises the sentence to a maximum of 14 years and/or a fine. A conviction under ss.330–333, breach of the law on appropriate consent by a money-laundering reporting officer and pre-judicing an investigation are all liable for up to six months in prison and/or a fine on summary conviction. On indictment this rises to five years and/or a fine.[30] The penalties for non-compliance with the provisions of the TA are a fine or up to six months' imprisonment on summary conviction, and a fine or up to 14 years on indictment.[31]

28 S.335(3)–(6) Proceeds of Crime Act 2002
29 S.342 Proceeds of Crime Act 2002
30 S.334 and s.336(6) Proceeds of Crime Act 2002
31 S.22 TA 2000

The Money Laundering Regulations 2007 (as amended)[32]

The laundering requirements here are imposed on: all banking and financial institutions, credit institutions, independent legal professionals (financial and real property transactions); auditors, insolvency practitioners, external accountants and tax advisers; trust or company service providers; estate agents; high value dealers and casinos; and a range of others who handle money or high value goods.

They also require that the identity of a new client be checked in any of the following situations: the creation of a business relationship; the carrying out of an occasional transaction; suspicion of money laundering or terrorist financing; and doubts being raised as to the documents obtained for the purposes of identification. The key thing is that it is carried out at the first reasonably possible time. While normally it should be done at the outset, there is some flexibility – for example, where the nature of the contact with the client makes it impractical. If the person dealing with the financial institution appears to be an agent, their identity must be checked as well as that of the principal.

Due diligence

The two-stage identity checking is well known and consists of an official document with a photo, such as a passport, and a second document with a home address. If the client is high-risk, it is appropriate to get additional information. In recent years, computer software has become available that supposedly checks on a client's identity and background. This operates with 'crawler' systems that check through the web for evidence of that person. This needs viewing with some circumspection, however, as it is easy enough for someone to plant such information on websites to await such a check. As seen, there are limits on when this is necessary and, in the case of solicitors, it only needs carrying out in 'financial or real property transactions', but in practice it is safest for it to be carried out with all new clients, because if this is not done when the new client crosses the threshold, it is unlikely it will be checked later on.

Corporate clients pose a more complex problem, as the only evidence of the company or limited liability partnership, and the people behind it, will be the information registered at Companies House, or the overseas equivalent. Company searches can provide data, but Companies House does not run security checks, so the information on its records should be viewed with caution if there are any grounds for concern. The position regarding corporate groups remains vague, but the safest approach is to determine whether the company is part of a corporate group and, if so, to determine the corporate family tree. It would seem sensible

32 As amended by the Money Laundering Regulations 2007/2298, 2007/3299 and 2012/2298

to then check on the ultimate holding company, as it is the people behind this who may be the real clients. Directors must be checked, as must 'controllers' (see below).

Enhanced customer due diligence and ongoing monitoring should be applied in any situation which presents a higher risk of money laundering or terrorist financing – for example, where the customer has not been physically present for identification purposes, or where unexpectedly large amounts of money are involved. Such extra checks could include ensuring there are additional identity-checking documents; supplementary measures to verify or certify the documents supplied; and that the first payment is carried out through an account opened in the customer's name with a credit institution.

Politically exposed persons

If a client is an individual who is or has been entrusted with certain prominent public functions, the person acting for them must be satisfied that the funds have an honest source. The range of people to whom this rule applies are: heads of state, heads of government, ministers and deputy or assistant ministers; members of parliament (and in federal states this probably includes regional parliaments); members of supreme or constitutional courts or of other high-level judicial bodies whose decisions are not generally subject to further appeal; members of courts of auditors or of the boards of central banks; ambassadors, chargés d'affaires and high-ranking officers in the armed forces (although 'high-ranking' is not defined); and members of the administrative, management or supervisory bodies of state-owned enterprises.

The category also extends to immediate family members, including spouses, partners, including anyone who would be regarded by their national law as effectively being a spouse, children (and this does not appear to be limited to legitimate children) and their spouses or partners, parents and, finally, persons known to be close associates, including anyone who is known to have joint beneficial ownership of a legal entity or legal arrangement, or any other close business relations with the person concerned, and anyone who has sole 'beneficial ownership' of a legal entity or legal arrangement which is known to have been set up for the benefit of the person concerned.

It needs to be said that this is not terribly realistic. How is a small or medium-sized firm expected to determine that their client is, for example, the partner of an illegitimate child of a member of the Indian regional parliament of Uttar Pradesh? Larger firms will potentially have the resources to check on the more prominent of the people on this list, but just as it was always possible for criminals to produce false documents indicating they are a different person with the same name, presuming they are using their real name in the first place, clients of a criminal disposition can do the twenty-first-century equivalent as well, which is to create a false audit trail of a fictional existence on the internet, as discussed above.

Beneficial owners

There is also a requirement that the 'beneficial owner' of funds be checked, and, in the case of a body corporate, this means anyone who directly or indirectly owns or controls more than 25 per cent of the shares or voting rights in the company, limited partnership or partnership. The value of this is questionable, as criminals will simply hold a lower percentage or use nominees to hold the shares or interest. In the case of a trust, checks must be carried out on anyone who is entitled to a specified interest in at least 25 per cent of the capital of the trust property and anyone who has control over the trust.

Know your client and ongoing monitoring

Professionals must carry out ongoing monitoring of clients, which is taken to mean the scrutinising of transactions undertaken throughout the course of the relationship including, where appropriate, the source of funds, to ensure that the transactions are consistent with the relevant person's knowledge of the customer, his business and risk profile. This is easy for solicitor and accountants acting on an ongoing basis, but for some professionals this may not be easy to achieve. Commercial banks, for example, find it much more difficult to monitor client activity beyond software monitoring of accounts. Follow-up contact by phone or in person can be made when unexpectedly large amounts show up in an account, but it is of limited effectiveness as a process.

Systems to prevent money laundering

All relevant personnel must have appropriate training, so that they are capable of determining whether a transaction is suspicious. It is also necessary for such people to have a reasonable knowledge of the relevant law. As already discussed, the Proceeds of Crime Act 2002 requires that a suspicious transaction report be made as soon as possible once a person acting in the course of their trade, profession or business knows or suspects[33] that someone is engaged in laundering. Unfortunately, the Act gives no guidance on what this state of mind means. The test seems to be an amalgam of objective and subjective, though in practice it is going to be determined by what a judge or magistrate deems to amount to this mental state.

The relevant legal definition of suspicion in this context was provided by Longmore LJ in *K Ltd v NatWest Bank*.[34] The person must 'think there is a possibility, which is more than fanciful, that the relevant facts exist. This is subject to the further requirement that the suspicion so formed should be of a settled nature.' This is a disturbingly wide basis on which professionals should be acting

33 There is an equivalent provision in s.19(1)(a) TA relating to terrorist funds.
34 [2006] EWCA Civ 1039

as unpaid state spies on their client base. In Switzerland, by way of comparison, banks are not required to report tax evasion, as it is not a crime there, nor are they required to report tax fraud, which is, unless the money is known to have come from an illegal source! The Swiss approach may involve far fewer reports being made, but the vast majority will be of genuine use to the authorities. In the EU as a whole, there seems to be a general trajectory towards progressively getting the widest range of people to make the maximum number of reports, despite the absence of any evidence that this approach is fruitful in terms of catching criminals.[35] Given that the Home Office's aim in creating a laundering reporting system was to provide a disincentive to crime by reducing its profit by reducing the pool of money available to finance future illegal activity, one can hardly regard the current system as a success.

Reporting procedures

It is necessary for firms to have in place systems whereby suspicious transactions are reported to the money-laundering reporting officer, officially termed the 'nominated officer'.[36] That person has the responsibility of determining whether an internal report warrants being passed on to the NCA. In instances where there is minor cause for concern that falls short of suspicion, and where the money-laundering reporting officer does not feel there is sufficient evidence to make a suspicious transaction report, best procedure is to make a file note of the reasons for concern. In due course, there may be an accumulation of minor issues that are felt to amount to suspicion, which can then lead to a report being made to the NCA.

Once a suspicious transaction report has been submitted, the NCA will then determine whether the reporting party can continue with the transaction. The NCA sometimes prefers the transaction to continue to facilitate its observation. The most useful case on reporting was *Squirrel Ltd v National Westminster Bank Ltd and HM Customs (Intervener)*,[37] where the High Court heard a request for the unfreezing of a bank account where NatWest had submitted a suspicious transaction report regarding a client, Squirrel Ltd, under s.328 Proceeds of Crime Act 2002. Having done so, the bank then blocked the account but felt it could not explain the reasons to the account holder because of the tipping-off provision in s.333. The Court determined that the bank had acted as required by law as all the law required of them was to make a report when they had reasonable grounds for suspicion. They were not required to become a detective agency. This does highlight a gap in the relevant law. What if Squirrel Ltd had needed funds to complete a property purchase or a business transaction? They could have lost a

35 For a useful discussion, see Chaikin, D. 'How effective are suspicious transaction reporting systems?' *JMLC* 2009 vol. 12, issue 3, pp. 238–253.
36 S.338(5) Proceeds of Crime Act 2002
37 (2005) EWHC 664

considerable amount of money through no fault of their own, and yet had no right to recompense.

Record keeping

The identity records must be retained for five years, commencing on the date when the business relationship ends, though given the requirements of the Limitation Act 1980,[38] firms in England and Wales will normally hold them for at least six.

Market abuse/insider dealing

The insider dealing and market abuse issues that the law and Financial Conduct Authority (FCA) regulations are seeking to deal with here are known to be disturbingly common. One analysis sponsored by the then Financial Services Authority estimated that approximately 28.9 per cent of trading announcements were preceded by insider dealing, as were 21.7 per cent of takeovers.[39] This was despite the fact that insider dealing, releasing insider information and encouraging others to carry out insider dealing have all been criminal offences since 1980. Between then and the creation of the civil offence of market abuse being created in 2003 there was an average of one successful criminal prosecution a year.

Insider dealing as a criminal offence

This is very similar to the civil offence of insider dealing, but the criminal offence is slightly narrower in that it does not extend to related derivative contracts and off-market transactions. In addition, there is no statutory criminal offence of attempting to carry out insider dealing. It is highly unlikely that someone would face both criminal proceedings under the Criminal Justice Act and a market abuse action under the Financial Services and Markets Act 2000. It would not fall the wrong side of the double jeopardy rule, as the market abuse action would be civil, but the FSA (as they then were) recognised the unsatisfactory nature of permitting something that is so close to double jeopardy, and announced that they would not bring proceedings if a criminal prosecution were taking place. It has to be said that the utilisation of criminal law has been so unsuccessful that it was the primary reason for the development of the civil offence discussed above. There have been few successful criminal prosecutions since insider dealing became a statutory criminal offence in 1980, and hardly any of these resulted in custodial sentences. The previous law, that of conspiracy to defraud, still exists, but has proved even less useful.[40]

38 S.5 Limitation Act 1980
39 Dublow, B. and Monteiro, N. 'FSA publishes measure of scale of market abuse.' March 2005
40 *R v de Berenger* (1814) 105 ER 536

The nature of the offences in the Criminal Justice Act 1993

There are three potential offences:

1) Insider dealing, which is committed where a party who is able to access unpublished price-sensitive information relating to a company, and which is likely to affect the price of the securities concerned,[41] then deals in those securities. The information does need not to have been accessed directly.
2) Encouraging others to deal, which occurs where the person doing the encouraging is an insider and unpublished price-sensitive information is involved.[42] It is sufficient that encouragement takes place; a transaction need not actually occur, though in practice cases have all related to situations where it has.
3) Disclosure, which consists of someone disclosing inside information outside the proper performance of their duties.[43] It is not necessary for a conviction for there to be evidence that the party disclosing intended it to be acted upon, as, were this not the case, successful prosecutions would be almost impossible.

What, then, is an 'insider'? Such a person is defined as someone who has inside information from an inside source, knowing this is the case.[44] The person concerned will need to have acquired the information as a result of being an employee, a director or a shareholder of an issuer of securities. It is not necessary for the crime to relate to shares in that company, though in practice it usually does. However, if the 'insider' is a professional adviser, such as an investment banker or external legal adviser or someone doing unrelated work for the firm on a temporary basis, such as a contractor, the company whose securities are involved is unlikely to be the direct employer. The law will apply to them in any event. The key issue is that the access to the information concerned should have arisen as a result of that person's employment, office or profession.

There are defences to protect those who work as analysts. Information is not regarded as inside information if it can be either readily acquired by those likely to deal in securities or acquired by those exercising due diligence.[45] However, the possibility of interpreting the description of information being accessed by virtue of the insider's employment excludes situations where an expert accesses information by virtue of his employment. There is no direct case on the point, but either *Grey v Pearson*[46] (golden rule) or *Heydon's Case*[47] (mischief rule) would assist.

41 S.52(1) and (3) Criminal Justice Act 1993
42 S.52(2)(a) Criminal Justice Act 1993
43 S.52(2)(b) Criminal Justice Act 1993
44 S.57 Criminal Justice Act 1993
45 S.58 Criminal Justice Act 1993
46 (1857) 6 HL Cas 61
47 (1584) 3 Co Rep 74

Secondary insiders are also caught, as are parties they pass the information on to, though this does not extend to making the information public. There is no requirement for the secondary insider to have taken any active steps to acquire the information. It is sufficient that they know that it was inside information and was obtained from an inside source, and that they then acted on it.

'Inside information' is 'specific information' that relates either to specific securities or a specific issuer of securities. If made public, the information should have a 'significant effect' on the price of any securities, though it does not need to be precise. The key issue is that it must not be publicly available. S.58 provides guidance on this. The first arises where information is published in accordance with the rules of a regulated market to inform investors and their advisers and is thus public information, where the information is set out in public records, where the information can already be readily acquired or where it can only be accessed by payment. Information can also be treated as publicly available even though it can only be worked out by experts or analysts, communication has only been to a section of the public, the information can only be found by observation, where it can only be accessed by payment and finally where the information is published abroad.

Securities

Securities have an idiosyncratic definition peculiar to the Criminal Justice Act.[48] They consist of shares and debt securities, which is widely defined and includes bonds, debentures and certificates of deposit. It also covers warrants, depositary receipts and derivative contracts (futures, options and contracts for differences). The securities concerned must either be listed on an official exchange of a State within the European Economic Area, or be admitted to dealing on, or have their price quoted on a regulated market.

Dealing

A person deals in securities if he acquires or disposes of the securities or procures an acquisition of the securities by another person.[49] It was determined in one case[50] that 'procure' means 'to produce by endeavour'. In none of these cases need the insider be proven to have benefited from the deal, though in practice this is obviously the normal motive.

48 See Sch. 2, Criminal Justice Act 1993
49 S.55 Criminal Justice Act 1993
50 AG's Reference (No. 1) of [175] QB 773

Defences

The defences fall into the categories of general and specific. The general defences are that the accused did not expect to make a profit or avoid a loss[51] – they took a position regarding the investment for another reason, such as buying shares as part of a takeover; where the accused reasonably believed that the information concerned was widely distributed enough to avoid prejudicing the interests of anyone else involved in the deal;[52] and where the accused can show that they would have entered into the arrangement in any event.[53] In the event of the accused being charged with disclosing price-sensitive information, the defences are that the accused did not expect anyone to deal in securities as a result of his disclosure;[54] or that the accused did not expect anyone to deal at a profit or avoid a loss as a result.[55]

The specific defences that apply are that market makers and dealers can plead that they were acting in good faith in the course of their business,[56] where it was market information and it was reasonable of the accused to act as they did. The third specific defence applies when it was market information which the insider acquired as a result of being involved in buying or selling securities.[57] Finally, the insider has a defence if they can show that they acted in line with the FCA's Price Stabilisation Rules.[58]

Penalties

The penalty on summary conviction is a maximum fine of £5,000 or imprisonment of up to six months, or both;[59] on indictment, an unlimited fine or imprisonment of up to seven years, or both.[60] Directors may be disqualified, as the crime is one which shows sufficient connection with corporate management.[61] Any profits may also potentially be seized under the Proceeds of Crime Act 2002. This permits[62] the Crown Court to order confiscation where two conditions are satisfied. The first is that the defendant has been convicted by the Crown Court, or committed to the Crown Court for sentencing, and the second is the

51 S.53(6) Criminal Justice Act 1993
52 S.53(1)(b), (2)(b) Criminal Justice Act 1993
53 S.53(1)(c), (2)(c) Criminal Justice Act 1993
54 S.53(3)(a) Criminal Justice Act 1993
55 S.53(3)(b) Criminal Justice Act 1993
56 Sch. 1, paras 1 and 2, Criminal Justice Act 1993. A market maker is someone who holds themselves out as operating in compliance with the rules of a regulated exchange, or under those of a prescribed market or Treasury-approved organisation.
57 Sch. 1, para. 3, Criminal Justice Act 1993
58 Sch. 1, para. 5, Criminal Justice Act 1993
59 S.61(1)(a) Criminal Justice Act 1993
60 S.61(1)(b) Criminal Justice Act 1993
61 *R v Goodman* [1994] 1 BCLC 349
62 S.6 Proceeds of Crime Act 2002

prosecutor or the Director of the NCA has asked the court to proceed under s.6 of the Proceeds of Crime Act 2002. Factors the Court will take into account are whether the defendant had a criminal lifestyle and whether s/he benefited from this. If the Court decides to proceed, they must then decide on the recoverable amount and make a confiscation order to that level. There is a statutory requirement[63] that the Court should take into account whether a victim of the conduct intends to start proceedings against the defendant, because if this is the case, a confiscation order should not be used if it would render the defendant incapable of compensating the victim.

It is worth adding that for the courts to have jurisdiction, the defendant must either have been within the United Kingdom when the act concerned was committed or the market where the investment was traded must be in the United Kingdom. Alternatively, the crime must have involved an intermediary who was situated in the United Kingdom; or, either the disclosure must have been made by the accused when they were situated in the United Kingdom, or the recipient of the information or of the encouragement to deal must have been situated in the United Kingdom.

Civil law issues other than the market abuse regime

Before moving on to market abuse, it is worth briefly mentioning that civil law issues can arise in the context of criminal insider dealing cases. For example, as a consequence of a party who has committed an insider dealing offence owing a fiduciary duty, where he is held to have acted as a constructive trustee, then any profit wrongly made will potentially belong to the company of which he is a director.[64] The courts have been quite imaginative in applying this principle, as can be seen from the cases of *Boardman v Phipps*,[65] *AG for Hong Kong v Reid*[66] and *Nanus Asia Co Inc v Standard Chartered Bank*,[67] where confidential information obtained in breach of an employee's duty of fidelity gave rise to a constructive trust over profits resulting from its use. If a third party in receipt of information should realise that the information was given to them in breach of a fiduciary duty, then the same principle could potentially apply. If the information is given in breach of confidence, then an action will lie on that basis and this will extend to employees as well as directors.

Beyond this, directors do not normally have a fiduciary obligation to the company or shareholders, but *Coleman v Myers*[68] suggests that they can acquire one where they are dominant directors in a small company. They must also declare

63 S.6(6) Proceeds of Crime Act 2002
64 *Walsh v Deloitte and Touche* [2001] UKPC 58
65 [1967] 2 AC 46, HL
66 [1994] AC 324, PC
67 [1990] HKLR 396
68 [1977] 2 NZLR 225

secret profits.[69] However, there does not appear to be a basis for shareholders or other dealers in securities claiming compensation because they traded with the insider dealer at what they may later believe to have been an unfair price, though in theory a criminal court could consider a compensation payment under s.130 of the Powers of Criminal Courts Act 2000.

Market abuse

Market abuse exists as part of the regime created by the Financial Services and Markets Act 2000 (as amended) (FSMA).[70] The Second Market Abuse Directive had no real impact in the UK, as it effectively exported the national approach to the EU and rendered certain categories of market abuse as criminal offences. In the UK this is already the case, as a result of the combined effect of the relevant parts of the Criminal Justice Act 1993, the Fraud Act 2006, conspiracy to defraud and ss.89–91 Financial Services Act 2012.

The essence of the regime is that certain types of behaviour are deemed to be in breach of the FSMA and can thus give rise to the FCA having the power to take steps against FCA-authorised persons and firms, together with anyone else who has committed market abuse.[71] Most commonly, the sanction is a fine, the scale of which is determined in part by the behaviour of the person or firm concerned and in part by the scale of their finances. A regulated person may be asked to return their licence to carry on regulated activities and in the case of authorised firms they can be required to.[72] In the case of individuals, the person may agree to co-operate with the FCA on this point and this is likely to assist in reducing the fine. Where the person facing enforcement proceedings for market abuse is regulated (and apart from the Shell case,[73] they always have been), there are additional potential sanctions. Specifically, these are removing, suspending or restricting a licence to carry on investment business, reprimanding in private or in public, sending a file to the Serious Fraud Office or Crown Prosecution Service, or, alternatively, commencing criminal proceedings themselves.[74] In the case of any party, the FCA can also publish a statement that someone has engaged in market abuse but add no additional penalty.[75] This has not been used as an approach, but theoretically it could be, where it was not appreciated generally at that point that such behaviour could amount to market abuse, but the FCA wished to mark this issue for future reference.

69 *Regal (Hastings) Ltd v Gulliver* [1942] 1 All ER 378 HL
70 Financial Services and Markets Act 2000 (Market Abuse) Regulations 2005, SI 2005/381 applying the first Market Abuse Directive
71 S.123 Financial Services and Markets Act 2000
72 Ibid.
73 Shell Petroleum and Trading Co. plc and The Royal Dutch Petroleum Co. NV, FSA enforcement action, 24 August 2004
74 S.401(2)(a) and 3(a) Financial Services and Markets Act 2000
75 S.123(3) Financial Services and Markets Act 2000

It should be borne in mind that the FCA Principles and Rules can also come into play. ENF 14.8 highlights the fact that a breach of the market abuse legislation will also be a breach of FCA Principle 5, requiring firms to observe proper standards of market conduct, which could result in the FCA taking enforcement action for a breach of the Principle. In addition, FCA Principle 7 requires firms to communicate with clients in a manner that is clear, fair and not misleading. COB 2.1.3 restates this, the main effect of which is that a private client affected by a failure to meet this rule will have a right of action under s.150 for any loss resulting. A consequence of FCA Principle 8[76] is that firms must create Chinese walls. Under COB 2.4.4 this may require a firm to avoid passing certain information from one person to another. Acting in conformity with this provides a defence against charges of market abuse, misleading statements,[77] against FCA enforcement actions and s.150 claims by private clients. Likewise, when a firm is required to act with knowledge of a fact, the effect of a Chinese wall in stopping someone in that firm from being in possession of that knowledge will not amount be an offence.

The market abuse civil offences

Market abuse is defined as

> behaviour (whether by one person alone or by two or more persons jointly or in concert) which –
>
> (a) occurs in relation to –
>
> (i) qualifying investments admitted to trading on a prescribed market,
> (ii) qualifying investments in respect of which a request for admission to trading on such a market has been made, or
> (iii) in the case of subsection (2) or (3) behaviour, investments which are rated investments in relation to such qualifying investments, and
>
> (b) falls within one or more of the types of behaviour set out in subsection (2) to (8).[78]

It will be noted that intention is not a factor.[79] The types of behaviour caught by the regime are as follows.

76 That a firm must manage conflicts of interest fairly, both between itself and its customers and between one customer and another.
77 S.397(2) and (3) Financial Services and Markets Act 2000
78 S.118(1) Financial Services and Markets Act 2000
79 MAR 1.2.3 G

Insider dealing

It is insider dealing where 'an insider deals, or attempts to deal, in a qualifying investment on the basis of inside information relating to the investment in question'.[80] This is essentially the same as the criminal offence discussed above, but here it is extended to cover an attempt to commit the offence.

Clearly, a key issue here is what an 'insider' is understood to be. It is wider than the categorisation used in the criminal law[81], and covers anyone who has inside information as a result of their membership or employment position in a company;[82] anyone who holds shares; anyone having access to the information through carrying out their employment or professional duties (these do not have to be inside the company concerned); information acquired as a result of criminal activities; or information obtained by other methods which they could reasonably be expected to have known would be inside information.

In this context 'inside information'[83] is information of a precise nature relating to qualifying investments which are not commodity derivatives, which is not generally available and relates directly or indirectly to the issuer of a qualifying investment. Also, if it was generally available, it would be likely to have a significant effect on the price of an investment. There is a different treatment for commodity derivatives.

Inside information can extend to that which has been received from a client in relation to a pending order in relation to anyone charged with executing orders concerning qualifying or related investments. The information must be of a precise nature, not be generally available and must relate directly or indirectly to an issuer of qualifying investments. If it were generally available, it must be likely to have a significant effect on the price of the qualifying investments or related ones. 'Precision'[84] means information which a reasonable investor would be likely to use as part of the basis of his investment decisions and which indicates circumstances or an event that exists, or is reasonably likely to, and is specific enough to enable conclusions to be drawn as to the effect on the price of qualifying investments or related ones.

The FCA[85] has its own guidelines in the Code of Market Conduct (MAR) and considers the following factors in determining whether information falls outside the definition of 'inside information'. If it is generally available, the FCA takes into account whether the information has been disclosed on a prescribed

80 S.118(2) Financial Services and Markets Act 2000
81 S.118B Financial Services and Markets Act 2000
82 This will include administrators.
83 S.118C Financial Services and Markets Act 2000
84 S.118C(5) Financial Services and Markets Act 2000
85 Issued pursuant to s.119 to provide guidelines as to what behaviour the FCA will regard as market abuse. S.122 makes clear that if behaviour takes place that does not amount to market abuse under the Code, then it is not market abuse for the purposes of the FSMA. Thus, if the Code were found to be in error, it would need to be amended before anyone could have civil proceedings taken against them.

market through a regulatory information service or in any other way in line with the rules of the market concerned; whether it could be obtained from public records; whether the information is otherwise generally available from such information, including where a fee has to be paid; whether the information can be obtained by observation without infringing confidentiality; and the extent to which such information can be obtained by analysis of publicly available information.[86]

The FCA also has its own view on what will amount to insider dealing for market abuse purposes. It falls into three main groupings: dealing on the basis of inside information that is not trading information; front running;[87] and an offeror in a corporate takeover entering into a transaction on the basis of inside information involving exposure to a price movement in the target company's shares other than for the takeover itself. This would extend dealing in derivatives in relation to the shares on behalf of the offeror.[88]

In determining whether someone's behaviour amounts to acting 'on the basis of' inside information, the FCA will have regard to whether the decision to deal was made before the person possessed the relevant inside information, if they dealt to satisfy a regulatory requirement or legal obligation that came into existence before they obtained the inside information, and whether the individual in possession of the inside information had any involvement with the decision to deal, or behaved in a way to influence it, or had any contact with those who were dealing.[89] If the FCA believes that the person did or did not act in line with a regulatory requirement, this will be a significant element in shaping their view as to whether or not the behaviour amounted to market abuse.[90]

So far,[91] to put this in context, of the 68[92] FSA and FCA enforcement actions on market abuse brought on a civil cases, 25 have been straightforward insider dealing cases. It is therefore far and away the most common type of market abuse.

Disclosure of inside information

This applies 'where an insider discloses inside information to another person otherwise than in the proper exercise of is employment, profession or duties'.[93] When determining whether or not someone could reasonably be expected

86 MAR 1.2.12 E

87 That is, trading on a person's own behalf ahead of a client order, while in possession of inside information, to take advantage of the expected price change in the investment concerned.

88 MAR 1.3.2 E

89 MAR 1.3.3 E

90 MAR 1.3.11 E

91 As at 31 May 2016.

92 In calculating this, joint actions are treated as one case.

93 S.118(3) ibid.

to know that information in their possession was inside information, the FCA is guided by whether or not a normal and reasonable person with inside information would or should have known that the person they received it from was an insider, and if a normal and reasonable person in the position of the person holding inside information would or should have known that it was inside information.[94]

Failure to observe proper standards of behaviour

This covers behaviour which is:

> based on information which is not generally available to those using the market but which, if available to a regular user of the market, would be, or would be likely to be, regarded by him as relevant when deciding the terms on which transactions in qualifying investments should be effected, and . . . is likely to be regarded by a regular used of the market as a failure on the part of the person concerned to observe the standard of behaviour reasonably expected of a person in his position in relation to the market.[95]

The FCA's view on whether a person's behaviour represents legitimate business falls into four categories, which, if satisfied, will cause the FCA to regard the transaction as legitimate: the extent to which the relevant trading is carried out to neutralise a risk arising out of their business; where a transaction is carried out on the basis of inside information concerning a client transaction that has been executed and where that information has not yet been required to be published by the exchange concerned or relevant regulations; where the trading is connected with a client transaction and has no impact on the price, or there has been adequate disclosure to the client who has not objected; or where the person's behaviour was reasonable by the proper standards of the market concerned bearing in mind any relevant legal or regulatory requirements and whether the transaction was carried out in a way that reflected the need for the market concerned to operate fairly and efficiently.[96]

What, then, does not amount to market abuse? Just carrying out client orders will not be, and it is probably also safe if the person acting possesses inside information that is not limited to trading information. Factors to consider are: whether the person has complied with the FCA Conduct of Business Rules and Code of Market Conduct (or where the party is overseas, the equivalent); whether the person agreed with a client to behave in a particular way; whether the person's behaviour appears to have been the effective carrying out of a client order; the extent to which the behaviour was reasonable by the standards of the market; or

94 MAR 1.2.8 E
95 S.118(4)(a) and (b) Financial Services and Markets Act 2000
96 MAR1.3.10 E

whether the trading was connected with a client and the trading had no impact on the price. Alternatively, whether there was adequate disclosure to the client that the deal would occur and they did not object.[97] Where takeover and merger activity is occurring, there is an obvious risk of market abuse in general and insider dealing in particular. However, trading while in possession of inside information as part of a public takeover or merger does not of itself amount to market abuse, because if it did, takeovers would be legally impossible without committing a criminal offence.[98]

The slightly unusual case of Casoni,[99] which involved market misconduct in the inappropriate distribution of research, fits into this legal category. Apart from that, it has not been a fertile area for enforcement actions.

Giving a false or misleading impression

Such behaviour will be regarded as having taken place where transactions are carried out other than for legitimate reasons and in line with 'accepted market practices' on the market concerned which

> give, or are likely to give, a false or misleading impression as to the supply of, or demand for, or as to the price of, one or more qualifying investments, or . . . secure the price of one or more such investments at an abnormal or artificial level.[100]

As far as the FCA is concerned, behaviour will be carried out 'in relation to' investments prior to an admission for trading or the commencement of trading if the act is in relation to them, and it continues to have an effect once the application has been made or it has been admitted to trading.[101] Refraining from action might amount to market abuse if the behaviour satisfies s.118(1)(a) and the person concerned has not carried out a legal or regulatory requirement, or if they gave rise to the impression that they would correct previous statements where necessary and have not done so.[102]

The FCA's key factors in determining whether market abuse by way of giving a false or misleading impression has taken place are: the extent to which the orders to trade given or transactions undertaken represent a significant volume of transactions in the relevant investment, bearing in mind the effect on price; the extent to which orders to trade given or transactions undertaken by someone with a significant buying or selling position leads to a significant change in the price

97 MAR 1.3.15 E
98 MAR 1.3.17 C
99 FSA Enforcement action, 20 March 2007
100 S.118(5)(a) and (b) Financial Services and Markets Act 2000
101 MAR 1.2.5 E
102 MAR 1.2.6 E

of the underlying investment, related derivative or underlying investment; whether the transactions led to a change in beneficial ownership; the extent to which orders to trade given or transactions undertaken include position reversals over a short period, a significant proportion of the daily volume of transactions in the relevant investment and might be associated with significant changes in the price. In addition, the extent to which orders to trade given or transactions undertaken are concentrated within a short time span, leading to a price change which is subsequently reversed; the extent to which orders to trade given change the representation of the best bid or the representation of the order book available to market participants are removed before they are executed; and the extent to which orders to trade are given or transactions are undertaken at or around a specific time when reference prices, settlement prices and valuations are calculated and lead to price changes which have an effect on this type of price and valuation.[103]

In determining whether behaviour amounts to securing an abnormal or artificial price level, the FCA considers three key factors: the extent to which the person has an interest, whether direct or indirect, in the price or value of the investment; the extent to which price, rate or option volatility movements and the volatility of these factors for the investment in question are outside their normal range; and whether a person has successively and consistently increased or decreased the bid offer he has made.[104]

As far as ascertaining whether abusive squeezes[105] have taken place, the FCA will consider the extent to which the person has been willing to limit their control or influence in order to help maintain an orderly market, and the price at which they are willing to do so. If the person was willing to lend the investment, there is less likelihood of it being an abusive squeeze. The extent to which the person's activity has caused settlement default on a bilateral or multilateral basis will also be a factor. The more widespread the risk of multilateral default, the greater the risk that it is an abusive squeeze. The extent to which prices under the delivery mechanisms of the market diverge from the prices for delivery will be a factor. Finally, the extent to which the spot or immediate market is unusually expensive compared with the forward market will correlate with the risk of an abusive squeeze. There are limits, though: having a significant degree of control of a market through ownership does not necessarily mean a squeeze is automatically abusive.[106]

103 MAR 1.6.9 E
104 MAR 1.6.10 E
105 This occurs where one party has a significant influence over the supply or demand or delivery mechanisms of a qualifying investment or the underlying product of a derivative contact, and also has a position in an investment under which such investments are deliverable, and engages in behaviour which distorts the price.
106 MAR 1.6.11 E–1.6.12 E

Fictitious devices

Carrying out transactions which employ fictitious devices or deception is a category of market abuse.[107] It can occur if a trader buys and sells simultaneously, to give the impression of trading taking place outside the normal price range, to benefit financially from an option. It can also occur where a trader buys a large volume of a contract just before close of trading to create a false price. Alternatively, it could occur where a trader holds a short position in an investment that will show a profit if it falls out of an index in which it is currently quoted, and the trader then places a large order to sell just before the close of trading. The manipulation here will be the attempt to create a false market, causing the investment to fall out of the index. It would also be market abuse if, at the end of a trading period, a trader places a large buy order on relatively illiquid shares to create a false price. Another example would be where a trader with a long position in exchange-traded contracts borrows a large amount of the cheapest ones and then either will not re-lend them, or only does so to those he believes will not re-lend to the market, to force those with short positions to have to deliver to satisfy their obligations contractual, forcing up the price as a result and leaving the trader making a profit.[108]

Market abuse by manipulating devices can occur in a number of ways. Perhaps the most obvious would be to take a position in an investment and then leak fictional information to the media and profit from the subsequent price movement. Another would be to enter into a transaction, or series of transactions, to conceal the ownership of an investment by hiding the real owner to get round disclosure requirements.[109] One method is known as 'pump and dump',[110] another as 'trash and cash'.[111]

Factors the FCA will take into account in determining whether manipulating devices have been used include whether orders to trade are given or transactions undertaken following the dissemination of false or misleading information by those people or others linked to them. Another is where orders to trade are given or transactions undertaken by people before or after those same people disseminate research which is biased in favour of their investments.[112] This is an area where there are extensive controls and requirements in the FCA Conduct of Business Sourcebook (COBS) to stop firms utilising the distribution of their research to move prices and take advantage of the fact.[113] The FCA realises that if research is being carried out for a firm's internal use, there is little danger of conflicts of interest arising, but if internal research papers to be used for the firm's own

107 S.118(6) Financial Services and Markets Act 2000

108 MAR 1.6.15 E–1.6.16 E

109 Nominee holdings do not fall foul of this, unless done for illicit purposes.

110 That is, taking a long position and then putting out misleading information to increase its price, following which the investment is sold at an artificially high price.

111 MAR 1.7.2 E. This consists of taking a short position in an investment and then putting out negative information to force down the price to make a profit.

112 MAR 1.7.3 E

113 See, for example, COBS 7.16.

advantage and then to be given to clients where it is reasonable to suppose it might influence the clients' investment decisions, market abuse will almost certainly be taking place. Where conflicts of interest arise, there is senior management responsibility for resolving the matter. The FCA believes that conflicts of interest can be satisfactorily determined by appropriately timed disclosure. Firms engaged in corporate finance business must have in place systems, controls and procedures suitable to the nature of their work. Provided they do this and act in line with COBS 5.10, they should not end up in breach of the market abuse laws.

Firms must also take reasonable steps to make sure that they have restrictions on own-account dealing by relevant staff to avoid a conflict of interest with clients and act in line with COBS 7.13. There are quite detailed and prescriptive rules relating to this.

Disseminating misleading information

Disseminating information which

> gives, or is likely to give, a false or misleading impression as to the supply of, or demand for, or as to the price of . . . qualifying investments, or . . . secure the price of one or more such investments at an abnormal or artificial level.[114]

In determining whether or not behaviour is improper disclosure amounting to market abuse, the FCA views the following as determining factors. First, whether the behaviour is permitted by the rules of market concerned or the Takeover Code, or whether the disclosure is accompanied by the imposition of confidentiality requirements on the person to whom the disclosure was made. In this instance, it must be reasonable to enable the person concerned to perform their proper functions, or is needed by a professional adviser to give advice on a transaction, or is reasonable to facilitate a transaction, or is reasonable and for the purpose of obtaining a commitment or expression of support, or, finally, that it is in fulfilment of a legal obligation.[115]

When determining whether there is misuse of information amounting to market abuse, the FCA is influenced by the extent to which the information is reliable, the closeness to its source of the person passing the information on; and, in addition, whether the information differs from that which is generally available, or where it relates to possible future developments which will require a disclosure in the future and the certainty that the development will happen, and there is no other material information generally available. In determining whether a regular user of the market would reasonably expect information to be disclosed or announced, the FCA is influenced by whether the information was disclosed in

114 S.118(7) Financial Services and Markets Act 2000
115 MAR 1.4.5 E

line with legal or regulatory requirements or if the information is routinely the subject of public announcements. Finally, is the behaviour based on information leading to possible future developments, where it is reasonable to believe that the information in question will become one of these categories?[116]

Market abuse by dissemination consists of behaviour such as knowingly or recklessly spreading false or misleading information about an investment through the media, or undertaking a course of business to give a false or misleading impression of an investment. Another would be where a person puts false or misleading information on the internet or submits false or misleading information to a regulatory information service. The FCA will consider whether a normal and reasonable person should have known that the information was false or misleading, or whether the person concerned actually did know. They will also form an opinion on whether the individuals responsible for disseminating information could only have known that the information was false or misleading if they had access to information the other side of a Chinese wall. If this is the case, it is only going to amount to abuse by dissemination if there is evidence the wall may have been breached. This is an area where good compliance can provide protection.[117]

FSA/FCA enforcement actions in this area have been Gower,[118] Osborne,[119] Hannam,[120] Cameron[121] and Goenka.[122] It is thus one of the commoner causes of regulatory enforcement. Perhaps the most unusual was the Shell case,[123] involving misleading statements regarding the level of reserves in their annual accounts and the failure to correct this.

Market distortion

Where not already covered above, such behaviour as is likely

> to give a regular user of the market a false or misleading impression as to the supply of, demand for, or value of, qualifying investments or . . . would be . . . regarded be a regular user of the market as behaviour that would distort, or would be likely to distort, the market . . . and the behaviour is likely to be regarded by a regular user of the market as a failure on the part of the person concerned to observe the standard of behaviour reasonably expected of a person in his position in relation to the market.[124]

116 MAR 1.5.6 E–1.5.7 E
117 MAR1.8.3 E–1.8.6 E
118 FSA Enforcement action 13 January 2011
119 FSA Enforcement action 26 February 2012
120 FSA Enforcement notice 27 February 2012, referred to Upper Tribunal
121 FSA Enforcement action 6 July 2010
122 FSA Enforcement action 9 November 2011
123 FSA Enforcement action 24 August 2004
124 S.118(8)(a) and (b)

The FCA will regard behaviour as amounting to market abuse by way of manipulating transactions where deals are done at the close of a market to mislead people as to the real value, such as wash trading[125] or painting the tape.[126] Examples of behaviour that the FCA will regard as amounting to market abuse in this context are: transactions where people act in collusion to secure a dominant position over the demand or supply of a qualifying investment to fix the price or create unfair trading conditions; or transactions where both buy and sell orders are entered into at the same time with the same price, quantity and party or different but colluding parties for non-legitimate reasons. Sometimes this can be acceptable if the trades are in line with those of the trading platform concerned, such as cross-trades. The FCA also regard it market abuse where small orders are entered into an electronic trading system at higher prices than previous bids, or lower ones than previous offers to move the price; abusive squeezes;[127] parties subject to a primary offering colluding in buying further amounts when trading commences so as to raise the price; transactions or orders used to stop the price falling below a certain level; and trading on a market or platform to improperly influence the price of the same or a related investment on another prescribed market.[128]

In this context, the issues the FCA will take into account in determining whether the behaviour concerned is legitimate are as follows. Is the person motivated by a desire to induce others to trade or to move the price of a qualifying investment? Is their motive illegitimate, or was the transaction executed in a particular way for the purpose of creating a false or misleading impression? Factors that are indications that behaviour is legitimate are whether the transaction is entered into pursuant to a prior legal or regulatory obligation, whether it is executed in a way which takes into account the need for the market to operate fairly and efficiently, the extent to which the transaction opens a new position increasing exposure to market risk and if the transaction complied with the rules of the relevant market. It is unlikely that market users, when trading in a manner and on a scale most beneficial to them, will be distorting the market and therefore committing market abuse. However, trading on prices outside the normal range will not always be an indication of market abuse, as this can happen as a normal part of trading.[129]

125 This takes place where the trade does not reflect a change in beneficial interest or market risk, or where there is, but the deal is between parties acting in collusion.

126 This covers entering into transactions that are shown on public display to give the impression of activity, and entering orders into an electronic trading system at prices that are higher than the previous bid or lower than the previous offer, and then withdrawing them before they are executed, to give a misleading impression of demand or supply.

127 This occurs where one party has a significant influence over the supply or demand or delivery mechanisms of a qualifying investment or the underlying product of a derivative contact, and also has a position in an investment under which such investments are deliverable, and engages in behaviour which distorts the price.

128 MAR 1.6.4 E

129 MAR 1.6.5 E, 1.6.6 E, 1.6.7 G and 1.6.8 G

Market abuse by misleading behaviour or distortion could be evidenced by the movement of physical commodity shares being manipulated to create a misleading impression as to the supply of or demand for a commodity or futures contract or the price of the same. The FCA will consider the following behaviour in determining whether this type of market abuse has occurred: the experience and knowledge of the people concerned; the structure of the market including reporting notification and transparency requirements; the legal and regulatory requirements that are applicable; the identity and position of the person concerned; and the extent and nature of the visibility of the activity. The FCA will also take into account whether the transaction was carried out pursuant to a pre-existing legal or regulatory obligation, whether it was executed in a way that took into account the need for the market to operate fairly and efficiently, and the characteristics of the market in question, taking into account any relevant law, rules and code of conduct. The position of the person concerned and the standards that can be expected from someone with that level of skill and knowledge will also be factors. It would protect the person under suspicion, if it transpired that the transaction complied with the rules of the market concerned. Finally, the protection provided where the necessary information was the other side of a Chinese wall from the person under suspicion will apply here as well.[130]

Perkins,[131] Alexander,[132] Swift,[133] Geddis,[134] Visser and Fagbulu,[135] Da Vinci Invest Ltd and others,[136] Goenka,[137] Coscia[138] and Carrimjee[139] are nine cases falling within this category. In a different way the share ramping in Betton,[140] Winterflood,[141] Kahn,[142] and Chaligné and Sejuan[143] fits into this category as well. The nine LIBOR actions (Martin Brokers, Robson, Stewart, Lloyds Bank, Bank of Scotland, Deutsche Bank, Barclays Bank, Ross and UBS) effectively belong more completely in this category than in any of the others, though, as with a number of cases, the facts sit across the boundaries of the civil definitions, although this instance saw proceedings brought as criminal cases as well as involving regulatory fines. With 22 cases, this is the second most common type of market abuse after insider dealing.

130 MAR 1.9.1 E–1.9.5 E
131 FSA Enforcement action 29 June 2010
132 FSA Enforcement action 14 June 2011
133 FSA Enforcement action 31 August 2011, upheld by Upper Tax Tribunal 28 January 2013
134 Upper Tribunal 2 September 2011
135 Upper Tribunal 15 August 2011
136 High Court injunction by FSA 31 August 2011
137 FSA Enforcement action 9 November 2011
138 FCA Enforcement action 22 July 2013
139 Upper Tribunal decision 8 August 2013
140 FSA Enforcement action 6 December 2010
141 [2010] EWCA Civ 423
142 FSA enforcement action 24 May 2011, plus High Court injunction
143 Upper Tribunal 28 September 2012

Encouraging others

There is also a secondary offence[144] of taking or refraining from taking any action which requires or encourages another person to engage in market abuse.

Miscellaneous cases

There are a number of actions that, although enforced against one or more of the above categories, or at least in some instances could have been, do not fit neatly in any category. These are Davidson and Tatham[145] (alleged failure to supply appropriate information under s.391(4), (6) and (7) and publishing inappropriate information), Davis and Parikh,[146] a case of failing to act with due, skill care and diligence while trading for a client, and W. H. Ireland,[147] an action involving insufficient market abuse controls. Two anomalous actions, Wolfson Microelectronics plc[148] and Entertainment Rights plc,[149] were both a failure to release inside information and perhaps belong in a different category.

Qualifying investments

These are investments in which activities amounting to market abuse can be carried out. The list is more extensive than that applicable to criminal insider dealing under the CJA 1993 and are defined[150] as: transferable securities; units in collective investment schemes; money market instruments; financial futures contracts including equivalent cash settled instruments; forward rate agreements; interest rate, currency and equity swaps; options; commodity derivatives; and any other instrument admitted to trading on a regulated market in a member state or for which a request for admission has been made. A regulated market is one of those established under the rules of a UK-recognised investment exchange and all other regulated markets.[151]

Safe harbours

Safe harbours are not defences as such, but, as their name implies, if a person or firm can show that they were placed there, then an offence will not have been committed. They apply in this instance where the behaviour conforms with a rule

144 S.123(1)(b) Financial Services and Markets Act 2000
145 Tribunal decision 7 September 2006
146 FCA Enforcement action 8 August 2013
147 FCA Enforcement action 23 February 2016
148 FSA Enforcement action 20 January 2009
149 FSA Enforcement action 23 January 2009
150 See Directive 2003/6/EC art. 1(3)
151 Prescribed Markets and Qualifying Investments Order, SI 2001 No. 96 as amended by the Financial Services and Markets Act 2000 (Market Abuse) Regulations 2005 No. 381, art. 4

which makes it clear that such behaviour is not market abuse, and where the behaviour conforms with the EU Regulation[152] implementing the Directive[153] regarding exemptions for buy-back programmes and stabilisation rules. Finally, it applies if it is carried out by someone acting on behalf of a public authority in pursuit of monetary authorities or policies with regard to exchange rates or managing public debt or foreign exchange.[154]

Jurisdiction

The jurisdictional elements limit the offence to acts carried out in the United Kingdom, or in relation to investments traded on a prescribed market in the United Kingdom, or for which a request for admission has been made and related investments in either case.[155]

Conclusions

We therefore now have a raft of laws and regulations designed to combat or at least reduce the incidence of money laundering, terrorist financing, insider dealing and the various categories of market abuse. There is just one problem: it seems to be having no discernible effect. That in itself is not a conclusive reason for not having the laws; breaking the speed limit while driving is illegal, yet it continues on an industrial scale. The fall-back position is to therefore to justify these laws on the basis that matters might be even worse without them. However, in the case of the laws discussed in this chapter, there is considerable intrusion into personal liberty. In the case of money laundering, this is quite significant. Every person who has bank or building society accounts, uses financial services or a very wide range of facilities involving money finds themselves being spied on. To make matters worse, the basis of this spying is an absurdly wide definition of 'suspicion', which seems to cover the mildest sense that something may be untoward. Suspicious transaction reports are then submitted to a government agency on an industrial scale to very little evident benefit. There seems to be no convincing evidence that this is resulting in a significant attack on drug gangs (the original target), organised crime or terrorism. Countries which have gone further and imposed a bulk cash transaction reporting requirement (the USA and Australia being obvious examples) seem to have fared no better. There seems to be evidence from past AUSTRAC reports[156] that the Australian Cash Transaction and Analysis Centre has been a less expensive organisation than others. However, monies recovered seem to have emanated from small-time tax evaders rather than serious

152 EC No. 2273/2003
153 2003/6/EC
154 S.118A(5) Financial Services and Markets Act 2000
155 S.118A(1)(b)(i)–(iii) Financial Services and Markets Act 2000
156 According to their most recent annual report for 2014–15, they had an annual operating deficit of AUS$8.4 million.

criminal gangs, and their extensive annual reports give little encouragement to the belief that a significant difference is being made to combating crime by their presence. The UK's National Crime Agency seems to fare no better on this front. Their most recent annual report[157] shows that 354,186 suspicious transaction reports were submitted, primarily (82.18 per cent) by banks with no other submitting group exceeding 4.23 per cent. An analysis of the annual report shows that of those reports where a request to continue acting was granted to the reporting firm, £107,951 was seized and £1,176,91 repatriated to HMRC, suggesting a similar situation to Australia. In cases where it was granted, £309,260 was seized. In the first group, there were 35 arrests and in the second, five, though no evidence is given as to how many of these arrests related to each other, nor is there any evidence as to how many arrests in previous years have since led to a conviction. The strongest arguments for any suspicious transaction reports are found on pages 29–31, where examples are given of those who have had monies reimbursed from criminals due to suspicions having been reported by third parties. What is less clear is how many of these would have been dealt with by other methods, such as normal police procedure or the victim seeking legal advice and redress. Certainly, there seems no evidence to support the industrial scale domestic spying which is taking place.

Turning to insider dealing and market abuse, the issues arising are less clear-cut. Very few would try arguing that insider dealing should be legal,[158] and the low number of successful prosecutions suggest that any law here will have limited effect. Perhaps its justification is that lawfully minded people will be very unlikely to now attempt insider dealing in the way that their predecessors pre-1980 might have been happy to. Common sense suggests that there is therefore probably a reductive effect, though it is impossible to find convincing evidence for this.

The civil 'offences' of market abuse, which include the insider dealing offences, do not in themselves amount to criminal offences, though in practice most will be breaches of either the Fraud Act 2006, conspiracy to defraud or sections 89–91 of the Financial Services Act 2012, according to whether there is fraudulent intent or a communication. Again, suspicious transaction reports will therefore be needed if a third party suspects criminal activity here, as it would with insider dealing, so there is an overlap with the issues raised by the money-laundering laws with regard to civil liberty intrusion. The scale of civil enforcement is clearly greater than criminal, but is still barely scratching the surface of the problem.

Overall, we therefore seem to be in the unhappy position of having a raft of criminal and civil enforcement laws that have significant impacts on the rights of the public, and very significant financial costs, especially when the compliance costs for those in the regulated sector are considered, but which provide the public with little determinable benefit to offset this. Nor does there seem to be an

157 For the year 2014.

158 Though some have: see Manne, H. G., *Insider Trading and the Stock Market*. The Free Press, New York, 1966, p. xiii, 274.

obvious solution. No one has provided evidence of an alternative legal approach that would be more effective, and legalising the areas covered would be unrealistic. The simplest solution might be to adopt a very restrictive definition of 'suspicious' for the purposes of transaction reports, and so limit the internal spying and reporting that is taking place. Then, at least, the downside of the laws discussed would be partly mitigated.

10 Independence and protection of auditors in the EU anti-money laundering framework

Rhian Dow and Umut Turksen

10.1 Introduction

Financial crimes are a major concern for the EU's single market[1] in general and the financial services community[2] in particular, as these malfeasant activities not only create serious, negative social and economic consequences for individual countries and the global community, but also threaten the integrity of the key actors (banks, accountants, auditors, etc.) in business. As a result, the socio-economic development of each jurisdiction is affected. It is known that the preferred medium for laundering the illicit funds is often legitimate financial institutions, and criminals often use professionals to help disguise and/or transfer their illicit gains.[3] Underlying reasons for this trend are the expertise,[4] experience, efficiency and relatively low cost of the services which the financial sector offers.

1 Directive (EU) 2015/849 of the European Parliament and of the Council of 20 May 2015 on the prevention of the use of the financial system for the purposes of money laundering or terrorist financing, amending Regulation (EU) No 648/2012 of the European Parliament and of the Council, and repealing Directive 2005/60/EC of the European Parliament and of the Council and Commission Directive 2006/70/EC, paras 1–28.

2 The communiqués from the United Nations, FATF, IMF, World Bank, governments, and banks indicate that there is a consensus on the international and dire consequences of money laundering. See: http://www.antimoneylaundering.ukf.net; The UK Parliament, http://www.parliament.uk/documents/upload/ctp81.pdf; and the World Bank, http://www.siteresources.wordlbank.org/EXTAML/Resources/396511-11465814227871/Reference_ Guide_ AMLCFT_2ndSupplement.pdf.

3 Masciandaro, D. Money laundering: the economics of regulation (1999) *European Journal of Law & Economics*, 7(3): 225–240; Gill, M. and Taylor, G. Preventing money laundering or obstructing business? Financial companies perspectives on know your customer' procedures (2004) *British Journal of Criminology*, 44(4): 582–594; Financial Action Task Force (FATF), *Mutual Evaluation Report* (MER) 2007 (available at: http://www.fatfgafi.org/dataoecd/14/7/38341173.pdf, accessed 2 December 2013); Sikka, P., Enterprise culture and accountancy firms: new masters of the universe (2007) *Accounting, Auditing and Accountability*, 21(2): 269–295; and Turksen, U. *et al.* Anti-money laundering law of Turkey and the EU: an example of convergence? (2011) *Journal of Money Laundering Control*, 14(3): 279–296.

4 OECD, *Bribery and Corruption Awareness Handbook for Tax Examiners and Tax Auditors* (OECD Publishing, 2013) p. 15.

Arguably, without these legitimate institutions and their actors (e.g. auditors, accountants and banks) the proceeds of crime cannot easily be laundered.[5]

The pressures and demands of a capitalist economy place accountants and auditors (AAs) in a particular relationship with the state. It is often the state that is responsible for organising and regulating this sphere, but it is the accountants and auditors, among other professionals, who become agents and leaders for achieving the aims and objectives of the state policy.[6] AAs ensure not only that financial activities and records are a true and fair reflection of the business concerned, but also that they are acting as crime detection and prevention agents of the state regulatory regimes.[7] The latter role serves two spheres: the internal business environment and integrity of the company; and the external crime prevention and law enforcement framework.

Mörth argues that the EU is going through a time when borders between the public and private sectors are being 're-evaluated, transferred and becoming more porous'[8] and the studies show that across the EU there are different approaches to public–private cooperation, which create different roles for private actors in the public sector.[9] Subsequently, bankers, accountants, compliance officers, auditors, etc. find themselves in the midst of legal and illegal financial activities, and thus have roles in the detection, prevention and reporting of illegal acts such as money laundering, fraud and corruption. The conduct and responsibilities of these professions are regulated by law, and states often rely on professionals to convey the socio-economic reality[10] in a given financial activity. Being experts, these professionals are also called upon to act to a certain extent as independent 'gate -keepers' of surveillance and law enforcement agents of the state.[11] It is therefore possible to assert that AAs are enablers for both criminal activities and crime prevention. While the AAs are assumed to be the guardians of society and are somehow expected to be in the front line of defence against financial crime,

5 Mitchell, A. *et al.*, *The Accountants' Laundromat* (Association for Accountancy & Business Affairs, 1998); Ehrenfeld, R. *Evil Money* (New York: Harper Books, 1992); Kochan, N., Whittington, B. and Compin, F. The role of accounting in money laundering and money dirtying (2008) *Critical Perspectives on Accounting*, 19: 592–602.

6 Booth, P. and Cocks, N. Power and the study of the accounting profession. In Cooper, D. J. and Hopper, T. M. (eds) *Critical Accounts* (London: The Macmillan Press, 1990), pp. 391–408; and Sikka, P. and Willmott, H. The power of 'independence': defending and extending the jurisdiction of accounting in the United Kingdom (1995) *Accounting, Organizations and Society*, 20(6): 547–581.

7 AAs are also needed in tracing funds (originating from illegal activities) back to their rightful owners.

8 Mörth, U. The market turn in EU governance: the emergence of public–private collaboration (2009) *Governance*, 22(1): 99–120.

9 Bergström, M., Svedberg Helgesson, K. and Mörth, U. A new role for for-profit actors? The case of anti-money laundering and risk management (2011) *Journal of Common Market Studies*, 49(5): 1043–1064.

10 Sikka and Willmott (1995), n. 6 above, pp. 550–556.

11 Wadsley, J., Painful perceptions and fundamental rights: anti-money laundering regulation and lawyers (2008) *Company Law*, 29(3): 65–75.

the success rate of convictions emanating from audits in relation to financial crime in some of the EU countries is extremely low.[12] For example, according to 2010 data, while suspicious activity reports submitted by AAs were in the several thousands in the UK, there were either no reports by the AAs in Germany, Denmark, Estonia, Portugal, or very few; 18 in Italy, six in Spain, five in Austria.[13] Subsequent conviction rates and types of sentences imposed also vary greatly across the EU.[14] It should not be underestimated that the methods employed by AAs may put a veil over money-laundering activities by encouraging the perception that companies are not corrupt and are accountable to various stakeholders.[15]

In order to establish an effective and a consistent anti-money laundering (AML) regime, the EU has created a number of legal instruments in the form of Directives,[16] which aim to harmonise different legal frameworks across the EU and transpose international guidance and recommendations of the Financial Action Task Force on Money Laundering (FATF)[17] into the EU.[18] These legal instruments require financial institutions and certain professions (including AAs) to undertake due diligence on clients and to report suspicious activities. Furthermore, AAs in particular are instrumental in assessing whether internal controls and risk-based AML measures are adequate and effective. Internal and/

12 For a comparative analysis of AML-related convictions rates across the EU, see: ECOLEF Project – The Economic and Legal Effectiveness of Anti Money Laundering and Combating Terrorist Financing Policy (2013) EC DG Home JLS/2009/ISEC/AG087; Eurostat (2013) Money Laundering in Europe, ISSN 2315–0807, p. 29.

13 Eurostat (2013).

14 Ibid., p. 72.

15 Sikka (2007), n. 3 above.

16 Article 288 of the Treaty on the Functioning of the European Union states: 'A directive shall be binding as to the result to be achieved upon each state to which it is addressed, but shall leave to the national authorities the choice of form and methods.' Accordingly, it could be argued that Directives are used to encourage harmonisation across the EU; however, they leave the method of achieving this to the Member States – hence Directives are considered to be binding as to the result.

17 The FATF Recommendation (22(d)) states that 'lawyers, notaries, other independent legal professionals and accountants' are required to meet the strict (customer due diligence) standards of the recommendations, 'when they prepare for or carry out transactions' for their clients related to: buying and selling of real estate; managing of client money, securities or other assets; management of bank, savings or securities accounts; organisation of contributions for the creation, operation or management of companies; creation, operation or management of legal persons or arrangements; and buying and selling of business entities. The Financial Action Task Force Recommendations, International Standards on Combating Money Laundering and the Financing of Terrorism & Proliferation, February 2012, available at: http://www.fatf-gafi.org/media/fatf/documents/recommendations/pdfs/FATF_Recommendations.pdf.

18 The Recitals 5 of the 3rd AML directive states that the Community should continue to take particular account of the recommendations of the FATF, as the foremost international body active in the fight against money laundering and terrorist financing. It is further emphasised that the 3rd AML directive should be in line with the new international standard brought about by the revised and expanded FATF recommendations.

or external reporting of suspicious activity during the auditing process is a form of whistleblowing or disclosure, as these persons are employed by the company concerned. A person who in good faith informs the public and the management authorities of the company about any illegal, corrupt and/or malfeasant activity is called a whistleblower.[19] Glazer and Glazer define a whistleblower as one who: (a) acts to prevent harm to others, not him or herself; (b) while possessing evidence that would convince a reasonable person.[20] The Parliamentary Assembly of the Council of Europe's Committee on Legal Affairs and Human Rights considers whistleblowing to be 'concerned individuals sounding the alarm in order to stop wrongdoings that place fellow human beings at risk'.[21] In the EU AML context, this definition is significant because the whole AML strategy rests on a risk-based approach.[22] Following its resolution in 2010, the Council of Europe also created a 'soft law' instrument, which recommends a set of measures to be put in place so as to protect whistleblowers.[23] According to this latest whistleblower protection framework, 'whistleblower' means any person who reports or discloses information on a threat or harm to the public interest in the context of their work-based relationship, whether it be in the public or private sector.

In the literature, one can also find a distinction between various whistleblowers, namely internal/insider (those with contractual relationship or employment with the organisation) and external/outsider whistleblowers (those who act independently of the organisation).[24] Whatever the definition may be,[25]

19 Srividhya, S. and Shelly, S. Whistle blowing protection – a watch dog for the organisation (2012) *International Journal of Social Science & Interdisciplinary Research*, 1(10) (available at: http://indianresearchjournals.com/pdf/IJSSIR/2012/October/17.pdf). It is important to note that there is distinction between whistleblowers and informants: informants use disclosure for clarifying their own role in the malfeasant activity or to reduce their liability. Whistleblowers, on the other hand, act because of the public interest and common good at stake, which includes performing legal duties and enforcement of the law.

20 Glazer, M. P. and Glazer P. *The Whistleblowers* (Basic Books, 1989) p. 4. In the literature, the most cited definition of whistleblowing is provided by Miceli and Near, who define whistleblowing as 'the disclosure of organisational member's (former or current) disclosure of illegal, immoral, or illegitimate practices under the control of their employers to persons or organizations that may be able to effect action', in Miceli, M. P. *et al. Whistleblowing in organizations* (Routledge, 2008), p. 6.

21 Parliamentary Assembly, Resolution 1729 (2010). Final version: http://assembly.coe.int/nw/xml/XRef/Xref-XML2HTML-en.asp?fileid=17851&lang=en.

22 The 4th EU AML Directive (2015/849) (e.g. Article 48(10)) requires European Supervisory Authorities to issue guidelines to competent authorities on the characteristics of a risk-based approach to AML/CTF supervision and the steps that supervisors should take when conducting supervision on a risk-sensitive basis: http://eur-lex.europa.eu/legal-content/EN/TXT/PDF/?uri=OJ:JOL_2015_141_R_0003&from=ES.

23 Council of Europe, Protection of Whistleblowers, Recommendation CM/Rec(2014) 7: http://www.coe.int/t/dghl/standardsetting/cdcj/CDCJ%20Recommendations/CMRec(2014)7E.pdf.

24 Brown, A. J. *et al. International Handbook on Whistleblowing Research* (Edward Elgar, 2014), pp. 7–8.

25 For a detailed analysis of various definitions of whistleblowing, see Brown ibid.

whistleblowing is generally seen as an important tool to counter corruption and financial crime and in enforcing laws, protecting the public and ensuring good governance and accountability,[26] as well as being an essential element of proper democratic system.[27] Despite the importance of whistleblowing for political, economic, social and legal development, the majority of whistleblowing legal instruments do not use the term 'whistleblowing'. It is argued that this is a result of negative historical connotations pertaining to whistleblowers, such as informants in repressive countries during the Cold War. Furthermore, several studies indicate that somewhere between half and two-thirds of whistleblowers are retaliated against and lose their jobs subsequently.[28] Nevertheless, for many years, whistleblowers had been seen as exceptional people who have high morals and are ready to sacrifice their reputation and careers in order to uphold organisational integrity.[29] This characteristic is still valid today, yet the legal developments in the EU's AML framework have meant that AAs must blow the whistle not because they, on a personal level, morally or ethically think it is right to do so, but because it is their professional legal duty. In other words, as far as the legal AML requirements go, personal discretion available to AAs is diminished. At the same time, legal protection for whistleblowers varies significantly in its scope and effect across the EU.

Given this legal duty to act and the potential retaliations or reprisals the whistleblowers could face, does the law provide adequate protection? Given the employee–employer relationship in which the AAs operate, is it possible for them to perform their duties in countering financial crime without fearing for the termination of their employment? In order to address these questions, there has been an impetus to create minimum standards for whistleblower protection at international level since the early 2000s. For example, Article 33 of the United Nations Convention against Corruption (UNCC) requires that

> each State Party shall consider incorporating into its domestic legal system appropriate measures to provide protection against any unjustified treatment for any person who reports in good faith and on reasonable grounds to the competent authorities any facts concerning offences established in accordance with this Convention.

Against this background, a number of studies indicate that reforms in whistleblower statutes in the USA and Australia in particular have improved the protection of

26 Dworkin, T. M. (foreword) in Brown, ibid.

27 Council of Europe, Protection of Whistleblowers, Recommendation CM/Rec (2014) 7, p. 5; Oakes, L. cited in Brown, A. J. *Whistleblowing in the Australian Public Sector* (ANU Press, 2008), p. 10.

28 Alford, S. F. *Whistleblowers: Broken Lives and Organisational Power* (Cornell University Press, 2001), ch. 2, p. 18.

29 Smith, R. Whistleblowers and suffering, in Brown, n. 24 above, p. 231.

the whistleblowers.[30] The Council of Europe also encourages countries to adopt whistleblower protection provisions. Article 9 of the Civil Law Convention on Corruption (CLCC) adopted by the Council of Europe stipulates that 'each Party shall provide in its internal law for appropriate protection against any unjustified sanction for employees who have reasonable grounds to suspect corruption and who report in good faith their suspicion to responsible persons or authorities'. It should be noted that unlike the loose requirement of 'shall consider' under the UNCC, the CLCC's requirement is to 'provide' protection substantively. The EU secondary legislation utilises the requirement for protection of the AAs by the use of the term 'should'. For example, Directive 2014/56/EU states:

> Whistleblowers can bring new information to the attention of competent authorities which may assist them in detecting and imposing sanctions for irregularities, including fraud. However, whistleblowers may be deterred from doing so for fear of retaliation, or may lack incentives to do so. Member States *should* therefore ensure that adequate arrangements are in place to encourage whistleblowers to alert them to possible infringements of this Directive or of Regulation (EU) No 537/2014 and to protect them from retaliation. [emphasis added]

Regulation (EU) No. 537/2014, on the other hand, makes no reference to protection of AAs. In the EU, very few countries have specific laws protecting whistleblowers.[31] It is not surprising that audits in the EU have not resulted in effective identification and prosecution of financial crime, and there seems to be inadequate protection for whistleblowers. Yet, to date, no comprehensive study of the whistleblower protection in the EU has taken place. This is perhaps evidence of the tension between EU Member States and the institutions of the EU and Europe (e.g. the EU Commission, Council of Europe, the European Court of Human Rights). The Parliamentary Assembly of the Council of Europe (PACE) asserted that the lack of harmonised whistleblower laws in Europe is mainly a result of 'deeply engrained cultural attitudes, which date back to social and political circumstances, such as dictatorship and/or foreign domination, under which distrust towards "informers" of the despised authorities was only normal'.[32]

30 Dworkin in Brown, n. 24 above.

31 Guyer, T. and Peterson, N. The current state of whistleblower law in Europe: a report by the Government Accountability Project (GAP), 08 May 2013. Report by the Parliamentary Assembly of the Council of Europe (PACE), 2009, which found that most European countries 'have no comprehensive laws for the protection of "whistle-blowers"'. European Developments, The Council of Europe resolution and recommendation on the protection of whistleblowers (2010) *Industrial Law Journal*, 39(4): 432–435.

32 Stephenson, P. and Levi, M. Council of Europe, The protection of whistleblowers: A study on the feasibility of a legal instrument on the protection of employees who make disclosures in the public interest, CDCJ(2012)9FIN, (20 December 2012); http://www.coe.int/t/dghl/standardsetting/cdcj/Whistleblowers/CDCJ(2012)9E_Final.pdf.

While these different attitudes exist across the EU, it can be argued that employees will report malfeasant activity if they can be assured that their disclosure will be taken seriously, that they will be protected against retaliation, and that their employer and regulatory authorities are serious about stamping out bad practices or unlawful activities.

This chapter comments on whether and to what extent the AAs in the EU are protected when they blow the whistle and report suspicious (financial crime) activity in the context of AML.[33] The 4th EU AML Directive[34] came into effect on 27 June 2015 and states that:

> There have been a number of cases where employees who have reported their suspicions of money laundering have been subjected to threats or hostile action. Although this Directive cannot interfere with Member States' judicial procedures, it is crucial that this issue be addressed to ensure effectiveness of the AML/CFT system. Member States should be aware of this problem and should do whatever they can to protect individuals, including employees and representatives of the obliged entity, from such threats or hostile action, and to provide, in accordance with national law, appropriate protection to such persons, particularly with regard to their right to the protection of their personal data and their rights to effective judicial protection and representation.

Furthermore, Article 61 of the Directive provides that Member States shall ensure that competent authorities establish effective and reliable mechanisms, which include, *inter alia*:

a) appropriate protection for employees or persons in a comparable position, of obliged entities who report breaches committed within the obliged entity;
b) clear rules that ensure that confidentiality is guaranteed in all cases in relation to the person who reports the breaches committed within the obliged entity, unless disclosure is required by national law in the context of further investigations or subsequent judicial proceedings;
c) persons in a comparable position, to report breaches internally through a specific, independent and anonymous channel, proportionate to the nature and size of the obliged entity concerned.

The 28 Member States of the EU have until June 2017 to implement the provisions of the 4th EU AML Directive. This Directive requires the EU to adopt

33 A comprehensive comparative analysis of various AML regimes across the EU has been conducted by the ECOLEF Project – The Economic and Legal Effectiveness of Anti Money Laundering and Combating Terrorist Financing Policy (2013) EC DG Home JLS/2009/ISEC/AG087.

34 See: http://eur-lex.europa.eu/legal-content/EN/TXT/PDF/?uri=OJ:JOL_2015_141_R_0003&from=EN.

a 'risk-based approach' to tackling money laundering (ML) at national and obliged entity (e.g. AAs) level. The EU's risk-based approach rests on four main pillars: intelligence; awareness; training; and periodic self-evaluation. If obliged entities are not able to report suspicious ML activities effectively, then this creates a great risk for the EU. Accordingly, this chapter comments on whether and to what extent the AAs in the EU are protected when they blow the whistle and report suspicious (financial crime) activity in the context of AML.[35] In the confines of this chapter, it is not possible to consider all 28 Member States of the EU. Rather, we have chosen several Member States in a hope to depict the general state of affairs across the EU and highlight main differences therein. While the EU AML framework has been evolving, the EU and various professional AA bodies have also endeavoured to ensure the integrity and independence of the AAs via legal instruments, code of ethics and self-regulatory practices.

10.2 The legal framework governing AAs

General policy direction pertaining to whistleblower protection (for both public and private disclosures) in Europe is outlined by the Council of Europe.[36] Accordingly, the normative framework envisaged to govern whistleblower protection requires *inter alia* that 'an employer should not be able to rely on a person's legal or contractual obligations in order to prevent that person from making a public interest report or disclosure or to penalise him or her for having done so'.

Currently, only four EU Member States have dedicated whistleblower legislation – the United Kingdom (UK), the Netherlands, Hungary and Romania. Of these four countries, only the UK has dedicated whistleblower protection laws that extend to all workers, in both the public and private sectors, including contractors and consultants.[37] The main reason for the slow development of whistleblower protection laws in the EU is argued to be the differences in employment law. For example, in the US an employment may be terminated 'at will' unless a statutory exception exists, whereas in most of the EU Member States an employer cannot terminate an employment contract without just cause. Accordingly, as whistle-blowing need not involve any misconduct, it would be difficult to establish a just cause to terminate the employment. In some EU countries, the threshold is even higher. For example, in France 'the employer must have a real and serious cause (*cause réelle et sérieuse*) for the termination of the employment agreement and must comply with all applicable dismissal procedures'.[38] While this approach may

35 A comprehensive comparative analysis of various AML regimes across the EU has been conducted by the ECOLEF Project, n. 33 above.

36 Council of Europe, Protection of whistleblowers, Recommendation CM/Rec(2014) 7.

37 Thad, M. G. and Peterson, N. F. *The Current States of Whistleblower Law in Europe* (2013) Government Accountability Project.

38 Moquet Borde & Lovells, *Doing Business in France* (1997) § 12.04 2–12, cited in Thad and Peterson, ibid.

be suitable for internal complaints mechanisms, it neglects the realities of external whistleblowing in the context of financial crime.

The EU whistleblower protection is further complicated by the fact that the EU's data protection laws may be incompatible with whistleblower laws in other countries such as the US Sarbanes–Oxley Act,[39] and by the increased number of European companies being registered in the US, thus being subject to US laws.[40] The 'data privacy' rules and prohibition of whistleblowers to appropriate company documents and provide them to regulators or to the press further hinder the development of EU whistleblower protection. Even within the EU's own regulations, the global accounting body the ACCA notes that there is potential for whistleblowing AAs to 'possibly face sanctions under one Directive for complying with the terms and intentions of another',[41] and calls for clarity on 'the exemption from prosecution for accountants who are acting not only in the public interest, but also under a legal and ethical obligation, in blowing the whistle on corrupt and unlawful practices when they discover them'.

With the globalisation of trade in general and the financial sector in particular, compliance with the laws in multi-jurisdictions is inevitable. Given that most money-laundering schemes involve multi-layered, multi-jurisdictional cover-ups, the lack of harmonised standards has a negative impact on both the effectiveness of AML regimes and whistleblowing practices.

10.3 The role of AAs

AAs, who may be employed either by companies as independent contractors or by accounting firms providing statutory external audit services to companies, are faced with perverse incentives and conflicting demands when it comes to the reporting of malfeasance by their employing or contacting organisation.

For both internal and external auditors, independence and objectivity are regarded as essential elements in performing their differing reporting functions, but are actually difficult to achieve in practice. As Tackett *et al.* ask, how 'can the auditor be independent of an entity when the entity has the right to fire the auditor and thereby damage the auditor's financial position?'[42]

39 Saelens, F. *et al.* The case of whistleblowing schemes in the European Union (2006) *European Company Law*, 3(4): 170–176. The US government has incorporated whistleblower protection provisions in nearly every piece of legislation in which US dollars will be spent or which are intended to protect the public from financial loss. This inevitably covers all anti-financial crime laws.

40 Sarbanes–Oxley Act 2002 and the Dodd Frank Act 2012.

41 ACCA senior manager tax and business law Jason Piper commenting on provisional EU inter-institutional agreement on the protection of trade secrets, 16 December 2015: http://www.accaglobal.com/uk/en/discover/news/2015/12/whistleblowing-protection.html.

42 Tackett, J., Wolf, F. and Claypool, G. Sarbanes–Oxley and audit failure: a critical examination (2004) *Managerial Auditing Journal*, 19(3): 340–350.

While the specific nature of the conflicts faced by AAs employed directly by and working within companies may differ from the dilemmas faced by external statutory auditors, most challenges to their collective abilities to report independently arise from some form of threat to their self-interest.

Public Concern at Work[43] recognises this 'practical dilemma' facing an AA who 'may elect not to make a public interest disclosure because they think it will not be in their own interests (be it, in the accountancy field, the loss of further business or concern for their professional reputation)'.

This presents a real challenge for auditors and, despite any legal protection afforded to them under various legislation, can be inferred from press reports of auditor firms being replaced following a client's discontent with supposedly independent but unfavourable audit reports.[44]

In the absence of specific legal protection for AAs under national AML legislation (see below), AAs must negotiate professional and ethical constraints, commercial concerns and diverse regulatory requirements in deciding whether and how to blow the whistle. There is evidence to suggest that despite legal requirements on AAs to make formal reports of fraud, money laundering and other economic crimes, relevant regulations and procedures are often not complied with, in some cases because of a lack of external auditor independence (see below).[45]

Ample literature and schools of thought support this suggestion that AAs' reporting independence is threatened when external auditors identify too closely with their clients/employers,[46] a situation which may arise from fear of losing the audit engagement or fees for provision of non-audit services, or even simply unconscious bias[47] from unduly lengthy tenure of the audit engagement.

43 Public Concern at Work (PCaW) response to the International Federation of Accountants (IFAC) exposure draft A Public Interest Framework for the Accountancy Profession (November 2010). PCaW is an independent charity providing confidential advice to members of the public with whistleblowing concerns.

44 For example: Ceres fires KPMG over financial report (2016) *Pacific Coast Business Times*, 23 February: http://www.pacbiztimes.com/2016/02/23/ceres-fires-kpmg-over-financial-report-statements.

45 See Hassink, H., Meuwissen, R. and Bollen, L. Fraud detection, redress and reporting by auditors (2010) *Managerial Auditing Journal*, 25(9): 861–881. Hassink *et al.*'s research among all audit partners of the top 30 Dutch audit firms found that Dutch regulatory requirements for auditors to report fraud in writing internally and externally were not met in the majority of instances.

46 The EU's Proposal for a Regulation of the European Parliament and of the Council on specific requirements regarding statutory audit of public-interest entities Brussels, 30.11.2011 COM(2011) 779 final 2011/0359 (COD) notes: 'Independence is neither assured nor demonstrable in a paradigm where audit has effectively become one of a plethora of commercial services. The lack of regular tendering of audit services and periodic rotation of audit firms has deprived audit of its key ethos: professional skepticism.'

47 See Bazerman, M. H., Loewenstein, G. and Moore, D. A. Why good accountants do bad audits (2002) *Harvard Business Review*, 80(11): 96–102 (134); Bazerman, M. H. and Moore, D. A. Is it time for auditor independence yet? (2011) *Accounting, Organizations and Society*, 36(4–5): 310–312.

Similarly, AAs working as internal auditor employees of companies also face economic interest threats to their freedom to report independently and objectively, although these may arise in different ways – for example, from the receipt of incentive-based compensation or through the use of the internal audit function as a training ground for future company managers.[48]

These remaining problematic issues have been reinforced by repeated public outcry over AAs' role in major corporate scandals, ranging from Enron's very public collapse in 2002 to the global financial crisis of 2007–08, which subsequently prompted a series of regulatory and professional reviews of auditor independence both in the US and Europe, culminating in the EU's recent regulatory changes of 2014–15.

The landscape of external audit has changed significantly since Mautz and Sharaf[49] first identified audit independence as one of audit's unsolved problems, and much of this change has been concentrated in the last two decades, largely as a response to a number of high-profile corporate and financial scandals in the UK, such as Maxwell pensions, Doncaster Council, Barlow Clowes, Barings Bank and BCCI, and the work of the Committee on Standards in Public Life, as well as scandals with global impact, such as the Enron scandal in the US.[50] While it is evident that the whistleblower protection particularly at the EU level has gained momentum following the Enron scandal and subsequent US legislation, few EU Member States have specific legal provisions protecting whistleblowers; hence it has been observed that the EU has a patchwork of legal protection for whistleblowers found in employment, criminal, media and anti-corruption laws.[51] Even in countries where protection may be found, this is scattered in various contexts such as employment, criminal, media and anti-corruption laws.[52] Unlike the protection regime provided by Sarbanes–Oxley 2002 and Dodd Frank Act 2012 in the US, the development and harmonisation of whistleblower protection in the EU have been slow. This is argued to be a consequence of different legal cultures, cultural attitudes and resistance to governance emerging from the EU and other regional organisations such as the Council of Europe and European Court of Human Rights.[53]

48 See Stewart, J. and Subramaniam, N. Internal audit independence and objectivity: emerging research opportunities (2010) *Managerial Auditing Journal*, 25(4): 328–360 for a comprehensive review of the literature in this area.

49 Mautz, R. K. and Sharaf, H. A. *The Philosophy of Auditing* (American Accounting Association Sarasota, Florida, 1961).

50 The Enron scandal gave rise to the well-known US statute, Sarbanes–Oxley, which has created compliance obligations that require audit committees to offer 'confidential, anonymous employee complain procedures', which in turn had implications for labour and data protection laws across the EU. For a detailed analysis, see: Dowling, D. C., Sarbanes–Oxley whistleblower hotlines across Europe: directions through the maze (2008) *The International Lawyer*, Spring: 1–57.

51 Stephenson and Levi, n. 32 above.

52 Ibid.

53 Ibid.

10.4 Nature and significance of audit independence

According to the International Federation of Accountants (IFAC) Code of Ethics, audit independence comprises two elements: independence of mind and independence in appearance. It defines the first of these components as the 'state of mind that permits the expression of a conclusion without being affected by influences that compromise professional judgement, thereby allowing an individual to act with integrity and exercise objectivity and professional skepticism'.[54] Independence in appearance is 'the avoidance of facts and circumstances' which would lead a 'reasonable and informed third party' to conclude that an auditor's, or an audit firm's, objectivity and professional scepticism had been ompromised.

It is worth noting, in this definition of independence, that neither element is given greater weight than the other by IESBA, implying that both may be considered equally important, and, further, that independence itself is significant only for the qualities it enables, namely objectivity and professional scepticism.

The EU legislation for AAs derives from two main instruments: a Directive (Directive 2014/56/EU),[55] which covers the statutory audit of annual and consolidated financial statements; and a Regulation (Regulation (EU) No. 537/2014),[56] which establishes further requirements in respect Public Interest Entities (PIEs). The Regulation and Directive are to be applied in all 28 EU Member States, and additionally in countries which are not EU Member States, but are Members of the European Economic Area (namely, Liechtenstein, Iceland and Norway). The Regulation sets out key requirements as well as a number of country options (see below), which provide Member States a degree of flexibility in implementing some of the changes. Member States have until 17 June 2016 to transpose the Directive into their domestic legislation, and to decide how to interpret the Regulation's baseline requirements at national level.

The Regulation is intended to address some of the specific threats to auditor independence, which have long vexed the profession and regulators, and exercised academic commentators. Its stated aims are to address conflicts of interest

54 The International Ethics Standards Board for Accountants, Code of Ethics, 2015, p. 47: https://www.ethicsboard.org/iesba-code.

55 Directive 2014/56/EU of the European Parliament and of the Council of 16 April 2014 amending Directive 2006/43/EC on statutory audits of annual accounts and consolidated accounts. The Directive and Regulation were the result of a lengthy consultative and legislative process, prompted by concerns raised about the role played by statutory auditors in the financial crisis, and will result in significant changes in the auditor–client company relationship, intended to ensure the independence of the statutory auditor from the audited company.

56 Regulation (EU) No. 537/2014 of the European Parliament and of the Council of 16 April 2014 on specific requirements regarding statutory audit of public-interest entities and repealing Commission Decision 2005/909/EC.

between the auditor and the shareholders of the audited company arising from, *inter alia*: the provision of non-audit services (NAS) by the auditor to an audited client; the familiarity between auditor and client which arises from long audit tenure; the current system whereby the audited company selects and pays its auditor; and the lack of choice of auditor resulting from market concentration.

10.5 Key aspects of the EU's regulatory framework

The Regulation applies to public interest entities and their statutory auditors and audit firms. Public interest entities (PIEs) are defined (by Directive 2006/43/EC) as any entity whose shares are traded on a regulated stock exchange in any Member State; credit institutions and insurance undertakings; and entities designated by Member States as PIEs because 'the nature of their business, their size and the number of their employees' gives them 'significant public relevance'.

Directive 2006/43 stipulates that

> Member States shall ensure that a statutory auditor or an audit firm shall not carry out a statutory audit if there is any direct or indirect financial, business, employment or other relationship – including the provision of additional non-audit services – between the statutory auditor, audit firm or network and the audited entity from which an objective, reasonable and informed third party would conclude that the statutory auditor's or audit firm's independence is compromised.

This provision, on its face value, seems to provide a sound independent mechanism for effective auditing. However, there are significant differences in how Member States have interpreted and applied this provision. As aptly observed by Ianniello,[57] these approaches range from strict regulation in certain jurisdictions (i.e. a total ban prohibiting the provision of non-audit services in France) to less restrictive practices, whereby the provision of non-audit services by auditors continue to be business as usual (e.g. in the UK, Finland, Spain, Portugal, Slovakia) or, as in Italy, certain non-auditing services are prohibited.

The flexibility and discretion conferred to Member States under the EU's regulatory framework permit over 50 options – some potentially significant. These are considered in Table 10.1 below.

57 Ianniello, G. The effects of board and auditor independence on earnings quality: evidence from Italy (2015) *Journal of Management and Governance*, 19: 229–253.

Table 10.1 Principal Member State options

Aspect	*Member State options*
Applicability of the EU regulations	May determine that the EU regulations (or some of them) are not applicable if a co-operative, savings bank or similar institution is required or permitted under law to be a member of a non-profit entity, as the auditor meets the independence requirements laid out in the regulations.
Audit fees	May adopt more stringent requirements than the 70% cap on non-audit services (NAS) and the 15% limit on the proportion of an auditor's total audit fees generated by a single audit client.
Prohibition of non-audit services	May prohibit other NAS. Can allow the provision of some of the prohibited services as long as: • There is no direct or material effect on the financial statements. • The auditor documents and explains the effect on the financial statements in the additional report to the Audit Committee. • The auditor complies with the independence requirements. Can establish stricter rules for undertaking NAS.
Audit report requirements	Can lay down additional requirements.
Additional auditor reporting	Can lay down additional requirements.
Report by the auditor to supervisors of PIEs	Can lay down additional requirements.
Record keeping by the auditor	Can require documents to be retained for more than five years.
Auditor appointment	Can decide a minimum number of statutory auditors in certain circumstances.
Duration of an audit appointment	Can set a shorter maximum period of audit engagement than ten years. Can extend the maximum period of audit engagement to 20 years and 24 years for sole audits and joint audits respectively.
Key audit partners	Can require audit partners to cease their participation in the statutory audit before seven years.
Ensuring that the provisions are applied	Can decide that the responsibility for ensuring that the provisions are applied is entrusted to a competent authority (for example the FRC).

Source: Mazars, 2015, p. 15[58]

58 Mazars, *Audit Reform for UK Listed Companies: a practical guide* (London: Mazars LLP, 2015).

10.6 Professional responses

After a period of intense lobbying, which resulted in the removal of some of the more controversial proposals (such as audit-only firms), large professional firms have greeted the regulatory changes with some reserve. KPMG[59] suggests that the EU changes go further than either the IESB guidelines on auditor independence or the US independence rules of the Securities and Exchange Commission, and 'constitute a redrawing of client-auditor relationships in the EU'.

Most concern, apart from the obvious self-interest objections raised by firms to mandatory auditor rotation and the prohibition of non-audit services, relates to the number of derogations, or options, available to Members States. KPMG[60] predicts that these 'have the potential to produce a complex patchwork of audit legislation', meaning that 'the final audit environment is unlikely to be uniform across the EU'. Ernst and Young (EY),[61] too, notes that 'it is likely, therefore, that implementation of the legislation will vary across the EU . . . its full impact remains to be seen'.[62]

The Federation of European Accountants (FEE) notes that the 'use of a Regulation should have resulted in a more certain and harmonised EU audit regulatory environment'.[63] However, divergence in the choices of Member State options will 'increase complexity and costs on business while the performance of the audit will not always be as smooth as it might be'.[64]

In terms of protection for whistleblowing AAs, the coverage is likely to be variable. So far, only Slovakia has specifically included consideration of this issue in its national legislation implementing the EU audit reforms.[65]

The fact the EU is far from establishing a fully harmonised auditing practice is further illustrated by individual national legal characteristics, which are examined below.

10.7 Country interpretations

10.7.1 United Kingdom

In the UK, the response to the conundrum of audit independence both predates the EU regulatory changes and, in some areas, outstrips them. Changes to the

59 KPMG, *EU Audit Reform: Redefining the Global Professional Services Market* (Zurich: KPMG International, 2014).
60 KPMG ibid.
61 EY, *Point of View: European Audit Legislation* (London: EY.com, 2014).
62 Ibid., p. 2.
63 FEE (2014), p. 8.
64 Ibid., p. 4.
65 The National Council of the Slovak Republic 423 Act of 11 November 2015 on Statutory Audit and on Amendments and Supplements to Act No. 431/2002 Coll. on Accounting, as amended, states that the 'obligation to maintain confidentiality shall not apply to the obligation to provide information according to this Act . . . or in order to prevent a crime from being committed.'

Companies Acts (2006) strengthened audit committees' oversight of auditor independence and reinforced auditors' personal responsibility. However, a fundamental threat to auditor independence remained – the near-oligopoly exercised over the audit of listed companies by the so called 'Big Four' accounting firms: KPMG, Deloitte, EY and PwC.

These huge global accounting and consulting firms dominate the audit of listed companies in the UK, auditing at least 96 per cent of the FTSE350.[66] This restricts companies' choice of auditor, causing long auditor–client relationships to develop. For example, Barclays announced last year that in response to pressure from the Financial Reporting Council (FRC) (see below), it would tender for a new audit firm, bringing to an end its relationship with its existing auditor, PwC (which had audited its books since 1896), by replacing it with another Big Four firm, KPMG.[67] In response to this issue, the UK Office of Fair Trading referred the supply of statutory audit services to large companies to the Competition Commission (CC) in October 2011 and in September 2012, the FRC revised the UK Code on Corporate Governance to include expectation that FTSE350 companies would put the external audit contract out to tender at least every ten years and extended auditor reporting. This requirement for rotation is more stringent than that of the EU. In September 2014, the Competition and Markets Authority (CMA), which has replaced the Competition Commission, published *The Statutory Audit Services for Large Companies Market Investigation (Mandatory Use of Competitive Tender Processes and Audit Committee Responsibilities) Order 2014*. The order takes into account the EU Regulation and Directive, and provides for the UK to take advantage of the derogation in the Regulation to allow a possible ten-year extension of the audit engagement, where a tendering process has been undertaken at the end of the initial ten-year period.

These measures go some way to ensure that auditors and auditing firms do not become a permanent feature and agents of the businesses, which they are supposed to audit independently. However, they do not necessarily provide enough protection from potential reprisals if and when auditors blow the whistle on the company.

The UK whistleblowing provisions, which have evolved within the common law tradition, have not normally given workers a general right to disclose information about their employment.[68] Even the revelation of non-confidential material could be regarded as undermining the implied duty of trust and give rise to an action for breach of contract. In relation to confidential information obtained in the course of employment, the common law again provides protection against

66 See: The Financial Direct 2016 Audit Fees Survey at: http://www.financialdirector.co.uk/wp-content/uploads/sites/28/cnt-import/accountancy-age/digital_assets/Audit_survey_for_web.pdf.

67 Helgren C. Barclays picks KPMG as first new auditor in 120 years, Reuters, 3 July 2015, http://uk.reuters.com/article/uk-barclays-auditor-kpmg-idUKKCN0PD14220150703.

68 Lewis, D. Ten years of public interest disclosure legislation in the UK: are whistleblowers adequately protected? (2008) *Journal of Business Ethics*, 82: 497–507.

disclosure through both express and implied terms. The duty of fidelity can be used to prevent disclosures while the employment subsists, and restrictive covenants can be used to inhibit the activities of former employees after the relationship has ceased. However, post-employment covenants will only be enforceable if they can be shown to protect legitimate business interests and are reasonable in all the circumstances. Even in the absence of an enforceable post-employment restrictive covenant, ex-employees are bound not to reveal matters learned in confidence during their employment.[69]

Where employees have allegedly disclosed confidential information in breach of an express or implied term, they may seek to invoke a public interest defence to a legal action. This has become available under the Public Interest Disclosure Act (PIDA) 1998. In relation to criminal acts, such as money laundering, it can be asserted that whistleblowing, disclosure and reporting would serve the public interest, which outweighs the employer's interest. Such a stance was also adopted by the European Court of Human Rights in the case of Heinisch,[70] whereby the Court held that the public interest disclosure deriving from criminal acts and the freedom of expression could not be held hostage to employer's interests. Accordingly, AAs should, at least in theory, be able to report without the fear of any retaliation. Yet such jurisprudence has not been instilled in the legal instruments in all EU Member States. Furthermore, the effectiveness of national legal instruments has been questioned. For instance, Lewis opines that while the PIDA has been hailed as model legislation, 'employers' interests have been given prominence' and whistleblowers have not been adequately protected.[71]

In the first ten years after PIDA came into force, it has been reported that the number of claims made under it annually increased from 157 in 1999 to 1761 in 2009.[72] This was still a small proportion (under 1 per cent) of all claims made to employment tribunals within that same period. More than 70 per cent of these claims were either settled or withdrawn without being subjected to a public hearing. The 22 per cent of the remaining cases were won. There is incomplete information on specific remedies awarded in these cases whereby, within the reported cases, the average compensation was £113,000 (the largest single compensation was over £3.8m) and the total of all awards was £9.5m.[73] Such claims also evidence that blowing the whistle is not a simple matter; often there is a counteraction by the employer and subsequently the employee, the whistleblower, has to resort to litigation to obtain a legal remedy.

Nevertheless, these remedies can be seen as a good element of a desired whistleblower protection regime and, indeed, PIDA has had an impact on the

69 See: *Hivac Ltd v Park Royal Ltd* [1946] Ch 169 and *Attorney-General v Guardian* [No. 2] 1990 1 AC.
70 *Heinisch v Germany* (28274/08).
71 Lewis, n. 68 above.
72 Stephenson and Levi, n. 32 above.
73 Ibid.

attitudes of and confidence in reporting malpractices in the UK. A survey conducted by Ernst and Young in 2007 found that 86 per cent of UK senior executives in multinationals felt free to report cases of fraud or corruption. At the same time the figure across mainland Europe was an average of 54 per cent. PIDA is not the only legal instrument to protect AAs. The UK Financial Reporting Council has published the UK Corporate Governance Code (CGC) in 2014, whereby the companies listed on the London Stock Exchange are required to ensure proper protection for AAs. Section C of the CGC sets out the general requirements for auditing, so that they are able to operate independently. However, there is no explicit mention of whistleblowing protection therein.

The most recent legal instrument which offers protection to disclosures involving money-laundering offences is the Serious Crime Act (SCA) 2015. Section 37 of the SCA provides an exemption for civil liability for money-laundering disclosures. Furthermore Section 50 states that the 'disclosure does not breach any obligation of confidence owed by the person making the disclosure or any other restriction on the disclosure of information (however imposed)'. While the SCA does not use the term 'whistleblower' as such, the overarching disclosure protection provisions are relevant and applicable for AAs.

As a global financial centre, the UK is seen as a petri dish for potential money launderers.[74] The UK possesses numerous legal instruments that deal with ML offences.[75] These include the Proceeds of Crime Act 2002 (PCA), the Terrorism Act 2000 (TA), both of which criminalise ML, and thereinafter the Money Laundering Regulations 2007 (Regulations), which impose – in addition to the PCA – obligations on the financial sector. The Serious Crime Act 2015 also contains provisions to combat ML. The statistics provided by the government indicate a robust and effective AML reporting system with many checks and balances emanating from AAs' practice.[76] At the same time, it is not clear how the UK intends to incorporate the 4th EU AML Directive into its AML framework. Relevant stakeholders are awaiting guidance and engagement from the government.[77] In any event, the protection of whistleblowers would be covered by the PIDA, thus enabling a good environment for ML disclosures.

74 HM Treasury, Preventing money laundering, http://www.gov.uk/government/publications/preventing-money-laundering; International Monetary Fund, United Kingdom: Anti-Money Laundering/Combating the Financing of Terrorism – Technical Note (International Monetary Fund. 2011).

75 For an overview of the UK AML laws, see: Harrison, K. and Ryder, N. *The Law Relating to Financial Crime in the United Kingdom* (Ashgate Publishing, 2013).

76 HM Treasury, The AML and CTF Supervision Report 2014 (updated on 24 March 2015), https://www.gov.uk/government/publications/anti-money-laundering-and-counter-terrorist-finance-supervision-reports/anti-money-laundering-and-counter-terrorist-finance-supervision-report-2013-14.

77 The Law Society, AML Policy Update, February 2016, http://www.lawsociety.org.uk/news/stories/policy-update-february-2016.

10.7.2 Italy

Italy already has a mandatory audit firm rotation of nine years[78] and Italian law recognises the independence of auditors, as well as a whistleblower protection in the context of financial crime. The law, containing 'Provisions for the prevention and repression of corruption and illegal practices in the public administration' (2012) provides that:

A. Except in cases of liability for calumny or defamation, a public servant who reports illicit conduct discovered in the course of his duties may not be sanctioned, dismissed or subjected to any discriminatory measure, direct or indirect, affecting his working conditions for reasons directly or indirectly related to the whistleblowing.
B. Without prejudice to the reporting requirements provided for by law, the identity of the informer may not be disclosed, without his consent, until such time as the disciplinary charge is contested.[79]

In cases involving a criminal offence (e.g. financial crime, money laundering), the obligation for public officials to notify the judiciary also implies the obligation to disclose (to this authority) the identity of the informer – which is necessary for the purposes of the investigation, as the Code of Criminal Procedure prohibits the use of anonymous complaints or reports. Furthermore, if it is found that the whistleblowing is liable to constitute calumny or defamation, the identity of the informer must be disclosed to the judiciary in charge of the proceedings, irrespective of any disciplinary action which may be taken.

While these provisions are welcome for whistleblower protection and independence, they only apply to public officials and neglect the private actors such as AAs. If a public servant would like to disclose money laundering or corrupt practices, the information can only be disclosed to their superior, the Judicial Authority or the Court of Audit. The identity of the whistleblowers cannot be revealed without their consent. It is important to note that whistleblower protection in Italy is not comprehensive and comes significantly short of countering financial crime because the law does not introduce new rules on the statute of limitations or any new criminal law provisions on false accounting and self-laundering (*autoriciclaggio*).[80] Corruption (which may include cover-up of money-laundering offences) in the private sector is designated as a crime in the Italian Criminal Code, but is covered by the Civil Code. While the recent legal

78 Ianniello, G. and Galloppo, G. Stock market reaction to auditor opinions – Italian evidence (2015) *Managerial Auditing Journal*, 30(6/7): 610–632.
79 Law No. 190 of 6 November 2012 on the prevention and repression of corruption and irregularities in the public administration, which came into force on 28 November 2012.
80 Italy to the EU Anticorruption Report, COM 2014, 38 Final, http://ec.europa.eu/dgs/home-affairs/what-we-do/policies/organized-crime-and-human-trafficking/corruption/anti-corruption-report/docs/2014_acr_italy_chapter_en.pdf.

reforms have tried to address the deficiencies related to financial crime in the context of corruption, limited liability arising from a lack of adequate supervision and narrow scope of prohibited activities hinder the potency of the law. GRECO reported that Italian accounting system does not comply with the Council of Europe Criminal Law Convention on Corruption, particularly because of the limited accounting requirements,[81] the setting of penalties and scope of false accounting offences.[82] Added to this inadequate environment is the speed of settling alleged offences. The slow pace and time-barred sanctions regime has resulted in very few successful prosecutions of financial crime in Italy. For example, it was reported that in 2011, out of 60 cases, only nine were investigated further and only three of these cases resulted in sanctions. Subsequently, the private actors such as AAs have neither specific recognition and obligation as key actors in countering financial crime nor any incentive and protection should they choose to report malfeasant activity. Even if they are protected by the law, the ineffective enforcement regime is not conducive for reporting suspicious ML activity.

The Italian AML regime (Legislative Decree 231/2007) is informed by the 3rd EU AML Directive (Dir. 2005/60/EC). In 2014, the scope of the AML regime was extended (by an amended to the Article 648 of the Penal Code) in order to encompass self-laundering activities, particularly with an emphasis on tax evasion. For the financial sector, the Bank of Italy issued 'Measures regarding the execution of organisational, procedural and internal auditing for the prevention of laundering' on 10 March 2011.[83] The AML regime in Italy has also seen a plethora of decrees and guidelines[84] addressing operational aspects of the financial sector, including due diligence methods, red flag indicators and reporting requirements. In addition, professional bodies such as Assirevi, the Italian Association of Accounting Auditors, published Document No. 181, 'Application of AML obligations to auditing companies' which comments on the requirements for AAs under the Legislative Decree no. 231 2007.[85] While these recent measures are in line with the FATF Recommendations and developments under the EU AML framework, they do not address the protection of AAs. They merely state

81 Only listed companies, state-owned companies and insurance companies are required to adhere to the accounting requirements.

82 GRECO Report – Italy, Joint First and Second Evaluation Rounds, 01 July 2013, https://www.coe.int/t/dghl/monitoring/greco/evaluations/round2/GrecoRC1&2(2011)1_Add_Italy_EN.pdf.

83 See: http://www.bancaditalia.it/compiti/vigilanza/normativa/archivio-norme/riciclaggio-terrorismo/decreto-leg-2312007/Provv_Organizz.pdf (in Italian).

84 For a detailed analysis of these measures, see: Grillo A. Anti-money laundering in Italy, 2014 Report, Compliance Net, 21 June 2015, http://www.compliancenet.it/documenti/150621-aml-in-italy-report-2014-v20.pdf.

85 Italian Association of Accounting Auditors, http://www.assirevi.it/documenti/Documento%20di%20ricerca%20n.%20%20181.pdf and http://www.compliancenet.it/assirevi-doc-181-normativa-antiriciclaggio-applicazione-alle-societa-di-revisione-20-maggio-2014.

the duties of AAs (e.g. Article 13 of the AML Decree and the Resolution No. 18802[86] issued by CONSOB on 01 February 2014).

10.7.3 Portugal

Portugal already has mandatory audit firm rotation shorter than EU requirements.

The Portuguese Labour Code protects public- and private-sector employees from unfair action by employers when reporting a crime, but to be reinstated they must file a complaint in court at their own expense. This in itself may deter any potential disclosure and reporting of suspicious activity and financial crime.

The Criminal Procedure Code obliges public officials to report any crime they discover while performing their duties. Yet there are no specific mechanisms in public institutions to ensure protection of whistleblowers and the types of reporting are restricted to financial activities (accounting, internal accounting controls, auditing, money laundering), bribery and corruption. While this focus may work well for countering financial crime, the scope of the current legal protection does not include private-sector employees, the judiciary or government or trade union officials. The biggest problem in whistleblower protection in Portugal is the fact that anonymous whistleblowing is prohibited.[87] The limited protection conferred to public-sector whistleblowers is deepened by a one-year limit on protections and the waiving of whistleblower anonymity if a suspected person is formally charged. Furthermore, there is no consolidated piece of legislation on whistleblowing or a central agency to oversee and coordinate disclosures or whistleblower protection.

The Portuguese Law No. 25/2008 has implemented the 3rd EU AML Directive. Articles 3 and 4 of this statute require AAs to take an active role in AML strategy. Independent auditing appears to underpin this strategy, yet the series of laws[88] enacted to address financial crime do not once mention the protection of persons who disclose information about actual or potential (suspect) ML activity. Article 20 of the AML law states that

> the disclosure of information in good faith by the entities subject to this law, in compliance with the duties laid down in Articles 16, 17 and 18, shall not constitute a breach of any duty of confidentiality, imposed by any legislative, regulatory or contractual provision, and shall not hold liable in any way the persons who disclose the information.

86 See: http://www.compliancenet.it/consob-disposizioni-adeguata-verifica-antiriciclaggio-revisori-21-febbraio-2014.

87 The Guidelines published by the Portuguese Data Protection Authority, 1 October 2009.

88 For a comprehensive list of legal instruments, see: FATF – Mutual Evaluation (Second Update) Report (Portugal) 2010, http://www.fatf-gafi.org/media/fatf/documents/reports/mer/PT_SecondUpdateReport_2010.pdf.

Disclosure of the identity of the person who made the report of suspicious activity faces a maximum penalty of three years' imprisonment or a fine (Article 20(b)). While this provision may protect the person disclosing information for a customer or a third party, it is unlikely to shield the AAs, because of the nature of their work and involvement with the company they are asked to audit, as well as the intimate and often privileged access to information available to them. At the time of the writing, it is not clear how Portugal intends to implement the 4th EU AML Directive.

10.7.4 Sweden

While Sweden does not have a specific piece of statute for whistleblower protection per se, retaliating against a whistleblower has been a criminal offence in Sweden since 1766. This key provision has informed labour, civil and criminal laws of the country and created a sound environment where disclosures can be made without the fear of reprisals. Both public and private employees are free to supply information to the press and disclose details of suspected malfeasant activities to the authorities. National or local governments are not permitted to investigate the identity of anonymous sources, nor may employees be fired or otherwise retaliated against. As long as a private-sector employee informs his employer first, he is free to report any wrongdoing to external organisations and persons. While the Swedish framework seems to be robust enough for effective disclosure, there are a number of shortcomings. Private companies are allowed to investigate who provided information to the media and can dismiss an employee (who leaked the information) on grounds of disloyalty. In contrast, public-sector employees and those employed by city-owned companies may anonymously pass on information to the media.[89] This creates unequal standing for whistleblowers and potentially hinders the protection regime for whistleblowers.

The Swedish Act 2009:62 on Measures to Prevent ML and Terrorist Financing is the main statute that governs the duties of AAs.[90] It has been reported that the Swedish government's recent reforms to its AML regime already comply with some of the requirements of the 4th EU AML Directive.[91] It is also clear that the Swedish AML law and policy are risk-based and report-oriented.[92] Yet, at the same time, it is not clear how exactly the whistleblower protection required by the Directive is going to be achieved.

89 Transparency International, Whistleblowing in Europe, 2013, http://www.stt.lt/documents/soc_tyrimai/2013_WhistleblowingInEurope_EN.pdf.

90 See: http://www.notisum.se/rnp/sls/lag/20090062.htm. Note that the Act was amended in August 2010.

91 See: https://www.bankinghub.eu/banking/finance-risk/finalization-4th-anti-money-laundering-directive. For example, the data retention rules require AAs to retain information for five years.

92 FATF, Mutual Evaluation (Fourth Follow-up) Report (Sweden) 2010, http://www.fatf-gafi.org/media/fatf/documents/reports/mer/FoR%20Sweden.pdf.

10.7.5 The Netherlands

The Netherlands already has mandatory audit firm rotation of eight years, permitted under regulatory changes, but is expected to change to ten years to comply with the EU regulation.

Whistleblower protection under the recent Whistleblower Regulation for Central Government and Police is particularly robust for the public sector in the Netherlands. Whistleblower protection for the private sector is governed by a system that is made up by a patchwork of rules and procedures, which is 'oriented towards protecting accused organisations rather than whistleblowers'.[93] This trend was evidenced by the initial judgment of the Amsterdam Court,[94] when a bank employee was told that he should have reported the problem internally first. Importantly, on appeal, the Dutch Supreme Court overruled this to a certain extent and opined that confidentiality and employee duties could *not* override the duty of honesty and trusteeship. In addition to this recent positive development in the Dutch whistleblower protection regime, there is a code of conduct under the umbrella organisation of the Labour Foundation. However, this is a voluntary mechanism, and it has been reported that many Dutch companies have not implemented independent reporting mechanisms.[95] The draft legislation, 'Bill on a House for Whistleblowers', which has been proposed recently, contains provisions that would protect disclosures if the suspicions are based on reasonable grounds, there is a public interest at stake, and due process is observed in handling the disclosures.

The Netherlands has implemented the 3rd EU AML Directive by the Act on the Prevention of Money Laundering and Financing Terrorism on 1 August 2008. Section 16 of this Act requires institutions to report unusual and suspicious transactions to the Financial Intelligence Unit Netherlands. The institutions are under a strict legal obligation to keep their reporting confidential. The reporting institution is not allowed to disclose its intention to report or the fact that a report has been made. Yet there are no specific rules as to protection of the whistleblowers. It is not clear whether and how the Dutch authorities intend to implement the requirements under the 4th AML Directive into Dutch legal system.

10.7.6 France

France already has joint audit regime – permitted under regulatory changes.

France does not have a specific legal instrument for whistleblower protection. France has been branded as 'an international oddity, having legislation that ostensibly protects employees of private companies but no law covering

93 Ibid.

94 LJN: BW9244, Hoge Raad, 11/04190, of 26 October 2012 and available at NJB 2012, 2254, RvdW 2012, 1341, and www.rechtspraak.nl.

95 Transparency International, n. 89 above.

government workers'.[96] While public-sector employees are required to report crimes to the Public Prosecutor, the law does not confer any protection against retaliation. Recent studies reveal that public officials who reported malfeasant activities were dismissed, ostracised or forced to take early retirement. Contracted workers, who make up 20 per cent of the overall workforce in the public sector, were also subjected to retaliation, whereby their contracts were not renewed or they were dismissed without due process.[97]

While, in the context of anti-corruption, France has tried to create a protection regime (under the 2007 Anti-Corruption Act) for whistleblowers who disclose information in 'good faith',[98] it failed to put in place an independent agency to conduct investigations, follow up allegations or collate data. Jurisprudence indicates that such protection only applies to reports of corruption-related crimes.[99] Furthermore, the French law does not offer any protection of the whistleblower's identity or stipulate particular methods for internal or external reporting channels. Suggestions by multinational companies to set up anonymous whistleblowing regimes have been struck down by rights to privacy and data protection laws.[100] In regards to AAs, reporting of financial crime in the context of accounting, banking and bribery is encouraged, and whistleblowing systems are regulated by the French Data Protection Authority. However, such regulatory overview is based on self-certification and subject to interpretation on a case-by-case basis.

The 3rd EU AML Directive was implemented by Ordonnance No. 2009–104 of 30 January 2009. While the reporting duties and procedures required by the French law are robust and mostly compliant with the FATF recommendations,[101]

96 Meyer, N. M., *Providing an Alternative to Silence: Towards Greater Protection and Support for Whistleblowers in the EU. Country Report: France* (France: September 2012), cited in Transparency International, n. 89 above.

97 Service Central de Prevention de la Corruption, Les dispositifs d'alerte: le whistleblowing (2011) *Rapport,* pp. 202–220, cited in Transparency International, n. 89 above.

98 French Labour Code 2007 states: 'No one can be prohibited to access a recruiting procedure or an internship or a period of training in a company, no employee can be sanctioned, dismissed or be subject to, direct or indirect, discriminatory measures, especially concerning salary, training, reclassification, appointment, qualification, professional promotion, relocation or renewal of contract, if he or she has disclosed, in good faith, either to his or her employer or to the judicial or administrative authorities, corruption-related offences that he or she would have discovered in exercising his/her functions. Any termination of contract which would be a result of this, any disposition or any contrary act would be void.'

99 Dassault Systems judgment (8 December 2009), cited in Sankowicz, D. and Henry, S. Update on whistleblowing in France, *Employment & Industrial Relations Law* (March 2012), http://www.paulhastings.com/docs/default-source/PDFs/update_on_whistleblowing_in_france.pdf.

100 Worlton, A. E. and Reynolds, J. French data protection authority blocks SOX whistleblower programs (2005) *Privacy in Focus,* July, http://www.wileyrein.com/publications.cfm?sp=articles&newsletter=4&id=1829, cited in Transparency International, n. 89 above.

101 See: FATF – Mutual Evaluation Report (France), 2010, http://www.fatf-gafi.org/countries/d-i/france/documents/mutualevaluationoffrance.html.

there is no mention of protection of reporters and whistleblowers in the AML legislation.

10.7.7 Spain

Spain has implemented the EU Directive 2006/43/EC into its domestic law, whereby the rotation of auditors is ensured.[102] Yet Spain lacks appropriate legislation to protect whistleblowers both in the public and private sectors. While all citizens are obliged to report criminal activity to authorities, there is no ensuing protection in terms of privacy, confidentiality or accountability. Consequently, there are very few instances of reporting and whistleblowing. Private-sector businesses are not obliged to implement any specific whistleblower protection schemes.

The Royal Decree 304/2014 contains the legal provision for Spain's AML policy and practice. Financial institutions, and their directors and employees, are protected from liability when disclosing information to the competent authorities in good faith under these rules (Article 23). In addition, financial institutions, and their directors and employees are prohibited from disclosing to the customer or third persons the fact that an SAR has been transmitted to the FIU or is (or may be) under review for crime prevention purposes. Spain also has rules which stipulate that under no circumstance can the FIU or any other competent authority or civil servant having access to such information reveal the identity of a reporting director, employee or agent. FIU's report to prosecutors and law-enforcement authorities cannot be directly incorporated into the judicial proceedings as this could reveal who the reporting party is (Article 46). While these are positive features of the AML regime in Spain, particularly when a customer or a third party is suspected of ML, it is not clear whether such provisions would apply to AAs reporting on their employees. Similar to other EU countries in the region (e.g. Portugal, France, Italy), Spain does not have any specific rules on protection of AAs in the context of AML nor is it clear whether and how the 4th EU AML Directive requirements on whistleblower protection will be implemented.

10.7.8 Germany

While employees in the public and private sectors cannot be arbitrarily dismissed for whistleblowing, Germany has no specific legislation on protecting them. According to a recent study, 44 per cent of federal, 36 per cent of *Länder* and 23 per cent of local or municipal authorities have a whistleblowing system in the

102 Ley 22/2015, de 20 de julio, de Auditoría de Cuentas Boletín Oficial del Estado, Núm. 173.

form of a hotline, website or ombudsman.[103] Similar to most EU countries, Germany does not have a specific statute that protects whistleblowers. Rather, numerous legal provisions are scattered across different legislation and in different contexts. For example, the German Data Protection Act (*Bundesdatenschutzgesetz – BDSG*) allows the data protection officer to report possible violations of the data protection rules to the authorities; the German Labour Protection Act (*Arbeitsschutzgesetz – ArbSchG*) allows employees to report possible threats of safety and health protection to the authorities, if an employer has not remedied previous internal complaints; the German General Equal Treatment Act (*Allgemeines Gleichbehandlungsgesetz – AGG*) provides for the employees' right to report possible discrimination to their employers and/or the Federal Anti-Discrimination Agency; and the German Works Constitution Act (*Betriebsverfassungsgesetz – BetrVG*) allows employees to complain about unfair treatment to their employers and/or the works council. The German Banking Act (*Kreditwesengesetz – KWG*) requires financial institutions to have a proper business organisation, including a mechanism which allows employees to report to an appropriate body within the company, any violations of the Regulation (EU) no. 575/2013, violations of the German Banking Act or any statutory orders issued in connection therewith, as well as criminal offences. While the employees who utilise such mechanisms are acting lawfully,[104] they are confined to internal reporting and there is no provision to ensure independent overview of the disclosure. It is clear that, similar to its neighbours, France and the Netherlands, there is no express whistleblowing law, and therefore individuals have to reply on piecemeal rights emanating from employment, criminal or anti-corruption laws. None of these deal with AML in particular, nor do they offer any extra layer of protection before or after any disclosure.

The German whistleblowing regime is further complicated by the fact that whistleblowers have to rely on the courts to determine whether they are entitled to protection against reprisal. This creates the unavoidable situation whereby the whistleblower must first report the alleged offence, wait for the employer's response and then seek legal protection from the courts. Taken on a case-by-case basis, the court judgments indicate that there are inconsistencies in this regard,[105] thus leaving whistleblowers vulnerable to reprisal.

The German AML legislation consists of the *Strafgesetzbuch* (Criminal Code), the *Geldwäschegesetz* (Money Laundering Act, hereinafter referred to as AML Act)

103 Salvenmoser, S. *et al.*, PricewaterhouseCoopers, cited in the EU Anti-corruption Report, 2014, http://ec.europa.eu/dgs/home-affairs/what-we-do/policies/organized-crime-and-human-trafficking/corruption/anti-corruption-report/docs/2014_acr_germany_chapter_en.pdf.

104 Brucklmeier L. Whistleblowing – what protection do employees have in Germany? (2015) *Lexology*, 15 May, http://www.lexology.com/library/detail.aspx?g=0e381c8c-94d5-4762-beed-2f0b0f3d9f1f.

105 Transparency International, n. 89 above.

and sector-specific laws such as the Banking Act.[106] Under the AML Act,[107] AAs have a duty to report suspicious activity and the overall AML strategy heavily relies on annual external audits. It has been noted that there is no systematic implementation of these duties in a harmonised manner.[108] IMF has stated that AAs are 'subject to strict professional secrecy obligations which contribute to a low level of reporting of suspicious transactions and complicate cooperation with investigative authorities'.[109]

The AAs supervised by the Federal Financial Supervisory Authority (BaFin)[110] and the *Länder*[111] play an important role in supervising financial institutions for compliance with AML/counter financing of terrorism requirements. AAs not only produce annual AML/CFT audit reports for all supervised institutions under a specific statutory authority and provide that report to the BaFin, but also carry out specific on-site AML/CFT inspections under the command of the BaFin.

The German Commercial Code requires all financial institutions to have their financial statements audited annually in compliance with the standards prescribed by the German Auditors Association.[112] The International Monetary Fund (IMF) report states that while the specific areas to be covered by the AAs are laid down in the Auditors Report Regulation, there are only limited agreed procedures or auditing standards for the work. The IMF opines that these regulations have now been outdated by the new AML Act and the introduction of the risk-based approach therein.[113]

Section 13 of the AML Act stipulates that anyone who reports to the law enforcement authorities a criminal offence (under Section 261 of the Criminal Code) 'cannot be held responsible' for the disclosure in question, unless it has been made in a deliberately false or grossly negligent manner. It has been stated that the notion of responsibility in this provision covers both criminal and civil liability for an employee who reports suspicious activities to his or her supervisor or an in-house unit responsible for filing suspicious activity reports.[114]

While the AML Act (Section 12) prohibits the disclosure of the fact that a suspicious activity report has been filed with the authorities, there is no provision that restricts disclosure of reporting institutions to share information among members of the same financial group, and between institutions that have a common interest in the transaction or the customer, provided that the other

106 Financial Action Task Force, *Mutual Evaluation Report Executive Summary: Anti-Money Laundering and Combating the Financing of Terrorism – Germany* (2010), p. 3.

107 *Gesetz über das Aufspüren von Gewinnen aus schweren Straftaten (Geldwäschegesetz – GwG)*, http://www.gesetze-im-internet.de/bundesrecht/gwg_2008/gesamt.pdf.

108 IMF Country Report No. 10/78, *Detailed Assessment Report on AML and CTF*, March 2010, https://www.imf.org/external/pubs/ft/scr/2010/cr1078.pdf, p. 13.

109 Ibid.

110 See: http://www.bafin.de/EN/Homepage/homepage_node.html.

111 The Federal Republic of Germany is a federal state made up of 16 constituent states, which are often referred to as the *Länder*.

112 See: http://www.idw.de/idw/portal/n589244/index.jsp.

113 IMF Country Report, n. 108 above.

114 Ibid.

institution is in an EU member State or ***a third country deemed to have equivalent AML/CFT standards*** (emphasis added). This waiver is problematic, both in terms of whistleblower protection and compliance with the FATF standards. The reporting actor is called upon to assess and form an opinion on the quality and state of AML mechanisms in other jurisdictions, a task which is even challenging for top experts in the field. Furthermore, the FATF recommendations prohibit any disclosure to third parties other than the competent authorities.[115]

The AML Act protects the identity of the ML compliance officers making the report to relevant agencies if the case is treated as a criminal case. Accordingly, the personal data of parties blowing the whistle are not stored at the financial intelligence unit or in the State Criminal Police Offices files available to other officers. It is not clear, however, whether this covers the AAs. Under Section 29(2) of the Banking Act, the AAs of credit institutions and financial services institutions are required to examine whether such institutions comply with the AML obligations under the AML Act, the Banking Act and EC Regulation 1781/2006. However, these obligations do not apply to branches of such institutions from other Member States of the EU. When AAs discover serious breaches of AML rules, they are obliged under Section 29 of the Banking Act to report the facts immediately to the BaFin, and in such cases the auditors are given statutory protection from any potential breaches of professional secrecy. While Germany seemingly has robust rules for protecting whistleblowers against breaches of secrecy requirements, it is not clear how Germany intends to incorporate the 4th EU AML Directive into its AML framework and whether the existing protection regime would satisfy the required EU standards under that Directive.

The overview of the whistleblower protection regime in the EU reveals that there is no fully fledged and harmonised mechanism for AAs. These trends in the EU are similar to those found in other affluent countries of the world. For example, a report on whistleblower protection in G20 countries[116] found that many countries fail to meet minimum international standards, such as independent reporting channels, including clear external avenues to third parties; anonymity; and internal disclosure mechanisms.

10.8 Recommendations as to how AAs should be empowered to report in the AML context

Whistleblowing and reporting are key instruments in exposing and countering all types of financial crime.[117] Having anti-money-laundering and/or anti-corruption

115 FATF Recommendations, 2012, p. 8, http://www.fatf-gafi.org/media/fatf/documents/FATF%20Standards%20-%2040%20Recommendations%20rc.pdf.

116 Wolfe, S. *et al.*, *Whistleblower Protection Rules in G20 Countries: The Next Action Plan*, 2014, http://transparency.org.au/wp-content/uploads/2014/06/Action-Plan-June-2014-Whistleblower-Protection-Rules-G20-Countries.pdf.

117 The infamous Panama Papers were provided by a whistleblower. See: The International Consortium of Investigative Journalists, https://panamapapers.icij.org/#_ga=1.115631748.34859270.1460118672.

laws alone is not enough for a successful strategy; ensuring enablers such as independent and effective reporting channels without fearing reprisals is equally important in creating a robust anti-crime environment in the work place as well as in the financial sector. While it is clear that in many EU Member States there is an absence of comprehensive whistleblower legislation, each legal system offers a degree of protection that may serve as an incentive.

This protection emanates from a variety of legal sources: employment law, civil service acts, human rights law, and witness-protection legislation, which confer protection on employees or witnesses to a crime. These patchworks of legislation may be interpreted, with some 'imagination', as whistleblower protection regimes available to certain types of people and disclosure of information. The obligation to report financial crime or suspicious activity to competent authorities is ensured by the EU legislation, but this does not mean that the person who files the report has a strong means to influence the legal process once it is launched. Disclosures or reports are typically made to a law enforcement agency or to a financial intelligence unit, and are investigated in an adminis-trative process if these agencies decide to pursue the case. In some jurisdictions, protection offered by the law can be invoked, not only when the evidence for a suspect or criminal activity is provided, but also when the identity of the whistleblower is disclosed. Even if the latter were not required, in light of the detailed financial details entailed in money-laundering schemes, typically available only to AAs and senior management of the company,[118] it would not be too difficult to infer from whom such information was derived, thus increasing the risk to AAs if suspicious activity reporting does not bear any results. While the EU AML regime emphasises a 'risk-based approach' in countering financial crime, the risk that obliged entities such as AAs are exposed to seems to be neglected. The success levels of the existing fragmented protection regimes are inconsistent across the EU.[119] Importantly, such a fragmented legal framework is linked to the AML regime and is not conducive to the EU's aim to create a harmonised AML regime, a fact recognised by the EU in its 4th AML Directive: 'Measures adopted solely at national or even at Union level, without taking into account international coordination and cooperation, would have very

118 The following were cited as some of the methods applied by AAs in the risk assessment process: monitoring movements in cash flows; comparison of movements of payables and receivables with business activity; identification of forged receipts and documents (e.g. over-reliance on copies rather than originals; checking the status of the firm against the government's company blacklist; financial analysis of the balance sheets for the last 2–3 years; correspondence with banks for intelligence gathering; frequent change of contact details of the client; identification of unrelated and unusual business activity in comparison to company's core business; credit rating and payback ability of the client; and investigation of company and owner's background. Turksen, U. Implications of anti-money laundering law for accountancy in the European Union – a comparative study, in Turksen *et al.* (eds) *Fighting Financial Crime in the Global Economic Crisis: Policy, Trends and Sanctions* (Routledge, 2014).

119 ECOLEF Project – The Economic and Legal Effectiveness of Anti Money Laundering and Combating Terrorist Financing Policy (2013) EC DG Home JLS/2009/ISEC/AG087.

limited effect.'[120] It is also worth noting that the EU envisages a 'holistic' attitude to the risk-based approach, since risk levels vary in different contexts.[121] Accordingly, the AML strategy must encompass enabling provisions for obliged entities (i.e. AAs) who have to report malfeasant financial activities.

AAs are employees and should be able to report any concerns they have about the financial dealings and standards of the companies they are responsible for. This is a basic right and a duty, recognised by the courts (e.g. in the UK under the Human Rights Act 1998), and should be available to all employees so that they can disclose information in the public interest. However, unlike most employees who may blow the whistle out of a moral conviction, the AAs have a statutory duty to report. It has been well documented that fear of losing clients is a significant factor in AAs' decisions to report suspicious activity.[122] A recent study involving AAs revealed that they fear losing the confidence of their clients, whereby if they were known as whistleblowers their clients would become cautious in sharing information with them, and this would result in the AAs facing difficulty in performing their normal duties.[123] Furthermore, interviewees highlighted the lack of trust and confidence in the suspicious activity-reporting mechanism, as the participant accountants were not convinced that the AML regime provided reasonable assurance and maintained confidentiality and privacy. Given the fact that whistleblower protection is less than adequate in numerous EU Member States, there is a great need to pay attention to the development and protection of accountants' 'independence'[124] in the context of fighting financial crime.

Given these fears and risks, there needs to be much more distance between the AA and the employer, so that true independence can be ensured and conflict of interest can be thwarted. Contractual duty and income emanating from the traditional employee–employer relationship does not aid AAs' ability to act freely and without fearing reprisal and damage to their reputation (should suspicious activity reported not amount to actual criminal activity).[125] This requires independence at the establishment stage of the contract for auditing services. For example, in a number of countries, notaries receive payment for the transactions and services they provide, yet the fees received go to a joint, central account, and

120 Directive (EU) 2015/849 of the European Parliament and of the Council of 20 May 2015 on the prevention of the use of the financial system for the purposes of money laundering or terrorist financing, amending Regulation (EU) No. 648/2012 of the European Parliament and of the Council, and repealing Directive 2005/60/EC of the European Parliament and of the Council and Commission Directive 2006/70/EC.

121 Ibid., para. 22.

122 Compin, F. The role of accounting in money laundering and money dirtying (2008) *Critical Perspectives on Accounting*, 19: 592–602.

123 Turksen, n. 118 above.

124 Sikka, P. and Willmott, H. The power of 'independence': defending and extending the jurisdiction of accounting in the United Kingdom (1995) *Accounting, Organizations and Society*, 20(6): 547–581.

125 It is not unusual for whistleblowers to face defamation charges if and when the disclosed information does not end in a successful conviction.

then an equitable share of the overall income is distributed to an individual notary public. This ensures that regardless of the volume and number of transactions that the notary public undertakes, there would be a shared income among all notaries. Such an approach could work in the context of AA appointments. In addition to the existing provision of rotational appointment of auditors, appointments via a regulated central body could also ensure a degree of protection, as the employer would not be able to choose a particular AA. Indeed, this would be a major overhaul for the industry, yet it would also ensure independence at the appointment stage.

The latest EU AML legislation requires Member States to establish effective and reliable protection mechanisms for AAs (among other professionals) during their tenure of delivering services.[126] This is a key element, which could determine or undermine the success of the EU's AML strategy and policy. The EU's AML policy needs to be more than a tepid statement or an enactment of a vague instrument to tick a box under a compliance regime (e.g. FATF Recommendations). Subsequently, Article 61 of the 4th EU AML Directive needs to be expanded to codify what specific measures are necessary to ensure that such envisaged protection is realised. For example, requirement of suspicious activity reporting (SAR) can be married with a protection clause whereby AAs are protected even if the suspicious activity does not amount to a breach of a legal obligation. It would also be advisable to create a provision whereby individuals are relieved from civil or criminal liability for making a disclosure of suspicious activity.[127]

Furthermore, in a number of Member States, whistleblower protection is only available to public-sector employees. Given the fact that AAs are serving the public interest while performing their duties in the private sector, there should be no difference in the treatment of private and public disclosures. Such a consistent approach would strengthen the trust in the system and could encourage AAs to engage with AML strategy.

10.9 Summary

This chapter examined the importance of independent reporting in the context of AML provisions applicable to AAs. In doing so, it identified the current state of affairs in relation to legal duties placed on AAs and critically examined whether AAs are able to report suspicious activity effectively. As a starting point, we identified the importance of AAs as one of the main gatekeepers and agents in countering financial crime. Subsequently, we outlined the legal framework in which they have to operate in the EU. While there are numerous external factors which affect AML strategy – *inter alia*, the volume of trade, number of companies and transactions involved, transnational and international nature

126 Ibid., Article 61.
127 Lewis D. Ten years of public interest disclosure legislation in the UK: are whistleblowers adequately protected? (2008) *Journal of Business Ethics*, 82: 497–507.

of business, the range of assets used to launder dirty money, and access to evidence – there are also inherent obstacles in relation to AAs' engagement with and reporting of suspicious activity. Independence and protection of AAs, both in terms of their initial recruitment and later in the duration of their tenure, are subject to various laws depending on in which EU Member State they operate. While the EU has endeavoured to harmonise its AML framework via a number of AML Directives and bring it to the level of internationally recognised best practices, we found by analysing numerous EU Member States laws that the protection of the key actors (obliged entities for AML) is given scant attention and differs tremendously. This trend is not conducive to creating a unified approach to countering financial crime in general and ML in particular.

Within the confines of a single chapter, it is not possible to make recommendations for each jurisdiction examined. Instead, we provided key recommendations that ought to inform the EU's AML legal framework. These include not only the recognition of the importance of independent SAR procedures, but also the creation of substantive provisions, codifying the elements of an effective protection regime for AAs.

11 Post-crisis regulation and prosecutions in financial crime: progress or paradox?

Gauri Sinha

11.1 Introduction

With the financial crisis[1] of 2008, two 'Rs' have emerged to the forefront: risk and regulation. The housing bubble in the United States is widely believed to have triggered the crisis; however, a deeper look reveals excessive risk-taking as the background to the crisis. A natural reaction to this 'living on the edge' attitude came about in the form of toughened regulation.

With this as the starting point, the author of this chapter asks a few crucial questions, starting with: has a stricter regime led to more effective regulation in financial crime? The answer lies in the analysis of the 'credible deterrence strategy' followed by the Financial Conduct Authority (FCA) in the United Kingdom that has led to an inefficient 'comply or explain' approach on the part of the regulated sector. This chapter argues that a move towards this tougher regulation is purely cosmetic and encourages regulated entities to follow a 'tick-box' approach. The underlying objective of the author is to counter the belief that excessive regulation leads to more efficient compliance of financial crime laws, and therefore a more stable financial system.

Looking at the crisis from the other side of the coin, why are individual prosecutions almost non-existent? Contributory factors, such as lack of resources for law-enforcement agencies, may give part of the answer; however, the author of this chapter contends that it is definitely not the most crucial factor.

Overall, excessive regulation and a shift towards corporate accountability in place of individual liability are misplaced, and are not capable of producing a deterrent effect. Prosecution or deferred prosecution of a corporation is mere

1 The International Monetary Fund describes a financial crisis as consisting of one or more of the following phenomena: substantial changes in credit volume and asset prices; severe disruptions in financial intermediation and the supply of external financing to various actors in the economy; large-scale balance-sheet problems (of firms, households, financial intermediaries and sovereigns); and large-scale government support (in the form of liquidity support and recapitalisation). See generally: S. Claessens and M. Ayhan Kose, 'Financial crises: explanations, types, and implications' (2013) International Monetary Fund Working Paper WP/13/28, 4, <https://www.imf.org/external/pubs/ft/wp/2013/wp1328.pdf> accessed 10 May 2016.

window-dressing, as a corporation does not have morality and therefore has no 'personality' which can be associated with liability. In analysing the above issues, the focus of the chapter remains the United Kingdom; however, in discussing the financial crisis and the (lack of) prosecutions, it is essential to traverse through the reaction of law enforcement to the issue of corporate accountability in the United States.

11.2 Post-crisis regulation and the move towards a risk-based approach

Much has been written about the causes of the crisis.[2] The IMF Working Paper recognises that, among the diversity of these writings, four common features of the causes can be identified:

(1) asset price increases that turned out to be unsustainable;
(2) credit booms that led to excessive debt burdens;
(3) build-up of marginal loans and systemic risk;
(4) the failure of regulation and supervision to keep up with financial innovation and get ahead of the crisis when it erupted.[3]

Failure in regulation remains one of the most mentioned causes.[4] It is widely believed that aggressive risk-taking was made possible due to relaxed regulation, contributing to the housing price bubble and leading to widespread financial distress when the bubble burst.[5]

The problems arising from a lack of regulation were particularly acute in the unregulated over-the-counter credit default swap[6] market. This lack of regulation, it is argued by Senator Tom Harkin, led to a situation where 'tools to manage and limit risk have turned out to magnify and amplify risk'.[7] Howard Davies looks at

2 The US housing market is seen by many as the root cause of the financial crisis. In the late 1990s, house prices grew rapidly in response to a number of contributing factors, including persistently low interest rates, over-generous lending and speculation. The bursting of the housing bubble, in addition to simultaneous crashes in other asset bubbles, triggered the credit crisis.

3 Claessens and Kose (n. 1 above) 4.

4 For an analysis of how weaknesses in regulation and supervision contributed to the crisis, see M. Cihak, A. Demirguc-Kunt, M.S.M. Peria and A. Mohseni-Cheraghlou, 'Bank regulation and supervision around the world: a crisis update' (2012) World Bank Policy Research working paper WPS6286, <http://documents.worldbank.org/curated/en/2012/12/17039335/bank-regulation-supervision-around-world-crisis-update> accessed 15 May 2016.

5 S.E. Harrington, 'Financial crisis, systemic risk and the future of insurance regulation' (2009) 76(4) *Journal of Risk and Insurance* 785.

6 Credit default swaps are a common form of credit derivative that may involve municipal bonds, emerging market bonds, mortgage-backed securities or corporate bonds, and have a fair amount of risk associated with them.

7 Senator Tom Harkin, Senate Committee on Agriculture, Nutrition and Forestry (Hearing on the Role of Financial Derivatives in Current Financial Crisis) 2008.

the problem of regulation from a more global perspective. In the lead-up to the crisis, he writes, regulators had not properly understood the way in which risks were transferred across borders and between different types of institution. The risk characteristics of new instruments designed to transfer risk were poorly understood.[8]

From the United Kingdom (UK) perspective, a statement issued by the House of Commons is pertinent in this regard: the Financial Services Authority (FSA) did not supervise Northern Rock properly. It did not allocate sufficient resources or time to monitoring a bank whose business model was so clearly an outlier; its procedures were inadequate to supervise a bank whose business grew so rapidly. In the case of Northern Rock, the FSA appears to have systematically failed in its duty as a regulator to ensure that Northern Rock would not pose such a systemic risk, and this failure contributed significantly to the difficulties, and risks to the public purse, that have followed.[9]

Analysing the role of regulation in the financial crisis, Adair Turner, the then chairman of FSA,[10] openly admits that the regulator made mistakes in the institution-specific supervision of Northern Rock. However, he adds that specific supervision would have made little difference to the 'shape and impact' of the crisis.[11] While the extent of the contribution of weak regulation in causing the crisis is debatable, the defensive approach of the FSA is clearly visible here.

Until the banking crisis, UK banking regulation could be described as 'light touch'. Nevertheless, with the regulator's shift from 'light touch' to 'intensive supervision' in the wake of the 2008 financial crisis, the FSA increasingly toughened its approach towards those it regulates. This may be a reflection of the defensive stance taken by Turner, as mentioned above. The FSA Chief Executive at the time,[12] Hector Sants, warned that the new regulatory regime would be more intrusive and direct than ever before: 'There is a view that people are not frightened of the FSA . . . I can assure you that this is a view I am determined to correct. People should be very frightened of the FSA.'[13] The 'credible deterrence' strategy, initiated by the FSA in 2009 and discussed later in this chapter, fits well

8 Howard Davies, 'Global financial regulation after the credit crisis' (2010) 1(2) *Global Policy* 185.

9 House of Commons Treasury Committee, *Fifth Report* (HC Session 2007–08), available at <http://www.publications.parliament.uk/pa/cm200708/cmselect/cmtreasy/56/5602.htm> accessed 25 April 2016.

10 Beginning April 2013, the FSA has now been split up into two separate regulatory authorities, the Financial Conduct Authority (hereinafter FCA) and the Prudential Regulation Authority (hereinafter PRA). However, the principal objectives of these organisations remain the same as the FSA. The modus operandi of the FCA also remains the same as its predecessor.

11 Adair Turner, 'The financial crisis and the future of financial crisis' (2009) <http://www.fsa.gov.uk/pages/Library/Communication/Speeches/2009/0121_at.shtml> accessed 10 May 2016.

12 Hector Sants held the position of the Chief Executive Officer of the FSA from 2007 to 2012.

13 'Be afraid, warns regulator Sants' *BBC News* (London, 12 March 2009) <http://news.bbc.co.uk/1/hi/business/7939619.stm> accessed 20 March 2016.

with this new-found purpose: it plans to create a consistent and more transparent framework for calculating financial penalties, which could mean some fines treble in size.[14] The author argues that the strategy translates into onerous burdens being passed on to the regulated sector as a means of transferring responsibility without focusing on the negative outputs. This is demonstrated both in the undefined and unguided risk-based approach.[15]

Against this background, this chapter embarks on the crucial journey to test the relationship dynamics between the FCA and its private-sector compliance partners. It is interesting to note that the move towards 'principles-based regulation' in financial crime was made by the FSA in 2006. The FSA describes principles-based regulation as meaning, where possible, moving away from dictating through detailed, prescriptive rules and supervisory actions on how firms should operate their business. It also means giving firms the responsibility to decide how best to align their business objectives and processes with the regulatory outcomes specified by the FSA.[16]

In the sphere of financial crime, this style of regulation translates into encouraging firms to adopt a risk-based approach by focusing their financial crime resources on areas of higher risk. That does not detract, however, from the need for firms to do their own analysis of where the risks lie. It is hoped that such an approach will, for example, ensure that lower-risk customers do not suffer from unduly burdensome procedures and requirements. On the other hand, it will ensure that firms undertake enhanced due diligence whenever that is required – that is, for customers and business lines that pose higher risk.[17]

The author believes that the risk-based approach has a dual consequence. On the one hand, it is true that the approach places the private sector at ease. On the other hand, and often much less emphasised, it can also be seen as creating more constraints for the private actors. The risk-based approach is based on the idea of risk assessment and risk management, as opposed to the previous rule-based approach.[18] While this new process lends a degree of flexibility, it also implies that regulated entities are expected to be able to categorise customers into low-/medium-/high-risk groups (for instance, while carrying out anti-money-laundering compliance), not only at the stage of acceptance but also on an ongoing

14 FSA, 'Enforcement financial penalties' (Consultation Paper July 2009) <http://www.fsa.gov.uk/pubs/cp/cp09_19.pdf> accessed 15 May 2016.

15 The principles-based regulation of the FCA, which has led to the application of the risk-based approach, is discussed later in this chapter.

16 FSA, 'Principles-based regulation' (FSA April 2007) <http://www.fsa.gov.uk/pubs/other/principles.pdf> accessed 10 May 2016.

17 FSA, 'Review of firms' implementation to a risk-based approach to anti-money laundering' (FSA March 2008) <http://www.fca.org.uk/static/documents/fsa-aml-implementation-review.pdf> accessed 20 May 2016.

18 B. Unger and F.V. Waarden, 'How to dodge drowning in data? Rule- and risk-based anti money laundering policies compared' (2009) 5 *Review of Law and Economics* 953.

basis.[19] Apart from carrying out continuous risk assessments, entities are also expected to constantly evaluate their relationships with present customers.[20] In line with this argument, Ross and Hannan observe that the risk-based approach is 'responsiblising' – it places private actors at the heart of crime prevention, hence transferring responsibility from public agencies to private agents.[21] Furthermore, Unger and Waarden state that the dangers associated with making risk assessments (such as false reporting or over-reporting) are also passed on to the private sector.[22] It is this argument of 'passing responsibility' by the regulator that encourages entities to follow a tick-box approach where seeming to comply gains more importance than actual efficient compliance.

The (in)effectiveness of this move towards a risk-based approach is also evident in the comparison of two thematic reviews on Anti-Money Laundering ('AML')[23] published by the FSA with an interval of ten years – 2001 and 2011.[24] Ironically, although the risk-based approach was fully immersed in law and regulation by 2011, the deficiencies in the AML structure of firms, as pointed out in the two reports remain remarkably similar. The FSA investigation in 2001 was carried out following the revelation that £1 billion of assets linked to the former military dictator of Nigeria, Sani Abacha, passed through banks in the UK. Out of the 23 banks that were investigated, significant weaknesses were revealed in 15 (65 per cent of the total sample), which related to, among others, inadequate senior management oversight of the account opening process for customers who could be classified as higher risk; and weaknesses in the verification of

19 See, for example, Article 8(1)(d) of the Third Money Laundering Directive (Directive 2005/60/EC) which requires: '[ongoing] monitoring of the business relationship including scrutiny of transactions undertaken throughout the course of that relationship to ensure that the transactions being conducted are consistent with the institution's or person's knowledge of the customer, the business and the risk profile, including, where necessary, the source of funds and ensuring that the documents, data or information kept are up to date'. These requirements are mirrored in the UK under Regulation 8, Money Laundering Regulations 2007.

20 See, for example: Articles 8(1)(a)–(c) of the Third Money Laundering Directive (Directive 2005/60/EC), where a number of customer due-diligence measures have been specified. These include questions and documentation of: identity; identification of the ownership structure and 'beneficial owner' of organisations; recognition of the client's objectives with the relationship and its 'intended nature'. These requirements are mirrored in the UK under Regulation 7, Money Laundering Regulations 2007.

21 S. Ross and M. Hannan, 'Money laundering and risk-based decision-making' (2007) 10 *Journal of Money Laundering Control* 106.

22 Unger and Waarden (n. 18 above).

23 'Anti-money laundering' has been employed by the author here as an example to denote the style of approach towards financial crime.

24 FSA, *The Money Laundering Theme: Tacking Our New Responsibilities* (FSA 2001) <http://www.fsa.gov.uk/pubs/other/money_laundering.pdf> accessed 10 April 2016; FSA, 'Banks' management of high money-laundering risk situations: how banks deal with high-risk customers (including politically exposed persons), correspondent banking relationships and wire transfers' (FSA 2011) <http://www.fsa.gov.uk/pubs/other/aml_final_report.pdf> accessed 10 April 2016.

the identity of beneficial owners of companies.[25] In June 2011 again, the FSA published the results of a thematic review into how banks in the UK handle customers who are high risk for money laundering, in particular where there is a risk of corruption.[26] The majority of banks in the FSA's sample failed to identify the source of wealth and source of income of clients who were senior foreign politicians, despite this being a clear legal requirement.[27] In conclusion, the report said that 'three quarters of banks in our sample, including the majority of major banks, are not always managing high-risk customers [effectively] and must do more to ensure they are not used for money laundering'.[28]

The crucial question that arises is: if concerns over accepting high-risk customers have not changed over a period of ten years, has there been any real progress since the inception of the risk-based approach? Killick and Parody explain that in the absence of public–private collaboration, the industry soon adopts whichever model is seen by the FSA as compliant, irrespective of its effectiveness and merit.[29] Following the same line of reasoning and echoing the concerns of the industry, the House of Commons Treasury Committee observed that after the FSA's thematic review, the regulator promised to be tougher on the banks it supervises, with a more stringent approach to inspection visits.[30] The Committee welcomed the FSA's commitment to take a more 'judgment-based' approach to supervision that allowed room for greater discretion from the supervisor.[31] However, the Committee also noted that:

> the FSA has concentrated too much on ensuring narrow rule-based compliance, often leading to the collection of data of little value and to box-ticking, and too little on making judgments about what will cause serious problems for consumers and the financial system.[32]

As a result, it is clear that this box-ticking approach to regulation needs to change. In *The Plan for Growth*, the government talks of 'a lower domestic regulatory burden' as one of its 'ambitions and measurable benchmarks',[33] while admitting

25 FSA 2001 (n. 24 above).
26 FSA 2011 (n. 24 above).
27 Regs 7 and 8, Money Laundering Regulations 2007.
28 FSA 2011 (n. 24 above) 4.
29 M. Killick and D. Parody, 'Implementing AML/CFT measures that address the risks and not tick boxes' (2007) 15 *Journal of Financial Regulation and Compliance* 210.
30 Treasury Committee, *Fixing LIBOR: Some Preliminary Findings: Second Report of Session 2012–13*, vol. 1 (HC 2012–13, 481-I) 87.
31 Ibid. 80.
32 Ibid. 87.
33 HM Treasury and Department for Business Innovation and Skills, The Plan for Growth (HM Treasury 2011) 6 <http://cdn.hm-treasury.gov.uk/2011budget_growth.pdf> accessed 16 April 2016.

that, '[g]uidance is often not provided, is provided after the regulation has come into force, or is not provided in a way that makes sense for businesses'.[34]

Focusing on two different sets of objectives also results in the shifting of blame for the inefficiencies of financial crime compliance from the public to the private sector and vice versa. Public authorities appear to suffer from a 'relentless culture of blame' that is coupled with an imbalance between social and economic concerns vis-à-vis the private sector.[35]

Gill and Taylor rightly point out that the problem is not that there is disagreement on the principles; instead, as the survey findings reveal, regulation is seen as important, even for the respondents who felt that existing procedures were deficient. The real challenge is to generate an effective and workable risk-based approach.[36] The consequence of the weaknesses in applying a risk-based approach results in a vicious circle – a firm is identified as possessing inefficient controls, the regulator fines the firm, and the firm reacts by seeming to comply to overcome the fear of the regulator.

In this scenario, the question that needs to be asked is: Is the 'comply or explain' approach, as part of this risk-based regulation, really working? It is to this deterrent approach of the regulator that the chapter now turns.

11.3 Credible deterrence strategy

Post-crisis, the new plans reflected FSA's determination to change behaviour and address concerns that firms are repeatedly failing to improve standards. They also aimed to ensure that fines better reflect the scale of the wrongdoing and that any profits made from the breaches are clawed back. Confirming this, Margaret Cole (Director of Enforcement at the FSA at the time) stated:

> These proposals are an important step in pushing forward our ethos of credible deterrence. By hitting companies and individuals in the pocket where it hurts, the fines will be a stark warning to others on what they can expect to pay for flouting our rules.[37]

Similarly, Martin Wheatley (Chief Executive at the FCA at the time) remarked:

34 Ibid. 20.

35 D. Lascelles, *Banking Banana Skins 2012: The System in Peril* (Centre for the Study of Financial Innovation 2012) 16 <http://download.pwc.com/ie/pubs/2012_banking_banana_skins.pdf> accessed 22 April 2016.

36 M. Gill and G. Taylor, 'Preventing money laundering or obstructing business? financial companies' perspectives on "know your customer" procedures' (2004) 44 *British Journal of Criminology* 582.

37 FSA, 'FSA proposes bigger fines to achieve credible deterrence' (Press release FSA/PN/091/2009, FSA 2009) <http://www.fsa.gov.uk/library/communication/pr/2009/091.shtml> accessed 10 May 2016.

> Simply put, credible deterrence is about taking tough, targeted, effective, public action against firms' and individuals' misconduct as a way of changing behaviours. We have been clear with industry that we have the resources and commitment to follow through with meaningful sanctions and that we are committed to achieving better outcomes . . . [ensuring] markets are clean and free from abuse.[38]

However, in the realm of financial crime, whether the increasing penalties have actually contributed towards 'cleaning the market' by having a deterrent effect as envisaged by Wheatley is a questionable matter. Against this background, it is first crucial to fully understand the meaning of the word 'deterrence' in crime studies. Jeremy Bentham and Cesare Beccaria are credited with some of the earliest formulations of criminal deterrence theory.[39] Beccaria wrote that the intent of punishment is to 'instill fear in other men'. Bentham was convinced that crime rose from the conscious, rational considerations of the individuals. Accordingly, a person contemplating the commission of a crime would undertake a cost–benefit analysis and would execute the criminal plan only if potential benefits sufficiently outweighed expected costs.[40] Under this assumption, the task of law-enforcement personnel and lawmakers was clear: the risks, or costs, for a potential criminal had to be so great that he would have far more to lose than to gain from committing a crime.[41]

The reality of this cost–benefit analysis and how it would be contrary to the perceived intention of having a deterrent effect can be seen clearly by delving deeper into some of the large fines levied by the FCA. The exponential increase in the amount of fines is evidenced by the £72 million fine imposed on Barclays Bank plc in November 2015, for failing to minimise the risk that it may be used to facilitate financial crime. When the author of this chapter studied the total profit made by Barclays in the same year (£2.1 billion),[42] it became clear that the fine is a mere 0.2 per cent of this fine. This is too low an amount to have a deterrent effect for a private firm that does not have interests in law enforcement in any case.

In other words, the cost of committing a crime is too low in the face of large profits earned and, as far as benefits are concerned, it is questionable how far the crime-prevention aims of law enforcement would match with the private regulated

38 Wheatley, M., 'The FCA – our vision for enforcement' (speech by Martin Wheatley, CEO designate of the FCA at the FSA's Enforcement Conference, FSA 2012) <http://www.fsa.gov.uk/library/communication/speeches/2012/0702-mw.shtml> accessed 10 May 2016.

39 C. Beccaria, *On Crimes and Punishments* (Macmillan 1963) (original work published 1764).

40 J. Bentham, *An Introduction to the Principles of Morals and Legislation* (Macmillan 1948) (original work published 1789).

41 J. Andenaes, *Punishment and Deterrence* (University of Michigan Press 1974) 7.

42 Barclays Bank Plc, 'Results announcement' (Barclays 2015) <https://www.home.barclays/content/dam/barclayspublic/docs/InvestorRelations/ResultAnnouncements/2015FYResults/20160301_FY15_Results_Announcement.pdf> accessed 12 May 2016.

sector. On this point, Reuter and Truman observe that collaboration between the public and private sector does not always flow naturally, because while the private sector may not welcome being co-opted by the government, law-enforcement agencies are also 'reluctant to take private businesses into its confidence out of fear of jeopardising its case, either prior to or during the prosecutorial stage'.[43] The reasons may lie in the difference between perception and reality, which brings to the forefront the tension between State sovereignty and 'neo-liberal governmentality'.[44] The State, being the sovereign power, 'imposes' laws and regulations on the private sector, due to which the private sector functions as a 'neoliberal' government, carrying out a series of surveillance practices.[45] Thus, while the issue of private–public exchanges within the broad context of crime control has been well accepted as a form of 'plural policing',[46] compliance with financial crime laws (for example, AML) involves a 'non-voluntary', public–private collaboration.[47] On an everyday basis, therefore, the public–private collaboration in the fight against financial crime remains marked by mutual wariness.[48] In economic terminology, the 'agency problem' seen between the government and firms also warrants a better collaborative effort between the two: while the government uses firms in order to access confidential information on customers, the latter are naturally inclined to be reluctant to provide such information, leading to the 'agency problem'.[49]

When calculating the quantity of a penalty, the FSA advocates assessing the value based on a mixture of factors outlined in its Decision Procedure and Penalties Manual (hereinafter 'DEPP'),[50] including: seriousness of the breach (DEPP 6.5A.2 G); the need for a deterrent effect (DEPP 6.5A.4 G); and any mitigating factors, including whether the firm was cooperative with the FSA (DEPP 6.5A.3 G). The value of the harm caused is usually assessed by looking at the revenues the firm has made from the particular product line (DEPP

43 P. Reuter and E. Truman, *Chasing Dirty Money: The Fight Against Money Laundering* (Institute of International Economics 2004) 176.
44 L. Amoore and M. Goede, 'Governing by risk in the war on terror' in L. Amoore and M. Goede (eds), *Risk and the War on Terror* (Routledge 2008) 5.
45 G. Favarel-Garrigues, T. Godefroy and P. Lascoumes, 'Reluctant partners? Banks in the fight against money laundering and terrorism financing in France' (2011) 42 (2) *Security Dialogue* 179.
46 B. Dupont, 'Governing security' in K. Kramar (ed.), *Criminology: Critical Canadian Perspectives* (Pearson 2011) 205.
47 B. Bowling and J. Sheptycki, *Global Policing* (Sage Publications 2011) 199.
48 P. Hardouin, 'Banks governance and public-private partnership in preventing and confronting organized crime, corruption and terrorism financing' (2009) 16 *Journal of Financial Crime* 199.
49 The agency problem arises when agents entrusted to look after the interests of their principal misuse this power for their own benefit.
50 FSA, *Decision Procedure and Penalties Manual* (Sections 6.5 and 6.5A of the FSA's Decision Procedure and Penalties Manual for the range of factors and criteria considered by the FSA in its decisions to impose financial penalties, FSA 2012) <http://fsahandbook.info/FSA/html/handbook/DEPP/6/5A> accessed 1 May 2016.

6.5A.2(1) G). This element of the penalty is calculated using a percentage of this revenue with a sliding scale, to take into account how serious the breach was (DEPP 6.5A.2(3) G). However, the top end of the scale is only 20 per cent of the revenue a firm has made from its misconduct (DEPP 6.5A.2(3) G). The DEPP manual is endorsed by the FCA on its current website.[51]

It may be interesting to compare this top end of the scale with the Barclays fine mentioned above, which is seen as one of the biggest fines for financial crime failings. On what basis did the FCA decide that imposing a fine that is a mere 0.2 per cent of the bank's profits would have a deterrent effect?

It is hardly surprising that if firms have the option between saying 'no' to suspect 'big business' and accepting the fines imposed by the regulator, many firms may see the latter as a cost of doing business. This has been reiterated by the FSA itself in its 2011 thematic review, wherein the FSA noted that 'a third of banks, including the private banking arms of some major banking groups, appeared willing to accept very high levels of money-laundering risk if the immediate reputational and regulatory risk was acceptable'.[52] The attitude is further confirmed by a Global Witness[53] submission to parliament, highlighting that compliance is seen all too often as a cost, rather than a profit centre. The 'downside' for firms is potentially small: seemingly large fines are in fact only a small fraction of profits; and there is only a very limited personal responsibility of individual employees.[54]

Killick and Parody succinctly capture the mood of the regulated fraternity when they note that, because of the fear of the regulator, many firms put into place robust and rigid frameworks that address every scenario, but mitigate none.[55] This was also observed by the FSA in its thematic review, wherein it noted examples of banks attempting to 'clean up' their act just before the visit. In one instance, a bank changed the status of numerous high-risk clients to low risk and, in another example, three banks added relevant information to their customer due-diligence files for the first time, very shortly before the FSA was visiting.[56]

Although imposed in the United States (US), it may be pertinent to analyse one of the biggest fines imposed on a UK bank so far for money-laundering failings. The UK-based bank admitted to a series of money laundering charges and was fined $1.9 billion by the US, the largest fine imposed for failings in

51 Ibid.

52 FSA 2011 (n. 24 above) 4.

53 Global Witness is an international NGO, established in 1993. Its goals are to expose the corrupt exploitation of natural resources and international trade systems, and to drive campaigns that end impunity, resource-linked conflict and human rights and environmental abuses.

54 Global Witness, *Submission to Parliamentary Commission on Banking Standards* (Global Witness 2012) <http://www.publications.parliament.uk/pa/jt201213/jtselect/jtpcbs/writev/ banking/bs17.htm> accessed 15 April 2016.

55 Killick and Parody (n. 29 above).

56 FSA 2011 (n. 24 above) 20.

AML compliance to date.[57] However, the author of this chapter evaluated the annual statements of HSBC for the year 2012 and deduced that the amount of profit gained by HSBC in that year was $20.6 billion.[58] This meant that the fine represented only about four weeks' earning for HSBC. It is hardly surprising that HSBC has been involved in a series of financial scandals thereafter. More recently, the bank has been exposed for helping hundreds of clients avoid and, in some cases, evade tax, through its Swiss private bank.[59] In January 2016, however, the FCA decided it would not pursue any formal action over the tax evasion scandal.[60] This is in stark contrast with what one would expect from the regulator in the wake of the recent 'Panama Papers' that have shockingly revealed that 'the files list more than 15,600 paper companies that banks set up for clients who wanted to keep their finances under wraps, including hundreds created by international giants UBS and HSBC'.[61]

The author also fails to comprehend how turning a blind eye on the part of the FCA is akin to a harsher or more effective post-crisis regulation. In fact, the paradox of the post-crisis regulation is that the conditions for excessive risk-taking still exist, albeit how the private sector responds to it has changed. Shielding failures from the eyes of the regulator assumes priority, translating into defensive compliance by the private sector. Unlike the FSA[62] and submissions by Global Witness,[63] which suggest that fines should be increased, this chapter does not argue to support this stand. Rather, it needs to be understood that more stringent fines are not an effective deterrent; instead, the focus changes to a 'tick-box exercise' and the objective of reducing crime through AML regulations recedes into the background. Levi pertinently points out how the 'trick of regulation is to minimise the illegitimate exploitation without wrecking the economic

57 A. Viswanatha and B. Wolf, 'HSBC to pay $1.9 billion U.S. fine in money-laundering case' *Reuters* (London, 11 December 2012) <http://uk.reuters.com/article/us-hsbc-probe-idUSBRE8BA05M20121211> accessed 14 March 2016.

58 HSBC, 'HSBC Holdings plc Annual Results 2012' (HSBC 2013) <http://www.hsbc.com/news-and-insight/2013/hsbc-annual-results> accessed 15 May 2016.

59 J. Dunkley, 'HSBC tax avoidance scandal: timeline of Britain's biggest banking leak', *Independent* (London, 18 February 2015) <http://www.independent.co.uk/news/business/comment/hsbc-tax-avoidance-scandal-timeline-of-britains-biggest-banking-leak-10054442.html> accessed 18 April 2016.

60 M. Kleinman, 'FCA ends probe into HSBC Swiss tax affair' *Sky News* (London, 4 January 2016) <http://news.sky.com/story/1616568/fca-ends-probe-into-hsbc-swiss-tax-affair> accessed 10 February 2016.

61 International Consortium of Investigative Journalists, 'Offshore links of more than 140 politicians and officials exposed' (ICIJ 2016) <https://www.icij.org/blog/2016/04/offshore-links-more-140-politicians-and-officials-exposed> accessed 18 April 2016.

62 FSA, 'FSA proposes bigger fines to achieve credible deterrence' (FSA press release FSA/PN/091/2009, FSA 2009) <http://www.fsa.gov.uk/library/communication/pr/2009/091.shtml> accessed 15 May 2016.

63 Global Witness (n. 54 above).

dynamism'.[64] Therefore, if 'escaping' fines or criminal penalties becomes the primary motivator for compliance, the risk-based approach, and, as a result, the role of the FCA, loses its real meaning. In the wake of these heavy corporate fines, individual prosecutions are almost non-existent and the few examples that exist still do not represent the entire picture behind individual accountability. The author goes deeper into this by analysing the Tom Hayes conviction for insider trading.

11.4 Commit a crime and claim a discount?

To take the point of inefficiencies behind these fines even further, the FCA, in recognition of the benefits of early settlement, offers a discount scheme.[65] The discount for early settlement is distinct from the credit a firm may receive for cooperation. Proactive cooperation is likely to result in reduced financial penalties in the majority of cases. It is interesting to note that the discount can be as much as 30 per cent and is available on a sliding scale, with 30 per cent being offered at the early settlement stage (Stage one).[66] Does this mean that the more cooperative a corporation is, the more 'incentivised' it is to commit a crime?

A recent case in point is when the FCA imposed fines totalling £1,114,918,000 ($1.7 billion) on five banks for failing to control business practices in their G10 spot foreign exchange (FX) trading operations: Citibank N.A. £225,575,000 ($358 million), HSBC Bank Plc £216,363,000 ($343 million), JP Morgan Chase Bank N.A. £222,166,000 ($352 million), Royal Bank of Scotland Plc £217,000,000 ($344 million) and UBS AG £233,814,000 ($371million). The banks agreed to settle at an early stage and therefore qualified for a 30 per cent discount under the FCA's settlement discount scheme.[67]

Failure to implement internal policies and procedures to comply with anti-money-laundering laws and regulations have also attracted several fines, starting with Royal Bank of Scotland, fined £5.6 million in 2010. At the time, this was the largest fine ever by the regulator for financial crime failings. Although the fine was initially decided at £8 million, here again RBS qualified for a 30 per cent reduction after it fully cooperated with the FSA.[68]

64 M. Levi, 'Money Laundering: Risks and Counter-Measures', in A. Graycar and P. Grabosky (eds), *Money Laundering in the 21st Century: Risks and Countermeasures* (Australian Institute of Criminology 1996).

65 FCA, 'Settlement and mediation' <http://www.fca.org.uk/firms/being-regulated/enforcement/how-we-enforce-the-law/settlement-mediation> accessed 15 May 2016.

66 Ibid.

67 FCA, 'FCA fines five banks £1.1 billion for FX failings and announces industry wide remediation programme' (FCA 2014) <http://www.fca.org.uk/news/fca-fines-five-banks-for-fx-failings> accessed 1 May 2016.

68 R. Wray, 'RBS handed FSA's biggest fine for lapses over money laundering rules' *Guardian* (London, 3 August 2010) <https://www.theguardian.com/business/2010/aug/03/royal-bank-of-scotland-fsa-biggest-fine> accessed 15 April 2016.

The idea of discounts has reached another level with the introduction of deferred prosecution agreements (DPAs). Simply put, a corporate deferred prosecution agreement is a way of imposing a term of probation before a conviction. The government files charges but then agrees to hold them in abeyance pending the company's successful completion of certain terms in the agreement for a period of time.

DPAs were introduced in the English legal system by Schedule 17 of the Crime and Courts Act 2013. In the US, DPAs have been a mainstream tool for US prosecutors dealing with corporate crime, particularly since the early 2000s. In the UK, in comparison, this is a much more recent phenomenon, with the first-ever DPA concluded only in 2015.[69]

According to the UK DPAs Code of Practice, an SFO prosecutor may invite a company to enter into DPA negotiations. Before such an invitation is extended, the prosecutor must be satisfied that: there is a reasonable suspicion that the company has committed an offence; there are reasonable grounds to believe that an investigation would establish a realistic prospect of conviction; and it is in the public interest to seek a DPA instead of a prosecution.[70]

It is the last element of public interest that particularly provokes the curiosity of the author. One of the public-interest factors, as laid out in the Code of Practice, for a prosecutor to consider while deciding *against* a DPA, is that the offending represents isolated actions by individuals – for example, by a rogue director.[71] This begs the question: if such directors are identified, why they are not prosecuted?

An ancillary issue is also one of individual rights that may be curtailed following the imposition of terms through DPAs. For example, a DPA often results in cooperation with the government's ongoing investigation (which obligates the company to make its employees available and includes privilege waivers). The author believes that, as a result, individuals who are really responsible for the alleged misconduct may be seen in fungibility with the rest of the employees, making it harder to trace the actual person/s responsible for the crime.

There is another crucial element of criminal law linked to DPAs that has not been actively researched yet, and it is one that makes an even stronger case for their misplaced application to corporate liability. The roots behind DPAs can be traced back to individual criminal liability, in the form of pre-trial diversion tools, as a way to handle juveniles without attaching a stigma to them for life as criminals.[72]

69 Serious Fraud Office, 'SFO agrees first UK DPA with Standard Bank, 30 November 2015' (SFO 2015) <https://www.sfo.gov.uk/2015/11/30/sfo-agrees-first-uk-dpa-with-standard-bank> accessed 15 April 2016.

70 Serious Fraud Office and Crown Prosecution Service, *Deferred Prosecution Agreements Code of Practice, Crime and Courts Act 2013* (SFO and CPS, 2013) <https://www.cps.gov.uk/publications/directors_guidance/dpa_cop.pdf> accessed 1 May 2013.

71 Ibid. 2.8.2 (iv).

72 E. Illovsky, 'Corporate deferred prosecution agreements: the brewing debate' (2006) 21(2) *Criminal Justice* 36.

This tool had no applicability to corporations until the 1990s. In this scenario, the author believes that it is presumptuous to think that individual deterrent behaviour would be similar to that of a corporation. As argued earlier in this chapter large fines are hardly a deterrent for criminal behaviour on the part of corporations, let alone a discount on that fine or a deferred prosecution. Once again, a criminal theory that is more suited to an individual is being blindly applied to a corporation.

Despite the corporation being a legal person, the differences between individual and corporate reactions to a crime could not be more stark: a corporation has no mind and therefore cannot experience guilt; it has no body, so cannot therefore act in a sense that is not entirely derivative. Punishing it would violate the fundamental principle that punishment must be imposed only on the actual offender; and the usual penalties envisaged within the criminal law are frustrated where the nature of the convicted party precludes imprisonment.[73] Admittedly, although this argument is far-fetched, the author sees merit in the reasoning. The separate legal personality of a company should not be construed to mean that it represents the same attributes as a natural person.[74]

The court has in few recent instances recognised the need to have a deterrent effect on the individuals working in the company as the ultimate objective of a financial penalty. A case in point is *R v Sellafield Limited / R v Network Rail Infrastructure Limited*,[75] where the court affirmed that the fine must be fixed to meet the statutory purposes, with the objective of ensuring that the message is brought home to the directors and members of the company (usually the shareholders). Another recent case in which the issue of deterrence in corporate punishment was dealt with is *New Look Retailers Limited v The London Fire and Emergency Planning Authority*.[76] In this case, the Court of Appeal asserted that, when passing sentence upon a corporation, it is appropriate for the judge to take into consideration the need for the fine to make an impact upon shareholders and senior managers.

The first ever deferred prosecution agreement in the UK was concluded on 30 November 2015 between ICBC SB plc and the SFO. The agreement, which was approved by the President of the Queen's Bench Division (the Rt Hon. Sir Brian Leveson), concerned a case of bribery in Tanzania that took place between November 2011 and March 2013. Standard Bank plc, which is a company

73 L.H. Leigh, *The Criminal Liability of Corporations in English Law* (LSE 1969).

74 The corporate personality of a company is different and separate from the promoters, directors or owners of the company. This is a widely known principle in law and has its source in the case of *Solomon v Solomon*. In this case, the court held that the corporate entity is different from the people who are in the business of running of the company. The misuse of this principle led to 'lifting of the corporate veil', wherein the shareholders or creditors of the company are protected if the company is engaged in any fraud or other criminal activities.

75 [2014] EWCA Crim 49 (CA).

76 [2010] EWCA Crim 1268 (CA).

that ICBC acquired only in 2015, was found to be involved in corrupt practices.[77] The judge held that, pursuant to Schedule 17, section 7(1) of the Crime and Courts Act 2013, the DPA was in the interests of justice and that its proposed terms were fair, reasonable and proportionate.[78]

This is a landmark decision, not only because the SFO's first application for a DPA was approved by the judiciary, but also because it was the first time in which a legal entity was charged in England and Wales with the offence of 'failure of commercial organisations to prevent bribery', as provided in section 7 of the Bribery Act 2010.

It is pertinent at this point to go back to the author's argument of fines being viewed as a cost of doing business. The complexity of calculating a fine in a DPA has also been underlined by the court: 'the most difficult assessment was as to the appropriate financial penalty which [. . .] must be broadly comparable to the fine that a court would have imposed following conviction after a guilty plea'.[79]

Specifically, in relation to the penalty imposed by the DPA at issue, considering that, by the end of 2014, ICBC's total assets amounted to about US$3 million and the Bank realised a net profit of about US$42 billion,[80] it appears evident that the monetary sanction of US$16.8 million cannot plausibly have any significant impact on the financial institution.

It has been suggested that DPAs may be used as an effective tool for corporate governance by including terms in the agreement relating to internal controls and policies, leading to more efficient compliance with financial crime laws.[81] While this could be a possibility, the author would like to reiterate that it should certainly not be used as an escape mechanism to replace individual prosecutions.[82]

11.5 Lack of individual prosecutions

Generally speaking, there are three ways of attributing liability to a corporation under English law. The first is vicarious liability, which English law limits to certain

77 *Serious Fraud Office v Standard Bank Plc* [2015] (Southwark Crown Court) <https://www.judiciary.gov.uk/wp-content/uploads/2015/11/sfo-v-standard-bank_Final_1.pdf> accessed 20 May 2016.

78 Ibid. 2.

79 Ibid. 16.

80 ICBC, *ICBC Business Review* (ICBC 2015) <http://www.icbc.com.cn/ICBC/About%20Us/Brief%20Introduction/brief%20introduction%20to%20icbc.htm> accessed 12 May 2016.

81 C. Grasso, *Peaks and Troughs of the UK Deferred Prosecution Agreement: The Lesson Learned from the First Ever DPA between the SFO and ICBC* (2016) Queen Mary University of London, School of Law Legal Studies Research Paper No. 223/2016 <http://ssrn.com/abstract=2748688> accessed 1 May 2016.

82 It must be noted here that, unlike the US, a DPA cannot be initiated against an individual in the UK.

regulatory offences.[83] The second theory is derived from the 'identification principle', which seeks to identify the senior management within a corporation as its 'brains', and renders the company liable for their acts of criminality. The third places corporate liability in the internal principles and procedures, which need to be in compliance with laws and regulations relating to financial crime. The first two theories clearly *derive* from an individual. Why, then, are there almost no prosecutions of persons who are actually responsible for a financial crime? Following from the discussion above, the author maintains that individual criminal prosecution is the only way to inject needed deterrence into a system that currently 'incentivises' fraudulent behaviour by corporations through means such as discounts and DPAs, as discussed above.

At first glance, it appears that the US has a much more effective enforcement[84] regime regarding individual prosecutions compared with the UK. The author holds the view that the reality, however, is fraught with several layers of window-dressing that need to be removed. Late 2013 was hailed as the first 'victory' of financial crisis prosecutions, with the conviction of Kareem Serageldin. Serageldin had been employed at Credit Suisse and, during the relevant time period of the fraud, he oversaw and managed a number of trading books in the securities department of the Investment Banking Division. Serageldin was indicted for artificially increasing the price of the bonds in order to create the false appearance of profitability of one of those trading books. The motivation for this lay in the prospect of enhancing his job performance and his eligibility for a promotion and bonuses from Credit Suisse.[85]

Behind that conviction, the reality was that, despite the government recommending a five-year maximum prison term, he was sentenced for only 30 months. The comment made by Judge Hellerstein is an indication of the systemic problem: 'Serageldin was in a place where there was a climate for him to do what he did . . . [i]t was a small piece of an overall climate inside that bank.'[86]

Contrary to popular belief, it has also been claimed that Serageldin's fraud really had nothing to do with the financial crisis. His crimes did not defraud investors or the public more broadly. Rather, his crimes defrauded Credit Suisse. Because of Serageldin's actions, the bank was unaware that one of its trading books was

83 Vicarious liability refers to a form of (derivative) liability where a legal person – for example, an employer – is liable on account of the wrongdoing of an employee.

84 It must be clarified here that the author is referring to an effective system of individual prosecutions, as opposed to the number of prosecutions.

85 Prosecution's Indictment in *United States of America v Kareem Serageldin* 12-cr-00089 2013 <https://www.justice.gov/archive/usao/nys/pressreleases/April13/SerageldinKareemPleaPR/U.S.%20v.%20Kareem%20Serageldin%20Indictment.pdf> accessed 1 May 2016.

86 R. Abrams and P. Lattman, 'Ex-Credit Suisse executive sentenced in mortgage bond case' *New York Times* (New York, 22 November 2013) <http://dealbook.nytimes.com/2013/11/22/ex-credit-suisse-executive-sentenced-in-mortgage-case/> accessed 15 May 2016.

significantly underperforming.[87] This is not to say that Serageldin should not have been convicted. This chapter simply seeks to argue that the real essence of individual prosecutions relating to financial crime has still not been realised.

At the time of writing, not a single high-level executive has been prosecuted in the UK for engaging in financial crime during the crisis. The limited number of prosecutions after the crisis still lacks the capability of having a potential deterrent effect, as the author later attempts to demonstrate by analysing the case study of Tom Hayes. At the outset, the US enforcement regime may seem more active and aggressive, but often the corresponding reasons for this are overlooked. The lack of resources is one such important factor. In comparison with the Department of Justice (DoJ),[88] the SFO is tiny, with a gross budget of less than £70 million.[89] In contrast, the DoJ's FY2017 enforcement budget stands at $29 billion, which is $265 million above the 2016 enacted level.[90].

The Bribery Act 2010 of the Westminster parliament should have brought about an increase in the activity of the Serious Fraud Office, particularly in view of the strict liability offence of commercial bribery under Section 7 of the Act. (A statutory defence of adequate procedures being in place to prevent bribery is available.) This increase in activity is unlikely to come about, bearing in mind the budget cuts that the SFO has had to face in the last few years.[91] Comment upon the financial resources available to the SFO was made by Sir John Thomas, President of the Queen's Bench Division on behalf of the Divisional Court in *Tchenguiz v Serious Fraud Office*,[92] when he said: 'The investigation and prosecution of serious fraud in the financial markets requires proper resources, both human and financial. It is quite clear that the SFO did not have such resources in the present case.' Further, it has been reported that despite receiving 2,508 tip-offs in 2014, only 12 new investigations were opened by the SFO, due to lack of resources.[93]

The larger point that the author is attempting to make here is that, although factors such as lack of resources do play a role, the fundamental issue of lack of

87 T. Haugh, 'The most senior Wall Street official: evaluating the state of financial crisis prosecutions' (2015) 9(2) *Virginia Law and Business Review* 153.

88 The Department of Justice is the primary federal criminal investigation and enforcement agency in the US.

89 SFO, 'Our funding and budget' (SFO 2016) <https://www.sfo.gov.uk/about-us/> accessed 1 May 2016. These are latest figures reflecting the 2015–16 budget.

90 Department of Justice, 'Budget and performance' (DoJ 2016) <https://www.justice.gov/about/budget-and-performance> accessed 15 April 2016.

91 L. Fortado and C. Binham, 'SFO chief set for extension after turning around agency', *Financial Times* (London, 2 December 2015) <http://www.ft.com/cms/s/0/204a43d6-98f6-11e5-9228-87e603d47bdc.html#axzz4A8kwIGCD> accessed 25 March 2016.

92 [2012] EWHC 2254 (Admin).

93 J. Dunkley, 'Serious Fraud Office failing to follow up thousands of tip-offs' *Independent* (London, 6 April 2015) <http://www.independent.co.uk/news/business/news/serious-fraud-office-failing-to-follow-up-thousands-of-tip-offs-10158889.html> accessed 10 April 2016.

individual prosecutions still remains a common factor both in the US and the UK. The author believes that the biggest reason behind this lies in the fact that the question of 'who' to prosecute is still not clear. For example, Serageldin's former employer, for one, is known to have revised its past financial statements to account for $2.7 billion that should have been reported. Lehman Brothers, AIG, Citigroup, Countrywide and many others also admitted that they were in much worse shape than they initially allowed. Merrill Lynch, in particular, announced a loss of nearly $8 billion three weeks after claiming it was $4.5 billion.[94] Against this background, why is it that we have only Serageldin as an example?

Taking a more recent example and going beyond the financial crisis, in May 2015 five global banks in the US – Citigroup, JPMorgan Chase, Barclays, the Royal Bank of Scotland and UBS – agreed to pay more than $2.5 billion in penalties for antitrust violations in the foreign exchange market.[95] In a chatroom where one of the schemes was hatched, one trader wrote: 'If you ain't cheating, you ain't trying.'[96] Though four banks pleaded guilty to criminal charges, no individual was sentenced to serve prison time.

There have been no notable high-level convictions for the financial crisis in the UK that can be compared with the Serageldin conviction, but the recent conviction of Tom Hayes, a former UBS and Citigroup derivatives trader, who became the first person to be convicted of LIBOR[97] offences, might help highlight the non-existence of individual prosecutions. Here the author finds an interesting parallel with the high-profile conviction of Serageldin in the US. While it may be too far-fetched to say that Serageldin and Hayes were 'scapegoats', there is still a big question to be asked: How was it possible for Serageldin and Hayes to be part of such an enormous financial scandal without the cooperation, or at least the knowledge, of management or other employees of the same level? Surely, the LIBOR scandal was just the tip of the iceberg, because the rigging of the $5.3-trillion-a-day Forex markets completely dwarfs the total $450 trillion value of financial contracts underpinned by LIBOR.[98] The 'ringmaster' of manipulation, Tom Hayes, pleaded not guilty in December 2013 to eight charges of fraud, instead, he insisted that he was operating in a 'grey area' where there were no rules

94 J. Eisinger, 'Why only one top banker went to jail for the financial crisis' *New York Times* (New York, 30 April 2014) <http://www.nytimes.com/2014/05/04/magazine/only-one-top-banker-jail-financial-crisis.html> accessed 18 May 2016.

95 Department of Justice, 'Five major banks agree to parent-level guilty pleas' (DoJ 2015) <https://www.justice.gov/opa/pr/five-major-banks-agree-parent-level-guilty-pleas> accessed 10 May 2016.

96 H. Sheffield, 'If you ain't cheating, you ain't trying: four global banks plead to felony charges of fixing the price of dollar and euros' *Independent* (London, 20 May 2015) <http://www.independent.co.uk/news/business/news/if-you-aint-cheatin-you-aint-trying-four-global-banks-plead-guilty-to-felony-charges-of-fixing-the-10264395.html> accessed 1 May 2016.

97 London Interbank Offered Rate, or LIBOR, is the average interest rate at which banks can borrow from one another.

98 'Libor: what is it and why does it matter?' *BBC News* (London, 3 August 2015) <http://www.bbc.co.uk/news/business-19199683> accessed 12 April 2016.

and that UBS distributed 'an instruction manual' on fixing LIBOR. Hayes is believed to have passed details of the UBS 'Guide to Publishing Libor Rates' to the Serious Fraud Office as part of his claim that manipulating the key interest rate benchmark was widespread.[99]

The sentencing remarks made by Justice Cooke point towards this rampant culture at UBS:[100]

> The conduct involved here is to be marked out as dishonest and wrong and a message sent to the world of banking accordingly. The reputation of LIBOR is important to the City as a financial sector and the banking institutions of the City. Probity and honesty is essential as is trust. The LIBOR activity of which you played a leading part put all that in jeopardy. The fact that others were doing the same as you is no excuse, nor is the fact that your immediate managers saw the benefit of what you were doing and condoned it and embraced it, if not encouraged it. The evidence established that when you arrived at UBS, some internal manipulation was going on, mostly in other currencies, of which you were essentially unaware but not external manipulation of Yen Libor of the kind which you engendered.

This is not to say that Tom Hayes was wrongly convicted for the LIBOR trade, but the author fails to understand how ignoring the 'immediate managers', as the judge puts it, is sending a strong signal to the banking industry.

The role of senior management has often been clearly identified. It may be pertinent here to revert to the fines imposed by the FCA on firms for financial crime failings as a part of their credible deterrence strategy, as mentioned earlier in this chapter. Taking the Barclays fine of £72 million as an example, the FCA found that senior management at Barclays engaged in financial crime risks associated with business relationships, regarding 'politically exposed persons' who should have been subject, not only, to enhanced levels of due diligence of monitoring but also due diligence checks of the business relationship by Barclays on on an ongoing basis. Also, in the Forex fine, the FCA is clear and certain that traders at different banks formed 'tight-knit groups', in which information was shared about client activity, to help them work out their trading strategies. These involved traders attempting to manipulate the relevant currency rate in the market, to ensure that the rate at which the bank had agreed to sell a particular currency to its clients was higher than the average rate it had bought that currency for in the market.

99 M. Dakers and agencies, 'Libor trial: Hayes handed over a UBS "instruction manual" on rigging' *Telegraph* (London, 18 June 2015) <http://www.telegraph.co.uk/finance/libor-scandal/11684438/Libor-trial-Hayes-handed-over-a-UBS-instruction-manual-on-rigging-prosecution-says.html> accessed 25 March 2016.

100 *Sentencing Remarks of Mr Justice Cooke* in *R v Tom Hayes* [2015] (Southwark Crown Court) <https://www.judiciary.gov.uk/wp-content/uploads/2015/08/r-v-tom-hayes-sentencing1.pdf> accessed 15 May 2016.

Looking at these prime examples that are significant representations of the 'credible deterrence strategy', it is paradoxical that although the involvement of senior management and employees of these firms is so clear, no single individual has been convicted. Resting on the 'success' of the Tom Hayes conviction is akin to making him the face of financial crime, while this is clearly not the case. In an attempt to provide a way forward, the author of this chapter suggests the criminal law principle of 'wilful blindness' as having potential application. In the US, Judge Rakoff also notes that prosecutors could ease their burden of proving intent by relying on concepts of 'willful blindness' or 'conscious disregard'.[101]

The principle is a well-established basis on which federal prosecutors have asked juries to infer intent in the US, including in cases involving complexities such as accounting rules, at least as esoteric as those involved in the events leading up to the financial crisis. And while some federal courts have occasionally expressed reservations about the use of the wilful blindness approach to prove intent, the Supreme Court has consistently approved it, as that Court stated most recently in *Global-Tech Appliances, Inc. v SEB S.A.*[102]

The doctrine of wilful blindness is well established in criminal law. Many criminal statutes require proof that a defendant acted knowingly or wilfully, and courts applying the doctrine of wilful blindness hold that defendants cannot escape the reach of these statutes by deliberately shielding themselves from clear evidence of critical facts that are strongly suggested by the circumstances. Dennis Barker explains that wilful blindness may apply only when a person believes the facts exist and deliberately avoids investigating further, in the hope of providing themselves with an escape route. This limited doctrine can reasonably be said to be an explanation of what is meant by knowledge as a matter of common sense, rather than a legitimate extension of the meaning of the term.[103]

In the UK, the principle is applied in cases where the defendant shuts his eyes to the obvious. This may also exist where the defendant deliberately refrains from making enquiries, the results of which he may not care to know.[104] In the case of *Westminster City Council v Croyalgrange*,[105] Lord Bridge said:

> It is always open to the tribunal of fact, when knowledge on the part of a defendant is required to be proved, to base finding of knowledge on evidence

101 N. Poser and J. Fanto, *Broker-Dealer Law and Regulation*, vol. 1 (2015 Supplement, 4th edn, Wolters Kluwer 2015) 12–40. Judge Rakoff is a US District Judge and is considered a leading authority on laws relating to white collar crime.

102 563 US 754, 131 S. Ct. 2060, 179 L. Ed. 2d 1167 (2011). The case considered whether a party, in order to 'actively [induce] infringement of a patent' under 35 U.S.C. §271(b), must know that the induced act constitutes patent infringement, or whether deliberate indifference to the existence of a patent can be considered a form of actual knowledge.

103 D.J. Baker, *Glanville Williams Textbook of Criminal Law* (4th edn, Sweet & Maxwell 2015) 156.

104 *Taylor's Central Garages (Exeter) v Roper* [1951] 2 TLR 284 (DC) 288–289 (Devlin J).

105 [1986] 2 All ER 353 (HL) 359.

> that the defendant had deliberately shut his eyes to the obvious or refrained from inquiry because he suspected the truth but did not want to have his suspicion confirmed.

In *R v Griffiths*, which was a case on handling stolen goods, knowing or believing them to be stolen, the Court of Appeal said that

> to direct the jury that the offence is committed if the defendant, suspecting that the goods were stolen, deliberately shut his eyes to the circumstances as an alternative to [directing them in terms of] knowing or believing that the goods were stolen is a misdirection; but to direct the jury that, in common sense and in law, they may find that the defendant knew or believed the goods to be stolen because he deliberately closed his eyes to the circumstances is a perfectly proper direction.[106]

This judgment was again cited with approval in *R v Saik.*[107]

The principle of 'knowledge' in criminal law has also been expanded in the draft Criminal Code, clause 18:

> A person acts . . . knowingly with respect to a circumstance not only when he is aware that it exists or will exist, but also when he avoids taking steps that might confirm his belief that it exists or will exist.[108]

To fully understand wilful blindness, this may be combined with another definition: 'The standard test of knowledge is – did the person whose conduct is in issue either know of the relevant circumstances or have no substantial doubt of their existence?'[109] The author suggests the application of this doctrine of wilful blindness to establish individual liability in corporate crime cases – for example, in the ones mentioned above – where the role of directors and senior management is clear.

11.6 The identification principle

The author argues that the identification principle is making it harder to take a step towards individual prosecutions. As legal persons, companies may be criminally liable for financial crime offences requiring *mens rea* by application of the identification principle. The identification principle essentially means that a

106 (1974) 60 Cr App R 14 (CA) 18.

107 [2006] UKHL 18, [2007] 1 AC 18 (HL) 46.

108 Law Commission, *A Criminal Law for England and Wales*, vol. 1, *Report and Draft Criminal Code Bill* (Law Com. No. 177, 1989) <https://www.gov.uk/government/uploads/system/uploads/attachment_data/file/235826/0299.pdf> accessed 13 May 2016.

109 Law Commission, *Report on Mental Element in Crime* (Law Com. No. 89, 1978) 58.

company would be liable for a serious criminal offence where one of its most senior officers had acted with the requisite fault. Expounded in the leading case of *Tesco Supermarkets Ltd v Nattrass*,[110] the application of this principle is limited to the actions of the 'Board of Directors, the Managing Director and perhaps other superior officers who carry out functions of management and speak and act as the company'. The identification principle acknowledges the existence of management or senior employees who are the embodiment of a company. As Lord Denning says in *HL Bolton Engineering Co Ltd v TJ Graham & Sons Ltd*:

> The state of mind of these managers is the state of mind of the company and is treated by the law as such . . . Whether [the] intention is the company's intention depends on the nature of the matter under consideration, the relative position of the officer or agent and other relevant facts and circumstances of the case.[111]

There are two problems that arise with this test: first, can the actions of the 'controlling mind' of the corporation necessarily be connected with the crime that has been committed? This is especially true when it comes to the size of a corporation – there is a much more complex process of delegation in larger companies, which may lead to the outcome that it is much easier to prove liability for smaller companies than for larger ones. Professor Gobert has stated that the doctrine 'fails to capture the complexity of the modern company'. By focusing on attributing the acts and state of minds of a limited range of senior people to the corporation, the identification doctrine fails to reflect the fact that, in modern corporations, a good deal of important policy or strategic decision-making may be decentralised, or regional rather than national.[112]

The problems in this test that targets only the top grade of a corporation has led to a reconsideration of *Tesco v Nattrass*, even where it applies to offences requiring proof of a mental element. The leading case in this regard is a decision of the Privy Council, *Meridian Global Funds Management Asia Ltd v Securities Commission*.[113]

Lord Hoffmann suggested that the directing mind model espoused in *Tesco v Nattrass* should not be regarded as the exclusive tool for attributing culpability to a company. The question of whose act and state of mind was to be attributed to the company was answered by 'applying the usual canons of interpretation, taking into account the language of the rule (if it is a statute) and its content and policy'.[114] This shows a progressive step from *Tesco*, which was focused on the

110 [1972] AC 153 (HL).
111 [1957] 1 QB 159 (CA) 172.
112 J. Gobert, 'Corporate criminality: four models of fault' (1994) 14(3) *Legal Studies* 393, 395.
113 [1995] 2 AC 500 (PC). An alleged breach of the securities legislation turned on whether the company had knowledge of the activities of its investment managers.
114 [1995] 2 AC 500 (PC) 507.

actions of the Board, whereas *Meridian* recognises the need for going beyond the Board and identifying the actual persons to whom the action can be attributed. However, it must be noted here that, surprisingly, *Meridian* has not yet been applied in an English case.[115]

In *Lennard's Carrying Co Ltd v Asiatic Petroleum Co Ltd*,[116] Viscount Haldane propounded the 'alter ego' theory, and distinguished that from vicarious liability. The House of Lords stated that the default of the managing director, who is the 'directing mind and will' of the company, could be attributed to him and he be held for the wrongdoings of the company. To capture it succinctly,

> a corporation is an abstraction. It has no mind of its own any more than a body of its own; its active and directing will must consequently be sought in the person of somebody who for some purposes maybe called an agent, but who is really the directing mind and will of the corporation, the very ego and centre of the personality of the corporation.[117]

It is true that companies are legal persons, but can we say the financial crime committed by a company is in isolation from the people working inside the company? Also, the current requirement to prove the directing mind and will requires the element of 'beyond reasonable doubt' in any case, so why is it not used in conjunction with wilful blindness to prosecute those who are actually responsible?

In truth, the original extremely narrow approach adopted by the judiciary, by which the criterion of identification was satisfied only when the criminal conduct was perpetrated by a person who was the real directing mind and will of the corporation, was later on mitigated. Indeed, it has been argued that, in appropriate cases, a person who is less elevated in the corporate hierarchy could potentially be considered the controller of a company. Such an approach, however, has been criticised, because it inevitably leaves uncertainty as to who will be regarded as a relevant person within the company structure.[118]

Wells digs deeper and acknowledges that, particularly in relation to criminal law, with its reliance on moral fault, there is still a struggle between the nominalists and the realists, a struggle that affects the rules by which responsibility is attributed. Since, in the nominalist view, the corporation does not exist apart from its members, any blameworthiness or responsibility can only derive from the culpability of an individual employee. That still leaves it to be decided whether the corporation will be responsible for all of its employees or only for some of them. For the realist, on the other hand, the corporation does represent

115 Michael Jefferson, *Criminal Law* (12th edn, Pearson 2015).
116 [1915] AC 705 (HL).
117 [1915] AC 705 (HL) 714.
118 P.L. Davies, S. Worthington, L.C.B. Gower and E. Micheler, *Gower & Davies' Principles of Modern Company Law* (2nd edn, Sweet & Maxwell 2008) 187.

something beyond the individuals comprising it, and this opens up completely different avenues for attribution.[119] In a separate piece of work, Wells holds that '[t]he variety in corporate form, reach and activity requires a flexible response both in terms of forms of regulation and in terms of corporate liability models'.[120] The author maintains that, while this discussion is important, what makes the identification principle particularly misplaced is the assumption that individual liability in the form of the identification principle can be imputed to a corporation. This is in tandem with the author's earlier argument that despite being legal persons, the deterrent behaviour of a corporation and an individual is completely different.[121]

It may be said that the Bribery Act 2010 has made a small step forward to overcome the difficulties in the identification principle. Section 7(2) of the Act attempts to separate individual from corporate liability by making it a defence for a corporation to prove that it had in place adequate procedures designed to prevent persons associated with it from undertaking such conduct. By doing so, it may be easier to establish liability on the person associated with the company who is engaged in the act of bribery. The definition of associated person is also not restricted to senior management or directors; instead, it extends to a corporation's agent, employee or subsidiary. However, given the failure of the implementation of the Bribery Act, as demonstrated earlier by the author in this chapter, it is questionable whether there will be any individual prosecutions at a time when even corporations are moving towards a deferred prosecution.[122] Moreover, financial crimes such as bribery, insider trading or money laundering each have different motivations, and independent reform is needed in all the areas separately. It is apt to conclude this section with a quote by J.A. Andrews:

> [W]here we use penal law to support fiscal, health and safety and other regulations, corporations must be brought within the system. On the other hand when we use the penal process to deter delinquency, we should recognise that companies are not delinquents, only people are.[123]

119 C. Wells, *Criminal Responsibility of Legal Persons in Common Law Jurisdictions* (Paper for the OECD Anti-Corruption Unit, OECD 2000) 2. <https://www.coe.int/t/dghl/monitoring/greco/evaluations/seminar2002/Wells_revised.pdf> accessed 30 April 2016.

120 C. Wells, 'Containing corporate crime: civil or criminal controls?' in J. Gobert and A.-M. Pascal (eds), *European Developments in Corporate Criminal Liability* (Routledge 2011).

121 The concept of vicarious liability that also holds a company responsible for the acts of its employees cannot be compared here. This is because when vicarious liability applies, the corporation is liable for the acts of all employees, even subordinate ones, whereas the identification principle is limited to the controlling officers and makes a company liable for *mens rea* offences. See Jefferson for a more detailed discussion on criminal law. Vicarious liability is used for regulatory offences in England and Wales that do not require proof of *mens rea*, including those which have due diligence defences.

122 So far, there have only been standalone individual prosecutions under the Bribery Act, and they do not relate to corporate liability.

123 J. Andrews, 'Reform in the law of corporate liability' [1973] *Criminal Law Review* 91, 94.

11.7 Conclusion

This chapter maintains that although failure in regulation and consequent excessive risk-taking remains one of the most cited causes for the 2008 financial crisis, there has been little progress since. This is paradoxical in the face of the plethora of regulations that the UK financial market now faces, which in financial crime translates into a risk-based approach. With the lack of public–private collaboration and divergent interests, this principles-based regulation has merely become a tick-box exercise for the regulated fraternity, where the focus is on 'seeming to comply' rather than actual compliance. The Credible Deterrence Strategy pursued by the FCA ignores the very component of deterrence itself, as increasing fines are becoming a cost of doing business for large firms. The author has demonstrated this by comparing the value of these fines with the profits earned by firms as stated in their annual accounts. The potential impact of these fines is further diminished with the large discounts offered by the regulator, and by deferred prosecution agreements. These last are seen by the author as an escape route to hide behind the inability to conduct successful individual prosecutions, which may even have the effect of 'incentivising' corporations to engage in financial crime.

Looking at prosecutions from the other end of the spectrum, the author also asks the bigger question about reasons for the lack of individual prosecutions. Why is it that practically no high-level executives have been prosecuted for their role in the financial crisis? Bringing a comparative element here, although it is true that the number of prosecutions is higher in the US, the lack of understanding of 'who to prosecute' still remains in both jurisdictions. In the UK, the Tom Hayes conviction for insider trading has been used as a case study to argue this point.

Besides analysing the lack of individual prosecutions, this chapter also makes some suggestions to move in the direction of change in this regard. The criminal law theory of 'wilful blindness' has been explored as having potential application to overcome this hurdle, along with getting rid of the identification principle to hold a corporation liable. The primary drawback in this principle is the focus on directors and top-tier management, which seems redundant in the age of multinational corporations where decision-making and accountability is a far more complex process. The only way of creating a deterrent effect is to target the actual person/s responsible for a crime.

12 The financial crisis and its relationship with white collar crime in the United States of America: time for the Feds to fight back?

Axel Palmer

> [R]egardless of how challenging it may be to make a case against individuals in a corporate fraud case, it's our responsibility at the Department of Justice to overcome these challenges and do everything we can to develop the evidence and bring these cases. The public expects and demands this accountability. Americans should never believe, even incorrectly, that one's criminal activity will go unpunished because it was committed on behalf of a corporation.[1]

12.1 Introduction

The purpose of this chapter is to critically assess the response of the United States of America (US) to financial crime, a key component of the financial crisis of 2008, which was considered to be 'the worst financial meltdown since the Great Depression'.[2] The political response to these events was in the hands of President Obama, who was inaugurated as President on 20 January 2009, his presidency ending eight years later in January 2017, which is significant because the responsibility to deal with the aftermath was in the hands of a single administration.

To put the challenge of dealing with the aftermath of the financial crisis[3] into perspective, Pontell *et al.*'s view was that '[t]he global meltdown [. . .] was

1 Department of Justice, 'Deputy Attorney General Sally Quillian Yates delivers remarks at New York University School of Law announcing new policy on individual liability in matters of corporate wrongdoing', 10 September 2015. https://www.justice.gov/opa/speech/deputy-attorney-general-sally-quillian-yates-delivers-remarks-new-york-university-school, accessed 4 March 2016.

2 Financial Crisis Inquiry Commission, *Final Report of the National Commission on the causes of the Financial and Economic Crisis in the United States. Official Government Edition*, January 2011, 3. http://cybercemetery.unt.edu/archive/fcic/20110310173545/http://c0182732.cdn1.cloudfiles.rackspacecloud.com/fcic_final_report_full.pdf, accessed 4 March 2016.

3 'A financial crisis occurs when people stop extending credit to other people because they fear that loans will not be repaid.' Eric A. Posner and Adrian Vermeule, 'Crisis governance in

influenced by a number of factors, including flawed financial policies law-breaking, greed, irresponsibility, and not an inconsiderable amounted concerted ignorance and outright stupidity.'[4]

This chapter will begin with the issues faced by President Bush in the closing months of his administration, examine the response of the new President Obama and then consider how the key federal authorities, the Department of Justice (DoJ) and the Securities and Exchange Commission (SEC), undertook their roles to supervise, regulate and protect consumers and individuals from financial abuse.[5]

12.2 What issues did President Bush face?

> For the first time in generations, Americans were questioning the safety of their money in banks. For the first time in more than 80 years, a generalized run on the nation's banking system was a real possibility. The nation was losing almost 800,000 jobs a month and household wealth had fallen by 17 percent – more than five times the decline in 1929.[6]

The US Department of the Treasury (US Treasury) recorded that '[t]he crisis began in the summer of 2007 and gradually increased in intensity and momentum the following year. A series of major financial institutions, including Countrywide Financial, Bear Stearns, IndyMac, and Fannie Mae and Freddie Mac failed.'[7] Then, on 15 September 2008, Lehman Brothers, a 150-year-old financial services firm, filed for bankruptcy as a consequence of being denied a bail-out by the federal government.[8] 'As Lehman fell, the remaining major investment banking firms in this country teetered on the edge of collapse as their funding sources were squeezed.'[9] President Bush's response on the day was that 'he is confident that the markets are resilient and can deal with the latest financial blows. "We are working to reduce disruptions and minimize the impact these financial market developments on the broader economy"',[10] followed by the rejoinder that

the administrative state: 9/11 and the financial meltdown of 2008' (2009) 76 *U Chi L Rev* 1613, 1619.

4 Henry N. Pontell, William K. Black and Gilbert Geis, 'Too big to fail, too powerful to jail? On the absence of criminal prosecutions after the 2008 financial meltdown' (2014) 61(1) *Crime, Law and Social Change* 1. Hereinafter, Pontell *et al.*

5 The Department of the Treasury, *Financial Regulatory Reform. A New Foundation: Rebuilding Financial Supervision and Regulation*. https://www.treasury.gov/initiatives/wsr/Documents/FinalReport_web.pdf, accessed 30 April 2016.

6 US Department of the Treasury, 'Initiatives, financial stability, about TARP'. https://www.treasury.gov/initiatives/financial-stability/about-tarp/Pages/default.aspx, accessed 12 April 2016.

7 Ibid.

8 Richard Holtzman, 'What's the problem Mr President? Bush's shifting definitions of the 2008 financial crisis' (2011) 86 (3/4) *International Social Science Review* 95.

9 See n. 6 above.

10 CNN, 'Lehman Brothers collapse stuns global markets', 15 September 2008. http://edition.cnn.com/2008/BUSINESS/09/15/lehman.merrill.stocks.turmoil/index.html?eref=edition, accessed 12 April 2016.

'[i]n the short run, adjustments in the financial markets can be painful for people worried about their investments and for employees of the firms'.[11] However, Holtzman's observation was that 'Bush's rhetorical response seemed out-of-step with the dominant public and media discourses on the financial crisis'.[12]

President Bush's response to the economic crisis was contained in three legislative measures: the Economic Stimulus Act 2008; the Emergency Economic Stabilization Act 2008; and the Housing and Economic Recovery Act 2008. The Economic Stability Act 2008 had as its objective to 'stimulate the economy and avoid or mitigate a recession'.[13] Deeds states that the Act had three main purposes: '(1) provide rebate checks [cheques] to American families; (2) provide incentives for businesses to invest in qualifying property; and (3) increase the loan limits for Fannie Mae, Freddie Mac and the Federal Housing Administration.'[14] Deeds' conclusion, though, is that this 'fairytale bipartisan piece of legislation',[15] which enjoyed cross-party support to be legislated in seventeen days, 'has not satisfied its purposes. American families, while maybe a little richer [. . .] are not in a safer financial condition. The government had good motives, but ended up spending $152bn on a plan that has not succeeded.'[16]

The next measure was the Housing and Economic Recovery Act 2008. This legislation contains a number of provisions not directly related to the economic crisis,[17] but it 'significantly strengthens the oversight and regulation of the government-sponsored enterprises [GSEs] Fannie Mae, Freddie Mac, and the Federal Home Loan Banks [. . .] and provides for the appointment of a conservator'.[18] The Housing and Economic Recovery Act 2008 responded to the severe crisis in the mortgage credit market by establishing the Federal Housing Finance Agency as the single regulator for Fannie Mae and Freddie Mac.[19]

11 Ibid.

12 Holtzman, n. 8 above, 96.

13 Johnny Deeds, 'The flawed logic of Congress in the Economic Stimulus Act of 2008' (2010) 12 *J L & Fam. Stud.* 299 (footnotes omitted).

14 Ibid., 300.

15 Ibid., 313.

16 Ibid., 313.

17 For an excellent and detailed commentary on the Act, see: Michael J. Novogradac and Glenn A. Graff, 'Impact of the Housing and Economic Recovery Act of 2008 on current and future low-income housing tax credit properties' (2008) 18 *J. Affordable Hous. & Cmty. Dev. L.* 47.

18 Cynthia M. Hajost, 'From oversight to conservatorship: what does the Housing and Economic Recovery Act of 2008 hold for GSEs Fannie Mae and Freddie Mac?' (2008) 18 *J. Affordable Hous. & Cmty. Dev. L.* 3.

19 'Previously, responsibility for oversight of the GSEs fell to two separate regulators: the Office of Federal Housing Enterprise Oversight (OFHEO) was responsible for oversight of the safety and sound-ness of the GSEs, and the Department of Housing and Urban Development (HUD) was responsible for oversight of the GSEs' obligation to help make mortgage financing more affordable and available for low- and moderate- income families.' Ibid., 5.

However, in early September 2008, both entities were placed in conservatorship,[20] which, as Emerson notes, although 'Congress provided the Treasury with authority for such an unprecedented action',[21] the Treasury's suggestion that

> merely providing his department with the authority would likely be sufficient to ward off the companies' collapse proved wrong. Instead, the credit crisis forced the Treasury essentially to take over Freddie Mac and Fannie Mae and, in so doing, expressly established the federal government as guarantor for their failing loan portfolios.[22]

The outcome was that the US Treasury provided $189.5bn in support at the outset of the conservatorships and an additional cumulative $187.5bn.[23]

These interventions, which Shah describes as *ad hoc,* proved to be insufficient;[24] at a time when '[a] financial crisis had been rolling on for months',[25] 'it took the direst of circumstances to propose [. . .] drastic action in the fall of 2008'.[26] The financial failure of Fannie Mae and Freddie Mac in September 2008 was then followed by the insolvency of AIG, after which 'Secretary Paulson had enough and sought new spending authority, proposing a single $700bn package that would serve as a co-ordinated economic intervention in the financial crisis'.[27] The outcome was the Emergency Economic Stabilization Act 2008 (EESA),[28] which aimed '[t]o provide authority for the Federal Government to purchase and insure certain types of troubled assets for the purposes of providing stability to and preventing disruption in the economy and financial system and protecting taxpayers'.[29] In the meantime, Lehman Brothers was allowed to fail 'with disastrous consequences because so many other firms [banks] had accounts with Lehman'.[30] The government was 'apparently persuaded by the scale of failures, the quite obvious contagion effect and independent evidence of a credit crunch, such as the

20 Federal Housing Finance Agency, 'Home / conservatorship / history of Fannie Mae & Freddie Mac conservatorships'. http://www.fhfa.gov/Conservatorship/Pages/History-of-Fannie-Mae--Freddie-Conservatorships.aspx, accessed 12 April 2016.

21 Chad D. Emerson, 'A troubled house of cards: examining how the Housing and Economic Recovery Act of 2008 fails to resolve the foreclosure crisis' (2008) 61 *Okla L Rev* 561, 582.

22 Ibid.

23 Federal Housing Finance Agency, n. 20 above.

24 Archit Shah, 'Recent developments: Emergency Economic Stabilization Act of 2008' (2009) 46 *Harv J on Legis* 569.

25 Ibid.

26 Shah provides a commentary on how the financial crisis developed. Ibid.

27 Ibid.

28 Emergency Economic Stabilization Act of 2008, Pub Law 110–343. The Act was signed into law on 3 October 2008.

29 Ibid.

30 Posner and Vermeule, n. 3 above, 1624.

extremely high rate of interest than banks began to charge each other for inter-bank loans'.[31]

The key element of EESA was the Troubled Asset Relief Programme (TARP). This was 'created to implement programs to stabilize the financial system during the financial crisis of 2008. It [. . .] is overseen by the Office of Financial Stability at the U.S. Department of the Treasury.'[32] The original purpose of TARP was to inject liquidity into the financial system by using it to purchase mortgage-related assets, because 'the government would help reduce uncertainty about banks' balance sheets, allowing them to borrow if they turned out to be insolvent'.[33] In the event, the US Treasury did not purchase troubled banking assets, relying instead on making equity purchases, together with using TARP funds 'to bail out the automakers in December 2008 and January 2009, based on the broad definition of "financial institutions" in the EESA'.[34] Eventually, the TARP funds were used: $250bn was committed in programmes to stabilize banking institutions; $27bn to restart credit markets; $82b to stabilize the US auto industry; $70bn to stabilize American International Group (AIG); $46bn to help struggling families avoid foreclosure.[35]

12.3 President Obama's response

The transition to President Obama brought a determination 'to build a new foundation for sustained economic growth'.[36] President Obama made plain his assessment of the task:

> This new foundation also requires strong, vibrant financial markets, operating under transparent, fairly-administered rules of the road that protect America's consumers and our economy from the devastating breakdown that we've witnessed in recent years. It is an indisputable fact that one of the most significant contributors to our economic downturn was a unraveling of major financial institutions and the lack of adequate regulatory structures to prevent abuse and excess. A culture of irresponsibility took root from Wall Street to Washington to Main Street. And a regulatory regime basically crafted in the wake of a 20th century economic crisis – the Great Depression – was

31 Ibid. 'For the first time in generations, Americans were questioning the safety of their money in banks. For the first time in more than 80 years, a generalized run on the nation's banking system was a real possibility. The nation was losing almost 800,000 jobs a month and household wealth had fallen by 17 percent – more than five times the decline in 1929.' US Department of the Treasury, n. 6 above.

32 US Department of the Treasury, n. 6 above.

33 Posner and Vermeule, n. 3 above, 1624.

34 Ibid., 1626.

35 US Department of the Treasury, n. 6 above.

36 The White House, 'Remarks of the President on Regulatory Reform' 17 June 2009. https://www.whitehouse.gov/the-press-office/remarks-president-regulatory-reform, accessed 30 April 2016.

> overwhelmed by the speed, scope, and sophistication of a 21st century global economy.[37]

President Obama painted a picture of misunderstood risks, easy money, lowering of standards and reward for recklessness rather than responsibility.[38] Furthermore, '[w]here there were gaps in the rules, regulators lacked the authority to take action. Where there were overlaps, regulators lacked accountability for their inaction.'[39] The government's response was a sweeping overhaul of the financial regulatory system,[40] with proposals to: 'Promote robust supervision and regulation of financial firms; Protect consumers and investors from financial abuse; Provide the government with the tools it needs to manage financial crises; Raise international regulatory standards and improve international cooperation.'[41] Not surprisingly, President Obama stated that 'enforcement will be the rule, not the exception',[42] which gave rise to the Fraud Enforcement and Recovery Act 2009.

12.3.1 Fraud Enforcement and Recovery Act 2009

The Fraud Enforcement and Recovery Act 2009 (FERA)[43] was President Obama's first legislation 'ostensibly combating the type of chronic misconduct which may have helped foster economic instability rather than merely combating the acute symptoms of such instability'.[44] The purpose of the Act is to 'improve enforcement of mortgage fraud, securities and commodities fraud, financial institution fraud, and other frauds related to Federal assistance and relief programs, for the recovery of funds lost to these frauds, and for other purposes'.[45] Reidy describes the measures introduced:

> A bipartisan Financial Crisis Inquiry Commission to examine the causes of the economic crisis, augments the False Claims Act, expands the definition

37 Ibid.
38 Ibid.
39 Ibid.
40 The White House, Remarks by the President in State of the Union Address, 24 January 2012. https://www.whitehouse.gov/the-press-office/2012/01/24/remarks-president-state-union-address, accessed 26 April 2016.
41 The Department of the Treasury, n. 5 above.
42 The White House, n. 40 above.
43 Pub Law 111–21.
44 Jon Reidy, 'The problem of "proceeds" in the era of FERA' (2010) 37(3) *Am J Crim L* 317, 318. The earlier American Recovery and Reinvestment Act 2009 was signed into law on 17 February 2009 and 'sets forth new restrictions on contracts and federal assistance agreements'. Kathryn T. Muldoon, 'Obstacles to economic stimulus: increased government oversight and the American Recovery and Reinvestment Act of 2009' (2010) 39(2) *Public Contract Law Journal* 285.
45 See n. 43 above.

> of 'financial institution' to better enable prosecution of mortgage-related offenses, establishes various mechanisms of recovery spending oversight and aims to increase the enforcement of financial fraud law.[46]

President Obama said that the Act would 'nearly double the FBI's mortgage and financial fraud program, allowing it to better target fraud in hard-hit areas'.[47] Furthermore, 'it provides the resources necessary for other law enforcement and federal agencies, from the Department of Justice to the SEC to the Secret Service, to pursue these criminals [and] bring them to justice'.[48] This legislation also plugs the gap in existing legislation by expanding the 'DOJ's authority to prosecute fraud that takes place in many of the private institutions not covered under current federal bank fraud criminal statutes – institutions where more than half of all subprime mortgages came from'.[49] The next section of the chapter concentrates on financial fraud and mortgage fraud in particular.

12.3.2 Financial Fraud Enforcement Task Force

President Obama, in his 2012 State of the Union speech, announced the creation of

> a special unit of federal prosecutors and a leading state attorney general to expand our investigations into the abusive lending and packaging of risky mortgages that led to the housing crisis. This new unit will hold accountable those who broke the law, speed assistance to homeowners, and help turn the page on an era of recklessness that hurt so many Americans.[50]

This initiative became the Residential Mortgage-Backed Securities Working Group with an objective to 'streamline and strengthen current and future efforts to identify, investigate, and prosecute instances of wrongdoing in the packaging, selling, and valuing of residential mortgage-backed securities'.[51] The former

46 Reidy, n. 44 above, 319.

47 The White House, 'Remarks by the president at signing of the Helping Families Save Their Homes Act and the Fraud Enforcement and Recovery Act', 20 May 2009. https://www.whitehouse.gov/the-press-office/remarks-president-signing-helping-families-save-their-homes-act-and-fraud-enforceme, accessed 30 April 2016.

48 Ibid.

49 Ibid.

50 Ibid.

51 Department of Justice, 'Attorney General Holder speaks at the announcement of the Financial Fraud Enforcement Task Force's new Residential Mortgage-Backed Securities Working Group', 27 January 2012. https://www.justice.gov/opa/speech/attorney-general-holder-speaks-announcementof-financial-fraud-enforcement-task-force-s, accessed 26 April 2016. The RMBS Working Group is a federal and state law-enforcement effort focused on investigating fraud and abuse in the RMBS market that helped lead to the 2008 financial crisis. The RMBS Working Group brings together more than 200 attorneys, investigators,

Attorney General Holder stated that he was 'confident that this new effort will improve our ability to ensure justice for victims; [and] help restore faith in our financial markets and institutions'.[52]

The establishment of the Working Group was accompanied by an explanation of previous endeavours, highlighting that some behaviour, however unethical or reckless, may not necessarily be criminal, a subject which commentators raise in relation to Department of Justice's subsequent sanctions. Holder said:

> Over the past three years, we have been aggressively investigating the causes of the financial crisis. And we have learned that much of the conduct that led to the crisis was [. . .] unethical, and, in many instances, extremely reckless. We also have learned that behavior that is unethical or reckless may not necessarily be criminal. When we find evidence of criminal wrongdoing, we bring criminal prosecutions. When we don't, we endeavor to use other tools available to us – such as civil sanctions – to seek justice. My number one commitment to the American people is that we will continue to devote significant resources to combating financial fraud and be as aggressive and creative as we can be in holding accountable those who, in violating the law, contributed to the financial crisis.[53]

The financial crisis was multi-faceted, involving not just banks and intermediaries but ratings agencies. In 2013, the Financial Fraud Enforcement Task Force

> announced the filing of parallel civil complaints [. . .] against the ratings agency Standard and Poor's (S&P) shedding a powerful light on conduct that went to the heart of the recent financial crisis. The [DoJ] alleged that from at least 2004 to 2007, S&P lied about its objectivity and independence. [. . .] [promised] that their ratings were based on data and analytical models reflecting the company's true credit judgment. In fact, [. . .] [S&P] regularly altered, or delayed altering, its ratings models to suit the company's own

analysts and staff from dozens of state and federal agencies including the Department of Justice, ten US Attorneys' Offices, the FBI, the Securities and Exchange Commission (SEC), the Department of Housing and Urban Development (HUD), HUD's Office of Inspector General, the FHFA-OIG, the Office of the Special Inspector General for the Troubled Asset Relief Program, the Federal Reserve Board's Office of Inspector General, the Recovery Accountability and Transparency Board, the Financial Crimes Enforcement Network, and more than ten state attorneys general offices around the country. Department of Justice, 'Bank of America to Pay $16.65 billion in historic Justice Department settlement for financial fraud leading up to and during the financial crisis', 21 August 2014. https://www.justice.gov/opa/pr/bank-america-pay-1665-billion-historic-justice-department-settlement-financial-fraud-leading, accessed 26 April 2016.

52 Department of Justice, n. 51 above.

53 Department of Justice, n. 51 above.

> business interests. [. . .] S&P issued ratings for certain CDOs that it knew were inflated at the time it issued them.[54]

In 2014, the Department of Justice announced

> a $16.65bn settlement with Bank of America Corporation [. . .] to resolve federal and state claims against Bank of America and its former and current subsidiaries, including Countrywide Financial Corporation and Merrill Lynch. As part of this global resolution, the bank has agreed to pay a $5bn penalty under the [FIRREA] [. . .] and provide billions of dollars of relief to struggling homeowners, including funds that will help defray tax liability as a result of mortgage modification, forbearance or forgiveness.[55]

The DoJ comment that the settlement 'attests to the fact that fraud pervaded every level of the RMBS industry, including purportedly prime securities' and that '[e]ven reputable institutions like Bank of America caved to the pernicious forces of greed and cut corners, putting profits ahead of their customers'.[56]

The DoJ, in its settlement with Morgan Stanley in 2016, stated that:

> Morgan Stanley acknowledged in writing that it failed to disclose critical information to prospective investors about the quality of the mortgage loans underlying its RMBS and about its due diligence practices. Investors, including

54 Department of Justice, 'Financial Fraud Enforcement Task Force Executive Director Michael J. Bresnick at the Exchequer Club of Washington, D.C.', 20 March 2013. https://www.justice.gov/opa/speech/financial-fraud-enforcement-task-force-executive-director-michael-j-bresnick-exchequer, accessed 26 April 2016.

55 'This settlement also resolves the complaint filed against Bank of America in August 2013 by the U.S. Attorney's Office for the Western District of North Carolina concerning an $850 million securitization. Bank of America acknowledges that it marketed this securitization as being backed by bank-originated "prime" mortgages that were underwritten in accordance with its underwriting guidelines. Yet, Bank of America knew that a significant number of loans in the security were "wholesale" mortgages originated through mortgage brokers and that based on its internal reporting, such loans were experiencing a marked increase in underwriting defects and a noticeable decrease in performance. Notwithstanding these red flags, the bank sold these RMBS to federally backed financial institutions without conducting any third party due diligence on the securitized loans and without disclosing key facts to investors in the offering documents filed with the SEC.' The settlement does not release individuals from civil charges, nor does it absolve Bank of America, its current or former subsidiaries and affiliates or any individuals from potential criminal prosecution. Department of Justice, n. 51 above.

56 Department of Justice, n. 51 above. A Residential Mortgage Backed Security (RMBS) is described as 'a type of security comprised of a pool of mortgage loans created by banks and other financial institutions. The expected performance and price of an RMBS is determined by a number of factors, including the characteristics of the borrowers and the value of the properties underlying the RMBS.' Department of Justice, 'Morgan Stanley agrees to pay $2.6 billion penalty in connection with its sale of residential mortgage backed securities', 11 February 2016. https://www.justice.gov/opa/pr/morgan-stanley-agrees-pay-26-billion-penalty-connection-its-sale-residential-mortgage-backed, accessed 27 April 2016.

federally insured financial institutions, suffered billions of dollars in losses from investing in RMBS issued by Morgan Stanley in 2006 and 2007.[57]

The Morgan Stanley settlement is instructive because the detailed statement of facts quoted by the DoJ highlighted behaviours which were deceptive or unfair: securitising 'underwater loans (loans that exceeded the value of the property);[58] securitising loans which did not meet the originators guidelines;[59] misrepresenting its due diligence processes.[60] The DoJ concluded that '[t]hrough these undisclosed practices, Morgan Stanley increased the percentage of mortgage loans it purchased for its RMBS, notwithstanding its awareness about "deteriorating appraisal quality" and "sloppy underwriting" by the sellers of these loans'.[61] To provide a flavour of the behaviours within Morgan Stanley, the DoJ quote comments such as:

> 'please do not mention the 'slightly higher risk tolerance' in these communications. We are running under the radar and do not want to document these types of things;'[62] and, 'Morgan Stanley's manager of credit-and-compliance due diligence was admonished to "stop fighting and begin recognizing the point that we need monthly volume from our biggest trading partners and that [. . .] the client [an originator] does not have to sell to Morgan Stanley".'[63]

Notwithstanding the DoJ's comments that it 'will not tolerate those who seek financial gain through deceptive or unfair means, and we will take appropriately

57 Department of Justice, n. 56 above.

58 'Morgan Stanley told investors that it did not securitize underwater loans (loans that exceeded the value of the property). However, Morgan Stanley did not disclose to investors that in April 2006 it had expanded its "risk tolerance" in evaluating loans in order to purchase and securitize "everything possible."' Department of Justice, n. 56 above.

59 'Morgan Stanley also told investors that it did not securitize loans that failed to meet originators' guidelines unless those loans had compensating factors. Morgan Stanley's offering documents "represented that '[the mortgage loans originated or acquired by [the originator] were done so in accordance with the underwriting guidelines established by [the originator]' but that 'on a case-by-case-basis, exceptions to the [underwriting guidelines] are made where compensating factors exist.'" Morgan Stanley has now acknowledged, however, that "Morgan Stanley did not disclose to securitization investors that employees of Morgan Stanley received information that, in certain instances, loans that did not comply with underwriting guidelines and lacked adequate compensating factors . . . were included in the RMBS sold and marketed to investors." So, in fact, "Morgan Stanley [. . .] securitized certain loans that neither comported with the originators' underwriting guidelines nor had adequate compensating factors."' Department of Justice, n. 56 above.

60 'Likewise, "Morgan Stanley also prepared presentation materials [. . .] that it used in discussions with potential investors that described the due diligence process for reviewing pools of loans prior to securitization," but "certain of Morgan Stanley's actual due diligence practices did not conform to the description of the process set forth" in those materials.' Department of Justice, n. 56 above.

61 Department of Justice, n. 56 above.

62 Ibid.

63 Ibid.

aggressive action against financial institutions that knowingly engage in improper investment practices',[64] there is no mention of action against individuals, other than a statement that 'Morgan Stanley promised to cooperate fully with any ongoing investigations related to the conduct covered by the agreement'.[65]

12.3.3 Dodd–Frank Wall Street Reform and Consumer Protection Act 2010

The 2008 financial crisis, as Ceresney comments, 'will be known as the modern financial system's *annus horribilis*'.[66] A natural consequence of a crisis is that 'citizens are asking angrily how this happened and who is to blame'.[67] This then invites the enquiry that '[a]midst this wreckage, as legislators consider proposals for sweeping regulatory reforms, prosecutors and regulatory agencies have begun the arduous and time-consuming process of determining whether any criminal wrongdoing led to the credit crisis'.[68] The outcome of this 'soul searching' was:

> The Dodd–Frank Wall Street Reform and Consumer Protection Act [Dodd-Frank][69] [. . .] [which] set out to reshape the U.S. regulatory system in a number of areas including but not limited to consumer protection, trading restrictions, credit ratings, regulation of financial products, corporate governance and disclosure, and transparency.[70]

The introduction to Dodd–Frank makes clear the legislation's intentions:

> To promote the financial stability of the United States by improving accountability and transparency in the financial system, to end 'too big to fail', to protect the American taxpayer by ending bailouts, to protect consumers from abusive financial services practices, and for other purposes.[71]

One particular aspect of Dodd–Frank is 'the Volcker Rule, [which] prohibits a bank from engaging in proprietary trading, and from acquiring or retaining an ownership interest in a hedge fund or private equity fund'.[72] The intent of the

64 Ibid.
65 Ibid.
66 Andrew J. Ceresney, Gordon Eng and Sean R. Nuttall, 'Regulatory investigations and the credit crisis: the search for villains' (2009) 46 *Am Crim L Rev* 225.
67 Ibid.
68 Ibid.
69 12 USC § 5322, which amends the Securities Exchange Act 1934.
70 US Securities and Exchange Commission, 'The laws that govern the securities industry'. http://www.sec.gov/about/laws.shtml#df2010, accessed 6 June 2016.
71 'Dodd–Frank Wall Street Reform and Consumer Protection Act.' Preamble. https://www.sec.gov/about/laws/wallstreetreform-cpa.pdf, accessed 6 June 2016.
72 The Dodd–Frank Wall Street Reform and Consumer Protection Act 2010, s. 619. 'The Volcker Rule is named after its main sponsor, Paul Volcker, who is a former Chairman of the Board of Governors of the Federal Reserve System and an economic adviser to the

Volcker Rule was to endeavour to replicate '[t]he US Banking Act of 1933, called the Glass–Steagall Act after its sponsors, [which] separated investment banking from retail banking by limiting the range and volume of securities-related transactions that the commercial entities could perform'.[73] This rule, though, does not merely affect US entities, but also applies to foreign banks and entities which have a branch or agency in the US, and clearly demonstrates the reach of US legislation.[74]

An additional outcome of the review of the 'financial crisis' was that the SEC recognised that more information on breaches of securities law was required, and it caused the SEC to promote the role of the 'Whistleblower'.[75] Dodd–Frank encourages whistleblowers to report suspected violations direct to the SEC 'Office of the Whistleblower'.[76] This will reward[77] such suppliers of information who are eligible to receive between 10 per cent and 30 per cent of any enforcement penalty in excess of $1 million that the agency ultimately recovers as a result of the report.[78] The largest reward was $30m, in 2014.[79]

President of the USA, Barack Obama'. Graeme Baber, 'A critical examination of the legislative response in banking and financial regulation to issues related to misconduct in the context of the crisis of 2007–2009' (2013) 20(2) *JFC* 237.

73 Baber, n. 72 above.

74 William E. Stern, 'Impact of the Volcker rule and related Dodd–Frank Act requirements on fund sponsors affiliated with non-US banking organisations' (2013) 4 *JIBFL* 229.

75 'Means any individual, or 2 or more individuals acting jointly, who provides information relating to a violation of this Act to the Commission, in a manner established by rule or regulation by the Commission.' Dodd–Frank Act 2010, s. 748(7).

76 The SEC established the 'Office of the Whistleblower', stating that the 'new whistleblower program is a part of our effort to enhance the agency's capacity to detect and prevent fraud'. US Securities and Exchange Commission, 'Speech by SEC Chairman: opening statement at SEC Open Meeting: Item 2 — Whistleblower Program', 25 May 2011. http://www.sec.gov/news/speech/2011/spch052511mls-item2.htm, accessed 6 June 2016.

77 'In addition to providing qualifying whistleblowers with a bounty, the Dodd–Frank Act protects whistleblowers in two other respects. First, it allows whistleblowers to remain anonymous up to the point of receiving their financial awards. Second, the Dodd–Frank Act allows whistleblowers to redeem their bounties unless they are convicted of a crime related to the reported FCPA violations.' Heidi L. Hansberry, 'In spite of its good intentions, the Dodd–Frank Act has created an FCPA monster' (2012) 102 *JCRLC* 195.

78 These percentages are typical when compared with other statutes with similar whistleblowing provisions, such as IRS Whistleblower Act and False Claims Act. Ibid. Carol M. Welu, 'A brave (but scary) new world: why private equity is not exempt from US and UK anti-corruption laws', 2 February 2011. http://www.squirepattonboggs.com/~/media/files/insights/publications/2011/02/china-outbound/files/squiresandersnewschinaoutboundenglishpdf/fileattachment/squiresandersnewschinaoutboundenglishpdf.pdf, accessed 6 June 2016. Robert S. Bennett, Hilary Holt LoCicero and Brooks M. Hanner, 'From regulation to prosecution to cooperation: trends in corporate white collar crime enforcement and the evolving role of the white collar criminal defense attorney' (2013) 68 *The Business Lawyer* 411.

79 Securities and Exchange Commission, 'SEC announces largest-ever whistleblower award' [$30m]. http://www.sec.gov/News/PressRelease/Detail/PressRelease/1370543011290#.VCktK77HthY. 'The SEC's whistleblower program has now awarded more than $62 million to 28 whistleblowers since the program's inception in 2011.' Securities and Exchange

However, Dodd–Frank was not the first attempt at encouraging 'informers to come forward with information about fraud against the [US] government in return for a share of the damages recovered'.[80] In 1863, pre-dating both conspiracy to defraud (1867) and mail fraud (1872), the False Claims Act empowered citizens to sue 'on behalf of the government for fraud against the government'[81] and share in the fruits of litigation: since 2009, the DoJ 'has recovered more than $13.3bn in False Claims Act cases'.[82] In 2012, the DoJ brought an all-time high of 647 whistleblower cases,[83] thus demonstrating the economic value of an incentivised whistleblower. Thus, the rewards from SEC clearly 'make it all the more likely that employees who notice such wrongdoing will take steps to bring it to light'.[84] However, this may be at the expense of reporting through companies' internal corporate risk management or governance channels. Indeed, the SEC 'reported receiving one to two "high value" tips per day, up from about a dozen a year prior to enactment of Dodd–Frank'.[85] Furthermore, there is also the risk of 'repeat bad faith' claims, as in a 2014 case where the SEC banned an individual who had knowingly made 196 award applications which were false, fictitious or fraudulent in pursuit of an award.[86]

Some eight years before Dodd–Frank, in the wake of 'a spate of financial/accounting scandals',[87] the Sarbanes–Oxley Act 2002 was enacted 'to protect investors by improving the accuracy and reliability of corporate disclosures made pursuant to the securities laws, and for other purposes'.[88] This was a 'Congressional response to revelations of several high profile accounting fraud

Commission, 'Whistleblower earns $3.5 million award for bolstering ongoing investigation', 13 May 2016. https://www.sec.gov/news/pressrelease/2016-88.html, accessed 17 May 2016.

80 Indira Carr, *Financial Fraud Law Report 4: The UK Bribery Act: Business Integrity and Whistleblowers* (Thompson Media 2012) 362.

81 Ibid., 369.

82 Department of Justice, 'Justice Department recovers $2.4 billion in false claims cases in fiscal year 2009; more than $24 billion since 1986', 19 November 2009. http://www.justice.gov/opa/pr/2009/November/09-civ-1253.html, accessed 6 June 2016. '$9.5 billion of those recoveries are from cases involving fraud against federal health care programs. Money goes back to the federal agency that was defrauded, replenishing federal funds and sending a message to potential scammers that ultimately they will be required to pay up to three times the amount of their fraud.' Department of Justice. 'Accomplishments under the leadership of Attorney General Eric Holder'. http://www.justice.gov/accomplishments, accessed 6 June 2016.

83 Ibid. 2016.

84 Bennett, LoCicero and Hanner, n. 78 above.

85 Hansberry, n. 77 above.

86 Securities and Exchange Commission, 'Final order'. https://www.sec.gov/about/offices/owb/orders/owb-multiple-final-051214.pdf, accessed 6 June 2016.

87 For example: Enron, Worldcom, Tyco, Arthur Andersen. Fred Yeager and others, 'US legislation designed to improve corporate governance: an exploration' (2010) 33(1) *Co Law* 25.

88 Sarbanes–Oxley Act of 2002. Preamble. http://www.iia-ru.ru/files/documents_open/Sarbanes-Oxley.pdf, accessed 6 June 2016.

cases including Enron, WorldCom, Tyco, [. . .] that resulted in mass destruction of investor value and loss of investor confidence in the integrity of the financial markets'.[89] Eventually, as Yeager notes, 'these cases led to criminal charges of company officials and the bankruptcy of Arthur Andersen LLP, at the time arguably the most prestigious independent auditing firm in the world', discussed later in this chapter.[90] Consequently, a key feature of Sarbanes–Oxley was provision for whistleblowers: first, anti-retaliation measures, 'which involves protecting whistleblowers from employer retaliation after they disclose wrongdoing';[91] second, a reporting arrangement which 'requires that corporations provide employees with a standardized channel to report organizational misconduct internally within the corporation'.[92] A further feature of Sarbanes–Oxley was increased sentences: 'the maximum penalty for wire and mail fraud from five years to twenty years imprisonment'.[93]

12.4 Fraud

The US government has, since enacting the Foreign Corrupt Practices Act 1977 (FCPA), given priority to combating economic crime, including the creation of the Financial Fraud Enforcement Task Force (FFETF) to strengthen efforts to combat financial crime arising from the 2008 financial crisis.[94] This followed an announcement in May 2009 that the DoJ 'has been given $330m to investigate any suspected instances of mortgage fraud and to pursue any potential prosecutions that arise from those investigations'.[95] At this stage, it is important to recognise that this does represent a change in US strategy, which, under Presidents

89 Yeager and others, n. 87 above.

90 Ibid.

91 Richard E. Moberly, 'Sarbanes–Oxley's structural model to encourage corporate whistleblowers' (2006) *BYU L Rev* 1107. Kiren Dosanjh Zucker, 'Cautionary tale for corporate whistleblowers: lessons from Federal Courts' decisions on Sarbanes–Oxley employee retaliation claims' (2011) 62(2) *Labor Law Journal* 81. The protection for an employee is not to be 'discharged, demoted, suspended, harassed or discriminated against in any other way'. George R. Salem and Laura M. Franze, 'The whistleblower provisions of the Sarbanes–Oxley Act of 2002'. http://apps.americanbar.org/labor/oshlcomm/mw/Papers/2003/salem.pdf, accessed 6 June 2016.

92 *Lockheed Martin Corp. v Administrative Review Board*, No. 11–9524, 2013 U.S. App. LEXIS 11159 (10th Cir. June 4, 2013). Moberly, n. 91 above. Salem and Franze, n. 91 above

93 Nicholas Ryder, *Financial Crime in the 21st Century* (Edward Elgar 2011) 107 (footnotes omitted).

94 Department of Justice, 'President Obama Establishes Interagency Financial Fraud Enforcement Task Force', 17 November 2009. http://www.sec.gov/news/press/2009/2009-249.htm, accessed 6 June 2016.

95 The White House, 'Reforms for american homeowners and consumers: President Obama Signs the Helping Families Save Their Homes Act and the Fraud Enforcement and Recovery Act', 20 May 2009. https://www.whitehouse.gov/the-press-office/reforms-american-homeowners-and-consumers-president-obama-signs-helping-families-sa, accessed 11 May 2016.

Clinton and Bush, had concentrated resources on the 'war on terror'.[96] Ceresney highlights that '[f]ollowing the September 11th attacks, the FBI shifted more than 1,800 agents, nearly one third of all agents in criminal programs, including many of those trained in financial investigations, to counterterrorism and intelligence duties'.[97] As a consequence, there were insufficient resources to deal with fraud and non-terrorism investigations.[98] Eventually, in 2008, 'the FBI announced operation "Malicious Mortgage", a multi-agency take down of more than 400 defendants charged with mortgage fraud schemes nationwide'.[99] This presaged the creation of FFETF. The purpose in creating the FFETF was:

> that no matter the office or agency – federal, state, or local; law enforcement or regulatory – all of us within government share a common desire and have a core obligation to do everything that we can do to protect the American public from the often devastating effects of financial fraud, whether it be mortgage fraud or investment fraud, grant or procurement fraud, consumer fraud or fraud in lending. And we know that *we can accomplish so much more by working together than working in isolated, compartmentalised silos.*[100]

President Obama's aim in creating FFETF is neatly encapsulated by stating that working together is better than in isolation. However, in terms of prosecuting economic crime, the US as a federal country[101] is not streamlined, hence the exhortation for agencies to work together:

> In the US, the picture is complicated even more by the Federal and state infrastructure. Federal agencies such as the [FBI] have jurisdiction over a wide range of different types of fraud and corruption, such as public sector fraud and corruption, mass marketing fraud and identity fraud.[102]

There are also the SEC, investment fraud; the Internal Revenue Service, tax fraud; the US Postal Inspectors, mail fraud; the US Secret Service, credit card fraud and currency fraud. This is on top of a state bureaucracy of law enforcement which is often as diverse and complex as at federal level.[103]

96 'On 24 September 2001 President George Bush proclaimed that "we will starve terrorists of funding", thus instigating the "financial war on terrorism".' Ryder, n. 93 above, 51.
97 Ceresney, Eng and Nuttall, n. 66 above.
98 Ibid.
99 Ibid.
100 Bresnick, n. 54 above (emphasis added).
101 '[H]aving or relating to a system of government in which several states form a unity but remain independent in internal affairs.' Oxford Dictionaries. http://oxforddictionaries.com/definition/english/federal, accessed 12 September 2013.
102 Mark Button and Jim Gee, *Countering Fraud for Competitive Advantage* (Wiley 2013) 52.
103 Ibid.

In the US 'the prevention of fraud is an essential part of many criminal statutes and it shows no signs of abating'.[104] However, as Podgor notes, the proliferation of fraud statutes is found to be 'problematic in that there is no specific group of statutes designated in the federal code as fraud statutes and no consistent definition'.[105] Podgor's view is that 'the term "fraud" is a "concept"'[106] and '[a]lthough fraud is not a crime in itself, fraud is an integral aspect of several criminal statutes'.[107] In the absence of a single fraud statute,

> there appears to be an acceptance of an 'I know it when I see it' approach. Judge Holmes of the Fifth Circuit stated that 'the law does not define fraud; it needs no definition; it is as old as falsehood and as versable as human ingenuity'.[108]

US Fraud statutes are either generic, such as 'conspiracy', 'mail' or 'wire' frauds, or specific, such as 'bankruptcy' fraud, 'healthcare' fraud and 'bank' fraud. At the 'generic' end of the spectrum, the 'focus of the [fraud] statute is almost exclusively on the fraud and not the object of the offense'.[109] Thus, 'the emphasis of the crime of mail fraud is the fraudulent conduct as opposed to the mailing'.[110] In a similar manner, 'a conspiracy to defraud does not require agreement to violate a specific statute'.[111] The statute 'Conspiracy to commit offense or to defraud the United States'[112] has been interpreted to be 'so elastic over the years that it can potentially encompass any conduct which a court views as "collusive and dishonest" if some federal rule or regulation was violated in the process'.[113] As such, it is easy to understand the sentiments of the often-quoted Judge Learned Hand, who in 1925 described the conspiracy statute as 'that darling of the modern prosecutor's nursery'.[114] The recognition of wrongdoing is one matter; the prosecution of wrongdoing is another and is in the hands of the federal authorities.

104 Ryder, n. 93 above, 103.
105 Ellen S. Podgor, 'Criminal fraud' (1999) 48 *Am U L Rev* 729.
106 Ibid.
107 Ibid.
108 Ibid. (footnotes omitted).
109 Ibid.
110 Ibid.
111 Ibid.
112 18 U.S.C. § 371 – Conspiracy to Defraud the United States.
113 Steven D. Gordon, 'The liability of colleges and universities for fraud, waste, and abuse in federally funded grants and projects' (1992) 75 *EDUc. L. REP* 13.
114 *United States of America, Appellee, v Fred Eubanks, Eugene Martinez, Leroy Jones, Henry D. Yanez, appellants.* United States Court of Appeals, Ninth Circuit. – 591 F.2d 513 Feb. 2, 1979. As amended 12 March 1979. http://law.justia.com/cases/federal/appellate-courts/F2/591/513/369568, accessed 6 June 2016, citing *Harrison v United States,* 7 F.2d 259, 263 (2d Cir. 1925) (Judge Learned Hand).

12.5 Response from the federal authorities

12.5.1 Department of Justice

The DoJ has 'control over all criminal prosecutions and civil suits in which the United States had an interest'.[115] The DoJ comprises 40 components, including the Criminal Division Fraud Section,[116] which 'plays a unique and essential role in the Department's fight against sophisticated economic crime. The Section is a front-line litigating unit that acts as a rapid response team, investigating and prosecuting complex white collar crime cases throughout the country.'[117] The role of the DoJ is protecting taxpayer dollars and consumers against financial fraud while ensuring competitive advantage.[118] The then Attorney General stated that they

> [h]ave charged and had sentenced a number of defendants involved in securities fraud and related investment fraud, mortgage fraud and Ponzi schemes. These defendants include CEOs, owners, board members, presidents, general counsel and other executives of Wall Street firms, hedge funds and banks.[119]

Although the DoJ state that they 'do not hesitate to bring charges against *anyone* [and] between 2009 and 2013, [they] charged more white-collar defendants than during any previous five-year period going back to at least 1994';[120] nevertheless the headlines are given to the significance of the penalties it imposes in 'over 60 cases against financial institutions since 2009, resulting in recoveries totalling over $85 bn'.[121]

The DoJ as primary regulator and prosecutor is supported by the investigative tools of the Federal Bureau of Investigation (FBI),[122] which is another division of the DoJ. Thus, the Attorney General has line-management responsibility for both investigation and prosecution. Financial intelligence is gained through FinCEN, which is part of the US Treasury.[123]

115 Department of Justice, '2014 budget'. https://www.justice.gov/sites/default/files/jmd/legacy/2013/11/11/fy14-bud-sum.pdf, accessed 6 June 2016.
116 Ibid.
117 Department of Justice, 'Criminal Division Fraud Section'. https://www.justice.gov/criminal/sectionsoffices/chart, accessed 6 June 2016.
118 Department of Justice 2016, n. 82 above.
119 Examples include: Allen, sentenced to 210 years' imprisonment for orchestrating $7 billion investment fraud; Barclays Bank $160m LIBOR violations. Department of Justice 2016, n. 82 above.
120 Department of Justice, 'Attorney General Holder Remarks on Financial Fraud Prosecutions at NYU School of Law'. http://www.justice.gov/opa/speech/attorney-general-holder-remarks-financial-fraud-prosecutions-nyu-school-law, accessed 6 June 2016.
121 Ibid.
122 Nicholas Ryder, *Financial Crime in the 21st Century* (Edward Elgar 2011) 102.
123 Financial Crimes Enforcement Network (FinCEN). http://www.fincen.gov, accessed 6 June 2016.

12.5.1.1 Department of Justice: enforcement mechanisms

The DoJ Criminal Division Fraud Section is responsible for authorising all FCPA criminal actions,[124] and 'develops, enforces, and supervises the application of all federal criminal laws except those specifically assigned to other divisions'.[125] Thus, the DoJ 'is solely responsible for criminal enforcement but may institute civil proceedings',[126] whereas the SEC can only institute civil proceedings, with any criminal prosecutions being referred to the DoJ.[127] The DoJ maintains a FCPA Unit and works with the FBI, whose 'International Corruption Unit has primary responsibility for international corruption and fraud investigations and coordinates the FBI's national FCPA enforcement program'.[128] The DoJ has instituted a new initiative: the Kleptocracy Asset Recovery Initiative to 'target and recover the proceeds of foreign official corruption that have been laundered into or through the United States'.[129] Their first success in 2012 was a $3 million restraining order against 'the former governor of the oil-producing Delta State in Nigeria' (Ibori) followed by another order for $4 million.[130]

In considering criminal penalties to be imposed for violation of FCPA, the DoJ also has the availability of 'the Alternative Fines Act',[131] which can double the fines provided for in the FCPA.[132] Furthermore, there is a procedure for

124 Department of Justice, 'Assistant Attorney General Lanny A. Breuer of the Criminal Division speaks at the Association of Certified Fraud Examiners Annual Conference San Diego – Tuesday, June 14, 2011'. http://www.justice.gov/iso/opa/ag/speeches/2011/ag-speech-110614.html, accessed 6 June 2016.

125 United States Department of Justice, 'About the division'. http://www.justice.gov/criminal/about, accessed 6 June 2016.

126 Frank J. Cavico and Mujtaba G. Bahaudin, 'Baksheesh or bribe: payments to government officials and the Foreign Corrupt Practices Act' (2010) 2(1) *JBSQ* 83.

127 Department of Justice and Securities and Exchange Commission, 'FCPA. a resource guide to the U.S. Foreign Corrupt Practices Act', 10. https://www.sec.gov/spotlight/fcpa/fcpa-resource-guide.pdf, accessed 6 June 2016 (hereinafter DoJ/SEC) 39.

128 DoJ/SEC, n. 127 above.

129 'Once fully implemented, this Initiative will allow the Department to recover assets on behalf of countries victimized by high-level corruption, building on the Justice Department's already robust enforcement of the Foreign Corrupt Practices Act. Through the Kleptocracy Initiative, the Department will ensure that corrupt leaders cannot seek safe haven in the United States for their stolen wealth. And, if we uncover such wealth, the Justice Department will forfeit and return this stolen money to its rightful owners – the people and governments from whom it was taken.' Department of Justice, n. 124 above.

130 Department of Justice, n. 124 above.

131 18 U.S.C. § 3571.

132 '[The alternative fines] provision is intended to enable federal courts to impose fines that will prevent convicted offenders from ***profiting from their wrongdoing***' (emphasis added). Court Listener, 'United States v. Sanford Ltd., Criminal No. 2011–0352 (D.C. 2012) District Court, District of Columbia'. https://www.courtlistener.com/opinion/2662147/united-states-v-sanford-ltd/?q=suitNature:Criminal%20Law,%20Sentencing%20and%20Punishment,%20Costs,%20Restitution, accessed 6 June 2016. The DoJ reports violations of FCPA where, in the settlement agreement, the Alternative Fines Act was considered. In *Alcatel-Lucent*, the Alternative Fines Act was used to set the fines parameter of up to twice

calculating the magnitude of fines, contained in the 'US Sentencing Guidelines',[133] which 'provide a very detailed and predictable structure for calculating penalties for all federal crimes, including violations of the FCPA'.[134]

The US has the ability to negotiate an outcome with the defendant.[135] In the US, the 'DoJ may agree to resolve criminal FCPA matters against companies either through declination or, in appropriate cases, a negotiated resolution resulting in a plea agreement, deferred prosecution agreement, or non-prosecution agreement'.[136]

In a plea agreement, 'the defendant generally admits to the facts supporting the charges, admits guilt, and is convicted of the charged crimes when the plea agreement is presented to and accepted by a court'.[137] For example, the publicly available letter detailing terms between DoJ and Siemens AG[138] shows a settlement where Siemens AG 'and three of its subsidiaries, pleaded guilty to FCPA-related violations. *The parent was not required to plead guilty to a bribery violation,* thereby likely avoiding mandatory debarment in Europe.'[139] In the US, a guilty plea does not result in automatic debarment from US government contracting, because an independent debarment authority will consider the issues.[140]

An alternative is a Deferred Prosecution Agreement (DPA), which operates as a 'Sword of Damocles',[141] in that the DoJ 'files a charging document with the

the base fine $48m, and the total agreed was $92m. Department of Justice, 'United States of America vs Alcatel-Lucent SA Deferred prosecution Agreement'. https://www.justice.gov/opa/pr/alcatel-lucent-sa-and-three-subsidiaries-agree-pay-92-million-resolve-foreign-corrupt, accessed 6 June 2016.

133 US Sentencing Commission, '2010 Federal Sentencing Commission Guidelines'. http://www.ussc.gov/Guidelines/2010_guidelines/index.cfm, accessed 6 June 2016.

134 DoJ/SEC, n. 127 above, 68.

135 Under Federal Rules of Criminal Procedure. Ibid., 74.

136 Ibid., 74.

137 Ibid., 74.

138 *United States v Siemens Aktiengesellschaft* Court Docket Number: 08-CR-367-RJL Plea Agreement dated 12 December 2008. https://www.justice.gov/sites/default/files/opa/legacy/2008/12/15/siemens.pdf, accessed 6 June 2016.

139 Robert W. Tarun and Peter P. Tomczak, 'A proposal for a United States Department of Justice Foreign Corrupt Practices Act Leniency Policy' 47 (2010) *Am Crim L Rev* 153 (emphasis added).

140 DoJ/SEC, n. 127, 70. Note: In the UK, the EU Public Sector Procurement Directive applies. The effect of this is that a commercial organization is excluded from participation in public sector contracts if convicted of fraud, bribery and corruption under Article 45. This provides the incentive to 'self report' to the SFO, with the prospect of negotiating an outcome and incurring a civil, rather than criminal, penalty. EU Public Services Procurement Directive 2004/18/EC Art. 45. Implemented in UK by the Public Contracts Regulations 2006, which provides revised rules for the procurement of supplies, works and services by public authorities. The Utilities Contracts Regulations 2006 implement the revised Utilities Directive (2004/17/EC) which provides, in a similar way, revised rules for procurement in the utilities sector. Office of Government Commerce, HM Treasury. http://www.hm-treasury.gov.uk/d/competitive_dialogue_procedure.pdf, accessed 6 June 2016.

141 'Sword of Damocles *n.* (also Damocles' sword) used by simile of an imminent danger, which may at any moment descend upon one.' ('Damocles, a flatterer, having extolled the happiness of Dionysius tyrant of Syracuse, was placed by him at a banquet with a sword

court, but simultaneously requests that the prosecution be deferred'.[142] The deferral, or not proceeding with the prosecution, is on the basis that the defendant pleads guilty, but in return for a fine or other penalties and agreement, as in the case of Daimler AG, to 'an independent compliance monitor for three years',[143] the DoJ agrees to dismiss the charges upon expiry of the agreement.[144] The attraction of a DPA is certainty, in the knowledge that a breach of the agreement would result in a criminal conviction, whereas 'a company's successful completion of a DPA is not treated as a criminal conviction'.[145]

A third agreement is a 'Non-Prosecution Agreement' (NPA). An NPA is less formal and restrictive than a DPA and, although the facts are disclosed, a charging document is not lodged with the court but left to lie on the prosecutor's file, to be activated if there is a breach of the NPA. This would include a tolling[146] agreement to stay any statute of limitations issues.

The use of a NPA is demonstrated in the 2013 agreement with Ralph Lauren Corporation (RLC), which had a subsidiary in Argentina.[147] The facts were that over a five-year period a manager of the subsidiary paid bribes and gifts totalling $593,000 to customs officials in Argentina to improperly obtain paperwork necessary for goods to clear customs and or avoid inspection;[148] payments were disguised and false invoices created. 'RLC did not have an anti-corruption program and did not provide any anti-corruption training or oversight with respect to its subsidiary in Argentina.'[149]

In parallel with the DoJ, the SEC also agreed an NPA, which was the first occasion both regulators completed agreements with the same company. The SEC's reasoning was '[w]hen they found a problem, [RLC] did the right thing by immediately reporting it [. . .] and providing exceptional assistance [. . .] [W]e will confer substantial benefits on companies that respond appropriately to

suspended over his head by a hair, to impress upon him the perilous nature of that happiness.') Oxford English Dictionary. http://www.oed.com/view/Entry/47084?redirectedFrom=sword+of+damocles#eid7417619, accessed 14 May 2013.

142 DoJ/SEC, n. 127 above, 74.

143 Tarun and Tomczak, n. 139 above.

144 *United States v Daimler AG* Court Docket Number: 10-CR-063-RJL. Deferred Prosecution Agreement dated 22 March 2010. https://www.justice.gov/sites/default/files/criminal-fraud/legacy/2011/02/16/03-22-10daimlerrussia-info.pdf, accessed 6 June 2016.

145 DoJ/SEC, n. 127 above, 70.

146 'A tolling agreement is an agreement to waive a right to claim that litigation should be dismissed due to the expiration of a statute of limitations.' US Legal.Com 'Definitions'. http://definitions.uslegal.com/t/tolling-agreement, accessed 6 June 2016.

147 Department of Justice, 'Ralph Lauren Corporation resolves Foreign Corrupt Practices Act investigation and agrees to pay $882,000 monetary penalty'. http://www.justice.gov/opa/pr/2013/April/13-crm-456.html, accessed 6 June 2016.

148 Securities and Exchange Commission, press release 22 April 2013. 'SEC announces non-prosecution agreement with Ralph Lauren Corporation involving FCPA misconduct'. http://www.sec.gov/news/press/2013/2013-65.htm, accessed 6 June 2016.

149 Department of Justice, n. 147 above.

violations and cooperate fully.'[150] The DoJ agreement gave credit for,[151] and rewarded, self-reporting by not prosecuting and, instead, entering NPAs with substantial fines. RLC have closed the Argentina operation.[152]

The DoJ has available the various options described above, as alternatives to criminal action. It also has a 'track record' of enforcement which has severe consequences that encourage a defendant to compromise rather than fight a case through the courts. The DoJ emphasise that 'fighting corruption is, and always will be, a core priority'.[153]

The ability of the DoJ to negotiate outcomes is graphically demonstrated by the differing experience of two of the world's major accounting firms: Arthur Andersen (AA) and KPMG.[154] In the fall-out of the Enron scandal,[155] the first criminal charge was also the first time a major accounting firm had been charged with obstruction of justice.[156] There was a marked difference between the experience of AA, which eventually had its guilty verdict overturned through Appeals to US Supreme Court and final withdrawal by the prosecution, and that of KPMG, which negotiated with the DoJ.[157]

The outcome of these two cases is that whereas 'KPMG remains a successful business to this day',[158] 'it was already too late for Arthur Andersen. Shortly after the indictment, the firm effectively collapsed.'[159] Thus, although it achieved a victory against the DoJ, it proved pyrrhic, because '[t]he company's right to a

150 Securities and Exchange Commission, n. 148 above (footnotes omitted).

151 The agreement gave credit for 'timely, voluntary, and complete disclosure of the conduct [. . .] extensive, thorough, and real-time cooperation with the Department, including conducting an internal investigation, voluntarily making employees available for interviews, making voluntary document disclosures, conducting a world-wide risk assessment, and making multiple presentations to the Department on the status and findings of the internal investigation and the risk assessment [. . .] early and extensive remedial efforts already undertaken – including conducting extensive FCPA training for employees worldwide, enhancing the Company's existing FCPA policy, implementing an enhanced gift policy as well as other enhanced compliance, control and anti-corruption policies and procedures, enhancing its due diligence protocol for third-party agents, terminating culpable employees and a third-party agent, instituting a whistleblower hotline, and hiring a designated corporate compliance attorney – and to be undertaken, including enhancements to its compliance program [. . .] and [. . .] agreement to provide annual, written reports.' Department of Justice 'Non prosecution Agreement' dated 22 April 2013. https://www.justice.gov/sites/default/files/criminal-fraud/legacy/2013/04/23/Ralph-Lauren.-NPA-Executed.pdf, accessed 6 June 2016.

152 Securities and Exchange Commission, n. 148 above.

153 Department of Justice, 'Acting Assistant Attorney General Mythili Raman delivers keynote address at the Global Anti-Corruption Congress', 17 June 2013. http://www.justice.gov/criminal/pr/speeches/2013/crm-speech-130617.html, accessed 6 June 2016.

154 Bennett, LoCicero and Hanner, n. 78 above.

155 Ibid.

156 Ibid.

157 Ibid.

158 Ibid.

159 Ibid.

jury trial was illusory, and the effect of the indictment was irreparable. Nothing from the Supreme Court could bring Arthur Andersen back from the dead.'[160] These examples show the value to firms in identifying breaches of the FCPA and taking the opportunity to negotiate a settlement with the DoJ.[161]

12.5.1.2 Department of Justice and Federal Bureau of Investigation response to financial crisis

> In the most basic ways, though, corporate misconduct isn't all that different from everything else DOJ investigates and prosecutes. Crime is crime. And it is our obligation at the Justice Department to ensure that we are holding lawbreakers accountable regardless of whether they commit their crimes on the street corner or in the boardroom. In the white-collar context, that means pursuing not just corporate entities, but also the individuals through which these corporations act.[162]

The DoJ view, as articulated by the Deputy Attorney General, is that 'individual accountability in corporate cases is so important – because it deters future illegal activity, because it incentivizes changes in corporate behavior and because it ensures that the people who engage in wrongdoing are held responsible for their actions'.[163] The rationale was that 'we cannot allow the flesh-and-blood people responsible for misconduct to walk away, while leaving only the company's employees and shareholders to pay the price [. . .] [N]othing discourages corporate criminal activity like the prospect of people going to prison.'[164] In other words, there is a deterrence effect of 'heads on pikes'.[165]

Notwithstanding these fine intentions, and bearing in mind that these comments were made in 2015 and not 2008, the DoJ accepts that there are limitations in pursuing financial fraud cases against individuals:

> In modern corporations, where responsibility is often diffuse, it can be extremely difficult to identify the single person or group of people who possessed the knowledge or criminal intent necessary to establish proof beyond a reasonable doubt. This is particularly true of high-level executives, who are often insulated from the day-to-day activity in which the misconduct occurs. Without an inside cooperating witness, preferably one identified early enough to wear a wire, investigators are left to reconstruct what happened

160 Ibid.
161 Ibid.
162 Department of Justice, n. 1 above.
163 Ibid.
164 Ibid.
165 Australian Prudential Regulation Authority, 'APRA speaks on Palmer'. (The report of John Palmer was commissioned by APRA [in 2001] to investigate its role into the collapse of HIH and tendered as evidence to the HIH Royal Commission.) http://www.apra.gov.au/MediaReleases/Pages/02_52.aspx, accessed 6 June 2016.

> based on a painstaking review of corporate documents, looking for a smoking gun that most financial criminals are far too savvy to leave behind. And since virtually all of these corporations operate worldwide, restrictive foreign data privacy laws and a limited ability to compel the testimony of witnesses abroad make it even more challenging to obtain the necessary evidence to bring individuals to justice.[166]

This may be seen as some 'special pleading' because, as Judge Rakoff questioned, 'Why have no high-level executives been prosecuted?'[167] Thus, 'the failure of the government to bring to justice those responsible for such colossal frauds bespeaks weaknesses in our prosecutorial system that need to be addressed'.[168]

The DoJ periodically issues instructions to attorneys.[169] Such an instruction in September 2015, the 'Yates Memorandum',[170] emphasises that 'fighting corporate fraud and other misconduct is a priority' of the DoJ.[171] The memorandum states that it is 'important that the [DoJ] fully leverage its resources to identify culpable individuals at all levels in corporate cases',[172] recognising that holding individuals to account 'is an important part of protecting the public [purse] in the long term'.[173] Yates set out six key steps,[174] some of which were new and some reflecting

166 Department of Justice, n. 1 above.

167 Jed S. Rakoff, 'The financial crisis: why have no high-level executives been prosecuted?' *The New York Review of Books*. http://www.nybooks.com/articles/2014/01/09/financial-crisis-why-no-executive-prosecutions, accessed 6 June 2016.

168 Rakoff, n. 167 above.

169 For earlier memoranda, see: Holder memorandum 1999, https://www.justice.gov/sites/default/files/criminal-fraud/legacy/2010/04/11/charging-corps.PDF; Thompson memorandum 2003, http://www.americanbar.org/content/dam/aba/migrated/poladv/priorities/privilegewaiver/2003jan20_privwaiv_dojthomp.authcheckdam.pdf; McNulty memorandum 2006, https://www.justice.gov/sites/default/files/dag/legacy/2007/07/05/mcnulty_memo.pdf; Filip memorandum 2008, https://www.justice.gov/sites/default/files/dag/legacy/2008/11/03/dag-memo-08282008.pdf, all accessed 30 April 2016.

170 Department of Justice, 'Individual accountability for corporate wrongdoing' (Yates Memorandum), 9 September 2015. https://www.justice.gov/dag/file/769036/download, accessed 30 April 2016.

171 Department of Justice, n. 170.

172 Ibid.

173 Ibid.

174 '(1) in order to qualify for any cooperation credit, corporations must provide to the Department all relevant facts relating to the individuals responsible for the misconduct; (2) criminal and civil corporate investigations should focus on individuals from the inception of the investigation; (3) criminal and civil attorneys handling corporate investigations should be in routine communication with one another; (4) absent extraordinary circumstances or approved departmental policy, the Department will not release culpable individuals from civil or criminal liability when resolving a matter with a corporation; (5) Department attorneys should not resolve matters with a corporation without a clear plan to resolve related individual cases, and should memorialize any declinations as to individuals in such cases; and (6) civil attorneys should consistently focus on individuals as well as the company and evaluate whether to bring suit against an individual based on considerations beyond

change of DoJ policy: full disclosure; investigators considering the role of individuals from the outset; civil and criminal attorneys working together; not releasing individuals from criminal or civil liability in corporate settlements.

The Attorney General and DoJ establish policy, but investigation lies with the FBI, a division of the DoJ, with a mission to be 'an intelligence-driven and a threat-focused national security organization with both intelligence and law enforcement responsibilities'.[175] The FBI makes the same points as the DoJ about the lack of high-level financial executives brought to justice.[176] In 2014, the FBI reported that they had 'more than 1,300 agents working roughly 10,700 white-collar crime cases. The number of corporate fraud cases we investigate has increased by roughly 65 percent since 2008.'[177] However, the challenge faced by the FBI is that in corporate fraud cases

> we have to examine the contents of someone's mind. My obligation as a prosecutor was to prove not that people engaged in a financial transaction that went south . . . not that they contributed to some enormous meltdown . . . but that when they did the things they did, they knew they were engaged in conduct that was criminal in nature.
>
> Unlike a drug case – which is about connecting people to a transaction – in nearly every white-collar case, it is clear who was involved in the transactions; the question is, 'What were they thinking?'
>
> Stupidity is not a crime. Risky behavior isn't a crime, no matter how many innocent people got hurt by that stupidity, greed, or recklessness. In this country, we put people in jail when we prove they knew they were doing something criminally wrong. That's hard, but it's right.[178]

Thus, it would be expected that the DoJ would address the issue of individual responsibility in a subsequent settlement. However, in Goldman Sachs, the DoJ trumpeted a $5bn settlement, which related to one of the causes of the financial crisis, notably the sale of Residential Mortgage Backed Securities. The settlement included $1.8bn to aid consumers harmed by its unlawful conduct, but preserves its rights to bring criminal charges.[179] Clearly, any criminal case is not certain to take place.

that individual's ability to pay.' Department of Justice, 'Individual Accountability for Corporate Wrongdoing', Yates Memorandum, n. 170 above.

175 Federal Bureau of Investigation, 'Quick facts'. https://www.fbi.gov/about-us/quick-facts, accessed 30 April 2016.

176 Federal Bureau of Investigation, 'James B. Comey, Director, Federal Bureau of Investigation, New York City Bar 3rd Annual White Collar Crime Institute, New York City, NY May 19, 2014'. https://www.fbi.gov/news/speeches/confronting-corporate-crime, accessed 30 April 2016.

177 Ibid.

178 Ibid.

179 Department of Justice, 'Goldman Sachs agrees to pay more than $5 billion in connection with its sale of residential mortgage backed securities', 11 April 2016. https://www.justice.

12.5.2 The Securities and Exchange Commission

The financial crisis of 2008 was not the first in US history. Indeed, a significant outcome of the earlier 'Great Crash of 1929'[180] and the ensuing 'Great Depression' was the establishment of the SEC.[181]

> When the stock market crashed in October 1929, public confidence in the markets plummeted. Investors large and small, as well as the banks who had loaned to them, lost great sums of money in the ensuing Great Depression. There was a consensus that for the economy to recover, the public's faith in the capital markets needed to be restored.[182]

The role of the SEC is regulation and enforcement of the US securities markets, and securities laws. The SEC's mission 'is to protect investors, maintain fair, orderly, and efficient markets, and facilitate capital formation'.[183] The SEC is governed by the Securities Act 1933, 'often referred to as the "truth in securities" law', which has two main objectives: first, to 'require that investors receive financial and other significant information concerning securities being offered for public sale'; and, second, to 'prohibit deceit, misrepresentations, and other fraud in the sale of securities'.[184] It also has powers under Securities Exchange Act 1934, Sarbanes–Oxley Act 2002, Dodd–Frank Act 2010 and Jumpstart Our Business Startups (JOBS) Act 2012.[185] The bedrock of the SEC's role has been to ensure that issuers of securities provide comprehensive, reliable and accurate reporting because '[m]aterially false or incomplete financial reporting saps investor confidence and erodes the integrity of our markets'.[186] What the 2008 financial crisis revealed to the SEC was that '[m]ost of these cases were not traditional financial reporting cases [. . .] Instead, these actions mostly focused on transactions in complex financial products like CDOs and RMBS that resulted in massive losses to investors.'[187] Prior to the financial crisis, the SEC had exhorted:

gov/opa/pr/goldman-sachs-agrees-pay-more-5-billion-connection-its-sale-residential-mortgage-backed; Department of Justice 'Settlement agreement'. https://www.justice.gov/opa/file/839891/download, both accessed 30 April 2016.

180 J.K. Galbraith, *The Great Crash 1929* (Penguin 1961).

181 US Securities and Exchange Commission, 'What we do'. http://www.sec.gov/about/whatwedo.shtml#create, accessed 16 March 2016.

182 Ibid.

183 Ibid.

184 Ibid.

185 Ibid.

186 Securities and Exchange Commission, 'Andrew Ceresney, Speech, the Directors Forum', 25 January 2016. http://www.sec.gov/news/speech/directors-forum-keynote-ceresney.html, accessed 17 March 2016.

187 Ibid.

> For corporate managers, remember, the integrity of the numbers in the financial reporting system is directly related to the long-term interests of a corporation. While the temptations are great, and the pressures strong, illusions in numbers are only that – ephemeral, and ultimately self-destructive.[188]

The SEC's concentration on civil action for accounting fraud led to them obtaining awards of '$450 million in monetary sanctions from 35 entities and individuals involved in the Enron fraud', and $750m in the WorldCom fraud.[189]

A major issue for the SEC was the discovery of the Madoff fraud (Ponzi scheme), which the judge described as 'extraordinarily evil': 'No other white collar case is comparable in terms of the scope, duration and enormity of the fraud and the degree of the betrayal.'[190] Bernard Madoff's Ponzi scheme defrauded investors of $65bn, and he received a prison sentence of 150 years.[191] The SEC was the regulator, and an inquiry into its lack of action concluded that:

> the SEC received more than ample information in the form of detailed and substantive complaints over the years to warrant a thorough and comprehensive examination and/or investigation of Bernard Madoff and BMIS for operating a Ponzi scheme, and that despite three examinations and two investigations being conducted, a thorough and competent investigation or examination was never performed.[192]

Nichols contends that 'Madoff was successful because: he understood the regulatory framework of the U.S. financial system and successfully exploited its gaps and weaknesses; and the [SEC's] enforcement efforts were abysmally inept.'[193]

188 Securities and Exchange Commission, 'Arthur Levitt, the "numbers game"' (28 September 1998), https://www.sec.gov/news/speech/speecharchive/1998/spch220.txt.

189 Securities and Exchange Commission, n. 186 above.

190 Federal Bureau of Investigation, 'Bernard Madoff sentenced to 150 years in prison', 29 June 2009. https://www.fbi.gov/newyork/press-releases/2009/nyfo062909.htm, accessed 12 May 2016.

191 Reuters, 'Madoff pleads guilty, is jailed for $65 billion fraud', 13 March 2009. http://www.reuters.com/article/us-madoff-idUSTRE52A5JK20090313, accessed 6 June 2016. Federal Bureau of Investigation, n. 190 above.

192 'The OIG found that between June 1992 and December 2008 when Madoff confessed, the SEC received six substantive complaints that raised significant red flags concerning Madoff's hedge fund operations and should have led to questions about whether Madoff was actually engaged in trading. Finally, the SEC was also aware of two articles regarding Madoff's investment operations that appeared in reputable publications in 2001 and questioned Madoff's unusually consistent returns.' Securities and Exchange Commission, Office of Inspector General, 'Investigation of Failure of the SEC to Uncover Bernard Madoff's Ponzi Scheme', 29 August 2009. https://www.sec.gov/news/studies/2009/oig-509.pdf, accessed 12 May 2016.

193 Cheryl Nichols, 'Addressing inept SEC enforcement efforts: lessons from Madoff, the hedge fund industry, and Title IV of the Dodd–Frank Act for U.S. and Global Financial Systems' (2011) 31 *Nw J Int'l L & Bus* 637.

Five years after the financial crisis, the SEC decided that as financial crisis issues had lessened, they should refocus their attention on financial reporting and auditing, by forming the Financial Reporting and Auditing Task Force (FRAud).[194] The purpose of FRAud is to 'concentrate on expanding and strengthening the [SEC] Division's efforts to identify securities-law violations relating to the preparation of financial statements, issuer reporting and disclosure, and audit failures'.[195] Furthermore, attention is given to Microcap fraud,[196] which is 'abusive trading and fraudulent conduct in securities issued by microcap companies, especially those that do not regularly publicly report their financial results'.[197] The SEC have also targeted '"gatekeepers," such as attorneys, auditors, broker-dealers, and transfer agents, and other significant participants, such as stock promoters and purveyors of shell companies'.[198]

The SEC is responsible for civil enforcement over 'issuers and their officers, directors, employees, agents', and has a 'specialized FCPA Unit'.[199] The emphasis for the SEC is on civil enforcement because, as Schipani notes, it 'has a wide variety of civil and administrative powers to address corporate fraud'.[200] The remedies available to it are financial penalties both in terms of fines and disgorgement of gains, together with preventing individuals from serving as directors or officers of public companies, and it may also suspend trading in a company's stock.[201]

> After the passage of Sarbanes–Oxley Act, the SEC may now also order a temporary freeze over payments the company is going to pay to its executives, and order CEOs and CFOs to forfeit any bonuses, incentive compensation and profits from the sales of securities when a company restates its financial statement due to misconduct.[202]

The SEC is judged on 'performance metrics', including case resolution: 'A case is considered "successfully resolved" if it results in a favorable outcome for the SEC,

194 Securities and Exchange Commission, n. 186 above.

195 Securities and Exchange Commission, 'SEC announces enforcement initiatives to combat financial reporting and microcap fraud and enhance risk analysis'. http://www.sec.gov/News/PressRelease/Detail/PressRelease/1365171624975, accessed 17 March 2016.

196 'The over-the-counter (OTC) market for securities, often referred to the microcap market, is designed for and comprised of companies with small amounts of assets and low stock prices.' Securities and Exchange Commission, 'Microcap fraud'. http://www.sec.gov/spotlight/microcap-fraud.shtml, accessed 17 March 2016.

197 Securities and Exchange Commission, n. 195 above.

198 Ibid.

199 DoJ/SEC, n. 127 above, 5.

200 C.A. Schipani, 'Falling off the corporate ladder: prosecution for financial fraud in the United States' (2011) 32(11) *Co Law* 336.

201 Ibid.

202 CEO – Chief Executive Officer; CFO – Chief Financial Officer. Ibid.

including through litigation, a settlement, or the issuance of a default judgment.'[203] Although the SEC states that it is a 'law enforcement agency',[204] tellingly, it confirms that '[i]n many cases, the Commission and the party charged decide to settle a matter without trial'.[205] In 2013, the SEC took 686 enforcement actions and imposed $3.4bn in 'monetary relief',[206] with a strategy to be more aggressive in enforcement and 'seeking stronger penalties, which raised the opportunity cost of malfeasance'.[207] The message conveyed to the market was clear: no institution is too large to be held to account and no violation is too small to escape scrutiny.[208]

12.5.2.1 SEC enforcement mechanisms

The SEC points to the significant number of enforcement actions which it has taken and the amount of financial monetary remedies in the form of disgorgement and penalties.[209] In 2013, there were 676 actions, resulting in monetary remedies of $3.4bn; in 2014, 755 actions and $4.16bn; and in 2015, 807 actions and $4.19bn.[210] The SEC states that 'it continued to build a strong record of first-of-their-kind cases that spanned the spectrum of the securities industry'[211] and draws comparison with the period 2005–2012, where the number of cases ranged from approximately 318 to 445, and monetary remedies ordered ranged from $1bn to $3.1bn.[212] The SEC Chair states that:

203 Securities and Exchange Commission, 'Strategic plan – fiscal years 2010–2015' (2011: 735 cases; $2.8bn). https://www.sec.gov/about/secstratplan1015.pdf, accessed 6 June 2016.

204 Securities and Exchange Commission, 'What we do'. https://www.sec.gov/about/whatwedo.shtml, accessed 18 May 2016.

205 Ibid.

206 Securities and Exchange Commission, *Fiscal Year 2013 Agency Financial Report*. https://www.sec.gov/about/secafr2013.shtml, accessed 12 May 2016.

207 Ibid., 17.

208 Ibid., 17.

209 SEC Enforcement actions: addressing misconduct that led to or arose from the financial crisis, as at 13 January 2016.

Number of entities and individuals charged = 198.
Number of CEOs, CFOs, and other senior corporate officers charged = 89.
Number of individuals who have received officer and director bars, industry bars, or commission suspensions = 53.
Penalties ordered or agreed to = >$1.93bn
Disgorgement and prejudgment interest ordered or agreed to >$1.47bn
Additional monetary relief obtained for harmed investors = $418m.
Total penalties, disgorgement, and other monetary relief = $3.76bn.

Securities and Exchange Commission, 'SEC Enforcement Actions'. http://www.sec.gov/spotlight/enf-actions-fc.shtml, accessed 17 March 2016.

210 Securities and Exchange Commission, 'SEC announces enforcement results for FY [to September] 2015'. https://www.sec.gov/news/pressrelease/2015-245.html, accessed 21 March 2016.

211 Ibid.

212 Ibid.

> Vigorous and comprehensive enforcement protects investors and reassures them that our financial markets operate with integrity and transparency, and the Commission continues that enforcement approach by bringing innovative cases holding executives and companies accountable for their wrongdoing sending clear warnings to would-be violators.[213]

SEC enforcement included actions against 'gatekeepers', including auditors, accountants and attorneys.[214] These actions include claims of violating the principle that auditors must be independent of their clients,[215] but they claim to have taken their first case against a major audit firm for 'non-independence' issues since 2009 against BDO for 'issuing false and misleading unqualified audit opinions about the financial statements [. . .] and five of the firm's partners, including national office personnel, for their roles in the deficient audits':[216]

> BDO agreed to admit wrongdoing, pay disgorgement of its audit fees and interest totaling approximately $600,000, and pay a $1.5 million penalty in addition to complying with undertakings related to its quality controls. The five partners also agreed to settle the charges against them.[217]
>
> Without admitting or denying the SEC's findings, [the five partners] agreed to be suspended from practicing public company accounting for varying periods [and agreed to pay penalties of $30,000, $15,000, and three of $10,000].[218]

The key phrases to note are: 'BDO agreed to admit wrongdoing' and 'without admitting or denying the SEC's findings'. The reason this is important is the

213 Ibid.

214 Ibid.

215 'Auditor independence rules require outside auditors to remain independent from their clients to ensure there is not even the appearance of a firm compromising its objectivity and impartiality when auditing financial statements.' Securities and Exchange Commission, 'SEC charges Deloitte & Touche with violating auditor independence rules', 1 July 2015. https://www.sec.gov/news/pressrelease/2015-137.html, accessed 22 March 2016.

216 Securities and Exchange Commission, n. 210 above.

217 Securities and Exchange Commission, 'SEC charges BDO and five partners in connection with false and misleading audit opinions'. https://www.sec.gov/news/pressrelease/2015-184.html, accessed 22 March 2016.

218 The SEC also conducted claims against officers and associates of the company, for whom the SEC provide further details: 'The SEC's complaint charges Pence with violating Section 10(b) of the Securities Exchange Act of 1934 and Rules 10b-5 and 13b2–2. The SEC is seeking permanent injunctions, disgorgement of ill-gotten gains plus prejudgment interest and penalties, and an officer-and-director bar. The SEC separately charged former General Employment CEOs Ronald E. Heineman and Salvatore J. Zizza with making materially misleading statements and omissions to BDO. Without admitting or denying the findings, they consented to SEC orders requiring them to each pay $150,000 penalties.' Securities and Exchange Commission, n. 217 above.

allegation that the SEC is keen to impose financial penalties to which firms and individuals are prepared to agree without admitting responsibility, which gives rise to conclusions that the SEC is more interested in monetary reward than prosecuting individuals.

12.5.2.2 SEC neither admit nor deny

Since 1972, the SEC has employed a settlement regime 'known generally as "neither admit nor deny"' (NAND).[219] This was 'a policy change that would form the foundation of its settlement regime for more than four decades'.[220] The outcome of the SEC's settlement arrangements, 'like many other civil settlements, typically require defendants to pay a penalty and return ill-gotten gains with interest'.[221] The difference between NAND settlements and others is that the defendant does not have to admit the charge, or subsequently deny the charge. The rationale for this arrangement, as Neumann identifies is that:

> NAND settlements yield valuable benefits to harmed investors, defendants and the SEC. NAND settlements allow both the SEC and defendants to avoid costly, time-consuming, and unpredictable litigation. NAND settlements also benefit defendants by minimizing their exposure to future class action suits and sparing them the public spectacle of a trial. On the other hand, NAND settlements benefit investors by efficiently punishing wrongdoers and quickly returning investor funds. Finally, NAND settlements benefit the SEC by allowing it to conserve limited resources and pursue a greater number of violations.[222]

The NAND regime overcame the difficulties previously seen, which 'did not bar defendants from publicly declaring that they were innocent and settled only to avoid costly litigation. Such post-settlement declarations of innocence made a mockery of the judicial process and embarrassed the SEC.'[223] These arrangements, which have stood for over forty years, have been regarded in a positive light by the SEC:

> It makes sense because the SEC can get relief within the range of what we could reasonably expect to achieve after winning at trial. By settling, the agency is able to eliminate all litigation risk, resolve the case, return money to

219 Matthew G. Neumann, 'Neither admit nor deny: recent changes to the Securities and Exchange Commission's longstanding settlement policy' (2015) 40 *J Corp L* 793, 797.
220 Ibid.
221 Ibid. (footnotes omitted).
222 Ibid. (footnotes omitted).
223 Ibid. (footnotes omitted).

> victims more quickly, and preserve our enforcement resources to redeploy to do other investigations – ordinarily, a significant win-win.[224]

Significantly, the SEC confirmed in late 2015 that the 'majority of cases continue to be resolved on a "neither admit nor deny" basis'.[225] The reason this is significant is that the courts have taken an interest in these settlements, in particular, as Neumann notes, 'the tenacious Federal District Court Judge Jed S Rakoff against the venerated Securities and Exchange Commission'.[226] In *SEC v Bank of America*,[227] Judge Rakoff

> found the SEC's proposed NAND settlement unacceptable [. . .] [for] the victims – Bank of America's shareholders who had been misled to the tune of $5.8bn would pay a $33m fine as a penalty for their own victimization. He questioned why the SEC did not seek a penalty against the lawyers who drafted the proxy statements instead [. . .] Judge Rakoff concluded by pointing to what he called a 'cynical relationship' between the SEC and Bank of America. A relationship where the parties were willing to shift the burden of the defendant's alleged wrongdoing to the victim-shareholders, and where the SEC would claim a hollow victory (a NAND settlement) at the 'expense [. . .] of the truth'.[228]

Other commentators have observed: 'The SEC has perhaps been too willing in the past to settle cases in which the defendants, both corporate and individual, neither admit nor deny wrongdoing. It justifies this practice because of the large number of cases it must investigate and the limited resources at its disposal.'[229] However, Judge Rakoff continued his theme in *SEC v Citigroup Global Markets*,[230] when presented with a draft 'Consent Judgment' for approval, commenting:

> the Court has spent long hours trying to determine whether, in view of the substantial deference due the SEC in matters of this kind, the Court can somehow approve this problematic Consent Judgment. In the end, the

224 Securities and Exchange Commission, Speech Mary Jo White 'Deploying the full enforcement arsenal', 26 September 2013. https://www.sec.gov/News/Speech/Detail/Speech/1370539841202, accessed 29 March 2016.

225 Securities and Exchange Commission, Mary Jo White 'Testimony on Examining the SEC's Agenda, Operations, and FY 2017 Budget Request Before the Committee on Financial Services United States House of Representatives Washington, D.C.', 18 November 2015. https://www.sec.gov/news/testimony/chair-white-testimony-sec-agenda-operations-2017-budget.html, accessed 29 March 2016.

226 Neumann (n 218) (footnotes omitted).

227 *SEC v. Bank of Am. Corp.*, 653 F. Supp. 2d 507, 507 (S.D.N.Y. 2009).

228 Neumann, n. 219 above (footnotes omitted).

229 Edward Greene and Caroline Odorski, 'SEC enforcement in the financial sector: addressing post-crisis criticism' (2015) 16(1) *Business Law International* 6.

230 *U.S. Securities and Exchange Commission v Citigroup Global Markets Inc* 827 F.Supp.2d 328 (S.D.N.Y. 2011).

> Court concludes that it cannot approve it, because the Court has not been provided with any proven or admitted facts upon which to exercise even a modest degree of independent judgment.[231]

Judge Rakoff was clearly antipathetic to the SEC assertion 'that, while the Consent Judgment must still be shown to be fair, adequate, and reasonable, "the public interest [. . .] is not part of [the] applicable standard of judicial review".'[232] Judge Rakoff's conclusion was that 'in any case like this that touches on the transparency of financial markets whose gyrations have so depressed our economy and debilitated our lives, there is an overriding public interest in knowing the truth'.[233]

In *Citigroup,* the issues are neatly summarised:

> Citigroup was able, without admitting anything, to negotiate a settlement that (a) charges it only with negligence, (b) results in a very modest penalty, (c) imposes the kind of injunctive relief that Citigroup (a recidivist) knew that the SEC had not sought to enforce against any financial institution for at least the last 10 years, [. . .], and (d) imposes relatively inexpensive prophylactic measures for the next three years. In exchange, Citigroup not only settles what it states was a broad-ranging four-year investigation by the SEC of Citigroup's mortgage-backed securities offerings, but also avoids any investors' relying in any respect on the SEC Consent Judgment in seeking return of their losses. If the allegations of the Complaint are true, this is a very good deal for Citigroup; and, even if they are untrue, it is a mild and modest cost of doing business.[234]

Judge Rakoff's conclusion in this judgment is, effectively, that for a financial institution, such arrangements with the regulator are an overhead, while for the SEC all they really obtain is a headline.[235] However,

> the SEC, of all agencies, has a duty, inherent in its statutory mission, to see that the truth emerges; and if it fails to do so, this Court must not, in the name of deference or convenience, grant judicial enforcement to the agency's contrivances.[236]

The SEC policy implementation demonstrates that it 'has not been shy about promoting its use of monetary punishments',[237] which are a key component of

231 *U.S. Securities and Exchange Commission v. Citigroup Global Markets Inc* (n 229) 330.
232 Ibid., 331.
233 Ibid., 335.
234 Ibid., 333.
235 Ibid., 333.
236 Ibid., 333.
237 Sonia A. Steinway, 'SEC "monetary penalties speak very loudly," but what do they say? A critical analysis of the SEC's new enforcement approach' (2014) 124 *Yale Law Journal* 209.

NAND agreements, but which prompts the question of criminal proceedings. Judge Rakoff, writing in a personal capacity, poses the question: 'The Financial Crisis: Why Have No High-Level Executives Been Prosecuted?'[238] In a postscript to the use of NAND agreements, it should be noted that the *Citigroup* decision was reversed upon Appeal,[239] which commentators considered was correct and emphasised that the courts should defer to the SEC. However, the Appeal court 'overcorrected by adopting a purely procedural test that will, practically speaking, result in the rubber-stamping of consent decrees'.[240] Judge Rakoff's response was that 'they who must be obeyed have spoken':[241]

> Nonetheless, this Court fears that, as a result of the Court of Appeal's decision, the settlements reached by governmental regulatory bodies and enforced by the judiciary's contempt powers will in practice be subject to no meaningful oversight whatsoever. But it would be a dereliction of duty for this Court to seek to evade the dictates of the Court of Appeals. That Court has now fixed the menu, leaving this Court with nothing but sour grapes.[242]

The courts having underlined that the SEC should be accorded deference, which is different from the position adopted in the United Kingdom, with its deferred agreements,[243] the focus of attention reverts to the SEC and how it deploys the remedies available to it.[244]

12.6 Conclusion

The financial crisis showed US regulation of financial conduct and markets to be deficient. The legislative endeavours of both the Bush and Obama administrations gave additional power to the federal agencies, the DoJ and SEC, and a brief to ensure that companies and individuals are held to account. The outcome, though, is that the DoJ and SEC appear to have concentrated on large-scale financial penalties to corporations rather than bringing individuals to account, leaving Rakoff's question 'Why have no high-level executives been prosecuted?' unanswered.

238 Rakoff, n. 167 above.

239 *Citigroup*, 752 F.3d; *SEC v Citigroup Global Mkts*, 827 F.Supp.2d 328, 332 (S.D.N.Y.2011), *rev'd*, 752 F.3d 285 (2d Cir. 2014).

240 Harvard Law Review, '*SEC v. Citigroup Global Markets, Inc.* Second circuit clarifies that a court's review of an SEC settlement should focus on procedural propriety.' 128 *Harv. L. Rev.* 1288. http://harvardlawreview.org/2015/02/sec-v-citigroup-global-markets-inc, accessed 30 March 2016.

241 *SEC. v. Citigroup Global Markets Inc.* 34 F.Supp.3d 379 (S.D.N.Y. 2014)

242 Ibid.

243 For a discussion on the first UK deferred prosecution agreement under the Crime and Courts Act 2013, see Axel Palmer and Nicholas Ryder, 'Is justice deferred, justice denied? Not necessarily'. *Financial Regulation International* 18 March 2016.

244 Steinway, n. 237 above, 209.

In the aftermath of the crisis, it was understandable that the first response of the US authorities would be to counter the threats to the US economy. However, President Obama did not ignore the deficiencies of pre-crisis regulation,[245] which the DoJ and SEC attempted to remedy by levying significant financial penalties. The fightback of the federal authorities has been long on rhetoric about individual accountability and that 'the public expects and demands this accountability',[246] but whatever the fine words, actions betray a satisfaction for its financial penalties, and in light of the crisis fading into the distance, public dissatisfaction appears to be on the wane. It remains to be seen whether the US public's worries about the criminal justice system operating unfairly is assuaged by higher income from fines. *Plus ça change.*

245 The White House, 'Remarks of the President on Regulatory Reform', 17 June 2009. https://www.whitehouse.gov/the-press-office/remarks-president-regulatory-reform, accessed 30 April 2016.

246 'But regardless of how challenging it may be to make a case against individuals in a corporate fraud case, it's our responsibility at the Department of Justice to overcome these challenges and do everything we can to develop the evidence and bring these cases. The public expects and demands this accountability. Americans should never believe, even incorrectly, that one's criminal activity will go unpunished simply because it was committed on behalf of a corporation. We could be doing a bang-up job in every facet of the department's operations – we could be bringing all the right cases and making all the right decisions. But if the citizens of this country don't have confidence that the criminal justice system operates fairly and applies equally – regardless of who commits the crime or where it is committed – then we're in trouble.' Department of Justice, n.1 above.

13 The National Crime Agency: a critical analysis of its potential impact on the UK's financial crime policy

Christopher Recker

Introduction

This chapter aims to home in on the key issues that surround the National Crime Agency (NCA) and the wider battle against financial crime. This chapter will first provide an overview of the legislative framework that governs fraud, money laundering, bribery and corruption and then introduce the regulators and law enforcement agencies (LEAs) of financial crime in the UK. This chapter will then consider the future of fraud, money laundering and bribery and corruption regulation in the UK, from the NCA's perspective. These issues will then be applied to the current problems faced by the regulators and LEAs of financial crime in the UK. This will allow a balanced analysis of the potential impact the NCA will have on the UK's financial crime policy. The chapter will then conclude and provide a balanced commentary on the success of the NCA and the extent to which it has impacted the UK's financial crime policy.

13.1 An introduction to financial crime and the National Crime Agency

13.1.1 The development of the NCA

> The NCA will transform our response to organised crime. It will tackle organised crime, defend our borders, fight fraud and cyber crime, and protect children and young people. This plan sets out the need and vision for the NCA – to be established in 2013 – and its scope, functionality and structure.[1]

The environment surrounding financial crime has drastically changed over the last decade. In 2012 it was estimated that organised crime cost the UK £20–40bn per year.[2] These figures had a direct effect on the Coalition Government's decision to

1 Home Office, 'National Crime Agency – a plan for the creation of a national crime-fighting capability' <http://www.homeoffice.gov.uk/publications/crime/nca-creation-plan>, accessed on 20 February 2012.

2 Home Office, 'Organised crime strategy' <http://www.homeoffice.gov.uk/crime/organised-crime-strategy/>, accessed on 28 February 2012.

'abolish the FSA and establish the NCA'.[3] Criminals are increasingly finding new ways of committing white-collar crime,[4] due to fast-paced technological advancements in almost all industries. However, it has been suggested that this 'gap from technological advancements must be filled with accountability and not technology'.[5] The implementation of the NCA is arguably a response to the ineffectiveness of previous financial crime and policing policy:

> The previous government tried to micro manage local policing but did not support forces effectively on national issues. We will change this. We will create a new NCA to lead the fight against organised crime, protect our borders and provide services best delivered at national level.[6]

The overarching intention is to ensure that 'a greater volume and complexity of economic crime cases can be tackled'.[7] It can be argued that because this agency was not formally operational until October 2013,[8] the introduction of the Financial Services Bill[9] served as the first step on the long road to financial crime prevention. Although it has been suggested that the implementation of the NCA was 'burdensome',[10] it is difficult to determine whether or not financial crime will be successfully combated as a direct result of improving financial intelligence and enforcement: 'the criminal sector is a lawless industry. Its activities are neither listed nor registered, but knowledge of them is crucial to shedding light on the sector's overall size.'[11] Of course, the NCA's tag-line provides a useful insight to its key objectives:

> Organised crime and cyber crime are some of the greatest threats to our national security. At present, there are over 5,500 organised crime groups impacting on the UK, comprising around 37,000 individuals. Serious and organised crime blights communities, ruins lives and costs the UK well over

3 A. Srivastava, I. Mason, M. Simpson and M. Litt, 'Financial crime' (2011) *COB*, 86(May), 1.

4 The term 'white-collar crime' was coined in 1939 during a speech given by Edwin Sutherland, and described as 'crime committed by a person of respectability and high social status in the course of his occupation'. Today, it generally refers to non-violent crimes usually committed in commercial situations for financial gain. Legal Information Institute, *White Collar Crime*, Cornell University Law School <https://www.law.cornell.edu/wex/white-collar_crime>.

5 Home Office, 'Policing in the 21st century: reconnecting police and the people' <http://www.official-documents.gov.uk/document/cm79/7925/7925.pdf>, accessed on 28 February 2012.

6 Ibid.

7 House of Commons debate in 2011 Hansard HC vol. 529 col. 233 (8 June 2011).

8 As established under the Crime and Courts Act 2013.

9 Financial Services Act 2012.

10 C. Warren-Smith, 'Regulatory: the year ahead' (2011) 161 *NLJ* 358.

11 R. Barone and D. Masciandaro, 'Organised crime, money laundering and legal economy: theory and simulations' (2011) *EJL&E*, 32(1), 115.

£20 billion each year. Our job is to disrupt and bring to justice those serious and organised criminals who present the highest risk to the UK.[12]

13.1.2 A review of the current legislation that relates to financial crime in the UK

To fully assess the potential impact that the NCA would have upon the UK's financial crime policy, it is necessary to consider the current laws that govern 'undesirable practices'.[13] Financial crime is defined as 'any offence involving fraud or dishonesty; misconduct in, or misuse of information relating to, a financial market; or handling the proceeds of crime'.[14] Under the Treaty on the Functioning of the European Union, EU Member States have an obligation to 'combat fraud and any other illegal activities that may affect the financial security of the Union'.[15] This has resulted in a common EU objective to eradicate financial crime, shown through the introduction of the Commission Anti-Fraud Strategy (CAFS) and proposals to amend the European Anti-Fraud Office (known as OLAF).[16] Furthermore, the EU has created a number of legal instruments that address money laundering and financing of terrorism.[17]

13.1.2.1 Fraud

Fraud is 'an act of deception intended for personal gain, or to cause loss to another party'.[18] Recent figures[19] have stated that the cost of fraud in the UK in 2010 was £38.4bn, more than twice the previous estimate of £13bn,[20] amounting to

12 'National Crime Agency – About us' <http://www.nationalcrimeagency.gov.uk/about-us>, accessed on 24 April 2016.

13 R. Tomasic, 'The financial crisis and the haphazard pursuit of financial crime' (2011) *FC*, 18(1), 7–8.

14 N. Ryder, *Financial Crime in the 21st Century: Law and Policy* (Edward Elgar Publishing 2011) 3; s.6(3) of the Financial Services and Markets Act 2000.

15 Treaty on the Functioning of the European Union (Treaty of Lisbon) Art. 325.

16 European Commission, 'Protection of the European Union's financial interests – fight against fraud – Annual Report 2010' COM (2011) 595 final <http://ec.europa.eu/anti_fraud/reports/commission/2010/EN.pdf>, accessed on 5 October 2011. Also see: European Anti-Fraud Office, 'EUROJUST and OLAF strengthen their co-operation in combating financial crime' <http://europa.eu/rapid/pressReleasesAction.do?reference=OLAF/11/11&format=HTML&aged=0&language=EN&guiLanguage=en>, accessed on 5 October 2011.

17 V. Mitsilegas and N. Vavoula, 'The evolving EU anti-money laundering regime – challenges for fundamental rights and the rule of law' (2016) *MJECL*, 1, 261.

18 Serious Fraud Office, 'What is fraud?' <http://www.sfo.gov.uk/fraud/what-is-fraud.aspx>, accessed on 12 October 2011.

19 National Fraud Authority, 'Annual Fraud Indicator – January 2011' <http://www.homeoffice.gov.uk/publications/agencies-public-bodies/nfa/annual-fraud-indicator/annual-fraud-indicator-2011?view=Binary>, accessed on 5 October 2011.

20 Policy Exchange, '*Fighting Fraud and Financial Crime, A New Architecture for the Investigation and Prosecution of Serious Fraud, Corruption and Financial Market*

approximately £765 per adult. The principle offences of fraud under the Fraud Act 2006 are defined as: committing fraud by false representation;[21] committing fraud by failing to disclose information when there is a legal obligation to do so;[22] and committing fraud by abusing one's position.[23] This was a new development on the back of the previous offences of fraud under common law and the Theft Act 1968, which had been 'manifestly unsuitable for complex fraud cases'.[24] The Fraud Act 2006 also created a 'general offence'[25] of fraud, which focused on the 'dishonest conduct' of the defendant.[26] However, there has been academic debate on the definition of 'dishonest' and whether or not 'creative accounting and exaggerated advertisements'[27] should be viewed as dishonest in relation to the Fraud Act 2006. From a commercial fraud and subsequent civil litigation perspective, recovery claims could be brought for breach of trust, breach of fiduciary duty, dishonest assistance, knowing receipt, conspiracy, conversion and in the tort of deceit.[28]

Fraud is committed in a variety of ways, *inter alia*:[29] insurance fraud;[30] mortgage fraud;[31] tax fraud;[32] and benefit fraud.[33] The US 9/11 Commission

Crimes <http://www.policyexchange.org.uk/assets/Fighting_Fraud_-_Mar_10.pdf>, accessed on 5 October 2011; for more fraud statistics, see: Fraud Advisory Panel, 'Facts and figures' <http://www.fraudadvisorypanel.org/new/fraud-facts-and-figures.php>, accessed on 12 October 2011.

21 S.2 of the Fraud Act 2006.

22 Ibid. s.3.

23 Ibid. s.4.

24 J. Pickworth, 'The Fraud Act 2006: a death knell for conspiracy to defraud – the "prosecutor's darling"?' (2009) *Euro. News.*, 64(Aug), 2.

25 Health Claims Bureau Group, 'Notes on the Fraud Act 2006' <http://www.hcbgroup.co.uk/files/FRAUD_ACT_2006_Paper.pdf>, accessed on 5 October 2011.

26 S.1 of the Fraud Act 2006.

27 J. Pickworth, 'The Fraud Act 2006: a death knell for conspiracy to defraud – the "prosecutor's darling"?' (2009) *Euro. News.*, 64(Aug), 3.

28 For a discussion and introduction into commercial fraud, see: Practical Law Company, *An Introduction to Commercial Fraud*, written and maintained by Clive Freedman QC and Harry Wright (both of 7KBW) <http://uk.practicallaw.com/0-509-2947>, accessed on 24 April 2016.

29 For more examples of how fraud is committed, see: Serious Fraud Office, 'The taxonomy of fraud' <http://www.sfo.gov.uk/taxonomy.swf>, accessed on 12 October 2011.

30 For an example of insurance fraud, see: Insurance Fraud Bureau, 'Man who faked his own death sentenced to six years' <http://www.insurancefraudbureau.org/files/press_release_pdfs/antony_mcerlean_sentenced_to_6_years_-_30.09.11.pdf>, accessed on 5 October 2011.

31 For an example of mortgage fraud, see: B. Draper, 'Real estate agent gets 20 months for mortgage scam' <http://www.businessweek.com/ap/financialnews/D9Q533600.htm>, accessed on 5 October 2011.

32 For an example of tax fraud, see: [Anon.], 'Mastermind behind booze tax fraud sent to jail' <http://www.leaderlive.co.uk/news/106742/mastermind-behind-booze-tax-fraud-sent-to-jail.aspx>, accessed on 5 October 2011.

33 For an example of benefit fraud, see: C. Ellicott, 'Traveller mother-of-9 claimed £63,000 benefits by saying she was living alone' <http://www.dailymail.co.uk/news/article-2045279/

Report[34] discovered that 9/11 had been partly funded by identity theft and immigration fraud, providing an example of how fraud has been used to fund serious criminal activities and terrorism. Fraudsters have adapted to social and technological advancements and are constantly developing new methods to commit fraud. In 2009, 20 per cent of UK web users had been the victims of fraudulent emails and 23 per cent of web users had been the victims of a phishing scam.[35] In September 2011, an online poker website was accused of defrauding poker players and was described as a 'global ponzi fraud scheme'.[36] Professional football has also been accused of being 'widely used for financial crime',[37] further demonstrating the development and wide spectrum of fraud in the UK.

Perhaps as expected with the increased use of smart phones, development of technology and reliance upon digital trading, the way in which fraudsters manipulate their victims has also changed.[38] These new issues and risks are great challenges for the police and regulatory authorities. Often, the true beneficiary of the fraud cannot be identified and/or the victim's money has been swiftly moved out of the jurisdiction. Barclays, in an effort to combat fraud against consumers, has aired a television advert highlighting how fraudsters can contact consumers, posing as genuine bank staff members, and request sensitive information (e.g. by asking for internet banking passwords, PIN numbers and other identification).[39] These challenges, of course, have to be appropriately combated and monitored by the regulatory agencies.

Fraud is controlled through several regulatory agencies, including the Serious Fraud Office (SFO), the National Fraud Authority (NFA) and the Financial Conduct Authority (FCA). The SFO is 'resourced to investigate allegations of

Traveller-mother-claimed-63-000-benefits-saying-living-alone.html?ito=feeds-newsxml>, accessed on 5 October 2011

34 9/11 commission report, 'The 9/11 Commission Report' <http://www.911commission.gov/report/911Report.pdf>, accessed on 5 October 2011.

35 The Get Safe Online Report – November 2010, *UK Internet Security: State of the Nation* <http://www.getsafeonline.org/media/Get_Safe_Online_Report_2010.pdf>, accessed on 5 October 2011; for more information on 'click fraud', see: L. Hoffmann, 'Guidelines for how to stop click fraud – or it just not stoppable?' (2011) *CTLR*, 17(7), 185–193.

36 The Wall Street Journal, 'Full Tilt Poker's Lederer, Ferguson accused of $US300m global ponzi fraud' <http://www.theaustralian.com.au/business/full-tilt-pokers-lederer-ferguson-accused-of-us300m-poker-fraud/story-e6frg8zx-1226142540690>, accessed on 5 October 2011; for more information on this, see: The Wall Street Journal, 'Full Tilt's collection woes bred alleged ponzi scheme' <http://online.wsj.com/article/SB10001424052970204422404576592813676923134.html>, accessed on 5 October 2011.

37 S. Ramage, 'Digital money, electronic fraud, new regulations and the old money laundering regulations' (2011) *Crim. Law.*, 200, 3.

38 For example, see: 'Action Fraud – latest scams to watch out for' <http://www.actionfraud.police.uk/news/latest-scams-to-watch-out-for-apr16>, accessed on 24 April 2016.

39 'TV AD Barclays – Fraud Smart: The Imposter' <https://www.youtube.com/watch?v=6yGvO-FefUc>, accessed on 24 April 2016.

major and complex fraud'.[40] The SFO will therefore only consider cases that involve a loss of £1m, affect the economy, are politically sensitive or are highly complicated.[41] The SFO has been criticised for having a lower conviction rate than the District Attorneys of New York and Manhattan.[42] However, it has been accepted that the SFO cannot 'get it right all the time'[43] and that the comparison with the US authorities may not be fair as these have been in operation for decades. In 2010–2011, the SFO stated that over £64m had been, or is due to be, returned to victims of fraud.[44] This is arguably a small figure in comparison with the estimated amount of fraud[45] that is committed within the UK annually. However, one only has to look at the recent failed convictions of many of the LIBOR defendants[46] to identify the pressure that the SFO is under to achieve positive results from its relatively modest, and publicly funded, budget.[47] Conversely, the extension of David Green's contract as Director of the SFO reinforces the SFO's commitment to combating serious and organised fraud and taking cases of public interest to trial.[48]

13.1.2.2 Money laundering

Money laundering is the process of 'concealing the illicit source of assets obtained or generated by criminal activity'.[49] It has been estimated that the amount of money laundered within the UK per annum is £19–48bn;[50] however, the Financial Action Task Force (FATF) states that it is impossible to

40 R. Wright, 'Fraud after Roskill: a view from the Serious Fraud Office' (2003) *JFC*, 11(1), 12–13.

41 Serious Fraud Office, 'What is fraud?' <http://www.sfo.gov.uk/fraud/what-is-fraud.aspx>, accessed on 5 October 2011.

42 J. De Grazia, *Review of the Serious Fraud Office, June 2008* <http://www.sfo.gov.uk/media/34318/de%20grazia%20review%20of%20sfo.pdf>, accessed on 5 October 2011.

43 R. Wright, 'Fraud after Roskill: a view from the Serious Fraud Office' (2003) *JFC* 2003, 11(1), 10–11.

44 Serious Fraud Office, 'Our Performance' <http://www.sfo.gov.uk/our-work/our-performance.aspx>, accessed on 5 October 2011.

45 National Fraud Authority, 'Annual Fraud Indicator – January 2011' <http://www.homeoffice.gov.uk/publications/agencies-public-bodies/nfa/annual-fraud-indicator/annual-fraud-indicator-2011?view=Binary>, accessed on 5 October 2011.

46 'Libor Defendants Acquitted (update)' <https://www.sfo.gov.uk/2016/01/29/libor-defendants-acquitted-update/>, accessed on 24 April 2016.

47 'SFO – About us' <https://www.sfo.gov.uk/about-us/#ourfundingandbudget>, accessed on 24 April 2016.

48 'Serious Fraud Office director has contract extended' < http://www.theguardian.com/business/2016/feb/09/serious-office-director-david-green-contract-extended>, accessed on 24 April 2016.

49 House of Lords Debate March 2011, 'The UK's record on legislation regarding bribery, tax avoidance, corruption and money laundering' <http://www.parliament.uk/documents/lords-library/LLN%202011-009%20BriberyFP.pdf>, accessed on 12 October 2011.

50 N. Ryder, 'The financial services authority and money laundering: a game of cat and mouse' (2008) *CLJ*, 67(3), 636–637.

produce a reliable figure.[51] The FATF[52] introduced recommendations to aid the prevention of money laundering[53] and produced mutual evaluation reports to 'monitor the progress of its members'.[54] The UK has been described as having a 'comprehensive legal structure to combat money laundering', evidenced by increasing prosecutions in this area.[55] However, in contrast, the UK is still referred to as a 'jurisdiction of primary concern'[56] for money laundering and some argue that this is because the UK regulates money laundering 'too heavily'.[57] Anti-money laundering regulations and checks in the UK are controlled by the FCA and suspicious activity reports and disclosures are made to the NCA. A disclosure, or suspicious activity report (SAR),[58] must be made if it is known, or there are reasonable grounds to suspect, that another party is engaged in money laundering.[59] The FCA has an obligation to reduce financial crime[60] and holds the power to prosecute for the offence of money laundering, as shown through the case of *R v Rollins*.[61] Part 7 of the POCA 2002 defines the three principal offences of money laundering as: concealing the proceeds of criminal conduct;[62] assisting another to retain the benefits of criminal conduct;[63] and the acquisition, use and possession of the proceeds of crime.[64] The consent regime[65] requires a firm to

51 Financial Action Task Force, 'Money laundering FAQ' <http://www.fatf-gafi.org/document/29/0,3746,en_32250379_32235720_33659613_1_1_1_1,00.html#howmuchmoneyislaundered peryear>, accessed on 12 October 2011.

52 For more information on the FATF recommendations, see: N. Jensen and C. Png, 'Implementation of the FATF 40 + 9 Recommendations: a perspective from developing countries' (2011) JMLC, 14(2), 110–120.

53 Financial Action Task Force, 'The 40 Recommendations' <http://www.fatf-gafi.org/document/28/0,3746,en_32250379_32236920_33658140_1_1_1_1,00.html>, accessed on 12 October 2011.

54 Financial Action Task Force, 'Mutual evaluations', <http://www.fatf-gafi.org/pages/0,3417,en_32250379_32236963_1_1_1_1_1,00.html>, accessed on 12 October 2011

55 Financial Action Task Force, 'Third mutual evaluation of United Kingdom of Great Britain and Northern Ireland' <http://www.fatf-gafi.org/document/9/0,3746,en_32250379_32236963_38917001_1_1_1_1,00.html>, accessed on 12 October 2011.

56 US Department of State, 'Major money laundering countries' <http://www.state.gov/p/inl/rls/nrcrpt/2006/vol2/html/62140.htm>, accessed on 27 October 2011.

57 J. Fisher, 'The anti-money laundering disclosure regime and the collection of revenue in the United Kingdom' (2010) *BTR*, 3, 262–263.

58 For more information on suspicious activity reports, see: R. Stokes and A. Arora, 'The duty to report under the money laundering legislation within the United Kingdom' (2004) *JBL*, May, 332–356.

59 S.330, s.331 and s.332 of the Proceeds of Crime Act 2002.

60 S.6 of the Financial Services and Markets Act 2000.

61 *R v Rollins* [2010] 1 *WLR* 1922. For more information on this case, see: The Financial Services Authority, 'former senior manager sentenced to 27 months in prison for insider dealing and money laundering' <http://www.fsa.gov.uk/pages/Library/Communication/PR/2011/010.shtml>, accessed on 12 October 2011; P. Ozin, 'Financial crime update', (2011) *BJIB&FL*, 26(1), 49–50.

62 S.327 of the Proceeds of Crime Act 2002.

63 Ibid. s.328.

64 Ibid. s.329.

65 Ibid. s.335.

restrict any further transactions with an individual or company under investigation until approval is given from NCA.

Operating in parallel to the POCA 2002, the EU's Third Money Laundering Directive[66] was implemented in the UK by the Money Laundering Regulations (MLR) 2007.[67] This introduced the 'risk based approach'[68] and the use of diligence methods such as 'Know Your Customer'.[69] This involves performing an identity check to ensure that funds originate from a 'legitimate'[70] source. However, it can be argued that 'identification is too easy to falsify'[71] and these requirements would, therefore, only succeed against 'amateurish attempts'[72] of money laundering. Institutions and professionals therein (as stipulated by the MLR) are also required to ensure that their employees are adequately trained to recognise and report any 'suspicious' transactions. This will include appointing a 'nominated officer',[73] who will liaise with the NCA and, if necessary, make an SAR. The nominated officer is under an obligation to make a disclosure to the NCA,[74] unless they fall within one of the exemptions or can show a 'reasonable excuse' for not making the disclosure.[75] There are currently no reported cases on what would constitute a 'reasonable excuse.' Therefore, if a disclosure were not made to the NCA, a nominated officer would be in breach of this obligation.[76] The FCA is able to impose a financial penalty on both firms and nominated officers for not having adequate anti-money-laundering provisions in place.[77] The case of *Shah v HSBC Private Bank (UK) Ltd*[78] raised the issue of how damaging the disclosure regime could potentially be. In particular, this regime can be most damaging on a regulated institution when

66 Directive (EC) 2005/60/EC of the European Parliament and of the Council of 26 October 2005 on the prevention of the use of the financial system for the purpose of money laundering and terrorist financing [2005] OJ L309/15.

67 Money Laundering Regulations 2007 SI 1992/1771.

68 M. Gill and G. Taylor, 'The risk based approach to tackling money laundering: matching risk to products' (2003) *Comp. Law.*, 24(7), 210–213.

69 Financial Services Authority, 'Discussion paper – reducing money laundering risk' <http://www.fsa.gov.uk/pubs/discussion/dp22_newsletter.pdf>, accessed on 12 October 2011.

70 N. Mugarura, 'The institutional framework against money laundering and its underlying predicate crimes' (2011) *JFR&C*, 19(2), 183–184.

71 M. Gill and G. Taylor, 'Preventing money laundering or obstructing business? Financial companies' perspective on "know your customer" procedures' (2004) *Brit. J. Criminol.*, 44(4), 591–592.

72 Ibid. 592–593.

73 HMRC, 'Appointing a nominated officer and training your employees' <http://www.hmrc.gov.uk/mlr/your-role/nominated-officer.htm>, accessed on 12 October 2011.

74 S.332 of the Proceeds of Crime Act 2002.

75 Ibid. s.330(6).

76 Ibid. s.330(4).

77 A. Srivastava, I. Mason, M. Simpson and M. Litt, 'Financial crime' (2011) *COB*, 86(May), 7–8.

78 *Shah v HSBC Private Bank (UK) Ltd* [2010] EWCA Civ 31. For more information regarding this case and legal privilege, see: P. Marshall, 'Does Shah v HSBC Private Bank Ltd make the anti-money laundering consent regime unworkable?' (2010) *BJIB&FL*, 25(5), 287–290.

there is a delayed decision from the Serious Organised Crime Agency (SOCA). It is, therefore, plausible to assert that this regime can also be a hindrance to firms, even though an increase in disclosures and convictions[79] has branded it as a 'success'.[80] 'Reputation risk'[81] could be argued to be part of the reasoning behind the British Banker's Association spending £250m each year to comply with money-laundering legislation.[82] This is because the fear of being 'shunned by legitimate enterprises'[83] and the 'loss of direct costs (loss of income) and indirect costs (withdrawal and possible legal costs)'[84] arguably outweigh the cost of complying with the legislation.

13.1.2.3 Bribery and corruption

Bribery, 'the corrupt payment, receipt or solicitation of a private favour of official action',[85] and corruption, 'when private gain is secured at public expense',[86] are both offences governed by the SFO[87] under the Bribery Act 2010. The SFO has the power to execute search warrants for the homes of suspects during an investigation, as confirmed in the case of *Burgin v Commission of Police of the Metropolis.*[88] It is estimated that these offences cost €120bn per annum across the EU,[89] a direct result of ineffective legislation, resulting in compliance challenges for Member States.[90] Throughout the EU, anti-corruption legislation has been

79 House of Lords Debate March 2011, 'The UK's record on legislation regarding bribery, tax avoidance, corruption and money laundering' <http://www.parliament.uk/documents/lords-library/LLN%202011-009%20BriberyFP.pdf>, accessed on 12 October 2011.

80 R. Stokes and A. Arora, 'The duty to report under the money laundering legislation within the United Kingdom' (2004) *JBL*, May, 352–354.

81 For more information on reputation risk, see: J. Harvey, 'Compliance and reporting issues arising for financial institutions from money laundering regulations: a preliminary cost benefit study' (2004) *JMLC*, 7(4), 333–346.

82 N. Ryder, 'The financial services authority and money laundering: a game of cat and mouse' (2008) *CLJ*, 67(3), 650–651.

83 United Nations Office on Drugs and Crime, 'Introduction to money laundering' <http://www.unodc.org/unodc/en/money-laundering/introduction.html?ref=menuside>, accessed on 12 October 2011.

84 J. Harvey, 'Compliance and reporting issues arising for financial institutions from money laundering regulations: a preliminary cost benefit study' (2004) *JMLC*, 7(4), 336–337

85 House of Lords Debate March 2011, 'The UK's record on legislation regarding bribery, tax avoidance, corruption and money laundering' <http://www.parliament.uk/documents/lords-library/LLN%202011-009%20BriberyFP.pdf>, accessed on 12 October 2011.

86 Ibid.

87 Serious Fraud Office, 'Bribery and corruption' <http://www.sfo.gov.uk/bribery--corruption/bribery--corruption.aspx>, accessed on 19 October 2011.

88 *Burgin v Commission of Police for the Metropolis* [2011] EWHC 1835 (Admin).

89 European Commission, 'Fighting corruption in the EU' COM (2011) 308 Final.

90 KPMG, *Global Anti-Bribery and Corruption Survey 2011* <http://www.kpmg.com/UK/en/IssuesAndInsights/ArticlesPublications/Documents/PDF/Advisory/23816NSS_Global_ABC_Survey.PDF>, accessed on 19 October 2011.

described as 'uneven and unsatisfactory',[91] thus causing additional difficulties for policing this offence.

The EU has previously introduced an 'anti-corruption report' to provide a system to 'periodically assess' corruption.[92] This aims to 'foster political engagement and help Member States to better enforce existing legislation',[93] because there is a 'lack of determination among politicians to combat corruption'.[94] The EU has also joined the UNCAC,[95] evidencing the recognition that corruption is a 'serious crime with cross-border dimension'.[96] It has now been recognised that, to prevent corruption, it is essential to utilise other financial crime provisions, such as anti-money-laundering standards,[97] in order to develop and combat both corruption and money-laundering laws.[98] It has been argued that bribery is particularly challenging to tackle because of its prevalence within certain industries.[99] In particular, and for example, it has previously been suggested that BAE Systems PLC paid over £1m in bribes to facilitate and secure an armaments contract.[100] If corporations regularly use bribery in the course of business, it is arguable that bribery and corruption are even larger challenges to overcome.

The Bribery Act 2010 introduced the offences of bribery[101] as: offering, promising or giving a bribe,[102] requesting, agreeing to receive or accepting a bribe,[103] bribing a foreign public official[104] and the failure of a commercial

91 European Commission, 'Fighting corruption in the EU' COM (2011) 308 Final.

92 European Commission, 'Establishing an EU anti-corruption reporting mechanism for period assessment' COM (2011) 3673 Final.

93 European Commission, 'Protection of the European Union's financial interests – fight against fraud – Annual Report 2010' COM (2011) 595 final.

94 R. Kay, 'European Commission announces new initiatives to tackle corruption' <http://www.globalregulatoryenforcementlawblog.com/2011/06/articles/government-investigations/european-commission-announces-new-initiatives-to-tackle-corruption/>, accessed on 19 October 2011.

95 For more information on UNCAC, see: United Nations Office on Crime and Drugs, 'UNODC's against corruption and economic crime' <http://www.unodc.org/unodc/en/corruption/index.html?ref=menuside>, accessed on 19 October 2011.

96 European Commission, 'Fighting corruption in the EU' COM (2011) 308 Final.

97 A. Bell, 'The Bribery Act: what's all the fuss about?' (2011) *LIM*, 11(2), 107–108.

98 I. Carr and M. Goldby, 'Recovering the proceeds of corruption: UNCAC and anti-money laundering standards' (2011) *JBL*, 2, 188–189.

99 R. Tomasic, 'The financial crisis and the haphazard pursuit of financial crime' (2011) *JFC*, 18(1), 9–10.

100 Ibid. For more information on the BAE corruption cases, see: Transparency International UK, 'Settlement of the BAE Systems corruption cases: significant issues of concern' <http://www.transparency.org.uk/all-news-releases/126-settlement-of-bae-systems-corruption-cases-significant-issues-of-concern>, accessed on 19 October 2011.

101 Berrymans Lace Mawer, 'BLM newsflash – Bribery Act 2010' <http://www.blm-law.com/2114/12169/objects/news/bribery-act-2010---are-you-ready-.html>, accessed on 19 October 2011.

102 S.1 of the Bribery Act 2010.

103 Ibid. s.2.

104 Ibid. s.6.

organisation to prevent bribery.[105] This statute 'reinforces the UK's reputation as a leader in the global fight against corruption'.[106] However, it has also been argued that 'a clear failure of the act is not providing resources for prosecutors to tackle international corruption'.[107]

It is arguable that the new 'corporate offence'[108] provides a clear demonstration of the UK and EU initiatives to combat bribery. This is because the 'corporate offence'[109] is an offence of strict liability, meaning that the prosecution will not need to prove that the business was aware of the bribery taking place, and instead would merely need to prove that the business failed to prevent it. The scope of this offence is particularly large, allowing the prosecution of 'anyone associated with the business, anywhere in the world'.[110]

Although this offence is relatively 'draconian',[111] s.7(2) allows the defence of providing 'adequate provisions' to prevent bribery. Guidance has been issued to provide principles that would satisfy this defence.[112] These principles are:[113] proportionate procedures, top-level commitment, risk assessment, due diligence, communication and monitoring.[114] However, and despite being a seemingly strong tool in the SFO's armoury, the first conviction under s.7 of the Bribery Act 2010 came nearly five years after its commencement.[115] It is difficult to determine what the position would have been had this conviction not come from a mere guilty plea on the part of Sweett Group Plc. The SFO now also has the power to enter into deferred prosecution agreements with those that it alleges have committed offences under the Bribery Act 2010. These agreements protect a company from a formal conviction in exchange for a financial penalty. The first two cases to cite s.7 of the Bribery Act 2010, both prior to Sweett Group Plc,

105 Ibid. s.7.

106 Ministry of Justice, 'UK clamps down on corruption with new Bribery Act' <http://webarchive.nationalarchives.gov.uk/+/http://www.justice.gov.uk/news/press-release-300311a.htm>, accessed on 19 October 2011.

107 D. Aaronberg and N. Higgins, 'All hail the Bribery Act – the toothless wonder!' (2011) *Arch. Rev.*, 6, 6.

108 S.7 of the Bribery Act 2010.

109 Ibid.

110 Berrymans Lace Mawer, 'BLM newsflash – Bribery Act 2010' <http://www.blm-law.com/2114/12169/objects/news/bribery-act-2010---are-you-ready-.html>, accessed on 19 October 2011.

111 A. Bell, 'The Bribery Act: what's all the fuss about?' (2011) *LIM* 2011, 11(2), 106–107.

112 S.9 of the Bribery Act 2010; Ministry of Justice, 'Guidance about procedures which relevant commercial organisations can put into place to prevent persons associated with them from bribing' <http://www.justice.gov.uk/downloads/guidance/making-reviewing-law/bribery-act-2010-guidance.pdf>, accessed on 19 October 2011.

113 Ministry of Justice, ibid.

114 Ibid.

115 'Sweett Group Plc sentenced and ordered to pay £2.25m after Bribery Act conviction' <https://www.sfo.gov.uk/2016/02/19/sweett-group-plc-sentenced-and-ordered-to-pay-2-3-million-after-bribery-act-conviction/>, accessed on 24 April 2016.

were compromised by way of a civil recovery settlement[116] and deferred prosecution agreement,[117] respectively. The lack of convictions under this section brings the effectiveness of this weapon into question.

However, of important consideration is the Coalition Government's decision to drop the prospect of an overarching offence, akin to s.7 of the Bribery Act 2010, for the 'failure to prevent economic crime'.[118] This decision was carefully considered owing to the apparent lack of successful convictions under s.7 of the Bribery Act 2010, and the challenges that come from identifying the directing mind and will of large corporate organisations for the purposes of criminal convictions. This statute 'consolidated'[119] the previous laws that governed bribery and corruption, and aimed to bring the UK into line with the bribery compliance regime[120] requested by the OECD.[121] However, it is difficult to assess whether it will go far enough and 'level the playing field for ethical British businesses'.[122] Therefore, 'the Bribery Act 2010, like the international conventions which it implements, is an important and welcome step, even if it must not be the final one'.[123]

13.2 The future of fraud regulation in the UK

13.2.1 Problems with the Serious Fraud Office

Fraud prosecutions in the UK have an entrenched history of being unsuccessful and running up large legal costs. The SFO,[124] in particular, has been criticised for

116 'Glenrothes cabling company pays £212,800 after reporting itself for failing to prevent bribery by a third party' <http://www.crownoffice.gov.uk/media-site/media-releases/1144-glenrothes-cabling-company-pays-212-800-after-reporting-itself-for-failing-to-prevent-bribery-by-a-third-party>, accessed on 1 May 2016.

117 'SFO agrees first UK DPA with Standard Bank' <https://www.sfo.gov.uk/2015/11/30/sfo-agrees-first-uk-dpa-with-standard-bank/>, accessed on 24 April 2016.

118 L. Clare and R. Elvin, 'Proposed new corporate offence dropped: failure to prevent economic crime' <http://www.anticorruptionblog.com/united-kingdom/proposed-new-corporate-offence-dropped-failure-to-prevent-economic-crime/>, accessed on 24 April 2016.

119 S. Sheikh, 'The Bribery Act 2010: Commercial organisations beware!' (2011) *ICCLR*, 22(1), 16.

120 Transparency International UK, 'Transparency International UK says the UK's record on enforcing foreign bribery rules is still un-impressive' <http://www.transparency.org.uk/all-news-releases/61-transparency-international-uk-says-the-uks-record-on-enforcing-foreign-bribery-rules-is-still-unimpressive>, accessed on 19 October 2011.

121 CMS Cameron McKenna, 'The evolving laws on bribery and corruption in England and Wales' <http://www.law-now.com/law-now/2009/anticorruptionevolvinglaws?cmckreg=true>, accessed on 19 October 2011.

122 M. Raphael, 'Be careful what you wish for' (2011) 161 *NLJ* 524.

123 R. Alexander, '"Bribery of a foreign public official" may cover a wider range than you might think' (2011) *Comp. Law.*, 32(4), 97.

124 For more information on fraud sentencing, see: M Levi, 'Hitting the suite spot: sentencing frauds' (2010) *JFC*, 17(1), 119–120.

the failed prosecutions of: the Maxwell Brothers, which cost the taxpayer between £20m and £30m;[125] Blue Arrow,[126] which cost the taxpayer £40m; and BCCI,[127] which ran up a total cost of over £200m.[128] In addition, the more recent case of LIBOR[129] has caused the SFO to come under further scrutiny for another set of failed prosecutions: 'there was no evidence, there was nothing. I think it was a sham, and I think they [the SFO] knew it was a sham. They didn't investigate properly, they didn't listen.'[130] However, it is worth noting that the SFO did secure the conviction of Tom Hayes, a former trader at UBS and Citigroup, in relation to the manipulation of the LIBOR rate.[131] When considering the above track record, it would not be unrealistic or unreasonable to state that the SFO certainly adopt a quantitative rather than qualitative approach to prosecutions.

In 2010/2011, the SFO held a budget of £35.9m[132] to tackle an area of white-collar crime estimated to cost around £38bn.[133] In 2015/2016 the core funding provided to the SFO was £33.8m, supplemented through 'additional funding' to provide a gross budget (as of 2 February 2016) of £62.2m. The 2010/2011

125 [Anon.], 'Litany of expensive fraud trials' <http://news.bbc.co.uk/1/hi/uk/4113134.stm>, accessed on 2 November 2011.
126 For more information on the Blue Arrow Case, see: [Anon.], 'SFO may discontinue Blue Arrow cases' <http://www.lawgazette.co.uk/news/sfo-may-discontinue-blue-arrow-cases>, accessed on 2 November 2011.
127 Serious Fraud Office, 'Bank of Credit and Commerce International' <http://www.sfo.gov.uk/our-work/our-cases/historic-cases/bank-of-credit-and-commerce-international-(bcci).aspx>, accessed on 5 October 2011; for more information on the BCCI failed prosecutions, see: A. Zuckerman, 'A colossal wreck – the BCCI–Three Rivers litigation' (2006) *CJQ*, 25(Jul), 287–311.
128 London Evening Standard, 'BCCI Trial could top £200m' <http://www.thisislondon.co.uk/news/article-9283430-bcci-trial-could-top-163200m.do>, accessed on 2 November 2011.
129 For a summary of the LIBOR scandal, see: 'New York Times – tracking the Libor scandal' <http://www.nytimes.com/interactive/2015/04/23/business/dealbook/db-libor-timeline.html?_r=0#/#time370_10900>, accessed on 24 April 2016.
130 G. Ruddick, 'Serious Fraud Office back in the dock after Libor acquittals' <http://www.theguardian.com/law/2016/jan/29/serious-office-back-in-the-dock-after-libor-acquittals>, accessed on 1 May 2016.
131 'SFO LIBOR Yen (Hayes)' <https://www.sfo.gov.uk/cases/libor-hayes/>, accessed on 1 May 2016.
132 S. Bowers, 'Financial fraud risks slipping under radar as SFO tackles bribery abroad' <http://www.guardian.co.uk/law/2011/jul/24/financial-fraud-sfo-overseas-bribery>, accessed on 2 November 2011; for more information on fraud budgets, see: Policy Exchange, 'Fighting fraud and financial crime, a new architecture for the investigation and prosecution of serious fraud, corruption and financial market crimes' <http://www.policyexchange.org.uk/assets/Fighting_Fraud_-_Mar_10.pdf>, accessed on 2 November 2011.
133 National Fraud Authority, 'Annual Fraud Indicator: January 2011' <http://www.homeoffice.gov.uk/publications/agencies-public-bodies/nfa/annual-fraud-indicator/annual-fraud-indicator-2011?view=Binary>, accessed on 28 November 2011.

gross budget, by comparison, was £40.1m.[134] While this is clearly a positive movement, and perhaps evidence of the increasing problem of fraud in the UK, the budget falls well short of the sheer severity of the cost of financial crime. The impact of a low budget could clearly hamper the SFO's ability to investigate and pursue potential fraudsters effectively and lead to inappropriate cases being taken to trial.

Although there has been no codified confirmation to date, it is entirely possible that the SFO may move to the NCA or the Economic Crime Agency (ECA). This would result in a greater amount of public funding being diverted to fewer financial crime agencies. It remains to be seen whether or not this would assist with the smooth operation and cooperation between these agencies. It has been suggested that additional taxation or a statutory levy on business may be used to fund this.[135] The influence that the current European regulatory bodies may have had on the NCA ought to be considered to allow an analysis of the developments in the UK's financial crime policy. The lack of an overarching European regime, combined with the limited scope that these organisations have, poses the larger question: How can fraud possibly be combated on an international or regional scale?

13.2.2 European fraud regulatory bodies

While the increase of fraud has damaged consumers on a 'national level',[136] financial crime has also created a vast array of problems on an international scale: 'in a global economy with integrated financial markets, new opportunities have opened up for all forms of illicit activity'.[137] In 2006, the EC recognised that fraud has cross-border nature and is a concern for the single market. This meant that enhanced cooperation between Member States and third countries were essential.[138] OLAF aims to protect the European budget by working with national

134 'SFO – About us – our funding and budget' <https://www.sfo.gov.uk/about-us/#ourfundingandbudget>, accessed on 1 May 2016.

135 J. Perry, R. Moulton, G. Barwick, R. Small, J. Green and N. Kay, 'The new UK regulatory landscape' (2011) *COB*, 84(Mar), 9.

136 T. Evans, 'Consumers losing £7 billion due to scams and fraud every year, says MP' <http://www.thisismoney.co.uk/money/bills/article-2059407/Consumers-losing-7billion-scams-fraud-year-MPs-say.html>, accessed on 16 November 2011.

137 Serious Fraud Office, *Serious Economic Crime: A Boardroom Guide to Prevention and Compliance* <http://www.seriouseconomiccrime.com/ebooks/Serious-Economic-Crime.pdf>, accessed on 16 November 2011. For a more detailed discussion of the EU's policy towards financial crime, see: E. Herlin-Karnell and N. Ryder, 'The robustness of EU financial crimes legislation: a critical review of the EU and UK anti-fraud and money laundering scheme' (2017) *European Business Law Review*, forthcoming.

138 European Commission, 'Concerning the need to develop a coordinated strategy to improve the fight against fiscal fraud' COM (2006) 254 final.

authorities to combat fraud.[139] However, the scope of OLAF is limited to fraud committed directly against the EU, and not individual Member States. It is therefore imperative that the NCA is able to interact and cooperate[140] with OLAF, when necessary, to help combat fraud against the EU.[141] OLAF has formed partnerships with the World Bank and the UN in the fight against fraud. This ensures that the €130bn budget of the EU is protected through the use of joint investigations.[142] However, OLAF can only investigate fraud against the EU when a request is made and, therefore, cannot actively seek to combat fraud, further evidencing the limited scope of OLAF. OLAF has previously launched a fraud enquiry against the European Medicines Agency.[143] Investigations of this nature could arguably damage consumer confidence (in this case in relation to the safety of medicines within the UK). This shows that OLAF values the prevention of fraud and corruption over the potential damage that could be suffered to consumer confidence. In 2010 fraud in the EU had increased by 109 per cent,[144] but in November 2011 the fight against fraud was described as a 'reassuring picture'.[145] Perhaps the process is encouraging, but it is difficult to provide clear evidence as to whether the EU initiatives will be greatly affected by the NCA. OLAF takes a different approach to fraud prevention by emphasising that a high number of fraud investigations do not equate to complete fraud protection.[146] It is also worth considering that combating fraud as a process consists of several stages: 'prevention is part of a cycle that begins with information on suspected irregularities, and is followed by investigation, detection and sanctions, before

139 OLAF, 'The first 10 years in the fight against fraud' <http://ec.europa.eu/anti_fraud/documents/publications-brochure/10_anniv_en.pdf>, accessed on 16 November 2011.

140 For more information on OLAF and co-operation with other international bodies, see: OLAF, 'International co-operation' <http://ec.europa.eu/anti_fraud/policy/international-cooperation/index_en.htm>, accessed on 18 February 2012.

141 European Commission, 'Communication from the Commission to the European Parliament, the Council, the European Economic and Social Committee, and the Committee of the regions and the Court of Auditors on the Commission Anti-Fraud Strategy' COM (2011) 376 final.

142 Europa Press Releases, 'World Bank and OLAF step up efforts to combat fraud and corruption in development. aid' <http://europa.eu/rapid/pressReleasesAction.do?reference=OLAF/11/14&format=HTML&aged=0&language=EN&guiLanguage=en>, accessed on 16 November 2011

143 J. Laurence, 'Drug watchdog in fraud investigation' <http://www.independent.co.uk/news/uk/crime/drug-watchdog-in-fraud-investigation-6258244.html>, accessed on 16 November 2011.

144 M. Banks, 'New report reveals "full scale" of EU fraud and waste' <http://www.theparliament.com/latest-news/article/newsarticle/new-report-reveals-full-scale-of-eu-fraud-and-waste/>, accessed on 17 November 2011.

145 European Commission Press Release, 'Fight against fraud: Commission publishes annual report' <http://europa.eu/rapid/pressReleasesAction.do?reference=IP/11/1133&type=HTML>, accessed on 17 November 2011.

146 OLAF Press Releases, 'MEMO Questions and Answers: OLAF's 2011 annual operations report' <http://ec.europa.eu/anti_fraud/press_room/pr/2011/13_en.html>, accessed on 10 March 2012.

leading to prevention actions themselves'.[147] A lack of an overall international law that would combat fraud further clouds the jurisdiction of all national and international regulatory agencies. It is essential that the fraud regulatory body within the UK is able to cooperate successfully on an international basis. Failure to do so could arguably be the downfall of combating fraud in the United Kingdom.

13.2.3 The Economic Crime Agency

Initially, the SFO was to be merged with elements of the FCA, the Office of Fair Trading (OFT) and the Crown Prosecution Service (CPS) fraud units to create the ECA.[148] This agency would operate in parallel with the renamed FCA, but may have to 'fight for prioritisation'[149] with certain prosecutions. The Attorney General stated that a decision has not yet been made on a new structure for economic crime.[150] Because of this, the ECA could be seen as a 'quick fix to a criminal activity that costs the economy £30bn per year'.[151] It has been stated that the SFO will not be broken up and will retain its powers relating to the investigation and prosecution of fraud.[152] However, the then Home Secretary, Theresa May, reserved the opportunity to reform the SFO in the future.[153] The Home Office believes that the introduction of an agency of this nature will greatly benefit the battle against financial crime: 'the creation of a new ECC as part of the NCA will also provide a more effective, better coordinated and intelligence-led response across all economic crime fighting agencies'.[154] The ECC, aimed at utilising and capitalising upon the NCA's 'intelligence picture',[155] has published a strategy to

147 Serious Fraud Office, 'Serious Economic Crime: A boardroom guide to prevention and compliance' <http://www.seriouseconomiccrime.com/ebooks/Serious-Economic-Crime.pdf>, accessed on 16 November 2011.

148 S. Hart and T. Webley, 'Proposed restructuring of UK agencies dealing with economic crime and fraud continues at pace' <http://www.globalregulatoryenforcementlawblog.com/2011/01/articles/government-investigations/proposed-restructuring-of-uk-agencies-dealing-with-economic-crime-and-fraud-continues-at-pace/>, accessed on 2 November 2011.

149 C. Conceicao and C. Ninan, 'Should the CPMA retain the power to prosecute market misconduct criminal offences?' (2010) 11 *JIBFL* 686.

150 House of Commons debate in 2011 Hansard HC vol. 527 col. 1293W (12 May 2011).

151 M. Raphael, 'Time is not right for an Economic Crime Agency' <http://www.guardian.co.uk/law/2010/jun/04/economic-crime-agency>, accessed on 2 November 2011.

152 J. Russell, 'Serious Fraud Office won't be scrapped, says Home Secretary' <http://www.telegraph.co.uk/finance/financial-crime/8564546/Serious-Fraud-Office-wont-be-scrapped-says-Home-Secretary.html>, accessed on 2 November 2011.

153 Frances Gibb, 'Serious Fraud Office given 12 months to save itself' *The Times* (London 8 June 2011) 5.

154 Home Office, 'Joining forces to fight fraud' <http://www.homeoffice.gov.uk/media-centre/news/fighting-fraud>, accessed on 9 November 2011.

155 Fact Sheet 2 of 12 on the National Crime Agency <https://www.gov.uk/government/uploads/system/uploads/attachment_data/file/98445/fs-nca-what-how.pdf>, accessed on 1 May 2016.

combat financial crime within the UK, to pursue, prevent and prepare.[156] It could be argued that the government has 'scored an own goal'[157] in relation to the development of the SFO by issuing unclear statements regarding the distribution of enforcement powers to the NCA and the FCA. This is because a shift in powers could potentially hinder prosecutions and 'the ability to educate through intelligent enforcement action'.[158] A lack of clarity of this nature could be seen as a weakness of the NCA. The 'sting in the tail'[159] is the option for the future review of the SFO, which could lead to its inevitable merger with the other regulatory agencies.

13.2.4 Joining forces – fighting fraud together[160]

Building upon developments by the NFA, the NFS[161] has an overall aim to 'restore consumer confidence'.[162] This strategy focuses on the reduction of fraud by strengthening the partnerships with other fraud agencies, such as the FCA, to reduce the level of fraud in the UK in the future. This is in line with the aims of the fraud review, which stated that 'the most important benefits will be the reduced fraud losses throughout the economy'.[163] However, it is difficult to clarify whether fraud could ever be reduced to such an extent that it would strongly affect the economy. The NFS claims to have greatly enhanced fraud prevention in the UK by increasing greater statutory provisions through the implementation of the Fraud Act 2006, as well as 'establishing a network of specialist fraud prosecutors'.[164] The benefits of this can arguably be evidenced by an increase in

156 Economic Crime Command <http://www.nationalcrimeagency.gov.uk/about-us/what-we-do/economic-crime>, accessed on 1 May 2016.

157 [Anon.], 'Government scores an own-goal in fight against white collar crime' <http://www.efinancialnews.com/story/2011-01-24/link-link-link>, accessed on 2 November 2011.

158 N. Holt, 'Lawyers warn shifting crime powers could hamper prosecutions' <http://www.moneymarketing.co.uk/regulation/lawyers-warn-shifting-crime-powers-could-hamper-prosecutions/1030542.article>, accessed on 2 November 2011.

159 S. Hart, 'UK's Serious Fraud Office survives – but for how long?' <http://www.globalregulatoryenforcementlawblog.com/2011/06/articles/securities-litigation/uks-serious-fraud-office-survives-but-for-how-long/>, accessed on 2 November 2011

160 Home Office, 'Fighting fraud together – the strategic plan to reduce fraud' <http://www.homeoffice.gov.uk/publications/agencies-public-bodies/nfa/fighting-fraud-tog/fighting-fraud-together?view=Binary>, accessed on 9 November 2011.

161 National Fraud Authority, 'The National Fraud Strategy: a new approach to tackling fraud' <http://www.insurancefraudbureau.org/files/misc_pdfs/nfsa_strategy_aw_11.03@2.pdf>, accessed on 28 November 2011.

162 J. Haines, 'The National Fraud Strategy: new rules to crack down on fraud' (2009) *Comp. Law.*, 30(7), 213.

163 North East Fraud Forum, *Fraud Review* <http://www.northeastfraudforum.co.uk/documents/FraudReview.pdf>, accessed on 12 February 2012.

164 National Fraud Authority, 'The National Fraud Strategy: a new approach to tackling fraud' <http://www.insurancefraudbureau.org/files/misc_pdfs/nfsa_strategy_aw_11.03@2.pdf>, accessed on 28 November 2011.

the amount of money confiscated in fraud cases during the first six months of 2011.[165] In October 2011, this strategy was furthered, aiming to reduce financial crime by more robust enforcement, prevention and awareness of fraud.[166] This strategy envisages achieving these targets by increasing financial intelligence and publishing regular reports to illustrate its progress.[167] However, the same report also stated that it might take until 2015 for the UK to achieve a position where it is 'resilient and less damaged' by fraud.[168] In 2016, fraud still remains a major and topical issue. It may be favourable that a strategy was developed to combat fraud, but was this timeframe too short to ensure that the UK achieved the intended targets? Fraudsters are constantly developing and evolving their methods in tandem with technological advancements,[169] and it would, therefore, be naive to assume that this would not continue to happen even with new fraud initiatives. This is even more prevalent with the current financial issues faced across the globe, in particular the fear of a 'lost decade'[170] from the debt crisis,[171] as well the extent of malfeasant activity that was revealed by the Panama Papers.[172] It is arguable that the UK does not have a large amount of time to build up a resilience to fraud; consumers alone are losing £7bn per year,[173] with the wider private sector estimated to lose around £12bn.[174] However, in contrast to these figures, it has been suggested that the UK could be losing up to £72bn each year from fraud.[175] KPMG

165 Fraud Advisory Panel, 'Facts and figures' <http://www.fraudadvisorypanel.org/new/fraud-facts-and-figures.php>, accessed on 28 November 2011.

166 Home Office, 'Joining forces to fight fraud' <http://www.homeoffice.gov.uk/media-centre/news/fighting-fraud>, accessed on 9 November 2011

167 Home Office, 'Fighting fraud together – the strategic plan to reduce fraud' <http://www.homeoffice.gov.uk/publications/agencies-public-bodies/nfa/fighting-fraud-tog/fighting-fraud-together?view=Binary>, accessed on 9 November 2011.

168 Ibid.

169 Ibid.

170 [Anon.], 'IMF chief warns of a "lost decade" for global economy' <http://www.bbc.co.uk/news/business-15649985>, accessed on 9 November 2011.

171 For more information on the debt crisis, see: A. Alexander, 'The cure that could kill off any recovery' <http://www.dailymail.co.uk/debate/article-2059155/European-debt-crisis-The-cure-kill-recovery.html>, accessed on 9 November 2011.

172 The International Consortium of Investigative Journalists, The Panama Papers, <https://panamapapers.icij.org>, accessed on 22 August 2016.

173 House of Commons Select Committee, 'MPs report on the system for enforcing consumer law' <http://www.parliament.uk/business/committees/committees-a-z/commons-select/public-accounts-committee/news/consumer-protection-report/>, accessed on 9 November 2011

174 National Fraud Authority, 'Fraud focus' <http://www.homeoffice.gov.uk/publications/agencies-public-bodies/nfa/fraud-focus-newsletter/fraud-focus-feb11?view=Binary>, accessed on 9 November 2011; for more information on the cost of fraud, see: Home Office, 'Fraud costs the UK over £38 billion, says the National Fraud Authority' <http://www.homeoffice.gov.uk/agencies-public-bodies/nfa/news/press-releases/fraud-costs-over-38-billion/>, accessed on 24 January 2012

175 North East Fraud Forum, *Fraud Review* <http://www.northeastfraudforum.co.uk/documents/FraudReview.pdf>, accessed on 12 February 2012

indicated that the amount of UK fraud in 2015 was £732m.[176] Financial crime increases during times of economic stress,[177] and this provides further evidence that these figures could still continue to increase if action is not taken soon.[178] This is further demonstrated by CIFAS stating that the UK is still vulnerable to fraud, despite the placement of current strategies.[179]

13.2.5 A culture of whistle-blowers?

Following the inception of the SFO, a number of commentators have argued that the new agency would reduce fraud,[180] thus putting greater pressure on the SFO to 'get tough'[181] over the next 12 months. However, with an 80 per cent conviction rate increase documented in April 2011, the SFO may be responding to this pressure.[182] The SFO has introduced a revised reporting regime[183] that aims to 'unmask fraud and bribery'[184] via a 'confidential hotline'[185] and an online form[186] that offers to protect the identities of whistle-blowers. However, this regime has been argued to be 'the repackaging of a service that has always existed'.[187] Richard Alderman, the former SFO Director, was particularly positive

176 O. Griffin, 'Fraud cost UK £732m last year' <http://economia.icaew.com/news/january-2016/fraud-cost-uk-732m-in-2015-kpmg-says>, accessed on 1 May 2016

177 [Anon.], 'Credit crunch fuels fraud cases' <http://news.bbc.co.uk/1/hi/business/7375091.stm>, accessed on 9 November 2011

178 For more information on fraud and the credit crunch, see: N. Dorn, 'The governance of securities: ponzi finance, regulatory convergence, credit crunch' (2010) *Brit. J. Criminol.*, 50(1), 23–45; A. Peters, 'Alarming increase in insurance fraud' <http://www.prweb.com/releases/2009/05/prweb2399334.htm>, accessed on 9 November 2011

179 CIFAS, 'Fraud rises' <http://www.cifas.org.uk/fraud_rises_novembereleven>, accessed on 28 November 2011.

180 Centre for Counter Fraud Studies, 'The financial cost of UK public sector fraud' <http://www.port.ac.uk/departments/academic/icjs/centreforcounterfraudstudies/documents/filetodownload,113045,en.pdf>, accessed on 9 November 2011.

181 R. Tomasic, 'The financial crisis and the haphazard pursuit of financial crime' *JFC* 2011, 18(1), 13–14.

182 Serious Fraud Office, 'Serious Fraud Office – more effective and costing less' <http://www.sfo.gov.uk/press-room/latest-press-releases/press-releases-2011/serious-fraud-office---more-effective-and-costing-less.aspx>, accessed on 18 February 2012.

183 Serious Fraud Office, 'SFO Confidential – giving us information in confidence' <http://www.sfo.gov.uk/fraud/sfo-confidential---giving-us-information-in-confidence.aspx>, accessed on 9 November 2011.

184 S. Dinneen, 'SFO: help us to unmask fraud' <http://www.cityam.com/news-and-analysis/sfo-help-us-unmask-fraud>, accessed on 10 March 2012.

185 Serious Fraud Office, 'How to report information to the Serious Fraud Office' <http://www.sfo.gov.uk/fraud/sfo-confidential---giving-us-information-in-confidence/how-to-report-information-to-the-serious-fraud-office.aspx> accessed on 9 November 2011.

186 Serious Fraud Office, 'SFO Confidential – provide information in confidence' <https://report.sfo.gov.uk/sfo-confidential---provide-information-in-confidence.aspx>, accessed on 9 November 2011.

187 S. Hart, 'SFO tells whistleblowers: it's good to talk' <http://www.globalregulatoryenforcementlawblog.com/2011/11/articles/government-investigations/sfo-tells-whistleblowers-its-good-to-talk/>, accessed on 9 November 2011.

about this new regime and how it would be put to use: 'I want whistle-blowers to feel comfortable about it and use SFO Confidential to help flush out fraud.'[188]

This was seen as a 'step in the right direction'[189] that would allow a greater amount of financial intelligence to be collected, resulting in an increase in fraud convictions. However, it is difficult to determine whether or not this regime will be branded a success, and whether fraud convictions will increase. Similarities have been drawn[190] between the new SFO confidential reporting regime and the measures available in the USA under the Dodd–Frank Act.[191] The provisions from this act allow a whistle-blower to be awarded up to 30 per cent of any fines, over a set amount, that are paid as a result of the provided information. When comparison is drawn, the question must be asked: Will whistle-blowers act selflessly in the UK? Or will this unincentivised regime simply take up valuable SFO time and resources?[192] The success of this service will surely have a large impact on whether or not the SFO is reformed. Of course, and a positive step in this direction, the implementation of the Enterprise and Regulatory Reform Act 2013 required that all whistle-blowing 'disclosures' be made in the public interest, so as to afford employees the protection under the Public Interest Disclosure Act 1998. The FCA also boasts fraud reporting and financial intelligence obligations for the regulated sector under the legally binding *FCA Handbook*,[193] as well as having a specific online form for those who have suffered shares fraud.[194] However, the various options available for reporting fraud can cause a certain degree of 'confusion and delay',[195] which could arguably be damaging to the entire reporting process.

188 Serious Fraud Office, 'Blow the whistle! New route for insiders to unmask fraud and bribery' <http://www.sfo.gov.uk/press-room/latest-press-releases/press-releases-2011/blow-the-whistle!-new-route-for-insiders-to-unmask-fraud-and-bribery-.aspx>, accessed on 9 November 2011.

189 C. Binham, 'SFO launches whistleblowing hotline' <http://www.ft.com/cms/s/0/11d2c6f6-04ae-11e1-91d9-00144feabdc0.html#axzz1dEFBIjt9>, accessed on 9 November 2011.

190 Ibid.

191 For more information on the Dodd–Frank Act, see: 'Clifford Chance, Dodd–Frank Wall Street reform and consumer protection act' <http://www.cliffordchance.com/content/dam/cliffordchance/PDF/Dodd-Frank_Memo_Revised_August.pdf>, accessed on 9 November 2011.

192 J. Meek, 'UK fraud whistleblowers need bounties, lawyers say' <http://www.risk.net/operational-risk-and-regulation/news/2125352/uk-fraud-whistleblowers-bounties-lawyers>, accessed on 13 March 2012.

193 Financial Services Authority, *FSA Handbook SYSC 6.3* <http://fsahandbook.info/FSA/html/handbook/SYSC/6/3>, accessed on 24 January 2012.

194 Financial Services Authority, 'Unauthorised firms reporting form' <http://www.fsa.gov.uk/Pages/Doing/Regulated/Law/Alerts/form.shtml>, accessed on 28 November 2011.

195 N. Ryder, *Financial Crime in the 21st Century: Law and Policy* (Edward Elgar Publishing Limited 2011) 137.

13.2.6 The future of fraud regulators

Fraud is developing to such a level that it is becoming increasingly difficult to combat.[196] In particular, vast opportunities have been created for fraudsters from the increasing use of internet banking and online shopping. Even though certain offences may be covered, from a financial point of view, through insurance companies or financial institutions, there is, ultimately, always a 'primary victim' of fraud.[197] The Fraud Advisory Panel has introduced 'indicators' to help employers to recognise fraud in a bid to prevent it.[198] However, fraud can be far subtler and more difficult to spot. While organisations such as OLAF and the NFA may be actively taking steps to counter fraud, in reality the picture is a different one. With fraudsters pushing boundaries to continue punishing and testing the private and public markets, it is difficult to see how fraud can be slowed down to such an extent that it could eventually be completely eradicated. It is also difficult to consider whether the NCA would really have as much of an impact on fraud as the government believes, or whether the SFO and other fraud regulatory bodies will retain their enforcement powers and render the NCA useless. Some firms are offering fraud-prevention services to help institutions and companies to combat fraud, even going as far as to state that the use of their service will equate to a 40 per cent reduction in lost revenue.[199] The difficulty seems to be that fraudsters are moving forward at a great pace, yet the process of introducing new legislation is painfully slow. It could be argued that because legislation takes time to be implemented, even with the NCA in place, new fraud may become difficult to combat. The reporting regimes in place that focus on 'whistle-blowers' are old and unincentivised, making it difficult to provide arguments for their complete success. The NCA may require even more power to tackle fraud in certain areas should fraud develop in specific ways, particularly in relation to cross-border fraud or fraud that did not originate within the UK, where 'individuals and/or public/private sector entities may be defrauded outside the UK or in internet transactions where, in the absence of a specified legal place of contract, it may be difficult to determine the location of the offence'.[200] One thing is for certain: the NCA will need to be dynamic to successfully adapt to constant variations in national and

196 K. Harrison and N. Ryder, *The Law Relating to Financial Crime in the UK* (Routledge, 2013) Ch. 4.

197 J. Burrows and M. Levi, 'Measuring the impact of fraud in the UK: a conceptual and empirical journey' (2008) *Brit. J. Criminol.*, 48(3), 304.

198 Fraud Advisory Panel, 'An introduction to fraud indicators' <http://www.fraudadvisorypanel.org/new/pdf_show.php?id=170>, accessed on 17 November 2011.

199 PKF Accountants and Business Advisers, 'The financial cost of fraud – what data from around the world shows' <http://www.pkf.co.uk/web/pkf.nsf/0/F459DDCCE5269C818025792D002A830E/$FILE/The%20Financial%20Cost%20of%20Fraud_WEB.pdf>, accessed on 9 November 2011.

200 J. Burrows and M. Levi, 'Measuring the impact of fraud in the UK: a conceptual and empirical journey' (2008) *Brit. J. Criminol.*, 48(3), 307–308.

global markets. A fraud investigation can be damaging to a company or individual's reputation, and a successful conviction would be even more devastating.

13.3 The future of money-laundering regulation in the UK

13.3.1 Financial services regulation and money laundering

Money laundering and financial crime have increased in times of economic hardship.[201] The failures of firms have resulted in an increased exposure to money laundering and a loss of confidence in the UK financial market.[202] BCCI, often described as having a criminal structure akin to an 'elaborate corporate spiders web',[203] was accused of being involved in many different forms of criminal activity. The involvement of money laundering in this scandal harmed and disfigured the financial services industry and jeopardised both market and public confidence.[204] Consequently, it has been argued that global capitalism has shown it is riddled with the 'shifting sands of risk and uncertainty',[205] and it is therefore no surprise that money laundering, in particular, greatly harms the financial services sector. This is because 'organized crime groups tend to invest a great deal of energy in diversifying money laundering procedures, from primitive to very complex schemes. Money laundering is the necessary interface between lawful and illicit markets.'[206]

This lack of public confidence could also arguably transfer to the methods by which the financial services are regulated. The mistakes made by the FSA, contributing to the failure of Northern Rock,[207] and resulting in it being nationalised and subsequently purchased by Virgin Money,[208] harmed public confidence. The bank was allowed to continue to make large losses, after the initial loss of

201 [Anon.], 'Credit crunch fuels fraud cases' <http://news.bbc.co.uk/1/hi/business/7375091.stm>, accessed on 9 November 2011.

202 Financial Services Authority Consultation Paper, *Financial Crime: A Guide for Firms* <http://www.fsa.gov.uk/pubs/cp/cp11_12.pdf>, accessed on 30 November 2011.

203 J. Kerry and H. Brown, 'The BCCI Affair' <http://info.publicintelligence.net/The-BCCI-Affair.pdf>, accessed on 19 December 2011.

204 A. Srivastava, I. Mason, M. Simpson and M. Litt, 'Financial Crime' (2011) *COB*, 86(May), 3.

205 J. Gray, 'Lessons from the BCCI saga for the current accountability debate surrounding Northern Rock' (2008) *JIBLR*, 23(2), 43.

206 R. Barone and D. Masciandaro, 'Organised crime, money laundering and legal economy: theory and simulations' (2011) *EJL&E*, 32(1), 119.

207 For more information on Northern Rock, see: The European Money and Finance Forum, *The Failure of Northern Rock: A Multi-Dimensional Case Study* <http://www.suerf.org/download/studies/study20091.pdf>, accessed on 19 December 2011.

208 P. Inman, 'Northern Rock sale to Virgin Money leaves tax payer with £400m bill' <http://www.guardian.co.uk/business/2011/nov/17/northern-rock-virgin-money-taxpayer>, accessed on 11 January 2012; for more information on the winding up of Northern Rock, see: S. Loizou, 'The Investment Bank Special Administration regime 2011 – a helping hand?' (2012) *JIBLR*, 27(1), 1–3; J. Gray, 'Northern Rock shareholders' challenge to basis

£1.36bn,[209] leading to accusations of the FSA being unaccountable.[210] The FSA was described as 'confused and inadequate',[211] perhaps falling in line with the Coalition Government's intentions to reform the organisation. This does not play well with public confidence, when considering that the FSA previously had a taxpayer-funded budget of £492m.[212] The 2015/2016 budget for the FCA was £479m.[213] The FCA has attempted to take a tough stance on issues such as financial crime, perhaps suggesting that it is trying to win back the lost confidence. This is demonstrated through the fine of £5.6m on the Royal Bank of Scotland Group for failing to have 'adequate systems and controls in place to prevent breaches of UK financial sanctions'.[214] Despite all of this, it still must be considered that

> whereas it did not fully live up to its pre-crisis reputation as a world-class regulator, the FSA remains a sophisticated, expert organization that has been operating at the highest levels in an intensely demanding field in which respect is not easily won.[215]

It is arguable that if the NCA creates a single all-powerful agency, public confidence will need to be upheld to ensure that it is able to operate to its full potential.

13.3.2 The UK's FBI and the Financial Intelligence Unit

It was suggested that the FSA would be merged with the other regulatory agencies to create a new and all-powerful 'FBI'-style agency,[216] the CPMA – now renamed the FCA.[217] Although SOCA was the closest agency that the UK had to a single

of compensation in nationalisation considered in High Court and Court of Appeal' (2009) *JFR&C*, 17(4), 467–475.

209 P. Aldrick, 'Northern Rock losses grow by more than £500m' <http://www.telegraph.co.uk/finance/newsbysector/banksandfinance/5710699/Northern-Rock-losses-grow-by-more-than-500m.html>, accessed on 19 December 2011.

210 House of Commons, 'Written evidence' <http://www.publications.parliament.uk/pa/cm201012/cmselect/cmtreasy/857/857fwe183.htm>, accessed on 19 December 2011.

211 C. Conceicao and C. Ninan, 'Should the CPMA retain the power to prosecute market misconduct criminal offences?' (2010) 11 *JIBFL* 686.

212 Financial Services Authority, 'Facts and figures' <http://www.fsa.gov.uk/Pages/About/Media/Facts/index.shtml>, accessed on 19 December 2011.

213 FCA Business Plan 2015/16, <http://www.fca.org.uk/static/channel-page/business-plan/business-plan-2015-16.html>, accessed on 1 May 2016.

214 Financial Services Authority, *Annual Report 2010/11* <http://www.fsa.gov.uk/pubs/annual/ar10_11/ar10_11.pdf>, accessed on 30 November 2011.

215 E. Ferran, 'The break-up of the Financial Services Authority' (2011) *OJLS*, 31(3), 458.

216 M. Hughes and D. Gardham, 'National Crime Agency head will be most powerful officer in UK' <http://www.telegraph.co.uk/news/8564002/National-Crime-Agency-head-will-be-most-powerful-officer-in-UK.html>, accessed on 14 December 2011.

217 G. Baber, 'A new approach to financial regulation: a step in the correct direction?' (2012) *Comp. Law.*, 33(1), 3.

regulatory and law enforcement body, its website previously stated that 'SOCA is not the UK's FBI'.[218] As of October 2013, SOCA ceased to exist and the NCA became responsible 'for leading the UK's fight to cut serious and organised crime'.[219] The NCA plays a different role in relation to financial crime regulation, in the form of the FIU, a legal requirement under EU law.[220] The FIU 'receives, analyses and disseminates financial intelligence'[221] from SARs to combat financial crime.[222] The UK is also a member of the Egmont Group,[223] which allows the UK to receive financial intelligence from other members to aid anti-money-laundering and financial crime practice. It was previously stated that the SOCA business model will be reviewed, 'ensuring firm foundations are laid for the NCA'.[224] In an initial draft bill the FCA, the 'son of the FSA',[225] was cited as the 'rule-making body'.[226] This draft bill also provided an 'integrity' objective that allows the FCA to make rules that address the risks of money laundering, with the intention of preserving the 'soundness, stability and resilience of the financial system'.[227] However, it was initially unclear whether the FSA would partially exist, retaining some of its strong prosecution and enforcement powers. Clearly, had this been the case, it would have negatively impacted the creation of the FCA, because the criminal sanction powers would need to come from elsewhere.[228] Accordingly, it was stated that 'the FSA's current enforcement priorities cannot

218 Serious Organised Crime Agency, 'Myths and misunderstandings' <http://www.soca.gov.uk/about-soca/how-we-work/myths-and-misunderstandings>, accessed on 14 December 2011.

219 The Serious Organised Crime Agency closed in October 2013: <https://www.gov.uk/government/organisations/serious-organised-crime-agency>, accessed on 1 May 2016.

220 Article 31, Directive (EU) 2015/849 of the European Parliament and of the Council, of 20 May 2015 on the prevention of the use of the financial system for the purposes of money laundering or terrorist financing, amending Regulation (EU) No. 648/2012 of the European Parliament and of the Council.

221 Serious Organised Crime Agency, 'What is the Financial Intelligence Unit?' <http://www.soca.gov.uk/about-soca/the-uk-financial-intelligence-unit>, accessed on 15 February 2012.

222 NCA 'How SARs are used to detect crime', <http://www.nationalcrimeagency.gov.uk/about-us/what-we-do/economic-crime/ukfiu>, accessed on 1 May 2016.

223 Egmont Group, 'The Egmont Group of Financial Intelligence Units' <http://www.egmontgroup.org/>, accessed on 15 February 2012.

224 Serious Organised Crime Agency, 'Serious Organised Crime Agency – Annual Plan 2011/12' <http://www.soca.gov.uk/about-soca/how-we-work/new-approaches>, accessed on 14 December 2011.

225 [Anon.] 'Reform of financial regulation gathers pace with son of the FSA' (2011) *Co. L.N.*, 297, 1.

226 G. Baber, 'A new approach to financial regulation: a step in the correct direction?' (2012) *Comp. Law.*, 33(1), 9.

227 HM Treasury, 'A new approach to financial regulation: the blueprint for reform' <http://www.hm-treasury.gov.uk/d/consult_finreg__new_approach_blueprint.pdf>, accessed on 14 December 2011.

228 HMRC, 'Review of the Money Laundering Regulations 2007: the Government response' <http://www.hmrc.gov.uk/mlr/mlr-review.pdf>, accessed on 14 December 2011.

be dismissed as those of a moribund regulator'.[229] Although the Coalition Government was initially non-committal on the exact time scale for the reforms and creation of the FCA, a policy document suggested that 'further refinement' would be needed before the end of 2012.[230] It could also be argued that the FCA is still trying to win over those who had lost confidence in the FSA: '[T]he FCA will aspire to command the respect of consumers and of the firms it regulates.'[231] Creating one powerful regulatory FBI-style agency may provide a strong sense of certainty for regulated firms and consumers, as well as making it easier for the government to allocate future powers to combat financial crime in the future, particularly in relation to the gathering of financial intelligence. The major criticism is that an agency of this nature would leave nowhere to turn should it get things wrong.[232] This is even more important when considering the cross-border nature of money laundering. It could arguably be difficult for one single agency to counter money laundering on more than one front.

13.3.3 International money laundering regulation and best practices

> The stakes are higher than ever for compliance. Money launderers are increasingly turning their attention to jurisdictions with lax anti-money laundering laws as well as to mid size financial institutions.[233]

One of the major problems with money laundering on an international scale is the lack of a universal law to help in the battle against financial crime. Instead, international money laundering regulation holds 'best practices',[234] all requiring the mutual support of other members in its prevention methods. Problems are beginning to appear because of globalisation and the 'instantaneous transfer of capital flowing across borders, along with the liberalization of financial markets'.[235] The cross-border nature of money laundering and other financial crimes create a greater need for cooperation and awareness among national regulators. This is because of the relatively liberal view of the financial markets, through free market

229 [Anon.] Travers Smith RIG, 'FSA enforcement action: themes and trends' (2011) *COB*, 87(Jun), 1.

230 Financial Services Authority, 'The Financial Conduct Authority – approach to regulation' <http://www.fsa.gov.uk/pubs/events/fca_approach.pdf>, accessed on 19 December 2011.

231 Ibid.

232 E. Lomnicka, 'The reform of consumer credit in the UK' (2004) *JBL*, Jan, 143.

233 Oracle Financial Services, *Best Practices for Anti-Money Laundering (AML): System Selection and Implementation* <http://www.oracle.com/us/industries/financial-services/062008.pdf>, accessed on 15 February 2012.

234 FATF, 'International best practices: managing the Anti-Money Laundering and Counter-Terrorist Financing policy implications of voluntary tax compliance programmes' <http://www.fatf-gafi.org/dataoecd/59/45/46252382.pdf>, accessed on 15 February 2012.

235 M. Arnone and L. Borlini, 'International anti-money laundering programmes: empirical assessment and issues in criminal regulation' (2010) *JMLC*, 13(3), 227.

capitalism, that society boasts today. Although free market capitalism can be beneficial and creates a vast array of opportunities for businesses and individuals, it also creates opportunities for criminals:

> As importantly, the speed and relative case with which funds may be transferred across borders has intensified the degree of contact along its filaments. While the intent of this model of world society was to highlight 'legitimised' transnational contacts, it has become evident that this cobweb is conducive to spreading security threats emanating from nearly all parts of the globe, as well as being rather effective at hiding the spiders that lurk within it.[236]

Extending the Vienna Convention,[237] which targeted illicit finance from drug-related crimes, the Palermo Convention[238] began to target illicit financing from 'serious organised crime'. Developing from this, the UNCAC aims to help member states set up an effective legal framework against money laundering, as well as increasing knowledge and expertise to counter financial crime.[239] A European Initiative from the European Supervisory Authorities suggests that a joint committee should be created to meet every two months with the purpose of discussing 'cross-sectoral consistency regarding measures combating money laundering'.[240] The FATF actively campaigns against money laundering by providing the 'minimum standards'[241] for its members through the 40 recommendations.[242] The FATF issues ongoing compliance reports[243] as a means of judging how its members are developing and whether or not they are still at risk from money laundering. The FATF also accepts the need for the 'widest

236 J. Wiener, 'Money laundering: transnational criminals, globalization and the forces of "redomestication"' (1997) *JMLC*, 1(1), 51.

237 United Nations, 'Vienna Convention on the law of treaties' 1969, <http://www.ilsa.org/jessup/jessup11/basicmats/VCLT.pdf>, accessed on 15 February 2012.

238 United Nations, 'Convention against transnational organized crime' 2000, <http://www.uncjin.org/Documents/Conventions/dcatoc/final_documents_2/convention_eng.pdf>, accessed on 15 February 2012.

239 United Nations Office on Drugs and Crime, 'Objectives of the Global Programme against Money-Laundering, Proceeds of Crime and the Financing of Terrorism' <http://www.unodc.org/unodc/en/money-laundering/programme-objectives.html?ref=menuside>, accessed on 19 December 2011.

240 P. Snowdon, 'The new European supervisory structure' (2011) *COB*, 83(Feb), 24

241 N. Jensen and C. Png, 'Implementation of the FATF 40 + 9 Recommendations: a perspective from developing countries' (2011) *JMLC*, 14(2), 113.

242 Financial Action Task Force, 'The 40 Recommendations' <http://www.fatf-gafi.org/document/28/0,3746,en_32250379_32236920_33658140_1_1_1_1,00.html>, accessed on 14 December 2011.

243 Financial Action Task Force, 'Improving Global AML/CFT Compliance: on-going process 28 October 2011' <http://www.fatf-gafi.org/document/42/0,3746,en_32250379_32236992_48966698_1_1_1_1,00.html>, accessed on 19 December 2011.

possible range of legal assistance and exchange of information'.[244] This combined with other organisations, such as the World Bank and the IMF,[245] which also actively campaign to prevent money laundering, conceivably creates a quasi-global initiative. However, this also paints a relatively clear picture on an international level. If the NCA does not continue to allow thorough and complete cooperation between other money-laundering regulatory agencies, the international regime is likely to fail.

13.3.4 The risk-based approach and cost of compliance

Two of the major criticisms of the anti-money-laundering regime in the UK are arguably the risk-based approach and the increasing costs of complying with anti-money-laundering provisions. However, the need for a system based upon risk is evidenced by the introduction of the Wolfsberg Principles.[246] The FCA uses a risk-based approach to 'allocate resources on a cost effective basis'[247] in relation to organisations physically threatened by money laundering. An approach based on 'risk' determines whether a transaction is lawful and preserves the integrity of a company. This is important because 'one of the company's most valuable assets is its integrity'.[248] Even though 'risk has always been an integral part of anti-money laundering policy',[249] it is difficult to provide a blanket approach in classing the levels of risk for certain businesses. An approach of this nature could be acceptable when declaring organisations that work mostly in cash or directly with money as high risk, such as currency exchange offices and money transmitters.[250] The government attempted to tackle this problem by debating the inclusion of a 'de-minimis exception' or 'financial threshold' for small business, defined by business with a VAT exclusive turnover of below €15,000.[251] The reasoning behind this is related directly to the high compliance costs of staying

244 Financial Action Task Force Guidance Document, 'International Best Practices – Managing the Anti-Money Laundering and Counter-Terrorist Financing Policy Implications of Voluntary Tax Compliance Programmes' <http://www.fatf-gafi.org/dataoecd/59/45/46252382.pdf>, accessed on 19 December 2011.

245 N. Mugarura, 'The institutional framework against money laundering and its underlying predicate crimes' (2011) *JFR&C*, 19(2), 186–189.

246 The Wolfsberg Group, 'Guidance on a risk based approach for managing money laundering risks' <http://www.wolfsberg-principles.com/pdf/Wolfsberg_RBA_Guidance_(2006).pdf>, accessed on 5 February 2012.

247 A. Veng Mei Long, 'Anti-money laundering measures in the United Kingdom: a review of recent legislation and FSA's risk based approach' (2007) *Comp. Law.*, 28(2), 40.

248 A. Simonova, 'The risk based approach to anti-money laundering: problems and solutions' (2011) *JMLC*, 14(4), 352.

249 M. Van den Broek, 'The EU's preventive AML/CFT policy: asymmetrical harmonisation' (2011) *JMLC*, 14(2), 172.

250 HMRC, *Anti-Money Laundering Annual Report to Her Majesty's Treasury 2010–2011* <http://www.hmrc.gov.uk/mlr/anti-mlr-report.pdf>, accessed on 14 December 2011.

251 HMRC, 'Review of the Money Laundering Regulations 2007: the Government response' <http://www.hmrc.gov.uk/mlr/mlr-review.pdf>, accessed on 14 December 2011.

up to date with legislation and procedures, and at times having a money-laundering reporting officer trained. The effectiveness of such exceptions was debatable, and this reflects the decision that no small business is low risk. Therefore, by merely using a fixed monetary threshold for classifying risk in this way, greater opportunities could open up for those wishing to commit money laundering.[252] Other problems with the risk-based approach came with the definitions and classifications of the regime:

> Some firms did not have a robust approach to classifying the money laundering risk associated with their clients. For example, one wholesale small firm classified all its clients as low or medium risk, despite the fact that most of them were based in Eastern Europe, North Africa and the Middle East. Another firm's risk-assessment procedures provided that the compliance officer or money laundering reporting officer would determine the risk category for each client and would record the basis of the assessment for each client. However, a file review showed no evidence that risk assessments had actually been carried out.[253]

It has been argued that 'anything other than a risk-based approach would be inappropriate, ineffectively prescriptive and generally cumbersome'.[254] Despite this, it has been suggested that certain procedures that help determine the level of risk, such as Know Your Client, have led to those wishing to move funds illegally 'getting around' these requirements by creating false identities.[255]

Compliance costs are enforced as both ongoing and specific anti-money-laundering policy costs that range between £600 and £52,000.[256] These costs have been argued to be 'disproportionate', with some organisations having to pay up to £1.3m to comply with anti-money-laundering rules.[257] Some firms are also offering training[258] on the relevant policies and legislation, but all costs have

252 Ibid.

253 Financial Services Authority, 'Review of firms' implementation of a risk-based approach to anti-money laundering (AML)' <http://www.fsa.gov.uk/pubs/other/jmlsg_guidance.pdf>, accessed on 19 December 2011.

254 HM Treasury, 'Review of the Money Laundering Regulations: summary of the call for evidence' <http://www.hm-treasury.gov.uk/d/mlr2007_summaryofevidence.pdf>, accessed on 14 December 2011.

255 A. Haynes, 'Are the anti-laundering laws failing?' (2011) 8 *JIBFL* 488.

256 Financial Services Authority, 'Financial crime: a guide for firms' <http://www.fsa.gov.uk/pubs/cp/cp11_12.pdf>, accessed on 19 December 2011.

257 [Anon.], '"Disproportionate" money laundering compliance rules cost big firms up to £1.3m' <http://www.legalfutures.co.uk/regulation/solicitors/disproporionate-money-laundering-compliance-rules-costs-big-firms-up-to-1-3m>, accessed on 15 February 2012.

258 SWAT UK, 'Anti-money laundering training and compliance' <http://www.swat.co.uk/Compliance/MoneyLaundering/MoneyLaunderingSupportAnOverview/tabid/289/Default.aspx?utm_source=WebButton-Compliance-AML&utm_medium=WebButton-Compliance-AML&utm_campaign=WebButton-Compliance-AML>, accessed on 19 December 2011.

some effect on business.[259] It is difficult to determine whether or not the NCA or the FCA will reduce compliance costs, or create relief for smaller firms to help them bear the burden of complying with anti-money-laundering legislation. Although the reduction of compliance costs was a key aim of previous anti-money-laundering strategies,[260] it is particularly challenging to determine whether it has been successful. Firms and organisations are still paying large fees in fear of the financial and reputation consequences that could arise from not doing so. Perhaps larger organisations will pay almost any price to uphold their reputation. The problem is the effect this has on smaller businesses that simply cannot afford to pay the costs. A financial threshold, on paper, would solve this problem; however, it is difficult to argue that money-laundering risk can be determined simply by turnover. Compliance costs are now calculated in relation to the size of each firm.[261] It is therefore arguable that steps are being made in the right direction to ensure that smaller firms are not adversely affected by high compliance costs.

13.3.5 The future of anti-money-laundering regulators

It is particularly important to note that money laundering has a great effect on economic growth and business.[262] This is because criminals are becoming increasingly 'agile at taking advantage of illegal opportunities from the economic downturn'.[263] The development of 'digital and electronic money'[264] has created a vast array of opportunities for those wishing to launder illicit assets. The need for criminals to be able to launder the proceeds of crime from illegal opportunities is essential: '[T]he stolen assets of a corrupt public official are useless unless they are placed, layered, and integrated into the global financial network in a manner that does not raise suspicion.'[265] It is difficult to tell the full extent of money laundering and how much damage it has done over the last few years. This is particularly

259 FATF, 'Anti-money laundering and terrorist financing measures and financial inclusion' <http://www.fatf-gafi.org/dataoecd/62/26/48300917.pdf>, accessed on 14 December 2011.

260 HM Treasury, 'Anti-Money Laundering Strategy – October 2004' <http://webarchive.nationalarchives.gov.uk/+/http://www.hm-treasury.gov.uk/media/D57/97/D579755E-BCDC-D4B3-19632628BD485787.pdf>, accessed on 25 February 2012.

261 Financial Services Authority, 'Financial crime: a guide for firms' <http://www.fsa.gov.uk/pubs/cp/cp11_12.pdf>, accessed on 19 December 2011.

262 Financial Action Task Force, 'Money laundering FAQ' <http://www.fatf-gafi.org/document/29/0,3746,en_32250379_32235720_33659613_1_1_1_1,00.html>, accessed on 19 December 2011.

263 Home Office, 'Extending our reach: a comprehensive approach to tackling serious organized crime' <http://www.soca.gov.uk/about-soca/how-we-work/new-approaches>, accessed on 14 December 2011.

264 S. Ramage, 'Digital money, electronic fraud, new regulations and the old money laundering regulations' (2011) *Crim. Law.*, 200, 1–3.

265 Financial Action Task Force, 'Laundering the proceeds of corruption' <http://www.fatf-gafi.org/dataoecd/31/13/48472713.pdf>, accessed on 14 December 2011

relevant when considering the loss in consumer and public confidence as a result of financial scandals.

While SOCA became redundant in October 2013, the FSA was 'rebranded' into the FCA but continued to operate under the FSA banner until 2013.[266] The challenges from the risk-based approach and compliance costs will also pose further hurdles to the development of the NCA. This, combined with the arguments against creating a single FBI-style agency, could be its inevitable downfall. Outside the UK, it could also be seen that a lack of cooperation could result in the beginning of the failure of global regulatory money-laundering incentives. The difficulties of ascertaining complete cooperation between different states and countries could be burdensome, and therefore it is imperative that the NCA is able to address this issue.

13.4 The future of bribery and corruption regulation in the UK

13.4.1 Bribery and corruption – 'a major brake on economic development'[267]

Bribery and corruption are arguably at the forefront of most financial crime incidents. Fraud and money laundering often involve corruption when attempting to conceal the proceeds of unlawful activities. This is because 'corruption is a method of shielding illegal activities from authorities'.[268] Bribery and corruption are therefore equally, if not more, damaging to the economy than other forms of financial crime:

> Bribery and corruption are damaging to democratic institutions and the governance of corporations. They discourage investment and distort international competitive conditions. In particular, the diversion of funds through corrupt practices undermines attempts by citizens to achieve higher levels of economic, social and environmental welfare, and it impedes efforts to reduce poverty. Enterprises have an important role to play in combating these practices.[269]

266 HM Treasury, 'A new approach to financial regulation: securing stability, protecting consumers' <http://www.hm-treasury.gov.uk/d/fin_fs_bill_policy_document_jan2012.pdf>, accessed on 15 February 2012; and Financial Services Act 2012.

267 Business Anti-Corruption Portal, 'UK public and private anti-corruption initiatives' <http://www.business-anti-corruption.com/anti-corruption-initiatives/partner-initiatives/united-kingdom/>, accessed on 18 January 2012.

268 M. Vere Van Koppen, C. J. De Poot, E. R. Kleemans and P. Nieuwbeerta, 'Criminal trajectories in organized crime' (2010) *Brit. J. Criminol.*, 50(1), 108–109.

269 OECD Guidelines, *OECD Guidelines for Multinational Enterprises – 2011 Edition* <http://www.oecd.org/dataoecd/43/29/48004323.pdf>, accessed on 10 March 2012.

This is why corruption can be referred to as the 'greatest single bane of our society today'.[270] When considering the costs and benefits of complying with other financial crime legislation, such as money laundering, firms are often afraid of the consequences of not complying and this, therefore, creates an additional 'fear factor'. However, it has been argued that 'firms should be cautious but not afraid of anti-corruption law'.[271]

Corruption can be involved in almost any, if not all, sectors of the economy. However, it could be argued that corruption is more likely to occur during particularly 'lucrative' business transactions and deals. This diversification is particularly demonstrated through the 2022 World Cup bid by Qatar, which has been littered with accusations of bribery and corruption.[272] Even more recently, corruption accusations within the governing body of football (FIFA) have led to suggestions that the corruption law in its home country, Switzerland, requires updating.[273] The arrests of Sepp Blatter and 14 other executives were carried out by the Swiss Police in dawn raids in May 2015 at the request of the US Government.[274] The cooperation between international agencies was crucial in staging the raids, providing further evidence as to how international co-operation is needed to combat financial crime. The actions that are being taken by corporations and organisations are certainly pointing towards the belief that 'bribery has no place in British businesses'.[275] Perhaps this reflects the benefits of ethical trading, particularly relating to building trustful relationships with clients, which has been argued to directly increase sales.[276] In 2011, and in relation to other countries, the UK was listed as 16th on the list of the most 'clean countries',[277] perhaps reflecting the changes that have come with the enactment

270 Transparency International UK, 'Corruption data' <http://www.transparency.org.uk/corruption-data#importanceofproblem>, accessed on 18 January 2012.

271 A. Durant, 'Gift horses' (2011) *LNB News* 11/07/2011 76.

272 [Anon.], 'Qatar could lose 2022 World Cup if corruption allegations proved, hints president Sepp Blatter' <http://www.telegraph.co.uk/sport/football/8525363/Qatar-could-lose-2022-World-Cup-if-corruption-allegations-proved-hints-Fifa-president-Sepp-Blatter.html>, accessed on 18 January 2012.

273 C. Bandel, 'FIFA inspires Swiss corruption law changes after bribery scandal' <http://www.businessweek.com/news/2012-01-19/fifa-inspires-swiss-corruption-law-changes-after-bribery-scandal.html>, accessed on 25 January 2012.

274 L. Siciliano and S. Jamieson, 'Fifa: a timeline of corruption – in 90 seconds' <http://www.telegraph.co.uk/football/2016/03/22/fifa-a-timeline-of-corruption---in-90-seconds/>, accessed on 1 May 2016.

275 UK Trade and Investment, 'Bribery and corruption' <http://www.ukti.gov.uk/export/howwehelp/overseasbusinessrisk/briberycorruption.html>, accessed on 18 January 2012.

276 Business Link, 'Ethical trading' <http://www.businesslink.gov.uk/bdotg/action/detail?itemId=1074299810&r.i=1074300562&r.l1=1073861169&r.l2=1073858854&r.l3=1074297694&r.s=sc&r.t=RESOURCES&type=RESOURCES>, accessed on 18 January 2012.

277 Transparency International, *Corruption Perception Index 2011* <http://cpi.transparency.org/cpi2011/results/>, accessed on 25 January 2012.

of the Bribery Act 2010. In 2015, the UK was listed as 10th,[278] perhaps evidencing the UK's efforts against financial crime.

13.4.2 The need for action – the Bribery Act 2010

The previous bribery and corruption laws came from various sources. It is therefore no surprise that modernisation was required to clarify the patchwork of common law and statutory offences.[279] Soon after coming into existence, the first conviction under the Bribery Act 2010 resulted in a court clerk[280] receiving a penalty fine and a six-year jail term.[281] However, this conviction will have 'little bearing on how complex overseas bribery cases will be dealt with',[282] because it does not touch upon the international jurisdiction of regulatory bodies. Instead, the SFO will now be 'under increased pressure to start its own action under the Bribery Act 2010'.[283] Guidance[284] has been issued in many forms prior to the implication of this statute, although some areas have not been clarified. In particular, the debate on the thin line between what is and what is not a bribe still awaits further clarification, something that may not be stated until relevant cases are brought by the SFO. It is still difficult to determine whether some actions are 'appropriate', such as taking a client to a sporting event, or whether this in

278 Transparency International, *Corruption Perception Index 2015* <http://www.transparency.org/cpi2015>, accessed on 1 May 2016.

279 Freshfields Bruckhaus Deringer, *Law Commission Report on Reforming UK Bribery Law* <http://www.freshfields.com/publications/pdfs/2009/feb09/24946.pdf>, accessed on 25 January 2012; for more information on the previous bribery and corruption laws, see: CMS Cameron McKenna, 'A Guide to existing bribery and corruption offences in England and Wales – April 2010' <http://www.cms-cmck.com/Hubbard.FileSystem/files/Publication/efae7aa0-f294-4801-b7e5-5ab4ed6b2675/Presentation/PublicationAttachment/9a8eda32-9471-412e-b1c8-32c27841fb3d/A%20guide%20to%20existing%20bribery%20and%20corruption%20offences%20in%20England%20and%20Wales_v2.pdf>, accessed on 25 January 2012.

280 *R v Munir Patel* (2011) Unreported and O. Bowcott, 'Court clerk becomes first person charged under the Bribery Act' <http://www.guardian.co.uk/law/2011/aug/31/court-clerk-charged-bribery-act>, accessed on 25 January 2012.

281 L. Roberts, 'Six year jail term for first person convicted under Bribery Act' <http://www.anticorruptionblog.com/uk-bribery-act/six-year-jail-term-for-first-person-convicted-under-the-uk-bribery-act/>, accessed on 25 January 2012; for more information on the first conviction under the Bribery Act 2010, see: E. O'Shea, 'First conviction proves Bribery Act has sharp teeth' (2011) *LNB News* 28/11/2011 43.

282 R. Kay and E. Osborne, 'UK Bribery Act first conviction – a damp squib?' <http://www.globalregulatoryenforcementlawblog.com/2011/10/articles/government-investigations/uk-bribery-act-first-conviction-a-damp-squib/>, accessed on 25 January 2012.

283 R. Kay, 'UK Bribery Act – first prosecution' <http://www.globalregulatoryenforcementlawblog.com/2011/09/articles/securities-litigation/uk-bribery-act-first-prosecution/>, accessed on 25 January 2012.

284 For more information on the use of guidance on the Bribery Act 2010, see: OECD, 'OECD statement on guidance for the Bribery Act' <http://www.oecd.org/document/39/0,3746,en_21571361_44315115_47468583_1_1_1_1,00.html>, accessed on 1 February 2012.

itself would be a bribe under the Bribery Act 2010.[285] Although the specifics of this statute are yet to be confirmed, the implications on the regulatory bodies that combat bribery and corruption are incredibly important; after all, 'any legislation is only as good as its enforcement'.[286] It is, therefore, essential that the interpretation of the Bribery Act 2010 results in a successful precedent set for future cases, as failure to do so could render the 'far reaching' powers under this statute largely ineffective.

In addition, the deficiencies identified with the s.7 offence of 'failing to prevent bribery' make it difficult to measure the direct success of the act. Ernst and Young comment that:

> After more than four years of debate, speculation and expectation since the Bribery Act came into force, Section 7 has been cited in three completed cases in the second half of 2015. While none of these cases provide extensive precedents of how Section 7 will be applied by the courts, the question of whether the Bribery Act has teeth is answered.[287]

13.4.3 Anti-bribery and corruption agencies in the UK

Although there are several different organisations that play a role in the fight against bribery and corruption,[288] the SFO and the FCA are the most important contenders. It is imperative that the SFO, as the 'principal enforcer of the Bribery Act 2010',[289] 'steps forward in anti-corruption measures, pushing the legislation to its limits'.[290] The aura of uncertainty that surrounds the SFO as a result of the introduction of the NCA does not bode well for this. This lack of certainty makes it difficult to determine where boundaries and jurisdictions will lie. However, Richard Alderman (the former SFO Director) influenced and developed the financial intelligence function of the SFO,[291] as well as clarifying that, even though

285 [Anon.], 'UK Bribery Act – practical guidance' <http://www.globalregulatoryenforcementlawblog.com/2011/02/articles/securities-litigation/uk-bribery-act-practical-guidance/>, accessed on 25 January 2012.

286 R. Alexander, 'The Bribery Act 2010 in force: an opportunity to be taken' (2011) *Comp. Law.*, 32(12), 353.

287 Ernst and Young Bribery Digest Special Edition – February 2016 <http://www.ey.com/Publication/vwLUAssets/EY-UK-Bribery-Digest-special-edition-February-2016/$FILE/EY-UK-Bribery-Digest-special-edition-February-2016.pdf>, accessed on 1 May 2016.

288 Business Anti-Corruption Portal, 'UK public and private anti-corruption initiatives' <http://www.business-anti-corruption.com/anti-corruption-initiatives/partner-initiatives/united-kingdom/>, accessed on 25 January 2012.

289 E. Davison, 'The principal enforcer' (2011) *LNB News* 08/02/2011 58.

290 Serious Fraud Office, 'Transparency International Anti-Bribery training launch – how effective is anti-bribery training?' <http://www.sfo.gov.uk/about-us/our-views/director's-speeches/speeches-2012/transparency-international-anti-bribery-training-launch---how-effective-is-anti-bribery-training.aspx>, accessed on 18 January 2012.

291 C. Monteith, 'Bribery Act 2010: Part 3: Enforcement' (2011) *Crim. L.R.*, 2, 119–120.

the ECC will not be undertaking the type of the work the SFO does, the SFO is very committed to helping the ECC.[292] The SFO seems to be setting up links to save itself, such as by 'working with business, not against',[293] and ensuring that it is able to use the new powers that it has been given under the Bribery Act 2010:

> First of all we engage with corporations on what is needed to bring about a real anti corruption culture in their organisations. This helps to promote and support ethical business activity. There will of course be those who have no intention of bringing about that sort of culture and so the other part of our activity concerns the work we are doing in identifying and bringing those individuals and corporations to court.[294]

The FSA has also played an important and active role in combating bribery and corruption. Before the introduction of the Bribery Act 2010, the FSA fined Willis Ltd for making payments to 'win business'[295] that totalled £27m.[296]

This shows that the FSA was 'flexing its muscles' in relation to bribery and corruption enforcement. This is arguably due to the enactment of the Financial Services Act 2012,[297] which announced the 'rebranding' of the FSA as the FCA, with an overarching aim to restore confidence in the UK financial system.[298] Perhaps the regulatory failure of the FSA, which contributed to the financial crisis, has created an aura of jealousy and retribution, which is pushing the FSA to 'clear its reputation' before the regulatory landscape changes. If the Bribery Act 2010 was able to work retrospectively, this incident may have been dealt with by the SFO. Suggestions have been made that the FCA would look into bribery in

292 Serious Fraud Office, 'Financial Crime Conference' <http://www.sfo.gov.uk/about-us/our-views/director's-speeches/speeches-2011/british-bankers-association.aspx>, accessed on 18 January 2012.

293 C. Monteith, 'Bribery Act 2010: Part 3: Enforcement' (2011) *Crim. L.R.*, 2, 114–116.

294 Serious Fraud Office, 'Financial Crime Conference' <http://www.sfo.gov.uk/about-us/our-views/director's-speeches/speeches-2011/british-bankers-association.aspx>, accessed on 18 January 2012.

295 Financial Services Authority, 'FSA fines Willis Limited £6.895 million for anti-bribery and corruption systems and controls failings' <http://www.fsa.gov.uk/pages/Library/Communication/PR/2011/066.shtml>, accessed on 25 January 2012.

296 Financial Services Authority, 'Willis Limited – Final Notice' <www.fsa.gov.uk/pubs/final/willis_ltd.pdf>, accessed on 25 January 2012.

297 HM Treasury, 'A new approach to financial regulation: securing stability, protecting consumers' <http://www.hm-treasury.gov.uk/d/fin_fs_bill_policy_document_jan2012.pdf>, accessed on 18 February 2012; Financial Services Bill (2012–2013) [278].

298 G. Baber, 'A new approach to financial regulation: a step in the correct direction?' (2012) *Comp. Law.*, 33(1), 6.

the banking sector.[299] However, because the SFO is the named enforcer[300] of the Bribery Act 2010, it is difficult to determine what direct role the FCA will play in countering bribery and corruption.

It has been argued that the SFO will only take on an extra '1–2 cases per year that go to court'[301] because of the Bribery Act 2010. This figure does not take into account the greater number of investigations that the SFO will hold because of the Bribery Act 2010,[302] and it is therefore not unreasonable to expect the true figure to be higher than this. Subsequently, many cases may have to be settled outside of court. However, it is difficult to determine whether or not the SFO would actually have the power to combat bribery and corruption, or whether this would transform into additional or fewer convictions. An alternative argument could be that the legislation has 'hit the ground running' and so reduced bribery and corruption to the extent that only a limited number of cases per year that go to court actually occur. One thing is for certain: 'Whether we have an SFO, an ECA, or some other animal, that organisation must have the tools to apply the new law.'[303] This is also imperative to the survival of the global initiatives that tackle bribery and corruption. Failure to hold the correct jurisdiction or power to apply the far-reaching rules of the Bribery Act 2010 could render a regulator virtually obsolete. In addition to the above, it has been suggested that amendments to the land registry to show the beneficial ownership of properties and unexplained wealth orders should be introduced to combat financial crime.[304] In addition, EU Directive 2014/95, to be introduced in the UK by December 2016, provides that certain companies with more than 500 employees will be required to comment upon bribery and corruption issues within their management reports. The writer predicts that these will be 'hot topics' over the coming years.

13.4.4 The risk of overseas corruption

The risk of corruption on a global level has been widely recognised.[305] Trading overseas can make it easier to hide illegal transactions from multi-jurisdiction-based organisations. This is because some of the businesses may not have representatives that are physically present in all aspects of a business deal, making it difficult to contain corruption, particularly if the country or jurisdiction is

299 R. Kay and T. Webley, 'FSA to investigate bribery in the banking sector' <http://www.globalregulatoryenforcementlawblog.com/2011/07/articles/government-investigations/fsa-to-investigate-bribery-in-the-banking-sector/>, accessed on 25 January 2012.

300 E. Davison, 'The principal enforcer' (2011) *LNB News* 08/02/2011 58.

301 C. Monteith, 'Bribery Act 2010: Part 3: Enforcement' (2011) *Crim. L.R.*, 2, 119–120.

302 Ibid.

303 M. Raphael, 'Be careful what you wish for' (2011) 161 *NLJ* 524.

304 Home Office, 'Biggest reforms to money laundering regime in over a decade' <https://www.gov.uk/government/news/biggest-reforms-to-money-laundering-regime-in-over-a-decade>, accessed on 1 May 2016.

305 Transparency International, *Corruption Perception Index 2015* <http://www.transparency.org/cpi2015>, accessed on 22 August 2016.

classified as having a 'high risk' of corruption. Extractive industries in a number of countries in Africa are identified as particularly susceptible to both bribery and corruption and thus classed as 'high risk'.[306] This can be evidenced by an incident in Southern Sudan that resulted in an £11m fine that was enforced by the SFO on Macmillan Publishers.[307] The EC has acknowledged that corruption costs the European economy around €120bn per year.[308] It has also been recognised that there are various different types of corruption, widening the playing field for those wishing to abuse economic and political systems:

> Individual Corruption: Corruption that primarily takes place in relations between individual citizens and public officials and authorities. Business Corruption: Corruption that primarily takes place in relations between companies and public officials and authorities. Political Corruption: Corruption that takes place in the higher echelons of public administration and on a political level.[309]

The SFO has been able to produce corruption indicators that help to identify bribery and corruption, such as abnormal cash payments. However, the SFO has accepted that 'corruption knows no bounds',[310] and that it is impossible to create an all-inclusive list of indicators. With entities such as the Organisation for Economic Co-operation and Development (OECD) overarching the SFO and FCA, many other countries have been amending their anti-corruption legislation. The UN also boasts a particularly strong anti-corruption campaign,[311] aiming to prevent corruption because it undermines 'social and economic development'.[312] In particular, the introduction of the 'Global Compact Anti-Corruption Principle'

306 OECD Guidance, 'OECD Due Diligence Guidance for responsible supply chains of minerals from conflict-affected and high-risk areas' <http://www.oecd.org/dataoecd/62/30/46740847.pdf>, accessed on 18 January 2012; OECD, 'Steps taken to implement the OECD convention on combating bribery of foreign public officials in international business transactions' <http://www.oecd.org/dataoecd/17/30/48362318.pdf>, accessed on 1 February 2012.

307 Serious Fraud Office, 'Action on Macmillan Publishers Limited' <http://www.sfo.gov.uk/press-room/latest-press-releases/press-releases-2011/action-on-macmillan-publishers-limited.aspx>, accessed on 1 February 2012.

308 BBC Democracy Live, 'Commission urged to tackle corruption' <http://news.bbc.co.uk/democracylive/hi/europe/newsid_9589000/9589857.stm>, accessed on 1 February 2012.

309 Business Anti-Corruption Portal, 'Country profiles' <http://www.business-anti-corruption.com/country-profiles/>, accessed on 18 January 2012.

310 Serious Fraud Office, 'Corruption indicators' <http://www.sfo.gov.uk/bribery--corruption/corruption-indicators.aspx>, accessed on 18 February 2012.

311 United Nations, 'Convention Against Corruption, Vienna convention' <http://www.unodc.org/documents/treaties/UNCAC/Publications/Convention/08-50026_E.pdf>, accessed on 18 February 2012.

312 United Nations Campaign, 'Against corruption today' <http://www.unodc.org/yournocounts/>, accessed on 1 February 2012

urges businesses to work together to fight against bribery and corruption.[313] This has even developed and led to the creation of an International Anti-Corruption Day on 9 December.[314] The development in international corruption law shows an important attitude shift, particularly in high-risk countries such as China and Russia.[315] The OECD requires its members to join the anti-bribery convention,[316] implementing a 'monitoring mechanism'[317] on a country-by-country basis. It is essential that the FCA and SFO are able to enforce a strong 'compliance and ethics program'[318] in accordance with the international bodies. If the NCA-'spawned' regulators are not able to co-operate and comply with the OECD and other international jurisdictions, fighting bribery and corruption on both a domestic and international levels will fail.

13.4.5 The future of bribery and corruption regulators

Regulatory bodies and LEAs at national level which are in charge of countering bribery and corruption need to be able to adapt to the changes on an international level. The implementation of the Bribery Act 2010 seems to be a step in the right direction, and an s.7 conviction instigated by the SFO is a clear evidence of this trend.[319] While the Financial Services Act 2012 confirmed that the FSA would be reformed,[320] there has been no formal confirmation of the reform of the SFO. Should the SFO be reformed as part of the NCA, this agency should retain the appropriate powers to combat and comply with all relevant conventions and organisations, particularly when considering how the methods of committing and reporting bribery and corruption are developing. An application for

313 United Nations, 'Anti-corruption' <http://www.unglobalcompact.org/Issues/transparency_anticorruption/>, accessed on 20 February 2012.

314 United Nations Office on Crime and Drugs, 'International anti-corruption day' <http://www.unodc.org/unodc/en/about-unodc/9-December.html?ref=menuside>, accessed on 1 February 2012.

315 Willis Executive Risks Alerts, 'Executive risks international update' <http://www.willis.com/documents/publications/Services/International/2011/ER_Alert_61_ER_Intntl_Update_10-11.pdf>, accessed on 1 February 2012

316 OECD, 'OECD convention on combating bribery of foreign public officials in international business transactions' <http://www.oecd.org/document/21/0,3746,en_2649_34859_2017813_1_1_1_1,00.html>, accessed on 1 February 2012.

317 Ibid.

318 Willis International Alert, 'Global anti-corruption rules take on a local flavour' <http://www.willis.com/documents/publications/Services/International/2011/IntlAlertAntiCorruption_54_Oct.pdf>, accessed on 1 February 2012.

319 SFO, 'Sweett Group PLC sentenced and ordered to pay £2.25 million after Bribery Act conviction', 19 February 2016, https://www.sfo.gov.uk/2016/02/19/sweett-group-plc-sentenced-and-ordered-to-pay-2-3-million-after-bribery-act-conviction>, accessed on 22 August 2016.

320 Financial Services Act (2012–2013) [278].

smartphones, entitled 'Bribespot',[321] allows organisations to see where bribery has been committed. However, this is also a method of being able to 'see what you can get away with', with the site providing an example of a €3 bribe that prevented a €30 fine for a motoring offence.[322] Some law firms[323] have been offering guidance and advice on the new legislation to their clients. It would seem that the changing attitude on an international level, particularly in high-risk areas, is also a step in the right direction, but, as is the similar situation with other regulators being reformed or replaced by the NCA, it is difficult to determine the exact picture until the reforms actually happen. The need for the SFO to retain the powers to interact and co-operate with other organisations will be paramount, and failure to do so could ignite the failure of the UK's anti-corruption regime.

13.5 A conclusion on the National Crime Agency and its potential impact on the UK's financial crime policy

13.5.1 The future of financial crime

While criminals are constantly developing new methods of breaching the walls of financial crime legislation in the UK, the UK is slowly reacting to prevent future incidents. The increasing use of the internet by consumers[324] has become paramount in this battle and this can be evidenced across all areas of white-collar crime. In addition, one of the major areas for development will surround the unlawful obtaining of data under s.55 of the Data Protection Act 1998, as the theft of data may well involve some form of associated financial crime. There are also inherent problems that come from some cultures and the ways in which financial crime legislation is tackled. In the Americas, some people believe that in the current economy bribery can 'sometimes be OK'.[325] It must also be considered that: 'Money laundering laws are very arbitrarily enforced in many countries and

321 S. Rubenfeld, 'New app lets people "check in" when bribes are paid' <http://blogs.wsj.com/corruption-currents/2011/05/17/new-app-lets-people-check-in-when-bribes-are-paid/>, accessed on 25 January 2012.

322 M. Panzarino, 'Bribespot lets people "check in" when they've been bribed' <http://thenextweb.com/apps/2011/05/17/bribespot-lets-people-check-in-when-theyve-been-bribed/>, accessed on 10 March 2012.

323 Osborne Clarke, 'Bribery Act 2010 – Get your business prepared' <http://www.osborneclarke.com/publications/services/employment-and-benefits/alert/2011/~/media/Files/publications/services/employment/bribery-act-2010-get-your-business-prepared.ashx->, accessed on 1 February 2012.

324 Action Fraud, 'The BBC has issued a warning over scam e-mail circulating' <http://www.actionfraud.org.uk/Heir-Hunters-scam-email-circulating>, accessed on 8 February 2012.

325 E. Alpert, 'Is bribery sometimes OK? How people answered across the Americas' <http://latimesblogs.latimes.com/world_now/2012/02/bribery-americas.html>, accessed on 8 February 2012.

since money laundering is a crime of motive, rather than one of specific activity, its enforcement is highly subjective, selective and politically biased.'[326]

The ever-developing battle against financial crime has been summed up by Lord Stevens; even though his statement refers expressly to corruption, it arguably equally applies to fraud and money-laundering regulation:

> Those of us who have been at the sharp end of investigating corruption have found it is exceedingly difficult, on occasions, to get to the truth of the matter. Complex laws don't allow you to drill down into the real substance and gain the evidence you need to convict people for the type of corruption we're talking about. I think the current laws regarding bribery and corruption have been adequately described as 'obscure, complex, inconsistent and insufficiently comprehensive'.[327]

Among other things, the legislators need to able to constantly adopt and develop legal provisions to tackle financial crime. This is more pressing today, as technological advancements and a changing social landscape present a flurry of opportunities for white-collar criminals.

13.5.2 The future of the National Crime Agency

It is arguable that the success of the NCA hinges on four main variables:

1. The receipt of the correct distribution of power, ensuring that influence can be exercised alongside other agencies (particularly in relation to the reform of both the FSA and SFO).
2. The receipt of sufficient enforcement powers, allowing the NCA to put up a 'successful' fight against all types of financial crime.
3. The ability to interact with other organisations both nationally and internationally.
4. The ability to operate on a reactive and proactive basis.

The Financial Services Act 2012[328] evidenced the beginning of the essential progression in the battle against financial crime. The uncertainty that surrounds the SFO has been particularly damaging and could be the inevitable failure of the fraud and corruption prevention regimes, assuming they are not adequately dealt with. A key question is whether or not the powers have been distributed evenly,

326 S. Ramage, 'Digital money, electronic fraud, new regulations and the old money laundering regulations' (2011) *Crim. Law.*, 200, 2.

327 Sky Sports News, 'Problem probe' <http://www1.skysports.com/football/news/12040/7496004/Problem-probe>, accessed on 8 February 2012.

328 Financial Services Act 2012 [278].

ensuring that the FCA becomes one of the primary combatants against financial crime in the UK:

> At the moment we do not have any powers because we are just going through the process of building a Bill. What is really important is we preserve many of the very good powers that I think were given to SOCA through the previous Act and make sure that where those still make sense they come through for NCA as well. Powers inevitably in law enforcement are hugely important.[329]

The development of these powers will ensure that the FCA and the reformed SFO will be able to remain as primary combatants in the ever-changing landscape that is financial crime prevention. This will also ensure that the FCA and SFO can develop without the need for long-winded time scales for passing new legislation when organised criminals discover new methods for breaching the prevention regime. Currently, the UK's financial crime legislation is reactive, and although this is beneficial and allows the law to be tailored to the current needs of the regime, the legislation will always be one step behind the criminals. The need for the NCA to be able to interact with the relevant global and European organisations (such as the SEC, FBI and Interpol) is paramount in ensuring that a strong compliance-based regime is upheld. Although many of these organisations do not hold the jurisdiction to combat financial crime that only emanates from the UK, should a European-wide crisis take place the NCA will need to be in pole position to assist in its combating. However, it must also be considered that it could be seen as ironic that other nations are looking to the UK, a nation that is currently undergoing a large reform of its financial crime policy, for 'prevention tips'.[330] The final question therefore remains: Was the NCA allocated the correct powers, allowing this entity to become proactive and be able to interact successfully with the relevant organisations? At this stage, it is difficult to answer; however, it can clearly be seen that unless this is adhered to, the NCA will become the name for the unnecessary reforms that were made to the UK's financial crime policy, creating an 'umbrella term' for the organisations that already existed within the UK. Perhaps this is a relatively negative view on the regulatory landscape that will come into play; the answer will not be known until the correct time comes and after all is said and done.

329 House of Commons Oral Evidence, 'Uncorrected transcript of oral evidence, Tuesday 17 January 2012' <http://www.publications.parliament.uk/pa/cm201012/cmselect/cmhaff/uc1553-i/uc155301.htm>, accessed on 8 February 2012.

330 T. Jones, 'Polish latest nation to visit UK for fraud prevention tips' <http://www.insuranceinsight.eu/insurance-insight/news/2143705/polish-nation-visit-uk-fraud-prevention-tips>, accessed on 8 February 2012.

14 Financial crises and financial crime: 'conscious coupling' and 'transformative understandings' of crime past, present and future

Sarah Wilson

The year 2017 will mark the tenth anniversary of the onset of the global financial crisis. During this decade, numerous accounts of the events leading to this have emerged, and, with these, a multitude of different ways seeking to recount or actually understand this 'once-in-a-lifetime' crisis[1] which had its roots in the US sub-prime mortgage crisis and transcended into the 'first crisis *of* globalisation'.[2] These narrative threads all in some way tell the story of extensive impropriety associated with widespread debt finance, which became exposed initially by the US sub-prime mortgage crisis. The origins of the US crisis lay in cuts in interest rates during 2001–03, in response to concerns about an economic downturn.[3] When combined with political support for democratising home ownership, this resulted in the aggressive pursuit of low-income groups by lenders, which was itself emboldened by historic house price patterns. This in turn attracted interest from investment banking, which, armed with statistics projecting continuing house price rises and relating to patterns of mortgage default, set about purchasing them and repackaging them into debt-based investment instruments/vehicles. In spring 2007, reports of significant losses being experienced in US investment banking started to 'spill over' to European institutions exposed to the now deeply troubled US sub-prime market. In September 2007, Bank of England Governor Mervyn King publicised that 'lender of last resort'[4] emergency assistance would be forthcoming for any bank experiencing short-term difficulties from extreme conditions, which first appeared likely to be short-lived. This provided a forecast

1 A. Haldane and V. Madouros, 'The dog and the frisbee' (Federal Bank of Kansas Economic Policy Symposium, Jackson Hole, Wyoming, 31 August 2012), 24.

2 G. Brown, *Beyond the Crash: Overcoming the First Crisis of Globalisation* (London: Simon & Schuster, 2010).

3 The policy pursued by Alan Greenspan, then head of the body responsible for setting interest rates, the US Federal Reserve Board.

4 Mervyn King's letter to the Treasury, 12 September 2007, and to then Chancellor Alistair Darling MP, 13 September 2007, referencing the iconic construct developed by Walter Bagehot (1873); see also the Bank of England's news release, 'Liquidity support facility for Northern Rock plc', 14 September 2007.

for how UK lender Northern Rock's request for Bank of England assistance – received on 13 September 2007 and announced the following day – marked the arrival of the global financial crisis in Britain.

Background and context

The difficulties experienced by Northern Rock flowed to a very significant degree from how the business of this (self-proclaimed) 'specialised lender' – and which lay in 'the provision of UK residential mortgages' – was funded by 'both the retail and wholesale markets',[5] and had been sustained through borrowing from its wholesale business.[6] Despite conscious expansion of its overseas market-base in order to manage this risk, the simultaneous seizure of all its key markets left it 'absolutely unable to finance [. . .] wholly illiquid assets', once the markets for mortgage-based securities closed.[7] This set of events would lead in turn to the institution seeking Bank of England emergency liquidity assistance, and being placed in partial public ownership. This was the first of three major banking failures, with RBS (Royal Bank of Scotland) and HBOS (Halifax Bank of Scotland) seeking emergency assistance in 2008, and with highly profiled enquiries for the latter two being published respectively in 2011[8] and 2013,[9] following the pattern of criticism set in 2008 by 'the run on the Rock'. In between these dates, a Consultation Paper from the Bank of England captured a mood for regulatory reform:

> The global financial crisis has demonstrated the need for fundamental reform of the financial system. The underlying structure of the international financial and monetary system is being re-evaluated. Whatever its structure, the prudential regulatory framework will need to be re-oriented to have a system-wide focus. And improvements need to be made to allow financial institutions to fail without imposing unacceptable costs on the rest of society.[10]

It *is* the case that seven years have now passed since this statement was made, some two years following the onset of the crisis. And even in 2009 the pace of reform and actually the likelihood of achieving reform merited by a 'once-in-a-lifetime' crisis was attracting criticism and even cynicism about the prospects of securing this. For some, humanity's immense capacity for convincing (and

5 Northern Rock, Community Report 2006, cited in the House of Commons Treasury Committee Report on Northern Rock: *The Run on the Rock*, HC 2007–8, 56–1, 9.

6 Ibid., 13, through expansion of its so-called 'originate to distribute' activity: terminology for securitising rather than holding ('originate to hold') assets/liabilities.

7 Ibid., 18.

8 FSA Board, *The Failure of the Royal Bank of Scotland* (London: FSA, 2011).

9 Parliamentary Commission on Banking Standards, *'An accident waiting to happen': The Failure of HBOS*, Fourth Report of Session 2012–13, HL Paper 144/ HC Paper 705.

10 Bank of England, *The Role of Macroprudential Policy: A Discussion Paper* (London: Bank of England, 2009), 3.

actually deluding) ourselves that 'this time is different' would prevent us learning valuable lessons from our previous experiences of crisis.[11] Further indication from this point in time that regulatory reform was unlikely to be either extensive and far-reaching or 'fast paced' arose from continuing economic downturn[12] and forces encouraging continuing 'as usual' rather than seeking radical change, as a financial services industry looked set to move from one 'exhausted grazing pasture' to the next.[13] Notwithstanding this, and recent suggestions that 'nothing has been learned'[14] from the crisis, regulators continue to insist that extensive reform remains a priority. This is evident as part of a continuing sustained critique on the role played by banks in bringing about the crisis; for example, where as part of a stinging attack on short-termism in banking corporate governance, and the role played by this in bringing about the crisis, the Bank of England's Chief Economist, Andy Haldane, insisted that the seeds of the financial crisis were sown by bankers 'borrowing too much' and doing so in many cases to chase 'higher return to remit to shareholders'.[15]

Even if the pace of *substantive* change might seem to remain painfully slow, post-crisis discourse *does* point to important and identifiable change in other related regards. This is evident in reflections such as those insisting that a new and aggressive financial culture wholly privileging profit maximisation over all else ensured that this time *was* different, and required responses configured accordingly.[16] This is also apparent in insistence that the crisis presents the opportunity and also the mandate for a fresh approach across the sweep of societal agendas, including the economy, and that human beings have the capacity to 'change course'.[17] This is readily apparent in new analytical directions which have emerged from the crisis, and which in distinctive ways can be regarded as responses to the assertion that that 'the crisis and the wrongdoing associated with it can be understood in a sophisticated way only by drawing upon many different academic and

11 C. Reinhart and K. Rogoff, *This Time Is Different: Eight Centuries of Financial Folly* (Princeton: Princeton University Press, 2009).

12 J. Stiglitz, *Freefall: Free Markets and the Sinking of the Global Economy* (London: Penguin, 2010).

13 Z. Bauman, *Living on Borrowed Time* (Cambridge: Polity, 2010).

14 See e.g. E. Dunkley, 'Banker bashing draws to an end as watchdog scraps review', *Financial Times* (London, 31 December 2015), reporting the views of John Mann MP.

15 Andy Haldane in an interview given to Duncan Weldon for BBC Newsnight, 24 July 2015: see http://touchstoneblog.org.uk/2015/07/andy-haldane-shareholder-primacy-is-bad-for-economic-growth.

16 D. O. Friedrichs, 'The financial crisis as white collar or economic, crime and the criminogenic architecture of Wall Street', *Economic Crime and the State in the Twentieth Century: A German–American Comparison*, German Institute of Historical Research, Washington DC, 14 April 2011, cited with permission.

17 R. Williams, speech accompanying the launch of R. Williams and L. Elliott (eds) *Crisis and Recovery: Ethics Economics and Justice* (Basingstoke: Palgrave, 2010), 28 September 2010, at http://rowanwilliams.archbishopofcanterbury.org/articles.php/941/crisis-and-recovery-book-launch-28th-september.

professional perspectives'.[18] Such viewpoints suggest the need for *analytical* approaches, which encourage examining these events and their impact using indices beyond traditional ones. In discourses for determining the onset and continuation *of* and recovery *from* periods of 'crisis', macroeconomic analysis emphasising data relating to GDP, import and export figures and rates of inflation and unemployment, etc. predominates, alongside increasing attention being paid to macroprudential assessments of financial system resilience through stress-testing and scenario analysis.[19] Alongside this, it has been suggested, can now be seen discernible newer strands of analysis which have become identified with the onset and continuation of this 'once-in-a-lifetime' crisis.[20]

Identification of the significance of 'transformation': substantive and intellectual reactions to the global financial crisis

From this sweep of new analytical approach, two trends are particularly notable. The first of these in many ways provides the most direct critique of conventional and primarily economics-focused analyses of periods of financial instability embodied in the parlance of 'crisis'. This is built on a very specific recent assertion that financial markets are social spaces as well as economic ones,[21] and of how periods of financial and wider instability impact hugely on social well-being and raise important issues for social justice.[22] This direction grafts effectively onto longer-standing critical assertions that the impact of business upon society ensures that its operations within society cannot be seen merely in economic terms.[23] In response also to how the global financial crisis is widely associated with failings in banking specifically, both in popular parlance[24] and in the orientation of regulatory reform,[25] socially focused analyses of the crisis are becoming attached to its impact

18 D. O. Friedrichs, 'Wall Street: crime never sleeps' in S. Will *et al.* (eds), *How They Got Away with It: White Collar Criminals and the Financial Meltdown* (New York: Columbia University Press, 2012), 4.

19 See e.g. Bank of England, *The Role of Macroprudential Policy: A Discussion Paper* (Macroprudential Discussion Paper, 2009). For general discussion, see E. Ferran *et al.* (eds) *The Regulatory Aftermath of the Global Financial Crisis* (Cambridge: Cambridge University Press, 2012); and E. Wymeersch *et al.* (eds) *Financial Regulation and Supervision: A Post-Crisis Analysis* (Oxford: Oxford University Press, 2012).

20 A. Haldane and V. Madouros, 'The dog and the frisbee', above n. 1.

21 R. Williams, speech, above n. 17.

22 As a pervading theme for Friedrichs, above n. 18; see also J. Welby, 'Repair or replace: where do we start among the ruins?' (Lecture for Finanzethikon, Zurich, 26 October 2012).

23 See e.g. L. E. Mitchell (ed.) *Progressive Corporate Law* (Oxford: Westview Press, 1995).

24 As evident in what has become known as 'banker bashing', widely to be found in the press; for example, the view that 'Banks are the biggest scroungers of public money – solutions will not simply materialise if we don't keep up the pressure', as expressed in S. Hundal, 'Why we need more banker bashing', *Guardian* (London, 7 February 2012).

25 As evident in the summary of the essence of post-crisis reform set out in Bank of England, *The Role of Macroprudential* Policy, above n. 10, 3.

for the poorest in society,[26] and even to assert that, leading up to the crisis, banking had become 'socially useless'[27] and demand that it must once again become 'socially use*ful*'.[28] It is the second identifiable strand of novel analysis of financial crises which pertains to this analysis. Here, it is argued that the global financial crisis has had a profound impact on how periods of crisis are analysed through the prism of 'financial crime'. And, moreover, a sizeable body of scholarship now testifies to increasing scholarly inclination to pursue enhanced understanding of financial crises – in terms of cause and effect – through analyses of financial *crime.*[29]

It is from this increasing, and increasingly identifiable, 'financial crisis–financial crime' nexus that the hypothesis of a 'conscious coupling' of these conceptualisations is now being advanced. As suggested, this is readily apparent in scholarly analysis of the financial crime, and where this can be found in legal scholarship from across a wide range of substantive interests, and also in cognate disciplines such as criminology/sociology,[30] and increasingly history;[31] and where 'newer' interest is also coming from anthropology[32] and neuroscience.[33] It is also the case that a 'conscious coupling' of the financial crisis with financial crime is also evident in policy calling for, and actually implementing, post-crisis regulatory reform. The latter can be found both in implicit references to the importance of the 'wrongdoing' associated with the crisis in the calibration of new responses – for example, in insistence that leading up to the crisis, within a financial services industry which served none but itself[34] – and in assertions that in a wider context of rising inequality, bankers became 'first among unequals'.[35] It is also evident in

26 See e.g. Centre for Social Justice, *Maxed Out: Serious Personal Debt in Britain*, November 2013; and Centre for the Study of Financial Innovation North East Credit Unions Report, *Helping the Financially Excluded: Supporting Credit Unions*, November 2012.

27 Lord Turner (then FSA Chairman), Mansion House Speech (London, 22 September 2009).

28 See perspectives from Bank of England Executive Director (and then head of Financial Stability, and now Chief Economist and Executive Director Monetary Analysis & Statistics), Andy Haldane; and Archbishop of Canterbury and subsequently Parliamentary Commission on Banking Standards member, Justin Welby: A. Haldane 'A leaf being turned: Occupy Economics, "Socially useful banking"' (Friends' House, London, 29 October 2012); and J. Welby, 'Repair or replace', above n. 22, and also 'How do we fix this mess? Long-term solutions to the financial crisis' (Westminster, 22 April 2013, accessible at http://www.archbishopofcanterbury.org/articles.php/5050/how-do-we-fix-this-mess-archbishop-justin-on-restoring-trust-and-confidence-after-the-crash).

29 See S. Wilson, review of N. Ryder, *The Financial Crisis and White-Collar Crime: The Perfect Storm?* (Abingdon: Routledge, 2014), Rutgers School of Law and School of Criminal Justice (2015) 'Criminal law and criminal justice books', http://clcjbooks.rutgers.edu.

30 E.g. D. O. Friedrichs, 'Wall Street', above n. 18.

31 E.g. S. Wilson, *The Origins of Modern Financial Crime: Historical Foundations and Current Problems in Britain* (Abingdon: Routledge, 2014).

32 J. Luyendijk, *Swimming with Sharks: My Journey into the World of the Bankers* (London: Guardian Faber, 2015).

33 J. Coates, *The Hour between Dog and Wolf: Risk-Taking, Gut Feelings and the Biology of Boom and Bust* (London: Fourth Estate, 2012).

34 See J. Welby, 'Repair or replace', above n. 28.

35 A. Haldane, 'A leaf being turned', above n. 28, 4.

direct references – for example, to 'extremely risky deals' in precipitating the onset of the crisis,[36] and actually to laws being broken during it.[37] It can also be located within narratives for new laws being put in place in the domestic sphere in order to punish wrongdoing and to prevent further infractions, such as new criminal liability for benchmark manipulation,[38] and in connection with a decision by a senior officer causing a financial institution to fail.[39]

In this regard, the academic scholarship which has emerged from the crisis shows how 'conscious couplings' of financial crime with financial crisis fall on a wide spectrum of analytical viewpoints. Many academic works suggest that the crisis is likely to influence approaches to financial crime enforcement very significantly in terms of intensifying enforcement interest in and prioritisation of financial crime.[40] A number of these perspectives point to distinct but clearly closely related views that the financial crisis is likely to affect very profoundly how financial crime is perceived and analysed.[41] In other perspectives, the 'conscious coupling' of financial crime with 'crisis' subsists even more powerfully in assertions that the *causes* of the financial crisis can be located in the occurrence of financial crime.[42] It is from this latter proposition of *causation* that the assertion of a further *consequences*-based relationship between financial crime and crisis arises, and one which is different again from those set out above. This posits that the crisis is capable of engendering 'transformative understandings' of crime.[43] The trope of 'transformation' in societal understandings of crime is premised on the causes-based theory that financial crime can be seen at the heart of the 'catastrophe' of 2007–08.[44] More is said about this shortly, and also about the nuances of this basic premise and its relationships with consequences-based analyses set out above. What remains to be clarified at this stage is what is actually meant by 'financial crime'.

Transformative understandings and fundamental conceptualisations: what is meant by 'financial crime'?

Exploring ideas of causation between financial crime and the financial crisis, and also proposing the latter as a moment capable of marking transformations in understandings of crime, is likely to place Friedrichs' work among the most influential to be generated by the crisis. Furthermore, Friedrichs' work also

36 HM Treasury, *Sanctions for the Directors of Failed Banks* (London, July 2012), 5–6, para 2.2 and Box 2A.
37 See S. Rustin, 'Andrew Tyrie: fresh from the HBOS debacle, now serious about reform', *Guardian* (London, 20 April 2013).
38 S.91 Financial Services Act 2012, as considered below in the main text.
39 S.36 Financial Services (Banking Reform) Act 2013, as considered below in the main text.
40 See e.g. R. Tomasic, 'The financial crisis and the haphazard pursuit of financial crime' (2011) *Journal of Financial Crime*, 18(1), 7.
41 See e.g. S. Wilson, *The Origins of Modern Financial Crime*, above n. 31.
42 See e.g. D. O. Friedrichs, 'Wall Street', above n. 18.
43 Ibid.
44 Ibid.

illuminates how financial crime might usefully be defined for these purposes. The need for illumination itself flows from how the terminology of 'financial crime' can be found to be commonly used, but is seldom explained.[45] This, in turn, is problematic, because 'financial crime' is also a term which can be widely applied across a spectrum of wrongdoing. It is also the case that there is also no internationally agreed definition of financial crime. In noting this in 2001, the IMF and World Bank set out some illustrative examples of what could be brought within the rubric of 'financial crime', considering the terminology of 'financial abuse'. The latter, it was suggested, could be widely applied instead of 'financial crime' in many instances, and that doing so would also capture the spectrum of approaches to configuring financial 'wrongdoing' across different States.[46] For analyses which speak of financial crime rather than financial abuse, there is a strong connection between financial crime and what is regarded as 'white-collar crime'. The term 'white-collar crime' is an example of how a technical and intellectually focused construct has crossed over into popular consciousness and become a 'public lexicon'.[47] However, even as a construct of sociology/criminology, 'white-collar crime' was contentious from the moment Edwin Sutherland coined it as the unlawful activity of persons of high social status and respectability, and committed in the course of occupation,[48] and has remained the subject of extensive criticism.[49] Notwithstanding, academic interest in financial crime specifically can be traced to Sutherland's classification of different species of white-collar crimes, where he included 'misrepresentations of asset values', approximating with 'fraud' and 'swindling'.[50]

From this, what might be called a 'white-collar crime–financial crime nexus'[51] can be seen in academic social science scholarship in the domestic sphere. It can also be seen utilised by UK authorities, as evident in former FSA Director Margaret Cole's insistence that the 'financial crime' of insider dealing was a very serious 'white-collar crime'.[52] This use of the terminology of 'financial crime' by the UK enforcement community can in turn be situated alongside definitions located not

45 See e.g. S. Wilson, 'Embedding responses to financial crime in nineteenth-century Britain: conform[ing] to the popular stereotype of "the criminal"' and challenging criminal and respectable identities', in *Crime, Identity and Economics: New Research and Approaches* (London: Institute of Historical Research, 2015).

46 IMF and World Bank, *Financial System Abuse, Financial Crime and Money Laundering – Background Paper* (Washington, DC: IMF, 2001), especially paras 5, 7 and 9.

47 S. Rosoff *et al.*, *Profit without Honor: White-Collar Crime and the Looting of America* (Upper Saddle River, NJ: Prentice Hall, 2010), especially 3–5.

48 E. H. Sutherland, *White-Collar Crime* (New York: Dryden Press, 1949), 9.

49 See e.g. D. Nelken, 'White-collar crime', in M. Maguire *et al.* (eds) *The Oxford Handbook of Criminology* (Oxford: Oxford University Press, 1994), 355.

50 Alongside duplicity in the manipulation of power – the double cross: see E. H. Sutherland, 'White-collar criminality' (1940) *American Sociological Review* 5, 3.

51 See e.g. S. Wilson, review of N. Ryder, above n. 29.

52 M. Cole, 'The FSA's approach to insider dealing', American Bar Association Speech, 4 October 2007.

only in social science, but actually in law itself. Here, legislation, setting out the regulatory regime for UK financial services, and the role of the regulator has, since 2000, defined financial crime as 'any offence involving (a) fraud or dishonesty, (b) misconduct in, or misuse of information relating to, a financial market, (c) handling proceeds of crime'.[53] And in focusing on 'crime in the commercial sphere',[54] this overview of the transformative effects of the financial crisis for financial crime suggests that much value lies in equating the conventional terminology of financial crime with Friedrichs' definition of 'finance crime'. This definition of 'large-scale illegality that occurs in the world of finance and financial institutions'[55] is capable of accommodating a range of individual research interests.[56] Its reference to illegality also signposts a return to considering why and how financial crime might be considered to have caused the financial crisis and why, as a consequence of this, 'transformative understandings' of crime might now transpire.

In the spirit of insisting that it is only through drawing upon many different academic and professional perspectives that a sophisticated understanding can be reached of the crisis and the wrongdoing associated with it, Friedrichs' analysis of the global financial crisis was likely to be nuanced. But he also proposed that 'fraudulent misrepresentations in many different forms and on many different levels' were clearly at its centre.[57] This latter observation's significance for this analysis flows from how, for Friedrichs, it pointed to the criminogenic architecture of high finance, and how this in turn both justified and also necessitated radical rethinking of the impact of crime on society.[58] Friedrichs' reference to 'architecture' sought to capture a milieu characterised by conditions 'that promote criminal activities and actions',[59] while the challenges of communicating such a message are clearly readily apparent to him. The stress being placed on changing or transforming conceptions of crime in societal consciousness required greater attention to be paid to harm emanating from high finance, alongside activities traditionally thought of as being 'socially injurious'.[60] For Friedrichs, societal

53 This is set out in the Financial Services and Markets Act 2000; the Financial Services Act 2012 added to this: '(d) the financing of terrorism'.

54 Lord Irvine, then Lord Chancellor, Law Commission, *Fraud and Deception: A Consultation Paper*, CP No. 155 (London: HMSO, 1999), para. 1.4.

55 D. O. Friedrichs, *Trusted Criminals: White Collar Crime in Contemporary Society* (Belmont: Thomson Wadsworth, 1996), 156.

56 See e.g. N. Ryder, *The Financial Crisis and White-collar Crime: The Perfect Storm?*, discussion of how this includes sub-prime mortgage lending (itself, alongside actual mortgage fraud) and predatory lending, alongside the flawed activities of Credit Rating Agencies, Ponzi schemes and the 'Financial War on Terror'.

57 D. O. Friedrichs, 'The financial crisis as white-collar or economic crime', above n. 16.

58 D. O. Friedrichs, 'Wall Street', above n. 18, 17 *et seq.*

59 Ibid., 20, 15.

60 The parameters for the State's interest in punishing and preventing socially injurious behaviour on the part of its citizens is classically expressed in G. Williams, *Textbook of Criminal Law* (London: Stevens and Son, 1983).

acceptance of this unconventional 'street crime'[61] required – as it did for Sutherland – emphasis on defining crime sociologically, so as to include activities beyond those that violated criminal laws, and which should be criminalised on account of their injurious nature.[62]

Reactions to financial crime – in times of transformation and predating it?

The theme of transformation running through Sutherland's work is evident in his aspiration for a 'unified' criminological theory,[63] which would ensure that activities he termed white-collar crimes would be perceived and enforced in ways which reflected their qualitative nature, rather than the status of their perpetrator. For Sutherland, notwithstanding that the workloads of the criminal courts did not reflect this,[64] white-collar crimes could be found distributed across a spectrum of *mala prohibita* and *mala in se*.[65] In the non-observance of this, Sutherland identified 'unorganised [societal] resentment' rather than positive societal affirmation that white-collar crimes did not merit or necessitate greater perceptual or enforcement attention.[66] Friedrichs' message is very much that the financial crisis is capable of mobilising public resentment towards financial crime; and that recalibrations of perceived 'harm' emanating from financial dealings are required to bring about requisite changes in public consciousness concerning what is permissible in this setting and what is not so. Here, 'transformative understandings of crime' were required in order to redress the position whereby 'activities with relatively mild harmful consequences for society are accorded much attention and treated harshly', while 'activities with demonstrably major harmful consequences for society are accorded little attention and only very selectively addressed'.[67] From this, Friedrichs hypothesised that societal indifference towards financial crime could break down and be replaced by levels of societal repugnance at the 'millions of lost homes, jobs and savings, along with broad and devastating effects on the physical and mental well-being of millions of people' being associated with the crisis and its aftermath.[68]

Friedrichs' commentary on the crisis – as one on the absence of 'collective consciousness' about the nature of crime in relation to harm'[69] – has strong echoes of Sutherland's work generally, and specifically his hypothesis of 'unorganised

61 D. O. Friedrichs 'Wall Street', above n. 18, 9.

62 Ibid., 15, with the most famous expression of this to be found in E. H. Sutherland, 'Is "white collar crime" crime?' (1945) *American Sociological Review*, 10, 132.

63 E. H. Sutherland, 'Is "white-collar crime" crime?', above n. 62, 132.

64 Ibid., 136–137.

65 Ibid., 139.

66 Ibid., 137–138.

67 D. O. Friedrichs, 'Wall Street', above n. 18, 20.

68 Ibid., 19–20.

69 Ibid., 20.

resentment'. Friedrichs' message, although clear and unequivocal, is located within a deeply divided branch of scholarship, characterised by a wide spectrum of views on what might be called white-collar crime's 'special nature'.[70] These divisions are also longstanding and emerged from criticism of Sutherland's work by his contemporary adversary Paul Tappan. In response to Sutherland's proposition that defining crime sociologically would bring it within the framework of 'crime' activity which *should* be classed as criminal, alongside that which already is so, Tappan not only replied that the only proper definition of crime arises from its prohibition using criminal law and enforcement through criminal processes, but also insisted that many of the activities that Sutherland wished to classify as crimes subsisted as part of the framework of accepted (and thereby legitimate) 'business practice'.[71] These divisions set in motion the 'special nature' of white-collar crimes, which has become a scholarly battleground for asserting that white-collar crimes are qualitatively different from 'conventional' crimes, because of several factors, including that they commonly arise as a secondary or 'collateral' consequence from prima facie lawful business activity,[72] or that purported difference drawn between them and 'ordinary' crimes is a socially constructed 'smoke screen', applied to 'explain' differences in perception and enforcement which cannot otherwise be justified[73] – and where the very latter proposition of 'bias' is itself highly contested.[74]

One area of scholarly agreement within this discourse is that 'white-collar crime' is one of the most highly contested sociological/criminological constructs ever. And while another of its rare qualities lies in how it has transcended intellectual interest and passed into public discourse, it is also the case that its location in public discourse mirrors divisions evident within academic scholarship.[75] This is evident in Friedrichs' regard for the financial crisis as a 'game changer' for societal attitudes towards financial crimes, and for how the magnitude of this global catastrophe would affect millions for many years to come.[76] Here, a narrative for 'banker blame' for the crisis, which emerged swiftly and easily from more generalised criticisms of a financial services sector that had served nothing and no one but itself, lies at the heart of Friedrichs' hypothesis of the crisis as a time that

70 See extensive discussion of this as a construct for analyses of white-collar crime in S. Wilson, *The Origins of Modern Financial Crime*, above n. 31.

71 P. Tappan, 'Who is the criminal?' (1947) *American Sociological Review*, 12, 96; see especially 96–100.

72 See e.g. D. Nelken, 'White-collar crime', above n. 49, 374.

73 Ibid., where Nelken considers this through discussion of 'seven types of ambiguity' associated with white-collar crime.

74 S. Wheeler *et al.*, 'Sentencing the white-collar offender: rhetoric and reality' (1982) *American Sociological Review*, 47, 641.

75 An example of the former can be seen in R. Tomasic, 'The haphazard pursuit of financial crime', above n. 40; and the latter in J. Symington, 'Challenging the culture of market behaviour', Speech, City and Financial Market Abuse Conference, 4 December 2012.

76 D. O. Friedrichs, 'Wall Street', above n. 18, evident in his references (e.g. at 20) to the harms, and themes of 'transformative collective consciousness' of crime.

will enable attitudes towards financial crime to transform. And echoes of Friedrichs' views on the capability of the crisis for rethinking societal concerns about crime and its impact, and the importance of doing so, are evident in how UK regulators have linked banker blame with criminal liability.[77]

More is said shortly about how the financial crisis might now be influencing approaches being taken to financial crime in its aftermath. This is pursued through considering briefly whether there is evidence of such a 'transformative movement' taking hold, and also the complexities entailed in assessing this, and how the latter might be linked to difficulties raised by the 'should' question. Here, the trope of 'transformation', as it is being used by Friedrichs, appears to signal Friedrichs' support for Sutherland's normative approach, and where the tradition of critique surrounding Sutherland's ideas and his legacy may raise questions about its currency and value in the search for new narratives for reacting to and calibrating responses for financial crime. However, it is also the case that Sutherland's ideas have endured across a timeframe now spanning seventy-five years, and they have arguably done more than simply endure. Indeed, there is evidence of a 'Sutherland revival' in more recent attempts to make sense of the perceptual and enforcement challenges presented by white-collar crime. Indeed, two of the most influential scholarly works to emerge during the last decade – in turn, theorising white-collar crime through prisms of 'lying, cheating and stealing'[78] and 'opportunity perspective'[79] – have posited that Sutherland is 'rightly remembered and venerated' for his critique of criminological theory and for stimulating criminologists' interest in societal vulnerabilities arising from structural inequality in criminal justice responses,[80] and how alternatives to this highly contested concept have failed to unite disciplinary and linguistic practices.[81]

The mechanics of 'transformation': new responses and 'collective [societal] consciousness'

In utilising this current intellectual appetite for acknowledging Sutherland's continuing importance generally, specifically in the context of financial crime, the importance which Friedrichs attaches to Sutherland's work is manifest in the former's entreaty for transformations in 'collective consciousness' of financial crime. Much can be learned from Sutherland's original work about *how*

77 See Andy Haldane's suggestion that there would be calls for bankers' 'heads on sticks', in Haldane, 'A leaf being turned', above n. 28, 6; and Andrew Tyrie's musings on bankers in 'orange jumpsuits', in S. Rustin, 'Andrew Tyrie: fresh from the HBOS debacle, now serious about reform', above n. 37.

78 S. P. Green, *Lying, Cheating and Stealing: A Moral Theory of White-Collar Crime* (Oxford: Oxford University Press, 2006); and M. L. Benson and S. S. Simpson, *White-Collar Crime: An Opportunity Perspective* (London: Routledge, 2009).

79 M. L. Benson and S. S. Simpson, *White-Collar Crime*, above n. 78.

80 Ibid., 87–88.

81 S. P. Green, *Lying, Cheating and Stealing*, above n. 78, 9–10.

'transformative understandings' of crime can be achieved. This entails understanding social processes involved in the recognition of behaviour as harmful and worthy of public rebuke and punishment by the State, and where Friedrichs' ideas on arousing 'community consciousness' about financial crime, which is different from that traditionally subsisting,[82] points to the value of Sutherland's views on how such a 'community consciousness' might be built:

> The relationship between the law and the mores tends to be circular. The mores are crystallized in the law and each act of enforcement of the laws tends to re-enforce the mores. The laws regarding white-collar crime, which conceal the criminality of the behaviour, have been less effective than others in re-enforcement of the *mores*.[83]

For Sutherland, effective criminal laws were ones which were extensively enforced, thereby giving them high visibility in society, where this helps to embed societal consensus around wrongdoing, and where, by contrast, ineffective laws do not generate this societal recognition. The long tradition of perception that financial crimes are under-enforced and unsuccessfully enforced within many jurisdictions would appear to evidence Sutherland's thinking in this regard, and this has inspired numerous academic perspectives on in/visibility of activities from societal consciousness of crime and enforcement of it.[84] In 1995, it was posited that '[n]o jurisdiction has had [. . .] great [. . .] success [using] criminal law in combating sophisticated abusive activity on its capital markets',[85] but a decade earlier Lord Roskill had noted that the largest and most cleverly executed crimes remained unpunished within the legal system of England and Wales.[86] And following the crisis, it has been suggested that financial crimes are 'among the most difficult crimes for the legal system to deal with, let alone control'.[87]

The difficulties associated with apparent lack of effectiveness of criminal enforcement in this sphere, identified in 1995 by Barry Rider, were those flowing from '[t]he standards and procedures of the traditional criminal justice system, which are necessary to ensure general civil and human liberties', presenting 'almost insurmountable barriers to the effective prosecution of economic crime'.[88] Applying Sutherland's theory of circularity between law and social mores to these activities, it becomes possible to see how financial crime becomes concealed

82 D. O. Friedrichs, 'Wall Street', above n. 18, 20.
83 E. H. Sutherland, 'Is "white-collar crime" crime?', above n. 62, 139.
84 See e.g. P. Davies *et al.* (eds), *Invisible Crimes: Their Victims and Their Regulation* (Basingstoke: Macmillan, 1999), especially the excellent summary of this conceptualisation given in P. Davies *et al.*, 'The features of invisible crimes', 3–28.
85 B. Rider, 'Civilising the law – the use of civil proceedings to enforce financial services law in the United Kingdom' (1995) *Journal of Financial Crime*, 3(1), 11, 13.
86 Lord Roskill, *Fraud Trials Committee Report* (London: HMSO, 1986), para. 1.6.
87 R. Tomasic, 'The haphazard pursuit of financial crime', above n. 40.
88 B. Rider, 'Civilising the law', above n. 85, 13.

from and thereby concealed *within* societal consciousness. Aubert's proposition in 1952 of the absence of harmony between law and social mores[89] is clearly understood in the domestic context, and can be seen very plainly in the Treasury's identification of difficulties associated with criminal enforcement in 2012. Without any reference being made to academic literature, this consultation reiterated very closely the problems identified by Rider in 1995, while looking to assert very strongly the value and the essence of criminal enforcement in the sphere of financial misconduct.[90] The Treasury was concerned with financial infractions of a highly specific nature, connected with 'extremely risky' conduct on the part of senior executives within financial institutions.[91] But these difficulties have been identified by the FSA in the context of its enforcement of market abuse, where this comprises insider dealing and market manipulation.

While the FSA's and now the FCA's interfacings with financial crime arise directly from its regulatory objectives, and ensure that it is not a 'mainstream prosecutor' of financial crime,[92] its then Director of Enforcement Margaret Cole opined in 2007 that its activities here were challenging, in ways which are identifiable with financial crime enforcement more broadly. Here, Ms Cole referred to the absence of a 'smoking gun', and the reality of being based on financial transacting, which is complex and not at all 'jury friendly'.[93] Furthermore, her insistence that market abuse is a financial crime which is a 'very serious white-collar crime', notwithstanding that it 'may not attract the immediate moral outrage of a violent crime against a person',[94] also shows an understanding of the essence of Sutherland's hypothesis of circularity between law enforcement and public consciousness of crime. This message is also clearly normatively configured, highlighting the importance of changing popular perceptions of these criminal activities, in ways which are identifiable with Friedrichs' more recent rendition of Sutherland's work. More recently still, Chancellor of the Exchequer George Osborne explained that those who 'commit financial crime should be treated like the criminals they are – and they will be'.[95] It can be argued that the Chancellor glossed over far too much the complexity belying his 'clear message' that there is to be 'no trade-off between high standards of conduct and competitiveness'. 'Far from it',[96] his recognition of the need for transformation in this sphere is evident,

89 V. Aubert, 'White-collar crime and social structure' (1952) *American Journal of Sociology*, 58, 263, 266.
90 HM Treasury, *Sanctions for the Directors of Failed Banks*, above n. 36, 15, paras 4.14–4.17.
91 Ibid., 5–6, para. 2.2, and Box 2A
92 References made to this during the FSA's lifetime include that of then CEO Hector Sants, in 'Delivering intensive supervision and credible deterrence', Reuters Newsmakers Event Speech (London, 12 March 2009).
93 M. Cole, 'The FSA's approach to insider dealing', above n. 52.
94 Ibid.
95 Rt Hon. George Osborne MP (then Chancellor of the Exchequer), Mansion House Speech (London, 10 June 2015).
96 Ibid.

alongside his allusion even to the transformative qualities of the financial crisis and its fall-out.

A new era of response to financial crime? And a time of 'transformation'?

The importance of a new era and time of transformation are readily apparent in how George Osborne's speech also remarked that '[t]he public rightly asks why it is that after so many scandals, and such cost to the country, so few individuals have faced punishment in the courts'.[97]

At this point it is pertinent to reflect on whether current domestic approaches to financial crime enforcement can properly be termed 'transformative'. In insisting that the financial crisis was capable of engendering transformations in community consciousness of crime, which would allow appropriate levels of societal recognition, that prima facie lawful financial dealings are capable of causing very significant harm for society, and also that this 'transformation' should occur, Friedrichs was also acutely conscious of how challenging achieving this would be. It would involve breaking down societal fixation with unlawful activities 'with relatively mild harmful consequences for society',[98] and require re-education on the causes and consequences of harm for society. Clearly the visible nature of much low-level 'street crime' lends itself easy political 'wins' arising from publicly focused reassurances about being 'tough on crime',[99] and it is not difficult to see how this becomes enmeshed in enforcement priorities, metrics and targets built on these. However, George Osborne's message also speaks to the perceived need to challenge traditional equations of the 'threat' of crime with crime which has been termed 'ordinary', 'traditional' and 'conventional' in nature and origin,[100] and to put in place responses which ensure that this happens.

In terms of whether there is any evidence of such a transformative movement occurring, the domestic context can reveal much about what indices of transformation might actually be, and also the complexity and nuance required to ascertain this. Very shortly after the Chancellor's 2015 Mansion House speech, CitiBank trader Tom Hayes became the first to be convicted of Libor manipulation, following the Libor-fixing scandal exposed in 2012.[101] This is what Andrew Tyrie MP – who had chaired the Parliamentary Commission on Banking

97 Ibid.

98 D. O. Friedrichs, 'Wall Street', above n. 18, 20.

99 As has become associated with the policy of the New Labour administration from 1997 to 2010.

100 All these terms can be found used in the academic literature on white-collar crime to illustrate the contrasts drawn between white-collar crime and other types of unlawfulness bearing criminal penalty.

101 See 'Trader jailed for 14 years over Libor rate-rigging', BBC News (London, 3 August 2015).

Standards appointed in the wake of the scandal – had forecast,[102] and while the acquittal of 'Lord Libor' Colin Goodman occurred not long afterwards,[103] this was part of a highly profiled and highly publicised series of prosecutions for alleged Libor and Euribor manipulations,[104] and for a time it looked as though prosecutions for Forex manipulations could also follow fines from US and UK regulators.[105] Moreover, not only was Tom Hayes' conviction upheld after his appeal against it, but the Court of Appeal took the opportunity to issue a stern warning that more criminal actions would follow, and so too would even sterner sentences, in order to reflect 'the serious harm caused and the need for deterrence' in response to those whose 'dishonest action not only damages financial markets but actually the general prosperity of the state'.[106] Tom Hayes has since been denied appeal to the Supreme Court,[107] and within one day of this being reported, new criminal liability for those whose decisions cause the failure of a financial institution, where dishonesty is not required, came into force in domestic law; namely, liability pursuant to s.36 Financial Services (Banking Reform) Act 2013.[108]

Furthermore, in response to the Libor scandal, a new specific crime of benchmark manipulation was created by virtue of s.91 Financial Services Act 2012. It was, of course, this legislation which created the new UK conduct regulator, the Financial Conduct Authority (FCA), as part of the new 'twin peaks'[109] regulatory regime, following the perceived failings of the Financial Services Authority exposed by the financial crisis.[110] The FCA has already secured six convictions for insider dealing in its short lifetime and is currently prosecuting a further six.[111] Post-legislative scrutiny of the Fraud Act 2006, published in 2012, has pointed to how the legislation – and, particularly, a centrepiece general fraud offence – is delivering on its intended objective of assisting the prosecution of fraud very

102 See S. Rustin, 'Andrew Tyrie: fresh from the HBOS debacle, now serious about reform', above n. 37.

103 See 'Not guilty verdict for Lord Libor', 25 Bedford Row (London, 1 February 2016).

104 See L. Fortado, 'UK prosecutors charge 10 with Euribor manipulation', *Financial Times* (London 3 November 2015).

105 See T. Wallace, 'Forex traders have been shocked into behaving themselves but it might not last, says BoE director', *Telegraph* (London, 23 July 2015); and 'SFO drops probe into price-rigging in foreign exchange', BBC News (London, 15 March 2016).

106 *Hayes v R* [2015] EWCA Crim 1944; para. 98.

107 H. Wilson, 'Libor-rigger Tom Hayes cannot go to Supreme Court', *The Times* (9 March 2016).

108 'Offence relating to a decision causing a financial institution to fail': see also Government News Story 'Senior bankers to face jail for reckless decisions' (London: HM Treasury, 7 March 2016).

109 See e.g. H. Sants, 'Delivering "twin peaks" within the FSA', speech at the British Bankers' Association briefing, London 6 February 2012.

110 As evident in a torrent of highly profiled criticism, exemplified and arguably set in motion in the HM Treasury Report, *The Run on the Rock*, above n. 5: see especially 3 and para. 190 at 81.

111 As evident in FCA Press Release, 'Two convicted of insider dealing in Operation Tabernula trial' (9 May 2016).

effectively;[112] interestingly, the new offence has been very successfully deployed in response to tax offending.[113] Taken together, these occurrences could persuasively be regarded as indices of a hardening of response to financial crime. This could also plausibly make them part of what helps to establish a virtuous cycle, in which social mores both lend support to greater criminal enforcement and are in turn reinforced by this. In this light, these occurrences could be regarded as evidence of a 'transformative movement' taking hold in relation to financial crime. However, the current vista is more nuanced and more complex than this.

The theme of transformation which is explicit in Friedrichs' work is also readily apparent in more implicit terms in Tomasic's forecast that the global financial crisis was likely to signal a retreat from the 'haphazard pursuit' of financial crime, underpinned by a hardening of attitudes towards it,[114] as a reaction to the perceived failings of 'light touch' regulation, alongside a stream of exposures of wrongdoing.[115] These post-crisis occurrences could quite plausibly suggest that what is being witnessed is not a time of transformation, let alone a 'transformative movement', but a continuation of an ad hoc – if not 'haphazard' – approach, identifying and reacting to the most egregious instances of misconduct. And, in this regard, the HSBC-Suisse alleged tax evasion exposures of February 2015 point to egregious conduct of significant magnitude. Just under one year after the exposés had generated reactions from highly profiled UK stakeholders, centrally Her Majesty's Revenue and Customs (HMRC), the Serious Fraud Office and the Financial Conduct Authority,[116] it was announced that following a 'deep dive'[117] into its Swiss private bank, HSBC would not face formal action by the FCA.[118] This was notwithstanding that these highly publicised accusations had followed others from 2013, implicating HSBC in money laundering in Mexico.[119]

Transformation of 'collective consciousness' or 'business as usual': concluding thoughts

Reactions to this outcome embraced both disappointment and surprise, especially so in the light of the severe rebuke received both by HSBC executives

112 Ministry of Justice Post-legislative assessment of the Fraud Act 2006: Memorandum to the Justice Select Committee (London, 2012).
113 Ibid., 6, para. 16.
114 R. Tomasic, 'The haphazard pursuit of financial crime', above n. 40.
115 Ibid., especially 7–8.
116 See '[HSBC bank] helped clients dodge millions in tax', BBC News (London, 10 February 2015).
117 See M. Kleinman, 'FCA ends probe into HSBC Swiss tax affair', Sky News (London, 4 January 2016).
118 J. Treanor, 'HSBC escapes action by City regulator following Swiss tax scandal', *Guardian* (London, 4 January 2016).
119 J. Thompson, 'HSBC "humbled" by magnitude of Mexico money laundering scandal', *Financial Times* (London, 24 May 2013).

and HMRC at the hands of the Public Accounts Committee, led by the formidable Margaret Hodge MP.[120] However, there are other occurrences which suggest against discounting the presence of a transformative movement from the outcome of HSBC-Suisse, or even from the plethora of 'settlements' in which financial institutions might have been seen to escape criminal enforcement.[121] This is on account of what might be regarded as a global 'transformative movement', and where current approaches to market abuse appear to support this. Here, it is the case that the UK's refocusing on criminal enforcement, in preference to administrative enforcement, in pursuit of the FSA/FCA policy of 'credible deterrence',[122] will surprise few with any sense of Britain's longstanding tradition of utilising criminal enforcement.[123] The position of the European Union is more interesting on account of the very definite philosophy in favour of administrative enforcement at the heart of the Market Abuse Directive 2003.[124]

In contrast, the European Commission and European Parliament have both stressed that the new Directive on Criminal Sanctions for Market Abuse (CSMAD 2014) is premised on the belief that 'Minimum rules on criminal offences and on criminal sanctions for market abuse are essential for ensuring the effectiveness of the EU policy on market integrity',[125] and fundamentally that criminal sanctions are considered to 'demonstrate a stronger form of social disapproval compared to administrative penalties'.[126] The recognition of high-frequency trading in the new Market Abuse Regulation (MAR) 2014[127] definition of market abuse can be seen in the recent US criminalisation of 'spoofing'.[128] The first conviction for this was secured in November 2015 in the case of Michael Coscia.[129] Furthermore, during 2016, US authorities successfully secured the extradition of UK 'Flash

120 See House of Commons Public Accounts Committee, 'HMRC representatives questioned on tax avoidance and evasion: HSBC', 23 March 2015.

121 E.g. Friedrichs' use of the 'case study' of Goldman Sachs, in D. O. Friedrichs, 'Wall Street', above n. 18.

122 See G. Wilson and S. Wilson, 'The FSA, "credible deterrence", and criminal enforcement – a "haphazard pursuit"?' (2014) *Journal of Financial Crime*, 21(1), 4.

123 See S. Wilson, *The Origins of Modern Financial Crime*, above n. 31.

124 Market Abuse Directive (MAD) 2003 (2003/6/EC), especially Article 14.

125 Directive 2014/57/EU of the European Parliament and of the Council of 16 April 2014: see European Commission Memo 'European Parliament's endorsement of the political agreement on Market Abuse Regulation' Brussels, 10 September 2013 http://europa.eu/rapid/press-release_MEMO-13-774_en.htm?locale=en, incorporating Frequently Asked Questions, including one (Q15) on 'Proposal for a Directive on Criminal Sanctions for Market Abuse'.

126 CSMAD 2014, Recital 6.

127 Regulation (EU) No. 596/2014 of the European Parliament and of the Council of 16 April 2014 on market abuse (market abuse regulation) and repealing Directive 2003/6/EC.

128 The new crime of spoofing was added to the Commodity Exchange Act 1936 by the Dodd–Frank Wall Street Reform and Consumer Protection Act 2010.

129 See 'US high-frequency trader convicted in first US "spoofing" case: Michael Coscia convicted of six counts of commodities fraud and six of "spoofing" in first criminal prosecution of banned trading practice', *Guardian* (London, 4 November 2015).

Crash' trader Narinder Singh Sarao to face spoofing charges pertaining to his alleged role in the fall of the Dow Jones Industrial Average in May 2010.[130] It is even the case that *US v Newman* and *US v Salman*[131] suggest the US Government is attempting to make inroads into the extensive permissible use of non-public information traditionally subsisting under US securities law, and embodied in narrowly drawn insider trading prohibitions. Taken together, tough US approaches to securities violations do speak persuasively to the presence of a transformative movement relating to financial crime.

The language of 'speaking persuasively' has been chosen deliberately and advisedly in relation to the presence of a 'transformative movement'. This has certainly been used in preference to language of 'demonstrating conclusively'. This is because, although it is the case that 2017 will mark a decade since the onset of the global financial crisis, it is too soon to determine whether it will set in motion a transformative movement that will bring about marked changes in the way financial crimes are perceived, and responses to them pursued and calibrated. It is likely that the short term will be characterised by occurrences suggesting that this is happening, and others which question whether it is. This is partly because, at present, even almost ten years following its onset, it remains unclear how transformative the crisis will be *at all*, in terms of delivering extensive and far-reaching regulatory reform more generally, and in affecting how ordinary citizens view the lives which they lead, and the pressures and entitlements which characterise this. This is the complex matrix within which any transformative movement relating to financial crime will be located, and within which it must be analysed. And as more indices of post-crisis financial enforcement become available for analysis, this will provide a new context for focusing on whether financial crime *should* attract greater societal animosity and greater enforcement attention. The study of financial crime continues to reveal structural ambiguities about financial crime, which are captured highly effectively in Aubert's seminal assertion for white-collar crime, that:

> [it] is of prime importance to develop and apply concepts which preserve and emphasize the ambiguous nature of white-collar crimes and not to 'solve' the problem by classifying them either 'crimes' or 'not crimes'. Their controversial nature is exactly what makes them so interesting from a sociological point of view.[132]

130 M. Dakers, 'Theresa May approves extradition of "flash crash" trader to the US', *Telegraph* (London, 28 May 2015).

131 *US v Salman* [2015] United States Court of Appeals 9 Cir. No. 14–10204 DC No. 3:11-CR-00625-EMC-1) [2015]; and *US v Newman and Ors* [2014] United States Court of Appeals 2d Cir. Nos 13–1837-cr (L), 13–1917-cr (con).

132 V. Aubert, 'White-collar crime and social structure', above n. 89, 266.

Index

For Product Safety Concerns and Information please contact our EU representative GPSR@taylorandfrancis.com
Taylor & Francis Verlag GmbH, Kaufingerstraße 24, 80331 München, Germany

www.ingramcontent.com/pod-product-compliance
Ingram Content Group UK Ltd.
Pitfield, Milton Keynes, MK11 3LW, UK
UKHW020022200926
475702UK00014B/2008
* 9 7 8 0 3 6 7 0 3 0 3 1 5 *